Western Civilization

Western Civilization

THE CONTINUING EXPERIMENT

THIRD EDITION

Volume A
To 1500

Thomas F. X. Noble
University of Notre Dame

Barry S. Strauss
Cornell University

Duane J. Osheim
University of Virginia

Kristen B. Neuschel
Duke University

William B. Cohen
Indiana University

David D. Roberts
University of Georgia

Houghton Mifflin Company   Boston   New York

Editor-in-Chief: Jean L. Woy
Sponsoring Editor: Nancy Blaine
Senior Development Editor: Jennifer E. Sutherland
Editorial Associate: Gillie Jones
Senior Project Editor: Christina M. Horn
Editorial Assistant: Marie Bernard-Jackson
Senior Designer: Henry Rachlin
Senior Production/Design Coordinator: Sarah Ambrose
Senior Manufacturing Coordinator: Sally Culler
Senior Marketing Manager: Sandra McGuire

Volume A cover image: *The Tragic Actor,* wall painting from Herculaneum. Photograph: Museo Archeologico Nazionale, Naples/Art Resource, NY.

Text credits begin on page A-17, which constitutes an extension of the copyright page.

Printed in the U.S.A.

Library of Congress Control Number: 2001131535

ISBN: 0-618-10212-4

1 2 3 4 5 6 7 8 9-WEB-05 04 03 02 01

Brief Contents

CONTENTS

CHAPTER 4

Alexander the Great and the Spread of Greek Civilization, ca. 350–30 B.C.   105

CHAPTER 5

Rome: From Republic to Empire, ca. 509–31 B.C.   137

CHAPTER 9

The Expansion of Europe in the High Middle Ages, 900–1300   275

CHAPTER 10

Medieval Civilization at Its Height, 900–1300   317

CHAPTER 11

Crisis and Recovery in Late Medieval Europe, 1300–1500   355

CHAPTER 12

The Renaissance   393

MAPS

DOCUMENTS

WEIGHING THE EVIDENCE

PREFACE

In the days devoted to writing this preface in February 2001, the British prime minister visited the president of the United States, and the American secretary of state visited the Middle East. American and British aircraft bombed Iraq, and U.S. officials made vigorous representation to the Chinese government about reports that they had furnished the Iraqis with radar technology and components. An American submarine on maneuvers in the Pacific surfaced without due caution and sank a Japanese fishing boat. Taliban militants in Afghanistan destroyed ancient Buddhist statues on the grounds that they offended Islam's strict prohibition of idolatry. The pope named forty-four cardinals from all over the world. With these kinds of subjects in the news in the dawning third millennium, one might well ask: Why study Western Civilization any longer?

For some five thousand years, a Western civilization has been growing, changing, reflecting on itself, and sharing ideas with its neighbors. The West alone is not civilized, of course, for there were ancient civilizations in China, India, and Africa. But the West is uniquely civilized in the sense that its ideas and institutions are distinctive. This is not to imply that the West is better or worse than the other civilizations with which it shares the earth. It is simply to emphasize the persistence of one ancient tradition alongside others. But does antiquity alone constitute a claim on the efforts of teachers and students?

We begin to answer that question by pointing out that everyone alive today has been influenced by Western Civilization. The West deserves to be studied because its tale is old and compelling but *demands* to be studied because its story has been central to the development of the world in which we live. Western institutions—most notably representative democracy and commercial capitalism—have spread to every corner of the world. Even capitalism's greatest rival, communism, is fundamentally Western. Western styles in architecture dominate the skylines of every major city in the world. Western popular culture, from movies and music to fast food, are found absolutely everywhere. Communications technologies, from cell phones to e-mail, are as global in spread as they are Western in origin.

Some people, inside and outside the West, have grave reservations about the extent of Western influence in the modern world. Some critics challenge Western religious, philosophical, political, and economic ideas at their core.

Others have no quarrel with Western ideas but regret that local cultures all over the globe are vanishing before a relentless Western onslaught. Still others wonder why Western achievements in political stability and economic prosperity cannot be more widely shared. In other words, to say that the West is dominant is only to state the obvious, not to insist that such domination is inevitable or desirable. But the sheer, unassailable fact of that domination makes the careful study of the West essential for informed, responsible participation in the modern world.

However ancient Western Civilization may be, and however pervasive its influence, the definition of the term itself is controversial. The "West" is sometimes understood in terms of geography and sometimes in terms of culture. Each understanding invites misunderstanding. For most people today, the "West" means western Europe. And yet western Europe was the heir of the peoples and cultures of antiquity. These included Mesopotamians and Egyptians, who were the ancestors of the West, as well as Greeks, Romans, Jews, and Christians, who were the founders of the West. These peoples all lived around the Mediterranean world, and it was those who came after them, who lived in Europe proper, who built the West. Within Europe, some might take the West to mean Paris, London, Vienna, Berlin, and Rome. Others would include Madrid, Dublin, St. Petersburg, Stockholm, Warsaw, and Budapest. Moreover, through exploration, war, and commerce, the "West" gradually imposed its influence on the whole globe. One thinks immediately of the Westernization of the North and South American continents, but Tokyo and Hong Kong, although undeniably Eastern, are strongly marked by Western influences. In short, the West has never been, and is not now, neatly confined to one area or people.

As a cultural phenomenon, "Western" implies many things: freedom and free, participatory political institutions; economic initiative and opportunity; monotheistic religious faiths; rationalism and ordered thought in the social, political, and philosophical realms; an aesthetic sensibility that aspires to a universal sense of truth and beauty. But westerners have felt free to evoke tradition as their guiding light and also to innovate brilliantly; to accommodate slavery and freedom simultaneously; to esteem original thought and to persecute people who deviate from the norm. "Western" indeed has meant many things in various places at different times.

More than a decade ago, the six authors of *Western Civilization: The Continuing Experiment* set out to create a textbook for a course that informs students about a tradition that has powerfully, although not always positively, affected everyone in the contemporary world. Although each of us found something to admire in all of the existing textbooks, none of us was fully happy with any of them. Convinced of both the inherent interest of Western Civilization and the importance of teaching the subject, we were nevertheless disconcerted by the celebratory tone of some books, which portrayed the West as resting on its laurels instead of creatively facing its future. We were disappointed with books that claimed "balance" but actually stressed a single kind of history. We regretted that so many texts were uneven in their command of recent scholarship. We aimed to address the full range of subjects that a Western Civilization book needs to address and to provide the student reader with interesting, timely material in a book that is handsome to look at—in short, a book that helps the instructor to teach and the student to learn.

In preparing the Third Edition, we profited from the experience of using the book, the advice and criticism of dozens of colleagues, and the reactions of thousands of students. We are pleased that fellow teachers have found our vision and approach to be sound and that students have found our material accessible. In this new edition we have incorporated many changes, but we have not abandoned our approach to the subject, our commitment to its importance (and interest!), and our dedication to the students and teachers who share the adventure of learning the subject.

Basic Approach

Western Civilization is a story. Therefore, we aimed for a strong chronological narrative line. Our experience as teachers tells us that students appreciate this clear but gentle orientation. Our experience tells us, too, that an approach that is broadly chronological will leave instructors plenty of room to adapt our narrative to their preferred organization, or to supplement our narrative with one of their own.

Although we maintain the familiar, large-scale divisions of a Western Civilization book, we also present some innovative adjustments in arrangement. For instance, Chapter 2 treats early Greece together with the whole eastern Mediterranean region in the period from about 1500 to 750 B.C. This approach links kindred cultures and respects chronological flow better than customary treatments, which take western Asia to a certain point and then backtrack to deal with early Greece. We present a single chapter on Late Antiquity, the tumultuous and fascinating period from A.D. 284 to 600 that witnessed the transformation of the Roman Empire into three successors: Byzantine, Islamic, and European. One chapter studies those three successors, thereby permitting careful comparisons. But we do assign chapters to some of the greatest issues in Western Civilization, such as the Renaissance, the age of European exploration and conquest, the Scientific Revolution, and the industrial transformation. Our twentieth-century chapters reflect an understanding of the last century formed in its closing years rather than in its middle decades. What is new in our organization represents adjustments grounded in the best scholarship, and what is old represents time-tested approaches.

In fashioning our picture of the West, we take two unusual steps. First, our West is bigger than the one found in most textbooks. We treat the Celtic world, Scandinavia, and the Slavic world as integral parts of the story. We look often at the lands that border the West—Anatolia/Turkey, western Asia, North Africa, the Eurasian steppes—in order to show the to-and-fro of peoples, ideas, technologies, and products.

Second, we continually situate the West in its global context. This is not a world history book. But just as we recognize that the West has influenced the rest of the world, so too we carefully acknowledge how the rest of the world has influenced the West. Silks and spices, algebra and pointed arches, poetic forms and religious ideas have all entered the West from Asia and Africa and left deep marks. We begin this story of mutual interaction with the Greeks and Romans, carry it through the European Middle Ages, focus on it in the age of European exploration and conquest, and analyze it closely in the modern world of industry, diplomacy, empire, and immigration.

Another approach that runs like a ribbon throughout this textbook involves balance and integration. Teachers and students, just like the authors of this book, have their particular interests and emphases. In the large and diverse American academy, that is as it should be. But a textbook, if it is to be helpful and useful, should incorporate as many interests and emphases as possible. For a long time, some said, Western Civilization books devoted excessive coverage to high politics—"the public deeds of great men," as an ancient Greek writer defined the historian's subject. Others felt that high culture—all the Aristotles and Mozarts—were included to the exclusion of supposedly lesser figures and ordinary men and women. In the 1970s books began to emphasize social history. Many applauded this new emphasis even as they debated fiercely what to include under this heading. We capture the Western tradition in its full contours, listening to the voices of all of those who have made durable contributions. Naturally, we have had to make choices about how and where to array key topics within our narrative. We have used two basic rules to guide our writing.

First, we deal with topics when they were historically significant, when they commanded a great deal of attention in the historical past, or when modern historians have been able to discover a lot of information about them. Our approach to the history of women is an instructive example. A glance at this book's table of contents and then at its index is revealing. The former reveals very few sections devoted explicitly and exclusively to women. The latter shows that women appear constantly in every section of this book. Is there a contradiction here? Not at all. Women have not experienced history in complete separation from men. We do not assume that Western Civilization is a male or a female story. But we do recognize that men have been seen as the dominant historical actors, and so, again and again, we turn to *gender* as a tool of historical analysis. This permits us to ask why, in certain political, economic, or social circumstances, either men or women were assigned or denied roles or opportunities.

Second, we have tried to be integrative. For example, when we talk about power we present the institutional structures through which power was exercised, the people who possessed power as well as the people who did not, the ideological foundations for the use of power, and the material conditions that fostered or hindered the truly or the would-be powerful. Similarly, when we talk of great ideas we describe the antecedent ideas from which seemingly new ones were built up, and we ask about the consequences of those ideas. We explore the social position of the authors of those ideas to see if this helps explain the ideas themselves or to gauge their influence. We try to understand how ideas in one field of human endeavor proved to be influential in other fields.

We invite the reader to look at our narrative as if it were a mosaic. Taken as a whole, our narrative, like a mosaic, contains a coherent picture. Viewed more closely, our narrative, like a mosaic, is made up of countless tiny bits that may have their individual interest but that do not even hint at the larger picture. Finally, just as the viewer of a mosaic may find his or her eye drawn especially to one area, feature, color, or style, so too the reader of this book will find some parts more engaging or

compelling than others. But it is only because there is, in this book as in a mosaic, a complete picture that the individual sections make sense, command our attention, excite our interest.

We ask, finally, that you note the subtitle of the book: "The Continuing Experiment." It was carefully chosen to convey our resolve to avoid a deterministic approach. For students and teachers, an appreciation of continuity and change, of unity and diversity, can foster sympathetic participation in our often bewildering world. We try to give individual actors, moments, and movements the sense of drama, possibility, and contingency that they actually possessed. We, with faultless hindsight, always know how things came out. Contemporaries often hadn't a clue. We respect them. Much of the fascination, and the reward, of studying Western Civilization lies precisely in its richness, diversity, changeability, and unpredictability. Moreover, and just as important, the experiment continues.

CHANGES IN THE THIRD EDITION

In preparing our Third Edition, we thought hard about our own experiences in using the book and we paid close attention to the advice given us by many instructors, both those who had used the book and those who had not. The authors of this book have always been attentive to how we organized its contents. But just as our understanding of great historical issues is not static, so too our thinking on the matter of how to present this history undergoes constant revision.

■ New Organization and Content

For this edition the most dramatic organizational changes will be found in the sections dealing with the Middle Ages, the nineteenth century, and the twentieth century. Chapters 9 and 10, on the period from 900 to 1300, have been completely reorganized and heavily rewritten. In the first two editions, each of these chapters was comprehensive in thematic coverage, and they split the period at the year 1150. In the Third Edition, each chapter treats the whole period from 900 to 1300. Chapter 9 covers economic and political history and includes the Crusades. Chapter 10 covers social, religious, and cultural developments.

Chapters 20 and 21 have been reversed. By presenting "The Industrial Transformation of Europe, 1750–1850" (formerly 21 and now 20) before "Restoration, Reform, and Revolution, 1814–1848," it has been possible to resolve some tensions that persisted through the first two editions. As but one example, our former discussion of workers and the working class in Chapter 20 suffered from a lack of economic, industrial background. Chapters 29 and 30 have been reorganized to accommodate both the inclusion of recent events and the altered perspectives that inevitably attend the unpredictable course of history's march. Chapter 29 now covers the years from 1949 to 1989, and Chapter 30 treats the years from 1989 to the present.

Chapters 1–6 contain new discussions of archaeological evidence, revised treatment of Judaism, expanded material on Spartan and Roman women, and new coverage of Roman law. Discussions of the social, political, and military struggles of late medieval Europe in Chapter 11 have been reorganized. There is new material on humanism in Chapter 12. Chapter 14 has a revised treatment of John Calvin and of the Reformation in Scandinavia and eastern Europe. Seventeenth-century Europe's complicated political history has been streamlined. Several aspects of the Scientific Revolution in Chapter 17 have been revised, and there is new material on Galileo and Newton. The treatment of France in Chapters 18 and 19 has been revised, with new material added on eastern Europe. The discussions of socialism and Marxism in Chapter 21 have been reorganized. Chapter 22 has a new treatment of the Canadian Confederation. All of the chapters on the twentieth century contain new material, and Chapter 30 incorporates contemporary coverage, for instance on the Russian regime of Vladimir Putin and the new parity laws for elections in France. In highlighting these changes, it is important to add that *every single chapter* finds new material inserted, old material deleted, and existing material reorganized.

■ New Approaches to Teaching and Learning

To make this book as accessible as possible to students, we have constantly been aware of its place in a program of teaching and learning. Each chapter begins with a vignette that is directly tied to an accompanying picture. The vignettes introduce the reader to one or more of the key aspects of the chapter. Then the reader encounters a thematic introduction that points clearly and in some detail to what will follow.

To make our chapter introductions even more effective, which means to give students greater confidence as they proceed through the book, we took four steps. First we placed on the first page of each chapter a succinct outline that immediately and dramatically tells the student reader what he or she is going to encounter in the following pages. Second, we put at the end of each chapter's introduction a list of three or four Questions to Consider designed to work with the introduction and outline to give the student a clear orientation to what will follow. Third, we added a list of Terms to Know—generally ten or twelve—that alert the student to people, events, or developments demanding special attention. As a complement to text coverage, a ready reference, and a potential study guide, all of the Terms to Know are defined in a Glossary at the back of the book. Fourth, as the reader begins to read the chapter proper, he or she will meet a general chapter chronology that serves as yet another orientation to the material contained in the chapter.

In addition to this fundamental attention to the opening of each chapter, we also sought to improve the book's teachability by adding a pronunciation guide. Whenever we use an unfamiliar name or term, we show the reader how to pronounce it. Instead of using the intricate rules of phonetics, we provided commonsense guides to pronunciation at the foot of the page.

Careful chapter summaries draw together major topics and themes and link the present chapter to the one that follows. To encourage students to strike out on their own historical discoveries, each chapter offers a few carefully selected suggestions for further reading. This book's website (discussed later) contains a lengthy, searchable list of additional readings.

■ New and Revised Features

In preparing this Third Edition, we paid particular attention to the book's features. Beginning with its first edition, this book has presented the two-page feature Weighing the Evidence at the end of each chapter. These features introduce students to the fascinating array of sources that historians use and invite them to think critically about the nature of historical information and inquiry. Each opens with a description of the evidence presented in the feature—sources such as images of Cleopatra, the Ravenna mosaics, a Renaissance painting, eighteenth-century political symbols, the layout of the British Museum, and pop art—and then permits the students to look over the shoulder of the historian to become active participants in the interpretive process. The sources examined are interesting and instructive in their own right, but the Weighing the Evidence features also contribute to the teaching program of the book. There are references to the features at appropriate points in the narrative, they contain cross-references to other sections or illustrations, and they support ongoing discussions.

Our Weighing the Evidence essays have been both distinctive and well received since the First Edition. Feeling no complacency about them, however, the authors prepared eight new ones, including "Gladiators," "Stained Glass," "The Modern City and Photography," and "Advertising."

Many textbooks have boxed documents. In four different respects we have taken special care with our documents for this edition. First, we have added forty-seven new documents. Second, we have included in every chapter at least one document that permits a gendered analysis of a key historical person or problem. Third, each chapter also includes a Global Encounters box, quoting either a Western person commenting on the non-Western world, or vice versa. These boxes further our intention to situate our story in its global context. Fourth, and finally, because some documents cry out for more discussion or context, the website for the book provides exercises to help students analyze one key document per chapter, as well as twelve of the Weighing the Evidence features.

To this edition we have added a distinctive new feature: an Information Technology box with an accompanying image. The book has six of these, detailing papyrus, paper, printing, newspapers, the telegraph, and the Internet. These boxes provide readers with interesting examples of how communication technology affected people's lives. For example, the box on printing discusses how the new technology dramatically reduced the price of books and helped promote literacy across Europe.

We have been conscious of how the book *looks* to the reader from the very beginning. In keeping with our desire to integrate the components of the book into a coherent whole, we carefully anchor the maps and photographs. The authors developed the maps in this book and wrote their captions. Moreover, for this edition there are eight new maps, including European Resources and Trade Routes, ca. 1100; Dominion of Canada, 1873; GDP per Capita in Europe, 2000; and Foreign-Born Population in Western Europe. In addition, nearly twenty of the carry-over maps have been significantly revised. The same is true of the pictures: the authors selected them and wrote all the captions. As part of our continuing quest to make all of the elements of the book work together, the authors replaced about one-third of the photos for the Third Edition and revised the captions of many others. All of the maps in the book are cross-referenced in the text, some several times, and many of the photos are also referred to directly. Our diverse array of boxed documents—five per chapter—are referred to and

tightly anchored in the text, and they support their surrounding discussion. As with the maps, familiar documents are blended with pleasing newcomers.

■ Formats

This book is flexible in format as well as substantive organization. Because schools use different academic calendars, organize Western Civilization courses according to different chronologies, and require or recommend different parts of the course, we issue this book in three formats:

- **One-volume hardcover edition** (Chapters 1–30)
- **Two-volume paperback:** Volume I: To 1715 (Chapters 1–17); Volume II: Since 1560 (Chapters 15–30)
- **Three-volume paperback:** Volume A: To 1500 (Chapters 1–12); Volume B: 1300–1815 (Chapters 11–19); Volume C: Since 1789 (Chapters 19–30)

Volume II begins with a comprehensive Introduction designed for students who did not take the first semester of the course or who are new to this book. It provides a survey of the course of Western Civilization from ancient times to the early centuries of the modern era. This Introduction has been streamlined, organized along more strictly chronological lines, and illustrated for the Third Edition.

SUPPLEMENTS

We have assembled with care an array of text supplements to aid students in learning and instructors in teaching. These supplements, including the website, *HM ClassPrep* instructor CD-ROM, *Test Items, Computerized Test Items, GeoQuest* interactive maps CD-ROM, and *Transparencies,* are tied closely to the text to provide a tightly integrated and comprehensive program. Student study aids and instructor course management materials are also available in WebCT E-Packs and Blackboard Course Cartridges.

The text-specific website contains a wealth of resources for students and instructors. For students, there are over forty web exercises, written by Christopher Carlsmith of Stanford University, relating to the boxed documents and Weighing the Evidence features in the text. Icons in the textbook direct students to the corresponding activities on the Houghton Mifflin website. Students can also test their knowledge of chapter content using *ACE* self tests and a comprehensive on-line study guide. To visit the site, begin at the Houghton Mifflin Company home page (**college.hmco.com**) and select the text and/or discipline.

Instructors will find a complete *Instructor's Resource Manual*, written by Sharon Arnoult of Midwestern State University, on the website, including learning objectives, annotated outlines, suggested lecture topics, discussion questions, classroom activities, and paper topics for each chapter of the text. The *Instructor's Resource Manual* also features suggestions for integrating the web exercises into your teaching.

Other website features include an extensive searchable bibliography to aid in student and instructor research, primary source selections, web links, and class presentation maps.

Each chapter of the *Test Items*, prepared by Diane Moczar of Northern Virginia Community College, offers a list of 10 to 20 key terms, 5 to 10 short-answer and essay questions, 2 or 3 map questions, and 40 to 50 multiple-choice questions. Answers to the multiple-choice questions are located at the end of the *Test Items*. We also offer a computerized version of the *Test Items*, enabling instructors to alter, replace, or add questions.

The full package of instructor materials is also available on an *HM ClassPrep* CD-ROM. The *Instructor's Resource Manual* and *Test Items* appear on the CD-ROM in their entirety, in addition to Powerpoint slides of the textbook maps and selected art images. The CD-ROM will function on either a PC or Macintosh platform. In addition, a set of overhead map *Transparencies* for the Western Civilization course is available on adoption.

The *GeoQuest* CD-ROM features thirty interactive maps and thirty presentation maps that illuminate the history of Western Civilization from ancient times to the present. Each of the interactive maps is accompanied by exercises with answers and essay questions. Different types of interactivity allow students to move at their own pace through each section. Four sample maps can be viewed on the Houghton Mifflin history website.

WebCT E-Packs and Blackboard Course Cartridges provide text-specific student study aids in customizable, Internet-based education platforms. Both platforms provide a full array of content delivery and course management features for instructors who wish to incorporate educational technology in their traditional classrooms or for those who are creating distance-learning courses.

ACKNOWLEDGMENTS

The authors have benefited throughout the process of revision from the acute and helpful criticisms of numerous colleagues. We thank in particular: **Sharon L. Arnoult,** Midwestern State University; **Pierre Cagniart,** Southwest Texas State University; **Eleanor A. Congdon,** Plymouth State College; **David Dean,** Carleton University; **Maribel Dietz,** Louisiana State University; **George Drake,** Grinnell College; **Janusz Duzinkiewicz,** Purdue University North Central; **Alan Fisher,** Michigan State University; **Peter A. Goddard,** University of Guelph; **Aaron Goldman,** San Jose State University; **Robert W. Hayman,** Providence College; **Charles J. Herber,** Emeritus, George Washington University; **W. Robert Houston,** University of South Alabama; **Gerald E. Kadish,** Binghamton University (SUNY); **Laurie Koloski,** College of William and Mary; **Lawrence N. Langer,** University of Connecticut; **Thomas F. Madden,** Saint Louis University; **Donald M. McKale,** Clemson University; **Shannon McSheffrey,** Concordia University; **Isabel Moreira,** University of Utah; **Mark Munn,** The Pennsylvania State University; **Christopher Oldstone-Moore,** Wittenberg University; **Mary R. O'Neil,** University of Washington; **Ron Palmer,** Jefferson Community College; **Joseph F. Patrouch,** Florida International University; **Craig Pepin,** Western Carolina University; **Thomas Lynwood Powers,** University of South Carolina, Sumter; **Carole Putko,** San Diego State University; **Paul Lawrence Rose,** The Pennsylvania State University; **John Rosser,** Boston College; **Raffael Scheck,** Colby College; **Bernard Schlager,** University of New Hampshire; **Thomas P. Schlunz,** University of New Orleans; **Eileen Soldwedel,** Edmonds Community College; **Alan E. Steinweis,** University of Nebraska, Lincoln; **Charles R. Sullivan,** University of Dallas; **Timothy M. Thibodeau,** Nazareth College of Rochester; **Kevin Uhalde,** Northern Illinois University; and **Leigh Whaley,** Acadia University.

Each of us has also benefited from the close readings and careful criticisms of our coauthors, although we all assume responsibility for our own chapters. Barry Strauss has written Chapters 1–6; Thomas Noble, 7–10; Duane Osheim, 11–14; Kristen Neuschel, 15–19; William Cohen, 20–24; and David Roberts, 25–30.

Many colleagues, friends, and family members have helped us develop this work as well. Thomas Noble wishes to thank Linda Noble for her patience and good humor. He is also grateful to John Contreni, Wendy

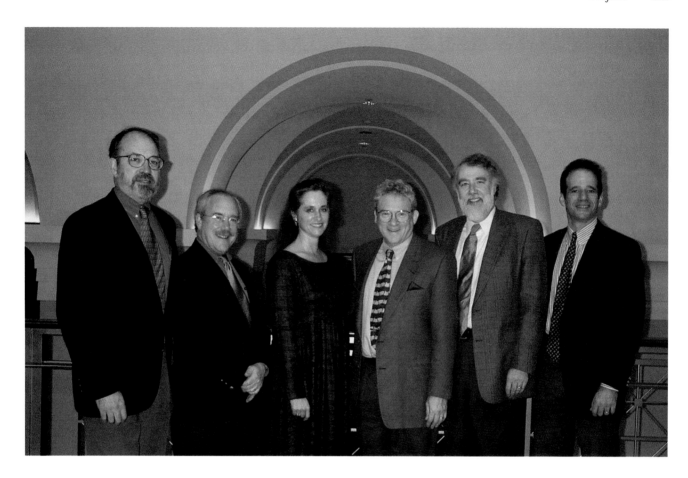

The Authors: Duane Osheim, Tom Noble, Kristen Neuschel, Bill Cohen, David Roberts, Barry Strauss

Davies, Thomas Head, Elizabeth Meyer, Julia Smith, Richard Sullivan, John Van Engen, Robert Wilken, and Ian Wood.

Barry Strauss is grateful to colleagues at Cornell and at other universities who offered advice and encouragement and responded to scholarly questions. He would also like to thank the people at Cornell who provided technical assistance and support. Most important have been the support and forbearance of his family. His daughter Sylvie, his son Michael, and, above all, his wife, Marcia, have truly been sources of inspiration.

Duane Osheim wishes to thank his family for support during the writing and revising of this book. He is also grateful to colleagues at the University of Virginia, who helped to clarify the many connections between Western Civilization and the wider world. He would specifically like to thank Erik Midelfort, Arthur

Field, Janis Gibbs, and Beth Plummer for comments and advice.

Kristen Neuschel thanks her colleagues at Duke University for sharing their expertise. She is especially grateful to Sy Mauskopf, Bill Reddy, John Richards, Tom Robisheaux, and Alex Roland. She also thanks her husband and fellow historian, Alan Williams, for his wisdom about Western Civilization and his support throughout the project, and her children, Jesse and Rachel, for their patience, joy, and curiosity.

William Cohen thanks his wife, Christine Mathieu, and his daughters Natalie, Leslie, and Laurel for their support and encouragement over the many years that this project has matured.

David Roberts wishes to thank Bonnie Cary, Linda Green, and Nancy Heaton for their able assistance and Joshua Cole, Karl Friday, Thomas Ganschow, John Haag,

Michael Kwass, John Morrow, Douglas Northrup, Miranda Pollard, William Stueck, Eve Trout Powell, and Kirk Willis, colleagues at the University of Georgia, for sharing their expertise in response to questions. He also thanks Beth Roberts for her constant support and interest and her exceedingly critical eye, and Ellen, Trina, and Anthony for their college-age perspective and advice.

The first plans for this book were laid in 1988, and over the course of thirteen years there has been remarkable stability in the core group of people who have been responsible for its growth and development. The author team remains intact. Our original Sponsoring Editor, Jean Woy, has become Editor-in-Chief for History, Political Science, and Economics but has never missed a meeting with us or weakened in her interest in and commitment to this book. Christina Horn, our Senior Project Editor, has been the wizard behind the curtain for all three editions. She understood from the beginning our desire to have maps, pictures, and boxes closely integrated with their pertinent text and she has never let us down. Our photo researcher, Carole Frolich, has been with us from the start, and she has always understood the spirit of this book and the wishes of its authors. When the Second Edition was in preparation, a Brief Edition was planned and produced. Our work on that version introduced us to Jennifer Sutherland, who then served as Senior Development Editor for the Third Edition. She entered quickly into the spirit of our book, but by casting a fresh eye on it she helped us see it again as if for the first time. Elizabeth Welch, our Senior Basic Book Editor for the first two editions, helped us to turn six voices into one and taught us how to write a textbook. We have now worked for several years with Nancy Blaine, our Sponsoring Editor, and we are most appreciative of her tireless energy and her faith in this book and its authors.

Although stability has been the hallmark of this project for years now, we are nevertheless delighted to acknowledge some people who came on board with the Third Edition. Sandra McGuire, Senior Marketing Manager, helped us to understand the many audiences for which we were writing. Gillie Jones, Editorial Associate, was masterful in managing the flow of manuscripts, disks, and e-mail attachments. Penny Peters designed the page layouts and created a pleasing visual effect. Henry Rachlin, Senior Designer, assembled diverse components into a book whose beauty truly facilitates its academic purpose.

Producing a successful textbook is hard work that makes high demands in terms of confidence, good humor, honesty, respect, and understanding. The authors of this book have been fortunate in their long and maturing relationship with their publishers.

Thomas F. X. Noble

ABOUT THE AUTHORS

Thomas F. X. Noble   After receiving his Ph.D. from Michigan State University, Thomas Noble taught at Albion College, Michigan State University, Texas Tech University, and the University of Virginia. In 1999 he received the University of Virginia's highest award for teaching excellence. In 2001 he became Robert M. Conway Director of the Medieval Institute at the University of Notre Dame. He is the author of *The Republic of St. Peter: The Birth of the Papal State, 680–825; Religion, Culture and Society in the Early Middle Ages; Soldiers of Christ: Saints and Saints' Lives from Late Antiquity and the Early Middle Ages;* and *Images and the Carolingians: Tradition, Order, and Worship.* Noble's articles and reviews have appeared in many leading journals, including the *American Historical Review, Byzantinische Zeitschrift, Catholic Historical Review, Revue d'histoire ecclésiastique, Speculum,* and *Studi medievali.* He has also contributed chapters to several books and articles to three encyclopedias. He was a member of the Institute for Advanced Study in 1994 and the Netherlands Institute for Advanced Study in 1999–2000. He has been awarded fellowships by the National Endowment for the Humanities (twice) and the American Philosophical Society.

Barry S. Strauss   Professor of history and Classics at Cornell University, where he is also Director of the Peace Studies Program, Barry Strauss holds a Ph.D. from Yale in history. He has been awarded fellowships by the National Endowment for the Humanities, the American School of Classical Studies at Athens, and the Killam Foundation of Canada. He is the recipient of the Clark Award for excellence in teaching from Cornell. His many publications include *Athens After the Peloponnesian War: Class, Faction, and Policy, 403–386 B.C.; Fathers and Sons in Athens: Ideology and Society in the Era of the Peloponnesian War; The Anatomy of Error: Ancient Military Disasters and Their Lessons for Modern Strategists* (with Josiah Ober); *Hegemonic Rivalry from Thucydides to the Nuclear Age* (co-edited with R. Ned Lebow); *War and Democracy: A Comparative Study of the Korean War and the Peloponnesian War* (co-edited with David R. McCann); and *Rowing Against the Current: On Learning to Scull at Forty.*

Duane J. Osheim   A Fellow of the American Academy in Rome with a Ph.D. in history from the University of California, Davis, Duane Osheim is a professor of history at the University of Virginia. A specialist in late medieval and Renaissance social and institutional history, he is the author of *A Tuscan Monastery and Its Social World* and *An Italian Lordship: The Bishopric of Lucca in the Late Middle Ages,* as well as numerous studies of religious values and rural life in late medieval Italy.

Kristen B. Neuschel   Associate professor of history at Duke University, Kristen Neuschel received her Ph.D. from Brown University. She is a specialist in early modern French history and is the author of *Word of Honor: Interpreting Noble Culture in Sixteenth-Century France* and articles on French social history and European women's history. She has received grants from the National Endowment for the Humanities and the American Council of Learned Societies. In 1988 she received the Alumni Distinguished Undergraduate Teaching Award, which is awarded annually on the basis of student nominations for excellence in teaching at Duke.

William B. Cohen   After receiving his Ph.D. at Stanford University, William Cohen taught at Northwestern University and Indiana University, where he is now professor of history. At Indiana, he served as chairman of the West European Studies and History Departments; he is currently Director of Graduate Studies for the History Department. A previous president of the Society of French Historical Studies, Cohen has received several academic fellowships, including a National Endowment for the Humanities and a Fulbright fellowship. Among his many publications are *Rulers of Empire; The French Encounter with Africans; European Empire Building; Robert Delavignette and the French Empire; The Transformation of Modern France;* and *Urban Government and the Rise of the City.* His current research is on the Algerian war and French memory.

David D. Roberts   After taking his Ph.D. in modern European history at the University of California, Berkeley, David Roberts taught at the Universities of Virginia and Rochester before becoming professor of history at the University of Georgia in 1988. At Rochester he chaired the Humanities Department of the Eastman School of Music, and he chaired the History Department at Georgia from 1993 to 1998. A recipient of Woodrow Wilson and Rockefeller Foundation fellowships, he is the author of *The Syndicalist Tradition and Italian Fascism; Benedetto Croce and the Uses of Historicism;* and *Nothing but History: Reconstruction and Extremity After Metaphysics,* as well as numerous articles and reviews.

Western Civilization

CHAPTER 1

The Ancestors of the West

O UTSIDE the city of Thebes in ancient Egypt, the kings maintained a village of workers to build and decorate royal tombs. Sennejdem°, a high-ranking Theban worker, was himself buried in a splendidly decorated tomb along with his wife Iynefert. In a scene from the tomb depicted to the left, Sennejdem is cutting wheat in the fields of the afterlife, where it grew higher than on earth. The painting illustrates many of humanity's early achievements: settled life, agriculture, technological innovation, representational art, writing (notice the symbols in the upper left corner of the painting), weaving (notice Sennejdem's pleated kilt), and religion.

Those achievements, which Sennejdem and Iynefert probably took for granted, were the most momentous inventions in human history. Approximately 100,000 years ago, the first modern humans evolved from humanlike ancestors. Human beings wrestled with an often-hostile environment, engaging in a continuing series of experiments, until beginning about 10,000 B.C. they learned how to plant crops and tame animals. The shift from a food-collecting to a food-producing economy dramatically increased the amount of human life that the earth could support. Between 3500 and 3000 B.C., human society became well organized in urban centers, supported by farmers in the surrounding territories, and able to keep written records: it had, in short, achieved civilization.

What we call Western civilization, however, was still more than two thousand years away. As a term *Western civilization* is imprecise, inviting disagreement about its definition and about the lands, peoples, and cultures that it embraces at any given time. In this book we give

---

Sennejdem (SEN-noo-tem)

Man harvesting wheat, Egyptian tomb painting.
(Erich Lessing/Art Resource, NY)

Origins, to ca. 3000 B.C.

Mesopotamia, to ca. 1600 B.C.

Egypt, to ca. 1100 B.C.

Widening Horizons: The Levant and Anatolia, 2500–1150 B.C.

Western civilization an evolving definition that permits comparison and reflection over time and space. In the strictest sense, Western civilization means the "West," and that, in turn, has traditionally meant the lands and peoples of western Europe.

Initially, however, the West embraced the Greek and Roman peoples, plus the foundational monotheistic religions of Judaism and Christianity. These first westerners in turn borrowed many ideas and institutions from the earlier civilizations of western Asia and Egypt. (These civilizations are sometimes referred to as the Ancient Near East.) Indeed, civilization began in those lands and came only relatively late to Europe.

Western Asia and Egypt contributed greatly to the cultures of Greece and Rome and to the religious visions of the Jews and Christians. Yet those earlier civilizations are sufficiently different from the West and its society, politics, and religion that they are better considered as ancestors or forerunners of the West rather than as its founders. (For a longer discussion of the definition of Western civilization, see the Preface.)

So, after briefly surveying the origins of the human species, the historian of the West must begin with the emergence of civilizations after 3500 B.C. in two great river valleys: the valley of the Tigris° and Euphrates° in Mesopotamia (today, Iraq and Syria), and the valley of the Nile in Egypt. Impressive in

their own right, Mesopotamia and Egypt influenced a wide range of other early civilizations in western Asia and northern Africa. Among them were the Hittites and the Syro-Palestinian city-states, whose own cultural contributions make them ancestors of the West as well. They are studied in this chapter. The Hebrews and the Greeks were also influenced by Mesopotamia and Egypt, but with the Hebrews and the Greeks, Western civilization begins, and so they are covered in Chapter 2.

QUESTIONS TO CONSIDER

- When, where, and how did modern humans evolve?
- How did people shift from a food-collecting to a food-producing economy?
- What is civilization? When, where, and why did it begin? What is Western civilization or the West?
- What did the civilizations of Egypt and western Asia contribute to the West between about 3500 and 1200 B.C.?

TERMS TO KNOW

hominids	Sumerians
hunter-gatherers	pharaoh
Neolithic Revolution	papyrus
cuneiform	Amarna reform
city-state	Ugarit

ORIGINS, TO CA. 3000 B.C.

THE earth is old; modern human beings are young; and civilization is a very recent innovation. Physical anthropologists, archaeologists, geneticists, and biochemists have made great strides in explaining human origins. Great disagreement still reigns nonetheless. Each decade seems to bring an

exciting new discovery that calls for the reassessment of previous theories.

We can be more certain about the series of processes, beginning around 10,000 B.C., that led to the emergence of civilization by 3500–3000 B.C. The period studied in this chapter includes both prehistory—the term often used for time before the invention of writing—and recorded history. Writing appeared last among the complex of characteristics that marks the emergence of civilization. Over a period of several thousand years, many humans abandoned a mobile existence for a sedentary one. They learned to domesticate animals and

---

Tigris (TY-gris)   **Euphrates** (yoo-FRAY-tees)

to cultivate plants. They shifted from a food-collecting economy to a predominantly food-producing economy. They developed the first towns, from which, over several millennia, the first urban societies slowly evolved. The result—the first civilizations, found in western Asia and Egypt—laid the groundwork on which later would be built the founding civilizations of the West: Greece, Rome, and ancient Israel.

■ The First Human Beings

Modern human beings, *Homo sapiens sapiens*—genus *Homo*, species *sapiens*, subspecies *sapiens*—first appeared within about 100,000 years ago (scholarly estimates vary). The human family, or hominids, are much older, however. The hominids include many ancient and extinct species, some of which are thought to be our evolutionary ancestors.

Africa, as current research argues, is the cradle of humanity. The first hominids appeared in Africa's tropics and subtropics over 4 million years ago. By 2.5 million years ago they had evolved into creatures who invented the first technology, simple stone tools. Prehistory is traditionally referred to as the Stone Age because stone was the primary medium from which hominids made tools. The hominids were migratory: not less than 1.6 million years ago and perhaps much earlier, they appeared in East Asia and the eastern edge of Europe.

The next important stage in human evolution is *Homo erectus* ("upright person"), a hominid with a large brain who used more complex stone tools and may have acquired language. The appearance of *Homo erectus* is usually dated to 1.8 million years ago, but a recent discovery in China may date *Homo erectus* as early as 2.25 million years ago. Slowly, separate *Homo erectus* populations in different places gave way to the gradual emergence of various archaic forms of *Homo sapiens*.

For many millennia humans struggled with the ebb and flow of glaciers. Their home was the Ice Age, as scholars refer to the period of fluctuating cycles of warm and cold, beginning about 730,000 years ago and ending only about 10,000 years ago. Early humans lived amid great contrasts in temperature, seasons, and landscapes, requiring considerable adaptation—but adapt they did.

Humans came late to Europe, though not as late as scholars once thought. Indeed, recent finds in Spain show the presence of archaic humans in Europe about 800,000 years ago. Beginning about 400,000 years ago, Europe was home to the ancestors of the best-known archaic people, the Neandertals. Fully evolved by 130,000 years ago, Neandertal people lived in Europe and western Asia for the following 100,000 years, to about 30,000

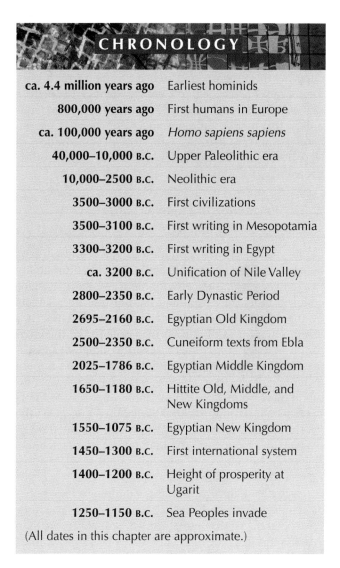

CHRONOLOGY

ca. 4.4 million years ago	Earliest hominids
800,000 years ago	First humans in Europe
ca. 100,000 years ago	*Homo sapiens sapiens*
40,000–10,000 B.C.	Upper Paleolithic era
10,000–2500 B.C.	Neolithic era
3500–3000 B.C.	First civilizations
3500–3100 B.C.	First writing in Mesopotamia
3300–3200 B.C.	First writing in Egypt
ca. 3200 B.C.	Unification of Nile Valley
2800–2350 B.C.	Early Dynastic Period
2695–2160 B.C.	Egyptian Old Kingdom
2500–2350 B.C.	Cuneiform texts from Ebla
2025–1786 B.C.	Egyptian Middle Kingdom
1650–1180 B.C.	Hittite Old, Middle, and New Kingdoms
1550–1075 B.C.	Egyptian New Kingdom
1450–1300 B.C.	First international system
1400–1200 B.C.	Height of prosperity at Ugarit
1250–1150 B.C.	Sea Peoples invade

(All dates in this chapter are approximate.)

years ago. Their strong and stocky physiques were perhaps an adaptation to the rugged climate of the Ice Age. The Neandertals were far from being the brutes they are usually imagined to be. They were, for example, among the first people to bury their dead, often with grave offerings—for example, flint, animal bones, or flowers—a practice that suggests they were sensitive enough to mourn their losses.

Neandertals, however, were not modern humans. Modern humans entered Europe about 40,000 years ago, having originated in Africa. Within 10,000 years, Neandertals had disappeared; whether through war or through disease or through intermarriage with modern humans, we do not know. The first modern humans tended to be taller and less muscular than Neandertals and other archaic people. They also used their hands more precisely and walked more efficiently, and they lived longer. With its high forehead and tucked-in face, the modern human skull is distinctive, but differences between the modern and archaic human brain are a matter of scholarly debate. Some archaeologists believe that Neandertals were capable of the same level of technology that modern humans achieved. What no one debates, however, is that, with the disappearance of Neandertals, it was modern humans who put into effect a revolution in culture.

■ The Revolution in Human Culture, ca. 70,000–10,000 B.C.

Before the emergence of modern humans and perhaps before Neandertals, people had relatively little ability to change the natural environment. Modern humans changed that. They exploited natural resources largely by means of technology and organization. Thus they began the process of human manipulation of the environment that—sometimes brilliantly, sometimes disastrously—has remained a leading theme of the human experience ever since. The key to this change was a dramatic increase in the amount and complexity of information being communicated—what might be called the first information revolution. The twin symbols of the revolution are cave paintings and notations made on bone, signs that humans were thinking about their environment and their experiences.

It was long thought that these dramatic changes began in Europe about 40,000 B.C.* Recently, however, they have been traced to southern Africa, probably more than 70,000 years ago. The discovery there of carefully worked bone tools and stone spearheads pinpoints the dawn of modern human technology. Still, it is not in Africa but elsewhere that we can best trace the early evolution of the modern human mind. Europe from about 40,000 to about 10,000 B.C. provides reliable evidence of the way of life and the culture of early human hunter-gatherer societies, complex organizations that survived by a food-collecting economy of hunting, fishing, and gathering fruits and

nuts. This period is sometimes called the Upper Paleolithic (Greek for "Old Stone") era. Then, around 10,000 B.C., western Asia offers evidence of a second revolution: the invention of a food-producing economy, consisting of the domestication of animals and the cultivation of crops. The period from about 10,000 to 3000 B.C. is sometimes called the Neolithic (Greek for "New Stone") era.

Archaeology tells us something about early people's way of life. So do analogies from contemporary anthropology, for even today a tiny number of people still exist in hunter-gatherer societies in isolated corners of the globe, for example, in the Kalahari Desert of Africa and in the Arctic. It is reasonable to speculate that early humans lived in small groups, numbering perhaps twenty-five to fifty persons, related by kinship or marriage. Early hunter-gatherers moved from place to place, following the seasonal migration of game, but by the eve of the invention of agriculture, some hunter-gatherers had settled down in villages. Hunting was largely a male preserve, while gathering nuts and berries fell into the female domain. Perhaps women brought their children with them as they worked or relied on kin or friends for childcare.

It was probably common for men and women to pair off, have children, and establish a family, much as marriage is a near-universal practice among humans today. Compared with other animals, humans produce extremely dependent infants requiring years of attention. In order to ensure the survival of the young to adulthood, men as well as women need to play a role in child rearing.

Early people found shelter by building huts or, frequently, by living in caves or rock shelters—hence our notion of the "caveman." Caves offered shelter, could be heated, and made a naturally good vantage point for observing prey and hostile humans. In the Upper Paleolithic era, about 30,000 years ago, caves were the site of the earliest representational art. The most spectacular Upper Paleolithic paintings discovered so far have been found in caves in southern France (for example, at Lascaux° and at Chauvet° Cave) and in Spain (at Altamira). European cave paintings of such animals as the bison, horse, reindeer, and woolly mammoth (a huge, extinct member of the elephant family with hairy skin and long, upward-curving tusks) attest to early human artistic skill. The presence of abstract shapes attests to an interest in symbols. The purpose of cave paintings is unknown, but perhaps they served as illustrations of myths or as attempts to control the environment through magic.

---

* We follow the traditional practice in the West of expressing historical dates in relation to the birth of Jesus Christ (actually, to a now discredited calculation of his birth date because in fact Jesus was not born in A.D. 1; see page 191). Dates before his birth are labeled B.C. (which stands for "before Christ") and dates after his birth are labeled A.D. (*anno Domini*, Latin for "in the year of the Lord"). A widely used alternate refers to these dates as B.C.E. ("before the common era") and C.E. ("of the common era").

Lascaux (lass-CO)   **Chauvet** (show-VAY)

Other early representational art includes engravings on stone of animals, birds, and stylized human females, as well as female figurines carved from ivory or bone. Usually represented with exaggerated breasts or buttocks, the carvings are called Venus figurines, after Venus, the Roman goddess of love. They may represent an attempt to control fertility through magic.

Upper Paleolithic craftsmanship is as impressive as the art. The early human tool kit included the first utensils in such easily worked materials as antler and ivory. Stone tools became longer and the first polished bone tools appeared, as did the first stone and bone spear points and the first bows and arrows. The presence of bone needles and awls (pointed tools for punching holes) implies sewing, probably of animal skins.

The existence of Upper Paleolithic artists and skilled craftspeople demonstrates at least a limited specialization of skills and division of labor: society required organization, albeit on a limited scale. Hunting was a communal enterprise. Related families are likely to have joined together in clans, which in turn may have formed tribes. It is often thought that each of these groups was patriarchal (literally, "ruled by the father"); that is, the family was governed by the father, the tribe by a male headman or chief. To be sure, some later myths (for example, among the ancient Greeks) argue that women were the rulers of prehistoric society. Today some historians see the possibility of matriarchy (literally, "rule by the mother") in the Venus figurines. There is, however, no firm evidence of matriarchy. Male chiefs probably did exist, as in later periods, but some tribes may have had no chief at all, following the decision of the community rather than an individual leader.

Chauvet Cave Art   This black-painted panel shows horses, rhinoceros, and wild oxen. This painting and others in the cave, discovered in 1994 in southern France, are over 30,000 years old, making them perhaps the oldest known paintings in the world.   *(Jean Cottes/Ministère de la Culture/Corbis Sygma)*

■ The Coming of Agriculture, ca. 10,000–5000 B.C.

The human discovery of agriculture was dramatic, meriting the name "Neolithic Revolution" that scholars sometimes give it. Yet if dramatic, the discovery spread slowly and unevenly. In most areas, hunting and fishing continued to be a major source of food, even though agriculture fed more people. Agriculture was first discovered sometime after 10,000 B.C. in western Asia, then discovered again independently in other parts of the world. By 5000 B.C. information about the new practices had spread so widely that farming could be found in many places around the world.

The story begins about 13,000 B.C., when humans began to specialize in the wild plants they collected and the animals they hunted. They had good reason to do so because hunter-gatherer society had become increasingly complex, and in some places permanent settlements had appeared. A settled existence probably produced more mouths to feed, stimulating the need for more food. The next step is not surprising: learning how to domesticate plants and animals.

People seem to have begun by domesticating dogs, which were useful in hunting. Then they learned to keep sheep, goats, and cattle. Next came farming. Humans learned first how to grow wheat and barley, then legumes (beans). With males occupied in hunting, it may well have been females who first unraveled the secrets of agriculture.

The earliest area of domestication is a zone of land stretching in a crescent shape west to east from what is today southern Jordan to southern Iran. Scholars call this region of dependable annual rainfall the Fertile Crescent (see Map 1.1). With domestication came small agricultural settlements, which were increasingly com-

Map 1.1   Western Asia   The Neolithic Revolution began after 10,000 B.C. in the Fertile Crescent, an arc-shaped region of dependable annual rainfall. In this area between the Tigris and Euphrates Rivers known as Mesopotamia, the world's first urban civilization took root about 3500–3000 B.C.

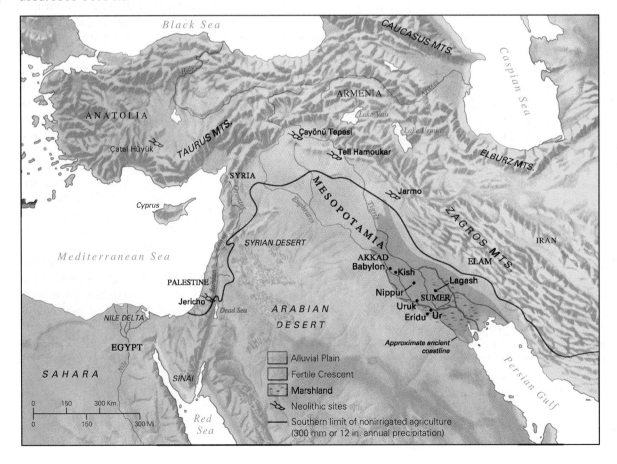

mon after 7000 B.C. Thus was born the farming village, probably the place that most people have called home since the spread of agriculture around the world.

Scholars once thought of Neolithic villages as simple places devoted to subsistence agriculture, with no craft specialization, and as egalitarian societies lacking social hierarchies. In recent years, new evidence and a rethinking of older information have altered this picture considerably. The Neolithic village site of Çayönü Tepesi° in eastern Anatolia, for example, provides evidence of metalworking (of copper) and specialization of labor (in bead making) from approximately 7000 to 6000 B.C. The site also contains the world's earliest known example of cloth, probably linen, woven around 7000 B.C. Other contemporaneous village sites reveal experiments in ironworking and craft specialization. Evidence points to long-distance trade between villages in pottery and in obsidian (a sharp volcanic glass used in tools). Artwork shows men wearing loincloths and headdresses, women wearing pants and halter tops, and both sexes wearing jewelry.

Consider the case of Jericho°, in Palestine near the Dead Sea (see Map 1.1), perhaps the oldest settled community on earth. A small village around 9000 B.C., by about 7000 Jericho had become a town surrounded by massive walls 10 feet thick and 13 or more feet high. The walls, about 765 yards long, probably enclosed an area of about 10 acres. The most prominent feature of the walls was a great tower 33 feet in diameter and 28 feet high with an interior stairway. Inside the walls lived a densely packed population of about two thousand people.

An even larger Neolithic town was Çatal Hüyük° in south central Anatolia (see Map 1.1). Its population of six thousand people in 6000 B.C. made it by far the largest settlement of the era. It was probably a trading center and perhaps a religious shrine. Carbonization from fire has preserved a wealth of artifacts attesting to Çatal Hüyük's sophistication, including woven fabrics, obsidian mirrors, wooden vessels, and makeup applicators.

Agriculture made human populations richer and more numerous, but the resulting concentrations of population bred disease and probably increased the scale of war. More men than ever before were available to fight because agriculture proved to be so efficient a source of food that it freed people for specialized labor. Some became craftsmen, some artists, some priests—and some warriors.

This is not to say that war in Neolithic times was sophisticated. Indeed, the phenomenon perhaps con-

sisted of group skirmishes and sporadic raids rather than systematic warfare. People added new weapons to the spear and the bow: the sling, the dagger, and the mace (a heavy war club). Spanish rock art shows a confrontation between two groups of archers, one following what seems to be a leader. The scene may be a ritual rather than a violent conflict, but we have physical cases of actual bloodshed. The earliest known evidence of organized warfare comes from a cemetery along the Nile River in the Sudan dating from 12,000 to 4500 B.C. The cemetery contains fifty-nine human skeletons, nearly half of whom died violently. Some were speared, some clubbed, and some killed by arrowheads. Some suffered multiple wounds. The victims include women and children.

◼ Neolithic and Copper Age Europe, 7000–2500 B.C.

Europe was one day to become the center of Western civilization, but the region lagged behind its neighbors at first. Innovations from the east reached Europe after 7000 B.C. and slowly transformed it. Europe was no empty vessel to be filled by eastern technologies, however: Europeans developed their own unique culture.

The term *Europe* refers to a vast peninsula of the Eurasian continent with several very distinct regions. Southern Europe is made up of a rugged and hilly Mediterranean coastal strip, linked to northern Africa and western Asia by the sea and by similarities in climate and landscape. High mountains are found in the Alps of south central Europe, from which chains of lower mountains radiate toward the southwest and southeast. Northern Europe, by contrast, consists in large part of forested plain, indented here and there by great rivers. In the southeast the plain, or steppe, becomes open and mostly treeless. The eastern boundaries of Europe are, in the north, the Ural Mountains and, in the south, the Caucasus Mountains. Georgia, Armenia, and Azerbaijan are all considered parts of Europe.

Before 7000 B.C., Europeans lived a traditional hunter-gatherer existence. Farming began in southeastern Europe around 7000 B.C., when migrants from western Asia introduced the settled way of life of the Neolithic village. That food-producing economy spread across Europe between about 6000 and 4500 B.C., borne alternately by colonization and by native adaptation of new technologies.

The farmers of Early Neolithic Europe (ca. 7000–ca. 4500 B.C.) were pioneers, living in hamlets or villages surrounded by larger hunter-gatherer populations. Not until 2500 B.C. did the majority of Europeans adopt a

---

Çayönü Tepesi (CHAH-yer-ner TEH-peh-see)
Jericho (JEH-rih-co) **Çatal Hüyük** (CHAH-tal Her-yerk)

food-producing way of life. Between 4500 and 2500 B.C., a give-and-take between pioneers and natives led to the development of regional cultures. This era of European prehistory is known as the Late Neolithic, or the Copper Age, because copper came into use on the Continent during this time, as did gold. Both metals were used primarily as status symbols: the most dramatic example is a Bulgarian burial site dating from about 4000 B.C. in which a 45-year-old man is buried with 990 gold objects as well as copper and flint weapons.

Between about 4500 and about 3500 B.C., Copper Age Europeans developed their own cultures in relative isolation from the more advanced East. For example, European metallurgy probably developed independently. On Europe's northern and western edges people began to set up megaliths—stone tombs and monuments—often of huge blocks. Such monuments may illustrate an awareness of time created by the spread of agriculture, with its seasonal rhythms.

Between about 3500 and 2500 B.C., Copper Age Europe grew in sophistication. The urbanization of Mesopotamia (in modern-day Iraq; see Map 1.1) had an impact on southeastern Europe, which supplied raw materials for western Asia. Greece underwent the greatest transformation, to the extent that it developed its own urban civilization by about 2000 B.C. (see Chapter 2). Elsewhere, especially in the Balkans, technological innovations came into use, from the wheel, to complex metal-casting, to wine cups (evidence of a new taste). The recent discovery of a Copper Age corpse preserved in the ice of the Italian Alps opens a window into northern Italian society of about 3200 B.C. (See the feature "Weighing the Evidence: The Iceman and His World" on pages 36–37.)

In western Europe stone monuments are the most dramatic cultural achievements. On the Mediterranean island of Malta, for example, people built elaborate temple complexes constructed of massive limestone blocks. In Britain, megalithic architecture reached its peak with Stonehenge, built in stages from about 2800 to 1500 B.C. This famous monument consists of a circle of stones oriented precisely on the rising sun of midsummer—a sign both of early Europeans' interest in the calendar and of their skill in technology.

Neolithic and Copper Age sculpture consists of many representations of females but few of males. Consider, for example, the ample, sculpted female figures found in Malta's temples. The enlarged buttocks and thighs of these statues might be symbols of fertility. Some scholars speculate that early Europeans wor-

The Maltese Female   This "Sleeping Lady," a terra-cotta statuette of the late fourth millennium B.C. from Malta, shows a reclining woman, perhaps a goddess or priestess. Her double-egg shaped buttocks are thought to symbolize fertility or regeneration.   *(Erich Lessing/Art Resource, NY)*

shiped goddesses until warlike invaders after 2000 B.C. brought male deities with them. The theory is, however, controversial.

■ The Emergence of Civilization, 3500–3000 B.C.

Civilization is derived from the Latin word *civitas*, meaning "commonwealth," or "city." The first civilizations, beginning in Mesopotamia and Egypt between 3500 and 3000 B.C., probably contained the first cities. What differentiated them from their predecessors, however, was not so much size (a city versus a town) as complexity. Civilization allowed human beings to think big. A large and specialized labor force, organized by a sufficiently strong government, made it possible to expand control over nature, pursue advances in technology, and trade and compete over ever widening areas. An elite class emerged that was able to pursue ever more ambitious projects in art and thought and to invent systems of writing. In short, the advent of civilization in the fourth millennium B.C. marked a major turning point. Thereafter, the human horizon expanded forever.

Civilization arose in Iraq, in the valley between the Tigris and Euphrates Rivers (see Map 1.1), a region that the Greeks named Mesopotamia (literally, "between the rivers"). At around the same time or shortly afterward, civilization also began in the valley of the Nile River in Egypt. Although these civilizations each developed largely independently, some borrowing between the two nonetheless took place.

Both Mesopotamia and Egypt are home to valleys containing alluvial land—that is, a relatively flat tract where fertile soil is deposited by a river. Otherwise, the two regions are quite different. Although the Nile Valley was easy to farm, much of the Tigris-Euphrates plain had to be tamed by would-be farmers. Every summer the Nile flooded in a relatively regular and predictable manner, bringing north to Egypt the waters of the monsoon rains of the Ethiopian highlands, where one of the river's sources—the Blue Nile—rises. The spring deluges of the Tigris and Euphrates were more sudden and less predictable. Moreover, the Nile's waters spread so broadly that it took less human effort than in Mesopotamia to irrigate most of the available farmland. In southern Mesopotamia, by contrast, most of the soil was alternately so dry or so marshy that agriculture would not have been possible without considerable irrigation and drainage—that is, the use of channels, dikes, or dams to control floodwaters and improve the fertility of the land. One Mesopotamian text describes a farmer as "the man of dike, ditch, and plow." Making matters worse, Mesopotamia was given to extreme heat and scorching winds.

Eye Idol   This tiny figurine, made from bone and named for its prominent eyes, may represent a person rather than a god. It comes from Tell Hamoukar in northeastern Syria (ca. 3500 B.C.), which is one of history's earliest cities.   *(Oriental Institute Hamoukar Expedition)*

Some scholars argue that the very hostility of Mesopotamia's environment generated the cooperation and control that civilization requires.

It has long been thought that the first cities developed in southern Mesopotamia. A recent discovery, however, suggests that cities were found in northern Mesopotamia too around the same time, that is, during the Uruk° Period (3800–3200 B.C.). An excavation at Tell Hamoukar° in northeastern Syria, near the Iraqi border, uncovered what appears to be a city of around 3500 B.C. The excavators found ovens and pottery, apparently used for large-scale food production, and they unearthed stamp seals and clay seal impressions, which may indicate a bureaucracy. A mud-brick fortification wall has tentatively been indentified. In short, several signs point to a city.

If cities developed simultaneously in northern and southern Mesopotamia in the mid-fourth millennium

---

Uruk (OO-rook)   **Tell Hamoukar** (tell ha-moo-CAR)

Uruk IV ca. 3100 B.C.	Sumerian ca. 2500 B.C.	Old Babylonian ca. 1800 B.C.	Neo-Babylonian ca. 600 B.C.	SUMERIAN Babylonian
				APIN epinnu plow
				ŠE še'u grain
				ŠAR kirû mountain
				KUR šadû orchard
				GUD alpu ox
				KU(A) nunu fish
				DUG karpatu jar

Figure 1.1   Early Mesopotamian Writing   The pictographs of early writing evolved into a system of phonetic syllables and abstract symbols. Simplified and standardized, this writing was *cuneiform,* or "wedge-shaped." Over time, it was adapted from Sumerian to Babylonian and other languages throughout western Asia.   *(Source: From* Babylon, *by Joan Oates. Published by Thames and Hudson Ltd., 1978. Used by permission.)*

B.C. they may share a common, earlier source: the Ubaid° culture of mid-fifth-millennium B.C. Mesopotamia. Many questions arise, among them whether Ubaid cities existed as early as 4500 B.C., a thousand years earlier than cities were thought to have first appeared. We will have to wait for future excavation and study to answer such questions.

The first cities emerged through a slow, incremental process of action and reaction. Labor became more specialized and agricultural production was maximized. When part of the population moves to a city, those who remain on the land must work harder or use better farming techniques or increase the amount of land under cultivation. In fourth- and third-millennium B.C. Mesopotamia, farmers did all three. Meanwhile, both the number and variety of settlements increased. Urban populations required the support of people in smaller units—towns, villages, and hamlets—clustered around a city.

Along with the growth of cities came the development of writing, about 3500–3100 B.C. in Mesopotamia. The development of writing from simple recordkeeping can be traced step by step. Before writing, Mesopotamian people used tiny clay or stone tokens to represent objects being counted or traded. By 3500 B.C., with 250 different types of tokens in play, the system had grown unwieldy enough for people to start using signs to indicate tokens. It was a short step to dispensing with the tokens and placing the signs on a clay tablet by making indentations in the clay with a reed stylus: writing. New words were soon added through pictographs (pictures that stand for particular objects). In time the pictographs evolved into ideograms—that is, abstract symbols that are no longer recognizable as specific objects and thus can be used to denote ideas as well as things.

In the centuries following its introduction, Mesopotamian writing became standardized. Scholars call the signs *cuneiform* from the Latin for "wedge-shaped," a good description of what early writing looks like (see Figure 1.1). In its first centuries, cuneiform was used almost entirely for economic records or commercial transac-

Ubaid (oo-BA-id)

tions. Then it was adapted to make brief records of offerings to the gods. By 2350 B.C. cuneiform had evolved into a mixed system of about six hundred signs, most of them phonetic (syllabic), with relatively few ideograms.

Experts used to think that writing began in Mesopotamia and spread to Egypt. Recent excavations, however, have found examples of early Egyptian writing securely dated to 3300–3200 B.C. In other words, Egyptian writing was independent: it was not derived from or related to cuneiform. Whether writing began in Egypt or Mesopotamia, therefore, is now an open question. What is clear, however, is that writing was invented to meet economic rather than creative needs. In Egypt the earliest writing includes records of the delivery of linen and oil as taxes to King Scorpion I. The writing consists of early *hieroglyphs* (literally, "sacred carvings"), a system of pictures and abstract signs that represent sounds or ideas, later to become more formal and standardized.

As we shall see, incising cuneiform on clay was much clumsier than writing with pen and ink on papyrus, as became possible in Egypt (see the feature "Information Technology: Papyrus"). Nonetheless, cuneiform was flexible enough to record the spoken language and to be used for poetry as well as for bookkeeping. Moreover, cuneiform became the standard script of various languages of western Asia for several thousand years. Clumsy it may have been, but cuneiform was writing, and writing is both a catalyst for change and the historian's best friend. Mesopotamia after 3000 B.C. was dynamic, sophisticated, and, best of all, intelligible to us.

MESOPOTAMIA, TO CA. 1600 B.C.

AFTER 3000 B.C. the people of Mesopotamia flourished. They experimented in government, in cooperation and conflict among different ethnic groups, in law, and in the working out of class and gender relations. Keenly aware of human limitations and vanity, they sought divine justice, as their literary and religious texts show. Their engineering skill, mathematics, and astronomy set ancient science on an upward path. In later centuries, Western civilization would build on these foundations, and then take off in new directions.

Archaeologists sometimes refer to the third and second millennia in the eastern Mediterranean and western Asia as the Bronze Age. In this period people mastered the technology of making bronze, an alloy of copper and tin, and bronze frequently replaced stone as a primary material for everyday use.

■ The City-States of Sumer

Though their culture is long dead, the Sumerians live on. Whenever someone today counts the minutes, debates politics, or quotes the law, the Sumerians live, for these are all legacies of that ingenious society.

The dominant inhabitants of Mesopotamian civilization in its first flowering are named Sumerians. Present in southern Mesopotamia by 3200 B.C. and probably earlier, the Sumerians entered their great age in the third millennium B.C., when their city-states enjoyed a proud independence (see Map 1.1).

The formative era of Mesopotamian civilization is known as the Uruk Period (ca. 3800–3200 B.C.) after one of its major archaeological sites. During the Uruk Period the Sumerians invented the wheel and the plow, planted the first orchards—of dates, figs, or olives—and developed the first sophisticated metal-casting processes. They built some of the first cities, for example, Uruk. They expanded the size of territories and populations, the scale of war, the complexity of society, and the power of government. Finally, as if to cap a period of remarkable change, at the end of the Uruk Period the Sumerians invented cuneiform writing.

Mesopotamian cities flourished in this era. By the period that scholars have named the Early Dynastic Period (2800–2350 B.C.), named for the first royal dynasties (ruling families), a large Mesopotamian city had grown to the point where it might cover 1,000 acres surrounded by more than 5 miles of walls, within which lived about fifty thousand people. Such a city was part of a network of thirty such city-states with a common culture, commerce, and propensity to make war on one another. Hence the city-states of Mesopotamia may be called the first civilization.

It was a land of cooperation and conflict. The Sumerian cities had much in common: language, literature, arts and sciences, and religion. Yet the cities often quarreled. In some cases conflict erupted over the boundaries of adjacent farmlands. The scarcity of fresh water also led to disputes among cities over water rights.

Each city had its own small urbanized area and a larger agricultural hinterland irrigated by canals. Cities traded with one another and with the outside world. The primary political units of southern Mesopotamia for most of the third millennium B.C., Sumerian city-states were an incubator of civilization.

How were the Sumerian city-states governed? A Sumerian might have responded that they were governed by the gods, for the Sumerians believed that the gods had created, and thus owned, everything on earth. Historians study human government, but the lack of

Papyrus

It grew in the marshes of the Nile River valley, a tall and graceful plant. Once it was picked, it might be eaten, woven into baskets or rope, used as construction material for lightweight boats or shelters, or burned for fuel or as incense. But, most important, this versatile vegetation generated a paperlike writing material that had a huge impact on ancient civilization. Today most paper comes from wood, following a technology developed in China. In the ancient West, however, people wrote on rolled sheets produced from an Egyptian plant. In fact, we derive our word *paper* from the name of the plant, *papyrus*. The Greeks called it *byblos*, from which came the Greek word for book and, eventually, our word *bible*.

Harvested papyrus was transformed into writing material by cutting the stalks into thin strips and laying them in a cross-hatched fashion to form sheets, which were then glued together into rolls, in which form it was sold. The roll was the standard form of both writing paper and books in ancient times. Although sizes varied, a typical roll was about 8 or 9 inches high by about 15 feet long (when unrolled). A sheet of paper was white, shiny, and smooth.

Rolls manufactured from papyrus became the primary writing material of the ancient world, outstripping all competing media. Papyrus was durable and easy to write on, which facilitated all written communication, from paying taxes to reading Plato. Even if they had had only stone or bone or animal skin to write on, humans would have made progress, but papyrus-making technology made things simpler. Progress requires a process of trial and error, which is easier to carry out on paper than in any other nonelectronic medium.

Unlike people in western Asia, where clay tablets were the standard writing medium, Egyptians wrote on papyrus, beginning around 3000 B.C. Carving cuneiform in clay with a reed stylus was cumbersome, but writing on paper with brush and ink was easy, flexible, and even elegant (see the photograph of the Egyptian *Book of the Dead* on page 26). Not only did papyrus allow Egyptians to develop several different written scripts, but it may also have helped stimulate the development of the alphabet. The first alphabet appeared in Egypt in the second millennium B.C., in a Semitic script with Egyptian influences. Although written on stone, that alphabet was probably developed through experimentation more easily done on papyrus.

People wrote everything on papyrus, from contracts to curses, from public documents to poetry, from trivial jottings to holy books. Highly prized because it was durable and flexible, papyrus grew more common than other writing materials available in antiquity, such as parchment (manufactured from animal skins), potsherds, stone, bone, or tablets of wood, wax, or clay. Although expensive for ordinary people, papyrus was cheap for the elites, who had a near-monopoly on literacy.

The papyrus plant has a tall triangular stem and a fluffy crown. It was often the subject of pharaonic art. Look, for example, at this painting from an Egyptian tomb of the fifteenth century B.C. The man on the right has poled the boat into a grove of papyrus plants. The man on the left is pulling a plant out by the stalk, while his coworker in the center is tying stalks into a sheaf.

Papyrus grew in several places around the Mediterranean, but in ancient times its main habitat was Egypt. The

evidence makes it difficult to say much with assurance about Sumerian government before the Early Dynastic Period.

Certainly in early times Sumerian temples were wealthy and powerful. A simple structure around 5000 B.C., the temple had become by 4000 B.C. an elaborate, monumental work of architecture built on a raised platform. Each city had at least one temple, the house of its patron god and the common symbol of the community. There is no evidence, though, for the once-prominent theory that the early Sumerian cities were temple-states, governed by priests.

By the beginning of the Early Dynastic Period around 2800 B.C., political power in a Sumerian city rested largely in the hands of its Council of Elders, whose members were probably wealthy landowners. Some scholars argue that the council shared power with a popular assembly, creating, in effect, a bicameral legislature and perhaps even a primitive democracy. The evidence is ambiguous, however, leaving it highly debatable whether ordinary people took part in Sumerian government.

In Sumer, as elsewhere in western Asia and Egypt throughout ancient times, ordinary people often faced

Nile Valley, particularly the delta, became the center of a vast international trade in papyrus in Greek and Roman times, from around 600 B.C. on. Yet the trade began much earlier, at least by around 1100 B.C., when it is known that paper was brought from Egypt to Phoenicia. In pharaonic times the manufacture of papyrus in Egypt may have been under royal supervision. The word *papyrus* itself may mean "that of the pharaoh."

The Classical Greeks got their papyrus from Egypt, at first possibly via the Phoenician port city of Byblos. The Romans considered papyrus to be "an indispensable necessity of public and private business," as one Roman writer put it. From Britain to Iraq, papyrus was in almost universal use during Greek and Roman times for more than a thousand years after 600 B.C.

Harvesting Papyrus   This Egyptian wall-painting, from a tomb of about 1450 B.C., shows boatmen gathering papyrus plants.   *(The Metropolitan Museum of Art [30.4.11])*

limits on their freedom. True, there seem to have been many free peasants. Yet these small "free" farmers often had to provide forced labor for the state as a kind of taxation—maintaining the vast Mesopotamian irrigation system, for example. There also seems to have been a large group of people who were only semi-free because they owned no land of their own but worked others' land. Finally, there were slaves, that is, people who could be bought and sold. Slaves were never very numerous in these societies because no large policing system existed yet to keep them from running away. Still, wealthy people usually had a few slaves to help in the household.

Slaves were usually brought from abroad as war booty or merchandise, although some slaves were local people who had been sold into slavery to pay off a debt; often they were children (especially daughters) sold by their parents.

By about 2700 B.C., political power shifted. It was a time of chronic intercity warfare, and the times demanded a strong hand. The new ruler was not a Council of Elders but rather a "big man" (*lugal*) or, less often, a "governor" (*ensi*)—that is, a king or, occasionally, a queen. The monarch was first and foremost a warrior. He claimed to be the earthly representative of the gods, a position that gave him general responsibility for his subjects' welfare. Accordingly, kings sponsored irrigation works, raised fortification walls, restored temples, and built palaces.

The earliest Sumerian kings, dating from the period 2700 to 2600 B.C., are Enmebaragesi of the city of Kish, his son and successor, Agga, and Gilgamesh° of Uruk, a hero of epic poetry whom many scholars consider a genuine historical personage. In the cities of Ur and Lagash, the king's wife was often a power in her own right. Kish was ruled by Ku-baba (r. ca. 2450 B.C.), the first reigning queen of recorded history.

Though warriors, Sumerian monarchs also recognized a responsibility for promoting justice. History's earliest known reformer of law and society was Uru-inim-gina, king of Lagash around 2400 B.C. Surviving documents describe Lagash as a society in which wealthy landowners encroached on the temples and oppressed the poor, and royal administrators mistreated ordinary people. The king's aims seem to have been both to correct abuses and to weaken independent sources of power threatening royal authority. Uru-inim-gina attempted to manage the bureaucracy, protect the property of humble people, and guard the temples. He also put into effect the first known wage and price controls. Uru-inim-gina's proclaimed intention was to promote impartial justice, a goal that he expressed in the formula "[the king] will protect the mother that is in distress, the mighty man shall not oppress the naked and the widow." If at the same time he also managed to increase his own power, then so much the better. As it turned out, Lagash was conquered only a few years after Uru-inim-gina's reign. His reforms nonetheless survived as the precedent for a long Mesopotamian tradition of royal lawgiving.

■ Conquest and Assimilation, ca. 2350–1900 B.C.

Mesopotamian cities faced competition from the surrounding peoples of the desert and the mountains. Poor and tough, these people coveted Mesopotamia's wealth. Some conquerors came directly from the hinterland to the walls of the city they were attacking; others climbed to power from within the Sumerian city-states. Both groups were sufficiently impressed by Sumerian culture to adopt a great many Sumerian customs and ideas. The most successful warrior-king was Sargon (r. 2371–2316 B.C.), an unusual figure who rose from obscurity to a high position under the king of Kish before founding his own

capital city, Agade°. Even more important, Sargon was a native speaker not of Sumerian but of Akkadian.

The Akkadians were originally a seminomadic people who lived on the edge of the desert. Shepherds, they moved their flocks with the seasons. Their language, Akkadian, belongs to the Semitic group of languages, which also includes Arabic and Hebrew. Scholars formerly believed that the Akkadians came directly from the desert to conquer Sumer, but it is now known that they had begun settling in the northern cities of southern Mesopotamia by the end of the Uruk Period. This northern part of southern Mesopotamia was known as Akkad.

As commander of one of history's first professional armies, Sargon conquered all Mesopotamia, and his power extended westward along the Euphrates and eastward into the Iranian Plateau. Rather than rule conquered peoples directly, the Akkadians generally were satisfied with loose control, as long as they could monopolize trade. They adopted Sumerian religion and wrote Akkadian in cuneiform.

Sargon's son inherited his throne. His dynasty boasted that it reigned over "the peoples of all lands" or "the four quarters of the earth." The Akkadian empire reached its greatest height in the reign of Sargon's grandson, Naram-sin (r. ca. 2250–2220 B.C.), but it did not survive the next reign. Sargon nonetheless proved to be one of western Asia's most influential figures. His dynasty's ideal of universal empire was one to which future conquerors would lay claim.

Sargon proved adept at using religion to legitimize his rule. A self-made monarch, he was sensitive to the charge of having stolen power. Indeed, he chose the throne name Sargon (Sharrum-ken in Akkadian) because it means "the king is legitimate." By claiming the status of the gods' representative on earth, Sargon strengthened his authority. He once paraded a defeated enemy in a halter before the temple and priests of Enlil, the chief Sumerian god, confidently proclaiming that Enlil was on his side.

Assimilation was another lasting Akkadian legacy. Although Sargon made Akkadian the official language of administration, he made politic concessions to Sumerian sensibilities. For instance, his daughter Enkheduanna°, whom he appointed high priestess at Ur and Uruk, wrote poetry in Sumerian, poetry powerful enough to be quoted often in later Sumerian texts. The first known woman poet, Enkheduanna described the union of Sumerians and Akkadians.

Gilgamesh (GIL-ga-mesh)

Agade (ah-GAH-day)   **Enkheduanna** (en-khe-du-AN-na)

Around 2200 B.C. the Akkadian empire broke up into a series of smaller successor states. Then, after a century of rule by invaders from the Zagros Mountains on the eastern border of Mesopotamia, the Sumerians returned to power under the Third Dynasty of Ur (2112–2004 B.C.). Far from stripping away all Akkadian influence, the revived Sumerian rulers spoke of themselves as "kings of Sumer and Akkad." It was a title that would have a long and potent history: for the next fifteen hundred years, many of the great kings of western Asia would label themselves, among other honorifics, "king of Sumer and Akkad." By using this title, the Sumerian kings of Ur showed that they recognized the existence of a composite, common Mesopotamian society.

This society survived renewed political turmoil around 2000 B.C. A new kingdom, under the rule of the Amorites, one of several raiding peoples, emerged around 1900 B.C. in southern Mesopotamia. The kingdom of the Amorites, Semitic-speakers, shared Mesopotamian culture and traditions. Babylon, northwest of Ur in the central part of Mesopotamia, became the Amorite capital. From Babylon, Amorite kings issued cuneiform decrees that, although written in a Semitic language, drew heavily on Sumerian material.

Akkadian Bronze   This stern-faced, life-size cast-bronze head, with its stylized ringleted beard and carefully arranged hair, shows Mesopotamian craftsmanship at its finest. Thought by some to be Sargon (r. 2371–2316 B.C.) or Naram-sin (r. ca. 2250–2220 B.C.), it was deliberately mutilated in ancient times.   *(Claus Hansmann, München)*

Plaque of Enkheduanna   This limestone disk depicts a procession of women, including Enkheduanna, daughter of King Sargon (r. 2371–2316 B.C.), a priestess and the first known woman poet.   *(University of Pennsylvania Museum, Philadelphia [neg. #S4-1399330, object #B16665])*

■ Hammurabi's Code

The most famous Amorite king, Hammurabi (r. 1792–1750 B.C.) ruled in Babylon about six hundred years after Sargon. Much of his forty-two-year reign was devoted to creating a Mesopotamian empire. A careful administrator who ushered in an era of prosperity and cultural flowering, Hammurabi is most famous for the text known as Hammurabi's Code. Although the work was less a "code" than a collection listing various crimes and their punishments—a kind of treatise on justice glorifying Hammurabi's qualities as a judge—we shall use the familiar name. Hammurabi's Code became both a legal and a literary classic, much copied in later times.

Hammurabi's Code offers a remarkable portrait of Mesopotamian society. The document contains nearly three hundred rulings in cases ranging from family to commercial law, from wage rates to murder. The administration of justice in Mesopotamia was entirely practical: we find no notion of abstract absolutes or universal principles, not even a word for "law."

Though occasionally less harsh than earlier law codes, which date as far back as around 2100 B.C., Hammurabi's Code was by no means lenient. Whereas earlier codes were satisfied with payment in silver as recompense for crime, Hammurabi's Code was the first to stipulate such ruthless penalties as mutilation, drowning, and impaling. It also introduced the law of retaliation for wounds: "If a man has destroyed the eye of a member of the aristocracy: they shall destroy his eye. If he has broken his limb: they shall break the (same) limb." Moreover, children could be punished for the crimes of their fathers. (See the box "Reading Sources: King Hammurabi Dispenses Justice.")

Inscribed in forty-nine vertical columns on a stone stele about 7½ feet high, and displayed in a prominent public place, Hammurabi's Code symbolized the notion that the law belonged to everyone. Although ordinary people could not read, it was possible for them to find a patron who could. Yet the societies of western Asia and Egypt were anything but egalitarian, and Hammurabi's society was no exception. Punishments there, as elsewhere, were class-based: crimes against a free person, for example, received harsher punishment than crimes against a slave or a semi-free person. Debt seems to have been a serious and widespread problem, frequently leading to debt slavery. Women could own and inherit property and testify in court. The overall direction of the code, however, was patriarchal: it enshrined the power of the male head of the family. For example, a son who struck his father had his hand cut off, while a woman who brought about the death of her husband "because of another man" was impaled on stakes.

■ Divine Masters

The Sumerians were polytheists—that is, they had many gods—and their gods (like the later gods of Greece) were anthropomorphic, or human in form. Indeed, Sumerian (and Greek) gods were thought to be much like human beings, by turns wise and foolish, except that they were immortal and superpowerful. Many Sumerian gods arose out of the forces of nature: An, the sky-god; Enki, the earth-god and freshwater-god; Enlil, the air-god; Nanna, the moon-god; and Utu (Semitic, Shamash), the sun-god. Other Sumerian gods embodied human passions or notions about the afterlife: Inanna (Semitic, Ishtar), goddess of love and war; and Ereshkigal, goddess of the underworld.

The Sumerians sometimes envisioned their gods holding an assembly, much like a boisterous Sumerian prototype. The Sumerians and Akkadians considered Enlil, city-god of Nippur, to be the chief god. The Babylonians replaced him with Marduk, city-god of Babylon.

Every Mesopotamian city had its main temple complex, the most striking feature of which was a *ziggurat*, or stepped tower. Constructed originally as simple raised terraces, ziggurats eventually became seven-stage structures. Unlike the pyramids of Egypt, ziggurats were not tombs but "stairways" connecting humans and the gods.

The keynote of Mesopotamian religion was a certain pessimism about the human condition. It is not surprising that the Mesopotamians, living in a difficult natural environment, regarded the gods with fear and awe. Although the gods communicated with humans, their language was mysterious. To understand the divine will, the Mesopotamians engaged in various kinds of divination: the interpretation of dreams, the examination of the entrails of slaughtered animals, the study of the stars (which stimulated great advances in astronomy, as we will see). By building temples, offering prayers and animal sacrifices, and participating in public rituals and processions, Mesopotamians hoped to appease their gods and discern their wishes.

Most people expected nothing glorious in the afterlife, merely a shadowy existence. It was thought that with a person's last breath, his or her spirit embarked on a long journey to the Netherworld, a place under the earth. More than one Mesopotamian text describes the Netherworld as the "Land-of-no-return" and "the house wherein the dwellers are bereft of light, / Where dust is their fare and clay their food, / Where they see no light,

⁊⅍ R E A D I N G   S O U R C E S

King Hammurabi Dispenses Justice

The Code of Hammurabi, king of Babylon (r. 1792–1750 B.C.), is one of the best-known documents of antiquity. Less a code than a treatise on justice, the text illustrates both the image of himself that the king wished to promote and the class and gender hierarchies of Mesopotamia in the second millennium B.C. The following excerpts are from the preface and body of the text.

[The gods] named me to promote the welfare of the people, me, Hammurabi, the devout, god-fearing prince, to cause justice to prevail in the land, to destroy the wicked and the evil, that the strong might not oppress the weak, to rise like the sun over the black-headed (people), and to light up the land. . . . I established law and justice in the language of the land, thereby promoting the welfare of the people. At that time (I decreed):

128: If a free man acquired a wife but did not draw up the contracts for her, that woman is no wife.

129: If the wife of a free man has been caught while lying with another man, they shall bind them and throw them into the water [that is, submit to the water ordeal, with the river as divine judge]. If the husband of the woman wishes to spare his wife, then the king in turn may spare his subject. . . .

170: When a free man's first wife bore him children and his female slave also bore him children, if the father during this lifetime has ever said "My children!" to the children whom the slave bore him, thus having counted them with the children of his first wife, after the father has gone to (his) fate, the children of the

first wife and the children of the slave shall share equally in the goods of the paternal estate, with the first-born, the son of the first wife, receiving a preferential share. . . .

196: If a free man has destroyed the eye of a member of the aristocracy, they shall destroy his eye. . . .

198: If he has destroyed the eye of a commoner or broken the bone of a commoner, he shall pay one mina [approximately one pound] of silver. . . .

202: If a free man has struck the cheek of an aristocrat who is superior to him, he shall be beaten sixty (times) with an oxtail whip in the assembly. . . .

237: When a free man hired a boatman and a boat and loaded it with grain, wool, oil, dates, or any kind of freight, if that boatman was so careless that he has sunk the boat and lost what was in it as well, the boatman shall make good the boat which he sank and whatever he lost that was in it.

Source: Adapted from James B. Pritchard, ed., *Ancient Near Eastern Texts Relating to the Old Testament,* 3d ed., with Supplement (Princeton, N.J.: Princeton University Press, 1969), pp. 164, 171, 173, 175–176.

residing in darkness."[1] The dead resided there permanently, though in some texts their spirits return to earth, often with hostile intent toward the living.

Archaeological evidence indicates a possible shift in such attitudes toward death, at least on the part of the Mesopotamian upper classes, by the late third millennium B.C. The kings and nobles of the Third Dynasty of Ur were buried with rich grave goods and with their servants, who were apparently the victims of human sacrifice following the master's death. Perhaps the rulers now expected to have the opportunity to use their wealth

again in a comfortable immortality, possibly influenced by Egyptian ideas (see pages 26–27).

■ Arts and Sciences

The people of Mesopotamia were deeply inquisitive. They focused on the beginning and the end of things. "How did the world come into being?" and "What happens to us when we die?" are perhaps the two fundamental questions of their rich literature. Consider, for example, the Babylonian creation epic known from its

⁂ R E A D I N G S O U R C E S

Heroism and Death in Mesopotamia

The Epic of Gilgamesh *sheds light on categories of gender and power in Mesopotamia. Men such as King Gilgamesh and his friend Enkidu have heroic adventures and risk death. Women lead quieter lives but are wiser and more realistic, as the following excerpts show.*

[Gilgamesh mourns the death of Enkidu.]
"Hear me, O elders and give ear unto me! It is for Enkidu, my friend, that I weep, Moaning bitterly like a wailing woman. The axe at my side, my hand's trust, The dirk in my belt, the shield in front of me, My festal robe, my richest trimming—An evil demon rose up and robbed me! O my younger friend, thou chasedst the wild ass of the hills, the panther of the steppe! We who have conquered all things, scaled the mountains, who seized the Bull and slew him, brought affliction on Hubaba, who dwelled in the Cedar Forest! What, now, is this sleep that has laid hold on thee? Thou art benighted and canst not hear me!" But he lifts not up his head; he touched his heart but it does not beat."

[Beginning lost. Gilgamesh is addressing Siduri, the ale-wife.]
"He who with me underwent all hardships—Enkidu, whom I loved dearly, who with me underwent all hardships—has now gone to the fate of mankind! Day and night I have wept over him. I would not give him up for burial—in case my friend should rise at my plaint—seven days and seven nights, until a

worm fell out of his nose. Since his passing I have not found life, I have roamed like a hunter in the midst of the steppe. O ale-wife, now that I have seen thy face, let me not see the death which I ever dread."

The ale-wife said to him, to Gilgamesh: "Gilgamesh, whither rovest thou? The life thou pursuest thou shalt not find. When the gods created mankind, death for mankind they set aside, life in their own hands retaining. Thou, Gilgamesh, let full be thy belly, make thou merry by day and by night. Of each day make thou a feast of rejoicing, day and night dance thou and play! Let thy garments be sparkling fresh, thy head be washed; bathe thou in water. Pay heed to the little one that holds on to thy hand, let thy spouse delight in thy bosom! For this is the task of mankind!"

Source: James B. Pritchard, ed., *Ancient Near Eastern Texts Relating to the Old Testament*, 3d ed., with Supplement (Princeton, N.J.: Princeton University Press, 1969), pp. 89–90.

 For additional information on this topic, go to http://college.hmco.com.

---

first line as *Enuma Elish*° ("When on high"). An epic poem is the story of heroic deeds, in this case the deeds of the gods of order, who triumphed over the forces of chaos. This poem also commemorates the political ascendancy of Babylon. The poem was recited annually during the New Year's festival by Babylonian priests. Another important Babylonian literary genre, known as wisdom literature, responded to life's vicissitudes with

precepts that are sometimes simple, sometimes sophisticated. It proved eventually to influence the wisdom literature of the Hebrew Bible.

The best-known example of Mesopotamian literature is the *Epic of Gilgamesh*. Frequently translated and adapted by various western Asian peoples, *Gilgamesh* may be a Sumerian work dating to about 2500 B.C. Gilgamesh, king of Uruk, was probably a real historical personage, but the poem primarily concerns his fictionalized personal life, in particular his painful pilgrimage from arrogant youth to wise maturity. The main themes

---
Enuma Elish (eh-noo-MAH EH-lish)

are friendship, loss, and the inevitability of death. Much of the poem discusses Gilgamesh's close relationship with Enkidu, who is first his rival, then his friend, and finally his educator. Enkidu's untimely death makes Gilgamesh aware of his own mortality. Distraught by his friend's passing, Gilgamesh goes on a vain quest for immortality. The *Epic of Gilgamesh* contains stories that presage the later biblical Eden and Flood narratives; there is little doubt but that those narratives found their way from Mesopotamia to the Hebrew Bible. (See the box "Reading Sources: Heroism and Death in Mesopotamia.")

The Mesopotamians made advances in mathematics, astronomy, medicine, and engineering. The Sumerians had two systems of numbers: a decimal system (powers of ten) for administration and business and a sexagesimal system (powers of sixty) for weights and mathematical or astronomical calculations. Like the Babylonians, we still divide hours by sixty today. Furthermore, our modern system of numerical place-value notation—for example, the difference between 42 and 24—is derived, through Hindu-Arabic intermediaries, from the Babylonian system. The Babylonians were adept at arithmetic and could solve problems for which we would use algebra. A millennium before the Greek mathematician Pythagoras (who claimed to have studied the Mesopotamian tradition) proved the validity of the theorem that bears his name, they were familiar with the proposition that in a right triangle the square of the longest side is equal to the sum of the squares of the other two sides. In the first millennium B.C. the Babylonians developed a sophisticated mathematical astronomy (see page 44). As early as the seventeenth century B.C., they made systematic, if not always accurate, recordings of the movements of the planet Venus.

In medical matters they demonstrated considerable critical ability. Physicians made advances in the use of plant products for medicines and in very rudimentary surgery. The Babylonians had a simple pregnancy test of moderate accuracy, for example, and their surgeons were experienced at setting broken bones. When they became ill, however, most people in Mesopotamia set more store by magic and incantations than by surgery or herbal medicine.

Mesopotamian sculptors, particularly the Sumerians, were adept and sophisticated. They did not produce realistic representations of reality—that was not their purpose. Rather, they aimed at creating symbols of religious piety or political or military power. Sumerian statues tend to be stiff and solemn. The head and face are carved in detail, and the body is neglected, sometimes little more than a geometrical form.

The most common type of Mesopotamian sculpture is relief sculpture, in which figures or forms are projected from a flat surface. Steles (upright stone slabs or pillars), plaques, and cylinder seals (small, carved stone or metal cylinders rolled over wet clay to make a stamp, indicating ownership) are all found.

Egypt, to ca. 1100 B.C.

 ROM Babylon to the valley of the Nile River was about 750 miles by way of the caravan routes through Syria and Palestine—close enough to exchange goods and customs but far enough for a distinct Egyptian civilization to emerge. As in Sumer, civilization in Egypt arose in a river valley, but Egypt was much earlier than Mesopotamia in becoming a unified kingdom under one ruler. Moreover, ancient Egypt survived as a united and independent kingdom for over two thousand years (to be sure, with some periods of civil war and foreign rule). Egypt made great strides in a variety of areas of human achievement, from the arts to warfare. Western civilization borrowed much from Egypt, especially in technology and religion.

■ Geography as Destiny

Ancient Egypt is a product of the unique characteristics of the Nile River (see Map 1.2). Egypt was "the gift of the Nile," to use the well-known phrase of Herodotus, a Greek historian who visited Egypt in the fifth century B.C.

Yet most of present-day Egypt is desert. Only about 5 percent is habitable by humans, including a few oases, the Nile Delta, and the Nile Valley itself, which extends about 760 miles from Cairo to Egypt's modern southern border: Upper Egypt, a long and narrow valley never more than about 14 miles wide. North of Cairo, in Lower Egypt, the Nile branches out into the wide, low-lying delta before flowing into the Mediterranean Sea.

The fertility of the Nile River gave ancient Egypt a prosperous economy and optimistic culture. The river's annual floods, which took place during late summer and autumn, were generally benign. With less human effort than was required in Mesopotamia, the floodwaters could be used to irrigate most of the farmland in the Nile Valley. As a result, Egyptian agriculture was one of the wealthiest in the ancient world. Bread and beer were the national staples.

Egyptian culture celebrated the Nile's bounty. "Hail to Thee, O Nile, that gushest forth from the earth and comest

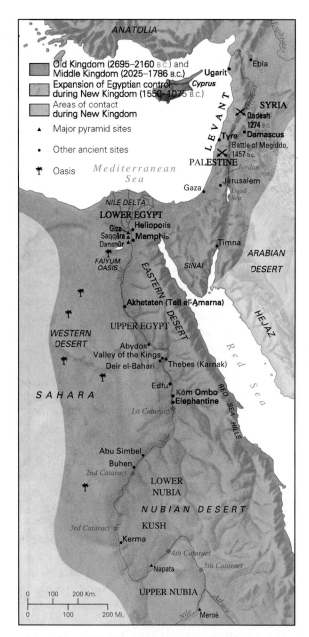

Map 1.2   Ancient Egypt and the Levant   The unique geography of the Nile Valley and its fertile soil left a stamp on ancient Egypt. Egypt enjoyed trade and cultural contact—and sometimes went to war— with nearby lands such as Nubia and the Levant.

to nourish Egypt!" So proclaims an ancient hymn that indicates the Egyptians' confidence in their natural environment. With its plentiful water and fertile land, Egypt suffered far less of the warfare that damaging floods and relative economic scarcity provoked in Mesopotamia.

Egyptian art and literature betray little of the despair over the unpredictability of the universe that developed in the harsher climatic conditions of Mesopotamia. The behavior of the Nile, furthermore, encouraged a static quality in Egyptian ideology. Change seemed undesirable. Even death appeared to be a minor event compared with the eternal regularity of the Nile, which may help explain the prominence in Egyptian religion of belief in the afterlife. In addition, the static outlook helped promote the idea of an absolute, all-powerful, and all-providing king—namely, pharaoh.

Early Egypt developed a distinctive civilization, with no major invasion for nearly 1,500 years after the beginning of the historical period around 3100 B.C. Just how isolated was early Egypt, however, and just how distinctive was its civilization? Debate has arisen in recent years about the relationship of Egypt with western Asia, Europe, and the rest of Africa. Before World War II, most Egyptologists tended to think of Egypt more as part of the Near East (that is, of the culture of western Asia) than as part of Africa. Many imagined that ancient Egyptians looked much like modern Europeans: part of "the Great White Race."[2] More recently, with the liberation after World War II of Europe's former African colonies and with the awakening of a growing interest in Africa by African Americans, some people have argued that Egypt was primarily African in character and that the ancient Egyptians were black.

The truth lies in between these two positions. Much of Egypt's earliest culture is African, as evidenced by both artifacts, such as Neolithic artwork and pottery, and ideas, such as the notion that the ruler represents the ancestors and guarantees the fertility of the soil. Yet in its late Neolithic era (ca. 3400–3050 B.C.), Egypt imported new styles and techniques in art, architecture, ceramics, and metallurgy from western Asia. As for the population, it seems from the fourth millennium B.C., if not earlier, to have consisted of Africans mixed with immigrants from western Asia. The Egyptians considered themselves a distinct ethnic and racial group, unlike their neighbors in Africa or elsewhere. Egyptians were generally darker skinned than the ancient peoples of Europe or western Asia but often lighter skinned than the peoples of Africa south of the Sahara. They included a considerable variety of skin colors and body types. The Egyptians of the southerly Upper Nile were more likely to have the dark skin and facial features characteristic of sub-Saharan Africans.

Egypt was in continual contact with other regions of Africa, particularly the neighboring areas of ancient Libya and Nubia (roughly, modern Sudan). The people of

Nubia, who were black Africans, borrowed from Egypt and were perhaps borrowed from in turn. Some scholars believe, for example, that the early Egyptian notion of monarchy originated in Nubia. In West Africa certain important institutions—including sacred royalty, the cult of the ram, and belief in the afterlife existence of a double of one's physical person—may possibly be of Egyptian origin.

■ Divine Kingship

Agriculture and settled village life emerged in Egypt around 5000 B.C. By 4000, villages had grown into towns, each controlling a strip of territory. About a thousand years later, around 3100 B.C., the Nile Valley had become one unified kingdom of Egypt, with a capital city perhaps at Memphis. We do not know precisely how this process unfolded. Egyptians writing after 3000 B.C. assumed that the Nile Valley had originally been home to two kingdoms roughly corresponding to Upper and Lower Egypt. Then, around 3100, Menes, king of Upper Egypt, is said to have conquered Lower Egypt and united the two into a single realm.

We do not know how much (if any) of this tradition is true. We *do* know that between about 5000 and 3100 B.C., Egyptian communities up and down the Nile Valley succeeded in clearing marshes and expanding the amount of land under cultivation, which in turn could support a larger population. By 3200 B.C., monumental architecture, writing, and kingship appeared. For several centuries Egyptians consolidated their institutions. Although few specifics are known about this Archaic Period (3200–2695 B.C.), it clearly laid the groundwork for the next era. Around 2700 B.C., a remarkable, distinctive, and relatively well-documented period of creativity began, the Third (2695–2600) and Fourth (2600–2500) Dynasties (that is, ruling families) of the Old Kingdom.

The history of third- and second-millennium B.C. Egypt is usually divided into three distinct eras of great prosperity: the Old Kingdom (2695–2160 B.C.), the Middle Kingdom (2025–1786 B.C.), and the New Kingdom (1550–1075 B.C.). Between the kingdoms, central authority broke down in the Intermediate Periods. Broadly speaking, the Old Kingdom was an era of spectacular creativity and originality, symbolized by the building of the Great Pyramids; the Middle Kingdom, an era of introspection and literary production; and the New Kingdom, an era in which Egypt's traditional isolation gave way to international diplomacy and expansion.

The early Egyptian government was the first government in recorded history to govern a large territory. Indeed, a chart of Egypt's power structure would be strictly hierarchical, resembling a pyramid, with a broad base of laborers and artisans supporting a small commanding elite. The occupant of the highest point of power was considered so important that for centuries Egyptians referred to the office rather than to the person, calling it "the Great House": in Egyptian, *per-aa,* or "pharaoh," as the ruler himself (or occasionally herself) was eventually called.

Egyptian kingship was sacred monarchy. In Mesopotamia, the king generally claimed to have been appointed by the gods. In Egypt, pharaoh was deemed to *be* a god. He was referred to as the "good god" in his lifetime and the "great god" after death. Considered the physical child of the sun-god Re, he was also equated with the sky-god Horus, and after dying he became Osiris, god of the underworld. Just as Egyptian myth recounted how the world was created when a god, sitting on a hill, made the waters recede, so pharaoh was thought to make the Nile rise and fall each year. (See the box "Reading Sources: Pharaoh the Divine and Invincible.")

A wall of language and ceremony separated kings from ordinary human beings. Egyptians did not speak "to" the king but rather "in his presence." He was outfitted with a variety of crowns, headdresses, and scepters. Pharaoh's exalted status was apparent on the occasion of a "glorious appearance" before his subjects, especially at the Sed festival or jubilee, a ceremony designed to rejuvenate the king's divine powers.

The most dramatic symbol of the king's divinity, however, was not a festival but a building—or, rather, a series of buildings—the pyramids. The ancients built thirty-five major and many smaller pyramids, of which the best known are the Great Pyramids of Giza—three gigantic, perfectly symmetrical limestone tombs constructed during the Fourth Dynasty. Nearly five thousand years after its construction, the pyramid of King Khufu (r. 2589–2566 B.C., better known by his Greek name, Cheops) is still the largest all-stone building in human history. Near the Great Pyramids stands the Great Sphinx, a human-headed lion carved out of a huge rock outcropping, perhaps representing Khufu's son, King Khafre (r. 2558–2532 B.C., Greek name, Chephren), for whom the second pyramid at Giza was built.

The pyramids were not just monuments to an ego, but temples where the king would continue to be worshiped and served in the afterlife. The structures served a political purpose as well. When the Great Pyramids were constructed, the kingdom of Egypt was still young and fragile. By carrying out an astonishingly large project focused on his person, the king made a statement of his

❧ READING SOURCES

Pharaoh the Divine and Invincible

Egypt's rulers presented themselves as god-kings. Excerpt (a), a selection from the grave stele of a high official of the Twelfth Dynasty of the Middle Kingdom (ca. 1850 B.C.), states pharaoh's divinity unhesitatingly. Excerpt (b), from an inscription about Amenhotep II (r. 1427–1400 B.C.), shows the emphasis that the warrior-pharaohs of the New Kingdom placed on their invincibility in combat—in sport as well as in battle.

(a)

Now, further, his majesty appeared as king as a goodly youth. When he had matured and completed eighteen years on his thighs in valor, he was one who knew every task of Montu [the war-god]; there was no one like him on the field of battle. He was one who knew horses: there was not his like in this numerous army. There was not one therein who could draw his bow. He could not be approached in running.

Worship King Nimaatre, living forever, within your bodies and associate with his majesty in your hearts. He is Perception which is in men's hearts, and his eyes search out every body. He is Re, by whose beams one sees. He is one who illumines the Two Lands more than the sun disc.

He is one who makes the land greener than does a high Nile, for he has filled the Two Lands with strength and life. The nostrils are chilled when he inclines toward rage, but when he is merciful, they will breathe the air. He gives food to them who are in his service, and he supplies them who tread his path.

(b)

Strong of arms, one who did not weary when he took the oar, he [Amenhotep II] rowed at the stern of his falcon-boat as the stroke [the rower who sets the pace] for two hundred men. When there was a pause, after they had attained half an iter's course [about two-thirds of a mile], they were weak, their bodies were limp, they could not draw a breath, while his majesty was (still) strong under his oar of twenty cubits [about 34 feet] in its length. He left off and moored his falcon-boat only after he had attained three iters [about 4 miles] in rowing without letting down in pulling. Faces were bright at the sight of him, when he did this.

Source: James B. Pritchard, ed., *Ancient Near Eastern Texts Relating to the Old Testament*, 3d ed., with Supplement (Princeton, N.J.: Princeton University Press, 1969), pp. 244, 431.

---

power: an eloquent, simple, and irrefutable statement. The sheer size of the Great Pyramids demonstrated the king's ability to organize a vast labor force. Indeed, it has plausibly been suggested that the encampment of workers at Giza represented the largest gathering of human beings to that date. Moreover, the pyramids and the rows of tombs surrounding them reinforced the hierarchical structure of Egyptian society, of which the king was the capstone. Only princes and select officials were given the privilege of erecting a tomb beside the royal pyramids, a privilege that Fourth Dynasty Egyptians viewed as a prerequisite to gaining access to eternal life. The principal

royal wives were permitted to be buried in small pyramids of their own.

In theory the king owned all the land, but in practice Egypt's economy was a mixture of private enterprise and centralized control. The king was thought to watch over Egypt carefully. In the Middle Kingdom, for example, he was represented as a good shepherd, appointed by the sun-god, Re, as one text says, "to keep alive the people and the folk, not sleeping by night as well as by day in seeking out every beneficial act, in looking for possibilities of usefulness." Even sleepless pharaohs needed help, however, and they delegated authority to a large group of

By the Middle Kingdom, even ordinary Egyptians believed they could enjoy immortality after death, as gods, as long as they could purchase for their graves funerary texts containing the relevant litanies. The texts emphasize ritual—incantations, magic spells, prayers—as the key to eternal life. Yet from time to time we find other texts, especially from the Middle Kingdom, that say that ritual is not enough: ethical behavior too is required. New Kingdom texts describe the details of a dead person's appearance before a divine court for judgment. Before forty-two judges of the underworld, the dead person declares his or her innocence of a variety of sins. A god then weighs the dead person's heart in the balance against a feather, symbol of *ma'at*, or truth. The sinless are admitted into eternal life in the kingdom of the blessed. The guilty, their heavy hearts devoured by a beast, suffer a second, final death.

Such absolute judgments were not found in daily life. Consider relations between the sexes. Egyptian women did not enjoy equal status with men, but they had a considerably greater measure of equality than women in other ancient societies, particularly in legal matters. As in Mesopotamia, so in Egypt a woman could buy or sell, bequeath or inherit, sue or testify in court, but a married Egyptian woman, unlike her eastern sisters, could do so without a male guardian's approval. A married woman in Egypt retained the status of complete legal independence. She could even own property without her husband's involvement. But how often did women exercise such privileges? Relatively little evidence of female property owners survives from Egypt. Although Egyptian women could work outside the home in a variety of enterprises, they were rarely managers. Women worked in agriculture and trade, in the textile and perfume industries, in dining halls, and in entertainment, and women served as priestesses of various kinds. Yet in Egypt, as elsewhere, women were expected to make the home the focus of their activities. So, although Egyptian women had more freedom outside the home than most ancient women, they exercised nothing like the freedom enjoyed by women in North America today.

■ Expansion, Reform, and Power Shifts, 1786–1075 B.C.

The humane attitudes of the Middle Kingdom were swept away after about 1700 B.C., when Semitic-speaking immigrants from Palestine—the Hyksos°, to employ the commonly used Greek term—conquered much of Egypt.

In many ways gentle conquerors, the Hyksos worshiped Egyptian gods, built and restored Egyptian temples, and intermarried with natives. As foreigners, however, the Hyksos were unpopular. Eventually a war launched from Upper Egypt, which had retained a loose independence, drove the Hyksos out.

The first restored Egyptian ruler of the New Kingdom was Ahmose° I (r. 1550–1525 B.C.). His proved to be a new Egypt indeed. The Hyksos had brought advanced military technology to Egypt, including the horse-drawn war chariot, new kinds of daggers and swords, and the composite bow. Made of laminated materials including wood, leather, and horn, the composite bow could hit a target at 600 yards. Having tasted foreign occupation, Egypt's new rulers determined to use such weapons in aggressive military campaigns abroad.

Warlike, expansionist, and marked by a daring attempt at religious reform, the New Kingdom's Eighteenth Dynasty (1540–1293 B.C.) has long held a special fascination for historians. One of the dynasty's memorable names is that of Queen Hatshepsut°. Widow of Thutmose II (r. 1491–1479 B.C.), Hatshepsut first served as regent for her young stepson and then assumed the kingship herself (r. 1479–1457 B.C.). Other Egyptian queens had exercised royal power before, but Hatshepsut was the first to call herself king. Some statues show her wearing a false beard, and some of her inscriptions refer to Hatshepsut as "he" not "she." Although Hatshepsut dispatched Egyptian armies to fight, her reign is best known for peaceful activities: at home, public works and temple rebuilding; abroad, a commercial expedition over the Red Sea to the "Land of Punt" (perhaps modern Somalia, in eastern Africa).

After her death, Hatshepsut was succeeded by her stepson, Thutmose° III (r. 1479–1425 B.C.). Late in his reign, he tried to erase his stepmother's memory by having Hatshepsut's statues destroyed and her name expunged from records—an attempt, perhaps, to cut off a claim to the throne by her supporters. A warrior-pharaoh, Thutmose III led his dynasty's armed expansion in western Asia and northern Africa. Thutmose won his greatest victory during his first campaign, at the Battle of Megiddo in Palestine in 1457 B.C. (see Map 1.2), where Egypt's triumph prevented the kingdom of Mitanni from expanding southward. Egypt now ruled an empire with territory in Nubia, Palestine, and Syria.

Empire brings power and power often causes conflict. So in imperial Egypt of the fourteenth century B.C., kings and priests struggled over authority. Consider the

Hyksos (HICK-sos)

Ahmose (AKH-mose) Hatshepsut (HAT-shep-soot)
Thutmose (THUT-mose)

Egyptian Queen   This elegant, red granite statue of the pharaoh Hatshepsut (r. 1479–1457 B.C.) is one of the few to depict her as a woman. She is usually shown as a man, complete with beard, to symbolize her royal power. Centuries later the proportions and carving techniques of Egyptian stone sculpture would influence the Greeks, although Greek artists chose less to copy the Egyptians than to try to outdo them (see the photo on page 82).   *(Brian Brake/Photo Researchers, Inc.)*

Amarna° reform, named for a major archaeological site at the modern town of Tell el-Amarna.

The Amarna reform was carried out by Thutmose III's great-great-grandson, King Amenhotep IV (r. 1352–1336 B.C.). Earlier, the god Amun-Re had become the chief deity of the New Kingdom. As supporters of the ideology of imperialism, his temple priests had been so richly rewarded with land and wealth that their power now rivaled pharaoh's own. Amenhotep IV's dramatic response was to forbid the worship of Amun-Re and replace him with the god Aten, the solar disk. Changing his own name to Akhenaten ("pleasing to Aten"), the king ordered the erasure of Amun-Re's name from monuments throughout Egypt. As a further step, Akhenaten created a new capital city in central Egypt at an uninhabited site at the desert's edge: Akhetaten (modern Amarna). The new town had a distinctive culture. Akhenaten's wife, Nefertiti, figures prominently in Amarna art, and she too may have played an important role in the reform.

The reform shifted power away from the priests and toward the king, but we need not doubt the reformers' sincerity. Contemporary literature suggests intense religious conviction in Aten as a benevolent god and one who nurtured not only Egypt but all countries. Although the Aten cult focuses on one god, only Akhenaten and his family were permitted to worship Aten directly; the rest of the Egyptian population was expected to worship the god through pharaoh.

Bold as the reform was, sustaining so dramatic a break with tradition proved impossible. After Akhenaten's death his son-in-law and successor, Tutankhaten (r. 1336–1327 B.C.) restored good relations with the priests of Amun-Re, which he signaled by changing his name to Tutankhamun. The Amun-Re cult was revived, the Aten cult was abolished, and the city of Akhetaten was abandoned. After Tutankhamun's death, the military exercised great influence over the remaining pharaohs of the Eighteenth Dynasty. Then, in 1291, a military officer founded a new dynasty as Ramesses° I (r. 1291–1289).

The Nineteenth (ca. 1291–1185 B.C.) and Twentieth (ca. 1185–1075) Dynasties are known as the Ramesside Era, from the most common name of the pharaohs. Though the era witnessed great warrior-pharaohs and builder-pharaohs, over time the kings lost power to the priests of Amun. Abroad, Egypt remained a formidable power, but it faced armed invasions, some of which required major efforts to repel (see page 34). In any case, many foreigners settled peacefully in the rich farmland of the Nile Delta, giving Egypt a more cosmopolitan character. Both their presence and the building of a great new city in the delta by the Ramesside kings led to a

---

Amarna (a-MAR-na)

Ramesses (RAM-zeez)

power shift within Egypt. When the Twentieth Dynasty ended in 1075, the New Kingdom ended with it, and regional conflict between the Nile Delta and Upper Egypt broke out.

■ Arts and Sciences in the New Kingdom

The Egyptians were superb builders, architects, and engineers. In addition to pyramids and irrigation works, they constructed monumental royal tombs, palaces, forts, and temples, and they erected looming obelisks. At their best, Egyptian architects designed buildings in harmony with the unique landscape—one of the reasons for the structures' lasting appeal. Their most original and enduring work was done in stone. Stone temples, for example, culminated in the imposing pillared structures of the New Kingdom. That period also saw the construction of rock-cut temples, the most famous of which is Ramesses II's (r. 1279–1213 B.C.) project at Abu Simbel (see Map 1.2). In front of the temples sit four colossal statues of Ramesses, also carved out of rock. Obelisks were slender, tapering pillars carved of a single piece of stone. Inscribed with figures and hieroglyphs, and usually erected in pairs in front of a temple, obelisks were meant to glorify the sun-god.

Throughout history, royal courts have excelled as patrons of the arts; the Egyptian court was one of the first and greatest. Egyptian craftsmen were master goldsmiths, glassmakers, and woodworkers. The major arts are well represented in tombs, which were decorated with rich, multicolored wall paintings, the first narrative depictions. Scenes of the gods, court ceremony, ordinary life, war, and recreation amid the crocodiles and hippopotamuses of the Nile Valley adorn subterranean walls. Like so much else in Egypt, painting had a religious purpose. Representations of living people were meant to perpetuate them in the afterlife.

Sculpture was another art form in which Egyptians excelled. Carved in stone, wood, or metal, Egyptian sculpture is a study in contrasts. The body posture is usually rigid and stiff, the musculature only sketchy; the face, in contrast, is often individualistic, the expression full of character and drawn from life. Statues represent kings and queens, gods and goddesses, husbands and wives, adults and children, officials, priests, scribes, animals. Mirroring broader cultural trends, statues of pharaohs underwent stylistic changes through the centuries. In the Old Kingdom, the royal expression was usually one of majesty and power, but in the Middle Kingdom, the king's face often appeared more human and weak. Statues of New Kingdom pharaohs often suggested imperial power, whereas Amarna sculptors emphasized introspective gazes and experimented with the grotesque. Eighteenth Dynasty sculpture often shows a striking interest in feminine beauty and grace.

Ancient Egyptian literature is notable for its variety. Religious subjects, historical and commemorative records, technical treatises in mathematics and medicine, and secular stories survive alongside business contracts and royal proclamations. A good example of Egyptian writing is the *Story of Sinuhe*, a Middle Kingdom prose tale. Sinuhe reveals both the charm of ancient Egyptian literature and its cultural chauvinism. (See the box "Global Encounters: Egyptian Attitudes Toward Foreigners.")

The vastness and variety of ancient Egyptian literature were made possible by the invention of a far more convenient medium for writing than the clunky clay tablets of Mesopotamia—papyrus. (See the feature "Information Technology: Papyrus" on pages 14–15.) Egyptian writing is best known for hieroglyphs. Elaborate and formal, hieroglyphs were generally used after the Archaic Period only for monuments and ornamentation. Two simplified scripts served for everyday use.

The people who built the pyramids had to be skilled at arithmetic and geometry. Egyptians were able to approximate pi (the ratio of the circumference of a circle to its diameter) and to solve equations containing one or two unknowns. Mathematical astronomy never reached the heights in Egypt that it reached in Babylon (see page 44), but the Egyptian calendar was a remarkable achievement. Based on observation of the star Sirius, the Egyptian calendar, with its 365-day year, approximates the solar calendar. Corrected to 365¼ days, it survives to this day as the calendar of Europe, the Americas, and much of the rest of the world.

Egyptian medical doctors were admired in antiquity and in demand abroad. They knew how to set a dislocated shoulder and used a full battery of splints, sutures, adhesive plasters, elementary disinfectants (from tree leaves), and burn treatments (fatty substances). A brilliant treatise, the Edwin Smith Papyrus, demonstrates their sophistication and rationalism. Dating from around 1750 B.C., the document claims to be a copy of an original from 2700 B.C. (the veracity of that claim is uncertain). Possibly a manual for the treatment of battlefield wounds, it is an ancient prototype of modern triage, dividing diseases into three categories: treatable, possibly treatable, and untreatable. In addition to signs of careful observation is tantalizing evidence that Egyptian doctors undertook postmortem dissection in order to understand the human body better.

Egyptian Attitudes Toward Foreigners

The story of Sinuhe is a well-known piece of Middle Kingdom prose literature. A court official, Sinuhe fled Egypt for Syria-Palestine after the assassination of the king. There he married the daughter of a tribal chief and became a successful chief himself. In his old age he received permission to return home. The tale demonstrates Egyptian curiosity about Palestine and Syria, at the same time revealing Egyptian cultural snobbery toward what another Egyptian text calls "the miserable Asiatic."

This decree of the King: . . . Come back to Egypt! See the residence in which you lived! Kiss the ground at the great portals, mingle with the courtiers! For to-day you have begun to age. You have lost a man's strength. Think of the day of burial, the passing into reveredness.

A night is made for you with ointments and wrappings from the hand of Tait [goddess of weaving]. A funeral procession is made for you on the day of burial; the mummy case is of gold, its head of lapis luzuli. . . . You shall not die abroad! Nor shall Asiatics inter you. You shall not be wrapped in the skin of a ram to serve as your coffin. Too long a roaming of the earth! Think of your corpse, come back! . . .

Copy of the reply to this decree:

The servant of the Palace, Sinuhe, says: In very good peace! . . . May the fear of you resound in lowlands and highlands, for you have subdued all that the sun encircles! . . .

Re [the sun-god] has set the fear of you throughout the land, the dread of you in every foreign country. Whether I am at the residence, whether I am in this place, it is you who cover this horizon. The sun rises at your pleasure. The water in the river is drunk when you wish. The air of heaven is breathed at your bidding. . . . This servant has been sent for! Your Majesty will do as he wishes! One lives by the breath which you give.

[Sinuhe returns to Egypt and is brought into the king's presence.]

Then the royal daughters were brought in, and his majesty said to the queen: "Here is Sinuhe, come as an Asiatic, a product of nomads!" She uttered a very great cry, and the royal daughters shrieked all together. They said to his majesty: "Is it really he, O kings, our lord?" Said his majesty: "It is really he!" . . .

His majesty said: "He shall not fear, he shall not dread! He shall be a Companion among the nobles. He shall be among the courtiers. Proceed to the robing-room to wait on him!"

I left the audience-hall, the royal daughters giving me their hands. We went through the great portals, and I was put in the house of a prince. In it were luxuries: a bathroom and mirrors. . . . Every servant was at his task. Years were removed from my body. I was shaved; my hair was combed. Thus was my squalor returned to the foreign land, my dress to the Sand-farers. I was clothed in fine linen; I was anointed with fine oil. I slept on a bed. I had returned the sand to those who dwell in it, the tree-oil to those who grease themselves with it.

Source: Miriam Lichtheim, *Ancient Egyptian Literature, Volume 1: The Old and Middle Kingdoms* (Berkeley: University of California Press, 1973), pp. 229–233.

WIDENING HORIZONS: THE LEVANT AND ANATOLIA, 2500–1150 B.C.

GYPT and Mesopotamia tend to capture our attention, but other early, nearby civilizations are, if less important, also significant contributors to the West. Not only were they the cradle of Western languages and writing systems, but they took part in the first international system of states, a forerunner of later international relations between the West and its neighbors. Let us look in particular at the city-states of the Levant°—that is, the geographic region known today as Syria and Palestine or Israel—and at a kingdom in Anatolia, today's Turkey.

Levant (le-VANT)

Map 1.3   The International System, ca. 1500–1250 B.C.   This era of competing kingdoms and city-states witnessed considerable war, especially between Egypt and the Hittites for control of Syria and Palestine. Yet it was also a period of international trade, diplomacy, and, from 1450 to 1300 B.C., peace.

■ The City-States of Syria-Palestine, ca. 2500–1200 B.C.

The discovery in 1974 of a huge cuneiform archive at Ebla° (modern Tell Mardikh) in northern Syria revolutionized our knowledge of one such city-state in the mid-third millennium B.C. Another Levantine city-state, Ugarit° (modern Ras Shamra), a cosmopolitan port, flourished in the second millennium B.C.

A prosperous city, Ebla was known for commerce and artisanry as well as scholarship. Its extensive cuneiform archives include the world's earliest known dictionaries. Sometime between 2500 and 2300 B.C., Ebla ruled a large kingdom, extending over much of Syria, and possibly containing as many as 250,000 people, of whom perhaps 30,000 lived in the city (see Map 1.3). Ebla's government fostered trade by negotiating commercial treaties and arranging dynastic marriages. The treaty between Ebla and Ashur, a city about 435 miles to the east, is the earliest known agreement between two states.

When diplomacy failed, Ebla resorted to war, with great success. Ebla's most notable conquest was Mari, a commercial competitor 300 miles downstream on the Euphrates.

Ebla was ruled by an oligarchy (a small, elite group) headed by fourteen regional governors who were probably also clan elders. The king, a sort of first among equals, was chosen by election rather than inheritance; his power was limited by the oligarchic council. Eblaites seem to have conceived of the state as a large family, the "children of Ebla." The queen and queen mother had significant government authority. The queen had her own properties, administered by officials who answered to her. If she was still alive, the queen mother, officially addressed as "the honored mother of the king," had considerable say in the succession.

Ebla fell to the Amorites around 2000 B.C. It remained a wealthy city, though much diminished in power. To find a much more vibrant city in Syria after 2000 B.C., we need only look at the coast and the city of Ugarit (see Map 1.3). Ugarit was a thriving Mediterranean port, especially around 1400–1200 B.C. Its cosmopolitanism made Ugarit

---

Ebla (EH-bla)   **Ugarit** (OO-ga-rit)

A Hittite Warrior This 6½-foot-tall figure was carved on the wall of an entry gate to the city of Hattusas, the Hittite capital, during the New Kingdom Period (1380–1180 B.C.). Fierce-looking, vigorous, and outfitted with battle ax, sword, kilt, and possibly mail shirt, he is designed to frighten away both human and supernatural enemies.   *(Ankara National Museum)*

is called Canaanite (from the Hebrew Bible, which calls Palestine "the land of Canaan"). The merchants of Ugarit, however, were often foreigners, and the bazaars echoed with a multitude of languages.

Ugarit played an important role in the spread of one of history's most important writing systems: the alphabet. Unlike the pictographic or syllabic systems of Mesopotamia, Egypt, and China, each sign in an alphabet stands for one and only one sound. In the 1300s B.C., scribes in Ugarit developed an alphabet. It was not the first alphabet, however. In Egypt, in the desert west of the Nile, limestone inscriptions have recently been found in a Semitic script with Egyptian influences. Dated to about 1900–1800 B.C., during the Middle Kingdom, the writing is now recognized as the earliest known example of an alphabet.

We do not know whether that alphabet was invented by Egyptians or by speakers of a Semitic language who were visiting Egypt. Nor do we know if that alphabet influenced Ugarit. What is clear is that Ugaritic scribes invented thirty cuneiform signs as an alphabet to write their Semitic language. Later adapted by the Phoenicians and, through them, the Greeks, the Ugaritic alphabet is the source of the Roman alphabet, used today by English and many other languages around the world.

■ The Hittites, 1650–1180 B.C.

Almost all the peoples of western Asia and Egypt whom we have discussed so far spoke a language belonging to the large Afro-Asiatic language family. But none of these languages survived antiquity in Europe. Instead, virtually every modern European language—as well as the dominant languages of Iran and India—are descendants of the long-lost proto–Indo-European language. These languages, from English and Russian to Iranian and Hindi, are said to belong to the Indo-European language family.

Indo-European speakers probably originated between 4500 and 2500 B.C. in southern Russia, in the region of the Dnieper and Volga Rivers. A warlike, mobile people, they emigrated east and west. The first speakers of an Indo-European language to establish a civilization in western Asia were the Hittites, who came to Anatolia some time before 1800 B.C. The Hittites were masters of the horse, which their warriors rode into battle. They ruled Anatolia from their city of Hattusas (modern Boghazköy). Rich in minerals and farmland, Anatolia provided a solid foundation for empire.

Hittite history is divided into several periods. The Old Kingdom (ca. 1650–1450 B.C.) was marked by the

distinctive among western Asian city-states. As a trading center it linked ships coming from the eastern Mediterranean island of Cyprus or the Anatolian ports with land caravans heading to Babylonia. The native inhabitants of Ugarit spoke a Semitic language. Their culture and that of large numbers of people in southern Syria and Palestine

Prayers of a Hittite Queen

Puduhepa, wife of Hittite king Hattusilis III (r. 1278–1250 B.C.), played an important role in state religious ritual and propaganda. The following selections from her recorded prayers show Puduhepa's official devotion to her royal husband as well as a belief, common in ancient religion, that women had a special closeness to the gods.

Prayer to the Sun-Goddess Herself

To the Sun-goddess of Arinna, my lady, the mistress of the Hatti lands, the queen of heaven and earth. . . . I, Puduhepa, am a servant of thine from of old, a heifer from thy stable, a foundation stone upon which thou canst rest. Thou, my lady, rearedst me and Hattusilis, thy servant, to whom thou espousedst me, was closely associated with the Storm-god of Nerik, thy beloved son. The place in which thou, Sun-goddess of Arinna, my lady, didst establish us was the residence of the Storm-god of Nerik, thy beloved son. How the earlier kings had neglected it, that thou knowest, Sun-goddess of Arinna, my lady. The earlier kings let fall into ruins even those countries which thou, Sun-goddess of Arinna, my lady, hadst given them. . . .

Sun-goddess of Arinna, my lady, yield to me, hearken to me! Among men there is a saying: "To a woman in travail the god yields her wish." Since I, Puduhepa, am a woman in travail and since I have devoted myself to thy son, yield to me, Sun-goddess of Arinna, my lady! Grant to me what I ask. Grant life to Hattusilis, thy servant [who was ill]! Through the Good-women and the Mother-goddess long and enduring years and days shall be given to him. Since thou, an exalted deity, holdest a place set apart from the gods, all the gods are subservient to thee, and no one appeals to thee in vain. In the assembly of the gods request thou the life of Hattusilis! May thy request be received with favor! Because thou, Sun-goddess of Arinna, my lady, hast shown favor to me and because the good of the land of its realm is close to thy heart, thou shalt enjoy the reverent worship of my family.

Prayer to Lelwanis [probably Ishtar]

. . . Hattusilis, that servant of thine, who is ill. In the presence of Sum. . . , the physician, they spoke charms over him. . . . If Hattusilis is accursed, and if Hattusilis, my husband, has become hateful in the eyes of you, the gods; or if anyone of the gods above or below has taken offence at him; or if anyone has made an offering to the gods to bring evil upon Hattusilis—accept not those evil words, O goddess, my lady! Let evil not touch Hattusilis, thy servant! O gods, prefer not our adversaries, our enviers, . . . to us!

Prayer to the Storm-God of Zippalanda

. . . This word, which I, Puduhepa, thy handmaid, have spoken in prayer, announce and relay thou to thy parents, Storm-god of Zippalanda, my lord! O god, my lord, yield to this word of mine! Because as a woman in travail I have in my own person made reparation to the god, my lord, intercede for me, god, my lord, with the Storm-god, thy father, and the Sun-goddess of Arinna, thy mother! Hattusilis, thy servant, wore himself out in the god's service; he gave himself body and soul to the restoration of Nerik, the beloved city of the god, my lord. So be thou, O god, my lord, favorably inclined toward Hattusilis, thy servant!

Adapted from James B. Pritchard, ed. *Ancient Near Eastern Texts Relating to the Old Testament*, 3d ed., with Supplement (Princeton, N.J.: Princeton University Press, 1969), pp. 393–394.

conquest and consolidation of Anatolia. The Middle Kingdom (ca. 1450–1380 B.C.) was a period of retrenchment and loss of territory. During the New Kingdom (ca. 1380–1180 B.C.) the Hittites first played an active role in international politics and then suffered a collapse in power. The Hittite empire reached its zenith in the New Kingdom, when it extended into Syria and northern Mesopotamia (see Map 1.3). Afterward came the Neo-Hittite era (ca. 1180–700 B.C.), when the Hittite empire had disintegrated into small successor states.

Old Kingdom Hittites could be characterized as a warrior society. A strong and boisterous nobility cultivated military virtues and kept the king weak. Ironically, queens were sometimes forceful and even enjoyed a measure of equality. The monarch was neither a god nor god's representative but rather first among equals. He was supported by an armed and mounted nobility who, in return for land, supplied him with troops and horses. The rising power of the nobility spelled trouble for central authority in the sixteenth century B.C., when conspiracy, feud, and assassination came close to destroying the Hittite kingdom. The powerful King Telepinu finally established himself and his family securely on the throne around 1500 B.C. In the Hittite New Kingdom the balance of power swung further in favor of the king, who was now addressed as "my Sun" during his lifetime and was deified after death.

Hittite queens and queen mothers had strong and independent positions, as at Ebla. Puduhepa°, wife of King Hattusilis° III (r. 1278–1250 B.C.), played a memorable role in state affairs. Puduhepa seems to have been the prime mover in the movement that made the Hurrian sun-goddess of Arinna (a shrine near Hattusas) the chief deity of the Hittite state. (See the box "Reading Sources: Prayers of a Hittite Queen.") Hattusilis publicly declared that he would not have rebelled against the previous king had Puduhepa not first dreamed of divine support for the coup.

Although the Hittites borrowed much of their religion from earlier civilizations, they developed political thought whose sophistication is quite original. Earlier peoples had kept lists and chronicles; Hittite annals are livelier, better argued, and more conscious of cause and effect. The royal annals of King Hattusilis III, for example, read in parts like a lawsuit, carefully pleading a justification of the king's actions. Hattusilis excused his usurpation of the throne by stating that the former king had unjustly stripped him of territory; furthermore, Hattusilis rebelled openly. Hittite treaties with subordinate states similarly argue their cases: each begins with an introduction providing historical background and justifying the relationship sworn to in the body of the text.

■ The First International System and Its Collapse, ca. 1500–1150 B.C.

The Hittites and New Kingdom Egyptians exercised great military power, yet what is even more remarkable about these states and others is their ability to make and

maintain peace. The years from about 1450 to about 1300 B.C. marked a period of peace among the great powers from Egypt to Anatolia and Mesopotamia— what historians call the first international system. The arts of peace are illustrated in surviving treaties and letters between monarchs, the most important of which comes from Amarna. The Amarna Archives (mid-fourteenth century), written in Akkadian cuneiform, illustrate formal communication among states. Rulers of great powers addressed each other as "brother," while Canaanite princes called pharaoh "my lord and my Sun-god" and assured him that they were "thy servant and the dirt on which thou dost tread." The texts reveal a system of gift exchange and commerce, politeness and formality, alliance and dynastic marriage, subjects and governors, rebels and garrisons. Two factors seem to have supported peace. First, shared values among kings created mutual respect and a willingness to compromise. Second, although no such concept as our balance of power existed then, a rough equality of power did prevail. Since no great power was likely to defeat the others, the parties avoided all-out war, preferring instead to compete by jockeying for allies among the small border states of Syria and Palestine.

But peace was not to last. By the late fourteenth century, Egypt and the Hittites were back at war. At the Battle of Qadesh in northern Syria in 1274 B.C., twenty thousand Egyptian troops faced seventeen thousand Hittites. Predictably, neither of the two evenly matched powers managed to conquer the other. Instead, they used resources that would soon be dearly needed for defense.

Between about 1250 and 1150 B.C., the international system came to a crashing end. From Mesopotamia to Greece, from Anatolia to Egypt, one state after another collapsed between about 1250 and 1150 B.C. Surviving evidence is fragmentary, but it suggests that both foreign and domestic problems led to the collapse. Raiders and invaders beset the eastern Mediterranean in this period. Called "Sea Peoples" by the Egyptians, they attacked both on land and at sea. We do not know precisely who they were. In addition, some evidence of regional famine and climatic change indicates that natural causes may have led to disruption and rebellion.

Whatever the cause, what followed would prove to be a different world. Yet the end of the international system did not result in the disappearance of ancient cultures. Although new peoples appeared and old peoples changed, both continued to borrow from the cultures that had flowered before 1250 B.C.

Puduhepa (pu-du-HE-pa)   **Hattusilis** (hat-tu-SIL-is)

Summary

THIS chapter covers not just the history of the ancestors of Western civilization but the very origins of civilization itself. Yet that milestone is only a small part of the vast era that ranges from the first hominids to the heirs of the great kingdoms of Egypt and western Asia after the collapse of the thirteenth century B.C. The achievements of this period may make it the most creative epoch in human history. First, probably beginning before 70,000 B.C., came the invention of human culture—that is, the development of communications to the degree that humans could cooperate to exploit their natural environment by means of technology and social organization. Next came the move from a food-collecting to a food-producing economy. After a series of independent discoveries beginning in the Fertile Crescent region of western Asia shortly after 10,000 B.C., food production spread to many places around the globe by 5000 B.C.

Over the thousands of years following the emergence of agriculture, we can trace the development of ever more complex organizations of human beings and ever increasing control of the natural environment, culminating in the emergence of civilization in Egypt and Mesopotamia after 3500 B.C. Elaborate though such large Neolithic towns as Çatal Hüyük or Jericho were, civilization marked a major step forward in sophistication. Civilization brought cities commanding the manpower, technology, and degree of labor specialization needed to build a monumental urban architecture and reshape the agricultural hinterland; civilization brought governments and armies controlling wide areas; civilization brought, finally, writing. By 3000 B.C. civilization was present in the Levant as well. Through trade networks, civilization affected a vast hinterland, including Europe. European societies, especially in southeastern Europe, were reshaped by trade with more advanced neighbors. European civilization emerged in the Aegean around 2000 B.C.

Mesopotamia and Egypt are the first and best remembered of the early civilizations. Their extraordinary achievements, later built on by the Greeks and Hebrews, laid the foundation for important Western concepts in government, religion, technology, art, and literature. It is hard to avoid the appearance of exaggeration when listing the inventions of Mesopotamia and Egypt, among them the first cities, kingdoms, and multi-ethnic empires; the first monumental architecture; the first advances in agriculture sweeping enough to support a large urban population; the first writing, and with it the first written attempts to explore the most profound subjects of life and death.

The years from 2000 to 1000 B.C. were a period of competition, exchange, and warfare among the various civilizations of the eastern Mediterranean region. They were also an era of further advance in literature and science. Then, the great kingdoms of the period collapsed, one after another, around 1250 to 1150 B.C.

It was not long before new states arose in Egypt and western Asia to replace those destroyed in the era of the Sea Peoples. In the first half of the first millennium B.C., new regions joined southern Mesopotamia, Egypt, the Levant, and Anatolia in making lasting contributions to the West: among them, Assyria (northern Mesopotamia), Persia, ancient Israel, and Greece. We turn to those regions in the next chapter.

■ Notes

1. James B. Pritchard, ed., *Ancient Near Eastern Texts Relating to the Old Testament*, 3d ed. (Princeton, N.J.: Princeton University Press, 1969), p. 107.
2. James H. Breasted, *The Conquest of Civilization* (New York: Harper & Bros., 1926), p. 112. Quoted in Brian Tierney, Donald Kagan, and L. Pearce Williams, eds., *Great Issues in Western Civilization from Ancient Egypt Through Louis XIV* (New York: McGraw-Hill, 1992), pp. 68–69.

■ Suggested Reading

Cunliffe, Barry, ed. *The Oxford Illustrated Prehistory of Europe.* 1994. An introduction to European material culture from the Paleolithic era to the early medieval period, with chapters written by a dozen archaeologists. Especially valuable for its treatment of the early period and for its integration of Greco-Roman civilization and the wider continental context.

Gurney, O. R. *The Hittites.* 3d ed. 1975. A sound introductory survey that pays close attention to the sources of evidence.

Hallo, William W., and William Kelly Simpson. *The Ancient Near East. A History.* 2d ed. 1998. A reliable and relatively up-to-date scholarly survey from the Paleolithic Age to the fourth century B.C., covering western Asia and Egypt.

Johanson, D. C. and Edgar B. *From Lucy to Language.* 1996. Excellent and relatively up-to-date introduction to human evolution, with outstanding photographs.

Murnane, William J. *The Penguin Guide to Ancient Egypt.* 1983. Both a well-illustrated travel guide and a scholarly, basic introduction.

Oates, Joan. *Babylon.* Rev. ed. 1986. A well-illustrated historical and archaeological introduction, from Sargon of Agade to the Greeks.

 For a searchable list of additional readings for this chapter, go to http://college.hmco.com.

The Iceman
and His World

On September 19, 1991, a German couple went hiking in the Italian Alps. At 10,530 feet above sea level, they thought they had left civilization and its problems behind until they stumbled on an unexpected sight: the body of a dead man lying in the melting ice. Nor was that their only surprise. At first they thought the corpse was the victim of a recent accident. When the authorities arrived, however, the body was discovered to be very old. A helicopter was ordered, and the body was brought to a research institute in Innsbruck, Austria. When the investigators were through, it was clear that the hikers had chanced upon one of the most remarkable archaeological discoveries of the century.*

He was 5,300 years old. The Iceman—as the corpse has become known—is a natural mummy, preserved under the snow: the oldest known remains of human flesh. If that weren't striking enough, consider the clothes and extensive gear that survived with him—they are a window into the European world of about 3200 B.C. The most difficult and most fascinating question is this: Who was the Iceman?

His body offers an introduction. Genetic testing shows that he was a European, a close relative of modern northern and alpine Europeans. Other tests indicate a difficult life. His growth was arrested by periods of illness, grave hunger, or metal poisoning. His teeth are badly worn, the result perhaps of chewing dried meat or, alternatively, of working leather. He may have undergone a kind of acupuncture; at any rate, he is tattooed, which in some cultures is a medical treatment rather than a form of decoration. He has several broken ribs, which indicates either damage under the ice, mishandling when the body was discovered, or an ancient accident or fight.

To get to know the Iceman better, however, we must go beyond his body to the artifacts found with it, which provide tantalizing clues to his social status. Look at the artist's drawing. A woven grass or reed cape lies over the Iceman's deerskin coat, which in turn covers a leather loincloth and garter, held in place by a leather belt. A fur hat, skin leggings, and calfskin shoes, stuffed with grass for insulation, complete his wardrobe. The Iceman and his contemporaries knew how to dress for the cold weather of the mountains.

The Iceman carries a rich tool kit. Notice his copper ax and 6-foot-long bow. A quiver (arrow case), two birch bark containers, a waist pouch, and—probably part of a backpack—a frame hang from his body. Among his items of equipment are flint tools (including a knife, a re-touching tool, and a scraper); a piece of net; two birch-fungus-like "polypores" threaded on a leather thong, probably used as a natural antibiotic; and fourteen arrows, all, oddly, broken. In short, it appears that the Iceman was equipped with a state-of-the-art mountain survival kit of his day.

What, however, was he doing on the mountain when he died? Scholars disagree. They all acknowledge that the Iceman probably reached the spot where he died from the south, since it is only from there—northern Italy—that the site was accessible in antiquity. What scholars differ about is the Iceman's occupation. Guesses range from a trader to hunter to metal prospector to shaman (a priest who uses magic).

Some argue that the Iceman was a refugee. His weapons point to violence, and so may his broken ribs. Perhaps he had retreated to the mountains from a fight. If so, it is not clear why he brought broken arrows or how he had time to pack his goods so carefully before fleeing; nor could it have been a small feat to climb mountains with broken ribs.

Perhaps the most convincing theory is that the Iceman was a shepherd. Since ancient times it has been

---

* The best brief introduction to the Iceman is Lawrence Barfield's "The Iceman Reviewed," *Antiquity* 68 (1994): 10–26, on which this discussion relies. See also Konrad Spindler, *The Man in the Ice* (New York: Harmony Books, 1994).

common for shepherds to move their flocks during the summer from the lowlands to greener pastures in the mountains, a pattern of migration known as *transhumance*. It has been suggested that the Iceman brought broken arrows with him to repair during his spare time. Perhaps he encountered a sudden snowstorm and died of exposure, perhaps after having broken his ribs in an accident.

If he was a shepherd, then the Iceman offers a rare illustration of the life of the kind of person who is not represented in most archaelogical sites: a person at the margins of society. Tombs usually yield the skeletons and grave goods of the elite, especially the urban elite: they rarely illustrate the lives of ordinary countryfolk. The Iceman's equipment suggests that he was not poor, but only his copper ax might indicate unusual status—and it is not a decisive index. Were the copper ax a show item, it might imply high status, but observe the Iceman's ax. It was set in a wooden handle and bound with leather, leaving little of the metal visible; it is, in short, a utensil rather than an ornament.

The copper ax is also the key to the Iceman's culture and its relationship with the wider world. Similar axes have been found in northern Italian tombs in Remedello, about 240 miles south of the Alps. Before the discovery of the Iceman, archaeologists believed that Italians learned the metalwork technology needed for such an ax from Anatolia, where similar pieces of metalwork are dated to approximately 2700–2400 B.C. Hence, the Remedello culture was usually also dated about 2700–2400 B.C. The discovery of the Iceman means that Remedello must be backdated by about five hundred years. It is clear, then, that by about 3200 B.C. northern Italians not only borrowed from the more advanced eastern Mediterranean areas but also created their own original technology and culture. So a small object (a copper ax), placed within a larger body of evidence (Italian and Anatolian metalwork), permits broad generalization about the interaction and independence of ancient cultures.

 For additional information on this topic, go to http://college.hmco.com.

Artist's Rendition of the Ice Man   *(New York Times Photo Sales)*

CHAPTER 2

The Sword, the Book, and the Myths: Western Asia and Early Greece

T HE bull in brick relief shown on the left symbolizes power even today, twenty-six hundred years after it was molded and glazed. About 4 feet high, this bull was one of several dozen figures of bulls and dragons that decorated the massive Ishtar Gate, which led through the inner town wall of Babylon° into the palace. The gate represents only a small part of a magnificent reconstruction of the city by the Neo-Babylonian° kings who ruled western Asia around 600–539 B.C.

Imagine the king's surprise had he known that under his nose an obscure prophet—we know him only as "Second Isaiah°"—was preaching a bold message to his compatriots, a conquered people living in exile in Babylon. Isaiah reminded them that Yahweh°, their god, was a god of justice and mercy—the one and only true god of the entire world—and that Yahweh had chosen the king of mountainous, backward Persia to conquer western Asia and redeem Yahweh's people. The Neo-Babylonian king might have laughed at the idea. Yet the Persians under Cyrus the Great conquered Babylon in 539 B.C. and proclaimed the freedom of Yahweh's people—the Jews—to return to Palestine and re-establish the Temple to their god in the city of Jerusalem°. They did so, and around this time they wrote down their religious and historical traditions in large sections of what would become the Hebrew Bible, or Old Testament.

Also in the sixth century B.C., Peisistratus°, the ambitious ruler of Athens, a tiny city-state a thousand miles northwest of Babylon, sponsored a literary project to preserve the religious and historical traditions of his people. The literary works whose texts were standardized under his patronage are the *Iliad* and *Odyssey*, the epic poems of

Babylon (BAB-eh-lon)   **Neo-Babylonian** (NEE-oh bab-eh-LONE-ee-an)
Isaiah (eye-ZAY-ah)   **Yahweh** (YAH-way)   **Jerusalem** (juh-ROO-suh-lem)
Peisistratus (pie-SIS-tra-tus)

Bull from Ishtar Gate, Babylon.   (Staatliche Museen zu Berlin, Museum für Vor- und Frühgeschichte/Bildarchiv Preussischer Kulturbesitz. Photo: Reinhard Saczewski)

Assyrians, Neo-Babylonians, and Persians, ca. 1200–330 B.C.

Israel, ca. 1500–400 B.C.

Early Greece, to ca. 725 B.C.

Homer, who had composed them about two centuries before.

Both the Hebrew Bible and the Homeric poems are deeply religious in outlook, but there the similarities end. The Hebrew Bible is monotheistic and focuses on the individual's subordination to God. Homer is polytheistic and glorifies the hero, who, though doomed to fail, aspires to godlike achievement. For most scholars the Bible and Homer represent two poles of Western civilization: the sacred and the worldly, the reverent and the heroic, holy writ and poetic craftsmanship.

Israel and Greece are, along with Rome, the founders of the West. Israel's holy book, the Hebrew Bible, founded the Western religious tradition. Greece, which founded the Western tradition of philosophy and politics, had its first great literary flowering in the works of Homer, whose epic poems are based on Greek myths.

The Neo-Babylonians, along with the other great empires of the era, the Assyrians and Persians, are ancestors of the West. Conquerors, they came to power by the sword, but once in power they spread civilization, serving as conduits through which the achievements of Mesopotamia were transmitted. They built great empires whose institutions were eventually transformed into notions of mass citizenship under law and justice in a universal empire by the third founder of the West, Rome.

The first half of the first millennium B.C., therefore, left a divergent legacy to the West. On the one hand, new empires arose that were more systematically organized, farther-flung, and more diverse ethnically than those created before. On the other hand, prophets, philosophers, and poets looked in new and deeper ways into the human soul.

In this chapter we look at the deeply influential developments in empire, religion, and thought forged in the first half of the first millennium B.C. At the same time, we consider the peaceful expansion in this era, through trade and colonization, particularly under the Phoenicians. Finally, we examine the material innovation that has earned the period the title "Iron Age."

QUESTIONS TO CONSIDER

- What made the first-millennium B.C. empires of the Assyrians, Neo-Babylonians, and Persians so much more effective than earlier empires?

- How did monotheism develop in ancient Israel, and what is its legacy today?

- What are the Homeric poems, and what light do they shed on the culture of early Greece?

TERMS TO KNOW

Assyrians	Israel
Neo-Babylonians	Torah
Persian Empire	covenant
monotheism	Minoans
Zoroastrianism	Mycenaeans
Phoenicians	Homer

ASSYRIANS, NEO-BABYLONIANS, AND PERSIANS, CA. 1200–330 B.C.

 ANCESTORS of the West, three great multiethnic empires emerged between the 800s and 500s B.C. Ruthless soldiers, brutal conquerors, and innovative administrators, the Assyrians established an empire in western Asia and Egypt during the ninth through seventh centuries B.C. They were followed in turn by a Neo-Babylonian empire in the late seventh and sixth centuries. However, neither of these was as successful or as durable as the empire of the Persians (ca. 550–330 B.C.). At its height the Persian Empire stretched from central Asia and northwest India in the east to Macedonia and Libya in the west (see Map 2.1). Persia's vast empire was loosely governed by a Persian ruling elite and its native helpers. Unlike the iron-fisted

Assyrians, the Persians were relatively tolerant and respectful of their subjects' customs. Many of Persia's kings were followers of Zoroastrianism, an ethical and forceful religion. A period of relative peace in most of Persia's domains from the 530s to the 330s B.C. fostered widespread economic prosperity.

Borrowing the administrative methods of the Assyrians and Medes° and the long-established officialdom of Babylon, the Persians built a new and durable imperial government. Their official art stressed the unity of the peoples of the empire under Persian leadership. Persian rule represented the greatest success yet in implementing the notions of universal kingship that dated back to Sargon of Agade (r. 2371–2316 B.C.; see page 16). In turn, Persia transmitted the trappings of absolute kingship to later ambitious rulers, from Alexander the Great to the caesars of Rome and from the Byzantine emperors to the Muslim caliphs.

■ Assyrians and Neo-Babylonians

The Assyrians, whose homeland was in what is today northern Iraq, spoke a Semitic language. For most of the second millennium B.C., they were a military and commercial power. Around 1200 B.C., the Assyrians' state collapsed during that era of international crisis (see page 34), but they held on to a small homeland of about 5,000 square miles, roughly the size of Connecticut. The toughened survivors emerged with an aggressive, expansionist ideology.

Assyria's greatest successes came in the eighth and seventh centuries. One by one, states large and small fell—Babylonia, Syria, the kingdom of Israel, Cilicia in southern Anatolia, even Egypt (though Assyrian rule there lasted only a generation). Assyria became the first state to rule the two great river valleys of the ancient Near East, the Nile and the Tigris-Euphrates (see Map 2.1).

The Assyrians were warriors. Ashur, their main deity, was a war-god. Theirs was an ideology of power, conquest, and control (see the box "Reading Sources: The Banquet of Ashurnasirpal II"). The key to Assyria's success was its army—from 100,000 to 200,000 men strong—which made an unforgettable impression on observers and foes. The Israelite prophet Isaiah of Jerusalem ("First Isaiah") said of Assyrian soldiers: "[Their] arrows are sharpened, and all their bows bent, their horses' hoofs are like flint, their chariot wheels like the whirlwind. Their growling is like that of a lion" (Isaiah 5:28–29). He might have added that Assyrian spearmen,

Medes (meedz)

CHRONOLOGY	
2000 B.C.	First Minoan palaces on Crete
1800–1550 B.C.	Height of Minoan civilization
1626 B.C.	Eruption of Thera volcano
1550 B.C.	Mycenaeans conquer Crete
1375 B.C.	Palace at Knossos destroyed
1400–1200 B.C.	Height of Mycenaean civilization
1250–1150 B.C.	Sea Peoples invade Palestine
1200 B.C.	Mycenaean palaces destroyed
ca. 1200–1000 B.C.	Israelites settle Palestinian hill country
ca. 1050–750 B.C.	Height of Phoenician city-states
1004–928 B.C.	Reigns of David and Solomon
ca. 725 B.C.	Homer
722 B.C.	Assyrians conquer kingdom of Israel
612 B.C.	Conquest of Nineveh ends Assyrian power
598 B.C.	Neo-Babylonians conquer kingdom of Judah
559–530 B.C.	Reign of Cyrus the Great
550–331 B.C.	Achaemenid Persian Empire
539 B.C.	Cyrus conquers Babylon; permits Jews to return to Palestine
ca. 425 B.C.	Judean assembly accepts the Torah

archers, and cavalrymen were equipped with weapons and armor of iron.

Thanks to new heating and cooling techniques, metal smiths in the ancient world produced an alloy of carbon and iron that was harder and more durable than bronze. It was also easier to obtain since iron ore is widespread—unlike tin, an essential element of bronze. Iron tools and weapons were often stronger and cheaper than their bronze predecessors, which opened up new technical and military possibilities.

Adding to its might, Assyria was the first major state to employ regular cavalry units (rather than charioteers)

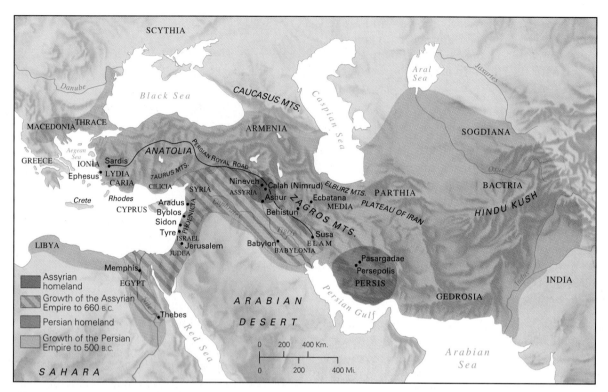

Map 2.1   The Assyrian and Persian Empires   In the 660s B.C. the Assyrians ruled the largest empire the ancient world had seen yet, extending from the Tigris to the Nile. The Persian Empire was even greater. Around 500 B.C. it reached from its heartland in southwestern Iran westward to Macedonia and eastward to India.

as the main strike force. The Assyrians were also excellent engineers, adept at taking walled cities by siege.

In addition, the Assyrians displayed superb organizational skills. The central standing army was supplemented with draftees conscripted from around the empire. Provinces were kept small to prevent the emergence of separate power bases, and independent-minded nobles were regularly checked by the kings.

To control the restive subjects of their far-flung empire, the Assyrians met rebellion with ferocious reprisals. Disloyal cities were attacked and, if need be, destroyed. Sculptured reliefs and inscriptions were set up to show, often in gruesome detail, the fate awaiting Assyria's enemies. We see or read of cities burned to the ground; of men flayed alive, even though they had surrendered, and walls covered with their skin; and of piles of human skulls. (See the feature "Weighing the Evidence: The Siege of Lachish" on pages 66–67.)

The Assyrians also engaged in mass deportation. They uprooted the people of a conquered country, resettled them far away—often in Assyria itself—and colonized their land with Assyrian loyalists. The so-called Ten

Lost Tribes of Israel—the people of the northern Israelite kingdom (see page 53)—were conquered by Assyria in 722 B.C., and many of them were transported to Mesopotamia, where they disappeared from history. (Those who remained in Israel mixed with colonists, and the new group became known, and scorned, as Samaritans.)

Assyrian policy was the result of careful calculation. The political goal was to punish rebellion, the economic goal to create a varied labor force. For example, although it is estimated that the Assyrians deported several million people, they deported not whole populations but a carefully chosen cross section of professions. They also deported entire families together, to weaken deportees' emotional ties to their former homes.

Another reason accounts for Assyria's success: the relative weakness of other powers. Egypt had been at the mercy of factions and invaders for much of the Third Intermediate Period (1075–656 B.C.). Around 950, for example, the kingship came into the hands of Libyan mercenaries. From the eighth century on, their rule was challenged in turn by invaders from the south, rulers of a new Nubian kingdom called Kush (see Map 1.2 on

❧ READING SOURCES

The Banquet of Ashurnasirpal II

This inscription comes from the palace of the Assyrian king Ashurnasirpal II (r. 883–859 B.C.) at his new capital city of Calah (Nimrud). The first two paragraphs illustrate the expansive claims to power of the Assyrian kings. The third shows the effort made to bringing in subjects from far and wide to the inaugural festival of the palace in order to awe them.

This is the palace of Ashurnasirpal, the high priest of Ashur, chosen by Enlil and Ninurta, the favorite of Anu and of Dagan who is destruction personified among the great gods—the legitimate king, the king of the world, the king of Assyria, son of Tukulti-Ninurta, great king, legitimate king, king of the world and king of Assyria—the heroic warrior who always acts upon trust-inspiring signs given by his lord Ashur and therefore has no rival among the rulers of the four quarters of the world; the shepherd of all mortals, not afraid of battle but an onrushing flood which brooks no resistance; the king who subdues the unsubmissive and rules over all mankind; the king who always acts upon the trust-inspiring signs given by his lords, the great gods, and therefore has personally conquered all countries; who has acquired dominion over the mountain regions and received their tribute; he takes hostages, triumphs over all countries from beyond the Tigris to the Lebanon and the Great Sea, he has brought into submission the entire country of Laqe and the region of Suhu as far as the town of Rapiqu; personally he conquered the region from the source of the Subnat River to Urartu. . . .

Ashur, the Great Lord, has chosen me and made a pronouncement concerning my world rule with his own holy mouth (as follows): Ashurnasirpal is the king whose fame is power! . . .

When I inaugurated the palace at Calah I treated for ten days with food and drink 47,074 persons, men and women, who were bid to come from across my entire country, also 5,000 important persons, delegates from the country Suhu, from Hindana, Hattina, Hatti, Tyre, and Musasir, also 16,000 inhabitants of Calah from all ways of life, 1,500 officials of all my palaces, altogether 69,574 invited guests from all the mentioned countries including the people of Calah; I furthermore provided them with the means to clean and anoint themselves. I did them due honors and sent them back, healthy and happy, to their own countries.

Source: Adapted from James B. Pritchard, ed., *Ancient Near Eastern Texts Relating to the Old Testament,* 3d ed., with Supplement (Princeton, N.J.: Princeton University Press, 1969), pp. 558–560.

---

page 22). Kushite pharaohs governed Egypt from around 719 until 656, when they withdrew back south. It was they who faced the Assyrian attacks in 671 and 667.

The conquest of Egypt marked imperial Assyria's greatest extent—and its overextension (see Map 2.1). A coalition army consisting of soldiers from a revived Babylonian kingdom and of Medes (who had formed a powerful state in Iran; see page 45) conquered Nineveh°, the Assyrian capital, in 612 B.C. and defeated the remnants of

the Assyrian army in battles in 609 and 605. Few of its subjects mourned the empire's passing.

The destruction of Assyria led to revival for Babylon, whose rulers attempted to revive the glories of Hammurabi's day (see page 18). For a short period, until the Persian conquest in 539 B.C., the Neo-Babylonian dynasty (founded in 626) and the Medes of Iran were the dominant military forces in western Asia. The Neo-Babylonian king Nebuchadrezzar° II (Nebuchadnezzar

---

Nineveh (NIN-eh-veh)

Nebuchadrezzar (neh-boo-khad-REZ-zar)

Assyrian King   This stern-faced, stone statue of Ashurnasirpal II (r. 883–859 B.C.) comes from a temple in his new capital city of Calah (Nimrud). He holds a scepter and flail (a tool for beating out grain from its husk), symbols of power. *(Courtesy of the Trustees of the British Museum)*

in the Hebrew Bible; r. 605–562 B.C.) conquered the king-dom of Judah (in southern Palestine) in 598 and de-stroyed Jerusalem, its capital, in 586. He deported many thousands of Judeans° to Babylon, an event remem-bered by Christians and Jews as the Babylonian Captiv-ity. Most of the rest of western Asia also fell to Nebuchadrezzar's troops. His most enduring achieve-

ment was rebuilding Babylon on a grand scale. In addi-tion to the city's numerous temples, shrines, and altars, he created the so-called Hanging Gardens celebrated by later Greek writers. They describe the structure as a large terraced complex that Nebuchadrezzar built for his queen, though it may have been a plant-covered ziggu-rat.

Neo-Babylonians and Assyrians both made great strides in astronomy. Their prime motive was not scien-tific but religious—that is, a belief in astrology (the study of the movements of heavenly bodies in the belief that they influence human affairs). Astrology led to advances in the scientific observation of the heavens. Assyrian priests had produced relatively accurate circular dia-grams (astrolabes) that showed the positions of the ma-jor constellations, stars, and planets over the course of the year. By 600 B.C., Assyrian and Neo-Babylonian as-tronomers could predict solstices, equinoxes, and lunar eclipses.

Astronomy in Mesopotamia reached its heights in the centuries after 500 B.C. The zodiac, a diagram show-ing the movement of the sun and planets relative to the constellations, was invented in Persian-ruled Babylon in the fourth century B.C. In the third and second centuries B.C., when Babylonia was under Hellenistic Greek rule, native scientists made impressive advances in mathe-matical astronomy, composing tables that could be used to calculate movements of the moon and planets. More sophisticated mathematical astronomy would not be produced in the West until the Scientific Revolution of the sixteenth century A.D.

Another western Asian society during this period was created by trade, not war. In both the Hebrew Bible and Homer, the Phoenicians° loom large as merchants and seamen, as "traders the world honored" (Isaiah 23:8). Phoenicians were Canaanites°, speakers of a Semitic language and heirs to the civilization that had prospered in Ugarit around 1400 B.C. (see page 32). After the inva-sions of the Sea Peoples and others around 1200 B.C., the Canaanites' once large territory was reduced to a narrow strip along the Mediterranean in the area of modern Lebanon and northern Israel (see Map 2.1). Between 1050 and 750 B.C., the inhabitants of the area flourished; historians call them, as did the ancient Greeks, "Phoeni-cians." Their purple-dyed textiles gave the Greeks their word for the color purple: *Phoenician.*

The Phoenicians were master shipbuilders and sailors. Around 600 B.C., their ships accomplished the first known circumnavigation of Africa. Around 450 B.C., they made the first known commercial sailing trip to the

---

Judeans (joo-DEE-unz)

Phoenicians (fuh-NEESH-anz)   **Canaanites** (CAY-nan-ites)

British Isles. Some scholars think they even reached Brazil. The most lasting Phoenician achievement at sea, however, was the planting of colonies in the Mediterranean, probably beginning in the ninth century B.C. Many of their colonies eventually became independent states. The greatest Phoenician colony was Carthage°, founded by the city of Tyre around 750 B.C. It was the major port city of the western Mediterranean for much of the next thousand years.

Phoenician traders introduced advanced material goods, slaves, and possibly law codes to the Greeks. It was probably from the Phoenicians, whose alphabet derived from Ugarit, that the Greeks adapted their alphabet.

Around 750 B.C., the Phoenician city-states lost their independence to the Assyrians, and in later years Neo-Babylonians, Persians, and other foreign conquerors followed. But Phoenician culture survived—at home, in the colonies, and among the many Mediterranean peoples influenced by it. The result, though unintended, was that Phoenician colonists exported the civilization of western Asia to the western Mediterranean.

■ Building the Persian Empire

A thousand miles east of Phoenicia, a great empire took root. Indo-European-speaking peoples, the Medes and the Persians arrived in western Iran probably around 1500 B.C. but perhaps not until 900 B.C. The two peoples were closely related in language and customs. The Medes lived in the central Zagros Mountains. The Persians made their homeland farther south in Anshan (modern Fars). At first the Medes ruled the Persians, but in 550 B.C., the tables were turned when the Medes were suddenly conquered by the young Persian king Cyrus the Great (r. 559–530 B.C.).

It took Cyrus only twenty years to conquer most of western Asia and much of central Asia. Within five years of his death in 530 B.C., his son and successor, Cambyses° (r. 530–525 B.C.), added Egypt and Libya. Cambyses' successor, Darius° (r. 521–486 B.C.), corraled northwestern India and Thrace. The frontier regions, especially Egypt, were often in revolt, and the attempt of Darius and his successor, Xerxes° (r. 486–465 B.C.), to extend Persian rule to Greece ended in failure (see pages 89–91). The Achaemenid° Persian Empire (named after a legendary founder, Achaemenes), nonetheless, survived for two hundred years, until a Greco-Macedonian army under

Phoenician Ivory   This delicately carved plaque of a cow and calf, just 3 inches high, illustrates the wealth of artistic talent at the disposal of the Phoenicians, whose civilization reached its peak between 1050 and 750 B.C.   *(Iraq Antiquities Department)*

Alexander the Great, king of Macedon (r. 336–323 B.C.), destroyed it.

Let us consider several reasons for the success of Achaemenid Persia. The first was military prowess. Persia was ruled by a warrior aristocracy whose traditional values, according to the Greek historian Herodotus, were "riding, hunting, and telling the truth." The state was able to field a huge army of about 300,000 men, conscripted from the various subject peoples. Although the resultant hodgepodge of soldiers from across the empire did not always fight as a unit, a crack infantry group, the 10,000 Immortals, provided a solid core. The Persians excelled as bowmen and cavalrymen. Following the Assyrians, they made cavalry into the decisive strike force of the battlefield, assigning a more minor role to chariotry. Persia was even more innovative at sea, where it had its subjects build the first great navy. Although Persians served as marines and sometimes as commanders, the rowers and seamen were usually Phoenicians or Greeks.

The second reason for Persia's success was political. Unlike the Assyrians, the Persians considered generosity and tolerance to be more effective than terrorism and brutality. As Cyrus prepared to attack Babylon, he

---

Carthage (CAR-thidge)   **Cambyses** (kam-BYE-seez)
Darius (dah-RYE-us)   **Xerxes** (ZURK-seez)
Achaemenid (ah-KEE-men-id)

❧ READING SOURCES

Cyrus and His Subjects' Gods

Although the Persians sometimes used brutal tactics, they preferred to gain their subjects' loyalty by gestures of goodwill, such as winning the favor of the religious leaders. Excerpt (a), a Babylonian inscription, demonstrates the political skill by which Cyrus the Great secured the surrender of Babylon in 539 B.C. without a battle. Excerpt (b), from the Hebrew Bible, records the favor that Cyrus showed to the Jewish exiles in Babylon.

(a)

He [Marduk] scanned and looked (through) all the countries, searching for a righteous ruler willing to lead him [i.e., Marduk] (in the annual procession). (Then) he pronounced the name of Cyrus, king of Anshan, declared him to be(come) the ruler of all the world. . . . And he [Cyrus] did always endeavor to treat according to justice the black-headed whom he [Marduk] has made him conquer. Marduk, the great lord, a protector of his people/worshipers, beheld with pleasure his [i.e., Cyrus's] good deeds and his upright mind (and therefore) ordered him to march against his city Babylon. . . .

I am Cyrus, king of the world, great king, legitimate king, king of Babylon, king of Sumer and Akkad, king of the four rims (of the earth), son of Cambyses. . . .

When I entered Babylon as a friend and (when) I established the seat of the government in the palace of the ruler under jubilation and rejoicing, Marduk, the great lord, [induced] the magnanimous inhabitants of Babylon [to love me], and I was daily endeavoring to worship him. My numerous troops walked around in Babylon in peace, I did not allow anybody to terrorize (any place) of the [country of Sumer] and Akkad. I strove for peace in Babylon and in all his other sacred cities.

(b)

In the first year of King Cyrus of Persia [539 B.C.] the Lord, to fulfill his word spoken through Jeremiah, inspired the king to issue throughout his kingdom the following proclamation, which he also put in writing: The decree of King Cyrus of Persia. The Lord the God of the heavens has given me all the kingdoms of the earth, and he himself has charged me to build him a house at Jerusalem in Judah. Whoever among you belongs to his people, may his God be with him; and let him go up to Jerusalem in Judah, and build the house of the Lord the God of Israel, the God who is in Jerusalem. Let every Jew left among us, wherever he is settled throughout the country, be helped by his neighbours with silver and gold, goods and livestock, in addition to the voluntary offerings for the house of God in Jerusalem.

Sources: Excerpt (a): Adapted from James B. Pritchard, ed., *Ancient Near Eastern Texts Relating to the Old Testament*, 3d ed., with Supplement (Princeton, N.J.: Princeton University Press, 1969), pp. 315–316. Excerpt (b): Ezra 1:1–3, in *The Oxford Study Bible: Revised English Bible with the Apocrypha* (New York: Oxford University Press, 1992).

portrayed himself as the champion of the traditional Babylonian deity Marduk, whose priests had been challenged as too powerful by the Neo-Babylonian kings. As a result, the Babylonians opened the city gates to the Persian army, allowing Cyrus to achieve that greatest measure of military success: victory without a battle. He also emphasized a sense of continuity with earlier Mesopotamian history in his adoption of the traditional

title of "King of Sumer and Akkad." Nor did Cyrus hesitate to break with Assyrian and Neo-Babylonian population transfers, as witnessed in his edict permitting the Jewish exiles in Babylon to return to Judea. (See the box "Reading Sources: Cyrus and His Subjects' Gods.")

The third reason for Persia's success was its skill at administration and organization. Darius played a crucial role in reorganizing the imperial administration and finances (military-minded Persians sneered at him as a "shopkeeper"). Like the Assyrian Empire, the Persian domain was divided into provinces, called *satrapies*°. Each of the twenty satrapies was a unit of administration and tax collection. For the first time, taxes could be paid with a stable, official coinage: the gold daric (named after Darius) and the silver shekel. Coins had been invented in the kingdom of Lydia in western Asia Minor in the seventh century B.C. Croesus (r. 560–547 B.C.), Lydia's king, was known for his wealth—hence the expression "rich as Croesus"—before Cyrus conquered him in 547 B.C.

The provincial governors, or *satraps*, were powerful, often quasi-independent figures. The empire had many centralizing forces to offset their autonomy, however. Each province had a royal secretary and was visited regularly by traveling inspectors known as "the king's eyes." A network of good roads radiated from the capital cities of Susa and Persepolis. The most famous road, the so-called Royal Road, stretched 1,600 miles from western Iran to western Anatolia (see Map 2.1). Covering the whole distance took most travelers three months, but the king's relay messenger corps could make the trip in a week, thanks to a series of staging posts furnished with fresh horses.

Another unifying element was a society that was law-abiding and prosperous. Darius proclaimed in an inscription that he had fostered the rule of law: "These countries [of the empire] showed respect toward my law; as was said to them by me, thus it was done." Although some scholars suggest that Darius turned the great body of traditional Babylonian case law into a new Persian code for the whole empire, evidence survives only for Egypt, where Darius ordered a codification of Egyptian law. Darius and other Persian kings helped create the conditions for compliance and security by taking an interest in the economy. For example, they opened to commercial traffic Persian roads and a canal connecting the Red Sea and the Nile.

Language, too, built unity. Not Persian, which relatively few people spoke, but Aramaic, the most widespread language of western Asia, became the empire's basic language of commerce and administration. A Semitic language related to Hebrew, Aramaic was first used by the Aramaeans°, a nomadic people who settled in northern Syria about 1100 B.C. and ruled an area extending into Mesopotamia before succumbing to Assyrian conquest about 725 B.C. The Aramaeans dominated the overland trade routes, which, combined with the simple and easily learned Aramaic alphabet, contributed to the spread of their language. Aramaic facilitated the devel-

Achaemenid Persian Silver   This silver rhyton (drinking vessel) is in the shape of a griffin, a mythological animal that is part lion and part eagle. Persian rulers commanded the talents of western Asia's best artists and craftsmen, silversmiths among them.   *(Courtesy of the Trustees of the British Museum)*

opment of literacy and recordkeeping. Aramaic would become the common language of western Asia for over a thousand years, until Arabic replaced it; Jesus Christ was to be its most famous native speaker.

■ The King of Kings

Despite its success, Persia's empire was fraught with several weaknesses. First, Cyrus had bequeathed a legacy as a charismatic war leader. Feeling the need to live up to his example, his successors sometimes undertook ambitious and expensive expeditions that failed, such as wars with the Scythians (a tough nomadic people in Ukraine) and the Greeks. Second, however mild Persian rule, however peaceful and prosperous, it was still rule by foreigners and it still involved taxation. Persian officials, military garrisons, and colonists were found—and were resented—in every corner of the empire. Native

satrapies (SAY-truh-peez)   **Aramaeans** (air-uh-MAY-unz) resentment, particularly in Egypt, and the independence of certain satraps led to intermittent provincial revolts.

The exaltation of the Persian king served as a counterweight to rebellious tendencies. From Darius on, the Persian monarch tried to overawe his officials with his majesty and might. The "King of Kings," as the monarch called himself, sat on a high, gold and blue throne, dressed in purple, decked out in gold jewelry, wearing fragrant oils and cosmetics, and attended by corps of slaves and eunuchs (castrated men employed in high positions). Although he was not considered a god, he had to be treated with reverence. Persians spoke of the king's *khvarna,* his "kingly glory," a mysterious aura of power. Anyone who came into the royal presence had to approach him with a bow to the ground, face down. Even when entertaining dinner guests, the king normally ate alone in a separate room, looking at the guests through a curtain. If, after dinner, the king wished to drink with his guests, he would sit on a golden-footed couch while they sat on the floor, and he and they would drink wine from separate casks.

Impressive as the court ceremonial was, Persian kings were not all-powerful. They were bound by the rule of law and by the considerable power of Persia's proud nobility, on whom they relied to fill the top administrative positions. Competing factions of ministers, wives, concubines, eunuchs, and sons often brought intrigue and discord to court, especially in the fourth century B.C., a time of frequent rebellion.

Royal authority was symbolized in the decoration of the great palaces at Susa and Persepolis, a project begun by Darius I and completed by his son and successor, Xerxes. The Susa palace, the larger of the two, reflected the universality of the empire in the variety of hands that built it. In an inscription, Darius points out that the cedar for the palace came from Lebanon, brought by Assyrians to Babylon and from there by Carians and Ionians (two peoples inhabiting western Anatolia; Ionians

Frieze at Persepolis   This sculptured relief lines the stairway to the audience hall of King Darius (r. 521–486 B.C.). It depicts Persian nobles, well groomed and formally dressed, carrying flowers for the New Year's feast.   *(Rony Jaques/Photo Researchers)*

were Greek) to Susa; the gold came from Sardis (western Anatolia) and Bactria; the silver and ebony from Egypt; the ivory from Ethiopia, India, and central Asia. Craftsmen from east and west took part in the construction. The Persepolis palace, too, displayed the heterogeneity of the empire in its architecture. The palace was placed on a terrace, as in Mesopotamia, but contained columned halls as in Egypt, with Assyrian-style column capitals or tops. In Persepolis, a frieze of sculpted relief panels lining a monumental stairway leading to the palace emphasized the king's vast power. The panels depict an endless procession of the peoples of the world paying homage to the King of Kings: from the nobility to the Immortals, to Median and Persian soldiers, to tribute-bearing subjects from the ends of the earth. The overall feeling of the scene is static, as if the Persian Empire would last forever.

■ Zoroastrianism

Like ancient Israel, Persia developed a highly ethical religion in the first millennium B.C. From obscure beginnings, Zoroastrianism° became the religion of Persia that persisted until the Muslim conquest in the seventh century A.D. Although largely extinct in today's Iran, an Islamic country, Zoroastrianism still survives in small communities elsewhere, primarily in India. Some scholars argue that Zoroastrian beliefs eventually influenced Judaism and Christianity, as well as Roman paganism and Indian Buddhism.

It is easier to describe ancient Zoroastrianism in broad strokes than in detail, partly because the religion changed radically over the course of its ancient history, and partly because relatively little information survives before A.D. 300. This much is clear: The religion was founded by a great reformer and prophet named Zarathustra° (Zoroaster in Greek). Zarathustra lived in eastern Iran. His teachings survive in the *Gathas* ("Songs"), a portion of the Zoroastrian holy book called the *Avesta*. Some scholars date Zarathustra as late as 550 B.C.; others prefer an earlier date, 750 or even 1000 B.C.

Zarathustra's society was dominated by warriors whose religion consisted of blood cults, violent gods, animal sacrifice, and ecstatic rituals in which hallucinogens were eaten. Zarathustra rejected such violent practices in favor of an inward-looking, intellectual, and ethical religion. He favored ceremonies involving fire, considered a symbol of purity. Zarathustra was not a strict monotheist like the Jews, but he did emphasize the power of one god over all people, the supremely good and wise creator of the universe, whom he called Ahura Mazda ("Wise Lord"). Unlike the Jews, Zarathustra considered the problem of evil to be virtually the central question of religion. If god was one, good, and omnipotent, how could evil exist?

Zarathustra's answer might be called *ethical dualism* (dualism is the notion of a grand conflict between good and evil). Ahura Mazda had twin children: the Beneficent Spirit and the Hostile Spirit. Each spirit had made a free choice: one for the "truth" and the other for the "lie"—that is, one for good and the other for evil. Every human being faces a similar choice between good and evil. "Reflect with a clear mind—man by man for himself—upon the two choices of decision, being aware to declare yourselves to Him before the great retribution," says Zarathustra.[1] Indeed, humanity is caught in a great cosmic struggle in which individuals are free to make a momentous choice. Zarathustra thus endowed humanity with great freedom and dignity. He distinguished between two states of being: the spiritual and the material. The more a person pursued spiritual purity, the greater was the person's ability to choose good rather than evil.

Zarathustra held a linear conception of history, similar to that in the Hebrew Bible. His religion is marked by a strong *eschatology* (interest in the end of the world) as well as *soteriology* (belief in a savior). He believed that one day, through an ordeal by fire, Ahura Mazda would judge all the people who had ever lived. Those who had chosen good would be rewarded, and those who had chosen evil would be punished. Then would follow a Last Judgment in which the dead would be transfigured and restored to a glorious bodily existence. There would be, Zarathustra promised, "long destruction for the deceitful but salvation for the truthful." The notion of a savior who would initiate the Last Judgment is an early Zoroastrian belief, if perhaps not a doctrine of Zarathustra himself.

In later centuries, Zarathustra's followers eased his uncompromising rejection of Iranian paganism. Under the leadership of priests, known as *magi*° in western Iran, the religion evolved and changed considerably. Lesser deities beneath Ahura Mazda were added to the Zoroastrian pantheon, in part to suit the religion to the needs of the huge, multicultural Persian Empire.

It is tempting to attribute Cyrus's policy of toleration to the ethical teachings of Zarathustra, but it is uncertain whether Cyrus was Zoroastrian. We are on firmer ground with later Persian kings, particularly Darius I, who had an image of himself alongside Ahura Mazda carved on

Zoroastrianism (zoh-roh-AS-tree-un-izm)
Zarathustra (zah-ruh-THOOS-truh)

magi (MAY-jye)

the face of an Iranian cliff. In an accompanying inscription Darius announces: "For this reason Ahura Mazda bore aid, and the other gods who . . . [exist], because I was not hostile, I was not a Lie-follower, I was not a doer of wrong—neither I nor my family. According to righteousness I conducted myself."[2]

ISRAEL, CA. 1500–400 B.C.

N the first millennium B.C. a small, often-conquered people turned imperialism on its head. Human achievement is meaningless, they argued; only the power of divinity matters. There is only one god, they said; all other gods are false. The one true god had revealed himself not to the awesome, imperialistic Assyrians but to the less powerful Hebrews—ancient Jews. They founded the Western tradition of religion. The God of ancient Israel eventually gave rise to the God of Christianity and of Islam as well as of modern Judaism.

The Hebrews, also known as Israelites, had existed as a people since about 1200 B.C. and perhaps for centuries earlier. They spoke a Semitic language.

■ The Hebrew Bible

As literature and as religious teaching, the Bible is unquestionably the most important book in Western civilization. As a source of history, however, it presents difficulties. Much of the Hebrew Bible (called the Old Testament by Christians) is based on written sources that probably date back at least as far as the early Israelite monarchy of about 1000 B.C. Other parts of the Hebrew Bible are probably the product of an oral tradition, and the nature, antiquity, and reliability of that tradition are the subject of much scholarly debate.

Archaeological evidence from the area of ancient Israel, a small number of inscriptions (almost all after 800 B.C.), and some information in Greek and Roman writings provides an alternative source of information. Yet little of that alternative evidence sheds light on the period before about 1200 B.C., and it offers only partial insight into the later period. The historian needs both to pay attention to the Bible and to consider its nature.

The Hebrew Bible reached something close to its current form a century or two before the birth of Christ. It consists of three main sections: (1) the Torah° (literally, "teaching"), also known as the Pentateuch, or five

Torah (TOE-rah)

books of Moses (that is, the first five books of the Bible); (2) the Prophets, that is, the "historical" books of the early prophets (Joshua, Judges, Kings, and Chronicles) and the books of the later prophets (Isaiah, Jeremiah, Ezekiel, and the twelve "minor prophets"); and (3) the Writings, various books of poetry, proverbs, and wisdom literature.

The books of the Hebrew (and Christian) Bible are canonical: one by one, each was accepted by established authority as sacred. Two key dates stand out in the canonization of the Hebrew Bible: 622 B.C. and about 425 B.C. On the first date, Josiah, king of Judah (see page 53), assembled "the entire population, high and low" to swear to obey "the scroll of the covenant which had been discovered in the house of the Lord" (the scroll probably was Deuteronomy, now the fifth book of the Torah). On the second date, a similar assembly of the people, called by the religious leader Ezra, swore to accept the five books of the Torah that had by then been assembled. The introduction of the Torah made its worshipers into what they have been ever since, "a people of the Book," as the Muslims would put it many years later. The written tradition and literacy became central to the Hebrews.

The Hebrews are the first people we know of to have a single national history book. That book was written not as secular history but as sacred history. It is the story of the working out of God's pact, or covenant, with the Hebrews, his chosen people. All ancient peoples told stories of their semidivine foundation. Only the Hebrews imagined the nation created by an actual treaty between the people and their God.

The central fact of human existence in the Hebrew Bible is God's covenant with the Hebrews. Because of the covenant, history has meaning. History is the story of the success or failure of the Hebrew people in carrying out God's commandments. The emphatic focus is on the individual: on individual people taking actions that have not just moral but military and political consequences that unfold over time.

Many of the themes, narrative details, and styles of writing in the Hebrew Bible derive from earlier cultures. The biblical Flood story, for example, seems to have been modeled on a similar flood in the *Epic of Gilgamesh* (see page 20). Biblical poems in praise of God are often similar to Egyptian poems in praise of pagan gods, and biblical wisdom literature (that is, works containing proverbs and rules of conduct) often recalls Egyptian or Babylonian parallels. In spite of such borrowings, the Hebrew Bible is dramatically different from its predecessors because it subordinates everything to one central theme: God's plan for humanity and, in particular, for his chosen people—the Hebrews.

Statuette of Bull   This bronze statuette of a Canaanite deity (ca. 1200–1100 B.C.) comes from a sanctuary in the hills of Samaria. At this time, most Israelites still worshiped pagan gods.   *(The Israel Museum, Jerusalem)*

■ The Emergence of Hebrew Monotheism, ca. 1500–600 B.C.

The earliest nonbiblical evidence of the Hebrews is an inscribed monument of the New Kingdom Egyptian pharaoh Merneptah (r. 1224–1214 B.C.). After a military expedition into Canaan° (that is, roughly, Palestine), the pharaoh declared triumphantly that "Israel is laid waste." Most scholars accept this as evidence of an Israelite presence in Canaan, but the question is, how did they get there? The Bible says that the Israelites settled Palestine by conquering its earlier inhabitants. Most scholars now reject that account. Archaeological evidence suggests, rather, a more complex process. Perhaps the Israelites were a combination of three groups: armed conquerors, shepherds who gradually entered the country and later settled down to farming, and dispossessed and oppressed Canaanites who rebelled against their masters.

From such sources the Israelites may have emerged. The Bible, however, tells a different story of Israelite origins. Although much of it is credible, none of it is confirmed by nonbiblical sources. Still, the biblical story of Israelite origins has been so influential in later Western

culture that we must examine it. If one follows the Bible, Hebrew history began sometime during the period 2000 to 1500 B.C. with the patriarchs, or founding fathers. Abraham, the first patriarch, migrated to Canaan from the city of Haran in northern Mesopotamia. A seminomadic chieftain, Abraham settled on territory north and west of the Dead Sea, where he grazed his herds. Seminomadic clans in the region frequently made long migrations in antiquity, so the biblical account of Abraham and his descendants, Isaac and Jacob, is plausible.

The Bible, however, emphasizes the implausible: Abraham's extraordinary decision to give up Mesopotamian polytheism for belief in one god. This god commanded Abraham to leave Haran; indeed, he made a treaty, or covenant, with Abraham. In return for Abraham's faith, said the god, "As a possession for all time I shall give you and your descendants after you the land in which you are now aliens, the whole of Canaan, and I shall be their God" (Genesis 17:8). Abraham was not a strict monotheist: Although he worshiped only one god, he did not deny the existence of other gods (see, for a comparison, the discussion of Akhenaten on page 28). Nevertheless, he took a giant step on the road to pure monotheism by coming to believe that only one god rules *all* peoples.

According to the Bible the next important step took place several hundred years later. In a time of famine in Canaan, many of Abraham's descendants left for prosperous Egypt. At first they thrived there, but in time they were enslaved and forced to build cities in the Nile Delta. Eventually, Moses, a divinely appointed leader, released the Hebrews from bondage in Egypt and led them back toward Canaan and freedom.

The Exodus ("journey out," in Greek), as this movement has been called, is a rare example of a successful national liberation movement in antiquity. Among those who accept its historicity, a date in the thirteenth century B.C. is frequently assigned to the Exodus. According to the Bible, the Exodus marked the key moment of another covenant, this time between the god of Abraham and the entire Israelite people. At Mount Sinai°, traditionally located on the rugged Sinai Peninsula between Egypt and Palestine, the Israelites are said to have first accepted as their one god a deity whose name is represented in Hebrew by the letters corresponding to YHWH. YHWH is traditionally rendered in English as "Jehovah," but "Yahweh" is more likely to be accurate. The Israelites accepted Yahweh's laws, summarized by the Ten Commandments. In return for obedience to Yahweh's commandments, they would be God's chosen people, his

Canaan (KAY-nan)

Sinai (SYE-nye)

&❧ READING SOURCES

The Covenant

The central event in the history of ancient Israel was the establishment, during the Exodus, of the covenant, or treaty, at Sinai (see Map 2.2) between God and his chosen people. Forty years later, just before his death, Moses addresses the Israelites and reminds them of their obligations and God's promise to bless their obedience.

Moses summoned all Israel and said to them: Israel, listen to the statutes and the laws which I proclaim to you this day. Learn them, and be careful to observe them. The Lord our God made a covenant with us at Horeb [Sinai]. . . .

These are the commandments, statutes, and laws which the Lord your God commanded me to teach you to observe in the land to which you are crossing to occupy it, a land flowing with milk and honey, so that you may fear the Lord your God and keep all his statutes and commandments which I am giving to you, both you, your children, and your descendants all your days, that you may enjoy long life. If you listen, Israel, and are careful to observe them, you will prosper and increase greatly as the Lord the God of your forefathers promised you. . . .

What then, Israel, does the Lord your God ask of you? Only this: to fear the Lord your God, to conform to all his ways, to love him, and to serve him with all your heart and soul. This you will do by observing the commandments of the Lord and his statutes which I give you this day for your good. To the Lord your God belong heaven itself, the highest heaven, the earth and everything in it; yet the Lord was attached to your forefathers by his love for them, and he chose their descendants after them. Out of all nations you were his chosen people, as you are this day. So now you must circumcise your hearts and not be stubborn any more, for the Lord your God is God of gods and Lord of lords, the great, mighty, and terrible God. He is no respecter of persons; he is not to be bribed; he secures justice for the fatherless and the widow, and he shows love towards the alien who lives among you, giving him food and clothing. You too must show love towards the alien, for you once lived as aliens in Egypt.

Source: Deuteronomy 5:1–2, 6:1–3, 10:12–19, in *The Oxford Study Bible: Revised English Bible with the Apocrypha* (New York: Oxford University Press, 1992).

"special possession; . . . a kingdom of priests, . . . [his] holy nation." (See the box "Reading Sources: The Covenant.")

The Ten Commandments are both more general and more personal than the laws of Hammurabi's Code. They are addressed to the individual, whom they commit to a universal standard. They emphasize prohibitions, saying more about what one should *not* do than about what one should do. The first three commandments establish Yahweh as the sole god of Israel, prohibit any sculpture or image of God, and forbid misuse of the divine name. The next two commandments are injunctions to observe the seventh day of the week (the Sabbath) as a day free of work and to honor one's parents. The sixth and seventh prohibit destructive or violent acts against neighbors, in particular adultery and killing. The final three command-ments regulate community life by prohibiting stealing, testifying falsely, and coveting another man's wife or goods. In contrast to the starkness of the Ten Commandments, an enormous amount of detailed legal material is also found in the Hebrew Bible.

Many scholars doubt whether Hebrew monotheism emerged as early as the thirteenth century. In any case, the Bible makes clear that many ordinary Hebrews remained unconvinced. For centuries afterward, many Israelite worshipers deemed Yahweh their greatest god but not their only god. Unready for the radical innovation that monotheism represented, they carried out the rituals of various Canaanite deities, whom they worshiped on hilltop altars. Forging a national consensus for monotheism took centuries.

Map 2.2 Ancient Israel   The Israelites settled in the Canaanite hill country west of the Jordan River and the Dead Sea after 1200 B.C. (*top map*). Control of Israelite territory after 928 B.C. was shared between two monarchies (*bottom map*): the kingdoms of Israel (conquered by the Assyrians in 722 B.C.) and Judah (conquered by the Babylonians in 598 B.C.).

From the thirteenth to the late eleventh century B.C., the Hebrews were governed by a series of tribal leaders, referred to as "judges" in the Bible, but eventually the military threat posed by the Philistines° persuaded the tribes to accept a centralized monarchy. The Philistines, one of the Sea Peoples, had captured the Palestinian coast in the twelfth and eleventh centuries and seriously endangered Israel. The first Israelite king, Saul (r. ca. 1020–1004 B.C.), had some success against them but eventually fell in battle along with his son, Jonathan. The next king, David (r. 1004–965 B.C.), a former mercenary captain for the Philistines, defeated them decisively.

David was Israel's greatest king. He extended the kingdom into parts of modern Jordan, Lebanon, and Syria and conquered the Canaanite city of Jerusalem, which he made Israel's capital. David's son and successor, Solomon (r. 965–928 B.C.), was also a great king, a centralizer who moved from a loose kingship toward a tightly organized monarchy. His most famous accomplishment was the construction of a magnificent Temple in Jerusalem. The Temple priesthood and sacrifices became the focus of the national cult of Yahweh. Previously, that focus had been a humble, movable wooden chest known as the Ark of the Covenant.

Solomon's reign represented the high-water mark of the power of the Israelite monarchy. Under his successors the monarchy was split into a large northern kingdom of Israel with a capital at Samaria and a smaller southern kingdom of Judah° centered on Jerusalem (see Map 2.2). In 722 B.C., the Assyrians conquered the kingdom of Israel and deported its inhabitants. Judah survived, first as a state controlled by Assyria and then as an independent power.

The religious history of the period of the two kingdoms (928–722 B.C.) and the Judean survivor-state (722–587 B.C.) is marked by an intense drive toward monotheism. The kings of Judah in the seventh century B.C., especially Hezekiah (r. 715–686 B.C.) and Josiah (r. 640–609 B.C.), aggressively attacked the worship of all gods other than Yahweh and all centers of Yahweh worship

Philistines (FILL-uh-steenz)   **Judah** (JOO-duh)

other than the Temple in Jerusalem. The kings also began the process of canonizing the Hebrew Bible. Ambitious and independent, Hezekiah joined in a revolt against Assyria that was brutally suppressed in 701 B.C. and almost cost him his kingdom (see the feature "Weighing the Evidence: The Siege of Lachish" on pages 66–67).

The Judean kings could not have succeeded without the help of the prophets, who were prominent from approximately 900 to 500 B.C. Seers uttering divinely inspired predictions were universal figures in ancient religion. No other culture of antiquity, however, has anything like the Hebrew prophets: charismatic, uncompromising, terrible figures who announced God's anger and ultimate forgiveness. The prophets remind us of the most radical spiritual teachings of Israel: absolute monotheism, an insistence on righteousness, contempt for materialism and worldly power, love of the powerless. They often supported the kings but did not shrink from confronting authority and insisting on uncompromising justice. Among them were Amos, a humble shepherd who preached the superiority of righteousness to ritual; Jeremiah, who prophesied the destruction of Jerusalem as punishment for the people's idolatry; and Isaiah, who predicted the coming of a savior who would inaugurate a new day of universal peace and justice.

A characteristic story of the prophets is the confrontation between Elijah, perhaps the most famous prophet, and Ahab, king of Israel (r. 871–852 B.C.). Ahab coveted the vineyard of one Naboth, but Naboth refused Ahab's offer to buy it. Spurred on by his wife, Jezebel, Ahab trumped up charges against Naboth, who was unjustly stoned to death. Ahab then confiscated the vineyard. God sent Elijah to declare to Ahab that, as punishment for committing murder, "dogs will lick [Ahab's] blood" and that of his family (1 Kings 21:19). In a remarkable scene, we witness not only Elijah's courage in confronting the king but also the king's surrender and repentance before Elijah's spiritual authority. Ahab (though not Jezebel) humbles himself and is spared, but his son and successor, King Ahaziah, who is equally wicked, is punished with a fatal injury. The Western tradition of civil disobedience owes much to the courage of the Hebrew prophets.

■ Exile and Return, 598–ca. 400 B.C.

The prophets prepared the people of Judah for survival by correctly predicting ruin and exile and promising that divine providence would guarantee return. The tenacity of the Judeans in clinging to this message was remarkable. Indeed, it needed to be, for between 598 and 586 B.C., the Neo-Babylonians conquered Judah, destroying

Jerusalem and the Temple. The cultural, political, and economic elite were deported to Babylon. Those who could, fled for Egypt. The dispirited remnant in Palestine shared their land with colonists from neighboring regions, with whom they intermarried and among whom their religion all but disappeared.

And that, given the usual fate of exiled and uprooted peoples in antiquity, should have been that. Yet not only did the Judeans in the Babylonian Captivity persevere in their religious loyalty; they actually returned to Palestine in large numbers.

The Neo-Babylonian rulers allowed Jewish deportees to continue to practice their religion. Jews* in Babylon were not slaves; rather they rented land on royal estates, and some became prosperous. Although some Babylonian Jews assimilated to local ways, many continued a Jewish religious life. Communal worship was observed in open places, perhaps with associated buildings. Some scholars argue that synagogues ("gatherings" in Greek), modest centers of prayer and study that have been the focus of Jewish worship ever since, first emerged in Babylon. It is also possible that the exiles put together the Torah in something like its current form. Elders led the community while prophets continued to speak out: two examples are Ezekiel, who preached the restoration of the Temple, and the man known to us only as "Second Isaiah" (Isaiah 40–66). Second Isaiah emphasized the universal aspect of the god of Israel, who made empires rise and fall and would bring the exiles home from far-off Babylon.

The Temple in Jerusalem was rebuilt around 515 B.C., only seventy years after its destruction. This remarkable turn of events was possible partly because of the Persians, who conquered Babylon in 539 B.C. and proclaimed the freedom of the Jews to rebuild their Temple in Jerusalem. Still, Persian benevolence would not have been enough if the Judean elite had not kept the faith burning among the exiles.

Second Isaiah's message points to a second important development among the exiles of Judah. As striking as the return to Palestine was the survival of large numbers of Judeans as an unassimilated people outside of Judah—in other words, as Jews. For the first time, membership in a community of worship was divorced from residence. Jewish communities flourished in Babylon, Persia, and Egypt, but the members often chose not to become Babylonians, Persians, or Egyptians. From the sixth century B.C. on, a majority of Jews were living outside Palestine, and the Jewish Diaspora ("dispersion") became a permanent fact of history.

---

*Strictly speaking, the terms *Jew* and *Jewish* are anachronistic before the fifth century B.C.

■ The People of the Covenant

A rough equality among the people of Israel, limited government, and the rule of law under God were all fundamental Israelite political notions. Eventually, they would become fundamental political ideals for many in the West, and they would be applied not only to Israelites but to all people.

According to Israelite belief, God made humans in his own image. Thus, all individuals were equal in a fundamental sense; all were bound by God's law. A king who disobeyed this law was illegitimate. Indeed, Israel was ambivalent at best about the institution of kingship, which was tolerated as an evil made necessary only by the country's many armed enemies. God's covenant with the Hebrews was a religious contract with political consequences, rendering God the only true king of Israel. Far from being gods themselves or even God's representatives, Israel's kings were merely God's humble servants.

Israelite egalitarianism was restricted to men. Israelite women usually could not own or inherit property, as women could in Hammurabi's Babylon; or sue in court, as women could in pharaonic Egypt; or initiate a divorce, as women could in Classical Athens (see page 88). The powerful goddesses of other ancient cultures were absent in Israel. Women participated in the rituals of early Israelite religion and the original Temple (ca. 940–586 B.C.) but were segregated in a separate women's courtyard in the rebuilt Temple (ca. 515 B.C.–A.D. 79) and absent from Temple ritual. Indeed, the perspective of the Hebrew Bible is predominantly male. Consider just two examples. First, of the 1,426 names in the Hebrew Bible, 1,315 are male; only 111 women's names appear, about 9 percent of the total.[3] Second, only men and boys can bear the sign of the Lord's covenant with Israel—that is, circumcision.

Nevertheless, Israelite women enjoyed honor as mothers and partners in running the household. The Hebrew Bible states that woman (as exemplified by Eve, the first woman) was created as "a suitable partner" for man (Genesis 2:18, 20). Reproduction and hence motherhood assume great importance in the Hebrew Bible; the Lord enjoins humans to "be fruitful and multiply" (Genesis 1:28). The Bible also commands that children honor both their father and their mother: the two parents are equal in parental authority (Exodus 20:12).

The Hebrew Bible sometimes displays sympathy for and insights into the strategies that women used to counter the abuses of male power. Rebecca, for instance, thwarts her husband Isaac's plan to give his blessing to their son Esau. As the eldest, Esau was entitled to this honor, but Rebecca preferred her younger son Jacob, and she saw to it that he and not Esau obtained her husband's blessing.

Only about a half-dozen women in the Hebrew Bible served as leaders of Israel, but that is more than in the literature of most other ancient cultures. Deborah (ca. 1125 B.C.), for example, a charismatic Israelite prophet, organizes an army that destroys the forces of a Canaanite commander. In a later book Esther, a Hebrew woman, becomes the wife of a Persian king whom the Bible calls Ahasuerus (probably Xerxes, r. 485–465 B.C.). Esther works ferociously at the Persian court to defeat a conspiracy to wipe out her people, and she saves them. The Book of Ruth (date uncertain) tells the story of a selfless and loyal woman, Ruth, who rescues her mother-in-law, Naomi, from ruin and poverty. The Bible celebrates Ruth as Naomi's "devoted daughter-in-law, who has proved better to you [Naomi] than seven sons." (See the box "Reading Sources: Ruth.")

Israelite culture prized women for their cunning, courage, and perseverance—qualities that allowed the people to survive. Military prowess was highly valued in men, but their inner qualities were appreciated as well. Schooled in defeat and exile, many Israelites came to the conclusion that "wisdom is better than weapons of war" (Ecclesiastes 9:18). Thus, the Hebrew Bible stresses God's primary interest in goodness of soul: "The Lord does not see as man sees; men judge by appearances, but the Lord judges by the heart" (1 Samuel 16:7). The God of Israel

Israelite Seal   This seal stone, which shows a roaring lion, was used by a man named Shema, an official of King Jeroboam of Israel. The stone was used to make an impression in hot wax, creating a seal on a document.   *(Reuben and Edith Hecht Collection, University of Haifa, Israel/Erich Lessing/Art Resource, NY)*

❧ READING SOURCES

Ruth

Some parts of the Hebrew Bible prohibit intermarriage. The Book of Ruth, however, praises marriage between Judean men and women from neighboring Moab (modern Jordan; see Map 2.2). This excerpt illustrates such unions, as it does the problem of food shortages, which were a special burden for widows.

Once, in the time of the Judges when there was a famine in the land, a man [Elimelech] from Bethlehem in Judah went with his wife [Naomi] to live in Moabite territory. . . .

Elimelech died, and Naomi was left a widow with her two sons. The sons married Moabite women, one of whom was called Orpah and the other Ruth. [After ten years the sons died.] . . . Then Naomi, bereaved of her two sons as well as of her husband, got ready to return to her own country with her daughters-in-law, because she had heard in Moab that the LORD had shown his care for his people by giving them food. . . .

Naomi said to her daughters-in-law, "Go back, both of you, home to your own mothers. May the LORD keep faith with you, as you have kept faith with the dead and with me; and may he grant each of you the security of a home with a new husband.". . . Then Orpah kissed her mother-in-law and took her leave, but Ruth clung to her.

"Look," said Naomi, "your sister-in-law has gone back to her people and her God. Go, follow her." Ruth answered, "Do not urge me to go back and desert you. Where you go, I shall go, and where you stay, I shall stay. Your people will be my people, and your God my God. Where you die, I shall die, and there be buried. I solemnly declare before the LORD that nothing but death will part me from you." When Naomi saw that Ruth was determined to go with her, she said no more.

[They returned to Naomi's hometown, Bethlehem, in Judah.]

Naomi had a relative on her husband's side, a prominent and well-to-do . . . [man named] Boaz. One day Ruth the Moabite asked Naomi, "May I go to the harvest fields and glean [collect excess grain] behind anyone who will allow me?" "Yes, go my daughter," she replied. So Ruth went gleaning in the fields behind the reapers. [She met Boaz in his fields.] . . .

Boaz said to Ruth, "Listen, my daughter: do not go to glean in any other field. Do not look any farther, but stay close to my servant-girls. Watch where the men reap, and follow the gleaners; I have told the men not to molest you. Any time you are thirsty, go and drink from the jars they have filled." She bowed to the ground and said, "Why are you so kind as to take notice of me, when I am just a foreigner?" Boaz answered, "I have been told the whole story of what you have done for your mother-in-law since the death of your husband, how you left father and mother and homeland and came among a people you didn't know before. The LORD reward you for what you have done. . . ."

[Eventually, Boaz marries Ruth; their great-grandson would be Israel's greatest king, David.]

Source: Ruth 1:1, 3–6, 8–9, 14–18; 2:1–3, 8–12, in *The Oxford Study Bible: Revised English Bible with the Apocrypha* (New York: Oxford University Press, 1992).

---

prized righteousness above wealth, might, sacrifice, or ritual.

One might say that Israelite law reflected a similar tension between power and righteousness. On the one hand, just as the God of Israel was omnipotent and jealous, so the law of Israel was meant to be comprehensive and forceful. Capital punishment existed for murder, rape, incorrigible rebelliousness of a son against his parents, adultery by a married woman (both she and her lover were to be executed), a woman's loss of her virginity before marriage, and other offenses. Harsh punishment was mandated for Canaanite towns taken by siege: the entire population was to be killed so as not to corrupt Israel with their religious practices.

Map 2.3   Aegean Greece   The Minoan civilization (height: ca. 1800–1550 B.C.) and the Mycenaean civilization (height: ca. 1400–1200 B.C.) flourished in turn in the second millennium B.C. Aegean region. The center of Minoan civilization was the island of Crete. A mainland people, the Mycenaeans conquered Minoan Crete around 1550 B.C.

On the other hand, by taking intention into account, Israelite law echoed a note already present in Mesopotamia. The so-called Law of the Goring Ox, for instance, allowed a person to go unpunished for owning an ox that gores a person to death, unless the owner knew beforehand that the animal was dangerous. If the owner did know, however, then the owner had to be put to death. Israelite law, moreover, demonstrated a belief in the sanctity of human life by prohibiting human sacrifice. An Israelite had to be ready in his or her heart (but *only* in his or her heart) to sacrifice his or her child to Yahweh, as Abraham was willing to sacrifice Isaac when Yahweh so commanded. After ascertaining Abraham's willingness to obey even to the point of sacrificing his son, Yahweh freed Isaac from the altar and supplied a ram as a substitute offering. Israelite monotheism thus rejected human sacrifice, as did the religions later derived from it.

EARLY GREECE, TO CA. 725 B.C.

HE Greeks founded the Western tradition in politics and philosophy. The ancient Greek genius was at its height in the era of the Greek city-states (ca. 700–300 B.C.), but it is already visible in the *Iliad*° and the *Odyssey*°, the epic poems of Homer (ca. 725 B.C.). Both are products of the first millennium B.C. Civilization, however, flourished in Greece a thousand years earlier, and Homer's works have roots in this earlier era. Most of what we know of this earlier period, called "Aegean° Greece" by scholars, is based on the discoveries of archaeologists. In particular, archaeology provides the evidence for the rise and fall of two monument-building, literate civilizations: the Minoans on the island of Crete and the Mycenaeans on the Greek mainland (see Map 2.3).

Iliad (IL-ee-ud)   *Odyssey* (ODD-uh-see)   **Aegean** (ih-JEE-un)

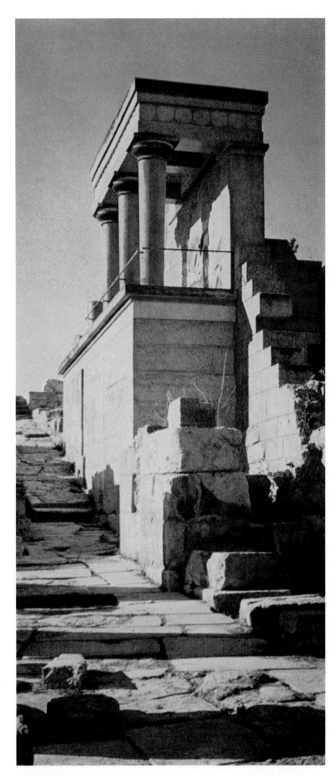

Palace of Knossos A paved ramp and (partially restored) portico are part of an entranceway to the palace. The tapered columns and combination of stone and timber are characteristic features of Minoan architecture. *(Dmitrios Harissiadis/Benaki Museum)*

■ The Minoans and Early Greece, 3000–1375 B.C.

Europe's first civilization appeared in Greece, on the Aegean island of Crete° around 2000 B.C. From there, civilization spread to the Greek mainland.

Civilization came relatively late to Greece, but in comparison with Egypt and even western Asia, Greece is not a hospitable land. Mountainous, and watered by few rivers, it contains little cultivable farmland. Although pastureland and forest are more abundant, one-third of the country is entirely unproductive. Most of the farmland, moreover, is to be found in upland plains, which are divided by mountains, making it difficult to concentrate a large labor force to work the land efficiently. The south enjoys a mild, Mediterranean climate but is quite dry. The north has a Balkan climate of hot summers and cold winters. The indented seacoast provides Greece with many harbors. Greece's geography influenced several recurring features of its history: contrasts between seafarers and mountaineers and between north and south, and the challenge of unifying so mountainous a terrain.

Agriculture preceded civilization in Greece. The first agricultural villages appeared shortly after 7000 B.C., bronze-making skills after 3000. After 3500 B.C., Greece became a supplier of raw materials for the new cities of western Asia. Both on the islands and the mainland, small towns appeared, sometimes fortified with stone walls, occasionally containing substantial stone and mud-brick structures. Between 3000 and 2400 B.C., people living on the Cycladic islands of the Aegean Sea produced exquisite marble sculptures and incised terra-cotta dishes.

Around 2000 B.C. civilization appears on Crete. Its origins are hotly debated, but we know that it was literate because Cretan writing has survived. It consists of a syllabary, or system of simple syllables that form words, known as "Linear A," and though we know its language is not Greek, we do not know what it is. The island of Crete is located on the sea routes between the Greek mainland, Egypt, and Anatolia. The archaeological record contains many signs of trade and cultural contact between Cretans and nearby peoples, from one of whom, perhaps, the Minoans were descended. The evidence for Minoan civilization is concentrated in Crete's palaces—monumental structures that first appeared at various locations on the island around 2000 B.C. After destruction by earthquake, the palaces were rebuilt on an even grander scale, to flourish especially during the period from 1800 to 1550 B.C. Scholars call the palace-builders

Crete (KREET)

and their civilization "Minoan°," after King Minos of later Greek myth. He was supposed to have ruled a great sea empire from his palace at Knossos (see Map 2.3). What the Minoans called themselves remains a mystery.

The Minoan palaces were not merely royal residences but centers of administration, religion, politics, and economics. Minoan palace bureaucrats supervised a large sector of the economy, just as their counterparts did in Ugarit, Egypt, the Hittite kingdom, and other ancient societies. The largest Cretan palace, as well as the first to be excavated, Knossos offers a striking example of Minoan civilization. The main building at Knossos covers 3 acres, the associated structures an additional 2 acres. The palace was built around a large central court, 180 feet long by 82 feet wide, probably used for public ceremonies. A mazelike structure surrounded the court. The palace had enormous staterooms, residence quarters, storage rooms, artisans' workshops, and bathrooms, interconnected by corridors, ramps, and stairways. Light wells admitted daylight, and brightly colored frescoes decorated the walls. Cretan architects were aware of palace architecture elsewhere in the eastern Mediterranean and may have borrowed from it, but precisely who influenced whom remains an open question.

The palaces make clear that the Minoans exploited Crete's considerable natural wealth in agriculture and timber. Archaeological and linguistic evidence indicates a widespread Minoan trading network from the Levant to Sicily. A Minoan settlement flourished on the Aegean island of Thera, 70 miles north of Crete (see Map 2.3). This settlement was destroyed in 1626 (or possibly 1628) B.C. by one of the most violent volcanic eruptions in history. So huge a catastrophe produced climate changes for several years, evident in the pattern of tree rings in ancient wood. That is why scholars can offer so specific a date for Thera's eruption.

From the lack of fortifications around Cretan palaces and the small amount of arms and armor found in burial sites, it appears that the Minoans lived in relative peace. Minoan frescoes show that women as well as men played important roles in cult and ritual. The women portrayed by Cretan artists are often beautiful, bejeweled, and elegant, the men often graceful and athletic. We see, for example, acrobats practicing the sport of bull jumping. Landscapes and animals are frequently illustrated. A statuette of a priestess holding a snake in either hand depicts Minoan interest in the relationship between humans and the natural world. In short, Minoan civilization gives an impression of peace, prosperity, and happiness. No wonder we sense a somewhat lost-Eden quality

Minoan (mih-NO-un)

Fresco at Thera   This detail of the so-called Fresco of the Ladies shows one of a pair of murals from a shrine. This festively costumed woman carries clothes and ornaments to a seated woman (not shown), perhaps a goddess.   *(The Ancient Art & Architecture Collection)*

about the violent and relatively sudden destruction of Minoan civilization. All of the palaces except Knossos were destroyed around 1550 B.C.; Knossos fell around 1375 B.C.

No shortage of theories has surfaced about the cause of the destruction, but the archaeological evidence strongly supports the notion of an invasion. But by whom? To find the answer, let us look to the Greek mainland.

■ The Mycenaeans, to ca. 1200 B.C.

A wave of destruction put an end to the Greek mainland's vigorous Copper Age (see page 10) around 2300 B.C. Centuries of relative poverty followed until, around 1700 B.C., signs of power and prosperity appear at a series of burial sites in central Greece and the Peloponnesus. The most dramatic are at Mycenae° (see Map 2.3), where the royal burials contain a treasure house of objects in gold and other precious metals. Many of the other cities in Greece that would later become famous, such as Athens and Thebes, were also thriving cities in this period.

The inhabitants of Mycenae, unlike the earlier inhabitants of the Greek peninsula, were Greek-speakers. They and the wider civilization they represent are called Mycenaean°. Just when and how the Mycenaeans got to Greece are tangled questions. Some scholars imagine migration, others invasion. Some believe the Mycenaeans' ancestors arrived as early as 2300 B.C., whereas others think it was not until 1700, more than a half-millennium later.

The Mycenaeans adopted and adapted technology, ideas, and art from their advanced neighbors in Crete, Egypt, Anatolia, and Syria-Palestine. The Mycenaeans traded with these neighbors. They also fought with them, for Mycenaean society was dominated by warrior-kings, raiders who exchanged booty to show off their wealth.

Around 1550 B.C. the mainland warriors achieved their greatest feat: the conquest of Crete. They destroyed most of the palaces but spared Knossos, which did not fall until about 1375 B.C. (we do not know the cause of that destruction). The warlike Mycenaeans had conquered the sophisticated Minoans. In turn, the Mycenaeans learned from their subjects and adopted a Minoan-style palace economy.

Mycenaean civilization was at its height between about 1400 and 1200 B.C. Kings lived in palaces whose storerooms were crammed with treasures. They traveled through their kingdoms on a network of good roads and

could muster rowers and ships. Mycenaean artists excelled at potterymaking and fresco painting, gold inlay work and ivory carving. Mycenaean builders constructed palaces, fortifications, bridges, huge vaulted tombs, and sophisticated drainage works.

Palace officials supervised considerable economic activity, often in minute detail, including agriculture, pasturage, and artisanry. Women and children as well as men were included in the labor force. Our knowledge of the palace economy comes primarily from thousands of clay tablets inscribed by palace scribes around 1200 B.C. They are written in a script scholars call Linear B, mostly an early form of Greek consisting of a combination of syllabary and ideograms (a system of symbols that stand for words or ideas).

Mycenaean merchants replaced Minoans in trade in the central and eastern Mediterranean. From Sicily to the Levant, they exported wine and scented oils and imported metals, ivory, and perhaps slaves. Mycenaean warriors engaged in activities ranging from raids and skirmishes to formal battles.

In the thirteenth century B.C., at the height of Mycenaean power, some unknown threat prompted the Mycenaean kings to fortify the palaces at Mycenae and elsewhere with stone walls. By 1200 B.C. most of the fortified sites had been destroyed. Afterward, only a few people continued to live in the old towns. It appears likely that Mycenaean Greece suffered from a combination of internal weakness and foreign invasion similar to that experienced by most of the eastern Mediterranean around 1250–1150 B.C., the era of the Sea Peoples (see page 34).

■ Between Mycenae and the City-States, ca. 1100–725 B.C.

The era from the fall of Mycenae to the rise of the Greek city-states was long referred to as the Greek Dark Ages. But that gloomy term is used less often as archaeology increases our knowledge of the period from roughly 1100 to 800 B.C. The evidence does, however, suggest a considerable depopulation in Greece from the twelfth through the ninth centuries B.C. It seems that rich and poor alike were worse off than in Mycenaean times.

After the destruction of the palaces around 1200 B.C., Mycenaean culture continued to flicker before finally fading in the early eleventh century. New peoples began to move into central and southern Greece around this time. They probably were the Dorians°, speakers of a Greek dialect who came from northern Greece. Their

---

Mycenae (my-SEE-nee)   **Mycenaean** (my-suh-NEE-un)   **Dorians** (DOOR-ee-unz)

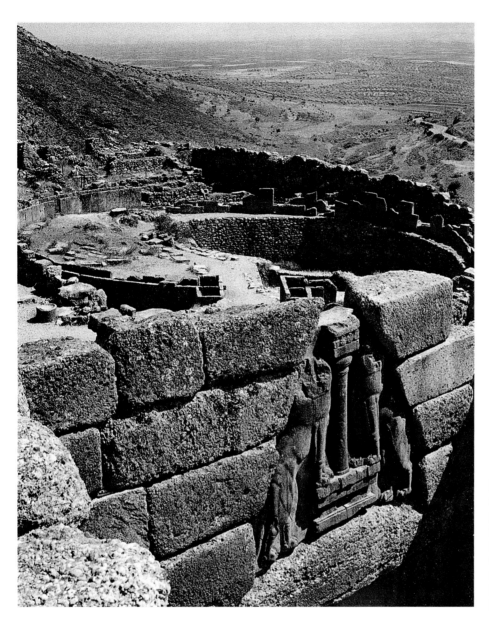

Lion Gate at Mycenae Carved about 1250 B.C. above the main gate of the citadel's massive walls, the lions—flanking a column, their front paws resting on altars—probably represent royal authority. Inside the walls is Grave Circle B, a royal burial site. *(Dmitrios Harissiadis/Benaki Museum)*

material culture was rougher and ruder than that of Mycenae's descendants; it boasts few distinctions besides the iron slashing sword and the long bronze fastener. The Dorians drove out or dominated the Mycenaean Greeks, turning much of central and southern Greece, including Crete, into Dorian centers. Among major settlements, only Athens maintained its independence. The city served as an asylum for Mycenaean refugees, many of whom migrated eastward around 1000 B.C. to the Aegean coast of Anatolia, which was destined to become an important center of Greek culture.

Greece from roughly 1100 to 800 B.C. was largely a poor and illiterate society of small towns and low-level agriculture and trade. Nevertheless, it produced notable painted pottery and preserved an oral tradition of poetry handed down from the Mycenaean era. After 800 B.C. a huge change came over Greece.

First of all, peace contributed to a sharp population rise, and the economy shifted from herding to farming, a more efficient source of food. Greek commerce, too, expanded, thanks in part to the impact of Phoenician traders.

Under pressure from rising population, Greeks founded colonies around the Mediterranean and the Black Sea beginning around 750 B.C. Meanwhile, trade and colonization inspired change at home. Dramatic new experiments in politics, warfare, and culture were attempted. It was the dawn of the era of the Greek city-state. We look at these changes in detail in Chapter 3. Here we focus on a milestone in literary artistry that heralded a new age: the epic poetry of Homer.

■ Homer and History

Had ancient Greece produced a Bible, the *Iliad* and *Odyssey* of Homer would have been its two Testaments. Only Hesiod°, a poet who lived around 700 B.C., enjoyed a comparable influence on later generations, but his poems (*Theogony* and *Works and Days*), though composed in the epic tradition, were shorter than Homer's and arguably less dramatic. But Greece did not have a Bible. Homer and Hesiod were poets, not priests. (As far as we know, the Greek world never had a priestly class comparable to that of Egypt or western Asia.) Although their poems inspired, moved, and educated the Greeks—a large part of a Greek boy's education consisted of learning to recite Homer from memory—they were not divine writ.

Homer was not a historian. He was a bard, a professional singer of heroic poetry—of songs praising the deeds of the great. Heroic poetry consciously glorifies and magnifies the actions of its subjects. In all likelihood, a great deal of tall tale colors Homer's stories of Achilles and Odysseus, of Helen and Penelope. We cannot even be sure that these men and women ever really existed.

Indeed, Homer lived neither in the age his poems are set in nor, for that matter, on the Greek mainland. Homer lived in Ionia, a region of the central western coast of Anatolia, perhaps in the city of Smyrna. Although we do not know just when he lived, it was not until centuries after the Trojan War, the pivotal event of his works. Most scholars today would date Homer to about 725 B.C. or later, a period of increasing change, growth, and ferment in Greece. Some scholars question whether there was just *one* Homer and argue that the *Iliad* and *Odyssey* are the works of two different poets.

The author of the poems worked in a continuous poetic tradition going back to the Mycenaean Age, from which he took stories, details, and language. Most scholars accept the theory that this tradition was oral, not written. Like oral poets elsewhere, Homer and his predecessors composed their poems as they sang them, making use of a stock of stories and formulaic expressions (such as the Greek equivalents of "swift-footed Achilles" and "grey-eyed goddess Athena"). In fact, Homer may have been illiterate.

Oral tradition gave Homer knowledge of a society that was long gone by his day. Although Homer studs his poems with accurate details of Mycenaean palace life, the ideology of his characters generally reflects the beliefs of his own, post-Mycenaean society.

Both in Mycenaean times and in Homer's day, the Greeks were polytheists. The gods of Greece are similar in many ways to the gods of Sumer. They share the foibles and foolishness of humanity but are immortal and far more powerful than humans. The gods figure prominently in early Greek poetry, but they are less powerful than Yahweh, less immediate, and less interested in the inner life of men and women. Already emerging at the beginning of the Greek cultural tradition was the belief that became the hallmark of ancient Greece: that "man is the measure of all things," as the thinker Protagoras would declare in the fifth century B.C.

The Greek gods of the first millennium B.C. were worshiped in Mycenaean times—offerings to them are recorded on Linear B tablets. Because they were thought to live on Mount Olympus, a 9,500-foot-high peak in northern Greece (see Map 2.3), the gods were called the Olympians. Hesiod's *Theogony* tells the story of the Olympians' birth and their triumph over an older generation of deities. The "household" of the Olympians—the early Greek pantheon was conceived of as a noble's household—included Zeus°, a sky-god and the "father of gods and men," and his consort, Hera; Zeus's brother, Poseidon, god of the sea, earthquakes, and horses; Ares, god of war; and Aphrodite, goddess of love. Also in the "household" were Zeus's children: Athena, goddess of wisdom and cunning; Hephaestus, god of craftsmen; Hermes, god of travelers and thieves; Apollo, god of disease and healing; and Artemis, goddess of the hunt, of maidens, and of childbirth.

Flawed and sometimes unpredictable, the Greek gods often seem childish, but the natural world they symbolized seemed equally inconstant to the ancients. The gods embody the values of a warrior society that put a premium on *aretê°*, or excellence, especially excellence in battle. The heroes in the *Iliad* and the *Odyssey* seek glory through military exploits. Homer's gods reward great warriors, but the gods insist on justice as well. Zeus punishes those who do evil—those who, for example, break oaths or give false judgments or violate the laws of hospitality. In the *Iliad,* the Trojan prince Paris sparks the Trojan War by abducting the beautiful Helen from her husband, the Greek king Menelaus, while he is a guest in Menelaus's household. In return, the Greeks attack Troy, a wealthy city in northwestern Anatolia. The gods destroy Troy as punishment for Paris's crime.

The *Iliad* and the *Odyssey* focus on the Trojan War and its aftermath. The *Iliad* is set in the tenth year of the conflict. The strain of fighting leads to a quarrel between Greek chieftains: Agamemnon, king of Mycenae and the leader of the expedition, and Achilles°, the greatest Greek warrior. The most prominent Trojans, King Priam

---

Hesiod (HEE-see-ud)   **Zeus** (ZOOS)   **aretê** (ah-reh-TAY)   **Achilles** (uh-KIL-eez)

and his eldest son, Hector, are less petty but will suffer the greater ruin. The *Odyssey* tells the story of the struggle of the Greek hero Odysseus° to return to Ithaca and to regain his kingship after a twenty-year absence, ten years in the war at Troy and ten years wandering homeward. It also focuses on the loyalty and ingenuity of Odysseus's wife, Penelope, who saves the household in her husband's absence, and the maturation of their son, Telemachus°, who helps his father regain his kingdom.

Homer puts as much emphasis on brains as on brawn; Odysseus, for example, is a man of intelligence and cunning, as well as strength. Homer argues, moreover, that the gods hold human beings to a code of justice, hospitality, and respect for parents. Finally, although the Homeric poems focus on the upper classes— and primarily on men—the poems have a strain of sympathy for ordinary people and for women. Indeed, they have a general sympathy for failure. Homer's heroes court death and often obtain it. Unlike the psalmist of the Hebrew Bible, a Homeric hero walks alone "through the valley of the shadow of death" (Psalm 23:4); he has no god to comfort, rescue, or redeem him. He knows that the gods ordain human life to be difficult and full of suffering. Human frailty, however, ennobles Homer's heroes.

Homer's princes are proud and jealous. In the *Iliad*, when Agamemnon is forced by divine command to return his "prize"—a girl captured in a raid—he demands that he take the "prize" of Achilles, his greatest warrior— that is, Achilles' girl. Achilles' response is to sulk in his tent while the Trojans drive his fellow Greeks to near-defeat. In the *Odyssey,* a group of nobles lives off the absent Odysseus's estate, waiting to see which of them Odysseus's wife (and ostensible widow) might marry. Odysseus's honor demands that he punish them by killing every last one. In both cases, Homer recognizes that the hero goes too far: Achilles' inaction leads to the death of his best friend, and ultimately to his own death; Odysseus's thirst for revenge leads to civil war.

■ World of the Heroes

Historians must distinguish between ideology and reality in Homer's poems. Homer focuses on the elite. Homeric warriors and their women hold aristocratic values and tend to look down on ordinary people. Scholarship shows, however, that society in Homer's day was more level and egalitarian. Except for a small number of traders and craft specialists who lived in towns, most people in the Greece of 725 B.C. lived in villages and hamlets. Most farmed or herded pigs, goats, or sheep, and most were free. The people of each community were called the *demos*°; the leading men, *basileis*°. *Basileis* means "kings," but it is more accurate to understand them as chiefs. No great difference of wealth existed between the basileis and ordinary free farmers.

Although the basileis took the lead in both government and war, the demos played a crucial role. Homer emphasizes contests between aristocratic champions, but his vivid battle scenes also include large companies of ordinary men fighting in mass combat in close formation. And if the basileis dominated Homeric government, the demos had at least a small say.[4]

The basic instruments of government that would exist for centuries in Greece appear in the *Iliad* and the *Odyssey*: generals, orators, judges, a council, and an assembly. When making decisions about war and peace, a council of elder basileis consults an assembly of the warriors. In this arrangement we see a fundamental principle of Greek government: the political community should be composed of the warriors.

Let us turn now to the ideology of Homer's basileis, which would greatly influence later generations in antiquity. In the epics, the chiefs make friendships and exchange goods across international boundaries. Greek and Trojan chiefs kill each other on the battlefield but rarely hate each other. Indeed, some are bound by hereditary ties of guest-friendship and so decline to fight each other. (See the box "Global Encounters: Greeks and Trojans.")

The main activity of Homer's basileis is warfare. The *Iliad* consists largely of a series of battlefield contests. Since women did not take part in battle, they are not presented on an equal footing with men. Yet Homer rarely criticizes women in general, as some ancient Greek writers would in later centuries. He shows considerable compassion for women, particularly in the *Odyssey*. Homer's women are weaker than men, but they are neither timid nor helpless. Penelope, for example, personifies female resourcefulness: by refusing to marry until she has finished weaving a shroud for Odysseus's elderly father, and then by unraveling every night what she has woven during the day, she puts the noble suitors off for years. She is as concerned with honor as any Homeric man. By refusing to accept an offer of marriage while Odysseus might still be alive, Penelope does honor to her own good name and to her husband's.

Homeric women play important roles in encouraging men or, in a more complex psychological process, in

---

Odysseus (oh-DIS-ee-us)
Telemachus (te-LEH-muh-kus)

demos (DEE-mus)　　**basileis** (bah-see-LAYS)

Greeks and Trojans

For Homer's aristocratic heroes, war was a struggle not of nations but of individual loyalties. Friendship and family ties mattered more than patriotism. As these excerpts from the Iliad *show, individual Greeks sometimes considered their enemies, the Trojans (and Trojan allies), to be respected rivals or even honored friends.*

Then looking darkly at [his commander, Agamemnon,] Achilles of the swift feet spoke:

"O wrapped in shamelessness, with your mind forever on profit, how shall any one of the Achaians [Greeks] readily obey you either to go on a journey or to fight men strongly in battle? I for my part did not come here for the sake of the Trojan spearmen to fight against them, since to me they have done nothing.

"Never yet have they driven away my cattle or my horses, never in Phthia where the soil is rich and men grow great did they spoil my harvest, since indeed there is much that lies between us, the shadowy mountains and the echoing sea; but for your sake, o great shamelessness, we followed, to do you favour, you with the dog's eyes, to win your honour and Menalos' from the Trojans.

"Now Glaukos, sprung of Hippolochos, and [Diomedes,] the son of Tydeus came together in the space between the two armies, battle-bent. Now as these advancing came to one place and encountered, first to speak was Diomedes of the great war cry: "Who among mortal men are you, good friend? . . . unhappy are those whose sons match warcraft against me."

Then in turn the shining son of Hippolochos answered: ". . . Hippolochos begot me, and I claim that he is my father; he sent me to Troy, and urged upon me repeated injunctions, to be always among the bravest, and hold my head above others, not shaming the generation of my fathers, who were the greatest men in Ephyre and again in wide Lykia. Such is my generation and the blood I claim to be born from."

He spoke, and Diomedes of the great war cry was gladdened. He drove his spear deep into the prospering earth, and in winning words of friendliness he spoke to the shepherd of the people [Glaukos]: "See now, you are my guest friend from far in the time of our fathers. . . . Let us avoid each other's spears, even in the close fighting. There are plenty of Trojans and famed companions in battle for me to kill, whom the god sends me, or those I run down with my swift feet, many Achaians for you to slaughter, if you can do it. But let us exchange our armour, so that these others may know how we claim to be guests and friends from the days of our fathers."

So they spoke, and both springing down from behind their horses gripped each other's hands and exchanged the promise of friendship; but Zeus the son of Kronos stole away the wits of Glaukos who exchanged with Diomedes the son of Tydeus armour of gold for bronze, for nine oxen's worth the worth of a hundred.

Source: The Iliad of Homer, trans. Richmond Lattimore (Chicago: University of Chicago Press, 1951), pp. 63, 156–159.

 For additional information on this topic, go to http://college.hmco.com.

bolstering a man's courage by playing the foil to his doubts and dreads. In the *Iliad*, Hector overcomes his own fears of battle by hearing his wife, Andromache°, express *her* terror at the thought of his dying and leaving her a widow and their infant son an orphan. Moreover, by taking the burden of hearth and home on herself, Andromache allows Hector to define masculinity as making war.

Andromache (an-DROM-eh-kee)

Loyalty to the family played an important role in social relations. A person's obligations to kin included the duty to avenge crime or murder. Friendship, cemented by an exchange of gifts, was another important social institution. Even humble peasants prided themselves on hospitality.

Such values served Homeric society well. Although they would survive in later centuries, they would be challenged after 700 B.C. by the increasing emphasis on public life as the Greek city-state evolved.

SUMMARY

THE first half of the first millennium B.C. witnessed dramatic developments among both the ancestors of the West and its founders. A new form of empire appeared. Multi-ethnic, far-flung, and claiming to be universal, such an empire would one day be brought into the Western tradition by Rome. The process began, however, among the West's ancestors in western Asia.

New military technology, the frank adoption of brutal and inhumane methods, and improvements in administration led to the creation of the Assyrian Empire, stretching from western Iran to Palestine and briefly even to Egypt. After short-lived hegemonies by Neo-Babylonians and Medes, the Persians established an empire that was larger, better organized, and more tolerant than the empire of the Assyrians. Heirs to Canaanite civilization of the second millennium B.C., the Phoenician city-states expanded across the Mediterranean Sea, less by military conquest than by trade and colonization.

The most important developments of the era, however, were not in commerce, weaponry, or imperialism but in new conceptions of the nature and meaning of human life. The Persians developed a new religion, Zoroastrianism, which emphasized ethics, dualism—that is, the conflict of good over evil with the eventual triumph of good—and redemption through a divine savior. The Israelites conquered Palestine and, even after losing it, held on to their identity by means of a tenacious belief in one god. They broke with tradition by insisting that their god was one, merciful, and just. Omnipotent, God gave history meaning and direction. The purpose of life, in the Israelite view, was to serve God by acting righteously. The new religion laid the foundation for Judaism as well as Christianity and Islam. The Jews wrote down their religious and historical traditions in a book that, along with the Christian New Testament, proved to be the most influential single text in the history of the West: the Hebrew Bible.

We know little of the ideologies of the Minoan and Mycenaean civilizations of the second millennium B.C., but their economies and governments seem to have been similar to those of the other palace-run states of the eastern Mediterranean. Yet by the first millennium B.C., the Greeks, like the Persians and the Hebrews, had broken with tradition, but with a greater emphasis on the human than on the divine. Homer's epic poems, which took shape approximately 725 B.C., focus on the fragile dignity of heroic human actions. Homer idealizes a society of aristocratic warriors seeking honor and glory. Although the Greek gods show favor to heroes, they display no transcendent interest in redeeming human souls. Men and women were doomed to die. Homer's legacy, therefore, was to glorify human heroism while recognizing the fleeting frailty of life. It was a legacy that raised as many questions as answers. In the middle centuries of the first millennium B.C., the Greeks would attempt to provide new solutions to Homer's problems. As we will see in the next chapter, their successes and failures in such diverse activities as politics and philosophy, war and art, literature and history, founded much of Western civilization.

■ Notes

1. S. Insler, *The Gāthās of Zarathustra: Acta Iranica*, 8 (Leiden, The Netherlands: E. J. Brill, 1975), p. 33.
2. Roland G. Kent, *Old Persian: Grammar, Texts, Lexicon* (New Haven, Conn.: American Oriental Society, 1950), p. 132.
3. Carol L. Meyers, "Everyday Life: Women in the Period of the Hebrew Bible," in Carol A. Newsom and Sharon H. Ringe, eds., *The Women's Bible Commentary* (Louisville, Ky.: Westminster/John Knox Press, 1992), p. 245.
4. Kurt A. Raaflaub, "Homer to Solon. The Rise of the *Polis*: The Written Sources," in Mogens Herman Hansen, ed., *The Ancient Greek City-State. Symposium on the Occasion of the 250th Anniversary of the Royal Danish Academy of Science and Letters, July 1–4, 1992, Historisk-filosofiske Meddelelser* 67, The Royal Danish Academy of Sciences and Letters (Copenhagen: Munksgaard, 1993), pp. 41–105.

■ Suggested Reading

Cook, J. M. *The Persian Empire.* 1983. A clear and readable introduction, updating earlier conclusions in the light of recent archaeological discoveries, particularly inscriptions.

Dickinson, Oliver. *The Aegean Bronze Age.* 1994. Perhaps the best single introduction to a vast and fascinating subject.

Finley, M. I. *The World of Odysseus.* Rev. ed. 1978. Essential introductory reading on the historicity, society, and ideology of the Homeric poems.

Moscati, Sabatino. *The World of the Phoenicians.* Translated by Alastair Hamilton. 1968. A general survey of politics, society, and culture, with more emphasis on the western than on the eastern Mediterranean.

Oates, J. *Babylon.* Rev. ed. 1986. A well-illustrated survey, from the period of Sargon to the Hellenistic Greeks, with a section on Babylon's cultural legacy.

Saggs, H. W. F. *The Might That Was Assyria.* 1984. A readable introductory history celebrating the Assyrians' achievements.

Shanks, H., ed. *Ancient Israel. A Short History from Abraham to the Roman Destruction of the Temple.* 1988. Short, readable essays by scholars offering up-to-date introductions to the subject.

For a searchable list of additional readings for this chapter, go to http://college.hmco.com.

The Siege of Lachish

From the distance, it looks like one of the foothills that surround it. Up close, though, it can be clearly seen for what it is: Tel Lachish, the mound of the biblical city of Lachish. It is a link in the chain of evidence that tells one of the most remarkable stories in biblical history.*

Lachish was a great city, a royal fortress, and second only to Jerusalem in its importance to the kingdom of Judah (928–587 B.C.). In 701 B.C. the Assyrians under King Sennacherib (r. 704–681 B.C.) besieged Lachish and took it by force. The siege of Lachish is unique in early biblical history for the wealth of independent corroborating sources. In addition to reports in the Hebrew Bible are many Assyrian written documents. Furthermore, Sennacherib commemorated his victory by depicting the siege and recording the spoils in carved reliefs that he erected in his royal palace at Nineveh. Finally, the mound itself has been excavated, allowing a striking comparison of the archaeological and pictorial evidence of a siege in the biblical period.

Originally a Canaanite town, Lachish was fortified by the Israelite kings because of its strategic location. It sits southwest of Jerusalem in the Judean foothills, dominating the road between the Judean hills to the east and the Philistine coast to the west (see Map 2.2). By the reign of King Hezekiah of Judah (r. 715–686 B.C.), one of the most prominent kings of the House of David, Lachish was a large garrison city constructed on a monumental scale. It included inner and outer rings of thick walls, a massive gate complex, many houses and shops, and, in the center, a palace-fort surrounded by earthen ramps.

Having seen Assyria turn the kingdom of Israel into an occupied province, Hezekiah knew that he was facing the greatest power of the region. Nevertheless, he joined Egypt and the Philistine cities in a revolt soon after Sennacherib came to the throne in 704 B.C. Sennacherib responded by attacking the rebels in 701. The Hebrew Bible states: "In the fourteenth year of the reign of Hezekiah, Sennacherib king of Assyria attacked and took all the fortified cities of Judah" (2 Kings 18:13). We can read the results of the campaign in one of Sennacherib's inscriptions:

"As to Hezekiah, the Jew, he did not submit to my yoke. I laid siege to 46 of his strong cities, walled forts and to the countless small villages in their vicinity, and conquered (them) by means of well-stamped (earth-) ramps, and battering-rams brought (thus) near (to the walls) (combined with) the attack by foot-soldiers, (using) mines, breeches as well as sapper work [that is, digging away foundations]." Hezekiah bowed to Assyrian power. He gave up territory (though not Jerusalem) and agreed to an increase in tribute, which now amounted to "30 talents of gold, 800 talents of silver, precious stones, antimony, large cuts of red stone, couches inlaid with ivory, elephant-hides, ebony-wood, boxwood and all kinds of valuable treasures, his own daughters, concubines, male and female musicians." So the Assyrian inscription records.

The Lachish reliefs (in Sennacherib's palace) offer a vivid picture of the attack on the city. Lachish was well fortified and well defended, but the Assyrians were experts in taking cities by storm. The reliefs show the camp of the attackers, Assyrian archers and slingers advancing on the city, battering rams and siege engines in action against the walls, flaming chariots thrown down by the defenders, and, after the city was taken, captives impaled on sharp stakes.

Look at the artist's reconstruction of an Assyrian assault on the city, based on the archaeological evidence. The soldiers are climbing a massive siege ramp that the Assyrians built against a "vulnerable" point in the city walls. The excavators of Lachish found the ramp, consisting of a level of stones cemented together over a core of boulders. It is the oldest siege ramp so far discovered in the ancient world. In and around the city the excavators found other evidence of the battle: hundreds of arrowheads, many slingstones, a number of pieces of bronze sheet mail used in armor, and what may be the crest of a helmet worn by one of the Assyrian spearmen shown attacking the city walls in the Lachish reliefs. Most dramatic, the excavators discovered about seven hundred skeletons, evidently civilians killed during the Assyrian attack and then buried in mass graves outside the city. Three of the individuals were trepanned; that is, they were operated on before death by removing a portion of their skulls. Perhaps this represents a last attempt, evidently futile, to save the lives of the wounded.

---

* In much of what follows about Lachish (LAH-kish), I rely on the discussion in David Ussishkin, *The Conquest of Lachish by Sennacherib* (Tel-Aviv: Tel-Aviv University, Institute of Archaeology, 1982).

Artist's Reconstruction of an Assyrian Assault on Lachish *(Drawing by Gert le Grange, from David Ussishkin,* The Conquest of Lachish by Sennacherib *[Tel Aviv: Tel Aviv University, Institute of Archaeology, 1982], p. 123. Reproduced with permission.)*

Detail of the Assyrian Conquest of Lachish, a Relief from the Palace of Sennacherib *(British Museum/ Erich Lessing/Art Resource, NY)*

The Lachish reliefs also depict rows of captives and deportees marching toward Sennacherib on his throne. Look at this detail of the relief, showing a large Judean family leaving Lachish for exile. They are allowed to bring cattle with them, and a woman and child are permitted to ride on a wagon. The Assyrians claimed to have deported 200,150 people from Judah, of whom many men ended up as slave laborers working on Sennacherib's palace.

As for Lachish, it was burned to the ground, as the excavations confirm. Sometime in the seventh century the city was restored and refortified. Lachish was destroyed again, however, in 598 B.C., during the first of two military campaigns in Judah by Nebuchadrezzar, the Neo-Babylonian king. The excavators found a group of pottery sherds with ink inscriptions (called *ostraca*) in old Hebrew script, dating to just before that destruction. This unique set of documents in classical Hebrew writing consists of letters to a man named Yaush, the military governor of Lachish. They testify, among other things, to the worship of Yahweh, to the signal system linking the fortresses of Judah, and to the practices of the scribal profession. Once again, the city's misfortune has proved illuminating to students of the past.

CHAPTER 3

The Age of the Polis: Greece, ca. 750-350 B.C.

I T is dawn. The light reveals a hillside in the city of Athens, a natural auditorium. Its rocky slopes, visible in the photograph opposite, would have been covered, beginning about 500 B.C., with wooden benches facing a platform cut into the rock. The six thousand men gathered there constitute a diverse group, ranging from farmers to philosophers, from dockyard workers to aristocrats. As they take their seats, these, the citizens of Athens, watch priests conducting prayers and offering a sacrifice. Then, all eyes turn to the individual who mounts the platform—a herald. His booming voice asks the question that marks the start of business: "Who wishes to speak?" Someone rises to address the assembly. It is the first democracy in history—and the central laboratory in this great experiment in participation.

The assembly meeting recalls the defining features of what was, in its era, the characteristic political institution in much of Greece: the *polis* (plural, *poleis*). Usually translated as "city-state," the polis is better understood as "citizen-state." The polis was the product of communal activities, whether in the assembly or the military or the theater, undertaken by its members—its citizens. Not every polis was a democracy, but every polis emphasized cooperative activities whose participants enjoyed at least a measure of equality. Every polis also sought a balance between the group and the individual, be that person the speaker or a military hero or a freethinker.

Balance is a difficult state to achieve, however, and the equilibrium of the polis was frequently disturbed by tension and exclusion. Paradox marked the polis. Greek democracy failed to grant equal rights to women or immigrants, and it depended on slave labor. Relations among poleis were less often a matter of cooperation than of war. Although the Greeks created magnificent religious architecture, a portion of their intellectual elite came to the conclusion that the gods were of little importance in explaining the universe. Although

Athenian Acropolis, with Pnyx Hill in foreground.
(Photo: Julia M. Fair)

one leading polis, Sparta, was a paragon of militarism, obedience, and austerity, scorning the life of the mind, another, Athens, prided itself on freedom and cultural attainments. Yet the Greeks made the most even of such tensions, exploring them in literary genres—tragedy, comedy, history, and philosophy—that focused on the polis as a central theme. Creative tensions also marked Greek achievements in sculpture, painting, and architecture.

The era of the polis proved to be a defining moment in Western history. Although the Greeks of this era borrowed much from neighboring cultures, they were remarkably original. In the mid-first millennium B.C., the monotheistic religious heritage of the West first emerged among the Jews. During that same era, the Greeks founded the Western tradition in a broad range of culture, including politics; philosophy; literary genres such as comedy, tragedy, and history; and the visual and plastic arts of painting, sculpture, and architecture.

QUESTIONS TO CONSIDER

■ What was the Greek polis, and why was its development a defining moment in Western civilization?

■ What was the nature of ancient Greek democracy?

■ What were the differences between Athens and Sparta, and what did each contribute to the Western experiment?

■ What were the limits of freedom and equality in the polis, and how did ancient Greek thinkers and writers explore those limits?

TERMS TO KNOW

polis	Pericles
Archaic Greece	Socrates
hoplite phalanx	Plato
Solon	Aristotle
Sappho	tragedy
Classical Greece	Herodotus
demokratia	Thucydides

SOCIETY AND POLITICS IN ARCHAIC GREECE, CA. 750–500 B.C.

HISTORIANS usually call the era in Greek history from roughly 750 to 500 B.C. the "Archaic period." In this context *archaic* refers to the style of sculpture in the two centuries before the "Classical period" (480–323 B.C.). Archaic Greece was a patchwork of hundreds of separate city-states, tribal leagues, and monarchies (see Map 3.1). Nevertheless, it displayed a distinctive style and outlook not only in art but also in politics, military arrangements, technology, economics, literature, and religion.

Although it was a period of paradox, the Archaic era laid the groundwork for much of lasting importance in Western civilization. Archaic Greece witnessed the simultaneous growth of individualism and a tight community spirit, the emergence of social cohesion despite a continual state of war, the coexistence of deep religious piety and the West's first nontheistic philosophy. The Archaic period also saw the origin of characteristic Western

types of governmental regimes—tyranny, oligarchy, and the first steps toward democracy—and of fundamental Western notions of citizenship and the rule of law.

■ Agriculture, Trade, Colonization, and Warfare

An observer of ninth-century B.C. Greece would hardly have predicted greatness of that poor, illiterate society of small settlements and low-level trade. Yet, as we saw in the discussion of Homer in Chapter 2, everything began to change in Greece in the eighth century. It was out of these changes that a new communal institution emerged: the polis°.

Change was a product of peace, which stimulated a sharp population rise. In response, the economy shifted from herding to farming, a more efficient source of food. Seeking new agricultural land in the rocky Greek peninsula, farmers terraced hillsides and drained marshes. The typical agricultural unit was the family farm. Most

---

polis (PO-liss)

farms were small and roughly equal in size, apparently a stimulus of social and political equality in Greece.

Greek commerce, too, was expanding. Shortly before 800 B.C., Greeks from the island of Euboea, perhaps following the example of Phoenician merchants and seafarers who had been casual traders in Greece for a century (see pages 44–45), established a trading post in Syria at Al-Mina on the mouth of the Orontes River, at the terminus of the chief caravan route from Mesopotamia (see Map 3.2). Shortly afterward, Euboeans established another trading post in the west, at Neapolis (now, the Bay of Naples) in Italy. In both east and west, Greek merchants sought iron and luxury goods. What they offered in return was probably silver, of which ancient Greece had rich deposits, and slaves.

From commerce it was but a short step to colonization in order to siphon off the extra mouths created by population growth. In colonization as in trade, the Greeks may have followed the example of the Phoenicians, who had begun establishing colonies probably in the ninth century B.C. Between about 750 and 500 B.C., the Greeks founded colonies throughout the Mediterranean and the Black Sea, planting nearly as many cities as already existed in Greece (see Map 3.2). Colonization in Italy and Sicily began in earnest around 750 B.C.; in the Chalcidice° in the northeast Aegean perhaps a generation later; in the Sea of Marmara about 680; in North Africa around 630; and in the Black Sea about 610. In the far west, Massalia (modern Marseilles) was established about 600. Southern Italy and Sicily, whose climate and landscape recalled the Aegean, were especially intense areas of Greek settlement, so much so that the Romans later called the region *Magna Graecia* ("Great Greece"). In the long run, Greek colonization proved to be of great importance for the spread of urban civilization westward, especially into Italy.

One important consequence of foreign contact was the introduction to Greece of the alphabet, borrowed from the Phoenicians. The first datable examples of the Greek alphabet were inscribed on pots in about 750 B.C. The alphabet spread rapidly and widely in the next century. Literacy underlay the achievements in poetry, philosophy, and the law that Archaic Greece has left behind. However, so few people at the time could read and write well that ancient Greek culture remained primarily oral culture.

Another consequence of foreign contact was the introduction of new military technology, which the

CHRONOLOGY

ca. 750 B.C.	Greek colonization of Magna Graecia begins
ca. 725 B.C.	Sparta conquers Messenia
ca. 675 B.C.	Pheidon becomes tyrant of Argos
ca. 625 B.C.	Sappho active as poet
594 B.C.	Solon is archon in Athens
ca. 560 B.C.	Pisistratus becomes tyrant of Athens
508 B.C.	Cleisthenes begins reforms in Athens
499 B.C.	Ionians revolt against Persia
490 B.C.	Battle of Marathon
480–479 B.C.	Persia invades Greece
477 B.C.	Delian League founded
460–429 B.C.	Pericles at peak of power
458 B.C.	Aeschylus's *Oresteia* first performed in Athens
431–404 B.C.	Peloponnesian War
395–386 B.C.	Corinthian War
399 B.C.	Trial of Socrates
371 B.C.	Battle of Leuctra

increase in wealth allowed Greeks to adopt. Social changes, furthermore, fostered new tactics on the battlefield. The result was the hoplite phalanx°, a tightly ordered unit of heavily armed, pike-bearing infantrymen. The phalanx not only became the dominant military force in Archaic Greece, but, with relatively few changes in equipment and tactics, it remained supreme on land in Greece, western Asia, and other Mediterranean regions for centuries, until its defeat by a Roman army in 197 B.C.

The phalanx emerged through a process of evolution rather than in a revolutionary leap. Before 800 B.C., single combat among the basileis appears to have decided battles. Around 800–750 B.C., armies began to include more men, fighting in close formation. Around

---

Chalcidice (kal-SID-uh-see)   **hoplite phalanx** (HOP-lite FAY-lanks)

Map 3.1 Archaic and Classical Greece The region of the Aegean Sea was the heartland of Greek civilization around 750–350 B.C. The mountainous terrain, rugged coastline, and numerous islands encouraged political fragmentation.

Map 3.2   Phoenician and Greek Colonization   Both the Phoenicians (beginning perhaps after 900 B.C.) and the Greeks (beginning around 750 B.C.) established numerous colonies on the coasts of the Mediterranean and Black Seas.

700 B.C. came new armaments. The result was the phalanx. The heavily armed infantryman (hoplite) of the fighting unit (phalanx) wore bronze armor on his shins and chest and a bronze helmet slit with a narrow opening for eyes and mouth. He carried a heavy wooden shield in his left hand. His weapons were a pike—a heavy wooden, iron-tipped thrusting spear at least 9 feet long—and a short, iron stabbing sword.

The men of the phalanx were arranged in close ranks, normally four to eight deep. Soldiers stood together in line, each man's shield overlapping his neighbor's. Hoplite combat involved set battles: head-to-head, army against army, all-or-nothing affairs, rather than individual skirmishes or guerrilla raids. Too unwieldy for Greece's mountains, the phalanx fought only in the plains. Battle usually consisted of an initial charge, followed by a grueling contest. The men in the front line pounded the enemy with their pikes while the men in the rear pushed forward. Finally one side would give way. The defeated ran away, if they could, while the victors staked their claim to the bloody field by erecting a trophy.

Greek hoplite warfare built on deep societal roots. Only independent men of means could afford hoplite armor. Thanks to the spread of the family farm, such men were common in Greece by around 700 B.C. Hoplites were amateur soldiers. Most were full-time farmers outside the fighting season, which lasted only for the summer months. The notion of the farmer-soldier, independent and free, would have a lasting impact in Western political thought. So would the warrior values of what became a way of life in Greece.

Aretê°, now translated as "excellence" or "virtue" but originally meaning "warrior prowess," was a central concept for the Greeks. In Homer, a warrior fought mainly for personal and familial honor (see page 63). By around 650 B.C., aretê referred also to the community. According to the poet Tyrtaeus (ca. 650 B.C.), the ideal soldier not only fights bravely but "heartens his neighbor by his words." Should he die, his death brings glory not only to

aretê (ah-reh-TAY)

Hoplites   A detail from a Corinthian vase of 625–600 B.C. shows pike-wielding hoplites closed in battle over a fallen comrade. In this image as elsewhere, Greek artists rendered warriors seminude and fighting in small groups, but in reality hoplites went into battle wearing heavy armor and fought in large units.   *(Louvre © R.M.N.)*

his father but also to his city and his countrymen. Although the battlefield remained the favored arena for displays of aretê, the assembly or the council house became increasingly acceptable as an alternative.

■ Emergence of the Polis

Paradoxes abound in the origins of the polis. The polis was both a product of the changes of the eighth century B.C. and itself a stimulus for change. As an urban settlement, the polis existed as early as the ninth or even the tenth century B.C. but its intense communal spirit did not emerge until around 700 B.C. In agriculture, the most important single profession, the prevalence of the family farm created a kind of rough social equality, which was reflected in a cultural emphasis on equality. Yet the polis rankled with social inequality as some grew rich on the profits of trade.

Polis came to denote not just a city but the community as a whole, corresponding roughly to a country or nation. One crude gauge of the centrality of the polis is the number, not to mention significance, of words the Greeks derived from it: among them, *polites* (citizen), *politeia* (constitution), *politeô* (to govern), *ta politika* (politics), and *politikos* (politician).

Most poleis° were small, many less than 100 square miles in size. Athens was one of the largest. Its territory, known as Attica (see Map 3.3), covered 1,000 square

poleis (PO-lays)

miles (approximately the size of Rhode Island). At its height (ca. 430 B.C.) the population of Athens was about 400,000, but a typical polis contained only between 5000 and 10,000 people. The philosopher Aristotle° (384–322 B.C.) wrote that an ideal polis should be small enough that the citizens know one another personally.

The polis consisted of two parts: the urban area, which usually was tiny, and the surrounding countryside, where most people lived. From the earliest times, the urban public space included both a defensible hill (preferably with a water supply), called a "high city" (*acropolis*°), and a "gathering place" (*agora*°) used as a marketplace and meeting place. At least one temple usually served as a focal point. After around 500 B.C. stone buildings, including council houses, theaters, covered porticoes, gymnasia, and baths, became increasingly common.

What distinguished the early polis, however, was not its buildings but its spirit. As the poet Alcaeus (b. ca. 630 B.C.) puts it, "Not houses finely roofed or the stones of walls well-built, nay nor canals and dockyards, make the polis, but men able to use their opportunity."

The Greeks came to call the polis a "common thing" (*koinon*). It was a shared commonwealth. It belonged to its people, not to a few nobles or to a king or a god. As early as about 700 B.C., important public documents were inscribed on stone. Acts of state were attributed not to a personified polis but to the community—for example, not to Thera but to "the Thereans," not to Sybaris but to "the Sybarites." The emphasis is on the plurality.

The emphasis was on equality as well. The early polis developed an ethos of measure and moderation. The ideal citizen was thought to be neither rich nor poor but of moderate means. All citizens should be roughly similar. Practice, however, proved different from theory, as the politics of the early polis makes clear.

■ Tyranny

Trade and colonization inspired change at home, for one thing, making increasing numbers of Greeks into seafarers. This was a critical development, for as the historian Thucydides (ca. 455–397 B.C.) argues, a sea power tends to be more dynamic and innovative than a land power. Seafarers are likely to come into contact with new ideas and institutions. In antiquity, ships moved more quickly and cheaply than land transport; thus, seafaring usually accelerated the rate of change.

One such change was Greece's growing wealth. To some extent, this wealth was general. The poet Hesiod, for example, records the increasing size and prosperity of the class of free farmers. Some individuals, however, grew far wealthier than others. Yet many of these newly rich lacked the status of the *basileis,* the elite of landowning families who monopolized political power and honor. In order to claim a share, the newly rich seem to have made common cause with the independent farmers who staffed the hoplite phalanx. The result was tyranny.

Tyrant, a term borrowed from the East, possibly from Lydia (a wealthy kingdom in Anatolia), originally referred not to an arbitrary and oppressive ruler but rather to a champion of the people. Having overthrown a narrow and entrenched aristocracy, tyrants were popular at first. *Tyrant* did not become a pejorative word before roughly 550 B.C., when the people soured on the second and third generation of tyrants.

Greek tyranny began in Argos, a polis in the northeastern Peloponnesus°, around 675 B.C. (see Map 3.1). The first tyrant was an Argive named Pheidon. By 660 tyranny had spread to nearby Corinth. Over the course of the seventh and sixth centuries B.C., all the major Greek poleis except Sparta became tyrannies.

Sources of evidence for the first tyrannies are poor, and much about the tyrants is debated by scholars. Yet it does seem that, in the seventh century B.C., wealthy men who had been denied political power rose on the shoulders of the hoplites and overthrew a narrow elite. They set up one-man rule, not in the name of the basileis, but on behalf of a much broader group: the prosperous farmers who fought in the phalanx.

Much of what the tyrants did, especially in the first generation, was popular and progressive. They stimulated the economy by founding colonies on trade routes, standardizing weights and measures, and encouraging the immigration of skilled craftsmen from other poleis. Corinth under the tyrant Cypselus (r. ca. 657–625 B.C.), for example, became the wealthiest city in Greece by exporting agricultural produce. Tyrants built temples and instituted festivals, providing both jobs and leisure-time activities.

When tyrants passed power on to their sons, however, the second generation tended to rule oppressively. Buoyed by the discontent of the demos, the basileis regrouped and tried to take back power. Thraysbulus of Miletus (ca. 600 B.C.), one second-generation tyrant, advised accordingly: To maintain power, a tyrant should

---

Aristotle (AR-is-tot-il)   **acropolis** (uh-CROP-uh-liss)
agora (AH-go-rah)

Peloponnesus (pel-uh-puh-NEE-suss)

"lop off the tallest ears of grain"—that is, execute or exile aristocrats in order to deny leaders to the opposition. But the tide of discontent was not to be stopped. Few tyrannies lasted beyond the third generation, when they were overthrown and replaced by oligarchy (literally, "rule by the few") or, less often, by democracy (literally, "power of the people"). By 500 B.C. tyranny had disappeared from most of Greece.

■ Sparta

Located in Laconia, a fertile valley in the south-central Peloponnesus, in the southern part of mainland Greece, Sparta seemed destined by geography for prosperity but not for glory. It was situated not at a crossroads or beside a great harbor but rather by rugged mountains that might have left it isolated (see Map 3.1). Yet Sparta proved to be an influential model of citizenship and constitutionalism, virtue and community, austerity and militarism.

The history of Sparta is not easy to write. Sparta was a closed military society, contemptuous of book learning, suspicious of foreigners, and secretive toward the outside world. Scholarship has lifted the veil a little, however. For example, Spartans believed that their unique system had been created at a stroke by the legendary lawgiver Lycurgus, who is supposed to have lived (according to the most common version) in the eighth century B.C. and whose charter for Sparta was a divine command. Nowadays, scholars argue for gradual innovations in Sparta rather than revolutionary change, for a process beginning around 650 B.C. and continuing for generations. And it is by no means clear that there ever was a Lycurgus. Let us consider the question of origins.

The foundations of Spartan society were laid around 650 B.C., when a three-part class system emerged. Helots°, unfree laborers who worked the land for their masters, were at the lowest level. In the middle ranks were *perioikoi* (roughly, "neighbors"), who were free but subordinate to the highest class. At the top stood Similars, who were the only full citizens. We do not know the number of helots, but we do know that they vastly outnumbered the other two classes.

Compared with individuals of the other classes, a Similar had a good life. If male and over 30, he had the right to attend the assembly and to hold public office. Each male Similar, moreover, was given a similar land allotment that was worked by helots, thereby freeing him to fight. As the name implies, Similars were alike but not equal. Wealthy Similars owned more land than the basic allotment.

Although Sparta is remembered as a conservative society, the idea of a large group of men sharing power was radical in its day. When the system began around 650 B.C., Similars numbered about nine thousand. What gave them their clout and prestige? The Similars were probably hoplites, the backbone of Sparta's army.

In the mid-seventh century B.C., Sparta was even more dependent on its army than was the average polis; the reason is the helots. Most helots were Messenians, whose fertile territory had been conquered by Sparta in about 725 B.C. Although the Messenians were Greeks, they were forced to labor for the conquerors. Sparta profited, but it now faced a security problem. The restive Messenian helots had to be policed, and a dramatic revolt sometime between 675 and 650 B.C. almost succeeded in expelling the Spartans. To keep Messenia, Sparta needed a crack army; to get that, Sparta needed to train, nourish, and glorify its soldiers. The political and economic result was to make all Spartan hoplites into Similars.

Sparta was no democracy, however. The ancients classified the Spartan government as "mixed" because it distributed power among the Similars through a combination of monarchy, oligarchy (that is, rule by an elite few), and popular government. The assembly of Similars constituted the popular element in the regime, but its powers were limited. Real power was shared among those Similars who were kings, elders, and *ephors* (overseers), men generally belonging to a few wealthy families.

The elite did not lead lives of luxury, however, at least not after around 550 B.C., when austerity became the order of the day. Society was re-ordered to promote the discipline and preparedness needed to maintain control of the helots. For example, Spartans' diet was famous for its simplicity. The preferred food was a black broth of pork cooked in its own blood and spiced with salt and vinegar. To discourage consumption, Sparta issued no coins; the official "currency" consisted of heavy and unwieldy iron skewers. Since the outside world was considered corrupt, Sparta engaged in little trade and admitted few foreigners to its territory—and they were subject to periodic expulsion.

Whereas other poleis offered little or no formal public education, Sparta schooled its sons from childhood to be soldiers—a system known as the *agoge*° ("upbringing"). Limited to male Similars, the agoge created a life cycle unique in Greece. At birth, babies were examined by public inspectors. Those who were considered deformed or unfit were "exposed"; that is, they were abandoned without food or shelter. The victims might die, but

---

helot (HEL-ut)

agoge (ah-go-GAY)

they might also be sold into slavery or even secretly adopted. (Other Greeks also practiced exposure of infants but the choice was a family matter, not public policy.) Surviving children were raised at home up to the age of 7, at which point boys left the family to be boarded with a "herd" of their age mates. For the eleven years from age 7 to age 18, a boy went through the rigorous training of the agoge. On the theory that good soldiers should be strong and silent, boys learned only enough reading and writing for practical ends—for example, for messages to and from military headquarters.

Many boys between the ages of 18 and 20 served in the *krypteia* (secret service), living covertly in the hills of Messenia, where they survived by hunting, foraging, and stealing. They spied on the ever-rebellious Messenian helots, whom they could kill with impunity because every year Sparta declared war on them. By age 20, all Similars had become hoplites, and they continued to serve in the army until age 60. Supported by helot labor, they devoted all their time to fighting and training the next generation.

Anything but democratic, Sparta ironically offered more opportunities outside the home to elite women than did other Greek states. For example, unlike most Greek girls, Spartan girls received a public education—limited, however, to physical training, which was thought to strengthen females for childbearing. Still, the sight of girls running, wrestling, and throwing the discus and javelin, which was common in Sparta, was unthinkable elsewhere in Greece. So was Sparta's unique recognition of the risks of maternity. Like Spartan men who died in battle, Spartan women who died in childbirth were allowed to have their names inscribed on their tombstones. All other Spartan burials were anonymous.

Spartan women were relatively more independent than women elsewhere in Greece. With the men consumed by military training or warfare, women ran the day-to-day operations of life, controlling the helot farm workers and servants, and raising the girls and the very small boys. Women married around age 20, men around 30. Newlyweds were supposed to spend only enough time together to produce offspring. Often neglected by their husbands, and having been schooled to assertiveness by youthful physical training outdoors, Spartan women also had the advantage of being able to inherit property, unlike Athenian women. (See the box "Reading Sources: Spartan Women.")

Beginning around 550 B.C., Sparta used its military might to build up a network of alliances (dubbed the "Peloponnesian° League" by scholars) in the Pelopon-

Spartan Woman   This bronze statuette (4¾ inches tall) from Laconia (ca. 530 B.C.) shows a woman running. Unlike other Greek women, elite Spartan women underwent physical education. Although their personal freedom was limited in Sparta, women suffered fewer restrictions than their counterparts in democratic Athens did.   *(National Archaeological Museum, Athens/Archaeological Receipts Fund)*

nesus and central Greece. It may seem paradoxical that a society that feared foreigners, as Sparta did, became the *hegemon°* (literally, "leader") of an extensive alliance system, but Sparta's fear made its leadership careful and deliberate. Sparta intervened in the wider world only to prevent threats from arising on the horizon. It used its power abroad when need be, but usually only after exhaustive debate and with utmost caution.

By around 500 B.C., all of the Peloponnesian poleis except Argos had alliances with Sparta, and in central Greece, Thebes came aboard shortly afterward. Allies swore "to follow Sparta wherever it may lead and to have the same friends and enemies." Until its breakup in the aftermath of the Peloponnesian War (431–404 B.C.; see page 91), the Peloponnesian League was the dominant

---

Peloponnesian (pell-uh-puh-NEE-shun)

hegemon (HEJ-uh-mahn)

Spartan Women

Spartan women were famous in antiquity for their remarkable freedom, but male observers differed as to whether the results were good or bad. In the following excerpts, Aristotle (384–322 B.C.) criticizes Spartan women, whereas Plutarch (ca. A.D. 50–120), a Greek scholar living in the Roman Empire, praises them.

Aristotle Complains

. . . the legislator [Lycurgus] wished the city as a whole to be hardy, and this is manifest in terms of the men; but he thoroughly neglected it in the case of the women, who live licentiously in every respect and in luxury. Wealth will necessarily be honored in a regime of this sort, particularly if they are dominated by women, as is the case of most stocks that are fond of soldiering and war. . . . This was the case with the Spartans, and many matters were administered by the women during the period of their [imperial] rule [405–371 B.C.]. And yet what difference is there between women ruling and rulers who are ruled by women? For the result is the same. . . .

Now this laxness concerning women appears to have arisen among the Spartans in a way that is quite reasonable. They spent much time away from their own land when they were at war. . . . As for the women, they say Lycurgus attempted to lead them toward the laws, but they were resistant, and he gave it up. . . . That what is connected with the women is not finely handled would seem not only to create an inappropriateness in the regime in its own terms, as was said earlier, but to contribute to their greed. For next to what has just been said, one must censure what pertains to the disparity in possessions. For it has happened that some of them possess too much property, and others very little; hence the territory has come into the hands of a few. . . . Indeed, nearly two-fifths of the entire territory belongs to women, both because many have become heiresses and because large dowries are given.

Plutarch Counters

Aristotle claims wrongly that he [Lycurgus] tried to discipline the women but gave up when he could not control the considerable degree of license and power attained by women because of their husbands' frequent campaigning. . . . Lycurgus rather showed all possible concern for . . . [women] too. First he toughened the girls physically by making them run and wrestle and throw the discus and javelin. Thereby their children in embryo would make a strong start in strong bodies and would develop better, while the women themselves would also bear their pregnancies with vigour and would meet the challenge of childbirth in a successful, relaxed way. He did away with prudery, sheltered upbringing and effeminacy of any kind. He made young girls no less than young men grow used to walking nude in processions, as well as to dancing and singing at certain festivals with the young men present and looking on. . . .

There was nothing disreputable about the girls' nudity. It was altogether modest, and there was no hint of immorality. Instead it encouraged simple habits and an enthusiasm for physical fitness, as well as giving the female sex a taste of masculine gallantry, since it too was granted equal participation in both excellence and ambition.

Sources: Aristotle, *The Politics,* trans. Carnes Lord (Chicago: University of Chicago Press, 1984), pp. 74–75; Plutarch, "Life of Lycurgus," in Richard J. A. Talbert, trans., *Plutarch on Sparta* (Harmondsworth, U.K.: Penguin, 1988), p. 24.

 For additional information on this topic, go to http://college.hmco.com.

land power in Greece and, after the defeat of Persia in 480 B.C., in the entire eastern Mediterranean.

Sparta exemplified community spirit and respect for law. The people of Sparta, as the historian Herodotus°

Herodotus (he-ROD-uh-tus)

(ca. 485–425 B.C.) quotes a Spartan king, "are free . . . , but not entirely free; for they have a master, and that master is Law, which they fear." Sparta was also an exemplar of equality—limited equality, to be sure, but equality extended to a wider group than ever before in Greece. The notion of the Similars, moreover, contains the germ of

Map 3.3   Attica   Mountains and plains alternate in the 1,000-square-mile area of ancient Attica. The Long Walls connecting Athens with the port city of Piraeus were built around 450 B.C.

the idea of the citizen: a free member of the political community who, unlike a subject, has rights as well as duties. Few other poleis could match the stability and sense of civic duty fostered by Sparta. In the realms of equality and citizenship, however, Sparta was eventually outstripped by Athens. In the realm of liberty, Athens wrote a new chapter in Western history.

■ Early Athens

Around 650 B.C. the basileis of the Pedion, or Attic, Plain (see Map 3.3), who proudly called themselves the Eupa-trids° ("well-fathered men"), ruled Athens. They served in one-year magistracies and afterward became life members of the Areopagus°, a council of elders named for its meeting place on the "hill of Ares." By its prestige,

this aristocratic council held the lion's share of power, both in politics and in justice, for it also served as a court. The demos° (the people) met in an assembly. Probably from early times on, the assembly had, in theory, supreme lawmaking power as well as authority over war and peace, but voting was by shouting, and few people challenged Eupatrid wishes.

By 632 B.C. the aristocrats faced trouble in Athens as elsewhere because of corruption, economic change, and assertive hoplites. A failed attempt that year to establish a tyranny left the forces for change eager. In 621 B.C. a loose coalition opposed to Eupatrid rule forced a codification of the laws, which were then issued in writing. This Code of Draco°, named for its main drafter, was infamous for its harsh provisions (hence the adjective *draconian*); it was written, a later commentator suggested,

---

Eupatrid (YOO-pat-rid)   **Areopagus** (ar-ee-OP-uh-gus)   **demos** (DEE-mus)   **Draco** (DRAY-co)

"not in ink but blood." Yet Draco's Code seems only to have whetted an appetite for change. A wealthy non-Eupatrid elite of hoplites was emerging, grown rich exporting olive oil. Some were merchants; most were prosperous farmers. They now wanted political power. As for ordinary Athenians, they typically worked small family farms. Over the years, bad harvests and soil exhaustion had sent many into debt. Those who had pledged their land as collateral became known as *hektemoroi* ("sixth-parters"), probably because they owed one-sixth of their crops to their creditors. Other farmers sank even further into debt and had only themselves or their children as collateral. Some ended up as slaves, sometimes sold abroad. Because both rich and poor Athenians had grievances against the Eupatrids, revolution was in the air. Enter Solon° (ca. 630–560 B.C.), who was appointed to the emergency position of sole *archon* (chief officer) for one year, probably 594 B.C. A Eupatrid who had become a merchant, Solon understood both the old and the new elite, and he was sympathetic to ordinary Athenians as well. As his surviving writings show, Solon was a moderate. He could have become tyrant, but he preferred to be a mediator; as such, he said, he "stood

with a strong shield before both parties [the common people and the powerful] and allowed neither one to win an unfair victory."[1]

Solon's reforms were comprehensive, spanning both economics and politics. He helped ordinary people by the "shaking off of burdens," measures that abolished the institution of hektemorage and probably canceled some debts. He also abolished the practice of making loans on personal surety and set up a fund to redeem Athenians who had been sold into slavery abroad. By freeing the hektemoroi, Solon ensured Athens a large class of independent small farmers.

Solon's other economic reforms were aimed at encouraging Athenian trade. To foster production of olive oil, a cash crop, he restricted all other agricultural exports. He changed Athenian weights, measures, and perhaps coins to conform to the most common Greek standard. The result was a commercial boom.

Solon made fundamental changes in Athenian government, too. He changed qualifications for office from birth to wealth, a boon to the non-Eupatrid elite. He established four census classes based on agricultural production. Most offices were reserved for men of property, but the poorest class, known as *thetes,* could participate in the assembly and courts. Solon probably established a Council of 400, which prepared the assembly's agenda.

Solon (SO-lun)

He is probably also responsible for regularizing council and assembly meetings and replacing the assembly's voice votes with the counting of hands.

Solon's moderation, respect for law, and liberation of the poor and downtrodden are milestones in Greek history. Yet, ironically, Solon's reforms had an unexpected byproduct—the growth of slavery in Athens. Though booming, the Athenian economy lost its cheap labor when Solon freed debt slaves and hektemoroi. The solution was to buy slaves abroad and import them to Athens. At the time, the island city-state of Chios was the center of the slave trade in Greece (see Map 3.2). After Solon, Athens along with Chios developed one of history's first large-scale slave systems. Slaves worked in agriculture, crafts, trade, and elsewhere in the economy. Unlike helots, slaves could be bought and sold and were often uprooted, and the system was better policed than in earlier societies.

If free Athenians had any moral doubts about slavery, they went unrecorded. Yet there was much dissatisfaction with Solon's reforms since his middle way satisfied neither Eupatrids nor champions of the free poor. After years of conflict, around 560 B.C. advocates of radical reform established a tyranny under Pisistratus° (ca. 600–528 B.C.). He and his sons held power for forty of the next fifty years.

Supported by the thetes, the Pisistratids exiled many Eupatrids and confiscated and redistributed their land. Pisistratus kept the façade of Solon's reforms while ensuring that loyal supporters held all key offices.

A stable regime, the tyranny witnessed prosperity at home and the expansion of Athenian influence abroad. Yet Pisistratus's dynasty lasted only two generations. A steadfast opponent of tyrants, Sparta deposed his son, Hippias, in 510 B.C. Athens's elites by birth and wealth were ready to establish an oligarchy, but the way was open for an unexpected development: the emergence of popular government.

THE CULTURE OF ARCHAIC GREECE

WHILE one trend in Archaic culture was communal solidarity, as reflected in the hoplite phalanx, another was quite the opposite: a growing elevation of individualism. Increased prosperity and mobility (social, geographic, and political) during the Archaic period encouraged the breakdown of old ties

and left some people with a sense of their uniqueness. Archaic poetry and sculpture both demonstrate this new consciousness of the self.

Meanwhile, although most Archaic Greeks celebrated religion, a small group of thinkers expressed religious doubts. While monumental stone temples and international centers for divination were being erected to honor the pantheon of gods, Greek thinkers began to move away from divine and toward abstract and mechanistic explanations of the universe. Their defection marked the start of the Western philosophical tradition.

■ Revealing the Self: Lyric Poetry and Sculpture

Between approximately 675 and 500 B.C., the dominant Greek literary form was lyric poetry. This genre consisted of short poems written in a variety of styles but sharing a willingness to experiment, sometimes by revealing private feelings, sometimes by commenting on contemporary politics (as in the poetry of Tyrtaeus). Epic poetry, by contrast, was longer, grander in theme and tone, and less personal.

Homer never speaks directly about himself, and Hesiod reveals only a few personal details. In contrast, Archilochus° of Paros (ca. 700–650 B.C.), the earliest known of the lyric poets, flaunts the self. Born on the Cycladic island of Paros, Archilochus was the son, perhaps the illegitimate son, of a noble. He was a mercenary soldier (that is, he fought for pay for a foreign country) and a colonist before returning home and dying in a hoplite battle against a neighboring island. The varied subjects of Archilochus's poetry include love, travels, and war. Much of his poetry is satire, sometimes mocking and ironic, sometimes vicious and abusive. Archilochus takes a cynical and detached view of hoplite ideals, freely admitting that he once tossed away his shield to escape the battlefield: "And that shield, to hell with it! Tomorrow I'll get me another one no worse."[2]

Sappho° of Lesbos (ca. 625 B.C.) is also famous as a private poet, one who composed unmatched descriptions of intimate feelings, among them love for other women. Sappho is one of the few women poets of antiquity whose work has survived—very little, unfortunately, but enough to show that she was educated, worldly, and versed in politics. Like a modern experimental poet, she uses language self-consciously. Sappho's sensuality comes through in a description of her feelings at seeing a woman whose company she wants talking with a man: her heart shakes, her tongue is stuck, her eyes cannot

---

Pisistratus (pie-SIS-trah-tus)

Archilochus (ar-KIL-uh-kus)   **Sappho** (SAF-oh)

see, her skin is on fire. "I am greener than grass," Sappho writes, "I feel nearly as if I could die."[3]

Sappho discusses female sexuality, a subject that Greek elite culture, dominated by males, tended to ignore. We know little about the sexuality of Greek women or of nonelite males. Among the male elite, romantic love in Archaic and Classical Greece was homosexual love or, to be precise, pederasty ("boy love"). The ideal relationship was supposed to involve a man in his twenties and a boy in his teens. The male elite was, strictly speaking, bisexual. By age 30, a man was expected to marry and raise a family. Perhaps bisexuality prevailed among elite females as well; Sappho, for example, eventually married and had a child.

Athenian Kore   This statue of a young woman (*kore*) exemplifies Archaic Greek sculpture's interest in the idealized human form. Note the slight smile, the carefully coiffed hair, and the elaborate clothes. Influenced by contemporary Egyptian statues, the Greek sculptors nonetheless created a new and original style.   *(Robert Frerck/Odyssey Productions)*

Another sign of Archaic Greece's interest in the personal is the growing attention paid to the depiction of the human body, both in painting (most of the surviving examples are painted pottery) and in sculpture. Archaic artists displayed increasing skill and sensitivity in depicting the human form. The rich marble deposits in Greek soil gave sculptors promising material; baked clay (terra cotta) and bronze were other common sculptural media.

Early Archaic marble sculpture (seventh century B.C.) was strongly influenced by the way Egyptian sculpture represented the human body. Like Egyptian statuary, early Greek sculpture tended to be formal and frontal. But over the course of the seventh and sixth centuries B.C., Greek sculptors experimented with a greater variety of poses and with increasing realism in showing musculature and motion. This realism, however, was expressed within limits, for the favorite subject of Archaic sculptors was not ordinary people but idealized, beautiful youth. Typical sculptural forms were the naked young man (*kouros*) and clothed young woman (*kore*), which often served as grave markers or monuments. The goal was to show people not as they were but as they might be.

■ Religious Faith and Practice

The Olympian gods who had been worshiped in the Mycenaean era survived in later ages, suitably adapted to fit new political and social conditions. In the Archaic period, accordingly, the Olympian gods became gods of the polis.

Although the Olympians were revered throughout Greece, each polis had its patron deity: Apollo at Corinth, Hera at Argos and Samos, Athena at Athens and Sparta. Each polis also had its favorite heroes or demigods—for example, Theseus, the legendary founder of Athens, and Heracles (Hercules), a favorite of Dorian cities such as Sparta and Thebes. Devotees considered it important to build a "house"—that is, a temple—for the local patron god or at least for his or her statue. The first temples were built of wood; the earliest stone temple, a temple of Apollo at Corinth, was built around 550 B.C.

Temples were rectangular structures with long sides on the north and south, short sides on the east and west, a colonnade around all four sides, and a pitched roof. The columns were based loosely on those of Egyptian architecture. Greek temples faced east so sunlight would illuminate the interior, which consisted of two rooms: a small treasury, open to the west, and a larger main chamber, in which a statue of the deity stood. The interior decoration of the temple was simple. Outside, however, brownish-red roof tiles, painted sculpture above the colonnade and in the pediments (the area between the gables and the front and rear doorways), and terra-cotta roof ornaments created a festive and lively effect. The bare white ruins seen today are misleading.

The emphasis on exterior rather than interior decoration in a Greek temple reflects the way the building was used. The main ceremony took place outside. A long altar stood in front of the temple and parallel to it. On feast days—and under the tyrants the number of such days was increased greatly, as a concession to the common people—temple priests would sacrifice animals (pigs, goats, lambs, and, less often, bulls) on the altar. Only the thighs would be burned for the gods. The rest of the meat would be boiled and distributed to worshipers.

As in other ancient cultures, so in Greece divination was an important element of religion. Divination was institutionalized in *oracles*, places where, it was believed, a god or hero might be consulted for advice. Of the various Greek oracles, that of Apollo at Delphi° (in central Greece) became the most prestigious and respected. At Delphi, Apollo spoke through the Pythia, a priestess who went into a trance. The utterances of Apollo of Delphi were famous among the Greeks for being ambiguous. Because different people might interpret them in different ways, Apollo could always be absolved after the fact if things did not turn out as the listener expected.

The oracle of Delphi was regularly consulted by poleis wishing to establish colonies. The oracle gave advice about the choice of location and the appropriate patron god or goddess, and it helped settlers draft new law codes. Delphi was also active in the search for new constitutions in the old poleis of Greece. Tradition says that Sparta based its government on a pronouncement of the Delphic oracle.

Archaic thinkers pondered the theme of divine justice. In Archaic literature we see less of the petty squabblings among the gods than in Homer and more of Zeus's majesty and justice. Although the wicked might seem to prosper, Zeus eventually punishes them or their descendants. "It never escapes him all the way when a man has a sinful spirit; and always, in the end, his judgment is plain," says Solon.[4]

Archaic writers delighted in portraying human emotions, but they had no confidence about the human ability to master emotions. In Archaic literature, people are weak and insignificant; their fortune is uncertain and mutable. Further, the gods are jealous of human success. People who aim too high are guilty of *hubris*—that is, arrogance with overtones of violence and transgression.

Hubris inevitably brings *nemesis,* "punishment" or "allotment." The safest course is for a person to be pious and humble.

So Archaic religion taught a humbling, even pessimistic, lesson. Yet religious teachings were not always heeded. The pages of Archaic history are full of examples of politicians, generals, athletes, merchants, and artists who aimed high and sought success with seemingly little worry, and no dire consequences. In Ionia° (the territory of the Greek cities along the central western Anatolian coast; see Map 3.2), one group of Greek thinkers made a radical break with Archaic religion and invented speculative philosophy.

■ The Origins of Western Philosophy

Abstract, rationalistic, speculative thinking emerged in Greece during the sixth century B.C. The first developments took place in Miletus, an Ionian city. It is often said that the thinkers of Miletus (the Milesians°) and their followers in other parts of Ionia invented philosophy. So they did, but we must be precise about what this means.

The Ionians were not the first to ask questions or tell stories about the nature and origins of the universe; virtually every ancient people did so. Nor did the Ionians invent science. They themselves conducted no experiments. By 600 B.C., moreover, science—including mathematics, astronomy, medicine, and engineering—had been thriving for over two thousand years in Egypt and Mesopotamia, a heritage with which the Ionians were familiar and from which they borrowed.

The real importance of the Ionians is as pioneers of rationalism. They began the movement away from anthropomorphic or divine explanations and toward an abstract and mechanistic explanation of the universe. They themselves did not make a clear distinction between reason and revelation, but they made it possible for later Greek thinkers to do so. Later Greek philosophers were rarely (if ever) atheists, but they took for granted what the Ionians labored to establish: the primacy of human reason.

The Ionians saw themselves as students of nature—*physis* (from which the word *physics* is derived). Although they also commented on morality and politics, their interest in natural phenomena is what makes the Ionians significant. In their own day, the Ionians were called "wise men" (*sophoi*); to a later generation, they were

---

Delphi (DEL-fye)

Ionia, Ionian (eye-OH-nee-uh, eye-OH-nee-un)
Miletus, Milesian (my-LEE-tus, my-LEE-zhen)

"lovers of wisdom," *philosophoi* (from which *philosopher* comes).

Thales°, the first Milesian thinker, made a name for himself by successfully predicting a solar eclipse in 585 B.C. He is credited with founding Greek geometry and astronomy. Little survives of his writings or those of the other Milesians, but it is clear that he created the first general and systematic theory about the nature of the universe. According to Thales, the primary substance, the element from which all of nature was created, was water. He emphasized the mobility of water and its ability to nourish life.

A reply was not long in coming. Around 550 B.C., Anaximander of Miletus wrote the first known book of prose in Greek, expounding his own philosophy of nature. He attacked Thales for oversimplifying and for failing to do justice to the dynamism of nature. Anaximander accepted Thales' monist assumption—that all matter originated from one primary substance—but he called the substance "the unlimited" or "the undefined" rather than water. A third Milesian, Anaximenes, replied that the primary substance might be unlimited but it was not undefined. It was air, whose properties of condensation and rarefaction symbolized the dynamic and changing nature of things.

Humble as these theories might seem today, they represent a dramatic development: an open and critical debate among thinkers, each of whom was proposing an abstract and rational model of the universe. Many scholars have speculated about the origins of this development. Why Miletus? Why the sixth century B.C.? There are no sure answers, although certain influences have been suggested. Among them are Miletus's contacts on the trade routes with sophisticated Babylon, the proximity of Ionia to non-Greek peoples and the resulting Milesian appreciation of variety and complexity, and the search for law and order in contemporary Greek political life and its extension to the philosophical plane.

In its second generation early Greek philosophy moved to other Ionian cities and then migrated westward across the Mediterranean. Heracleitus° of Ephesus (ca. 500 B.C.) proposed fire as the primary substance. Although fire was ever changing, it had an underlying coherence. According to Heracleitus, this paradox nicely symbolized the nature of the universe. He summed up the importance of change by the aphorisms "All things flow" and "You cannot step into the same river twice." The universe witnessed a constant struggle of opposites, yet an essential unity and order prevailed. To describe this order, Heracleitus used the term *logos*. This key concept of Greek philosophy is difficult to translate: among other definitions, *logos* can mean "word," "thought," "reason," "story," or "calculation."

Heracleitus's contemporary, Pythagoras° of Samos, was both a rationalist and a religious thinker. On the one hand, Pythagoras was a mathematician who discovered the numerical ratios determining the major intervals of the musical scale, that is, the range of sound between high and low. It is less certain if, as tradition has it, he discovered the so-called Pythagorean theorem—that in a right triangle the hypotenuse squared is equal to the sum of the squares of the other two sides.

On the other hand, Pythagoras believed that the purity of mathematics would improve the human soul. Just as he had imposed numerical order on the musical scale, so could philosophers understand the entire universe through number and proportion. The resulting knowledge was no mere academic exercise but a way of life. He devoted himself to "observation" or "contemplation"—to *theoria* (from which *theory* comes).

In Croton in Magna Graecia (southern Italy), Pythagoras founded a religious community. Its members observed strict secrecy, but it appears that they abstained from meat because they believed in the kinship of all living things. They also believed in the reincarnation of the human soul, though not necessarily into a human body. Pythagoras is said to have stopped a man from beating a dog because he recognized from the barking that the dog was the reincarnation of a friend who had died.

The early Greek philosopher whose work is most fully preserved is Parmenides° of Elea in Magna Graecia. Parmenides (b. ca. 515 B.C.) completely distrusted the senses. He believed that reality was a world of pure being: eternal, unchanging, and indivisible, comparable to a sphere. To Parmenides, change was a mere illusion. Parmenides, therefore, is the first Western philosopher to propose a radical difference between the world of the senses and reality. This fundamental strain of Western thought would be taken up by Plato and his followers and then passed to Christianity.

To sum up, in philosophy as in so many other endeavors, the Archaic Greeks were great borrowers and even greater innovators who left a profound mark on later ages. By the late sixth century B.C., Archaic Greece was poised on the brink of a revolution that would give birth to the Classical period of Greek civilization.

Thales (THAY-leez)
Heracleitus (her-uh-CLY-tus)

Pythagoras (py-THAG-uh-russ)
Parmenides (par-MEN-uh-deez)

CLASSICAL GREECE

T HE word *democracy* comes from the Greek word *demokratia°*, coined in Athens early in the fifth century B.C. *Demokratia* literally means "the power *(kratos)* of the people *(demos)*." A modern democracy is characterized by mass citizenship, elections, and representative government. Athenian demokratia, in contrast, was a direct democracy in which elections mattered less than direct participation; citizenship was narrowly restricted; women were excluded from politics; resident aliens could almost never become citizens; and citizens owned slaves and ruled an empire. Modern democracies may cover a huge territory, but Athens encompassed only 1,000 square miles. Modern democracies tend to emphasize individual rights. Athens, in contrast, often placed the community first. In spite of these differences, Athenian demokratia established principles that are enshrined in democracy today: freedom, equality, citizenship without property qualifications, the right of most citizens to hold public office, and the rule of law.

The young democracy's greatest achievement was to spearhead Greece's victory over the Persian invaders in 480 B.C. After that victory, Athens became Greece's leading sea power. Yet Sparta remained the superior land power, and the two poleis were soon locked in a cycle of competition and war. The result nearly destroyed Athenian democracy while, even more serious, it undermined Greece's very independence.

■ The Development of Demokratia, 508–322 B.C.

Tyranny often gave way to oligarchy—to government by wealthy men, both Eupatrids and non-Eupatrids. In Athens after Pisistratid rule, however, conditions were ripe for revolution. Solon had left a society of independent small farmers, while the Pisistratids had strengthened the ranks of immigrants and weakened the Eupatrids. Elite leaders nonetheless tried to establish an Athenian oligarchy. We may imagine strong popular opposition.

Ironically, a Eupatrid, a member of the Alcmeonid clan by the name of Cleisthenes° (d. ca. 500 B.C.), led the revolution. Originally Cleisthenes aimed to head the oligarchy, but his rivals shut him out of power. He turned then to the demos, whose leader he became. The watchwords of the day were *equality* and *mixing.*

Frightened by the assertive populace, the oligarchs called for Spartan military assistance, but to no avail: Cleisthenes rallied the people to victory. The Athenian triumph proved, in Herodotus's opinion, "that equality is an excellent thing, not in one way only but in many. For while they were under a tyranny, [Athenians] were no better at fighting than any of their neighbors, but once they were rid of tyrants they became by far the best."[5]

Cleisthenes extinguished Eupatrid power once and for all by attacking its local bases of support. For example, he abolished the four traditional tribes and apportioned the people among ten new tribes. Immigrants and their descendants, who had been excluded from the old tribes, now joined natives in the new tribes. The tribes formed the basis of a new Council of 500 to replace Solon's Council of 400. The council was divided into ten tribal units, each serving as a kind of executive committee for one of the ten months of the civic year.

The centerpiece of the government was the assembly, some of whose members, emboldened by the new spirit of equality, now spoke up for the first time. The new Council of 500, like its predecessor, prepared the assembly's agenda, but assemblymen felt free to amend it. Only the Areopagus council remained a privileged preserve.

The last and most unusual part of the Cleisthenic system was ostracism, a sort of annual *un*popularity contest that received its name from the pieces of broken pottery *(ostraka)* on which the names of victims were chiseled. The "winner" was forced into ten years of exile, although his property would not be confiscated. Ostracism was meant to protect the regime by defusing factionalism and discouraging tyrants. Judging by Athens's consequent political stability, it worked.

In 508 B.C. the poorest Athenians had relatively little power in Cleisthenic government. They lacked the financial means, the political consciousness, and the self-confidence needed to engage in politics. Changing conditions by the 450s rendered Athens even more democratic. During that period, the oldest principle of Greek politics came to the fore: Whoever fights for the state governs it. To counter the Persian threat against Greece in the 480s (see page 91), Athens built a great navy. The standard ship was a trireme°, an oared warship rowed by 170 men on three decks. The core of the rowers consisted of Athenian thetes. Just as hoplites supported new regimes in Greece after 700 B.C., so rowers supported new regimes in Greece after 500 B.C.

---

demokratia (deh-mo-kra-TEE-uh)
Cleisthenes (KLICE-the-neez)

trireme (TRY-reem)

Greek Trireme   The *Olympias* is a hypothetical reconstruction of an Athenian war galley of about 400 B.C. Rowed by 170 oarsmen arranged on three decks, the trireme fought by ramming an enemy ship with the bronze ram attached to its bow.   *(Courtesy of the Trireme Trust)*

A second revolution occurred around 461 B.C., when Ephialtes (d. ca. 460 B.C.) and his young associate, Pericles° (ca. 495–429 B.C.), targeted the last bulwark of privilege, the Areopagus. They stripped away the council's long-standing supervisory powers over the regime and redistributed those powers to the Council of 500 and the people's court. The decade of the 450s saw another innovation: payment for public service, specifically for jurors, who received a half-drachma (perhaps a half-day's wages) for a day of jury duty. Eventually other public servants also received pay. Conservatives complained bitterly because they perceived, rightly, that state pay made political activity by poor people possible. State pay was, an Athenian said, "the glue of demokratia."

Demokratia became closely connected with Pericles, who inherited the constituency of Ephialtes after his assassination around 460 B.C. For much of the next thirty years, Pericles dominated Athenian politics. An aristocrat who respected the common people, an excellent orator who benefited from an education in philosophy, an honest and tireless worker, a general who led in peace as well as war, Pericles was a political giant. Under his leadership, demokratia became firmly entrenched as the government and way of life in Athens.

Athenian democracy survived, with occasional oligarchic intrusions, for 150 years after Pericles' death. During those years it became more institutionalized and cautious, but it also became more thoroughly egalitarian.

■ How Demokratia Worked

Unlike most modern democracies, Athenian demokratia was direct and participatory. Pericles once claimed that in Athens "people pay attention both to their own household and to politics. Even those occupied with other activities are no less knowledgeable about politics."[6] This is part boast, but only part. Large numbers of ordinary citizens attended the assembly from time to time and held public office or served on the Council of 500 for a year or two. (See the box "Reading Sources: The Debate on Democracy.")

The instruments of government are easily sketched. The central institution was the assembly. Open to all male citizens over age 20, assembly meetings were held in the open air, on a hillside seating several thousand on benches (see the photograph on page 68). In the fourth century B.C. the assembly gathered a minimum of forty times per year, about once every ten days.

Pericles (PAIR-ih-kleez)

❧ READING SOURCES

The Debate on Democracy

Characters in Greek drama often discuss general principles. In this excerpt from Euripides' tragedy The Suppliant Women *(ca. 420 B.C.), Theseus, legendary king of Athens, and a herald from Creon, tyrant of Thebes, debate the merits of democracy.*

Herald

What man is tyrant in this land? To whom / Must I give the word I bring from Creon, ruler / In Cadmus' country [Thebes] . . . ?

Theseus

One moment, stranger. / Your start was wrong, seeking a tyrant here. / This city is free, and ruled by no one man. / The people reign, in annual succession. / They do not yield the power to the rich; / The poor man has an equal share in it.

Herald

That one point gives the better of the game / To me. The town I come from is controlled / By one man, not a mob. And there is no one / To puff it up with words, for private gain, / Swaying it this way, that way. . . . / The people is no right judge of arguments. / Then how can it give right guidance to a city? / A poor man, working hard, could not attend / To public matters, even if ignorance / Were not his birthright. When a wretch, a nothing, / Obtains respect and power from the people / By talk, his betters sicken at the sight.

Theseus

. . . Nothing / Is worse for a city than a tyrant. / In earliest days, before the laws are common, / One man has power and makes the law his own: /Equality is not yet. With written laws, / People of small resources and the rich / Both have the same recourse to justice. Now / A man of means, if badly spoken of, / Will have no better standing than the weak; / And if the little man is right, he wins / Against the great. This is the call of freedom: / "What man has good advice to give the city, / And wishes to make it known?" He who responds / Gains glory; the reluctant hold their peace. / For the city, what can be more fair than that?

Source: Adapted from Euripides, *The Suppliant Women*, trans. Frank Jones, in *Euripides IV: The Complete Greek Tragedies*, ed. David Grene and Richmond Lattimore (Chicago: University of Chicago Press, 1958), pp. 73–74.

The assembly heard the great debates of the day. It made decisions about war and peace, alliance and friendship; it conferred honors and issued condemnations; it passed decrees relating to current issues and set up commissions to revise fundamental laws. In the assembly great orators addressed the people, but everyone, however humble, was theoretically entitled to speak.

The judicial branch consisted of courts, which, with a few exceptions, were open to all citizens, no matter how poor. Aristotle or a member of his school comments that "when the people have the right to vote in the courts, they control the constitution." Juries were large, commonly consisting of several hundred men chosen by lottery; small juries, it was felt, were easily bribed. After a preliminary hearing, cases were decided in a single day.

The executive consisted of the Council of 500 and some seven hundred public officials (also, under Athens's empire in the fifth century B.C., several hundred others living abroad). All male citizens over age 30 were eligible to serve. Most public officials were chosen by lottery, which put rich and poor, talented and untalented, on an equal footing. To guard against installing incompetents or criminals, all officials had to undergo a scrutiny by the council before taking office and an audit after the term. Most magistracies, moreover, were boards, usually of ten men, so even if a bad man managed to pass this scrutiny, he would be counterbalanced by his colleagues. Only generals and treasurers were chosen by election.

Athens had a relatively weak executive, and no chief executive such as a president or prime minister.

Generals and orators led assembly debates, and sometimes exercised great influence, but ordinary people set the agenda and made the decisions by taking votes at each assembly meeting. On the local level, every deme (county) had an annually chosen executive and a deme assembly of all citizens.

So novel and populist a system of government has not been without critics, either in antiquity or today. Some have charged that the Athenian people were uneducated, emotional, and easily swayed by oratorical tricks. Others say that demokratia degenerated into mob rule after the death of Pericles. Still others complain about the lack of a system of formal public education, which denied many citizens equality of opportunity.

The copybook of Athenian democracy does have some blots in its history, particularly in the heat of wartime. The Peloponnesian War (431–404 B.C.) witnessed several Athenian atrocities and judicial murders. Yet these were exceptions: In its roughly two hundred years of existence, Athenian demokratia was generally stable, law-abiding, and fair-minded.

■ Metics, Women, and Slaves

Another serious charge against Athenian demokratia is that it was democracy for a small elite only. Adult male citizens never accounted for more than one-tenth of the population, approximately 40,000 out of a total population—men, women and children, resident aliens, and slaves—of about 400,000. To become a citizen, at age 18 a boy had to prove that he was the legitimate son of a citizen father and a citizen maternal grandfather. Girls were never officially registered as citizens. Although the term *citizeness* existed, Athenian citizen women were usually referred to as "city women." As for resident aliens, whether male or female, they rarely attained citizenship.

In the fifth and fourth centuries B.C., Athens had a large population of foreigners. Some were transient. Others were officially registered resident aliens, or *metics°*. Metics came by the thousands from all over the Greek world and beyond. Some, like Aristotle (a native of a Greek colony in Macedonia°), were attracted by the city's schools of philosophy, but most came because of its unparalleled economic opportunities. Metics could not own land in Athens, and they had to pay extra taxes and serve in the Athenian military. Nevertheless, they prospered in Athenian commerce and crafts.

Athenian women generally led restricted lives. They were excluded from politics and played only a modest role in commerce as small retailers. They rarely received an education, not even in physical fitness as at Sparta. In legal and contractual matters Athenian women were almost always required to be represented by a male guardian.

Yet perhaps Athenian women led less restricted lives than it might seem. Let us distinguish between theory and practice. Paradoxically, the more power was distributed among the male citizenry, the more hostile to women's freedom did Athens's citizen ideology become. Greek males believed that the more honor a woman brought the man who won her, the more danger she might bring by tempting outsiders to seduce her. Hence demokratia promulgated an ideal of seclusion for women.

Practice, however, was another matter. As Aristotle asks rhetorically, "How is it possible to prevent the wives of the poor from going out?" *Poor* is a synonym for *ordinary* in ancient Greek. Ordinary women could not stay at home because they had to run errands, draw water, and sometimes even help make ends meet. Ordinary houses, moreover, were small and cramped, and in the Mediterranean heat women could not stay inside all the time.

Women played a major role in Athenian religion. They were priestesses in more than forty major cults. They participated each year in many festivals, including several reserved for women only. One such festival, the Thesmophoria, a celebration of fertility held each autumn, featured a three-day encampment of women on a hillside in the city, right beside the Athenian assembly amphitheater. Women attended public funeral orations in honor of soldiers who had died fighting for Athens, and probably attended plays.

We occasionally get glimpses, sometimes more, of Athenian women resisting or working behind the scenes to correct male mistakes. An inheritance case reveals a woman go-between interceding among her quarreling male relations. Greek comedy shows women mocking male pretensions and establishing sisterly friendships. A woman who brought a large dowry into a marriage could use it and the threat of divorce to influence her husband (the dowry had to be returned to the woman's father or guardian if there was a divorce). In short, Athenian women had some access to the world outside the household and some influence within the household. There existed, nonetheless, a real disparity in power between men and women.

One small group of noncitizen women, *hetairai* or courtesans (that is, prostitutes patronized by men of

---

metic (MEH-tik)   **Macedonia** (mah-suh-DOE-nee-uh)

wealth and status) sometimes had unusual access to power. The most famous example is Aspasia°, an educated woman from Miletus, who for many years was the mistress of Pericles, to whom she bore a son. Aspasia and Pericles gathered around them a glittering circle of thinkers and artists. Some say that Aspasia even influenced Pericles' political decisions.

Turning to slavery, that institution was widespread in democratic Athens. Some slaves served in agriculture, some labored under miserable conditions in Athenian silver mines, and some were engaged in commerce or the military (where some rowers were slaves). Most, however, worked as domestics or in small workshops as, for example, metalworkers or furniture makers. The vast majority of slaves were non-Greek. Most were prisoners of war; some were victims of pirates or debtors from states where, unlike Athens, citizens might still end up in debt-slavery. Thrace (roughly, modern Bulgaria) and Anatolia were the main sources of slaves, but some slaves came from North Africa and other Mediterranean regions.

The living conditions of slaves were usually poor and in the silver mines abysmal. Emancipation, however, was more common in Athens than in the American South before 1865. A few ex-slaves even rose to positions of wealth and power in Athens. A striking and unusual case is that of Pasion (d. 370 B.C.). Originally a slave employee of a banking firm, he bought his freedom and became the wealthiest Athenian banker of his day, as well as an Athenian citizen.

Athenian demokratia lacked many features of modern democracy: among them, a notion of universal human rights, the possibility for immigrants to become citizens, gender equality, the abolition of slavery, and public education. To its small citizen body, however, Athenian demokratia offered extraordinary freedom, equality, and responsibility, and a degree of participation in public life seldom equaled. Demokratia was a model of what democracy could be, but not of who could take part.

■ The Persian Wars, 499–479 B.C.

In 500 B.C. Sparta, hegemon of the Peloponnesian League, was the most prominent power of the Greek mainland. Across the Aegean Sea in Anatolia, the Greek city-states had been under Persian rule for two generations, since Cyrus the Great's conquest in the 540s. In 499 B.C., however, events began to unfold that not only would revo-

Aspasia (uh-SPAY-see-uh)

Women at Work   This Classical vase painting shows women filling jugs with water at a fountain and carrying the jugs back home. Fetching water was daily work for women, often slaves, which the women in this scene may well be. *(Louvre © R.M.N.)*

lutionize that balance of power but would throw the entire eastern Mediterranean into two hundred years of turmoil.

Led by Miletus, the Ionian Greek city-states rose in revolt against Persia in 499 B.C. Athens sent troops to help, but despite initial successes Athens reconsidered the alliance and withdrew its forces. The Ionian coalition broke down thereafter and was crushed by Persia. Miletus was besieged and destroyed, but otherwise Persia was relatively lenient in Ionia.

Upstart Athens, however, could not go unpunished. In 490 B.C., Darius I sent a large naval expedition to Athens carrying about 25,000 infantrymen and 1,200 cavalrymen (with horses). They landed at Marathon, some 24 miles from the city of Athens (see Map 3.3). Athens sent 10,000 men (including 1,000 allies) to defend Marathon. A great battle ensued.

Persian overconfidence and the superiority of the Greek phalanx over Persia's loosely organized infantrymen won Athens a smashing victory: Persia suffered 6,400 casualties, Athens only 192. (The story, unconfirmed, that a messenger ran from the battlefield to the city of Athens with the news, "Rejoice, we conquer!" is the inspiration for the modern marathon race, a slightly

The Enemy as Barbarian

Classical Greeks no longer regarded the enemy as honored rivals, as Homer's heroes had regarded Trojans. Rather, they looked down on the enemy as a barbarian. Greece's archenemies, the Persians, were portrayed as indulgent, effeminate, emotional, slavish, cruel, and dangerous. Consider the contrasting portraits of Persians and Greeks in these excerpts from the historian Herodotus's account of Persia's invasion of Greece in 480 B.C.

The Persians

He [King Xerxes of Persia] then prepared to move forward to Abydos, where a bridge had already been constructed across the Hellespont from Europe to Asia. . . . It was here not long afterwards that the Greeks under Xanthippus the son of Ariphron took Artayctes the Persian governor of Sestos, and nailed him alive to a plank—he was the man who collected women in the temple of Protesilaus at Elaeus and committed various acts of sacrilege. This headland was the point to which Xerxes' engineers carried their two bridges from Abydos—a distance of seven furlongs. . . . The work was successfully completed, but a subsequent storm of great violence smashed it up and carried everything away. Xerxes was very angry when he learned of the disaster, and gave orders that the Hellespont should receive three hundred lashes and have a pair of fetters thrown into it. And I have heard before now that he also sent people to brand it with hot irons. He certainly instructed the men with the whips to utter, as they wielded them, the following words: "You salt and bitter stream, your master lays this punishment upon you for injuring him, who never injured you. But Xerxes the King will cross you, with or without your permission. No man sacrifices to you, and you deserve the neglect by your acrid and muddy waters"—a highly presumptuous way of addressing the Hellespont, and typical of a barbarous nation. In addition to punishing the Hellespont Xerxes gave orders that the men responsible for building the bridge should have their heads cut off. This unseemly order was duly carried out. . . .

The Greeks

To the Spartan envoys . . . [the Athenians] said: "No doubt it was natural that the Lacedaemonians [Spartans] should dread the possibility of our making terms with Persia; nonetheless it shows a poor estimate of the spirit of Athens. Were we offered all the gold in the world, and the fairest and richest country the earth contains, we should never consent to join the common enemy and bring Greece into submission. There are many compelling reasons to prevent our taking such a course, even if we wish to do so: the first and greatest is the burning of the temples and images of our gods—now mere heaps of rubble. It is our bounden duty to avenge this desecration with all the power we possess—not to clasp in friendship the hand that wrought it. Again, there is the Greek nation—the common blood, the common language; the temples and religious ritual; the whole way of life we understand and share together—indeed, if Athens were to betray all this it would not be well done. We would have you know, therefore, if you did not already know it, that we will never make peace with Xerxes so long as a single Athenian remains alive."

Source: Herodotus, *The Histories*, trans. Aubrey de Sélincourt (Baltimore: Penguin, 1954), pp. 429, 550.

longer distance of about 26 miles.) After the battle, Athens experienced a burst of confidence that propelled it to power and glory.

Meanwhile, Persia sought a rematch. After Darius's death in 486, his son and successor, Xerxes, amassed a huge force of about a thousand ships and several hundred thousand soldiers and rowers, vastly outnumbering potential Greek opposition. Athens, under the leadership of Themistocles (ca. 525–460 B.C.), prepared by building a fleet of two hundred ships. Athens joined

Sparta and twenty-nine other Peloponnesian poleis in a Hellenic League of defense, with Sparta in overall command. Most poleis either stayed neutral or, like Thebes and Argos, collaborated with Persia. The Greeks had over three hundred ships and about fifty thousand infantrymen.

Persia invaded Greece in 480 B.C. and won the opening moves. At the narrow pass of Thermopylae in central Greece (see Map 3.1), the Persians outflanked and crushed a small Spartan army, who died fighting to the last man, including their king Leonidas. This sacrifice added to the Spartan reputation for courage but left the road south open. Abandoned by its defenders, Athens was sacked.

The tide then turned. The Greeks lured the Persian fleet into the narrow straits between Athens and Salamis. The Persians could not use their numerical superiority in this confined space, and the Greeks had the home-base advantage. The result was a crushing Persian defeat under the eyes of Xerxes himself, who watched the battle from a throne on a hillside near the shore.

Because their sea links to the Levant had been cut, Xerxes and the remainder of the Persian fleet left for home. Soon afterward the united Greek army under Spartan leadership defeated Persian forces on land at Plataea (just north of Attica; see Map 3.1) in 479 B.C. At about the same time, the Greek fleet defeated a reorganized Persian fleet off the Anatolian coast near Mycale. The victorious Greeks sailed the coast and liberated the Ionians. Not only did Persia fail to conquer the Greek mainland, but it also lost its eastern Aegean empire.

Greeks did not remember the invader fondly. After 480 they thought of Persians not merely as enemies but as barbarians—that is, cultural inferiors. (See the box "Global Encounters: The Enemy as Barbarian.") At the same time, Greeks became more conscious of their own common culture.

■ Struggles for Hegemony, 478–362 B.C.

The Greek unity forged by the struggle against Persia was fragile and short-lived. What followed was a constant struggle in diplomacy and war among city-states, usually arranged in leagues under hegemons.

Following the Greek victory over Persia, Athens expanded its power as hegemon of a new security organization. Founded on the island of Delos in the Aegean Sea, the so-called Delian League aimed both at protecting Greek lands and at plundering Persian territory. The number of allies grew from about 150 in 477 B.C. to about 250 in 431 B.C. at the height of the league.

Fearful as ever of entanglements outside the Peloponnesus, Sparta preferred to leave the Aegean to Athens. Many Spartans nonetheless watched with unease and jealousy as Athenian power boomed.

Afraid of the new titan, the major allied states rebelled, one by one, beginning with Thasos in 465 B.C., but Athens crushed each rebellion. Sometimes after surrender, rebels were executed and their wives and children were sold into slavery. Allied complaints began to stir Sparta. A conflict between Greece's greatest land power, Sparta, and Greece's greatest sea power, Athens, started to look all but inevitable.

The Peloponnesian War, as this conflict is known today, came in 431 B.C. and lasted intermittently until 404. The war proved bloody and bitter. Battles between huge fleets, economic warfare, protracted sieges, epidemic disease, and ideological struggle produced a devastating war. It was clear that the Greeks could not maintain their unity against Persia; indeed, they appeared to be destroying themselves. (See the box "Reading Sources: Pericles' Funeral Oration.")

In this era both democratic Athens and oligarchic Sparta sought to promote their respective ideologies. Some unfortunate states became ideological battlegrounds, often at great cost of life. In Corcyra (modern Corfu; see Map 3.4), for example, bloody civil war marked a series of coups and countercoups in the 420s B.C.

Given Spartan supremacy on land and Athenian mastery of the sea, it is not surprising that the Peloponnesian War remained undecided for a decade and a half. The balance of power shifted only after an Athenian blunder, an expedition to conquer Sicily (415–413 B.C.) that became a quagmire and then a disaster, leading to total defeat and thousands of Athenian casualties. In the aftermath most of the Athenian empire rose in revolt. Persia re-emerged and intervened on Sparta's side—in return for Sparta's restoration of Ionia to Persia, an ironic counterpoint to Sparta's role in driving Persia from Greece in 479. Athens, nevertheless, was sufficiently wealthy and plucky to hold out until 404 B.C.

Sparta won the Peloponnesian War, but establishing a new Greek order proved beyond its grasp. Trained as soldiers not as diplomats, never fully reconciled to using sea power, lacking the oratorical skills valued by other Greeks, sure of themselves and contemptuous of others, Spartans made poor leaders. Sparta took over Athens's former empire and quickly had a falling-out with its allies, Persia, Corinth, and the Boeotian° city-states, especially Thebes.

Boeotia, Boeotian (bee-O-shuh, bee-O-shun)

🙠 READING SOURCES

Pericles' Funeral Oration

The historian Thucydides reports that in winter 431–430 B.C., at the end of the first year of the Peloponnesian War (431–404 B.C.), Athens's leading politician, Pericles (ca. 495–429 B.C.), gave a speech at the public funeral of the Athenians who had died fighting that year. Pericles used the occasion to celebrate Athens's way of life.

Our constitution does not copy the laws of neighboring states; we are rather a pattern to others than imitators ourselves. Its administration favors the many instead of the few; this is why it is called a democracy. . . .

Further, we provide plenty of means for the mind to refresh itself from business. We celebrate games and sacrifices all the year round, and the elegance of our private establishments forms a daily source of pleasure and helps to distract us from what causes us distress; while the magnitude of our city draws the produce of our world into our harbor, so that to the Athenian the fruits of other countries are as familiar a luxury as those of his own.

If we turn to our military policy, there also we differ from our antagonists. We throw open our city to the world, and never by alien acts exclude foreigners from any opportunity of learning or observing, although the eyes of an enemy may occasionally profit by our liberality; trusting less in system and policy than to the native spirit of our citizens; while in education, where our rivals from their very cradles by a painful discipline seek after manliness, at Athens we live exactly as we please, and yet are just as ready to encounter every legitimate danger. . . .

We cultivate refinement without extravagance and knowledge without effeminacy; wealth we employ more for use than for show, and place the real disgrace of poverty not in owning to the fact but in declining the struggle against it. . . .

In short, I say that as a city we are the school of Hellas; while I doubt if the world can produce a man, who where he has only himself to depend upon, is equal to so many emergencies, and graced by so happy a versatility as the Athenian.

Source: Robert B. Strassler, ed., *The Landmark Thucydides, A Comprehensive Guide to the Peloponnesian War* (New York: Touchstone, 1996), pp. 112–114.

In addition, Sparta suffered a vast decline in the number of citizens. The original nine thousand Similars of the seventh century B.C. had dropped to about only fifteen hundred in 371 B.C. The main problem seems to have been greed. Rich Spartans preferred to get richer by concentrating wealth in fewer hands rather than open the elite to new blood. Thousands of men could no longer afford to live as elite soldiers.

The result was military disaster. In 371 B.C. the Boeotian army crushed the Spartans at the Battle of Leuctra, killing a thousand men (including four hundred Similars) and a Spartan king. In the next few years Boeotia invaded the Peloponnesus, freed the Messenian helots, and restored Messenia to independence, after some 350 years of bondage. It was a fatal blow to Spartan power, but Boeotia, too, was exhausted and its main leaders, Epaminondas (d. 362 B.C.) and Pelopidas (403–364 B.C.), were dead. None of the Greek city-states had been able to maintain hegemony.

Nothing better demonstrates the fatal excess of individualism in classical Greece and the absence of cooperative virtues than the wars of the city-states in the fourth century B.C. They accomplished nothing but leaving a weakened Greece prey to outsiders.

Map 3.4   Greece in the Peloponnesian War   During the long and bloody Peloponnesian War (431–404 B.C.), much of the Greek world was divided in two camps: one led by Sparta, the other by Athens.

THE PUBLIC CULTURE OF CLASSICAL GREECE

HE word *classical* means "to set a standard." The culture of Greece between 480 and 322 B.C. proved so influential in the later West that it may justly be called classical. Classical Greek culture was public culture. Poets were not inward-looking or alienated figures. Rather, to quote the Athenian playwright Aristophanes° (ca. 455–385 B.C.), they were "the teachers of men" who commented on contemporary public debate. (As the quotation might also suggest, men, especially citizens, dominated public life.) Dramas were performed in a state theater at state religious festivals. The philosopher Socrates° (469–399 B.C.) discussed philosophy in marketplaces and gymnasia. It was not private individuals but the public that was the major patron of sculpture and architecture.

Public life, accordingly, is the central theme of Classical Greek art and literature. In tragedy, for example, regardless of the particular hero or plot, the same character always looms in the background: the polis. The Classical historians Herodotus, Xenophon, and especially Thucydides focus on public affairs rather than private life. Classical philosophy ranged from biology to metaphysics; however, politics was undoubtedly its central focus.

Aristophanes (air-ih-STOF-uh-neez)

Socrates, Socratic (sock-ruh-TEEZ, suh-KRAT-ik)

The Parthenon The temple of Athena Parthenos ("the Maiden") on the Athenian Acropolis, the Parthenon was dedicated in 438 B.C. One of the largest and most complex Greek temples, it was built of fine marble. The partially restored ruins symbolize the wealth, power, and greatness of classical Greece. *(William Katz/Photo Researchers)*

■ Religion and Art

A hallmark of Classical culture is the tension between the religious heritage of the Archaic period and the worldly spirit of the Classical age. The Classical period was a time of prosperity, political debate, and military conflict. "Wonders are many on earth, and none more wondrous than man," said the Athenian tragedian Sophocles° (ca. 495–406 B.C.). Yet Sophocles was a deeply religious man who also believed that people were doomed to disaster unless they obeyed the laws of the gods. Sophocles mirrored a widespread debate, for he knew his countrymen well. He was not only a popular playwright but also a general, state treasurer, priest, and friend of Pericles.

Classical religion was less sure of itself than its Archaic predecessor. A few people even questioned the very existence of the gods, although most Greeks wanted religion to be adapted to the new age, not discarded altogether. Thus, Athenian religion was tailored to the needs of a democratic and imperial city. In the 440s B.C., under Pericles' leadership, Athens embarked on a vast, ambitious, and expensive temple-building project, using Delian League funds and serving as a large public employment program. Temples were built in and around the city, most notably on the Athenian Acropolis. (See the feature "Weighing the Evidence: The Parthenon" on pages 102–103.)

Classical sculptors completed the process begun by their Archaic forebears of mastering the accurate representation of the human body. In anatomical precision, Classical Greek sculpture was the most technically proficient sculpture the world had seen. Like Archaic sculpture, it was not, however, an attempt to portray humans "warts and all," but an idealization of the human form.

To adapt religion to a new age, new cults were introduced. The most popular was the worship of Asclipius, god of healing. Traditionally a minor figure and considered a son of Apollo, Asclipius became enormously popular in his own right beginning in the late fifth century B.C., perhaps in response to the high mortality of the Peloponnesian War. Outside Athens, large shrines to

Sophocles (sof-uh-KLEEZ)

Asclipius at Epidauros (in the Peloponnesus) and Cos (an island off the Anatolian coast) became pilgrimage centers in the fourth century B.C. for ailing people in search of a cure.

■ The Sophists and Socrates

Success in democratic politics required a knowledge of oratory. This demand was met in the late fifth century B.C. by the arrival in Athens of itinerant professional teachers of *rhetoric,* the art of speaking. They were known as Sophists° (from a word meaning "to instruct" or "make wise"). Sicilian Greeks invented rhetoric around 465 B.C. by drawing up the rules of argument. For a fee—rarely small and sometimes astronomical—Sophists taught young Athenians the art of speaking. Their curriculum consisted not only of rhetoric but also of the rudiments of linguistics, ethics, psychology, history, and anthropology—in other words, any aspect of "human nature" that might help an aspiring politician. Within a few years most ambitious young Athenians of prosperous families were studying with Sophists.

At their best, Sophists sharpened young minds. Athenian tragedians, historians, and philosophers all benefited from sophistic teaching. Protagoras (b. ca. 485 B.C.), perhaps the best-known Sophist, summed up the spirit of the age in his famous dictum "Man is the measure of all things"—an appropriate credo for the interest in all things human that is apparent in Classical literature and art. There is, however, a more troubling side to the Sophists. As teachers of rhetoric, they taught respect for success, not for truth. Thus, they acquired a reputation as word-twisters who taught men how to make "the weaker argument defeat the stronger."

Much to the distress of conservatives, Sophists drew a distinction between *nomos,* a word that means "law" or "convention," and *physis,* which means "nature." The distinction had revolutionary potential. In general, Sophists had little respect for the established order, or nomos. They considered it mere convention. A great man trained by a Sophist might rise above convention to realize the limitless potentialities of his nature, or physis: If he used his skill to overturn democracy and establish a tyranny, so much the worse for democracy. Indeed, the Sophists trained both unscrupulous democratic politicians and many of the oligarchs who launched coups d'état against Athenian democracy at the end of the fifth century B.C. As a result, *sophist* became a term of abuse in Athens and remains so to this day.

Classical Greek advances in rhetoric, therefore, were as problematic as they were brilliant. The Sophists had a wide-ranging effect on many different branches of thought. Consider, for example, the work of the philosopher Democritus° (b. ca. 460 B.C.), a native of the northern Greek polis of Abdera but a visitor to Athens. Democritus was not a Sophist, but he shared the common Sophistic notion that the reality of nature was far more radical than conventionally thought. He concluded that all things consisted of tiny, indivisible particles, which could be arranged and rearranged in an infinite variety of configurations. He called these particles *atoma,* "the uncuttable" (from which the word *atom* is derived).

The physicians of the Aegean island of Cos are known as Hippocratics, from Hippocrates° (b. ca. 460 B.C.), the first great thinker of their school. If they were not directly influenced by the Sophists, they shared similar habits of thought. Like the Sophists, the Hippocratics were religious skeptics. They considered disease to be strictly a natural phenomenon in which the gods played no part. Hippocratic medicine was noteworthy for its methodology, which emphasized observation and prognosis (the reasoned prediction of future developments). The Hippocratics were the most rigorously naturalistic physicians to date, although no more successful in healing illness than earlier practitioners.

In the fifth century B.C. not all thinkers welcomed the conclusions of the Sophists. Perhaps their most notable critic, and the greatest of all fifth-century philosophers, was Socrates (469–399 B.C.). Unlike the Sophists, he charged no fees, had no formal students, and did not claim to teach any positive body of knowledge. In fact, his basic thesis was negative: the radical ignorance of most people, including himself. His only superiority, he believed, was his awareness of his ignorance. Unlike the Sophists, most of whom were metics, Socrates was an Athenian citizen.

Socrates, however, resembled the Sophists in his intense interest in political theory. Like any good Athenian citizen, Socrates served in the military—as a hoplite during the Peloponnesian War. He had his doubts about democracy, which he criticized for inefficiency and for giving an equal voice to the uneducated. He preferred rule by a wise elite. Nonetheless, Socrates was too loyal an Athenian to advocate revolution.

Yet Socrates made many enemies because of his role as a self-styled "gadfly": Socrates stung the pride of

Sophist (SOF-ist)

Democritus (dee-MOCK-ruh-tus)
Hippocrates, Hippocratics (hih-POK-ruh-teez, hih-puh-KRAT-iks)

Athens's leaders by demonstrating their ignorance. Mistakenly considered a Sophist by the public because of his unconventional opinions, in 399 Socrates was tried, convicted, and executed by an Athenian court for alleged atheism and "corrupting the young." The Athenian public soon had second thoughts, and the trial of Socrates is usually considered one of history's great miscarriages of justice, as well as one of Athenian democracy's greatest blunders.

Socrates was trained in the Ionian natural philosophy tradition. He went beyond it, as the Roman thinker Cicero later said, by bringing philosophy "down from the heavens into the streets"; he changed the emphasis from the natural world to human ethics. Like most Greeks, Socrates believed that the purpose of life was the pursuit of aretê. Unlike his contemporaries, however, he did not consider aretê to be primarily excellence in battle or in public life but, rather, excellence in philosophy. One became good by studying the truth, which is part of what Socrates meant by his saying "Virtue (aretê) is knowledge." He also meant that no one who truly understood goodness would ever choose to do evil.

Such an outlook downgrades the importance of willpower or the emotions in shaping action, but it makes education into the cornerstone of society. Teach people well, according to Socrates, and they will behave morally. Socrates has gone down in history as an inspiring teacher despite his protestations of not teaching anything. His emphasis was not on research or writing—Socrates refused to write anything down. He believed that truth could be found only in persons, not through books—that philosophy requires a thoughtful verbal exchange. His favorite technique was to ask people difficult questions. Pedagogy that relies on inquiry is still called the "Socratic method."

■ Plato and Aristotle

Because Socrates never wrote anything down, we are dependent on others for our knowledge of him. Fortunately for us, he inspired students who committed his words and ideas to paper. Socrates' most distinguished student, and our most important source for his thought, was Plato° (427–348 B.C.), who in turn was the teacher of Aristotle (384–322 B.C.). Together, these three men laid the foundations of the Western philosophical tradition. They were thinkers for the ages, but each was also a man of his times.

Socrates grew up in confident Periclean days. Plato came of age during the Peloponnesian War, a period cul-

minating in the execution of Socrates. Shocked and disillusioned, Plato turned his back on public life, although he was an Athenian citizen. Instead of discussing philosophy in public, Plato founded a private school in an Athenian suburb, the Academy. Plato held a low opinion of democracy, and when he did intervene in politics, it was not in Athens but in far-off Syracuse (in Sicily). Syracuse was governed by a tyranny, and Plato hoped to educate the tyrant's heir in philosophy—a vain hope, as it turned out.

In an attempt to recapture the stimulating give-and-take of a conversation with Socrates, Plato did not write straightforward philosophical treatises but, rather, dialogues or speeches. All of Plato's dialogues have more than one speaker, and in most the main speaker is named "Socrates": Sometimes this figure is the historical Socrates, sometimes merely a mouthpiece for ideas Plato wished to explore.

A voluminous writer, Plato is not easily summarized. The word that best characterizes his legacy, though, is *idealism*, of which Plato is one of Western philosophy's greatest exponents. Like Parmenides, Plato believed that the senses are misleading. Truth exists but is attained only by training the mind to overcome common-sense evidence. The model for Plato's philosophical method is geometry. Just as geometry deals not with this or that triangle or rectangle but with ideal forms—with a pure triangle, a pure rectangle—so the philosopher could learn to recognize purity. A philosopher would not be misled by, for example, comparing aretê in Athens, Sparta, and Persia; a philosopher would understand the meaning of pure, ideal aretê. No relativist, Plato believed in absolute good and evil.

Philosophy is not for everyone, according to Plato. Only a few people have the requisite intelligence and discipline. In the *Republic*, a dialogue that is perhaps his best-known work, Plato demonstrates the nature of his idealism and its political consequences. He envisioned a society whose elite would study philosophy and attain enlightenment. They would understand the vanity of political ambition but would nonetheless accept the responsibility of governing the masses. Plato never makes clear precisely why they should assume this burden. It is possible he was enough of a traditionalist, in spite of himself, to consider a citizen's responsibility to the polis to be obvious. In any case, Plato's ideal state was one in which philosophers would rule as kings, benevolently and unselfishly. (See the box "Reading Sources: Plato on Philosopher-Kings.")

Plato explored the details of such a state in the *Republic* and in other dialogues, particularly the *Laws*. It is not clear how wedded he was to specific details; indeed, some of them may have been meant merely to shock or

---

Plato (PLAY-toe)

Plato on Philosopher-Kings

Plato (427–348 B.C.) in his masterpiece, The Republic, *argues that the ideals of justice can never be reached until philosophers put aside their books and run the government—and until politicians step aside to let them do so. The following fictional discussion between Socrates and Glaucon (Plato's brother) shows just how unusual such an ideal community would be and just how hard it would be to establish.*

And I said: Cities will have no respite from evil, my dear Glaucon, nor will the human race, I think, unless philosophers rule as kings in the cities, or those whom we now call kings and rulers genuinely and adequately study philosophy, until, that is, political power and philosophy coalesce, and the various natures of those who now pursue the one to the exclusion of the other are forcibly debarred from doing so. . . .

. . . The uneducated who have no experience of truth would never govern a city satisfactorily, nor would those who are allowed to spend their whole life in the process of educating themselves; the former would fail because they do not have a single goal at which all their actions, public and private, must aim; the latter because they would refuse to act, thinking that they have settled, while still alive, in the faraway islands of the blessed.—*True.*

It is then our task as founders, I said, to compel the best natures to reach the study which we have previously said to be the most important, to see the Good and to follow that journey upward. When they [the best natures] have accomplished their journey and seen it sufficiently, we must not allow them to do what they are allowed to do today. —*What is that?*

To stay there, I said, and to refuse to go down again to the prisoners in the cave [that is, ordinary people who live unenlightened lives], there to share both their labours and their honours, whether these be of little or of greater worth.

Are we then, he said, *to do them an injustice by making them live a worse life when they could live a better one?*

You are again forgetting my friend, I said, that it is not the law's concern to make some one group in the city outstandingly happy but to contrive to spread happiness throughout the city, by bringing the citizens into harmony with each other by persuasion or compulsion, and to make them share with each other the benefits which each group can confer upon the community. The law has not made men of this kind in the city in order to allow them to turn in any direction they wish but to make use of them to bind the city together. —*You are right, I had forgotten.*

Source: G. M. A. Grube, trans., *Plato's Republic* (Indianapolis: Hackett Publishing Company, 1974), pp. 133, 171–172.

to satirize. An overall picture emerges, however. The ideal state would be like a small polis: self-sufficient and closed to outside corrupt influences like Sparta, but committed to the pursuit of things intellectual like Athens. Society would be sharply divided into three classes—philosophers, soldiers, and farmers—with admission to each class based on merit rather than heredity. Poetry and drama would be strictly censored. Plato advocated public education and toyed with more radical notions: not only gender equality but the abolition of the family and private property, institutions that he felt led to disunity and dissension.

Plato's ideas have always been controversial but almost never ignored. Even in his own day, most people considered Plato far too radical. The writings of his great student Aristotle were more to contemporary tastes. Originally from Macedonia, Aristotle spent most of his life in Athens, first as a student at the Academy, then as the founder of his own school, the Lyceum°. Like Plato, Aristotle wrote dialogues, but none has survived. His main extant works are treatises, largely compilations by students of his lecture notes. One of the most wide ranging of intellectuals, Aristotle had a voracious appetite for knowledge and for writing. His treatises embrace politics, ethics, poetry, botany, physics, metaphysics, astronomy, rhetoric, zoology, logic, and psychology.

Although influenced by Plato's idealism, Aristotle was a far more practical, down-to-earth thinker. His

Lyceum (lie-SEE-um)

Aristotle This bronze bust, found in a Roman-era villa in the Italian city of Herculaneum, is said to represent the great Classical philosopher. The statue has the dignified and pensive look betokening one of the giants of ancient Greek thought. *(Alinari/Art Resource, NY)*

father had been a doctor, which may account for Aristotle's interest in applied science and in biology and the biological method. Unlike Plato, Aristotle placed great emphasis on observation and fieldwork and on classification and systemization.

Aristotle agreed with Plato about the existence of absolute standards of good and evil, but he emphasized the relevance of such standards to everyday life. Unlike Plato, Aristotle considered the senses important guides; change, he believed, was not an illusion but rather an important phenomenon. Aristotle's view of change was teleological—that is, he emphasized the goal (*telos* in Greek) of change. According to Aristotle, every organism changes and grows toward a particular end and is an integral and harmonious part of a larger whole. The entire cosmos is teleological, and each and every one of its parts has a purpose. Behind the cosmos was a principle that Aristotle called "the unmoved mover," the supreme cause of existence.

Aristotle defined an object's aretê as the fulfillment of its inherent function in the cosmos. The aretê of a horse, for example, was to be strong, fast, and obedient; the aretê of a rose was to look beautiful and smell sweet. As for the aretê of a human being, Aristotle agreed with Plato: Only the philosopher achieved true aretê. As a

pragmatist, however, Aristotle did not imagine philosophers becoming kings. Not that he advocated democracy, which he considered mob rule. Instead, Aristotle advocated a government of wealthy gentlemen who had been trained by philosophers—not the best regime imaginable but, in Aristotle's opinion, the best one possible.

Aristotle believed that men had stronger capacities to make judgments than women and so should rule over them. He condemned states like Sparta that accorded power to women. (See the box "Reading Sources: Spartan Women" on page 78.) Hence, Aristotle would be cited in later centuries to justify male dominance. Ironically, however, Aristotle was more enlightened on gender issues than most contemporaries. For example, he believed that since women played a crucial role in the family, they should receive education in morality.

Aristotle may be the single most influential thinker in Western history. His scientific writings not only were the most influential philosophical classics of Greek civilization, and of Roman civilization as well, but remained so during the Middle Ages in the Arabic and Latin worlds. It took nearly two thousand years before serious rivals challenged Aristotle's intellectual supremacy.

■ Athenian Drama

Perhaps the greatest art form that emerged in the polis was drama. Modern comedy and tragedy find distant ancestors in the productions of Athens's theater of Dionysus, named for the god of unrestraint, liberation, and wine. Comedy and tragedy began in religious festivals honoring Dionysus (also known as Bacchus) but quickly became an independent forum for comment on public life. Ancient drama was poetry, not prose. Because it highlighted the relation of the individual to the community, drama proved to be the most suitable poetic medium for the ideology of the polis.

According to ancient tradition, tragedy was first presented at the Dionysian festival in Athens by one Thespis in the 530s B.C. (hence the word *thespian* for "actor"). The first surviving tragedy dates from the 470s, the first surviving comedy from the 420s. A play in the fifth century B.C. consisted of a chorus (a group of performers working in unison) and three individual actors who played all the various individual speaking parts. Plays were performed in an open-air theater on the south hillside of the Acropolis. Enormously popular, drama spread all over Greece, and eventually most poleis had a theater.

Classical Athenian tragedy was performed at the annual Dionysia in March. Each playwright would submit a trilogy of plays on a central theme, plus a raucous farce to break the tension afterward. Comedies, which were

Theater at Delphi   Open to the air, an ancient Greek theater contained tiers of stone benches above a circular area where the action took place, behind which backdrops could be erected. The audience often had a view of stirring scenery that, at Delphi, included the temple of Apollo and the valley below.   *(Vanni/Art Resource, NY)*

independent plays rather than trilogies, were performed both at the Dionysia and at a separate festival held in winter. Wealthy producers competed to outfit the most lavish and impressive productions. Judges would award prizes for the best plays—a typical reflection of Greek competitiveness.

Tragedy is not easy to define, except generally: a serious play with an unhappy ending. Perhaps a short tag from the playwright Aeschylus° can be said to sum up tragedy if anything can: *pathos mathei,* "suffering teaches." The essence of tragedy is what has been called the tragic sense of life: the nobility in the spectacle of a great man or woman failing but learning from failure. In *Oedipus the Tyrant* (ca. 428 B.C.) by Sophocles, for example, the hero unknowingly kills his father and unknowingly marries his mother. Oedipus cannot escape the consequences of his deeds, but he can react to his fate with dignity and heroism; he can try to understand it. Oedipus loses his power as tyrant and goes into exile, but he retains a degree of honor. He executes his own punishment by blinding himself. As Aristotle observed, tragedy derives its emotional power from the fear and pity that it evokes and from the purification of the senses *(katharsis)* that it leaves in its aftermath.

The great period of Attic tragedy began and ended in the fifth century B.C. Aeschylus (525–456 B.C.), Sophocles (ca. 495–406 B.C.), and Euripides° (ca. 485–406 B.C.) were and are considered the three giant playwrights. Although other tragedians wrote plays, only the works of these three men (or, rather, a small fraction of their works) have survived. Aeschylus was perhaps the most pious of the three. His plays—notably the trilogy of the *Oresteia* (the *Agamemnon,* the *Libation Bearers,* and the *Eumenides*), the only surviving tragic trilogy, dating from 458 B.C.—take as their central question the justice of Zeus. The subject is the myth of the house of Atreus—in particular, the murder of King Agamemnon by his much-wronged wife, Clytemnestra, and her murder in turn by their son, Orestes, avenging his father. Aeschylus casts this primitive saga into an epic of the discovery of justice. In fulfillment of the will of Zeus, Athena puts an end to vengeance killings and institutes the supposed first court of law: the court of the Areopagus in Athens.

Sophocles, too, was interested in divine justice. His tragedies focus on the relationship between the individual and the community. Heroic individuals have a spark of the divine in them, but their towering virtues are threats to ordinary people. In *Antigone* (ca. 442 B.C.), for example, the heroine refuses to compromise with injustice. Her late brother had committed treason, for which his corpse is denied burial—the standard Greek punishment. Antigone, however, insists on following a higher law, Zeus's law, which demands that all bodies be buried. Turmoil, disorder, and death ensue, but Antigone stays true to principle.

Of the three tragedians, Euripides is the least traditional and the most influenced by the Sophists. His plays reflect the disillusionment of the Peloponnesian War era. Euripides was more impressed by divine power than by divine justice. The central gods of Aeschylean drama are Zeus the father and Apollo the lawgiver, while Sophocles

Aeschylus (ESS-kih-luhs)   **Euripides** (yoo-RIP-uh-deez)

focuses on semidivine heroes, but Euripides' major deities are Dionysus and Aphrodite, goddess of erotic passion. In *Medea* (431 B.C.), for example, Euripides dissects the feelings of love, jealousy, and revenge that drive a woman to murder her own children in order to take revenge on her faithless husband (the children's father). In the *Bacchae* (406 B.C.), an arrogant young king named Pentheus is punished for refusing to recognize the power of Dionysus (Bacchus). When he goes to the hills to spy on drunken women called Bacchae who are worshiping the god, he ends up as their prisoner. Driven to frenzy by Dionysus, the women do not recognize the king; Pentheus's own mother, one of the Bacchae, mistakes him for an animal and kills him.

The changes in tragedy from Aeschylus to Euripides reflect the changes in Athens as first imperial arrogance and then the Peloponnesian War took their moral toll. Aeschylus's confidence in the goodness of the community gives way first to a focus on the individual struggling to be good and then to a fundamental doubt about the possibility of goodness. The civic order, celebrated so confidently at the end of the *Oresteia* (458 B.C.), looks less certain in Sophocles' *Oedipus* (ca. 428 B.C.) and by the time of Euripides' *Bacchae* (406 B.C.) seems terrifyingly weak.

Comedy, too, was invented in Athens in the Classical period. Like tragedy, comedy offers a moral commentary on contemporary Athenian life. Unlike tragedy, which is usually set in the past and takes its characters from mythology, Athenian comedy (the so-called Old Comedy) is set in the present and pokes fun at politicians and public figures. Whereas tragedy is generally serious and sad, comedy is light, biting, and humorous.

The greatest writer of comedy in the fifth century B.C. was Aristophanes (ca. 455–385 B.C.). His extant plays are lively, ribald, even scatological, and full of allusions to contemporary politics. Aristophanes loved to show the "little guy" getting the better of the powerful and women deflating the pretensions of men. In *Lysistrata* (411 B.C.), his best-known play, he imagines the women of Greece stopping the Peloponnesian War by going on a sex strike, which forces the men to make peace.

■ Historical Thought and Writing

Like drama, history flourished in the exciting intellectual atmosphere of classical Athens. Indeed, its two greatest historians, Herodotus (ca. 485–425 B.C.) and Thucydides° (ca. 455–397 B.C.), are among the founders of history-

---

Thucydides (thoo-SID-uh-deez)

writing in the West. This judgment is not meant to discount the contributions of, for example, the Hittites or Hebrews, or the chronicles, inventories, and genealogies of early Greece. Herodotus and Thucydides, however, are more rationalistic than their predecessors, and their subject matter was war, politics, peoples, and customs—what we think of as the stuff of history-writing today. Indeed, the word *history* comes from a word used by Herodotus, *historiai*, meaning "inquiries" or "research."

The works of Herodotus (*The Histories*) and Thucydides (*The Peloponnesian War*) have unifying themes. The thread through *The Histories* is the cyclical rise and fall of empires. Herodotus sees the Persian Wars as merely one episode in a vast historical drama. Again and again, hardy, disciplined peoples conquered their neighbors, grew wealthy, were corrupted by a life of luxury, and were eventually conquered in turn. Success made people arrogant, driving them to commit injustices, which were eventually punished by Zeus. The breadth of Herodotus's vision is noteworthy. A native of Halicarnassus (a polis on the southwestern coast of Anatolia; see Map 3.4), Herodotus traveled widely, eventually settling in Athens. He wrote not only about Greeks but also about Persians, Egyptians, and a host of other peoples in Europe, Asia, and Africa. (See the box "Global Encounters: The Enemy as Barbarian" on page 90.)

Only a child at the time of the Persian Wars, Herodotus gathered information by interviewing older people in various countries as well as by checking what limited written public records existed. Herodotus also wrote about previous centuries and places he had not visited, but with uneven accuracy. He could rarely resist a good story, and alongside solid research are tall tales, unconfirmed accounts, and myths.

Thucydides, however, by contrast, prided himself on accuracy. He confined himself mainly to writing about an event that he had lived through and participated in: the Peloponnesian War. A failed Athenian general, Thucydides spent most of the Peloponnesian War in exile, carefully observing, taking notes, and writing.

Like Herodotus, Thucydides was influenced by the grandeur of Classical tragedy. He also shows the signs of the sophistic movement, especially in the finely crafted speeches he includes. Thucydides' great theme is the disastrous effect of war on the human soul. His case study, the Peloponnesian War, proved that war is a harsh teacher: It strips away the veneer of civilization and reveals the savagery of human nature. In Thucydides' opinion, Periclean Athens had been a high point in the history of civilization. The strain of prolonged war, however, destroyed Athens's moral fiber as well as its empire.

SUMMARY

WESTERN philosophy, science, politics, sculpture, painting, and literary genres such as comedy, tragedy, and history all emerged in Archaic and Classical Greece. The focus of ancient Greek life was the city-state, or polis. Though small, exclusive, often factionalized, and rarely capable of achieving unity in a large area, the polis may be unparalleled in its ability to foster individual creative genius. At the same time, the polis promoted the idea that public duty is more important than private advantage.

Paradox was the hallmark of the polis. The Greeks invented democracy while at the same time limiting the freedom of women and immigrants, oppressing slaves, and engaging in imperialism. Although the Greeks originated the concept that natural phenomena have natural causes, they nonetheless recognized the power of the irrational—be it divine whims or human emotions. With its democracy, freedom, and high culture, Athens stands for one aspect of the achievement of the polis; with its hierarchy, militarism, and austerity, Sparta stands for another.

Athens reached its peak under Pericles, whose leadership in the mid-fifth century B.C. ushered in a time of empire, prosperity, and cultural greatness. The major tragedians were all active, and the sophistic movement was at its most optimistic and progressive. Periclean Athens was unique, not only for the sheer concentration of talent, but also for the sense that the state, the cultural elite, and the people were united in a common purpose.

Although later times witnessed a fall from that state of grace, they did not suffer any decline in creative achievement. The outbreak of the Peloponnesian War in 431 B.C. marked the beginning of a century in which Greek warfare was more brutal than before. Yet this century also delighted in the comedies of Aristophanes, devoured the history-writing of Herodotus and Thucydides, and debated the philosophy of Socrates, Plato, and Aristotle.

By the end of the fourth century, as we shall see in Chapter 4, the polis was to lose its independence to a powerful monarchy. In succeeding years, new cities in western Asia and Egypt would amass the wealth and power to challenge such old centers as Athens as cultural capitals. Yet the culture that flourished in the new sites was Greek culture. The polis lost its freedom but gained a central place in the legacy of the West.

■ Notes

1. Excerpt from a poem by Solon, quoted in Aristotle, *Constitution of Athens*, trans. Barry S. Strauss.
2. Charles Rowan Beye, *Ancient Greek Literature and Society,* 2d ed., rev. (Ithaca, N.Y.: Cornell University Press, 1987), p. 78.
3. Ibid., p. 79.
4. Adapted from Richmond Lattimore, trans., *Greek Lyrics,* 2d ed. (Chicago: University of Chicago Press, 1960), p. 19.
5. Herodotus, *The Histories,* trans. Barry S. Strauss.
6. Thucydides, *The Peloponnesian War,* trans. Barry S. Strauss.

■ Suggested Reading

Beye, C. R. *Ancient Greek Literature and Society.* 2d ed. 1987. A witty and readable analysis from Homer to the Hellenistic era.

Biers, W. *The Archaeology of Ancient Greece: An Introduction.* Rev. ed. 1987. A clear presentation of the achievements and variety of archaeological excavation in Greece.

Boardman, John. *The Greeks Overseas: Their Early Colonies and Trade.* 4th ed. 1999. The standard introduction, authoritative, vivid, updated, and beautifully illustrated.

Cartledge, Paul, ed. *The Cambridge Illustrated History of Ancient Greece.* 1998. Twelve fine essays by leading scholars on subjects ranging from the natural environment to the status of women to philosophy, featuring lively writing and excellent photos.

Connolly, Peter, and Hazel Dodge. *The Ancient City: Life in Classical Athens and Rome.* 1998. Connolly's gorgeous illustrations and outstanding reconstructions distinguish this introduction to daily life in the two cities.

Hansen, Mogens Herman. *Athenian Democracy in the Age of Demosthenes.* 1991. An authoritative introduction to Athenian democracy that places the political system in its social context.

Martin, Thomas. *Ancient Greece from Prehistoric to Hellenistic Times.* 2000. A readable and scholarly introduction, emphasizing politics and war.

Osborne, Robin. *Greece in the Making, 1200–479 B.C.* 1996. Excellent, detailed, scholarly, up-to-date, and very stimulating history of Greece from the end of the Mycenaean world to the end of the Archaic period.

Pomeroy, Sarah B. *Goddesses, Whores, Wives, and Slaves: Women in Classical Antiquity.* 1975. An overview of women in politics and society in Greece, the Hellenistic world, and Rome, and still the best introduction to the subject.

Pomeroy, Sarah B., Stanley M. Burstein, Walter Donlan, and Jennifer Tolbert Roberts. *Ancient Greece: A Political, Social, and Cultural History.* 1999. A balanced introduction from the prehistoric to Hellenistic periods, with special emphasis on classical Greece.

 For a searchable list of additional readings for this chapter, go to http://college.hmco.com.

The Parthenon

The Parthenon, completed in 432 B.C., dominates both the skyline of Athens and the historical imagination of the West. The building's fine marble and classical proportions symbolize the free, confident, and united society that one might expect of Periclean Athens, the world's first democracy (see the photograph on page 94). A close look, however, suggests a more complex story. The Parthenon's sculpture offers glimpses of the tensions behind the classical façade.

The temple of Athena Parthenos ("the Maiden"), as the Parthenon is formally known, was a public project of Greece's wealthiest city-state, leading naval power, and premier democracy. Athenians spared no expense on its construction. Sculpture included a gold and ivory statue of the goddess Athena inside the temple and, on the outside, statuary in each pediment (the triangular space under the eaves) and sculptured reliefs running around the building above the exterior and interior colonnades.

So lavish a program of art demonstrated Athenian wealth but also served an educational purpose: to illustrate basic Athenian values. Because every Athenian male was expected to fight for the city when called on, militant competition is a central theme. Above the exterior colonnade, for example, ninety-two separate panels of relief sculpture depict gods and heroes fighting such foes as giants and centaurs. The sculpture above the interior colonnade is not so easily characterized, however.

The interior sculpture forms a continuous band, or frieze, around the four sides of the building. Warriors aplenty, primarily cavalrymen but also hoplites and charioteers, compose the line-up. See the detail from the west wall. Two riders are illustrated here: one turning and signaling, the other taking control of a rearing horse. Naked youths, they embody the ideal of strong bodies in the service of the polis. The long hair worn by the first rider, popular among the upper classes, was a reminder that Athenian cavalrymen were aristocrats.

The Parthenon Frieze, Detail from the West Wall *(Courtesy of the Trustees of the British Museum)*

The Parthenon Frieze, Detail from the East Wall *(The Louvre)*

Not all of the men in the interior frieze are warriors, though, and women, too, are depicted. See the detail from the east wall. Look at the four women shown here. Like the riders, they are young and in pairs, but there the similarity ends. The women are on foot, clothed, and in solemn procession. The heavy folds of their robes, the hands held at the side, and the expression on the one visible face all suggest calm and decorum.

From both of these pieces we may detect Athenian commonplaces about gender. Young women were expected to be maidenly, reserved, and modest. Their bodies were to be kept private. Young men were expected to be outgoing and assertive. Although men wore clothes in public, they exercised naked in gymnasia, wrestling grounds, and stadiums, competing in a healthy activity considered to be effective preparation for war.

The historian finds subtler messages in the two scenes. For example, however constrained the role of women, their very presence in the frieze is significant. Women were not permitted to attend the Athenian assembly, but they participated in the rituals and festivals that played so large a role in Athenian public life. Notice, for instance, the two girls shown in the back who are carrying ritual vessels.

One group of people is notably absent from the frieze: Athenian rowers. The oarsmen who manned Athens's warships, though poor, were the city's most loyal supporters of democracy. Why are they not depicted on a temple built by vote of Athens's popular assembly, the disbursements for whose construction were inscribed in stone and posted nearby so that any citizen could inspect the handling of public funds?

The answer depends on knowing precisely what the frieze as a whole depicts, but that knowledge—despite the fame of the Parthenon and the relative wealth of documentation from Periclean Athens—is embarrassingly shaky. Most scholars argue that the subject is the Pan-Athenaic procession, held once every four years to honor Athena. The people depicted are said to be the people of Athens—a daring novelty, considering that all previous Greek temple sculpture was restricted to gods, heroes, and mythological figures.

Yet if the scene is the Pan-Athenaic procession, how are we to explain the absence of certain well-known features of that procession—for instance, a large ship model? Some scholars prefer to view the scene as an illustration of a legend from the early history of Athens, a period in which rowers played little role in the Athenian military. Still, there are many nautical motifs in Athenian myth, motifs the Athenians could have chosen to illustrate if they had wished to celebrate the rowers.

Clearly, the Athenians preferred to depict hoplites and horsemen. Some might conclude that Athens was not as democratic as it claimed to be. Another explanation is that Athenian rowers, despite all their political assertiveness, admired the ideal of the hoplite and appreciated good horsemanship, and that conservative traditions died hard even in democratic Athens.

A ROUND 275 B.C. a grand procession made its way through the stadium and along the broad avenues of Alexandria, the capital city of Egypt. The attractions included exotic animals from Ethiopia, Arabia, India, and Greece; floats carrying statues of gods, kings, and personifications of cities; soldiers in armor and women in finery; and gold and silver every- where, in crowns, cups, and jewelry. At the center of the parade was the likeness of the man who had founded Alexandria, Alexander the Great himself. He was shown much as we see him on the silver coin shown on the left, which was minted in Alexandria: a young man in classical pro- file and wearing an elephant skin on his head, symbol of a career of conquest that had taken Greek-speakers into Egypt and across western and central Asia as far as India. To the kings of Egypt, the dynasty of the Ptolemies, Alexander was a symbol of power and authority, so it is no wonder that they featured him in the parade that they sponsored.

Alexander had created new realities of power in barely a dozen years (336–323 B.C.) as king of Macedon°. A northeastern Greek king- dom that had previously been only a fringe power, Macedon rose me- teorically under King Philip II (r. 359–336 B.C.) to become the leading military power in Greece. Philip was a brilliant and ambitious gen- eral, but his son and successor, Alexander the Great, outstripped him.

Alexander laid the foundations of a new Greek world: the world of the Hellenistic° period (323–30 B.C.), in which Hellenic, or Greek, lan- guage and civilization spread and were transformed. This era was dis- tinct in many ways from the preceding Hellenic period (ca. 750–323 B.C.). In Hellenistic times, Macedonians and Greeks replaced Persians

---

Macedon, Macedonian (MAH-seh-don, mah-seh-DOE-nee-un)
Hellenistic (hel-len-IS-tik)

Alexander the Great, silver coin from Alexandria.
(Fitzwilliam Museum, Cambridge/Dagli Orti/The Art Archive)

Alexander the Great and the Spread of Greek Civilization ca. 350–30 B.C.

as the ruling people of Egypt and western Asia. Large numbers of Greek-speaking colonists moved south and east. Governed by Macedonian dynasties, Egypt and the Levant became integral parts of the Greek world and remained so until the Arab conquest in the seventh century A.D. Greek-speaking kingdoms thrived briefly as far east as modern Afghanistan and Pakistan. At times the new ruling elite was open to natives who learned Greek and adopted Greek ways, but more often the natives were excluded and exploited.

Conquest put huge amounts of wealth into Greek hands. Alexander and his successors built great new cities: Antioch° in Syria, Pergamum° in Anatolia, Seleucia° in Mesopotamia, and, greatest of all, Alexandria in Egypt. Trade increased and expanded southward and eastward. In political life, individual cities continued to be important, but federal leagues (that is, unions of city-states) and monarchies ruled most of the Greek-speaking world.

Material and political expansion led to unanticipated cultural changes, which may be summarized as a turn inward. Frequently finding themselves among strange peoples, the Greeks sought comfort in new philosophies, religions, and modes of literary and artistic expression. Many of these new cultural forms emphasized people's emotions and intentions, not simply their actions. Science, meanwhile, flourished under royal patronage, as did the emerging discipline of literary criticism. The prestige of royal women tended to promote improvements in the overall status of Greek women.

Hellenistic Greeks boasted of having created one world, a common or ecumenical region (from the Greek *oikoumene*°, "inhabited [area]"). In truth, that world was complex. Native cultures flourished, while Greeks adapted and Hellenized a number of Egyptian and Asian deities.

Hellenistic Greek contact with one native culture in particular—Judaism—proved to have a lasting impact on the West. Under the impact of the Greeks, Judaism became more self-conscious and placed a greater emphasis on salvation, martyrdom, and individual study and prayer. Some Jews resisted Greek culture, others adopted it, and still others resolved to convert Greeks to Judaism. Reshaped by its contacts with the Greeks, Hellenistic Judaism was poised to transform Western religion.

QUESTIONS TO CONSIDER

- How did Macedon conquer both the Greek city-states and the Persian Empire, and what new states emerged as a result?

- How did Greek civilization spread during the Hellenistic era, and what distinguished it from the civilization of the preceding Classical period?

- What power did women, slaves, and native peoples have in Hellenistic society?

- What new philosophies, religions, and modes of literary and artistic expression were developed in the Hellenistic period?

TERMS TO KNOW

Macedon	Stoics
Philip II	Epicureans
Alexander the Great	Maccabees
Hellenism	mystery religions
Alexandria	
Antioch	
Ptolemies	
Seleucids	
Antigonids	

Antioch (AN-tee-ock)   **Pergamum** (PUR-guh-mum)
Seleucia (seh-LOO-she-uh)
oikoumene (oy-koo-men-AY)

PHILIP AND ALEXANDER

HE Hellenistic world was founded by two conquerors: Philip II of Macedon (382–336 B.C.) and his son, Alexander III, known as Alexander the Great (356–323 B.C.). After a century of indecisive warfare among the Greek city-states, Philip swept south and conquered them in twenty years; in even less time Alexander conquered Egypt and all of western Asia as far east as modern Pakistan. The legacy of these impressive conquests was to spread Greek civilization and to change it, both of which consequences were revolutionary developments.

■ The Rise of Macedon

Macedon was a border state, long weaker than its more advanced neighbors but capable of learning from them and ultimately of conquering them. Though rich in resources and manpower, Macedon lacked the relatively efficient organization of the polis. It included both tribal groups and scattered cities. Several dialects of Greek were spoken, some unintelligible to southern Greeks, who considered Macedonians "barbarians" (from the Greek *barbaros*, meaning "a person who does not speak Greek"). Ordinary Macedonians lived rough, sturdy lives, while the king and the royal court inhabited a sophisticated capital city: at Pella they sponsored visits by leading Greek artists and writers. Philip confounded Greek stereotypes of Macedonian barbarism by turning out to be a brilliant soldier and statesman—a man of vast ambition, appetite, and energy. A hard drinker, vain, and a man with numerous wives and lovers, he was also an excellent orator and general. Philip's goals were to make himself dominant in Macedon and then, after neutralizing opposition in Greece, to conquer the Persian Empire, or at least its holdings in Anatolia. He accomplished all but the last.

The instrument of Philip's success was his army, a well-trained, professional year-round force. Macedon, with its plains and horses, was cavalry country, and Philip raised cavalry to a new level of importance. In battle, the Macedonian phalanx would first hold the enemy phalanx until the cavalry could find a weak spot and break the enemy line. Then the phalanx would attack and finish the job. Macedonian hoplites carried extra-long pikes to keep the enemy at a distance. Philip also mastered the technology of siegecraft, raising it to a level unseen since Assyrian days (see page 42).

Philip used his army effectively. After capturing the lucrative gold mine of Mount Pangaeum in Thrace (the

CHRONOLOGY	
359–336 B.C.	Reign of Philip II of Macedon
ca. 342–292 B.C.	Life of playwright Menander
338 B.C.	Greece falls to Philip at Battle of Chaeronea
336–323 B.C.	Reign of Alexander the Great
331 B.C.	Battle of Gaugamela completes Persian defeat
322–275 B.C.	Wars of the Successors
313 B.C.	Zeno founds Stoic philosophy in Athens
312 B.C.	Seleucus I conquers Babylon
304 B.C.	Ptolemy I king of Egypt
294 B.C.	Museum founded in Alexandria
276 B.C.	Antigonus Gonatas king of Macedon
263 B.C.	Kingdom of Pergamum founded
ca. 246 B.C.	Parthia revolts from Seleucids
ca. 245 B.C.	Bactria gains independence
244–222 B.C.	Reforms of Agis and Cleomenes in Sparta
ca. 225 B.C.	Eratosthenes of Cyrene calculates earth's circumference
217 B.C.	Battle of Raphia brings Palestine under Ptolemies
167–142 B.C.	Maccabean revolt in Judea
146 B.C.	Antigonid Macedonia becomes a Roman province
64 B.C.	Seleucid Syria becomes a Roman province
30 B.C.	Ptolemaic Egypt becomes a Roman province

region east of Macedon), he turned to the Greek city-states nearby. Olynthus, the most important, fell in 348 B.C. Led by the Athenian Demosthenes° (ca. 385–322 B.C.), the main Greek city-states prepared to make a stand.

Demosthenes (de-MOSS-thuh-neez)

Demosthenes was a superb orator, but his attempts to forge a unified force came too late. By 338 B.C., when an Atheno-Theban army met the Macedonians, Philip had already won over much of the Greek world through diplomacy, bribes, and threats. His complete military victory at Chaeronea in Boeotia was followed up with a lenient settlement in which all the Greeks except Sparta acknowledged Philip's hegemony (see Map 4.1). The Greeks would rebel against Macedon more than once, but always in vain, until they fell under the even greater power of Rome. The day was over when the polis could decide the fate of the eastern Mediterranean.

In 336 B.C. Philip was murdered by a disgruntled courtier, and the invasion of the Persian Empire fell to his 20-year-old son, Alexander, the new king.

■ Alexander the Conqueror

Alexander III of Macedon (r. 336–323 B.C.) is as famous in art as in literature, in romance as in history, in Iran or India as in Europe or America. Yet the evidence for the historical Alexander is almost as problematic as that for the

historical Socrates or Jesus. After Alexander's untimely death at age 32, contemporaries wrote histories and memoirs, but none has survived. Several good historical accounts, based on earlier texts, are extant, but none was written less than three hundred years after Alexander's day. (See the box "Reading Sources: Virtues and Vices of Alexander the Great.") Alexander, moreover, was not only a legend in his own time but a master propagandist. Many of the incidents of his life took place in remote regions or among a few individuals, and they tended to grow with the telling.

Still, Alexander's virtues are clear. He was charismatic, handsome, intelligent, and well educated; as a teenager he had Aristotle himself as a private tutor. Alexander was ruthless as well as cultured. He began his reign with a massacre of his male relatives, but he brought a team of Greek scientists along with him on his expedition through the Persian Empire. Although he destroyed peoples and places, Alexander founded twenty cities. One of those cities was born in 331 B.C., at the site of a fishing village in the northwestern part of Egypt's delta. Alexander and his advisers planned a great trad-

Alexander Mosaic   This detail of a Roman-era mosaic from Pompeii shows Alexander the Great in battle, probably at Issus. Shining in his battle armor, Alexander is bareheaded, with a wide-eyed, intense gaze betokening his power. The larger scene includes the Persian king Darius, fleeing in his chariot.   *(Scala/Art Resource, NY)*

Map 4.1   Conquests of Philip and Alexander   Between 359 and 323 B.C., the armies of Macedon conquered first the Greek city-states and then the Persian Empire. Macedonian power extended from Greece and Egypt eastward to modern Pakistan.

ing center to replace Tyre, whose inhabitants had been killed or enslaved by the Macedonians who stormed the town in 332 B.C. The new city, called Alexandria, later grew into the largest city in the Mediterranean.

For all his varied interests, however, Alexander was first and foremost a warrior. Battlefield commander of the Macedonian cavalry at age 18, he devoted most of the rest of his life to warfare. As a leader of men, Alexander was popular and inspiring, and he shared risks with his troops. He knew the value of propaganda and took pains to depict his expedition to the Greek city-states as a war of revenge for Persia's invasion of Greece in 480 B.C. instead of what it actually was: the onslaught of Macedonian imperialism. He loved the colorful gesture. He began his expedition to conquer Persia in 334 B.C. by sacrificing animals to the gods at Troy, a site evoking Homer's heroes.

On the eve of invasion, Persia vastly outnumbered Macedon on both land and sea. Darius III of Persia was rich; Alexander's treasury was virtually empty. The Macedonian expeditionary force was short on supplies. The peoples in Persia's multi-ethnic empire were restive, but so too were Alexander's Greek allies, the mainstay of his fleet. One of Darius's advisers proposed a naval campaign to raise a revolt in Greece and force the Macedonians home. How then did Alexander propose to conquer Persia?

The answer was the Macedonian army. Although Alexander invaded Anatolia with only about thirty-five thousand men, they were the fastest marching, most experienced, and most skilled army in the eastern Mediterranean. If Persia would fight the Macedonians in a set battle, Alexander might be confident of victory—and it appeared that Persia would indeed fight. Persian elite

Virtues and Vices of Alexander the Great

Writing in the second century A.D., four centuries after Alexander's death, the historian Arrian composed from earlier accounts what is now the best surviving history of Alexander. A military man himself, Arrian appreciated Alexander's skills but was not blind to his flaws.

Alexander died in the 114th Olympiad, in the archonship of Hegesias at Athens [June 323 B.C.]. . . . He had great personal beauty, invincible power of endurance, and a keen intellect; he was brave and adventurous, strict in the observance of his religious duties, and hungry for fame. Most temperate in the pleasures of the body, his passion was for glory only, and in that he was insatiable. He had an uncanny instinct for the right course in a difficult and complex situation, and was most happy in his deductions from observed facts. In arming and equipping troops and in his military dispositions he was always masterly. Noble indeed was his power of inspiring his men, of filling them with confidence, and, in the moment of danger, of sweeping away their fear by the spectacle of his own fearlessness. When risks had to be taken, he took them with the utmost boldness, and his ability to seize the moment for a swift blow, before the enemy had any suspicion of what was coming, was beyond praise.

Doubtless, in the passion of the moment Alexander sometimes erred; it is true he took some steps towards the pomp and arrogance of the Asiatic kings: but I, at least, cannot feel that such errors were very heinous, if the circumstances are taken fairly into consideration. For, after all, he was young; the chain of his successes was unbroken, and, like all kings, past, present, and to come, he was surrounded by courtiers who spoke to please, regardless of what evil their word might do. On the other hand, I do indeed know that Alexander, of all the monarchs of old, was the only one who had the nobility of heart to be sorry for his mistakes.

Source: Arrian, *The Campaigns of Alexander,* trans. Aubrey de Sélincourt. Rev. J. R. Hamilton (Harmondsworth, England: Penguin, 1971), pp. 395–396.

 For additional information on this topic, go to http://college.hmco.com.

ideology impelled the army to face the enemy head-on. Darius, moreover, was a new monarch and a usurper and so under pressure to prove himself in the field. As expected, Macedon crushed the enemy. The war was decided in three great battles (see Map 4.1): at the Granicus River in Anatolia (334 B.C.), at Issus in Syria (333 B.C.), and at Gaugamela in Mesopotamia (331 B.C.). Darius fled into Iran and was deposed, assassinated, and replaced by a man whom Alexander captured and executed. By 328, Alexander's claim to be king of Persia was sealed with blood and iron.

Having conquered the Persian heartland, Alexander turned eastward. The last seven years of his career are marked by three themes. First is the continuing and, in Alexander's mind, apparently open-ended military campaign. He pushed his army not only into the eastern parts of the Persian Empire but beyond, into modern Pakistan, which had not been controlled by Persia since the early fifth century B.C. The Macedonians won a major

victory there in 326 B.C. near the Hydaspes River (modern Jhelum River) over the army of King Porus, a force employing as many as two hundred elephants (see Map 4.1). Alexander's infantry suffered considerable casualties before inflicting enough wounds on the elephants to make them uncontrollable. Alexander prepared to continue eastward, perhaps as far as the Bay of Bengal, but his exhausted and homesick men had other plans. They mutinied beside the Hyphasis River (modern Beas River, near the modern Indo-Pakistani border) and forced Alexander finally to turn back. He reached Persia in late 325 B.C.

The second theme of Alexander's later career is his increasing despotism. After conquering Persia, Alexander turned on the Macedonian nobility, among whom he feared potential rivals, for Macedonian nobles had a tradition of rebelling against strong kings. The years after 330 B.C. are marked by conspiracy trials, purges, and assassinations. The most spectacular took place in 328 in

Map 4.2   Hellenistic Kingdoms, Leagues, and City-States, ca. 240 B.C.   After Alexander's death, his empire lost its political unity. Great new cities and kingdoms arose in the lands he had conquered.

Maracanda (modern Samarkand, located in Uzbekistan) when, after a drunken quarrel, Alexander himself murdered Cleitus, one of his senior commanders.

Another sign of Alexander's growing despotism was his demand for the trappings of Persian kingship. After conquering Persia, for example, he made independent-minded Greeks and Macedonians bow down before him. He required that the Greek city-states deify him. "If Alexander wishes to be a god, let him be," was the concise reply of the Spartans, but Alexander had now set a precedent for both Hellenistic monarchs and Roman emperors.

The third theme of Alexander's later career is his novel policy of fusion. After returning from the Indian subcontinent, Alexander began training an army of thirty thousand Iranians and dismissed a large number of Macedonian troops. He forced his main commanders to marry Iranian women, just as he did himself. In 324 B.C. Alexander staged a grand banquet in Mesopotamia for nine thousand, at which he prayed for "concord and a partnership in rule between Greeks and Persians." Such actions were a sharp break with the traditional Greek belief in their national superiority. Aristotle, for example,

had referred to the peoples of western Asia as fit only to be slaves. Alexander's policy probably owed less to idealism than to a desire for a new power base independent of the Macedonian nobility.

Alexander died in Babylon in June of 323 B.C., a month before he turned 33, probably of malarial fever, although some contemporaries suspected poison and some historians have suggested drunkenness. Alexander did not designate a successor. His wife, pregnant at his death, would give birth to a son and heir, but he was shunted aside by the Macedonian generals, who began a long and bloody round of wars over the spoils of empire. It took approximately fifty years of fighting, from 322 to 275 B.C., to make clear that three large kingdoms—Macedon (under the Antigonid dynasty), Ptolemaic° Egypt, and the Seleucid° realm—would inherit most of Alexander's empire. The rest was divided among small kingdoms, federal leagues, and independent city-states (see Map 4.2).

Ptolemaic (tol-eh-MAY-ik)   **Seleucid** (seh-LOO-sid)

111

In the long run, Alexander's life was far more influential than his death. His conquests did nothing less than lay the foundations of the Hellenistic world. It is ironic to measure in such impersonal terms the achievements of one who, more than most people in history, exemplifies individual success. Whether it was exalting a savior or debunking a hero, much of Hellenistic culture centered on the myth of heroism that Alexander had engendered. Historians who insist the individual is insignificant will rarely have a more challenging refutation than Alexander.

THE HELLENISTIC KINGDOMS, 323–30 B.C.

VARIETY, flexibility, and the creation of a new elite to transmit Greek culture compose the Hellenistic political legacy. Hellenistic political units ranged from multi-ethnic kingdoms to small, ethnically homogeneous city-states (see Map 4.2). The Greek peninsula saw both a monarchy with republican pretensions and experiments in federalism and in social revolution. In Asia and Egypt, a new ruling elite emerged consisting both of Greeks and Macedonians and of natives. Although the first group tended to dominate high office, natives were by no means excluded. The immigrants wanted land, wealth, or adventure. Their paths were smoothed by a new ideology that identified being Greek less with loyalty to an individual city than with participation in a common Greek civilization.

Although the Hellenistic world became relatively peaceful after 275 B.C., conflict among the kingdoms continued. Generally waged at a low level of intensity, with bribes and diplomacy as weapons, the conflict nonetheless sometimes broke out into major battles. A number of small states emerged in Anatolia, notably Pergamum, whose wealthy rulers were patrons of literature and art, and Galatia°, carved out by Celtic invaders from Europe.

■ Colonialism, Greek Style

Many Greeks and Macedonians emigrated from home during the fourth and third centuries B.C., but we do not know how many. The few available statistics indicate a significant migration but not a mass exodus. By the second century B.C., the colonizing impulse had diminished in Greece and Macedon, but a large number of Jews left war-torn Palestine, particularly for Egypt. Ptolemaic Egypt and the Seleucid realm were also the most common destinations for Greek and Macedonian migrants.

Greek migrants could take advantage of a new definition of being Greek that had begun to emerge even before Alexander's conquests. Disappointed by the narrow and self-destructive localism of the Greek city-states, Isocrates° (428–338 B.C.), an Athenian teacher of rhetoric, sought a wider horizon. Isocrates redefined the meaning of Greek identity. He promoted the idea that Greece was not a collection of city-states but, rather, a civilization. "The people we call Hellenes," that is, Greeks, he wrote, "are those who have the same culture as us, not the same blood."[1]

The ideal of Greek culture made it easier for the migrants to maintain a Greek identity. For that matter, it was now possible for foreigners to become Greek by learning the Greek language and literature. The number of Hellenized foreigners was relatively small, yet their very existence marked a break from the Classical polis, where even a resident genius such as Aristotle could not obtain Athenian citizenship because he was not of Athenian descent.

The Greek language also served as a common denominator, along with Aramaic, both of which became the languages of trade in the eastern Mediterranean. To get a sense of the importance of Isocrates' redefinition of Hellenism, consider that one of the most famous Greek-speakers of all antiquity was Paul, the Christian apostle who was born a Jew in Tarsus, a city in southern Anatolia.

Immigrants sought to realize dreams of prosperity or adventure. Although agriculture was the main economic pursuit, trade, industry, finance, administration, and military service also offered opportunities. The large Ptolemaic bureaucracy needed administrators and tax collectors.

In the Ptolemaic and Seleucid realms, administration was a joint effort of both immigrants and natives. The Macedonian conquerors might have preferred to rely on Macedonians and Greeks, but their territories never attracted enough immigrants from "home" to make that possible. Besides the new rulers needed both the goodwill and the local knowledge of the people whom they had conquered. Thus, the upper echelons of government were dominated by Greek and Macedonian

---

Galatia (guh-LAY-shuh)

Isocrates (eye-SOCK-rah-teez)

immigrants and their descendants, but native elites held governmental positions as well. Especially after about 200 B.C., some natives served the new rulers as administrators or soldiers, usually in low- or mid-level positions but sometimes in high office. Others worked in the traditional native administrative structures that survived largely intact in the new kingdoms, for example, as judges or village headmen or priests.

Consider, for example, soldiers. To create a permanent, hereditary military group living in the countryside, Ptolemy° I settled his soldiers on land allotments. Native Egyptians were excluded from the army at first but served as policemen. By the second century B.C., however, the dynasty turned to native Egyptians as a new source of soldiers. In return for military service, natives now received land, tax breaks, and the right to call themselves Hellenes. Their Hellenism sometimes merely scratched the surface, but sometimes it went deeper.

An Egyptian named Plenis, a villager in middle Egypt in the late second century B.C., is a good example of this cultural cross-fertilization. Plenis was a tenant farmer on a royal estate and a priest in a local Egyptian cult. His horizon was not narrow, however; like his father before him, Plenis served as a soldier in the Ptolemaic army. Plenis, moreover, could write Greek as well as Egyptian, and he even used a Greek name: Dionysius, son of Kephalas.

Temples, which often administered large estates, represented important sources of native power. Priests shaped local opinion and were in a position, therefore, both to enjoy considerable independence and to demand royal patronage. Both Ptolemies and Seleucids complied: from Babylon to Edfu, money poured into temple-building and renovation.

The Seleucids addressed the security needs of their far-flung realms by establishing over seventy colonies extending to central Asia. Some colonies were civilian, but most were military, composed of retired or reserve soldiers, mostly Greeks or Macedonians, but also including Jews and other non-Greek peoples. Colonists received land allotments. Greek-style public buildings were erected, and some cities were laid out according to a rectilinear grid plan reminiscent of the Classical polis. The gymnasium attained a great practical and symbolic importance as both the center of Greek culture and the preparatory school for entry into the elite. The Hellenistic gymnasium offered education in literature, philosophy, and oratory as well as athletics.

Ptolemy (TOL-eh-mee)

Singing African   This Hellenistic bronze figurine shows a black African, perhaps an Ethiopian, playing a musical instrument (now missing). The lithe body and emotionalism of the work are typically Hellenistic. Africans were a common subject for the sculptors of Alexandria, whence this piece may have come.   *(Bibliothèque Nationale de France)*

Some Seleucid colonies developed into flourishing cities. For example, Greek cities dominated the Syrian coastline and much of Anatolia until the coming of Islam in the seventh century A.D. Greek urbanization should not create the false impression, however, that the Seleucids were motivated by some civilizing mission. They were not. They established colonies to increase their power.

Tanagra Figurine A terra-cotta (baked clay) statuette of around 320 B.C. shows a modestly dressed woman, wearing a hat and carrying a fan. Named for its place of manufacture in Greece, this popular style of figurine demonstrates the Hellenistic taste for ordinary, household themes. *(Staatliche Museen zu Berlin, Antikensammlung/Bildarchiv Preussischer Kulturbesitz)*

■ Economic Expansion

Immigration and colonization were not the only sources of new economic opportunities. At the beginning of the Hellenistic era, Alexander turned the huge gold and silver reserves of Persia into coinage and released it onto the market virtually all at once. Although Alexander's action stimulated a rapid inflation lasting about seventy-five years, it also had the positive effect of greatly stimulating commerce. In particular the economy of Hellenistic Egypt became highly monetarized, even on the village level. Barter continued to exist in Egypt, but the widespread presence of money served to increase the production and circulation of goods, helping to render Egypt an economic powerhouse. Another stimulus to trade was the creation of thriving new Hellenistic cities, especially Alexandria with its great harbors, canals, marketplaces, and infrastructure of banks, inns, courts, and shipbuilding facilities.

During Hellenistic times, trade and commerce tended to shift from Greece proper to Anatolia and Egypt (see Map 4.3). The island of Rhodes, located off the southwest tip of Anatolia, grew into a major trading center, especially for grain. This development was the result of excellent harbors; a location on the merchant routes between Asia, Africa, and southeastern Europe; and a superb fleet. The Rhodian aristocracy grew rich off taxes and duties, wisely reinvesting a portion of the profits in naval infrastructure (such as arsenals and dockyards) and in campaigns against pirates. Egypt too had many products to trade. Grain was the most important, but textiles, glass, papyrus (from which a kind of paper was produced; see the feature "Information Technology: Papyrus" on page 14), and luxury goods were also significant. Egyptian goods were sold throughout the Mediterranean. A network of canals connecting Alexandria to the Nile and the Red Sea beyond also made possible active trading with Sudan, Arabia, and India.

The Seleucid kingdoms controlled rich trade routes to Arabia, India, and central Asia. Commerce was facilitated by good roads, safe sea travel between the Persian Gulf and India, and a unified royal coinage. The Seleucids traded agricultural goods and manufactured products such as textiles, glassware, and metalwork for spices from India and Arabia. In the first century B.C. they even had trade contacts with China, whose silk garments reached the Mediterranean. The kingdom of Pergamum, which stretched inland from Anatolia's northwest coast, exported the agricultural products of the rich hinterland it controlled, as well as the local gray-blue building stone and, as an alternative to Egyptian papyrus, parchment.

Map 4.3　The Eastern Mediterranean, ca. 200 B.C.　The great Hellenistic powers contended for control of this vibrant, turbulent, and prosperous region. Conflict centered on Palestine and the Aegean islands, the rulership of which frequently changed hands.

Slavery was an important part of the Hellenistic social and economic scene. Although war and piracy were the main sources of enslavement, some people were born into slavery. In Sicily and southern Italy, slaves worked huge plantations, but eastern Mediterranean slaves were commonly found in the household or in administration, and in cities rather than in the countryside. Many unfree laborers worked on farms in Egypt and western Asia. Following the pre-Greek traditions of those regions, they were generally tenant farmers tied to kings or potentates rather than outright slaves.

On some plantations, conditions for slaves were harsh enough to lead to mass uprisings. It was not unusual, however, for domestic or administrative slaves to buy their freedom, sometimes using savings they were allowed to keep, sometimes borrowing money from the master or from friends (see the box "Reading Sources: Macedonian Slaves Buy Their Freedom"). Greeks enslaved fellow Greeks, but often, it seems, with guilty consciences; they frequently made special efforts to help Greek slaves win their freedom. Even in bondage, therefore, Greeks had special privileges.

■ **Macedon and Greece**

Macedon was the last of the three great Hellenistic kingdoms to emerge from civil war after Alexander's death. Not until 276 B.C. was Antigonus Gonatas, grandson of Alexander's general Antigonus the One-Eyed, established firmly on the throne. His Antigonid° dynasty

---

Antigonid (an-TIG-on-id)

📖 READING SOURCES

Macedonian Slaves Buy Their Freedom

This marble inscription of either 280 or 235 B.C., from the city of Beroia in Macedonia, records the manumission of about a dozen slaves. Note that the slaves had to pay for their freedom, that they had to continue to serve their mistress, Attinas, for the rest of her life, and that they ran the risk of re-enslavement.

In the reign of King Demetrios, seventh and twentieth year, month Peritios, in the priesthood of Apollonides the son of Glaukios. Payment for their freedom was made by Kosmas, Marsyas, Ortyx to Attinas, daughter of Alketas, for themselves and their wives, Arnion, Glauka, Chlidane, and for their children, both those now alive and any that may later be born, and for all their possessions, each fifty gold *staters* [coins]; and Spazatis for herself and her possessions paid gold *staters,* twenty-five of them. And for them if they remain with Attinas while Attinas lives and do whatever Attinas orders, and Attinas dies, they may depart to wherever they wish. And it shall not be possible for Alketas nor Alketas' wife nor the descendants of Alketas nor Lareta to seize them or their wives or their children or Spazatis or to reduce

[them] to slavery or to take away anything of their possessions on any pretext nor by another on their behalf. But if not, they shall be free and the one attempting to reduce them to slavery shall pay for each person one hundred gold *staters* and to the king another hundred for each person. And if anyone from their possessions takes [something], he shall pay double the value of that which he took from them. [But if] they do not remain and do not do whatever Attinas orders, they and [their] wives and their [children], while Attinas [lives, for the] one not doing [thus], his freedom shall be invalid. . . .

Source: Adapted from Stanley M. Burstein, *The Hellenistic Age from the Battle of Ipsos to the Death of Cleopatra VII* (Cambridge: Cambridge University Press, 1985), pp. 73–74.

---

lasted about a century, when the conquering Romans made Macedon first a republic and then a Roman province.

True to the traditions of Macedon, the Antigonids projected an image of simplicity and toughness. Like Philip II and Alexander the Great, Antigonus immersed himself in the culture of the Greek city-states, partly because he admired it, partly because it brought him prestige. As a young man, Antigonus had studied the new school of Stoic philosophy in Athens (see page 128). As king, he devoted himself to the Stoic dictates of duty, describing his office as "noble servitude" and his diadem as a mere "rag." Antigonus shared the traditional Macedonian ambition to dominate the Greek city-states, but he faced rival powers. Besides Ptolemaic Egypt, there was the kingdom of Epirus in northwestern Greece and two new federal leagues in the south, the Aetolians° (north of

the Corinthian Gulf) and the Achaeans° (in the Peloponnesus; see Map 4.3).

The federal leagues were more tightly organized than Classical Greek military leagues (such as the Peloponnesian League) and larger than the Boeotian League, a fourth-century B.C. federal alliance that had covered a relatively small territory. The new leagues permitted some participation by ordinary men but were dominated by the wealthy; they were not democracies.

Yet the leagues interest us as models of federalism that would one day influence the founders of the United States. The Aetolians, for example, practiced proportional representation by population in a federal council for constituent cities. The Achaeans successfully balanced local and federal authorities. Constituent cities kept their own constitutions while recognizing federal jurisdiction. The federal government consisted of a

---

Aetolians (ay-TOL-ee-unz)

Achaeans (uh-KEE-unz)

governing general (both president and commander-in-chief) and ten subordinate magistrates, an executive council, and a general assembly.

Athens, less successful than Sparta in maintaining independence, repeatedly experienced Macedonian rule. Through a combination of war and diplomacy, however, Athens won periods of freedom from the late fourth to the mid-second century B.C., when Rome held sway over Greece. Athens remained a vibrant democracy until the late third century B.C., when the oligarchic upper classes finally won the upper hand for good.

Extremes of wealth and poverty, problems of debt, and class conflict challenged Hellenistic Greece. The decline of democracy enabled the wealthy to contribute less to the public good in taxes and to amass private fortunes. The result was sometimes class conflict, but the elite usually made just enough concessions to avoid full-scale revolution.

Sparta was an exception. In the late third century B.C. a social revolution was launched from above by Agis and Cleomenes, two Spartan kings working together. After defeat in the fourth century B.C., Sparta had become impoverished (see page 92). The reformers now offered debt relief, a redistribution of land, and a restoration of Classical Spartan austerity and equality. Popular in Sparta, the revolution threatened to spread elsewhere. Peloponnesian oligarchs called in Macedonian forces, which crushed Sparta in 222 B.C. and ended the revolution.

■ Ptolemaic Egypt

The wealthiest, the most sophisticated, and the longest lasting of the Hellenistic kingdoms was Ptolemaic Egypt. One of Alexander's great generals, Ptolemy (d. 283 B.C.), became governor of Egypt in 323 B.C. and proclaimed himself king in 304. His dynasty lasted until Rome annexed Egypt in 30 B.C., after the suicide of the last of the line, Queen Cleopatra (see page 126). By contrast, Macedon was absorbed by Rome a century earlier, in 146; Pergamum was annexed in 133; the Seleucid kingdom succumbed to Rome in 64.

Unlike the Antigonids, the Ptolemies did not pursue the simple virtues but rather gloried in wealth and grandeur. Ptolemy I showed the way to his successors when he had Alexander's funeral procession hijacked on its way to Macedonia and established a tomb and then a cult in the capital city, Alexandria—a Greek hero-shrine in the land of the pyramids. Ptolemy I made arrangements to have himself proclaimed "Savior God" after his death; his successors, less reticent, took divine honors while still alive.

The most important Ptolemaic borrowing, however, was the pharaonic tradition of royal intervention in the economy, which the Ptolemies combined with Greek customs of literacy and the use of money rather than barter. The result was a highly complex and profitable economy. Putting to use the science of the Museum, the great institute in Alexandria (see page 121), the Ptolemies sponsored irrigation and land reclamation projects, the introduction of new crops (for example, new varieties of wheat), and the greatly expanded cultivation of old ones (such as grapes for wine).

Most of the people of Egypt made their living in agriculture, either as independent small farmers or as tenants on large estates. Government enriched itself through taxes, rents, demands for compulsory labor, state monopolies (on such diverse items as oils, textiles, and beer), and various internal tolls and customs duties. The result was boom times under strong kings and queens in the third century B.C. Egypt became the most prosperous part of the Hellenistic world, and Alexandria became the wealthiest, most populous city in the Mediterranean, as well as its literary capital (see Map 4.3). In the second century B.C., however, continued economic prosperity was derailed by decline. Weak kings, bureaucratic corruption, inflation of the currency, and the end of Greek immigration created conditions for revolt.

Since pharaonic times, tendencies toward regional independence had bedeviled Egypt's government. The Ptolemaic period was no exception. Regional unrest stirred in the 240s and then mushroomed after the Battle of Raphia in 217 B.C., a struggle in Gaza between the Ptolemies and Seleucids for control of Palestine. The Ptolemies won, but only by enrolling thousands of Egyptians in the Macedonian phalanx, responding to a shortage of Greek mercenaries. Emboldened by their new military power, people in Upper Egypt soon broke into armed revolt against the government in far-off Alexandria. Rival kings appeared in the south, and unrest continued for about a century.

To advance their cause, the rebels inflamed anti-Greek sentiment. High taxes and regional rivalries, however, probably carried more weight than nationalism in the minds of most people. Although friction between immigrants and natives sparked from time to time, most Egyptians accepted the Ptolemies as pharaohs as long as they brought peace and prosperity. (See the box "Global Encounters: Egyptians versus Greeks in a Temple.")

Nor did the Ptolemies allow national sentiment to stand in the way of reasserting their power. In 196 B.C., for example, Ptolemy V Epiphanes celebrated his coronation in full pharaonic ceremonial in Memphis. Egyp-

Egyptians versus Greeks in a Temple

This second-century B.C. *papyrus, a petition to the authorities from a Greek worshiper of Serapis, provides insight into relations between Greeks and Egyptians in Hellenistic Egypt. It shows how Greeks lived in the temple at Memphis in order to worship Serapis, a Hellenized Egyptian god (see page 129). It also depicts violence and hostility across ethnic lines.*

To Dionysius, general and one of the "friends" [of the king], from Ptolemy son of Glaucias, a Macedonian, one of those "held in detention" [that is, on a voluntary, religious retreat] for twelve years in the great Temple of Serapis in Memphis. As I have suffered grave injustice and my life has been frequently endangered by the temple cleaners whose names are listed below, I am taking refuge with you in the belief that in this way I would best secure justice. For on . . . [November 9, 161 B.C.] they came to the temple of Astarte, which is in the sanctuary, and in which I have been living "in detention" for the number of years mentioned above; some of them had stones in their hand and others sticks, and they tried to force their way in, in order to seize the opportunity to plunder the temple and to put me to death because I am a Greek, like men laying a plot against my life. But when I anticipated them and shut the door of the temple, and shouted to them to withdraw in peace, they did not go away even so. When Diphilus, one of the worshipers held "in detention" by Serapis besides me, expressed indignation at their conduct in such a temple, they pushed him back, handled him very roughly and beat him up, so that their lawless brutality was clear for all to see. When these same men treated me in the same way in . . . [November 163], I immediately addressed a petition to you, but as I had no one to look after the matter further, they were let off scot-free and became even more arrogant. I therefore ask you, if you please, to order them to be brought before you, so that they may receive the punishment they deserve for all these misdeeds. Farewell.

[There follows a list of seven non-Greek names, of which six are Egyptian and one possibly Anatolian.]

Source: Adapted from M. M. Austin, *The Hellenistic World from Alexander to the Roman Conquest: A Selection of Ancient Sources in Translation* (Cambridge: Cambridge University Press, 1981), pp. 434–435.

---

tian priests commemorated the occasion in a decree written in Egypt's traditional language of kingship in a trilingual inscription (Greek, hieroglyphic, and demotic—ordinary—Egyptian). This inscription, discovered by French soldiers in 1798 and dubbed the Rosetta Stone (named for the place where it was found), led to the modern European deciphering of hieroglyphics.

Despite the frictions, evidence points to native-settler cooperation, especially in the countryside, where intermarriage and bilingualism became common. Many an ordinary Greek became fully assimilated to Egyptian ways, and even wealthy, sophisticated, urban Greeks adopted a smattering of Egyptian customs. The Egyptian calendar, Egyptian names, and mummification were all in use. By 98 B.C., assimilation was evident in the cultural

hybrid of a group of 18- and 19-year-old male youths who received traditional Greek military and literary training but prayed to Egypt's crocodile-god.

■ Seleucids and Attalids

The kingdom founded by Alexander's general Seleucus° (ca. 358–281 B.C.) experienced shifting borders and inhabitants. The Seleucid kingdom began when Seleucus took Babylon in 312 B.C. and ended in 64 B.C. when Syria became a Roman province. Many territorial changes occurred in between. The first three kings ruled a domain stretching from the Aegean to Bactria° (modern

---

Seleucus (suh-LOO-kus)   **Bactria** (BACK-tree-uh)

Afghanistan), but by the early second century B.C., most of the Iranian Plateau and lands eastward had been lost. At its height, in the third century B.C., the Seleucid kingdom had three nerve centers: Ionia (in western Anatolia), with a capital at Sardis; Syria, with a capital at Antioch; and Babylonia, whose capital was Seleucia-on-the-Tigris (near modern Baghdad; see Map 4.2).

Unlike the compact Nile Valley with its relatively homogeneous population, the far-flung and multi-ethnic Seleucid lands presented an enormous administrative challenge. To govern such a conglomerate, the kings took over the Persian system of satraps (provincial governors), taxes, and royal roads and post (see page 47), to which they added an excellent army trained according to Macedonian traditions, a common coinage, and a Hellenistic ruler cult. The chief Seleucid innovation was the establishment of colonies. Greek and Macedonian

soldiers and administrators dominated, but natives also filled bureaucratic slots.

The greatest Seleucid city was Antioch, which became one of the wealthiest and most luxurious of all eastern Mediterranean cities; only Ptolemaic Alexandria outstripped it. The intellectual and artistic capital of Greek Asia in Hellenistic times, however, was not Antioch but Pergamum, in northwestern Anatolia (see Map 4.3).

The rulers of Pergamum, the Attalid dynasty of kings, carved out a small kingdom that became independent of the Seleucids in 263 B.C. and fell into Roman hands in 133 B.C. The Attalids made Pergamum into a showplace of Greek civilization, a would-be second Athens. As in Athens, public building was focused on a steep acropolis. The upper city of Pergamum was laid out on hillside terraces rising to a palace and fortified citadel. One of the terraces housed the famous Pergamum Altar, a huge

Panel from Pergamum Altar   This frieze (ca. 180–150 B.C.) decorating the podium of the altar of Zeus illustrates the war of the gods and the giants, imparting a heroic dimension to the battles of the Attalid kings and the Celts. The theme of Greeks versus barbarians recalls the sculpture of Athens's Parthenon, suggesting that Pergamum was the successor to Athens as the champion of Greek civilization.   *(Art Resource, NY)*

A Greek-Influenced Indian Statue This figure of a *bodhisattva* ("enlightened one") belongs to the Gandharan school, which was heavily influenced by Hellenistic sculpture. The statue's proportions, facial features, and draped clothing particularly recall Hellenistic motifs, suggesting that it may be the work of a Greek sculptor. *(Royal Ontario Museum)*

monument to an Attalid victory over the Celts, who first invaded Anatolia in 278 B.C. and whose advance the Attalids checked. They could not, however, stop the Celts from settling in central Anatolia, where they created their kingdom of Galatia.

Pergamum was famous for its sculptors and for a library second only to Alexandria's. Pergamene writers focused on scholarship to the exclusion of poetry, perhaps as a result of the influence of Stoic philosophers, who disapproved of poetry's emotionalism.

■ The Greco-Indian Interaction

The Seleucids' hold on Alexander's vast eastern domains turned out to be temporary. A new Persian dynasty, the Parthians°, achieved independence in the mid-third century B.C. and over the next century carved out an empire extending westward into Mesopotamia. But to the east, Bactria remained Greek, if not Seleucid. From the mid-third century B.C., an independent Greek Bactria prospered (see Map 4.2).

Vivid evidence of Greek colonization in Bactria comes from the site of Aï Khanum (its ancient name is unknown) in northern Afghanistan. This prosperous and populous city contained many reminders of Greece, among them a gymnasium, theater, and library. A pillar in the gymnasium was inscribed in the mid-third century B.C. with 140 moral maxims from Delphi in Greece, over 3,000 miles away.

In the second century B.C., Bactrian kings extended their rule into the Indus River valley and the Punjab, a region with a modest Greek presence since the fifth century B.C., when the Persians settled Greek mercenaries there. Virtually no literary evidence survives, but monuments and, particularly, coins demonstrate Greco-Indian cultural interaction. For example, some coins from the second century B.C. show bilingual inscriptions in Greek and Indian languages. Their designs include a variety of Indian religious motifs, such as the lotus plant, symbol of Lakshmi, goddess of wealth and good fortune. Indians admired Hellenistic astronomy; one text goes so far as to say that Greek scientists should be "reverenced like gods."

The Hellenistic world seems to have intrigued King Asoka° (r. ca. 270–230 B.C.), who ruled almost the entire subcontinent, the largest empire in India to date. Asoka is best remembered as a religious reformer. A convert to Buddhism, he played a major role in its spread, which proceeded under the slogan of *dhamma*, that is, morality or righteousness. One of his inscriptions records "victory" by dhamma, "where reigns the Greek king named Antiochus, and beyond the realm of Antiochus in the lands of the four kings named Ptolemy, Antigonus, Magas, and Alexander," which is generally thought to refer to embassies to the Hellenistic kingdoms.[2]

The envoys apparently found few converts, for it is difficult to find any trace of Buddhism in Hellenistic Greek culture, at least outside the Greco-Indian kingdoms. There, one of the most powerful Greek rulers, Menander Soter Dikaios (r. ca. 155–130 B.C.), may have converted to Buddhism in the mid-second century B.C.

Parthians (PAR-thee-unz)   **Asoka** (uh-SO-kuh)

But certain aspects of Indian religion *did* interest Greek intellectuals around the Mediterranean in Hellenistic and Roman times, especially India's powerful currents of asceticism, mysticism, and monasticism. Observers on Alexander's expedition, Hellenistic envoys, merchants, and philosophers in search of Eastern wisdom—all served as conduits between East and West. One of the most influential was Megasthenes, a Seleucid ambassador to the court of Asoka's grandfather, who published his *Indika*, a description of India, around 300 B.C.

Yet the degree to which this interest influenced Greek and Roman culture is debatable. Although ancient writers mention Greek or Roman philosophers who were attracted by Indian culture, modern scholars tend to be cautious. The ancients had a weakness for tall tales and stories of exotic inspiration. Consider, for example, the following reports. Pyrrho of Elis, founder of the Hellenistic philosophical school of skepticism (see page 128), supposedly based his notion of the imperturbable sage on one Calanos, an Indian whom Pyrrho saw step calmly on a funeral pyre when Pyrrho was part of Alexander's expedition. Around A.D. 40, one Apollonius of Tyana, a pagan religious thinker, is supposed to have traveled to India to study with its sages. Two centuries later the great Neo-Platonic philosopher Plotinus (A.D. 235–270) is reported to have traveled with the Roman emperor Gordian's army eastward, hoping in vain to reach India. Some scholars see Indian influence in Plotinus's mysticism and pantheism, but others dismiss these various reports.

Central Asian nomads overran Bactria in the late second century B.C. The Hellenistic kingdoms of India and Pakistan, however, survived until about the time of Christ, and some Greek communities lasted until the fifth century A.D. The Gandharan sculptors who flourished in a formerly Greek-ruled region in about A.D. 200 used Greek artistic techniques to depict Buddhist subjects, which might suggest the impact of Indian culture on the remaining Greek population.

THE ALEXANDRIAN MOMENT

B Y the first century B.C., Alexandria was a city of a half-million or more inhabitants. It was one of the largest, wealthiest, and most important cities in the world. The bulk of the population were Egyptian, but Greeks and Jews made up large minorities, and no one would have been surprised, in this cosmopolitan center, to see an Indian or a Celt, an Italian or a Persian.

The capital of Egypt, Alexandria was also perhaps the most important place where Greek culture was spread and transformed in the Hellenistic era. At the same time, it was a mix of ethnic cooperation and conflict. Underwater archaeologists, for example, looking for submerged parts of the city in Alexandria harbor, have found Egyptian sphinxes and obelisks as well as Greek statues. Written sources portray a picture of social change in the elite, an increase in leisure time, a growth in educational opportunities for both sexes, royal patronage of culture, and the value of even a limited knowledge of Greek literature as the ticket to advancement.

■ The Anti-Epic Temperament

In 294 B.C. King Ptolemy I invited the deposed tyrant of Athens, Demetrius of Phalerum, to found an institution of culture in Alexandria. A writer himself, Ptolemy was no less sincere because the new foundation would bring him prestige and keep his engineers up to date on new technology for warfare and agriculture. Demetrius had studied with Aristotle's successor at the Lyceum, Theophrastus° (ca. 370–288 B.C.), a practical man interested in compiling and cataloging knowledge.

The new institution was called the Museum (literally, "House of the Muses," or the home of the female deities who inspired creativity). The Museum was a residence, study, and lecture hall for scholars, scientists, and poets. One of its key components was the Library, in its day the largest repository of Greek writing in the world. In the third century B.C.—at the height of the Ptolemaic kingdom—the Library contained 700,000 papyrus rolls, the equivalent of roughly 50,000 modern books. Its nearest competitor, at Pergamum, contained less than a third as many rolls.

The Library reflects an increase in the size of the Hellenistic reading and writing public. As independence vanished, city-states converted their military training programs for 18- and 19-year-old men into educational programs in literature and philosophy. The names of over a thousand writers of the Hellenistic era survive, and after 300 B.C., anthologies, abridgments, and school texts proliferated.

Although modeled on Athens's Lyceum, the Museum represented a departure from the public culture of the Classical period. The denizens of the Museum were an elite, dependent on royal patronage and self-consciously Greek, as if to set up a barrier against Egyptians. At the Museum, culture was an object of study, not a part of

---

Theophrastus (the-uh-FRAS-tus)

civic life as it had been in Classical Athens. A witticism of Timon, a philosopher from the Peloponnesus who lived in the third century B.C., rings true: "In Egypt, land of diverse tribes, graze many pedants, fatted fowls that quarrel without end in the hen coop of the Muses."

Before we examine Alexandrian literature further, it is worth noting how greatly Hellenistic Athenian literature diverged from Classical culture. The greatest Hellenistic Athenian writer, and a figure of international renown, was Menander° (ca. 342–292 B.C.). He was the master of a style of comedy called "New Comedy," as distinguished from the "Old Comedy" of Aristophanes, which had flourished a century earlier (see page 100). Where Old Comedy was raucous and ribald, New Comedy was restrained; where Old Comedy focused on public matters such as war and politics, New Comedy was domestic and private. New Comedy epitomized the turn away from public life in Hellenistic times.

Menander wrote over seventy plays, but only one complete work has survived, *Dyskolos* (*The Grouch*). There are also substantial excerpts from several other comedies as well as Roman imitations. The elements of Menander's skill and popularity shine through. Witty and fluent, he favored stock plots and stock characters: the boastful soldier, the clever slave, the dashing but inept young man, the sweet maiden, and the old miser. Within those limitations, Menander created realistic and idiosyncratic characters. As a Hellenistic critic asked rhetorically: "O Menander and Life, which of you imitated the other?"

Like Menander, Alexandrian writers spurned public themes, but in Alexandria the characteristic literary figure was not the playwright but the critic. He was a professional man of letters, as likely to write literary history as poetry. His works tended to be scholarly, even pedantic; they were refined, erudite, subtle—in a word, courtly. Prime concerns of the critics were establishing a literary canon and standardizing the texts of the canonical authors. Adopted by the Romans, Alexandrian critical standards have influenced the West to this day.

Of the three greatest Alexandrian writers, two—Callimachus° (305–240 B.C.) and Apollonius° of Rhodes (b. ca. 295 B.C.)—worked at the Library; the third, Theocritus° (ca. 300–260 B.C.), probably lived on a stipend from the Ptolemies. Popular for centuries, Callimachus was probably the most influential, the complete Hellenistic poet. A native of Cyrene (see Map 4.2) who came to Alexandria as a schoolteacher, Callimachus found a position in the Library. There he composed a virtually universal history of all recorded Greek (and much non-Greek) knowledge.

A prolific writer, Callimachus generally preferred short to long poems: "Big book, big evil," was his maxim. Earlier Greek poets were usually austere and public minded; Callimachus preferred the private, the light, and the exotic. "Don't expect from me a big-sounding poem," he writes; "Zeus thunders, not I."[3] Callimachus was expert at the pithy statement in verse, the epigram.

The Causes, Callimachus's masterwork (of which little survives), is at seven thousand lines his one long poem, but it is a collection of brief vignettes rather than a unified narrative. The central theme is the origins of festivals, customs, institutions, and names, many of them obscure. Arcane diction and complex allusions abound. Only an elite could understand such writing, but Callimachus was an elitist. "I detest all common things," he states.

Another major Alexandrian writer was Callimachus's student, Apollonius of Rhodes. Tradition claims that Apollonius retired to Rhodes after his epic poem *Argonautica*° (*Voyage of the Argo*) was poorly received. The subject is the legend of Jason and the heroes who travel on the ship *Argo* to Colchis, at the far end of the Black Sea, in pursuit of the Golden Fleece (the skin of a winged ram). With the help of the Colchian princess Medea, who falls in love with Jason, the heroes succeed and return home safely after numerous adventures.

Apollonius devotes much of the poem to a discussion of the roots of various names, cults, and customs. The main novelty, however, is a fundamental and pervading doubt about the very possibility of heroism. Apollonius's Jason is no Achilles, no Odysseus. Homer describes Odysseus as "never at a loss"; Apollonius describes Jason as "helpless." Men move the action in the *Iliad* and the *Odyssey*; Jason depends on a woman, Medea, for his success. Indeed, much of the *Argonautica* focuses on Medea and in particular on her love for Jason. With the exception of the works of Sappho, previous Greek poetry generally either ignored female eroticism or presented it in a hostile light. Apollonius's work illustrates both the improved status of women in Hellenistic ideology and the great interest of the age in the inner life of the emotions. All in all, the *Argonautica* is less a traditional epic than an anti-epic.

Like Callimachus, Theocritus, a native of Syracuse, wrote short, polished poetry. He composed thirty-one subtle and refined poems, conventionally known as idylls. The best-known of the poems focus on country life. They are the first known pastoral poems; indeed,

---

Menander (meh-NAN-der)   **Callimachus** (kah-LIH-muh-kus)
Apollonius (ap-uh-LO-nee-us)   **Theocritus** (the-OCK-rih-tus)

Argonautica (ar-go-NAW-tih-kuh)

Street Musicians   The lively scene of a mixed group of young and old, male and female, recalls the jaunty mimes popular with the Hellenistic public. A mosaic of about 100 B.C., the artwork comes from a private villa in the Greco-Italian city of Pompeii.   *(Museo Nazionale, Naples)*

Theocritus probably invented the genre. Theocritus's pastorals explore nature, but always self-consciously, always with the city in mind. His peasants and shepherds are marvelously cultured, more like townspeople on an excursion than true rustics. Through his Roman admirers, Theocritus's love of nature has exerted a powerful hold on the Western literary imagination.

Outside the Museum, Alexandria had a lively popular culture, much of it Egyptian or influenced by Egyptian models. A glimpse of it is afforded in the seven surviving mimes, or farces, of an obscure writer named Herondas or Herodas. Although written in literary Greek, they discuss commonplace subjects—shopping for shoes, tourism, lawsuits, and beatings at school—and titillating themes such as adultery and prostitution. Lively, bawdy, and funny, filled with the grit of everyday life in the third century B.C., they are a reminder of just how specialized the culture of the Museum was.

■ Advances in Science and Medicine

The Ptolemies not only reaped practical benefits in military and agricultural technology from their Museum, but they became the patrons of a flourishing period in the history of pure scientific inquiry. They also unwittingly promoted a split between philosophy and science that has characterized much of Western culture since. Antigonid patronage of ethical and political philosophy helped keep Athens pre-eminent in those fields. The study of science, in contrast, tended to shift to Alexandria. The rulers of Pergamum and, far to the west, Syracuse, a flourishing Hellenistic city in Sicily, were great patrons of science as well. Wealth, improved communications and literacy, continued warfare, and cross-fertilization between Greek and non-Greek traditions, especially Greek and Babylonian astronomy, were all catalysts of Hellenistic science.

Some of the best-known figures of Hellenistic science were mathematicians. In his *Elements,* the Alexandrian Euclid (active ca. 300 B.C.) produced a systematic exposition of geometry, hugely influential in both Western and Islamic civilizations. A Sicilian Greek, Archimedes° of Syracuse (287–212 B.C.), did original work on the geometry of spheres and cylinders, calculated the approximate value of pi (the ratio of a circle's circumference to its diameter), and made important discoveries in astronomy, engineering, optics, and other fields. Archimedes was as great an inventor as he was a theoretician. One of the most important of his innovations was the water snail, also known as Archimedes' screw: a device to raise water for irrigation. Invented by Archimedes during a stay in Egypt, the screw made it possible to irrigate previously barren land, as did the ox-driven water wheel, another Ptolemaic invention.

Advances in mathematics promoted advances in astronomy. Aristarchus of Samos (active ca. 275 B.C.) is known for his heliocentric hypothesis, which confounded tradition by having the earth revolve around the sun, instead of the sun around the earth. He was right, but Hellenistic astronomy lacked the data to prove his theory, so its rejection was not unreasonable at the time. Eratosthenes° of Cyrene (active ca. 225 B.C.) was saddled with the frustrating nickname of "Beta" (the second letter of the Greek alphabet) because he was considered second best in every branch of study. This "second best" nonetheless calculated through simple geometry an extraordinarily accurate measurement of the earth's circumference.

Hellenistic medicine thrived in Alexandria. Both Greece and Egypt had long-established medical traditions. Egyptian drugs, and possibly Egyptian doctors' knowledge of the eye as well as their emphasis on measurement, helped stimulate Alexandrian medical progress, as no doubt did the mere fact of cross-fertilization. The key to medical advance, however, was the dissection of human cadavers in Alexandria, a first in the history of science. In Greece, as in many ancient societies, religious tradition demanded that dead bodies not be mutilated. But in the frontier atmosphere of early Alexandria, this traditional taboo lost much of its force. Although Egyptians did not practice dissection, they did practice embalming, which may have helped Alexandrian Greeks overcome the prohibition against cutting open the human body. Ever supportive of research, the Ptolemies provided corpses to Greek scientists for dissection. Indeed, they had condemned criminals sent from prison for live dissection by scientists. The practice, only a short-lived experiment in the early third century B.C., outraged many writers in antiquity, just as today it would be considered an atrocity.

The leading scientific beneficiary was Herophilus° of Chalcedon (ca. 320–250 B.C.), a practicing physician in Alexandria. Among his achievements was the recognition (against Aristotle) that the brain is the center of the nervous system, a careful dissection of the eye, the discovery of the ovaries, and the description of the duodenum, which he named (*duodenum* is a Latin translation of a Greek word meaning "twelve fingers," describing the organ's length). In addition, Herophilus developed a detailed theory of the diagnostic value of measuring pulse rates.

Hellenistic technology has long fascinated and frustrated scholars. The great engineers invented both numerous engines of war and various "wonderworks" to amuse the royal court. Among the latter were mechanical puppets and steam-run toys. Given these advances, why did the Greeks achieve neither a scientific revolution along the lines of the one begun in the early modern era by such thinkers as Copernicus and Galileo, nor an industrial transformation, such as was ushered in by the steam engine around A.D. 1800? Historians are not entirely sure but can venture a guess. Greek machine-making technology was not as sophisticated as that of eighteenth-century Europe. The prevalence of slavery in antiquity, moreover, discouraged the invention of labor-saving machines; steam was used only for playthings and gadgets. A related point is the elitist bias of Greek intellectual life. After Archimedes' death, for example, it was claimed that although he had written copiously on theoretical matters, he never bothered to write about his mechanical inventions because he considered them "ignoble and vulgar."

Perhaps the most important point is the Greek attitude toward nature. Whereas Jews and Christians learned from the Bible that human beings have dominion over nature, thereby making possible the conclusion that it is appropriate to conquer nature, the Greeks thought in more restricted terms. They believed that nature set limits, that a virtuous person tried to follow nature, not subdue it. Thus, Greek engineers were not inclined to make the revolutionary changes that their modern counterparts have promoted.

Archimedes (ar-kuh-MEE-deez)
Eratosthenes (er-uh-TOSS-the-neez)

Herophilus (her-AH-fih-lus)

■ Men and Women in Art and Society

Like Hellenistic literature, Hellenistic art attests to changing male attitudes toward women and toward gender issues. The portrait of Jason and Medea in Apollonius's *Argonautica* makes fun of masculine pretensions and celebrates the triumph of female intelligence. It also presents a sympathetic portrait of a woman's romantic desire for a man, as does Theocritus's work. In the Classical period, depictions of romantic love were generally restricted to male homoeroticism. Accordingly, statues of naked males were common, but women were almost always depicted clothed. Hellenistic sculpture, by contrast, affords many erotic examples of the female nude.

There are indications that the Hellenistic Greek male of the elite was much more willing than his Classical predecessor to see lovemaking as a matter of mutuality and respect. Classical vase-painting often depicts heterosexual lovemaking with the mood lusty and explicit. In Hellenistic vase-painting, in contrast, the emphasis is more often on tenderness and domesticity. Hellenistic men wrote with sensitivity about satisfying a woman's needs and desires. The vogue in Hellenistic art for representations of Hermaphrodite°, the mythical creature who was half female and half male, may suggest a belief that the feminine was as important a part of human nature as the masculine.

Many a Hellenistic artist or writer seems to be as interested in emotion as in action and to focus on the inner as much as on the outer life. Hellenistic art often depicts women, children, and domestic scenes. Representations of warriors are as likely to focus on their unrestrained emotions as on their soldierly self-control.

Hellenistic women enjoyed small improvements in political and legal status and considerable improvements in economic and ideological status. A number of reasons explain these advances. First, Greek women, particularly in the elite, benefited from the spread of monarchy. For one thing, queens and princesses in royal courts had power and prestige that had been denied women in city-states. For another, under monarchy the notion of the loyal and prosperous subject replaced that of the independent citizen-warrior. Citizens in the Classical polis had been encouraged to be aggressive and exaggeratedly masculine to the point of hostility to women. Subjects in Hellenistic monarchies were meant to cultivate the more passive and reflective virtues of legalism, obedience, and economic enterprise. Because

---

Hermaphrodite (her-MAF-ro-dyte)

Aphrodite of Cnidos   This 7½-foot-tall marble statue is a Roman copy of an original by Praxiteles (ca. 350–330 B.C.). Perhaps the most famous of Hellenistic female nudes, the statue was housed in a special shrine where it could be viewed in the round to accommodate all the interest it generated.   *(Vatican Museums)*

℘ READING SOURCES

The Power of Hellenistic Women—and Its Limits

These two inscriptions commemorate prominent women. The first, written about 218 B.C. in the city of Lamia, honors Aristodama of Smyrna. Note that although Aristodama is free to perform in public, her brother Dionysios probably traveled with her as her official guardian. The second inscription, from the city of Priene, perhaps in the first century B.C., recalls Phile, who funded an aqueduct and was rewarded with public office.

Aristodama

. . . With good fortune. Resolved [by the city] of the Lamians. Since Aristo[d]ama, daughter of Amyntas, a citizen of Smyrna in Io[nia], epic poetess, while she was in our city, gave several [public recitations] of her poems in which the nation of the Aetolians [and] the People's ancestors were worthily commemorated and since the performance was done with great enthusiasm, she shall be a proxenos [diplomatic representative] of the city and a benefactress, and she shall be given citizenship and the right to possess land and [a house] and the right of pasture and inviolability and security on land and sea in war and peace for herself and her descendants and their property for all time together with all other privileges that are given to other proxenoi and benefactors. And Diony[sios], her brother, and his descendants shall have the rights of a proxenos, citizenship, [inviolability]. . . .

Phile

[Phil]e, daughter of Apollonios and wife of Thessalos, the son of Polydektes, having held the office of stephanephoros [magistrate], the first woman [to do so], constructed at her own expense the reservoir for water and the city aqueduct.

Source: Adapted from Stanley M. Burstein, *The Hellenistic Age from the Battle of Ipsos to the Death of Cleopatra VII* (Cambridge: Cambridge University Press, 1985), pp. 59, 86–87.

Greek men associated these virtues with women, their respect for female qualities tended to increase. Also, in the new cities, as in many a frontier society, women more often were permitted to inherit and use property than in old Greece.

It was an era of powerful queens: Olympias, Alexander the Great's mother, played kingmaker after her son's death. Arsinoe II Philadelphus was co-ruler of Egypt with her husband (who was also her brother) for five years at the height of Ptolemaic prosperity around 275 B.C. The most famous Hellenistic woman, Cleopatra VII, was queen of Egypt from 51 to 30 B.C. Although she was the lover of two of the most powerful men in the world, the Romans Julius Caesar and Mark Antony, Cleopatra was no exotic plaything. Rather, she was a brilliant and ambitious strategist who nearly succeeded in winning a world empire for her family. (See the feature "Weighing the Evidence: Images of Cleopatra" on pages 134–135.)

Writers in the new Hellenistic cities often described freedom of movement for women. Theocritus and Herondas, for example, show women visiting a temple or a show. Nor did Hellenistic men, even in Athens, obey Pericles' injunction not to speak of women, even good women. In Hellenistic Athens, aristocratic fathers put up inscriptions in honor of their daughters who had participated in the cult of Athena. Although women generally continued to need a male guardian to represent them in public, in some situations, at least in Egypt (where the evidence is most plentiful), a woman could represent herself. A woman could petition the government on her own behalf. Widows and mothers of illegitimate children could give their daughters in marriage or apprentice their sons. A few cities granted women citizenship or even permitted them to hold public office.

Some Hellenistic cities admitted women to the gymnasium, previously a male preserve. Heretofore only

Sparta had promoted physical education for women, but by the first century A.D., women were even competing in the great Pan-Hellenic games. Gymnasia were also centers of education in music and reading. One consequence of growing literacy was the re-emergence of women poets and the first appearance of women philosophers in the West. Before dying at age 19, Erinna, who lived on the Aegean island of Telos during the late fourth century B.C., wrote the *Distaff,* a poem in memory of her childhood friend Baucis. This three-hundred-line poem, famous in antiquity, described the shared experiences of girlhood. Hipparchia° of Maroneia (b. ca. 350 B.C.), like her husband Crates of Thebes, studied Cynic philosophy. The Cynics, like another philosophical school, the Epicureans, supported a measure of equality between women and men. Hipparchia and Crates led an itinerant life as popular teachers and the Hellenistic equivalent of counselors or psychologists.

Much of the explanation for the relative freedom of elite women lies in the new economic power of this group. The new cities generally imposed fewer restrictions on women's economic roles than had Classical poleis such as Athens. In many cities women could sell land, borrow money, and decide whether their husbands could make loans or contracts on the strength of their dowries. Free women could manumit slaves as well. (See the box "Reading Sources: The Power of Hellenistic Women—and Its Limits.")

The role reversals of male and female in Hellenistic art and literature, therefore, are indicators of genuine social change. Hellenistic women never attained the equality that sometimes exists between men and women today, but they did enjoy genuine though limited improvements in status. Men and women played new roles in a changed, complex world. The new Hellenistic philosophies and religions attempted to address that complexity.

THE TURN INWARD: NEW PHILOSOPHIES, NEW FAITHS

THE events of the Hellenistic era—emigration, a trend from independent city-states to monarchies and federal leagues, new extremes of wealth and poverty, and contact with foreign peoples and customs—all these generated uncertainty. In response, Greek culture was spread and transformed. As literacy expanded, more Greeks than ever before could participate in cultural debate. New philosophies and religions arose to meet new spiritual concerns, generating ideas that would be influential for centuries.

The meeting of Jews and Greeks proved to be just as significant. Challenged by Greek conquest, Greek colonization, and their own migration to Greek lands, Jews alternately embraced Hellenism and engaged in resistance, both cultural and armed. In the process, first Judaism and then Hellenism were changed forever.

■ Cynics, Stoics, Epicureans, and Skeptics

Although the polis lost its military and political preeminence in the fourth century B.C., philosophy continued to thrive. It was, however, much changed. With the city-state losing significance as a focus of loyalty, and with the Greek-reading public growing in size and geographic extent, Hellenistic philosophy paid less and less attention to politics. Moreover, as we have seen, Hellenistic science tended to become a separate discipline from philosophy. What was left as the prime subject of philosophy was ethics, the discovery of the best way to live. The essence of the good life, most philosophers agreed, was finding peace of mind, or freedom from troubles. Hellenistic philosophers won wide followings; indeed, for many people, primarily in the elite, philosophy became a way of life, even a religion.

Several competing philosophical schools emerged. The first to attract attention was Cynicism°. Never a widespread philosophy, Cynicism is nonetheless important as a precursor of the two most popular doctrines, Stoicism and Epicureanism. Finally, Skepticism rejected the main philosophies as mere dogmatism and proposed instead a commonsense attitude toward ethics.

The first Cynic was Diogenes° of Sinope (ca. 400–325 B.C.). An exile in Athens, Diogenes developed a philosophy that rejected all conventions. People find happiness, he decided, by satisfying their natural needs with simplicity. Accordingly, Diogenes chose a life of poverty. A beggar in rags, he delighted in shocking conventional morality. Famous for wit and shamelessness, he was nicknamed "Dog" (*kuon*) because the Greeks considered dogs to be shameless animals; his followers were called "Doglike" (*kunikoi,* whence the name *Cynic*).

Although he founded no school, Diogenes cast a wide shadow. Among those whom he indirectly influenced was Zeno (335–263 B.C.), who began one of the

---

Hipparchia (hih-PAR-kee-uh)

Cynicism (SIN-uh-sizm)   **Diogenes** (dye-AH-juh-neez)

most important philosophical systems of antiquity: Stoicism°. Zeno came to Athens in 313 B.C. from Citium in Cyprus, a multi-ethnic city; he was possibly of Phoenician origin. Influenced by both Cynicism and Socratic philosophy, Zeno developed his own doctrines, which he taught in the *Stoa Poikile* ("Painted Porch," whence the name *Stoic*), a public building.

Like Plato and Aristotle, Zeno sought an absolute standard of good on which to base philosophical decisions. He found it in the divine reason (*logos*), which he considered the organizing principle of the universe and the guide to human behavior. The best life was a life in pursuit of wisdom—that is, a life of philosophy. Only that rare and forbidding figure, the Sage, could truly attain wisdom; ordinary people could merely progress toward it. What was required was study and the attempt to be free from all passion.

Stoicism may seem harsh. It is not surprising that *stoical* has come to describe austere indifference to pain. In some ways, however, Stoicism was comforting. First, freedom from passion was meant to bring peace of mind and happiness. Second, unlike Plato, the Stoics were empiricists—that is, they trusted the evidence of the senses, an attitude that they thought would inspire confidence and security. Third, the common share in divine logos entailed a common human brotherhood—led, to be sure, by a Greek-speaking elite. Fourth, because brothers have a duty to one another, the Stoics argued that a good person should play an active role in public life.

Like Hellenistic poets or portraitists, the Stoics emphasized the inner life. They believed that intentions matter. This Stoic belief was an important departure from Greek tradition, which tended to emphasize the outcome of an action, not its motivation. Stoicism also departed from traditional Greek localism, embracing a more cosmopolitan outlook. "This world is a great city, [and] has one constitution and one law," wrote Philo of Alexandria (30 B.C.–A.D. 45), a Stoic and a Jew. Many Stoics believed in a natural law or law of nations—that is, that overarching and common principles governed international relations.

With its emphasis on duty and order, Stoicism became popular with Greek ruling elites, both Macedonian kings and their opponents in city-states and leagues. Stoicism would enjoy even greater success with the Romans, who found its strictures congenial to their own stern morality and who used its concept of a universal state to justify their empire. A great deal of Stoicism was later embraced by early Christian writers.

Epicurus (341–270 B.C.), an Athenian citizen, founded his philosophical school at around the same time as Zeno founded Stoicism. There were other similarities: Both schools were empiricist and materialist (that is, they tended to trust the evidence of the senses), both sought peace of mind, and both inspired widespread followings. Epicurus, however, taught not in a public place but in a private garden. Whereas the Stoics encouraged political participation, Epicureans counseled withdrawal from the rough and tumble of public life. "Calm" and "Live in hiding" are famous Epicurean° maxims.

Epicurus's materialism is based on the atomic theory of Democritus (see page 95). It envisions a thoroughly mechanistic universe in which the gods exist but play no active role in events. Individuals need fear neither fickle deities nor an unhappy afterlife because the soul is merely a combination of atoms that ceases to exist after death. What might be the purpose of life in such an unheroic universe? The answer was the avoidance of pain and pursuit of pleasure. The latter component of Epicureanism was called hedonism (from *hedone*, Greek for "pleasure"), but not, as the word has come to mean today, indulgence in food, drink, or sex. Instead, Epicureans meant intellectual pleasure. Friendship and fraternity were Epicurean ideals—the private analogs, as it were, of Stoic brotherhood.

The Epicureans raised eyebrows and sometimes ire, occasionally suffering persecution by the state. They were accused of atheism and sensuality; to this day, *epicurean* connotes a fondness for luxury and pleasure. Classical Greek philosophy defined virtue as the highest good. The Epicurean emphasis on pleasure, even spiritual pleasure, seemed perverse to some. Yet Epicureanism was simple, sure of itself, practical, and offered both friendship and a sense of community. It became a popular philosophy, especially among the wealthy.

Skepticism° was founded by Pyrrho of Elis (ca. 360–270 B.C.), a Greek who traveled with Alexander to India. Like Stoics and Epicureans, Skeptics sought peace of mind. They rejected those thinkers' conclusions, however, on the grounds that they were dogmatic—that is, based not on positive proof but merely on opinion (*doxa*). Considering the senses unreliable, Skeptics rejected the commonsense approach of Stoics and Epicureans. They preferred to suspend judgment on the great philosophical questions (hence our term *skepticism* for a doubting state of mind). Whoever was able to do so could accept the customs of the community, avoid politics, and thereby obtain peace of mind.

Stoicism (STO-ih-sizm)

Epicurean (eh-pi-kyuh-REE-un) **Skepticism** (SKEP-tih-sizm)

■ The Mystery Religions

The traditional Greek religion of the Olympian gods came under attack on every front in the Hellenistic era. First, the newly divinized kings stole the spotlight. Second, Hellenistic philosophers, like their Archaic and Classical predecessors, criticized the Olympians as primitive, unsophisticated, and immoral; their critique reached an ever widening audience. A third attack came from science and scholarship. Around 300 B.C., Euhemerus of Messene wrote in his *Sacred Scripture* that Zeus, Ouranos, and Kronos were not divine beings but merely great kings of the past who were rewarded with deification, much as a Hellenistic monarch might be. Debunking the Olympians became a popular literary pastime. For instance, Poseidon was said to be worshiped as the sea-god because he had been the first shipbuilder, and Hades, god of the dead, was said to have invented burial rites.

The Olympians retained their temples, but the rituals seemed hollow and antiquarian. What was to replace them? Of the several new religious movements that marked the age, three stand out: the divinization of kings, the cult of Tyche (Fortune), and the mystery religions.

Under the Ptolemies and Seleucids, the ruler-worship that Alexander had demanded became standard procedure. Many subjects no doubt considered the divinity of their king or queen merely a patriotic formality. Others treated the divinized monarch as something like a patron saint who could intercede in heaven. The old Greek city-states, especially the democracies, bristled at ruler-worship. "To transfer to men the honor due to the gods," the Athenian playwright Philippides (active ca. 300 B.C.) wrote, "is to dissolve the democracy."

He might have said much the same about the Hellenistic cult of Tyche° (Fortune or Luck), often worshiped as a goddess, sometimes as the protector of a particular city. The most famous example was the Tyche of Antioch, personified as a statue of a woman wearing the battlements of the city on her head as a kind of crown—a very popular statue, to judge by the many copies found around the Hellenistic world.

The third major Hellenistic trend, the mystery religions, offered similar solace to that of the philosophical schools: ethical guidance, comfort, release from worries, reassurance about death, and a sense of unity. Unlike philosophies, however, they achieved their goals through the revelation of secret doctrines, or "mysteries," into which worshipers were initiated. Long a feature of Greek religion, mystery cults grew in popularity during Hel-

A Cretan Dream Interpreter in Egypt   A painted stele (ca. 200 B.C.) advertises the services of a Greek in Memphis near the temple of Serapis, a Greco-Egyptian god. The inscription and pediment are Greek, while the pilasters, women, and sacred bull (facing an altar) are Egyptian. *(Egyptian Museum, Cairo)*

lenistic times. Consider the cult of Demeter at Eleusis, a town just outside the city of Athens. Demeter was the goddess of fertility. Her daughter, Persephone, supposedly spent half the year in the underworld, among the dead, but came back to earth each spring. As told to initiates, the myth symbolized the promise of a blessed afterlife. The precise details of the ritual remain unknown to this day. What is clear is that they included fasting, ritual bathing in the sea, a procession, and a torch-lit ceremony in the great hall at Eleusis.

Various new mystery religions from outside Greece became more popular, particularly the Hellenized Egyptian cults of Serapis and of Isis. Created under Ptolemy I, Serapis° was meant to combine Osiris, the Egyptian god of the afterlife, with Apis, the god of the Nile flood. Serapis also suggested Pluto, the Greek god of the underworld.

Tyche (TOO-kay)

Serapis (SEH-ruh-pis)

Bronze Coin with Menorah   This issue of Mattathias Antigone (r. 40–37 B.C.), the last Hasmonean king, is an early example of the use of the seven-branched candelabrum as the symbol of the Jewish people. A similar candelabrum was used in the Temple of Jerusalem.   *(Erich Lessing/Art Resource, NY)*

Hence, it is an early example of the common Hellenistic practice of religious syncretism, or fusion. Despite its roots, Serapis-worship had little appeal to native Egyptians, but the god became popular in the Greek world as patron of healing and sailing.

Another traditional Egyptian deity, Osiris's wife, Isis°, also became a popular Greek and, later, Roman goddess. Called the Goddess of Ten Thousand Names, Isis was said to symbolize all the female deities of antiquity. Hers was a cult of the afterlife and of the suffering but tender and loving mother; she was particularly popular among women. Thus, under Ptolemaic sponsorship, ancient Egyptian cults were recast and spread throughout the Greek-speaking world, circulating such notions as the suffering mother, the Last Judgment, and blessed eternal life after death. Early Christianity was much influenced by such Greco-Egyptian religious notions, but it was more directly the product of debate and ferment within Hellenistic Judaism.

Isis (EYE-sis)

■ Hellenistic Judaism

Few consequences of Alexander's conquests had so lasting an impact as the mixing of Greeks and Jews. Even before Alexander took Judea from the Persians in 332 B.C., the two peoples were in occasional contact, but in the Hellenistic era, their fates became intertwined. The Greeks governed Judea and then lost it to a Jewish independence movement. Meanwhile millions of Jews settled in Egypt, Syria, Anatolia, and Greece.

Changed by its contact with Greek culture, Hellenistic Judaism placed a greater emphasis on salvation, martyrdom, and individual study and prayer. Jewish responses to Greek culture varied: they ranged from admiration to resistance to outreach—that is, the desire to convert Greeks to Judaism. In its creative ferment, Hellenistic Judaism proved to have a long-lasting impact on the West.

Hellenistic Judea was governed first by the Ptolemies until 200 B.C., afterward by the Seleucids, until the establishment of an independent Jewish state in 142 B.C., which came under Roman suzerainty in 63 B.C. The Greeks were not absentee rulers. Rather, they estab-

❧ READING SOURCES

The Jews Struggle over Hellenism

Greek colonists introduced Hellenic customs to Palestine in the second century B.C. The Jewish response varied greatly, from eager assimilation to violent resistance, as is demonstrated by the following selections from the First Book of Maccabees, written around 100 B.C. The book is considered part of the Bible by some Christians but not by Jews.

At that time, lawless men arose in Israel and seduced many with their plea, "Come, let us make a covenant with the gentiles around us, because ever since we have kept ourselves separated from them we have suffered many evils." The plea got so favorable a reception that some of the people took it upon themselves to apply to the king, who granted them liberty to follow the practices of the gentiles. Thereupon they built a gymnasium in Jerusalem according to the customs of the gentiles. . . . They joined themselves to the gentiles and became willing slaves to evil-doing. . . .

The king [Antiochus IV] wrote to all his kingdom, for all to become one people and for each to abandon his own customs. All the gentiles agreed to the terms of the king's proclamation. Many Israelites, too, accepted his religion and sacrificed to idols and violated the Sabbath. . . .

Many Israelites strongly and steadfastly refused to eat forbidden food. They chose death in order to escape defilement by foods and in order to keep from violating the Holy Covenant, and they were put to death. Indeed, very great wrath had struck Israel. . . .

[An Israelite sacrifices to Zeus.] When [the Jewish priest] Mattathias saw this, he was filled with zeal and trembled with rage and let his anger rise, as was fitting; he ran and slew him upon the altar. At the same time he also killed the king's official in charge of enforcing sacrifices, and he destroyed the altar.

Source: The First Book of Maccabees 1:11–15, 41–43, 62–64; 2:24–25, in *The Anchor Bible,* vol. 41 (New York: Doubleday, 1976).

lished a large number of Greek colonies in and around Judea, especially under the Seleucids. Many Jews, especially wealthy ones, adopted some degree of Greek culture. Not all of these so-called Hellenizers abandoned Judaism. Indeed, some reshaped Jewish traditions to appeal to a Greek audience. Yet some Hellenizers abandoned Jewish customs altogether for the Greek gymnasium, theater, and political institutions. With the help of the Seleucid king Antiochus IV Epiphanes (r. 175–163 B.C.), Jewish Hellenizers in 175 B.C. had Jerusalem proclaimed a Greek polis, renamed Antioch, like many a Seleucid city; they even built a gymnasium at the foot of the Temple Mount. In 167 B.C. they went further by outlawing Sabbath observance, prohibiting circumcision, and rededicating the Temple to Olympian Zeus.

The traditionalists, however, resisted. Aided by the political ineptitude of their opponents, who raised taxes, they rallied the Jewish masses into opposition. Soon a guerrilla revolt began in the countryside, led by the Hasmonean family, also known as the Maccabees, whose successes are celebrated today by Jews during the religious holiday of Hanukkah. (See the box "Reading Sources: The Jews Struggle over Hellenism.")

The guerrilla movement developed into a disciplined armed uprising, which forced the Seleucids to tolerate an independent state under the Hasmonean dynasty. Religiously conservative at home, the state was expansionist abroad, conquering nearby territories such as the Galilee and forcing their inhabitants to convert to Judaism.

During the struggle over Hellenism, new elements of lasting significance became part of Judaism. First, the Jews developed a literature of spiritual resistance to the foreigner. This literature was apocalyptic—that is, it claimed to reveal dramatic, heretofore secret truths. Drawing on both biblical and Mesopotamian traditions, Jewish apocalyptic writing predicted a future cataclysm, when a royal redeemer would evict the foreigner and establish a new kingdom of Israel. The redeemer was often identified with another notion that first became popular in this era: the Messiah (literally, "anointed one"), someone anointed with oil signifying his election as king, a descendant of King David, who would save Israel. Another new aspect of Hellenistic Judaism was martyrdom, the notion of the holy sacrifice of one's life for a religious cause. There was also a growing belief in a final judgment day and resurrection, when God would raise the meritorious dead to live again on earth in their own bodies.

Hellenistic Judaism was far from monolithic. Various sects each proposed its own version of Judaism. Among these sects were the Sadducees° ("righteous ones"), a wealthy establishment group for whom the rituals of the Jerusalem Temple were the heart of Judaism. Their opponents, the Pharisees° ("those who separated themselves"), insisted on the validity of the oral tradition of interpretation alongside the written law of the Hebrew Bible and the Temple rituals. The Pharisees proposed a kind of democratization of Judaism, emphasizing study and prayer in small groups. A third group was the Essenes°, generally identified with the Qumran° community in the Judean desert (see page 192). As for the Hellenizers, although some were merely status seekers, others sincerely wished to combine Jewish ethical monotheism with the cosmopolitan spirit of Hellenistic civilization. They wanted, in short, to bring Jewish teachings to non-Jews, or Gentiles ("the nations").

Most Jews of the Hellenistic era lived outside Judea. The Diaspora had spread into (among other places) Syria, Anatolia, the Greek mainland, and Egypt, where a strong Jewish presence during the Persian period grew even stronger, particularly in Alexandria. Jews served the Ptolemies as soldiers, generals, bureaucrats, and tax collectors. They also prospered in private enterprise. Jewish success, as well as their maintenance of a separate culture, led to hostility among ordinary Greeks and Egyptians. Such attitudes spawned the first anti-Semitic

literature as well as sporadic violence that at times broke into riots and persecution. Yet there was also considerable admiration among Greek intellectuals for what they saw as Jewish virtue and antiquity.

Greek was the common tongue of Diaspora Jews. Between around 300 and 100 B.C. in Alexandria the Hebrew Bible was translated into Greek. Known as the Septuagint, or Seventy, from the number of translators who, legend has it, labored on the project, this text made the Bible accessible to a Jewish community increasingly unable to understand Hebrew or Aramaic. In later centuries, the Septuagint became the Old Testament of Greek-speaking Christians.

Foreign conversions and immigration into the Diaspora began to change the meaning of the word *Jew*. The word came to mean less "inhabitant of Judea" than "practitioner of Judaism." In short, *Jew* came to denote as much a religion as a nation.

Summary

HE major legacy of the Hellenistic age was its culture. This Greek-speaking culture—which now extended across the Persian Empire and encompassed Egypt—was dominated by inhabitants of or immigrants from old Greece and their descendants. The broad-minded ideas of Isocrates smoothed the way for the Greeks of different city-states to unite in kingdoms but offered less hope to others. We must not lose sight, however, of the continued flourishing of native cultures in the multi-ethnic kingdoms of the Ptolemies and Seleucids. Although Greeks and Macedonians dominated these regimes, they never imposed homogeneity, either in politics or in culture.

The most important Greek cultural development of the age was a retreat from a complex of values associated with the citizen-warrior ideal of the Classical city-state. The polis came under the shadow of federal leagues and kingdoms; philosophers questioned the very point of political activity. The hero gave way to the antihero, often a man whose success was dependent on the kindness and love of a woman. The female nude became as important a subject for sculptors as the male nude. Hellenistic women were freer than their predecessors in their movement and their ability to hold property and have some say in public life.

Stoic philosophers were far more interested in intention (versus action) than were their Classical predecessors. Yet their interest in the subject pales before that of the Jews, new actors on the Greek stage. Judaism placed an emphasis on the interior dialogue between humans and the divine that was more radical than anything in the Greek tradition. Some Greeks admired Jewish ethics, but few were willing to accept Jewish laws and rituals. Greeks did, however, borrow from other native religions. Hellenistic religion, therefore, was an exception to the general Greek indifference to native culture. The common denominator of the new religious teachings was a close, personal relationship with a savior-god who would guarantee comfort, peace, and eternal life after death.

Ironically, these very doctrines brought their Greek adherents closer to Hellenistic Judaism, which preached righteousness and justice in this life and the hereafter through subordination to the truth of the one and only God. The Jewish doctrine of messianic kingship might even have reminded Greeks of their own ruler cults. Imperceptibly, Hellenic and Hebraic were drawing closer. Under the Roman successor state, which we examine in Chapters 5 through 7, Hellenism and Judaism would be combined in a new and powerful form: Christianity.

■ Notes

1. Isocrates, "Panegyricus," trans. H. I. Marrou, in *A History of Education in Antiquity,* trans. George Lamb (New York: Mentor Books/New American Library, 1956), p. 130.
2. Romila Thapar, *Aśoka and the Decline of the Mauryas* (Oxford: Oxford University Press, 1961), p. 256.
3. Quoted in Charles Rowan Beye, *Ancient Greek Literature and Society,* 2d ed., rev. (Ithaca, N.Y.: Cornell University Press, 1987), p. 265.

■ Suggested Reading

Bowman, Alan K. *Egypt After the Pharaohs.* 1986. An excellent and highly readable introduction to the social history of the Ptolemaic and later periods.

Cohen, Shaye. *From the Maccabees to the Mishnah.* 1987. An excellent introduction by a distinguished scholar of Second Temple Judaism.

Grant, Michael. *From Alexander to Cleopatra: The Hellenistic World.* 1982. A lively and readable introduction, at its best on cultural history.

Green, P. *Alexander to Actium: An Essay in the Historical Evolution of the Hellenistic Age.* 1989. A collection of elegant essays synthesizing scholarship on a wide variety of topics in political, cultural, and social history.

Long, A. A. *Hellenistic Philosophy: Stoics, Epicureans, Sceptics.* 2d ed. 1986. A concise critical analysis of the main ideas and methods of thought of the major Hellenistic philosophers.

Walbank, F. W. *The Hellenistic World.* Rev. ed. 1993. A fine introduction, especially to political history, by a leading scholar of Polybius.

Wood, Michael. *In the Footsteps of Alexander the Great.* 1997. An engaging story that retraces Alexander's path today while it narrates his history; magnificent color photos of seldom-seen sites.

 For a searchable list of additional readings for this chapter, go to http://college.hmco.com.

Images of Cleopatra

"Cleopatra's nose: if it had been shorter, the whole face of the earth would have changed," wrote the French philosopher Blaise Pascal (1623–1662). He does Cleopatra an injustice. It was not a pretty face and classical features that enabled her to win the throne of Egypt (r. 51–30 B.C.), to obtain first Julius Caesar and then Mark Antony as ally and lover, and finally to come close to gaining control of the Roman Empire. Intelligence, daring, charm, and extraordinary diplomatic skill account for Cleopatra's success.

Let us consider the queen's manipulation of her public image—no mean task, given the fragility of Ptolemaic power in the first century B.C. Within Egypt, the monarch had to satisfy several different ethnic groups. Most important were the Greeks and Macedonians—who dominated government, the military, and the economy—and the native Egyptian majority. Daughter of Ptolemy XII (r. 80–51 B.C.), Cleopatra was supposed to rule jointly with her brother, but they had a falling-out. She wrested the throne from him and then from another brother and thus had to assert her legitimacy. Also, Ptolemaic Egypt had to project an image of unity to the Romans, who were threatening to annex it as they had the other Hellenistic monarchies.

Cleopatra, like earlier Ptolemaic monarchs, met these challenges by presenting two faces to the world. To the Greeks and Romans she was a Hellenistic monarch; to the Egyptians she was an ancient pharaonic queen. Look first at the bronze coin of Cleopatra issued at Alexandria probably in the 30s B.C. The queen is shown as a young woman. Her hair, tied in a bun at the nape of her neck, is in the so-called melon style often seen in Hellenistic female portraits. She wears a diadem (royal headband), its ends hanging behind her neck. More commonly worn by Hellenistic kings than by queens, the diadem signifies Cleopatra's claim to authority.

So does the queen's profile. She is portrayed with a prominent chin, a large mouth, and a rugged nose. These features may not be the standard attributes of beauty, but they are precisely the features that mark coin portraits of Cleopatra's father. By emphasizing Cleopatra's physical similarity to her father, the portrait artist perhaps subtly suggests her right to sit on his throne.

The side of the coin not shown here is far from subtle: its legend states clearly in Greek, "Queen Cleopatra."

The illustration is of an eagle and thunderbolt and a double cornucopia (horn of plenty) entwined with a diadem. The eagle and thunderbolt recall the Greek god Zeus, and the two cornucopias suggest fertility and prosperity. All are recurrent symbols of Ptolemaic royalty. The coin thus portrays Cleopatra as a Greek monarch, the worthy heir of her father. It would have been an effective image in Alexandria, a city dominated by Greeks and visited by Romans, but not in the countryside, especially south of the Nile Delta, in Upper Egypt, an area that was primarily Egyptian. Following dynastic custom, Cleopatra changed her image there.

In Upper Egypt, earlier Ptolemies frequently had been represented in stone in traditional pharaonic style, and they were great restorers of ancient Egyptian temples and builders of new ones. Look at the sculptural relief from the temple of the Egyptian cow-goddess Hathor at Dendera in Upper Egypt. The temple was a monumental structure initiated and underwritten by Ptolemy XII. Cleopatra, his daughter, added an enormous relief on the outside of the rear wall. Carved into the stone are two persons carrying offerings for Egyptian deities. The persons are Cleopatra (*left*) and her son Ptolemy XV Caesar, who ruled with his mother from 44 to 30 B.C. Alleged

Bronze Coin of Cleopatra   (*Courtesy of the Trustees of the British Museum*)

to be the illegitimate son of Julius Caesar, Ptolemy XV was commonly known as Caesarion or "little Caesar." At Dendera, however, he and his mother are shown neither as Romans nor as Greeks but as Egyptians.

Look closely at Cleopatra. She wears a long body-hugging robe. On her head is a royal headdress with symbols of the Egyptian gods: the lyre-shaped cow horns and sun-disk of Hathor, the tall plumes of Isis, and the ram's horn of Amon. Caesarion is shown as a pharaoh, wearing the double crown of Upper and Lower Egypt. Mother and son offer incense to the local deities. The small figure between Caesarion and Cleopatra is his *ka*, or soul.

Cleopatra's face is in profile but otherwise has very little in common with her portrait on the Alexandrian coin. Although the features are stylized pharaonic commonplaces, the shape of her head perhaps echoes the elegant and graceful relief portraits of Hatshepsut (r. 1479–1457 B.C.), the most famous female pharaoh before Cleopatra.

Cleopatra commissioned other artworks and monuments in the native style in the Nile Valley. This was the custom of her dynasty, and Cleopatra had absorbed its traditions, but she stands second to none of the Ptolemies in shrewdness and subtlety. She was the only Ptolemaic monarch to learn to speak Egyptian, and she was the only one to come even close to gaining the upper hand over Rome. As the artifacts shown here indicate, she was able to put on an Egyptian face as easily as a Greek one, but she never lost sight of her true interests.

Relief of Cleopatra and Caesarion *(Erich Lessing/ Art Resource, NY)*

CHAPTER 5

Rome: From Republic to Empire ca. 509–31 B.C.

ERE is the Roman Forum. The photograph takes us from an arch celebrating military triumph to the ruins of, first, a public hall; then, behind it, a temple; and, in the rear, the remains of buildings on the Palatine Hill. On this hill, shepherds founded the city of Rome, and on this hill, centuries later, emperors lived. We see, in short, the civic center of the city destined to give the Western world many of its fundamental ideas about government and empire.

The ancient Romans were a practical people. Virgil (70–19 B.C.), for example, the greatest Roman poet (see pages 179–180), celebrates not his countrymen's artistry or cultivation but rather their pragmatic accomplishments:

> For other peoples will, I do not doubt,
> still cast their bronze to breathe with softer features,
> or draw out of the marble living lines,
> plead causes better, trace the ways of heaven
> with wands and tell the rising constellations;
> but yours will be the rulership of nations,
> remember, Romans, these will be your arts:
> to teach the ways of peace to those you conquer,
> to spare defeated peoples, tame the proud.[1]

The Romans turned an Italian city-state into one of the largest empires in history, including all the countries of the Mediterranean as well as large parts of western Asia and of northern and central Europe. By holding this empire for centuries and by promoting prosperity in every corner, Rome planted in what would become Britain, France, Germany, and Spain (among other places) the seeds of the advanced civilizations of the Mediterranean.

The Forum, Rome.
(Mike Yamshita/Woodfin Camp & Associates)

137

Rome is no less important for its influence on the Western civic tradition. Much of the modern vocabulary of politics, from *president* to *inauguration* to *forum*, can be traced back to Rome. After an early period of monarchy, Rome was for centuries a republic (Latin, *res publica*, literally "public thing") before becoming essentially a monarchy again under the Caesars. The Roman Republic mixed popular power with government controlled by wealthy landowners. The government was divided into three branches, which created a system of checks and balances that tended toward consensus. The result was efficiency and, for centuries, stability.

Roman politicians sought to control ordinary citizens but in some ways were more flexible than Greek democrats: unlike Greece, Rome extended its citizenship to a large population, first throughout Italy and then across its entire empire. The modern nation-state with its mass citizenship owes much to Rome. Indeed, although Rome was not democratic, modern democracy—that is, popular government with a large population, whose officials are elected by the people—has roots in the Roman Republic as well as in the Greek city-state.

Fueled by fear, ambition, and greed, Roman expansion generated its own momentum. Rome's arrogance matched its success: in consolidating power over huge territories, the Romans committed atrocities, enslaved whole peoples, and destroyed cities with little provocation. Ironically, military success slowly undermined both Rome's political stability at home and the socioeconomic basis of its army. Meanwhile, the Romans showed great open-mindedness in borrowing from other societies, in particular from the Greeks, to whom the Republic owed great cultural debts. Also fascinating is the shrewdness and generosity with which the Romans shared their citizenship with the elites whom they had conquered, thereby winning their loyalty and strengthening Rome's grip on their territories.

Historians conventionally divide the Republic into three periods: Early (509–287 B.C.), Middle (287–133 B.C.), and Late (133–31 B.C.). This chapter begins with the origins of the city of Rome in the early first millennium B.C. and then traces the Republic from its foundation to its imperial conquests to its collapse under their weight. Success spoiled Rome. The unintended consequences of conquest on Rome's society, politics, and culture led to a revolution that, in the century beginning in 133 B.C., saw the Republic's downfall.

QUESTIONS TO CONSIDER

■ How was the Roman Republic governed, and to what degree did that government shape the later political tradition of the West?

■ How much access to power did women, conquered peoples, and slaves have in Roman society?

■ How did Rome acquire an empire that stretched from Britain to Iraq?

■ What were the unintended consequences of conquest on Rome, and how did they lead to revolution that destroyed the Republic?

TERMS TO KNOW

Latin	triumph
res publica	legion
Etruscans	Gracchi
senate	Caesar
paterfamilias	Cicero
Punic Wars	Cato the Elder

BEFORE THE REPUBLIC, 753–509 B.C.

HE ancient Romans believed that their city was founded on April 21, 753 B.C., by Romulus, a descendant of refugees from the Trojan War. Although the name "Romulus" supplies a convenient etymology for "Rome," little stock can be placed in this story. Nevertheless, archaeology provides a kind of confirmation. The first evidence of buildings in Rome comes from the eighth century B.C. A simple village of farmers and shepherds—a collection of huts—was established then on the Palatine Hill, one of the seven hills on which Rome would cluster and the place where tradition puts the settlement of 753 (see inset, Map 5.2, on page 150).

Archaeological evidence does not mean that we have to accept mythology as history, but it does revive basic questions: What were Rome's origins, and how did it grow? Are seeds of Roman greatness visible in its early history? By examining the data of archaeology and of those elements in ancient historiography that seem to be based on accurate tradition, we can answer these questions, at least in outline.

■ Archaic Rome and Its Neighbors

Italy is a long peninsula, shaped roughly like a boot, extending about 750 miles from the Alps into the Mediterranean (see Map 5.1). In the far north, the high Alps provide a barrier to the rest of Europe. To the east, the Adriatic Sea separates Italy from modern Slovenia and Croatia; to the west, the Tyrrhenian Sea faces the large islands of Sardinia and Corsica (and the smaller but iron-rich island of Elba) and, beyond, the coasts of France and Spain. Off the "toe" of the Italian boot, and separated from the mainland by a narrow, 3-mile strait of water, is the large island of Sicily, rich farm country in ancient times. Sicily is only 90 miles from North Africa. In short, Italy is centrally located in the Mediterranean. It was both a target for conquerors and a springboard for conquest.

Italy contained some of the ancient Mediterranean's most fertile and metal-rich land. From the alluvial watershed of the Po and Adige Rivers in the north, the agriculturally rich plains of Etruria° (modern Tuscany), Latium° (the region of Rome), and Campania (the region of Naples) unfold southward down Italy's west coast. Although the Apennine° Mountains run north–south along most of the Italian peninsula, they are low com-

---

Etruria (ee-TROO-ree-uh)   **Latium** (LAY-shum)
Apennine (AP-puh-nine)

CHRONOLOGY

753–509 B.C.	Monarchy (traditional dates)
509–287 B.C.	Early Republic
449 B.C.	Law of the Twelve Tables
338 B.C.	Latin League dissolved; Roman citizenship extended
289 B.C.	First Roman coinage (traditional date)
287–133 B.C.	Middle Republic
264–146 B.C.	Punic Wars
240 B.C.	First play produced at Rome
197 B.C.	Rome defeats Macedonian phalanx
146 B.C.	Rome destroys Carthage and Corinth
133–31 B.C.	Late Republic
133–121 B.C.	The Gracchi
107–78 B.C.	Marius and Sulla
66–62 B.C.	Pompey's eastern campaigns
63 B.C.	Consulship of Cicero
58–51 B.C.	Caesar conquers Gaul
44 B.C.	Caesar assassinated
31 B.C.	Antony defeated at Actium; Octavian in power

pared with the Alps and contain many passes, permitting the movement of armies.

In the first millennium B.C., Italy was a hodgepodge of peoples and languages. They included the Etruscans in the north, Greek colonists in southern Italy and in Sicily, and such mountain peoples as the Sabines and the Samnites. Latium was home to a number of small Latin-speaking towns, one of them Rome. In the fifth century B.C. another important people arrived on the Italian scene: Celts (called Gauls by the Romans), large numbers of whom crossed the Alps and settled in northern Italy after roughly 500 B.C. Most of these various peoples spoke Indo-European languages, of which Latin, the language of the Romans (as well as other peoples of Latium), was one.

Rome's location in Italy was central and protected. Rome is located in Latium, which is about half-way

Latium

0   15 Km.
0   15 Mi.

Lake Sabatinus

Arno

Tiber

Veii •

Tibur •

AEQUI

• Gabii

• Rome

Anio

Tiber

L A T I N S

Tusculum •

• Praeneste

H E R N I C I

• Anagnia

Ostia •

Lake Albanus

Mt. Albanus

Lake Nemorensis

Trerus

• Lavinium

Tyrrhenian Sea

• Cora

Ardea •

• Norba

V O L S C I

Satricum •

• Privernum

Antium •

☐ Roman territory, ca. 500 B.C.

ALPS

VENETI

Adige

Po

• Mantua

LIGURES

ETRUSCANS

• Spina

Felsina (Bologna) •

• Ravenna

A d r i a t i c   S e a

ILLYRIA

Ligurian Sea

Faesulae •

Arno

Volaterrae •

• Arretium

UMBRI

PICENTES

Populonia •

ETRURIA

• Perusia

• Clusium

Elba

Vetulonia •

• Volsinii

A P E N N I N E S

SABINES

ETRUSCANS

SAMNITES

APULI

LIGURES

Alalia •

Vulci •

Tarquinii •

• Veii

• Caere

• Rome

Tiber

LATINS

LATIUM

Corsica

CAMPANIA

Capua •

Cumae •

Neapolis (Naples)

MESSAPII

Puteoli •

• Herculaneum

Pithecusae

• Pompeii

OSCI

• Tarentum

Bay of Naples

Sardinia

LUCANI

Gulf of Tarentum

SARDI

Tharros •

• Sybaris

T y r r h e n i a n   S e a

BRUTTII

Carales •

• Croton

M A G N A   G R A E C I A

M e d i t e r r a n e a n   S e a

Messana •

Panormus •

SICANI

SICULI

Sicily

Utica •

Cape Bon

• Acragas (Agrigentum)

• Syracuse

Hippo Regius •

Carthage •

NORTH AFRICA

0   50   100 Km.
0   50   100 Mi.

Malta

☐ Etruscans of Etruria

☐ Expansion of Etruscans

☐ Greeks

☐ Carthaginians

OSCI Other peoples

Etruscan Tomb Painting
This wall painting from Tarquinia shows a married aristocratic couple at a banquet. The style of the figures is derived from Greek art, but the depiction of husband and wife dining on the same couch is characteristically Etruscan. *(National Museum, Tarquinia/Scala/Art Resource, NY)*

down the Italian peninsula. Located 15 miles inland on the Tiber°, the largest river on Italy's west coast, Rome had access to the sea. A midstream island makes Rome the first crossing place upstream from the Tiber's mouth, offering the Romans freedom of movement north and south. Yet strategically, Rome was protected. It was far enough from the sea to be safe from raiders and pirates. And its seven hills offered a natural defense.

In the seventh century B.C., Archaic Rome (as the pre-Republican period is called) began to change from a large village into a city. In this era Rome saw its first stone houses, its first public building, and its first forum or civic center. In the sixth century, streets, walls, drains, temples, and a racetrack followed. What caused the transformation? Probably the key factor was contact with

---

Tiber (TY-ber)

Map 5.1 Early Italy and Region of City of Rome
Early Italy comprised a variety of terrain and peoples. Rome was located in the central Italian region of Latium. The Alps separate Italy from northern Europe. The Apennine mountain range runs almost the entire length of the Italian peninsula. Much of the rest of Italy is fertile plain.

Magna Graecia°, the Greek colonies to the south (see Map 5.1). Established in the eighth and seventh centuries B.C., the colonies transported westward the sophisticated urban civilization of the eastern Mediterranean.

More controversial is the impact of Rome on its neighbors to the north, the Etruscans°. The twelve Etruscan city-states were organized in a loose confederation centered in Etruria. They grew wealthy from the mining of iron, copper, and silver, from piracy, from trade, and from a network of influential Etruscan emigrants throughout central Italy, possibly including Rome's last three kings (traditionally dated 616–509 B.C.).

Most scholars argue that the Etruscans conquered pre-Republican Rome and left a significant cultural and material legacy. Recent research, however, suggests a pattern of cross-fertilization and emigration rather than conquest; it further argues that the Etruscan legacy in Rome was superficial. According to this new view, to the extent that any outside culture influenced Archaic Rome, it was the Greeks—who also influenced the Etruscans and other central Italian peoples, for that matter. The Etruscan city-states were similar to Rome; they were its peer, not its elder sibling.

Magna Graecia (MAG-nuh GREE-shuh)
Etruscans (ee-TRUS-kunz)

Since most societies resist outside influence, it makes sense to downplay the Etruscan impact on Rome, as the new theory argues. Yet too little evidence survives from Archaic Rome to allow a firm conclusion. Likewise, our inability to decipher the Etruscan language (which is neither Indo-European nor Semitic) also dictates caution. At least we can be certain of some things about the Etruscans: They were great artists, for example, and Etruscan elite women had high status compared with their Greek or Roman counterparts. Etruscan women kept their own names, and Etruscan children bore the names of both parents. In addition, Etruscan elite women were permitted to attend athletic contests in spite of the presence of naked male athletes.

■ The Roman Monarchy

Tradition says that Rome was ruled by seven kings before the foundation of the Republic. Although the number of kings may be a later invention, their existence is undoubted. In addition to traces of the monarchy in Republican institutions, there is archaeological proof: a form of the Latin word *rex* ("king"), for example, has been found inscribed on a Roman monument from the early sixth century B.C. The king's power, called *imperium* (from *imperare*, "to command"), was very great, embracing religious, military, and judicial affairs.

The king was advised by a council of elders, called the "fathers" (*patres* in Latin) or the "senate" (*senatus*, from *senex*, "old man"). In theory the senate was primarily an advisory body, but in practice it was very powerful. Senators were the heads of the most important families in Rome, so the king rejected their advice at his peril. Romans spoke of the senate's *auctoritas*, a quasi-religious prestige.

Most senators were patricians°, as early Rome's hereditary aristocracy was known. The rest of the people, the bulk of Roman society, were called plebeians°. Plebeians were free; most were ordinary people, though some were wealthy. Patricians monopolized the senate and priesthoods, and they did not intermarry with plebeians.

The whole people, probably both patricians and plebeians, met in an assembly organized in thirty local units, or *curiae*, hence the name *curiate assembly*. Though the assembly's numbers were large, its powers were limited. Before becoming law, resolutions of the assembly required approval by the senate.

Early Rome was a class-based society, but it was open to foreigners. Among others, Etruscans, Sabines,

and Latins—as the inhabitants of other Latin-speaking towns are called—came to settle in Rome. The Tarquins, whose family is traditionally said to have provided two kings of Rome, including the last, may have originally come from Corinth. Unlike Athenians, who tried to hide the presence of immigrants in their country by a myth of indigenous origins, Romans openly discussed their mixed roots. Foreigners at first had low status, but they gained equality around 550 B.C., for pragmatic purposes. Rome needed soldiers to fight its wars; in order to expand the body of loyal infantrymen, the immigrants were granted citizenship—a reform traditionally associated with King Servius Tullius (578–535 B.C.).

Servius probably introduced to Rome the hoplite phalanx (see page 71), with immigrants included in its ranks. The changes in the army contributed to the process that, within several generations of Servius's reform, took Rome from monarchy to republic.

GOVERNMENT AND SOCIETY IN THE EARLY AND MIDDLE REPUBLICS, CA. 509–133 B.C.

RADITION says that the Roman Republic was established in 509 B.C., when the kings were overthrown. Nowadays, scholars envision a long process rather than a single, dramatic upheaval. In either case, the new Republic was destined to have a unique influence on Western political institutions, so it is worth a close look.

The Republic differed from the monarchy in two basic ways. First, the Republic stood for liberty, which for the Romans meant both freedom from the arbitrary power of a king and freedom to participate in public affairs. Second, the Republic was a commonwealth, in Latin, *res publica*°, literally "public thing," as opposed to *res privata*, "private thing," as the Romans characterized monarchy. As a kingdom Rome belonged to the royal family, but as a republic it belonged to the Roman people. In theory, the Roman people was sovereign—that is, the people ruled the state.

But which people? This is a key question because the Romans did *not* embrace another principle that might seem to follow from liberty: equality. Rather, they believed in order, balance, and competition, all of which are central themes of Roman Republican history. Roman

---

patricians (puh-TRIH-shunz)   **plebeians** (pleh-BEE-unz)

res publica (rays POO-blee-kuh)

society and culture, moreover, were conservative. Once the young Republic had its new values in place, it tried to maintain those values over the centuries with little change. Nor did the Republic give up entirely on the old values of the monarchy. Rather, it continued some of those values.

■ What Kind of Republic?

The Early Republic (509–287 B.C.) witnessed centuries of social and political conflict. The Middle Republic (287–133 B.C.) was a shorter period of relative stability and consensus. Then social and political conflict broke out again with a vengeance in the Late Republic (133–31 B.C.), ultimately rendering the Republic a terminal blow.

The best and most even-handed ancient analyst of Roman politics is the historian Polybius° (ca. 200–118 B.C.). A Greek and former hostage who lived in Rome, Polybius observed his adopted city with an outsider's discerning eye. Polybius argued that in the Middle Republic of his day, Rome was a "mixed constitution," balancing the power of the masses with the authority of the elite. The fortunate result was a strong and stable state.

Underlying Polybius's appraisal is a division of Roman political institutions into three branches: executive, deliberative, and legislative. Influenced by the Romans, the American founders adopted a similar division, but with the legislative and deliberative functions combined and a judicial branch added. In Rome, various magistrates of the executive branch administered justice, in addition to their other responsibilities. The Roman senate, which made up the deliberative branch, was far more influential than the U.S. Senate, although during the Republic the Roman senate could not make law. The Roman legislative branch consisted of several popular assemblies.

The three parts of the Roman constitution, then, were the magistrates, the senate, and the people. For Polybius, the assemblies were a democratic element in Rome's constitution; the senate, an oligarchic element; and the magistrates, a royal element.

Not all historians agree with Polybius. His critics argue that he was misled by the democratic façade of Rome's several popular assemblies. In the last analysis, they maintain, the Roman oligarchy controlled the state. The oligarchs monopolized high office, both civil and military; rigged elections; dominated proceedings in the senate; set the course of cultural life; and controlled religion in a society that knew no separation of church and state.

Polybius (po-LIH-bee-us)

Although these criticisms contain some truth, they overstate the case. Rome experienced real political competition and a real need to court the voters; all laws were debated in public meetings, often fiercely debated; candidates for office ran ambitious campaigns, which suggests that the results were not rigged; the people's representatives could veto any action taken by public officials; and freed slaves became citizens, which was rarely true in a democratic Greek state such as Athens. Of course the wealthy elite had considerable power, but that power was limited, which means that, as Polybius writes, the Roman political system was balanced and competitive.

In short, Rome was a mixed constitution. It was not always a stable society, however. Let us survey Rome's political institutions and then examine the conflicts of the Early Republic and the compromises that resolved them in the middle era. We will turn to the revolution that destroyed the Late Republic at the end of this chapter.

■ Political Institutions

Executive power lay in the hands of Rome's magistrates. They were more powerful and more elite figures than their counterparts in Greek democracies. Magistrates were elected to office by the Roman people rather than chosen by lottery, as in Greek democracy. Election required extensive campaigning, which in turn necessitated money and connections, but also an ability to persuade the people. Magistracies were time-consuming jobs, but offered no salary, unlike public office in Greek democracy. Thus, only a wealthy elite few could afford to be magistrates.

Eager for strong, effective magistrates but ever fearful that power might lead to corruption, Rome imposed the principles of *collegiality* and *annuality* on its officials. Every magistrate was accountable to one or more colleagues, and the tenure of office was only one year. The chief magistrates were eventually called consuls, of which there were two. Each consul had the power to veto the other's actions. Like the former king, each consul had *imperium,* the power to issue commands and order punishments, including execution.

From about 500 B.C. to about 300 B.C., other magistracies emerged to assist the consul as administration grew more complex. In addition to those annual magistrates were two censors, older men elected once every few years for eighteen-month terms. At first their job was to supervise the census, the military register of citizens that recorded each man's property class. Later, the censors

A Clear Sign of Power   The lictor, or official, depicted in this bronze statuette (ca. first century A.D.) accompanied Roman magistrates, who had *imperium*, the power to issue punishments resulting in execution. That power is visible in the fasces he holds—an ax in a bundle of wooden rods bound with straps.   *(Courtesy of the Trustees of the British Museum)*

became, as it were, supervisors of public morals, since they could punish "bad" citizens.

The Republic's government adapted flexibly to trying circumstances. In times of emergency, for example, the Republic turned power over to a single magistrate. The dictator, as he was called, made decisions that were beyond appeal, but he held office for only six months.

The deliberative branch of the Roman constitution consisted of the senate, which guided and advised the magistrates. During most of the Republic, the senate consisted of three hundred men, each of whom served for life. In the third century B.C. and later, every senator was a former magistrate. Senators possessed great authority. They supervised public expenditures and were for all practical purposes in charge of foreign policy.

The legislative branch of the constitution consisted of four popular assemblies: the curiate assembly, the centuriate assembly, the council of the plebs, and the tribal assembly. Like the political system as a whole, Roman assemblies combined democratic and nondemocratic features. On the one hand, all decisions were made by majority vote, and only after speeches had been heard or campaigns conducted. Assembly meetings were often preceded by public meetings, typically in the forum, in which issues were debated in lively discussion. Women, free noncitizens, and even slaves could attend. On the other hand, voting took place by groups and those groups were unrepresentative. Furthermore, in contrast to Greece, in Rome assembly participants stood rather than sat down and received no salary for attendance.

Although the curiate assembly of the monarchy survived, in the Republic it was relegated to a largely ceremonial role. The centuriate assembly held real power: it elected magistrates, voted on laws and treaties, accepted declarations of war and peace, and acted as a court in cases of treason, homicide, and appeals from the magistrates' decisions. This assembly offered popular participation but under strict control. The assembly was divided according to wealth into census classes of fighting men. The classes voted in order of wealth. First came the equestrians, or cavalrymen, then five classes of infantrymen, and finally the *proletarii* ("breeders"), men too poor to provide their own arms. Because the equestrians and the first class of infantry—the wealthiest men—constituted a majority, in many elections the four remaining classes of infantry and the proletarii did not vote at all.

The two other assemblies were the council of the plebs and the tribal assembly. The latter supplanted the former; in fact it became Rome's main legislative body in the third century B.C., outstripping the centuriate assembly in making laws. To understand the evolution and workings of the tribal assembly, we turn now to the class conflicts in Rome during the fifth through third centuries B.C.

■ Conflict of the Orders

The Early Republic was a crucible. Social and political conflict, usually considered a struggle between the patrician and plebeian orders, severely tested the Roman state between 494 and 287 B.C. A relatively stable state emerged, one that assigned the leading role to a widened elite (though still a relatively narrow one) while offering a measure of popular power. As Rome reached a domestic political consensus, it presented an ever stronger military front to its external opponents. By 300 B.C., Rome was ready to grow from local power to dominance in Italy and then the Mediterranean.

Tradition gives Rome only 136 patrician families in 509 B.C., but they dominated the Early Republic. The plebs, in contrast, comprised masses of poor peasants and a tiny number of men who, though wealthy, were not patricians; there were plebeian artisans, traders, and shopkeepers, but they composed only a small part of the population. In their own ways, the various plebeian groups each wanted to break patrician power. Wealthy plebeians wanted unrestricted access to high office, from which they had been largely excluded. Ordinary plebeians demanded relief from debt, redistribution of land, and codification and publication of the law. For a century and a half, the two groups of plebeians made common cause, writing an important chapter in the history of political resistance.

Debt and hunger loomed large in the Early Republic. A form of debt-bondage called nexum° forced a free man who defaulted on a loan to work off what he owed, often for the rest of his life. Plebeians wanted nexum abolished. The average peasant farm was too small to feed a family, rendering most peasants dependent on public land for farming and grazing. Time and again throughout Republican history, however, public land was occupied by the wealthy, who denied or restricted access to the poor. The only plebeian hope was to change the system.

The story of the plebs in the fifth century B.C. was one of solidarity. They organized themselves as kind of a state within the state, complete with their own assembly (the council of the plebs) and officials (the tribunes of the plebs). The decisions of the council of the plebs, called *plebiscita* (from which *plebiscite* comes), were

binding only on the plebs; they did not receive the full force of law for over two hundred years. Yet the plebs did not retreat. On several occasions during the Early Republic they resorted to secession: the plebs as a whole left the city, often for the Aventine Hill, where they stayed until their grievances were addressed (see inset, Map 5.2).

The ten tribunes°, elected annually by the plebs, were the people's champions. A tribune's house stood always open to any plebeian who needed him, and he could not leave the city limits. Inside the city of Rome, a tribune also had the right to veto any act of the magistrates, assembly, or senate that harmed plebeians. In return, the plebs swore to treat the tribunes as sacrosanct and to lynch anyone who harmed them.

Impressive as plebeian activity was, the patricians had formidable resources with which to oppose them. They controlled important priesthoods and had many supporters in the military. Furthermore, the new tribal assembly, created around the same time as the council of the plebs, used a system of representation that heavily favored landowners such as patricians. The tribal assembly elected lower magistrates and, like the centuriate assembly, voted on laws and acted as a court of appeals.

Nevertheless, the plebeians pressed onward, wringing concession after concession from the patricians, until finally the patricians retreated: they decided to neutralize the opposition by meeting the main demands of the plebeian elite. The outcome was a new, combined patrician-plebeian nobility. The patricians had wisely decided to compromise to preserve most of their privileges. The personnel changed, but the elite continued to have great power in Rome.

The specific events in the patrician-plebeian conflict follow two lines of development: concessions to wealthy plebeians and concessions to poor ones. A key moment came in 449 B.C. with publication of the law code known as the "Twelve Tables," eventually, if not at first, on twelve bronze tablets in the Forum. By modern standards, the code was primitive and severe, but its very existence was a plebeian victory because published law became accessible and dependable. Unfortunately, the complex legal procedure remained a secret of the priests for another 150 years, which ensured that no poor man could go to court without the help of a patron.

Continued plebeian pressure slowly yielded other gains through the fourth century B.C. Around 445 B.C., the patricians accepted patrician-plebeian intermarriage, but it took nearly another eighty years, until 367 B.C., until they agreed to plebeian consuls. That same

---

nexum (NEKS-em)

tribunes (TRIB-yoonz)

Shrine of a Wealthy Household This painting from Pompeii shows the spirit of the paterfamilias in a toga, which is wrapped around his head in keeping with Roman procedures of sacrifice. He is flanked by the spirits of departed ancestors. A snake symbolizes fertility. *(Alinari/Art Resource, NY)*

of political authority. In theory, though not always in practice, the Roman household was an authoritarian institution governed by a male; thus, the familia is an example of patriarchy.

The legal head of the familia was the *paterfamilias*°, the oldest living male—usually the father in a nuclear family, though occasionally the grandfather or, in cases of unusual longevity, the great-grandfather. According to Roman law, the paterfamilias had supreme power within the household. Although he was supposed to call a council of senior male relatives to consult on major decisions, he was not required to follow their advice. He had the right to sell family members into slavery and the rarely used power to kill an errant wife or child. A son, no matter how old, was always legally subject to the authority of a living paterfamilias. Only the paterfamilias, moreover, could own property free and clear. Thus, a 30-year-old man might be under the authority of his paterfamilias and dependent on him for an allowance.

Roman respect for the paterfamilias stemmed from Roman esteem for ancestors, who were more important than in Greek culture. All patricians and some plebeians belonged to a *gens*° (plural, *gentes*), a kinship group that traced its ancestry back to a purported common ancestor. All Roman males had a personal and family name, and patricians and elite plebeians also had a third (middle) name, indicating their gens: for example, Gaius Julius Caesar, whose personal name Gaius was followed by the gens name Julius and the familia name Caesar.

In theory, the paterfamilias was the focus of power in the household, but practice was more complex. The sources are full of fathers who showed affection, love, and even indulgence toward their children. Moreover, Roman women usually married in their late teens and men in their late twenties. Given the low life expectancies, it was common for a man of 25 to have already buried his father. Many, perhaps even most, adult males were independent of a paterfamilias.

Unlike men, Roman women never became legally independent, even on the death of a paterfamilias. Instead of receiving a personal name, a daughter was called by the name of her father's gens. For example, Gaius Julius Caesar's daughter was called Julia; if Caesar had had a second daughter, she would have been Julia Secunda ("Julia the Second"). Although fathers were expected to support all male children, they had to support only the first of their daughters. In other words, they were free to "expose" additional daughters—that is, leave them in the open to die or, as was perhaps more likely, to

year saw a debt-relief law, and nexum was finally abolished in 326 B.C.

Finally, in 287 B.C., the merging of patrician and plebeian orders culminated in a law that made decisions of the council of the plebs and the tribal assembly binding on the whole community. Rome's new, combined patrician-plebeian elite was based on wealth, not heredity. The overwhelming majority of Romans remained excluded, but they had won important concessions too: freedom from nexum, access to the published laws, increased power for their assembly, and, most important, protection from arbitrary power via the tribunes.

The problems of poverty continued, but during these same Early Republican years the poor began to find another form of relief in the new land that Rome acquired through conquest.

■ **The Roman Household**

The Latin word *familia* is broader than the English word *family*. Better translated as "household," it connotes slaves, animals, and property, as well as the members of a nuclear family and their ancestors or descendants. The familia was the basic unit of Roman society. A center of both production and consumption, it was also a model

paterfamilias (PAH-ter-fah-MIL-ee-us) gens (jenz)

The Rape of Lucretia

The historian Livy attributes the founding of the Roman Republic to outrage over the rape of the aristocratic woman Lucretia by Sextus Tarquinius, son of King Tarquinius Superbus. Though of dubious historicity, the story reveals a great deal about Roman attitudes toward gender, honor, and their political implications.

[A guest in Lucretia's house in her husband's absence, Sextus Tarquinius demands that she sleep with him.] But all in vain; not even the fear of death could bend her will. "If death will not move you," Sextus cried, "dishonor shall. I will kiss you first, then cut the throat of a slave and lay his naked body by your side. Will they not believe that you have been caught in adultery with a servant—and paid the price?" Even the most resolute chastity could not have stood against this dreadful threat.

[After being violated by Sextus Tarquinius, Lucretia summons her husband and father.] "In your bed, Collatinus, is the impress of another man. My body only has been violated. My heart is innocent, and death will be my witness. Give me your solemn promise that the adulterer shall be punished—he is Sextus Tarquinius. He it was who last night came as my enemy disguised as my guest, and took his pleasure of me. . .

"What is due to him," Lucretia said, "is for you to decide. As for me, I am innocent of fault, but I will take my punishment. Never shall Lucretia provide a precedent for unchaste women to escape what they deserve." With these words she drew a knife from under her robe, drove it into her heart, and fell forward, dead.

Her father and husband were overwhelmed with grief. While they stood weeping helplessly, Brutus [aristocrat and family friend] drew the bloody knife from Lucretia's body, and holding it before him cried: "By this girl's blood—none more chaste till a tyrant wronged her—and by the gods, I swear that with sword and fire, and whatever else can lend strength to my arm, I will pursue Lucius Tarquinius Superbus, his wicked wife, and all his children, and never again will I let them or any other man be King in Rome."

Source: Livy, *The Early History of Rome,* trans. Aubrey de Sélincourt (Harmondsworth, England: Penguin, 1971), pp. 98–99.

---

be adopted or raised as a slave. A father also arranged a daughter's marriage and provided her with a dowry. In theory, again, the customs suggest a most severe relationship, but the evidence shows considerable father-daughter affection, including married daughters who sought advice or aid from their fathers.

Most women in early Rome married *cum manu*° (literally, "with hand")—that is, they were "handed over" to their husbands, who became their new paterfamilias. Even so, Roman wives and mothers had more prestige and freedom than their counterparts in Classical Greece. Legends of early Rome mention some who were peacemakers, negotiators, or catalysts of quarrels among men. (See the box "Reading Sources: The Rape of Lucretia.") Roman women regularly shared meals and social activities with their parents and were expected to take an interest in their husbands' political lives.

---

cum manu (kum MAN-oo)

■ Patrons and Clients

Patron (derived from *pater,* "father") means "defender" or "protector." *Client* means "dependent." Roman society consisted of pyramidal patron-client networks. Most patrons were in turn clients of someone more powerful; only a very few men stood at the top of the pyramid. To the Romans, justice meant not that patron and client treated each other as equals but rather that they showed each other respect and fulfilled mutual obligations.

Various paths led to the status of client. A peasant in need of help on his farm might ask a wealthy neighbor to become his patron. A manumitted slave became the client of his former owner. A conquered foe became the client of the victorious general. The status of client or patron was hereditary.

Patron and client might help each other in various ways. A patron might provide a client with food or with property for a dowry. He might settle disputes or provide legal assistance. In return, a client owed his patron respect and service. He escorted his patron in public on important occasions—possession of a large clientele signified prestige and power. If his patron sought political office, the client voted for him and urged others to do so. If his patron needed money, the client was obligated to contribute, perhaps to an election campaign or to pay fines or ransoms.

Cloaked in an elaborate language of goodwill, the patron-client relationship was considered a matter of *fides*° ("good faith" or "trustworthiness"). Romans spoke not of a client submitting to a patron's power but rather of a client "commending himself" to the patron's fides. A patron spoke not of his clients but of his "friends," especially if they were men of standing or substance.

A patron was supposed to put his clients before his kin by marriage; only blood or adoptive relations were to take precedence. According to the Twelve Tables, a patron who defrauded his client was accursed and subject to death with impunity.

Patronage played an important role in Roman domestic politics, but it was not decisive. For example, a wealthy patron expected his humble clients to vote as he wished, but he abused them at his peril. If a man's clients grew discontented, they might find a new patron. Patronage was relatively more important in foreign affairs. Experience as patrons schooled Roman leaders in treating the peoples they conquered as clients, often as personal clients. Moreover, the Roman state sometimes took foreign countries into its collective fides—much as a patron did a client—thus allowing Rome to extend its influence without the constraints of a formal alliance.

■ Religion and World-View

If we knew nothing about early Roman religion, we could deduce much about it from the familia and patronage. We could expect to find an emphasis on powerful fathers and binding agreements, and both are indeed present. The task of a Roman priest, whether an official of the state or an individual paterfamilias, was to establish what the Romans called the "peace of the gods." Roman cults aimed at obtaining the gods' agreement to human requests, at "binding" the gods—the Latin term for which is *religio*.

The earliest Roman religion was animistic; that is, it centered on the spirits that, the Romans believed, haunted the household and the fields and forests and determined the weather. The Lares, the spirits of departed ancestors, guarded the house, and the Penates watched over stored grain. The spirit of the hearth was Vesta; of the door, Janus; of the rain and sun, Jupiter (later identified with the Greek sky-god and the father-god Zeus); of the crops and vegetation, Mars (later identified with the Greek war-god Ares). The Romans believed that these spirits needed to be appeased—hence the contractual nature of their prayers and offerings. Over the years, as a result of Greek influence, anthropomorphism (that is, the worship of humanlike gods and goddesses) supplanted Roman animism.

Roman state religion grew out of house religion. Vesta, the hearth-goddess, became goddess of the civic hearth; Janus, the door-god, became god of the city's gates; Jupiter became the general overseer of the gods; and Mars became the god of war. When trade and conquest brought the Romans into contact with foreign religions, the Romans tended to absorb them. The senate screened and sometimes rejected new gods, but by and large Roman polytheism was tolerant and inclusive.

The Republic sponsored numerous priestly committees, or colleges, to secure the peace of the gods. Originally restricted to patricians, most of the highest priesthoods were opened to plebeians by law in 300 B.C. Although some priesthoods were full-time jobs, most left the officeholder free to pursue a concurrent career as a magistrate or a senator. The two most important priestly colleges were the augurs°, who were in charge of foretelling the future from omens and other signs, and the pontiffs, who exercised a general supervisory function over Rome's numerous rituals, sacrifices, offerings, prayers, temples, and festivals. The chief pontiff, the *pontifex maximus*°, was the head of the state clergy. He was chosen by election. The pontiffs alone controlled the interpretation of the law until the fourth century B.C. The Romans allowed priests to interpret the law on the theory that an offense against humans was also an offense against the gods.

The system provided for only two colleges of priestesses: those of Ceres, goddess of fertility and death, and those of the Vestal Virgins. The six Vestals tended the civic hearth and made sure that its fire never went out. They served, as it were, as wives of the whole community, as guardians of the civil household. The Vestals were the only Roman women not under the authority of a paterfamilias. Chosen between the ages of 6 and 10 by the pontifex maximus, they had to remain virgins for thirty years or face death. The Vestals' chastity was considered an index of male honor and so was watched closely.

---

fides (FEE-days)

Roman ideology promoted simple and austere farmers' virtues—discipline, hard work, frugality, temperance, and the avoidance of public displays of affection even between spouses. Such virtues underlined the difference between the Republic and the kings with their luxury and sophistication. At the same time, these virtues papered over class distinctions between rich and poor and so promoted stability.

Other Roman ideals included the supreme virtue of the household, *pietas*—devotion and loyalty to the familia, the gods, and the state. Household duties and gender obligations were defined clearly. Women were to be modest, upright, and practical. Men were to project *gravitas* (weight, seriousness), never lightness or levity. A serious man would display self-control and constancy, the ability to persevere against difficult odds. The masculine ideal was *virtus* (literally, "manliness"), which indicated excellence in war and government.

Roman men who attained virtus considered themselves entitled to the reward of *dignitas,* meaning not only public esteem but the tangible possession of a dignified position and official rank—in short, public office. The ultimate test of virtus, however, was in battle. Rome's wars supplied ample occasion to display it.

FROM ITALIAN CITY-STATE TO WORLD EMPIRE, CA. 509–133 B.C.

 T the beginning of the Republic (ca. 509 B.C.), Roman territory comprised about 500 square miles. By 338 B.C., Rome controlled the 2,000 square miles of Latium and was moving north into Etruria and south into Samnite country. Three-quarters of a century later, in 265 B.C., Rome controlled all of the Italian peninsula south of an imaginary line from Pisae (modern Pisa) to Ariminum (modern Rimini), an area of about 50,000 square miles (see Map 5.2). By 146 B.C., Roman provinces included Sicily, Cisalpine Gaul (northernmost Italy), Sardinia, Corsica, and Spain (divided into two provinces). Once-great Carthage was the Roman province of Africa (roughly, modern Tunisia), and once-mighty Macedon was the province of Macedonia, whose governor was also effectively in charge of Greece. The Seleucid kingdom was free but fatally weakened. Rome was the supreme power between Gibraltar and the Levant. It was the greatest empire of the ancient West. How and why had Rome, from its humble beginnings as a local power, reached this breathtaking height?

◼ Republican Expansion: The Conquest of Italy, ca. 509–265 B.C.

Romans maintain that they conquered an empire without ever committing an act of aggression. When war was declared, a special college of priests informed the gods that Rome was merely retaliating for foreign injury. True, the Romans were frequently attacked by others, but often only after provocative behavior by Rome had left its rivals little choice.

Rome's early conquests reveal many of its lasting motives for expansion. No doubt lust for conquest played a part, as did fear and hatred of outsiders, but self-control and shrewdness were stronger Roman characteristics. Greed, particularly land-hunger, was a perennial theme. Sometimes a domestic political motive was at work, for foreign adventure was a convenient way of deflecting plebeian energies. Perhaps the most significant factors, however, were the personal ambitions of a warrior elite and the presence of conflict in early Italy.

Victory in battle promised both prestige and booty and the political success that might follow. Military achievement brought unique acclaim. For example, certain victorious generals were allowed to celebrate a triumph; no such ceremony rewarded the feats of peacemakers or distinguished judges or other public benefactors. The triumphant general rode a chariot through the city to the temple of Jupiter on the Capitoline Hill. He was accompanied by his troops, by the spoils of victory including famous captives, and by the magistrates and senators. (See the box "Reading Sources: A Roman Triumph.")

The harsh reality of Italian politics also ruled against pacifism. Without the willingness to fight, Rome could never have maintained its freedom. Yet what began as a pragmatic response to present dangers hardened into a habit of meeting even remote threats with force. In the fourth century B.C., having gained control of Latium, Rome considered the Samnites of central and southern Italy to be a potential threat. In the third century B.C., once Rome controlled Italy, it felt threatened by the powerful Carthage. After Carthage, the threat of Macedon was squelched, and after Macedon, Seleucid Syria, and so on.

Though flexible and far-reaching, Roman diplomacy sometimes ended up in war. Rome made formal alliances with some states, granting protection in return for obedience and troops or ships when needed by Rome. Short of a formal commitment, however, Rome might accept a state "into its fides"—that is, treat the state as a client. The result was only a moral, and not a legal, commitment, which sometimes sufficed to frighten

Rome

FIELD OF MARS

QUIRINAL HILL

VIMINAL HILL

CAPITOLINE MT.

Senate House

Forum

Regia

Temple of
Jupiter

Tiber Island

ESQUILINE MT.

PALATINE
MT.

CAELIAN MT.

Hills of Rome

Circus
Maximus

AVENTINE
MT.

Servian Wall

ALPS

Extent of Roman Italy by 218 B.C.

Aquileia

Verona

Adige

Cremona

Po

Placentia

CISALPINE GAUL

Bononia

Genua

Ariminum
(Rimini)

Pisae
(Pisa)

Arno

Florentia

Fanum Fortunae

Ancona

*Ligurian
Sea*

Arretium

UMBRIA

Castrum Truentinum

PICENUM

ETRURIA

Populonia

Saturnia

Elba

ILLYRIA

Castrum Novum

Tiber

Corsica

Aleria

Reate

Corfinium

Veii

Rome

SAMNIUM

Appian Way

LATIUM

Arpinum

*Adriatic
Sea*

APULIA

Tarracina

Beneventum

CAMPANIA

Venusia

Barium

Capua

Misenum

Appian Way

CALABRIA

Brundisium

Neapolis
(Naples)

LUCANIA

Tarentum

Paestum

*Gulf of
Tarentum*

Tyrrhenian Sea

Thurii

Sardinia

Croton

BRUTTIUM

Neapolis

Carales

Mediterranean Sea

Messana

Locri

Rhegium

Lilybaeum

Sicily

Syracuse

Utica

*Cape
Bon*

Hippo Regius

Carthage

Malta

NORTH AFRICA

0   50   100 Km.

0   50   100 Mi.

Roman territory (full citizens)

Roman territory
(citizens without suffrage)

Roman allies

Latin colonies

Carthaginian possessions

■ Greek cities

━━ Major roads by 100 B.C.

A Roman Triumph

The Roman triumph symbolizes the prestige flowing from military success in Rome; it also demonstrates the senate's attempt to control victorious generals. This description is drawn from the Epitome of Zonaras, *a Byzantine historian of the twelfth century* A.D. *Zonaras drew his material on Rome from Plutarch (ca.* A.D. *50–120) and Dio Cassius (second–third century* A.D.*).*

When any great success worthy of a triumph had been gained, the general was immediately saluted as imperator by the soldiers, and he would bind sprigs of laurel upon the *fasces* [bladed axes bundled in rods, carried as a symbol of authority] and deliver them to the messengers who announced the victory to the city. On arriving home he would assemble the senate and ask to have the triumph voted him. And if he obtained a vote from the senate and from the people, his title of *imperator* was confirmed. . . .

Arrayed in the triumphal dress and wearing armlets, with a laurel crown upon his head, and holding a branch in his right hand, he called together the people. After praising collectively the troops who had served with him, and some of them individually, he presented them with money and honored them also with decorations. . . . A large part of the spoils also was assigned to the soldiers who had taken part in the campaign. . . .

After these ceremonies the triumphant general would mount his chariot [with his children and rela-

tives]. . . . A public slave . . . rode with the victor in the chariot itself, holding over him the crown of precious stones set in gold, and kept saying to him, "Look behind!" . . . Thus arrayed, they entered the city, having at the head of the procession the spoils and trophies and figures representing the captured forts, cities, mountains, rivers, lakes, and seas—everything, in fact, that they had taken. . . . When these adjuncts had gone on their way, the victorious general arrived at the Roman Forum, and after commanding that some of the captives be led to prison and put to death, he rode up to the Capitol. There he performed certain rites and made offerings and dined in the porticoes up there, after which he departed homewards towards evening, accompanied by flutes and pipes.

Source: From Naphtali Lewis and Meyer Reinhold, eds., *Roman Civilization: Selected Readings,* vol. 1: *The Republic and the Augustan Age,* 3d ed. (New York: Columbia University Press, 1990), pp. 230–231.

any would-be aggressor from harassing Rome's new friend. If not, Rome had to go into battle to prove its trustworthiness as a patron.

Military success requires tenacity, discipline, and flexibility—all qualities that Rome cultivated. Roman organizational ability and love of order made the Roman military camp a much more regular and systematic place than anything seen since Assyrian days. Beginning in the

Map 5.2   Roman Italy, ca. 265 B.C.   Rome controlled a patchwork of conquered territory, colonies, and allied states in Italy, held together by a network of treaties and of roads. The city of Rome (*inset*) was built on seven hills beside the Tiber River.

fourth century B.C., Rome began to reward its soldiers with regular pay; this and the distribution of conquered land improved morale. Two other points are even more significant: the willingness to utilize foreign military technology and the combination of generosity and firmness with which Rome treated its allies.

Borrowed from the Greeks in the sixth century B.C., the hoplite phalanx suited Rome on the relatively level ground of Latium but fared poorly in the rugged Apennines against the Samnites. Following a major defeat in 321 B.C., the Romans adopted with great success the Samnites' equipment and tactics.

Unlike the phalanx, which overpowered the enemy by fighting as one thickly massed unit, a Roman legion was flexible and adaptable. Legions were drawn up into three lines, thirty maniples ("handfuls"), and sixty centuries (literally "hundreds," although the number of men per century varied); and each century was commanded by a centurion. A legion marched in a checkerboard pattern, leaving gaps in the lines. In battle each line closed its gaps as it attacked in turn. Unlike hoplites, who engaged the enemy at short range, legionnaires first threw their javelins at long range. Then, having broken the enemy's order, they charged and fought with sword and shield. The semi-independence of the maniples, each with its own commander and banner, created a more maneuverable army than that of the phalanx and one better suited for mountain fighting. When Rome's

legions beat the Macedonian phalanx decisively in 197 B.C., military history entered a new era.

Rome was the leading power among the Latins, whom it led in an alliance known as the Latin League. Rome was first among equals, but the citizens of even the humblest Latin state had reciprocal rights of intermarriage and commerce with Romans and the right to become a citizen of another state by migrating there. Under Roman leadership the Latin League successfully defended Latium's borders against a series of enemies during the fourth and fifth centuries B.C. But eventually Rome had to confront a bitter two-year-long Latin revolt (340–338 B.C.).

The year 338 B.C. marked a turning point. Defeated peoples in the ancient world were often executed, deported, or enslaved. Victorious against the Latins, Rome, by contrast, pursued generosity. The Latin League was dissolved. Some of its member states were annexed, and their inhabitants became Roman citizens; others retained independence and alliance with Rome though no longer with one another. The non-Latin allies of the former rebels were also annexed by Rome, but they received the unique halfway status of "citizenship without suffrage." They shared the burdens of Roman citizenship but also all the rights except the vote; they also retained the right of local self-government. The settlement of 338 B.C. broke new ground by making it possible for Rome and its former allies and enemies to live together on the basis of relative equality.

The settlement also set a precedent for future Roman expansion. As Rome conquered Italy, a number of privileged Italian cities (called *municipia*) received the status of citizenship without suffrage. Others remained independent but were tied to Rome by perpetual alliance. Romans often annexed a portion of the land of these states.

If municipia were the carrots of Roman imperialism, the stick was a network of military roads and colonies crisscrossing Italy, allowing Rome to keep an eye on

Bronze War God   This elegant, fourth-century B.C. Etruscan bronze, thought to represent Mars, the god of war, shows the metal breastplate worn by a warrior of that era.   *(Scala/Art Resource, NY)*

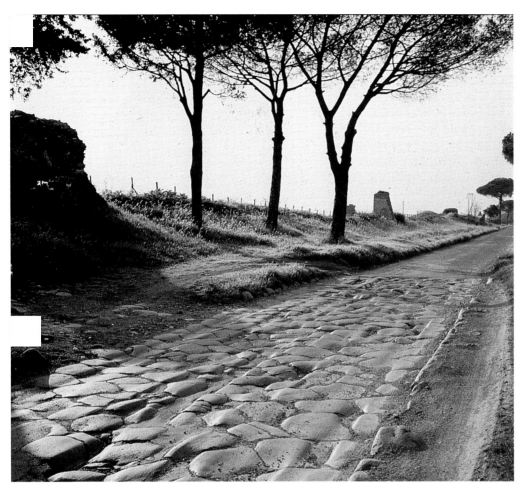

The Appian Way   Named for the censor Appius Claudius Caecus, who proposed its construction, Rome's first great road was built in 312 B.C. during the Samnite Wars. It originally ran 132 miles from Rome to Capua and was extended an additional 234 miles, probably by 244 B.C., to Brundisium, on Italy's southern Adriatic coast.   *(F. H. C. Birch/Sonia Halliday Photographs)*

potential rebels. Roman roads allowed the swift movement of troops and linked the growing network of colonies. Colonies were established in strategically vital areas. The inhabitants, Roman and Latin, owed military service to Rome.

In later years, Italians would complain about treatment by Rome, but compared with inhabitants of Roman provinces outside Italy, they had a privileged status. Romans too would complain about allied demands for equality, but Rome received from its allies a huge and seemingly inexhaustible pool of military manpower. The allies staffed the Roman armies that conquered Samnites, Etruscans, and Gauls, all of whom came into the Roman orbit by the early third century B.C. Manpower abundance won Rome's war (280–276 B.C.) against the Greek general

Pyrrhus° of Epirus (319–272 B.C.), an adventurer who intervened in southern Italy. Although Pyrrhus won battle after battle, he was unable to match Roman willingness to sustain thousands of casualties time and again. Pyrrhus's seeming victories, therefore, turned out to be defeats, which sent him home to Greece disappointed and left us with the expression "Pyrrhic victory."

As for Rome, by 265 B.C. it emerged as the ruler of all of Italy south of the Pisae-Ariminum line (see Map 5.2). One might say that Rome unified Italy, although Italy was less a unity than a patchwork of Roman territory and colonies and of diverse cities, states, and peoples each allied to Rome by separate treaties.

Pyrrhus (PIR-us)

◼ Rome Versus Carthage: The Punic Wars, 264–146 B.C.

The conquest of Italy made Rome one of two great powers in the central Mediterranean. The other was Carthage°. Founded around 750 B.C. by Phoenicians from Tyre, Carthage controlled an empire in North Africa, Sicily, Corsica, Sardinia, Malta, the Balearic Islands, and southern Spain. (The adjective *Phoenician* is *Punicus* in Latin, hence the term *Punic°* for Carthaginian.) Like Rome, Carthage was guided by a wealthy elite, but it was mercantile in character rather than agrarian. Rome was a land power, Carthage a sea power. Rome had virtually no navy. Carthage, on the other hand, commanded a great war fleet, and its merchant ships dominated the western Mediterranean and played a major role in the East.

Carthage was an economic powerhouse. The Carthaginians exploited the mineral-rich mines of Spain. They were the first Mediterranean people to organize large-scale plantations of slaves for the production of single crops. Even though the Romans zealously wiped out most of Carthaginian elite culture, they did make sure to preserve one Carthaginian classic: a multi-volume work on agriculture by Mago. Translated from Punic into Latin by order of the senate, Mago's treatise had enormous impact on Roman landowners, who, with the importation of massive numbers of slaves, adopted the plantation system in Italy (see page 157).

Carthage boasted brilliant generals, especially in the Barca family, whose most famous member was Hannibal° (247–183 B.C.). Carthage might have been a handicapper's favorite at the outbreak of its long wars with Rome in 264 B.C., yet the end result was disaster for Carthage. A combination of Carthaginian weaknesses and Roman strengths accounts for the outcome.

Unlike Rome, Carthage did not have a citizen army. The commanders were Carthaginian, but most of the soldiers were mercenaries and so of questionable loyalty. A second difference in the two states lay in the treatment of allies. Rome treated the Italians with considerable respect and tolerance. Carthage showed contempt for its allies, who repaid the favor by revolting whenever they had the chance. Third, although Carthage's military manpower resources were considerable, they were not as great as Rome's.

At the start of the Punic Wars, Rome had no navy or commanders to match the Barca family, but it proved

---

Carthage (CAR-thidge)   **Punic** (PYOO-nik)
Hannibal (HAN-uh-bull)

Punic Mask   This grey terra-cotta mask comes from Carthage and dates to the third or second century B.C. Masks like these were placed in tombs to keep evil spirits away.   *(Bardo Museum/The Ancient Art & Architecture Collection)*

adaptable, tenacious, and ruthless. To win the First Punic War (264–241 B.C.), for example, Rome not only built a navy but outlasted the enemy in a long, bloody, and exhausting conflict. After initially granting a mild peace treaty, Rome took advantage of later Carthaginian weakness to seize Sardinia and Corsica and to demand an additional indemnity.

Forced to give in to these treacherous exactions, Carthage decided to build a new and bigger empire in Spain, beginning in 237 B.C., under Barca family leadership. Hannibal's father, the general Hamilcar Barca (d. 229 B.C.), had gone undefeated in the First Punic War, and is said to have raised his son to seek a rematch. With Spain's rich deposits of silver and copper at its disposal, Carthage once again posed a credible threat to Rome. In the mid-220s, an ever watchful Rome challenged Carthaginian power in Spain through a Roman client there. The new Carthaginian commander, 27-year-old Hannibal Barca, was not to be cowed, however, and the Second Punic War ensued (218–201 B.C.).

Carthage was willing to risk war because Hannibal promised a quick, cheap, and easy victory. Because Carthage no longer had a fleet, the Romans felt secure in Italy; Hannibal surprised them by marching overland to Italy, making a dangerous passage across the Alps. A tactical genius, Hannibal reckoned that with his superior generalship he could defeat the Romans in battle and cause them enormous casualties, and he was right. Hannibal's forces dominated the battlefield. Among his victories was the Battle of Cannae in Apulia (southeastern Italy) where, in 216 B.C., Carthage gave Rome the bloodiest defeat in its history, killing perhaps thirty thousand Romans.

A crushing Barca success, but huge casualties alone could not bring Rome to its knees. Nor did Rome's allies revolt en masse, as Hannibal had hoped. Most stood by Rome, which had treated them relatively benignly in the past and which now threatened rebels with terrible reprisals. Roman pragmatism, moreover, showed itself able to deal with crisis. After Cannae, Rome's leadership accepted a cautious strategy of harassment, delay, refusal to fight, and attrition. Hannibal was stymied by an enemy who lost battles but refused to surrender. Nor did Hannibal have the power to take the city of Rome.

In the meantime, Rome had bought valuable time to regroup. A new military star emerged: Publius Cornelius Scipio° (236–183 B.C.), a Roman who finally understood Hannibal's tactics and matched them. First Scipio conquered Carthage's Spanish dominions, and then he forced Hannibal back to North Africa for a final battle in 202 B.C. near Zama (in modern Tunisia). Scipio won the battle and gained the surname Africanus ("the African"). As for Hannibal, he played a prominent role in Carthaginian politics for about a decade, until Rome forced him into exile in Syria. In about 183 B.C., after taking part in the Seleucids' unsuccessful war against Rome, he committed suicide rather than face extradition to Rome.

The peace settlement of 201 B.C. stripped Carthage of its empire. Yet soon its economy rebounded, reviving old Roman fears of Carthage's political ambitions. In the Third Punic War (149–146 B.C.), Rome mounted a three-year siege under the leadership of Scipio Aemilianus (185–129 B.C.), finally destroying the city of Carthage in 146 B.C. Approximately a century later, Carthage was resurrected as a Roman colony and became one of the empire's greatest cities. In the meantime, it was left desolate, its people killed or enslaved.

Rome emerged from the Punic Wars as the greatest power in the Mediterranean. It had acquired new provinces in Sicily, Sardinia, Corsica, Spain, and North Africa (where Carthage's former territory was annexed as the province of Africa). The road to further conquest seemed to lead in all directions.

Scipio (SIP-ee-o)

■ Victories in the Hellenistic East, ca. 200–133 B.C.

Most countries would have savored peace after such an ordeal as the Punic Wars, but Rome immediately leaped into a long conflict in Greece and Anatolia. Its aims were to weaken the power of Macedon, which it feared might threaten Rome one day, especially since the Macedonian king Philip V (r. 221–179 B.C.) had made an alliance with Hannibal after Cannae. Rome won a relatively quick and easy victory when in 197 B.C. the legions crushed the Macedonian phalanx at Cynoscephalae in central Greece (see Map 5.3).

Rome had hoped to impose a patron-client relationship on Greece and Macedon, thereby avoiding having to sustain a permanent military presence, but that hope failed. The independent-minded Greeks chafed at Roman domination. Several years of miscommunication and intrigue followed, only to lead to renewed wars. First the Seleucids, under the ambitious king Antiochus III (r. 223–187 B.C.), challenged Rome for hegemony on the Greek peninsula. It was in this war that Hannibal took a small, doomed part. Roman forces made short work of the enemy. Driven out not only from Greece but from Anatolia as well, the Seleucids in effect recognized Roman supremacy in the Mediterranean (188 B.C.).

Then came another two rounds of war that pitted Rome against Macedon and various Greek states (171–167 and 150–146 B.C.). Victorious in both wars, Rome deprived the Greeks and Macedonians of their independence. Wherever democracy had survived in Greece, it was replaced with oligarchy. In 146 B.C., Rome destroyed Corinth, one of Greece's wealthiest cities, as a warning against further rebellion. Greece then suffered Roman neglect and taxation for nearly two hundred years.

By annexing Carthage, Macedon, and Greece in the mid-second century B.C., Rome created a dynamic for expansion around the entire Mediterranean. Before the century was over, southern Gaul was annexed, and Rome had gained a foothold in Asia. The kingdom of Pergamum (northwestern Anatolia) had supported Rome throughout Rome's wars in the east. When Attalus III of Pergamum died without an heir in 133 B.C., he surrendered his kingdom to the Roman people, who made it into a province of Asia.

Two great Hellenistic states remained independent: the Seleucid kingdom and Ptolemaic Egypt (see Map 5.3). Roman ambassadors and generals frequently interfered in their affairs, however, and no one was surprised when, in the first century B.C., they too were annexed by Rome.

156

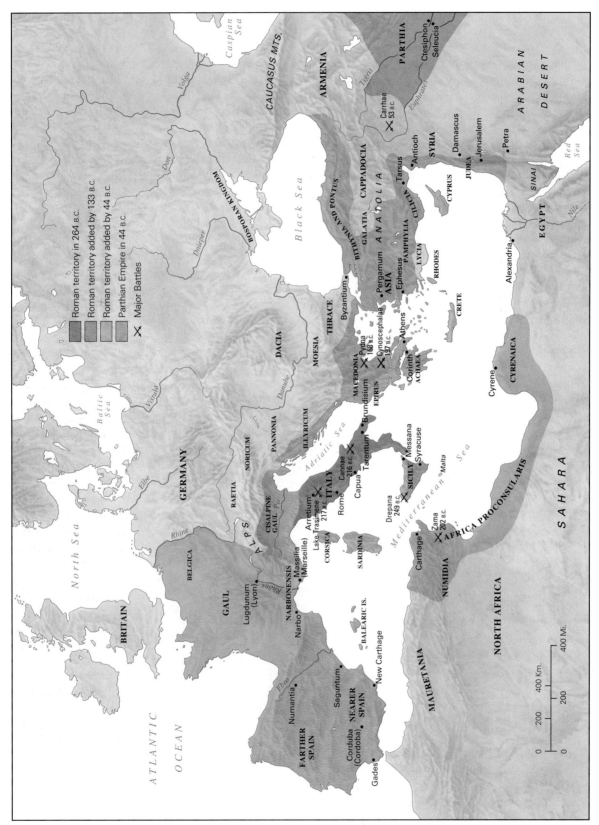

Map 5.3 Roman Expansion, 264–44 B.C. Wars against Carthage, the major Greco-Macedonian powers, Gauls, Germans, and other peoples brought Rome an empire on three continents.

■ The Socioeconomic Consequences of Expansion

Expansion led to enormous and unintended changes in Rome's society, economy, and culture. Already wealthy, the Roman elite now came into fabulous riches. Huge profits awaited the generals, patrons, diplomats, magistrates, tax collectors, and businessmen who followed Rome's armies. In Italy, most profits were in the form of land; in the provinces, not only in land, but in slaves, booty, and graft. One of the worst grafters, Gaius Verres, governor of Sicily from 73 to 71 B.C., was prosecuted by Cicero (see page 166), then beginning his oratorical career, for allegedly extorting tens of thousands of pounds of silver from his province. But even Cicero skimmed off several thousand pounds of silver as governor of the province of Cilicia (southern Anatolia) from 51 to 50 B.C.

The first Roman coinage, traditionally dated to 289 B.C., facilitated commercial transactions. Previously, the Romans had made do with barter, uncoined bronze, and cast bronze bars, but now they imitated the workmanship and style of Greek coins. Equally prominent in the homes of wealthy Romans were Greek metalwork, jewelry, art objects, and other luxury goods. Conservatives bemoaned the decline of traditional Roman austerity, but they fought a hopeless rear-guard action. (See the feature "Weighing the Evidence: Luxury Goods and Gender Wars in Rome" on pages 170–171.)

Ordinary Romans needed no reminder of the virtues of austerity, for they did not share in the elite's profit from Roman expansion. Indeed, a century of intensive warfare—from the outbreak of the Punic Wars in 264 B.C. to the destruction of Carthage and Corinth in 146 B.C.—strained the lot of the Roman people to the breaking point. Hannibal's invasion left much of the farmland of southern Italy devastated and Italian manpower considerably reduced. Yet most people might have rebounded from these problems within a generation or two, if they had not faced other serious troubles.

Conscription had become the norm. The average term of military service between ages 17 and 46 was six years; the maximum term was twenty years. Because experienced legionnaires were at a premium, commanders were loath to release them from service. But the longer a man was away in the army, the harder it was for his wife and children to keep the family farm running. With help from a patron, they might be able to make do, though most patrons in fact added to the problem through the introduction to Italy of large-scale agricultural entrepreneurship. Those who sought wealth monopolized Italian farmland, imported huge numbers of slaves, and brought ruin on the free peasantry of Italy.

The last two centuries B.C. witnessed the transformation of Roman rural society from a society of independent farmers to one in which slave labor played a major role. By the end of the first century B.C. Italy's slave population was estimated at 2 to 3 million, about a third of the peninsula's total. Prisoners of war and conquered civilians provided a ready supply of slaves. Most worked in agriculture or mining, and their treatment was often abominable; the fewer house slaves were usually better off.

Wealthy Romans wanted to invest in large landed estates, or *latifundia*°, worked by slaves. These estates were either mixed farms (most often devoted to cultivating vines, olives, and grain) or ranches (establishments where animals were raised for meat, milk, and wool). One devotee of the latter was the prominent conservative Marcus Porcius Cato° (234–149 B.C.), known as Cato the Censor. Cato argued that there were only three ways to get rich: "pasturage, pasturage, and pasturage." All a would-be entrepreneur needed was land. Conquests had gained Rome a plenitude of land in Italy. Called public land, it belonged to the Roman people, but an individual was legally entitled to claim about 320 acres as his own. Many entrepreneurs flouted the law, however, and grabbed large chunks of public land for pasturage. They often forced families of absent soldiers off private land, either by debt foreclosure or by outright violence. Sometimes families would leave the land for the city, but usually they stayed as tenants.

Before about 170 B.C., poor Romans were sometimes able to find land in colonies. By 170 B.C., however, Rome had established all the colonies in Italy that its security demanded, so this avenue of escape from poverty was closed. A displaced farmer who wanted to compete in the labor market would have found it difficult to underbid cheap slave labor; in any case, Roman ideology frowned on wage labor by citizens. Nor was it practical for a poor farmer to sue a wealthy patron who seized his land, because a plaintiff himself had to bring the accused into court.

The situation of the Italian peasantry was becoming increasingly miserable by the mid-second century B.C. As one modern scholar has put it, "In conquering what they were pleased to call the world, the Romans ruined a great part of the Italian people."[2]

---

latifundia (lat-uh-FUN-dee-uh)
Cato (KAY-toe)

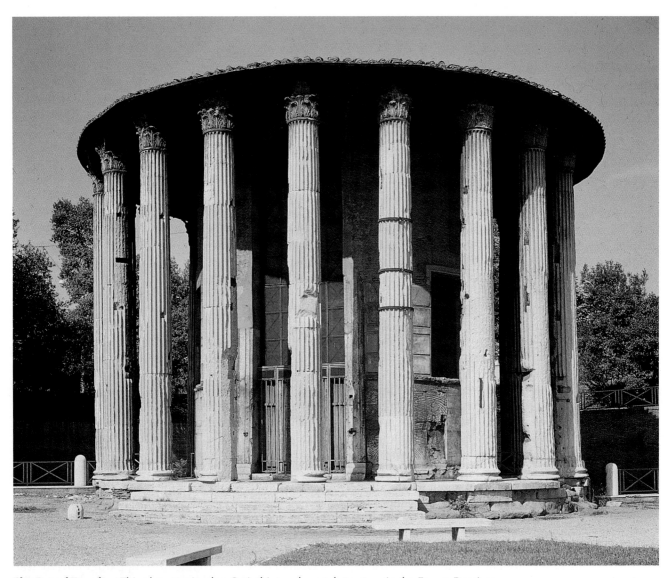

The Round Temple This elegant, circular, Corinthian-columned structure in the Forum Boarium in Rome, built around 150–100 B.C., is the oldest surviving marble temple in the city. Greek in style, it is an example of Roman borrowing from sophisticated Hellenistic culture. *(Scala/Art Resource, NY)*

■ The Impact of Greece on Rome and Its Empire

Rome learned much from its new encounters with foreign peoples—and from none more than the Greeks. Wealthy Romans cultivated interests in Greek art, literature, rhetoric, and speculative thought; poor and rich alike enjoyed Greek drama. Before the mid-third century B.C., Roman literature was virtually nonexistent. An oral tradition of songs, ballads, and funeral oratory kept alive the deeds of the famous, for writing was generally restricted to commercial and government records and inscriptions. In short, the Romans conquered Italy without writing about it.

Contact with the Greek cities brought changes. Large numbers of Roman soldiers in Magna Graecia (southern Italy and Sicily) were introduced to comedy, tragedy, mimes, and sophisticated song lyrics, and many developed a permanent taste for them. It is no accident that the first production of a drama at Rome took place in 240 B.C., the year after the end of the First Punic War. Afterward, the annual production of such dramas became standard procedure.

No one could accuse the Romans of rushing headlong into a new age, however. The authorities continued to have their doubts about theater, which seemed excessively emotional and probably corrupt. They did not allow the building of a permanent theater in Rome until 55 B.C., insisting that the wealthiest city in the Mediterranean make do with makeshift wooden structures. Nor did the Roman elite readily become playwrights or poets. The first gentleman-poet in Rome, Lucilius (180–102 B.C.), did not arrive until the second century B.C., and he was a Latin, not a Roman. His predecessors, the founders of Latin literature, were all of low social status; little of their work survives.

The two great early Latin playwrights are Titus Maccius Plautus (ca. 254–184 B.C.) and Publius Terentius Afer, today known as Terence (ca. 195–159 B.C.). Both of them wrote comedies on the model of the great Greek comic playwright Menander (see page 122). Plautus was an Umbrian and a poor man who learned his Latin in Rome; Terence was a North African slave, educated and freed in Rome. Twenty-one plays by Plautus and six by Terence survive. Plautus's plays are generally earthy slapstick farces. They are invariably set in Greece, not Rome, in part out of escapism (many were written during the Second Punic War), in part out of the censorial demands of the Roman authorities. They nonetheless reveal much about Roman society. Terence's plays are more subtle than Plautus's, indicating the growing sophistication of Roman theatergoers.

Latin prose developed more slowly than did poetry and drama. The first histories by Romans, composed after the Second Punic War, were written in Greek, for Latin lacked the vocabulary or the audience for history. Cato the Censor was the first historian of Rome to write in Latin. His *Origines,* of which we have only remnants, recounted Roman history from the origin of the city to about 150 B.C. The earliest surviving Latin prose work is Cato's *On Agriculture.*

In the traditional education of a Roman aristocrat, parents and close family friends played the primary role. Although this practice continued, in the second century B.C., wealthy Romans began acquiring Greek slaves to educate their sons in Greek language and literature. Soon Greek freedmen began setting up schools offering the same subjects. Before long, similar Latin grammar schools also opened.

One of the forms of Greek literature that appealed most to the practical-minded Romans was rhetoric. Roman orators studied Greek models, and many would say that they eventually outdid the Greeks. Cato was the first Roman to publish his speeches, and he also wrote a book on rhetoric. Both gave impetus to the spread of sophisticated rhetoric in Rome.

Scipio Aemilianus, conqueror of Carthage in 146 B.C., had a distinguished political and military career. He was also patron of a group of prominent statesmen and soldiers who shared his love of Hellenism. Among the writers whom they supported were the playwright Terence, the poet Lucilius, the historian Polybius, and the Stoic philosopher Panaetius (ca. 185–109 B.C.). The Stoic emphasis on duty, wisdom, and world brotherhood appealed both to Rome's traditional ideology and to its more recent acquisition of empire. Yet not all Romans shared Scipio's admiration of Greek culture: Cato, for example, was famously ambivalent.

Cornelia, Scipio Aemilianus's mother-in-law, was an educated lover of Hellenism who wrote letters that existed several hundred years later as examples of elegant Latin prose. Her villa in the resort of Misenum on the bay of Naples was well known for the distinguished guests whom she received there. When her husband, an outstanding statesman and general, died, Cornelia chose to remain a widow. One of the men who tried to change her mind was no less a figure than the king of Egypt. The widow spent her time managing her own estate and supervising the education of her two sons, the future tribunes Tiberius and Gaius Gracchus (see page 161).

Although Cornelia's privileges were extraordinary, she is nonetheless a reminder of the opportunities that imperial expansion offered to wealthy Roman women. Marriage practices are one example of change. Few women were married *cum manu* anymore, that is, handed over by their fathers to their husbands. A woman's father or nearest male relative, not her husband, was most likely to be her paterfamilias, which meant that a husband's control over his wife's dowry was limited. The result was more freedom, at least for wealthy women.

Cornelia is also a reminder of the fundamental conservatism of Roman society. Although we know the years of birth and death of numerous elite Roman males of the second century B.C., we do not know Cornelia's. Nor did her literary interests entail any neglect of home and family. Cornelia bore twelve children, though only three of them lived to adulthood (such was the reality of infant mortality even for the wealthiest Romans).

THE REVOLUTION FROM THE GRACCHI TO THE CAESARS, 133–31 B.C.

CITIZEN of the Roman Republic in the mid-second century B.C. might have looked forward to a long and happy future for his country, unaware that the Republic—after 350 years of expansion—was about to begin a century of domestic and foreign unrest that would bring down the whole system. Why and how did the Republic collapse? More than a century of warfare weighed heavily on the ordinary people of Italy—the Romans and allied peasants whose farms were ruined while they were off fighting. The Roman elite was bitterly divided over what to do about the problems of the peasants. One group wanted to redistribute land on behalf of the poor; another group had no sympathy for them.

By the Late Republic the city of Rome was crowded and populous: scholars estimate the number of inhabitants to have reached 1 million by the end of the first century B.C. The government had to take charge of the grain supply. But elite politicians exploited the issue for partisan purposes. Once before, during the struggle between the patrician and plebeian orders in the Early Republic, the elite had been similarly divided and had resolved its differences through compromise (see page 145). The Late Republic, however, was an age of individualism, sophistication, and cynicism. Ambitious nobles were no longer willing to subordinate themselves to the community. Thwarted from above, it was not long before competing armies of land-hungry peasants were marching across Italy.

■ The Gracchi

Many Romans fretted over the military dimension of the agrarian crisis. In modern societies, draftees are often the poorest people. In Rome, military service was a prestigious activity, so a property qualification was imposed and the poor were not drafted. As fewer and fewer potential soldiers could afford to own property, however, during the second century it became necessary to reduce the property qualification several times. By 150 B.C., a conscript had to own property worth only 400 denarii—roughly a small house, a garden, and some personal belongings. If the peasantry continued its decline, Rome would either have to drop the property qualification for the military altogether or stop fielding armies. Clearly, something had to be done.

Into the breach stepped Tiberius Sempronius Gracchus° (d. 133 B.C.), one of the ten tribunes for the year 133 B.C. (See the box "Reading Sources: Tiberius Gracchus on Rome's Plight.") The son of Cornelia and a distinguished general and ambassador (whose name Tiberius shared), Tiberius belonged to the eminent Gracchi° family. He seemed an excellent spokesperson for a group of prominent senators who backed land reform. He proved, however, to be arrogant and overly ambitious. In pursuit of his goals he deposed one of his fellow tribunes, Octavius, an opponent of reform, and thereby shocked and angered conservatives.

Tiberius's proposed law restored the roughly 320-acre limit to the amount of public land a person could own (plus an exception for a man with two sons, who was allowed to hold about 667 acres). A commission was to be set up to repossess excess land and redistribute it to the poor, in small lots that were to be inalienable—that is, the wealthy could not buy them back. The former landowners would be reimbursed for improvements they had made, such as buildings or plantings.

The proposal was moderate, but wealthy landowners repudiated it outright. Many senators suspected that Tiberius wanted to set himself up as a kind of superpatron, buoyed by peasant supporters. The senate was in fact more disturbed by Tiberius's methods than by the substance of his proposed law because those methods threatened the senate's power. In addition to deposing Octavius, Tiberius, when the bill became law, intervened in the senate's bailiwicks of foreign affairs and finances by earmarking tax receipts from the new province of Asia to finance land purchases. Finally, Tiberius broke with custom by running for a second consecutive term as tribune. While the tribal assembly prepared to vote on the new tribunes, some senators led a mob to the Forum and had Tiberius and three hundred of his followers clubbed to death.

This shocking event marked the first time in the Republic that a political debate was settled by bloodshed in Rome itself. The ancient sources agree that it was the beginning of a century of revolution. Tiberius's killers had not merely committed murder, but had attacked the traditional inviolability of the tribunes. Yet over the next century public violence grew as a weapon of politics in the Republic. The land commission went ahead with its work, even without Tiberius. His younger brother, Gaius°

Tiberius Gracchus (ty-BEER-ee-us GRAK-us)
Gracchi (GRAK-eye)   **Gaius** (GUY-us)

Tiberius Gracchus on Rome's Plight

In 133 B.C. Tiberius Gracchus proposed to confiscate from wealthy landowners public land possessed in excess of the legal limit and to redistribute it to poor Roman citizens. The proposal, and Tiberius's unorthodox methods of getting it passed into law, sparked a controversy that led to his murder. Plutarch (ca. A.D. 50–120) discusses Tiberius's motives and paraphrases one of his speeches.

His brother Gaius recorded in one of his writings that when Tiberius on his way to Numantia [in Spain] passed through Etruria and found the country almost depopulated and its husbandmen and shepherds imported barbarian slaves, he [Tiberius] first conceived the policy which was to be the source of countless ills to himself and to his brother. But it was the people themselves who chiefly excited his zeal and determination with writings on the porticoes, walls, and monuments, calling on him to retrieve the public land for the poor.

. . . Tiberius, fighting for an honorable and just cause with an eloquence that would have dignified even a meaner cause, was formidable and invincible whenever, with the people crowding around . . . , he took his place and spoke in behalf of the poor. "The wild beasts that roam over Italy," he said, "have their dens, each has a place of repose and refuge. But the men who fight and die for Italy enjoy nothing but the air and light; without house or home they wander about with their wives and children. Their commanders lie when they exhort the soldiers in battle to defend sepulchers and shrines from the enemy, for not one of these many Romans has either hereditary altar or ancestral tomb; they fight and die to protect the wealth and luxury of others; they are styled masters of the world, and have not a clod of earth they can call their own."

Source: Plutarch, *Life of Tiberius Gracchus,* in Naphtali Lewis and Meyer Reinhold, eds., *Roman Civilization: Selected Readings,* vol. 1: *The Republic and the Augustan Age,* 3d ed. (New York: Columbia University Press, 1990), pp. 251–252.

(d. 121 B.C.), ready to continue Tiberius's work, became tribune himself in 123 B.C. Gaius expanded Tiberius's coalition, adding to it supporters from the equestrian order and the urban populace, mainly composed of slaves and freedmen. He gave the plebs cheap grain at subsidized prices. The equestrians were wealthy, landed gentry, similar to senators in most respects except for their failure to have reached the senate; they yearned for political power. A small but important group of equestrians was engaged in commerce and tax collection in the provinces. The senate regulated their activities through the so-called extortion courts, which tried corruption cases. Gaius staffed those courts with equestrians. Alluding to the new equestrian power, Gaius remarked, "I have left a sword in the ribs of the senate."

Gaius's ultimate aims are unclear, but one thing is certain: he posed a dangerous threat to the senate's power. He sponsored an extension of his brother's agrarian law, new colonies, public works, and relief for poor soldiers. Eventually Gaius ran aground on a plan to include the Italian allies as beneficiaries of agrarian reform—a farsighted notion but one unpopular with the Roman people, who were jealous of their privileges. Gaius was denied a third term as tribune in 121 B.C. (he had won a second the previous year). Soon his supporters engaged in violent scuffling with their opponents. The senate responded to his action by passing a declaration of public emergency, empowering the magistrates to use any means necessary to protect the state.

One of the consuls had Gaius and 250 of his followers killed. Another 3,000 Gracchans were executed soon thereafter. Within a few years, the Gracchan land commission was abolished. It is estimated that approximately 75,000 citizens had been given land. The law, however, was amended to permit the resale of redistributed land, and with the wealthy poised to buy land back, the settlers' future was uncertain. The senatorial oligarchy was back in control.

Or so it seemed. In fact, Roman politics had become an unstable brew. In time, it became clear that the Gracchi had divided the political community into two loose groupings. On one side were the *optimates°* ("the best people"), conservatives who asserted the rule of the senate against popular tribunes and the maintenance of the estates of the wealthy in spite of the agrarian crisis. On the other side were the *populares°* ("men of the people"), who challenged the rule of the senate in the name of relief of the poor. The populares were not democrats. Like the optimates, they were Roman nobles who believed in hierarchy, but they advocated the redistribution of wealth and power as a way of restoring stability and strengthening the military.

■ Marius and Sulla

By 100 B.C., Rome's agrarian crisis had become a full-scale military crisis, too. Roman armies under senatorial commanders fared poorly, both in Numidia (modern Algeria) and in southern Gaul against Germanic invaders (see Map 5.3). The situation was saved by an outsider to established privilege, an equestrian named Gaius Marius° (157–86 B.C.), the first member of his family to be elected consul, for 107 B.C. This "new man" proved to be a military reformer and a popularis. Marius made several moves to streamline and strengthen the Roman army: Camp followers were reduced in number, and individual soldiers were made to carry their own equipment. To meet the Germans, who attacked in overwhelming waves, maniples—the tactical subunits of a legion—were reorganized and combined into larger units called cohorts, rendering the army firmer and more cohesive. Most important, Marius abandoned altogether the property qualification for the military. As a result, Roman soldiers were no longer peasants doing part-time military service but rather were landless men making a profession of the military.

Politically they became a force to be reckoned with. As an indispensable general, Marius demanded and won six elections to the consulship, unconstitutional though that was. Furthermore, after winning the wars in North Africa and Gaul, Marius championed his soldiers. In 100 B.C. he asked that land be distributed to them. The senate refused but its victory was temporary. The poor recognized that only military leaders such as Marius desired to meet their need for land. As a result, ordinary Romans, who were all now eligible for the army, transferred their loyalty from the senate to their commander.

The Republic was weak, and it became weaker still as a result of two new wars. First, its Italian allies rose against Rome in a bloody and bitter struggle from 91 to 89 B.C. known as the "Social War"—that is, war with the *socii* ("allies"). The allies fought hard, and Rome, in order to prevail, had to concede to them what they had demanded at the outset: full Roman citizenship. The war wrought devastation in the countryside, further destabilizing the Republic. The other conflict of this period pitted Rome against Mithridates (120–63 B.C.), a rebellious king in northern Anatolia. Mithridates conquered Roman territory in western Anatolia and slaughtered the numerous Italian businessmen and tax collectors there. Once again a military man rose to save the day for Rome: Marius's rival and former lieutenant, Lucius Cornelius Sulla° Felix (ca. 138–78 B.C.), consul for the year 88 B.C., patrician and optimas.

Yet Marius was jealous, and his troops and Sulla's fought a civil war over the issue of the command against Mithridates. Sulla's forces won the first round by marching on Rome, but after they departed for the East, Marius's men retook the city and settled scores. Victorious over Mithridates, Sulla returned to Italy in 83 B.C. for a final reckoning. Sulla defeated Marius's men (minus Marius himself, who had died in 86), then sealed his victory with proscription: that is, he had posted the names of his political opponents, as many as two thousand men. Their land was confiscated, their sons disenfranchised, and they were executed. Sulla settled his veterans, about eighty thousand men, on land in Italy from which he had expelled entire communities that had opposed him.

Having assumed the long-dormant office of dictatorship—now, unconstitutionally, for life—Sulla attempted to restore the senatorial rule of pre-Gracchan days. To this end, he greatly weakened the tribunate and strengthened the senate, whose size he doubled, from about three hundred to about six hundred members.

---

optimates (op-tee-MAH-tayz)
populares (pah-poo-LAH-rayz)   **Marius** (MARRY-us)

Sulla (SUL-luh)

Bust of Julius Caesar   This marble sculpture accurately conveys the conqueror's firmness of expression and perhaps his intelligence—but not his looks, since Caesar was bald.
(Vatican Museums/Scala/Art Resource, NY)

The most long-lasting of Sulla's measures was his reform of the courts. He abolished trials before popular assemblies and equestrian-staffed courts. Criminal cases were now heard before one of seven standing courts, whose juries were composed of senators. Although later Roman criminal law evolved considerably, it was founded on Sulla's actions. Generally only wealthy people had access to the standing courts; alleged crimes involving ordinary people were heard before lesser magistrates.

Sulla retired in 79 B.C. and died a year later. His hope of restoring law and order under the senate died with him. Within ten years, the old powers of the tribunes had been restored. Discontent smoldered among the men whose land Sulla had confiscated. Equally serious, many senators, aspiring to what Sulla had done and not to what he had said, pursued personal power, not the collective interests of the senate.

■ Pompey and Caesar

New would-be Mariuses or Sullas now arose. The dominant leader of the seventies and sixties B.C. was the optimas Pompey° the Great (106–48 B.C.), a brilliant general and a supporter of Sulla. Young Pompey went from command to command: he put down an agrarian rebellion in Italy and a rebellion in Spain, cleared the Mediterranean of pirates, defeated Mithridates again, and added rich conquests to the empire in Anatolia, Syria, Phoenicia, and Palestine. In the fifties B.C. the tide began turning in favor of Gaius Julius Caesar° (100–44 B.C.), an even more gifted general and politician—indeed, perhaps one of history's greatest. A popularis, Caesar had family connections to Marius and his supporters. Caesar's career depended on his dazzling oratory, his boldness, and his

Pompey (POM-pee)   **Caesar** (SEE-zer)

sheer talent at war and politics. Caesar conquered Gaul, gained a foothold in Britain, and laid the foundations of Roman rule in Egypt (see Map 5.3).

While the elite of the Late Republic struggled to maintain order and secure power, ordinary people struggled for survival itself. Violence had become a way of life in rural Italy. Many once-prosperous farmers, dispossessed peasants, and runaway slaves ended up as robbers or bandits. It was also an era of slave revolts, the most serious of which lasted from 73 to 71 B.C. under the leadership of Spartacus, a Thracian slave who had been a gladiator. An able commander, Spartacus beat nine separate Roman armies in two years before finally suffering defeat. At the same time, Rome also faced major wars in Spain and Anatolia.

Roman women were sometimes pawns, sometimes partners in the political careers of Pompey and Caesar. In 80 B.C., for example, Pompey divorced his first wife to advance his career by marrying Aemilia, Sulla's stepdaughter. Aemilia was not only married at the time but pregnant by her first husband. Soon after her divorce and remarriage, she died in childbirth. Caesar took many mistresses, among whom was the queen of Egypt, Cleopatra (see pages 134–135). Caesar had a penchant for certain Egyptian institutions, such as the Egyptian calendar, and he toyed with becoming a monarch himself, an inclination that Cleopatra perhaps encouraged. Another of Caesar's mistresses was Servilia, stepsister of Marcus Porcius Cato (Cato the Younger, 95–46 B.C.), great-grandson of the famous censor (see page 157). She was also mother of Brutus, the man who would eventually help murder Caesar.

Pompey was an optimas, Caesar a popularis, but the two of them agreed that they, not the senate or the assemblies, should dominate Rome. Each man's ambition was more important to him than any political principles. In 60 B.C. they entered into a pact with a third ambitious noble, Marcus Licinius Crassus (d. 53 B.C.). Known today as the "First Triumvirate," this coalition amounted to a conspiracy to run the state. Their individual ambitions rebuffed by the senate, each man had an agenda that could be achieved by pooling resources in the triumvirate: for Pompey, ratification of his acts in the East and land for his veterans; for Caesar, who became consul for 59 B.C., a long period of command in Gaul and a free hand in his behavior there; for Crassus, a rebate for the tax collectors of Roman Asia, whom he championed, and eventually a command in Syria to make war on Parthia (the revived Persian Empire).

Having achieved its goal, the triumvirate did not long survive, but its very existence shows how little the Republic now meant. Crassus died in an inglorious defeat at Carrhae in Syria in 53 B.C., tarnished further by the Parthians' successful capture of Roman legionary standards (see Map 5.3). Frightened by Caesar's stunning victories in Gaul, Pompey returned to the senatorial fold, now led by Cato the Younger. Cato and his supporters stood for the traditional rule of the senatorial oligarchy. In 49 B.C. they ordered Caesar to give up his command in Gaul, but instead Caesar marched on Italy with his army. Italy's northern boundary was marked by a tiny stream called Rubicon; when Caesar defiantly crossed it, he declared, "The die is cast." Indeed it was, for civil war. Caesar swept to victory against the senate's army, led by Pompey, at Pharsalus in Greece in 48 B.C. Pompey fled but was assassinated. The complete destruction of the senate's forces took until 45 B.C.

The years of civil war took Caesar from Spain to Anatolia. During the fighting he showed the qualities that made him great: he was fast, tough, smart, adaptable, and a risk-taker. He was a diplomat too, offering mercy to any of his enemies who joined him. A talented writer, Caesar published two books about his military campaigns: *On the Gallic War* and *On the Civil War,* the latter appearing after his death. These works glorified Caesar's conquests and defended his decision to wage civil war. (See the box "Global Encounters: Caesar on the Gauls.")

Back in Rome, Caesar sponsored a huge number of reforms. His political goal was to elevate Italians and others at the expense of old Roman families. To achieve this, Caesar conferred Roman citizenship liberally, on all of Cisalpine Gaul (northernmost Italy) as well as on certain provincial towns. He enlarged the senate from six hundred to nine hundred, adding his supporters, including some Gauls, to the membership. Caesar sponsored social and economic reforms too, including reducing debt and founding the first colonies outside Italy, where veterans and poor citizens were settled. He undertook a grand public building program in the city of Rome. Caesar's most long-lasting act was to introduce the calendar of 365¼ days, on January 1, 45 B.C. Derived from the calendar of Egypt, it is known as the Julian calendar.

Caesar did not hide his contempt for Republican constitutional formalities. By accepting a dictatorship for life he offended the old guard; by flirting with the title of king he infuriated them. With one eye toward avenging Crassus and another toward equaling the achievements of Alexander the Great, Caesar made preparations for a war against Parthia, but in vain. His career ended abruptly on March 15, 44 B.C. (the Ides of March by the Roman calendar), when sixty senators stabbed him to death. The assassination took place in the portico attached to the Theater of

Caesar on the Gauls

Julius Caesar (ca. 100–44 B.C.) advertised his achievements in conquering Gaul (58–51 B.C.) in his Commentaries on the Gallic War. *The book focuses on battles and negotiations, but here Caesar discusses the society of the Gauls (also known as Celts). He depicts the inhabitants as superstitious and belligerent.*

In the whole of Gaul two types of men are counted as being of worth and distinction. The ordinary people are considered almost as slaves: they dare do nothing on their own account and are not called to counsels. When the majority are oppressed by debt or heavy tribute, or harmed by powerful men, they swear themselves away into slavery to the aristocracy, who then have the same rights over them as masters do over their slaves. Of the two types of men of distinction, however, the first is made up of the druids (priests), and the other of the knights.

The druids are involved in matters of religion. They manage public and private sacrifices and interpret religious customs and ceremonies. Young men flock to them in large numbers to gain instruction, and they hold the druids in great esteem. For they decide almost all disputes, both public and private: if some crime has been committed, if there has been murder done, if there is a dispute over an inheritance or over territory, they decide the issue and settle the rewards and penalties. If any individual or group of people does not abide by their decision, the druids ban them from sacrifices. This is their most severe punishment. Those who are banned in this way are counted among the wicked and criminal: everyone shuns them and avoids approaching or talking to them, so as not to suffer any harm from contact with them. . . .

Druids are not accustomed to take part in war, nor do they pay taxes like the rest of the people. . . . The principal doctrine they attempt to impart is that souls do not die but after death cross from one person to another. Because the fear of death is thereby set aside, they consider this a strong inducement to physical courage. Besides this, they debate many subjects and teach them to their young men—for example, the stars and their movements, the size of the universe and the earth, the nature of things, and the strength and power of the immortal gods.

The second class is that composed of the knights. When necessity arises and some war flares up—which before Caesar's arrival used to happen almost every year, so that they were either on the offensive themselves or fending off attacks—they are all involved in the campaign. Each man has as many retainers and dependents about him as is appropriate to his status in terms of his birth and resources. This is the sole form of power and influence they know.

The whole of the Gallic nation is much given to religious practices. For this reason those who are afflicted with serious illnesses and those who are involved in battles and danger either offer human sacrifice or vow that they will do so, and employ the druids to manage these sacrifices. For they believe that unless one human life is offered for another, the power and presence of the immortal gods cannot be propitiated.

Sources: Julius Caesar, *Seven Commentaries on the Gallic War with an Eighth Commentary by Aulus Hirtius,* trans. Carolyn Hammond (New York: Oxford University Press, 1996), pp. 126–128.

 For additional information on this topic, go to http://college.hmco.com.

Pompey, in front of a statue of Pompey himself, where the senate was meeting that day. It had been eighty-nine years since the murder of Tiberius Gracchus.

The assassins called themselves Liberators, believing that they were freeing themselves from tyranny just as the founders of the Republic had done centuries before. Indeed, one of the chief conspirators, Marcus Junius Brutus (ca. 85–42 B.C.), claimed descent from Lucius Junius Brutus, traditional leader of the revolt against the Tarquins that was thought to have established the Republic. Like his co-conspirator Gaius Longinus Cassius (d. 42 B.C.), Brutus had been a magistrate, military officer, and provincial administrator.

The assassination of Caesar threw Rome back into turmoil. Civil war followed for the next thirteen years, first between the Liberators and Caesar's partisans and then between the two leading Caesarians. The final struggle pitted Mark Antony (Marcus Antonius, ca. 83–30 B.C.), Caesar's chief lieutenant and the man who inherited his love affair with Cleopatra, against Octavian (Gaius Julius Caesar Octavianus, 63 B.C.–A.D. 14), Caesar's grandnephew and adopted son and heir to Caesar's name and his huge fortune. At first it looked as if Antony had the upper hand because Octavian was young and inexperienced, was not a general, and was cursed with poor health. Octavian was, however, a man of unusual cunning and prudence. His forces defeated Antony and Cleopatra at the naval battle of Actium (off northwestern Greece) in 31 B.C.; their suicides followed shortly. The Roman world held its breath to see how Octavian would govern it.

■ The World of Cicero

Marcus Tullius Cicero° (106–43 B.C.) is one of the best-known figures of all antiquity. Like Marius, he was a wealthy equestrian from the central Italian town of Arpinum who, as consul (in 63 B.C.), became a "new man." Cicero was an optimas and defender of the senate, though ready for compromise with the equestrians, from whose ranks he himself had arisen. He made his name by successfully leading the opposition to Lucius Sergius Catilina, a down-and-out patrician who organized a debtors' revolt in Etruria; the army smashed the rebellion.

Cicero was intelligent, ambitious, and talented. As a young man he studied philosophy and oratory in Greece. As a result, he produced elevated and serious writings. Never as original as Plato or Aristotle, Cicero

---

Cicero (SIS-er-o)

nonetheless was crucial in making the Latin language a vessel for the heritage of Greek thought. A prolific writer, Cicero produced over a hundred orations, of which about sixty survive; several treatises on oratory; philosophical writings on politics, ethics, epistemology (the study of the nature of knowledge), and theology; poetry, of which little survives; and numerous letters. After his death in 43 B.C., his immense correspondence was published with little censored. The letters and speeches provide a vivid, detailed, and sometimes damning picture of politics.

Politics in the Late Republic was loud and boisterous. The elite prided itself on free speech and open debate. In senate deliberations, court cases, and public meetings in the Forum that preceded assembly votes, oratory—sometimes great oratory—was common. Few orators in history, though, have matched Cicero's ability to lead and mislead an audience by playing on its feelings. He knew every rhetorical trick and precisely when each was appropriate.

Because of increased freedom and greater educational opportunities, during the Late Republic it was possible for elite women as well as men to study oratory. Private tutors were common among the aristocracy, and girls often received lessons alongside their brothers. Girls sometimes also profited from a father's expertise. A particularly dramatic case is that of Hortensia, daughter of Quintus Hortensius Hortalus (114–50 B.C.), a famous orator and rival of Cicero. An excellent speaker herself, Hortensia defied tradition by arguing successfully in the Roman Forum in 42 B.C. against a proposed war tax on wealthy women.

Cicero pilloried one elite woman who enjoyed considerable freedom: Clodia (b. ca. 95 B.C.). Sister of the notorious populist gang leader Clodius and wife of optimas politician Metellus Celer (d. 59 B.C.), Clodia moved in Rome's highest circles. Cicero accused her of poisoning her husband (the charge was unprovable). She is better remembered from the poems of Catullus (ca. 85–54 B.C.), where she is called Lesbia. In passionate and psychologically complex verse, Catullus describes the ups and downs of their affair, which Clodia eventually ended.

Ordinary people lacked the education and freedom to express themselves in the manner of a Catullus or Hortensia, but a less civilized means of expression was open to them: the political gang. Brawls and violence between the rival groups of Clodius, a supporter of Caesar, and Milo, a supporter of the senate, became increasingly common in the fifties B.C. As dictator, Caesar abolished the gangs. (See the box "Reading Sources: Cicero in Defense of Milo.")

❧ READING SOURCES

Cicero in Defense of Milo

On January 18, 52 B.C., a brawl between the rival gangs of Clodius and Milo on the Appian Way left Clodius dead. Cicero himself defended Milo, a fellow optimas, but Milo was convicted and exiled. As this excerpt shows, Cicero's speech to the jury reveals both the violence of Late Republican life and the elegance of his rhetoric.

As subsequent events demonstrated, his [Clodius's] plan was to take up a position in front of his own country manor, and set an ambush for Milo on the spot. . . .

Meanwhile, Milo . . . attended the Senate on that day, until the meeting was concluded. Then he proceeded to his home, changed his shoes and his clothes, waited for the usual period when his wife got ready, and then started off at just about the time when Clodius could have got back to Rome if it had been his intention to return at all on the day in question. But instead he encountered Clodius in the country. . . .

And so at about five in the afternoon, or thereabouts, he found himself confronted by Clodius before the gates of the latter's house. Milo was instantly set upon by a crowd of armed men who charged down from the higher ground; while, simultaneously, others rushed up from in front and killed the driver of the coach. Milo flung back his cloak, leapt out of the vehicle, and defended himself with energy. But meanwhile the people with Clodius were brandishing their drawn swords, and while some of them ran towards the coach in order to fall upon Milo from the rear, others believed he was already slain and began to attack his slaves who had been following behind him. A number of those slaves of Milo's lost their lives defending their master with loyal determination. Others, however, who could see the fight round the coach but were unable to get to their mas-

ter's help, heard from Clodius' own lips that Milo was slain, and believed the report. And so these slaves, without the orders or knowledge or presence of their master—and I am going to speak quite frankly, and not with any aim of denying the charge but just exactly as the situation developed—did what every man would have wished his own slaves to do in similar circumstances.

The incident, gentlemen, took place exactly as I have described it. The attacker was defeated. Force was frustrated by force; or, to put the matter more accurately, evil was overcome by good. Of the gain to our country and yourselves and all loyal citizens, I say nothing. It is not my intention to urge that the deed be counted in favor of Milo—the man whose self-preservation was destined to mean the preservation of the Republic and yourselves. No, my defense is that he was justified in acting to save his life. Civilized people are taught this by logic, barbarians by necessity, communities by tradition; and the lesson is inculcated even in wild beasts by nature itself. . . . That being so, if you come to the conclusion that this particular action was criminal, you are in the same breath deciding that every other man in the history of the world who has ever fought back against a robber deserves nothing better than death. . . .

Source: Cicero, "In Defense of Titus Annius Milo," in *Selected Political Speeches of Cicero,* trans. Michael Grant (Harmondsworth, England: Penguin, 1969), pp. 232–234.

Cicero's works provide evidence of a crucial development in the practice of Roman law. Often unheralded, what Cicero's contemporaries did was invent the notion of the legal expert, a person devoted to explaining and interpreting the law. Roman law needed interpretation because it was complex and intricate. Much of it was the work not of legislators but of magistrates, who issued annual statements setting forth how their courts would work. The result was unsystematic and sometimes contradictory and cried out for someone to make sense of it.

Enter the jurisconsults, legal interpreters who emerged in the third and second centuries B.C. At first they had no special standing, but in the first century they became true jurists; their interpretations began to be considered authoritative. No earlier Mediterranean society had a professional class of legal experts, but no earlier society had faced issues as complicated and turbulent, or had grown to 3 million citizens, as the Roman Republic did in the mid-first century B.C. The Western tradition of legal science has its roots in Rome.

Rome's political system, unlike its legal system, did not adapt flexibly to changing circumstances. The disenfranchised of the Late Republic had reasonable goals: land for those who had fought for their country and admission to the senate of a wider group. Yet the old elite resisted both. Cicero's solution was to build on Sulla's reforms by uniting the senatorial and equestrian orders and by widening the Roman ruling class to include the elite of all Italy. The expanded ruling class could close ranks and establish *otium cum dignitate,* "peace with respect for rank." Cicero's proposed new order was distinctly hierarchical.

In the turbulent times of the Late Republic, the Roman elite often turned to the Hellenistic philosophers. The poet Lucretius° (ca. 94–55 B.C.) describes the Epicurean ideal of withdrawal into the contemplative life in a long didactic epic called *On the Nature of Things.* Most elite Romans, however, including Cicero, preferred the activist philosophy of Stoicism (see page 128). Cicero put forth a generous view of human brotherhood. He argued that all people share a spark of divinity and are protected by natural law. Consequently, all persons have value and importance and should treat others generously. Such ideas would be influential in the new Roman Empire when, under the leadership of Augustus, fair treatment of provincials was a major theme. For Cicero, however, these ideas existed more as theory than as practice.

Cicero did not hide his lack of sympathy for his fellow citizens who were poor. In one speech he castigated "artisans and shopkeepers and all that kind of scum"; in a letter he complained about "the wretched half-starved populace, which attends mass meetings and sucks the blood of the treasury." Cicero also made his disdain for democracy clear: "The greatest number," he said, "should not have the greatest power."

Elitist as Cicero's views were, they were by no means extremist. Cassius, Brutus, and the other Liberators had little interest in even Cicero's limited compromises.

Lucretius (loo-CREE-shus)

Their stubbornness proved to be their downfall, for dispossessed peasants and ambitious equestrians transferred their loyalties to Julius Caesar and, later, to Augustus. One of Caesar's supporters, Sallust (86–ca. 34 B.C.), wrote biting and bitter works of history that indicted the greed and corruption of the optimates, whom he blamed for the decline of the Republic. In any case, peace was not restored, for the generation of Liberators was wiped out in renewed civil war and a new generation emerged, weary for peace.

SUMMARY

 ROME was destined to provide Western civilization with many basic notions about government and empire, but Rome sprang from humble origins. A central Italian village at first, Rome was urbanized after contact with more sophisticated neighbors. Rome became a monarchy and then a republic. It practiced imperialism with almost unlimited success, but ultimately the weight of empire brought down first the social system and then the political regime.

The Republic was a mixed constitution. It combined popular power with control by an oligarchy. In its first centuries, the oligarchy displayed flexibility and wisdom. It proved able to accommodate not only the competitive instincts of the aristocracy and the recently rich but also the land-hunger of the common people. The old aristocracy of the patricians opened its ranks to the newly ambitious leaders of the plebeians and also made room in the government for popular representation. The engrained hierarchy of the Roman social and cultural system helped keep politics stable.

The elite channeled popular energies into protecting the young Republic from its numerous rivals in central Italy. Rome consolidated its control of that region by wisely treating its allies with a mixture of firmness and generosity. By extending Roman citizenship, Rome gave them a stake in continued Roman hegemony. Having disposed of its nearest enemies, Rome mounted a quest for absolute security, a quest that led to conquest in Italy and the rest of the Mediterranean. Greed and ambition, as well as fear, were powerful motives of expansion.

Having defeated all opponents near and far, Rome seemed to have won absolute security by the mid-second century B.C. Yet its strength was deceptive. Contact with Greek culture liberated the Romans from ruder, peasant ways but also loosened previous restraints. A huge influx of slaves made acquisition of large estates profitable. The Italian peasantry was already weakened by conscription and the devastation of farmland, and the elite was arrogant from its military success. Thus, it became easy for the strong to confiscate the land of the weak. The result was a growing and dangerous social instability with military and political ramifications. At the very moment of triumph, the Republic was in grave danger.

Members of the Roman elite, rather than displaying that talent for compromise that had made the Republic great, refused to share their wealth with the poor. The poor, however, got their revenge by throwing their support to new patrons, military leaders who raised private armies to win land for their followers and glory for themselves. By the first century B.C., the Republic had collapsed under the weight of political maneuvering, judicial murders, gang warfare, and civil war. The time was right for the last of the private commanders—Octavian—to recreate the Roman state under his leadership as Augustus, first of the emperors. In the next chapter we examine the world that he remade.

■ Notes

1. *The Aeneid of Virgil*, trans. Allen Mandelbaum (Berkeley: University of California Press, 1971), pp. 160–161.
2. P. A. Brunt, *Social Conflicts in the Roman Republic* (New York: Norton, 1971), p. 17.

■ Suggested Reading

Barker, H., and T. Rasmussen. *The Etruscans*. 1997. Excellent historical introduction and guidebook, written with gusto.

Beard, Mary, and Michael Crawford. *Rome in the Late Republic: Problems and Interpretations*. 2d ed. 1999. An unusual and innovative approach to the subject, emphasizing sociocultural and institutional analysis more than narrative.

Brunt, P. A. *Social Conflicts in the Roman Republic*. 1971. A fine, non-Marxist view of the importance of class conflict throughout Republican history.

Cornell, T. J. *The Beginnings of Rome: Italy and Rome from the Bronze Age to the Punic Wars (c. 1000–264 B.C.)*. 1995. A readable and ambitious survey combining archaeological and literary evidence, often in support of iconoclastic conclusions.

———, and J. Matthews. *Atlas of the Roman World*. 1982. A readable introduction to Roman history written by two scholars; the maps and photos are beautiful, among the best available.

Crawford, Michael. *The Roman Republic*. 2d ed. 1993. The best short introduction, sophisticated, lively, and concise.

Dixon, Suzanne. *The Roman Family*. 1992. A good historical study in complexity, strongly aware of the difference between the myth and reality of the Roman family, and nicely written.

Ward, A. M., F. M. Heichelheim, and C. A. Yeo. *A History of the Roman People*. 3d ed. 1998. The best introductory textbook, scholarly and readable.

 For a searchable list of additional readings for this chapter, go to http://college.hmco.com.

Luxury Goods and Gender Wars in Rome

The carefully wrought gold earrings shown here represent the height of fashion in the central Mediterranean around 200 B.C. Hellenistic taste favored such gold hoop earrings embellished with inlaid colored glass. This set, moreover, displays one of the favorite decorative motifs of the goldsmiths of Magna Graecia in southern Italy during this period: the dove. The artist has crafted the doves as pendants: note how each dove hangs from the earring and stands on a small base trimmed with a garland. Two inches tall, the earrings are miniature sculptures. A Roman woman might wear such jewelry proudly, certain that it bespoke not only good taste and wealth but also the power of her city to command the best artistry of the Greek world.

Not all Romans, however, looked with favor on such finery. Some said it represented not Roman success but decadence. While some observers saw, reflected in the gold, the sight of Greek craftsmen dancing to Roman tunes, others perceived a scene of corruption and wastefulness. Both men and women in the Roman elite began to indulge a taste for luxury in the third century B.C., but women came in for special criticism.

Conservatives considered women's luxuries to pose a special threat to society because they represented not only foreign influence but a threat to right order in the household. If women controlled the economic power to purchase luxury goods, where, then, was the authority of the paterfamilias? More open-minded Romans defended women's contributions to society and their right to the recognition that luxury goods betokened. A debate on women's luxuries raged in Rome around 200 B.C. Let us examine both its historical background and the position of its most famous participant, the conservative champion Marcus Porcius Cato (234–149 B.C.), known as Cato the Censor.

From their first conquest in Magna Graecia in the third century B.C., Romans began to bring home Greek artists and craftsmen and their works. The trickle of art flowing toward Rome is said to have become a flood when Roman armies entered Greece and Anatolia. The simple and frugal elite of traditional Roman ideology began to give way in the third century B.C. to lovers of the good life.

The new wealth and new tastes created a luxury goods industry in Rome. Traditionalist opinion was shocked. Not that Rome lacked wealthy households before 300 B.C. Rather, before then Republican ideology had successfully frowned on conspicuous consumption and display. Now it became common for elite men to wear rings and their wives and daughters to don jewelry as well as fine clothes and cosmetics and—a particular sign of wealth and honor—to ride in carriages. Hannibal's invasion of Italy put the brakes on luxury, however, because it forced Romans to adopt austerity for the duration of the war. In 215 B.C. the Oppian Law put limits on the gold and fine clothing women could own and on their privilege of riding in carriages.

Twenty years later, in 195 B.C., when the emergency had passed, a proposal was made to repeal the law. Elite women demonstrated in favor of repeal. According to the historian Livy, Valerius (one of the consuls for 195) supported their position:

> Women cannot claim magistracies or priesthoods or triumphs or military decorations or awards or the spoils of war. Cosmetics and adornments are women's decorations. They delight and boast of them and this is what our ancestors called women's estate.*

Enter Cato, the other consul for 195 and an advocate of traditional Roman values of austerity. Livy reports that Cato denounced luxury goods as signs of Greek corruption and women's license, even perhaps of women's eventual equality. Although some scholars doubt whether Cato ever so criticized the Greeks, there

---

*Trans. E. Fantham in Elaine Fantham, Helene Peet Foley, Natalie Boymel Kampen, Sarah B. Pomeroy, and H. A. Shapiro, *Women in the Classical World: Image and Text* (New York: Oxford University Press, 1994), p. 261.

Hellenistic Earrings, Gold and Inlaid Glass

(Harriet Otis Cruft Fund. Courtesy of the Museum of Fine Arts, Boston)

is no doubt about his hostility to luxury. As censor in 184 B.C., he assessed taxes on luxury goods and slaves at ten times their market value in order to discourage their use.

Nor is there any doubt about the degree of male worry about women's wealth in Cato's Rome—even though the repeal of the Oppian Law eventually passed in 195 B.C., over Cato's opposition. For example, a character in the play *Pot of Gold*, by Cato's contemporary Plautus, condemns wealthy wives with their "fine clothes and jewelry . . . and maids and mules and coachmen and footmen and pages and private carriages."** In 186 B.C., nine years after the repeal of the Oppian Law, some elite women were found guilty of participation in alleged orgies of the god Bacchus (the Greek Dionysus). Seventeen years later, in 169 B.C., a law was passed forbidding the wealthiest Roman men from leaving more than half of their property to a daughter, in order to prevent the loss through marriage of most of a family's wealth.

**Ibid.

How can we explain such attention by the government to the behavior of elite women? The answer in large part is that war and empire had brought such women new power, power that elite men feared. While those men had often spent years abroad fighting Rome's wars, their wives had learned how to run households. The enormous wealth brought home from those wars often ended up as dowries. Women had the right to retain control of part of their dowries, which sometimes made them wealthier than their husbands. Cato complained that some wives went so far as to lend money to their husbands and then send slaves to reclaim the interest.

So the museum-piece earrings that now win our admiration as works of art once stirred up gender wars that rocked the Roman elite. They remind us how rich in unanticipated consequences was Rome's imperial success. Nonetheless, they must not blind us to the imbalance of wealth in Rome. As the carriages of wealthy women rolled by, the vast majority of Roman women could only stand and watch, hoping to catch a glimpse of gold.

CHAPTER 6

Imperial Rome

31 B.C.–A.D. 284

THE imperial family of Rome walks in stately procession to a sacrifice: Livia, wife of Augustus, first of the emperors; his daughter, Julia; Julia's husband, Agrippa; and various cousins and in-laws and their children. They are formally dressed in togas and gowns, heads wreathed. The men and women gaze seriously; the boys and girls have impish looks, betraying thoughts of mischief as they hold their parents' hands. They are all carved in stone, one of several sculptured reliefs decorating the walls of a public monument in Rome. Dedicated on Livia's birthday in 9 B.C., the monument shown here illustrates the propaganda themes of the new regime, among them the happy family as symbol of peace after generations of civil war. The senate, which had commissioned the monument, called it the *Ara Pacis Augustae,* or Altar of Augustan Peace.

Having made peace was no idle boast on Augustus's part. Not only did he end the Roman revolution, but he began a period of two hundred years of prosperity and stability in the Roman Empire. Augustus took advantage of Rome's war-weariness to create a new government out of the ruins of the Republic. Like the builders of the Early Republic's constitution, Augustus displayed the Roman genius for compromise. He had superb political instincts. Although Augustus retained the final say, he shared a degree of power with the senate. He made financial sacrifices to feed the urban poor and distribute farms to landless peasants. He ended Rome's seemingly limitless expansion and stabilized the borders of the empire. He began to raise the provinces to a status of equality with Italy.

Augustus and the Principate,
31 B.C.–A.D. 68

The Roman Peace and Its Collapse,
A.D. **69–284**

Early Christianity

Ara Pacis (detail), Rome.
(Scala/Art Resource, NY)

The *pax Romana*° ("Roman peace"), at its height between A.D. 96 and 180, was an era of enlightened emperors, thriving cities, intellectual vitality, and artistic and architectural achievement in an empire of 50–100 million people. Yet it was also an era of slavery. More positively, the Roman peace was a period of heightened spirituality. In the peaceful and diverse empire, ideas traveled from people to people, and the religious beliefs of an obscure sect from western Asia began to spread around the Mediterranean and into northern Europe. The new religion was Christianity.

After 180, Rome slowly passed into a grim period marked in turn by bad emperors, civil war, inflation, plague, invasion, and defeat. After reaching a nadir around 235–253, Rome's fortunes began to improve under a series of reforming emperors who would forge a stronger and vastly different empire.

QUESTIONS TO CONSIDER

- How did Augustus lay the foundations of the new, imperial government that would replace the Roman Republic? Why was he so successful?

- What was life like in the era of the Roman peace?

- How was the Roman Empire shaken by the crisis of the third century A.D., and how did it survive?

- What were the origins of Christianity in Palestine, and how did the new religion spread around the Roman world?

TERMS TO KNOW

Augustus
Principate
Livia
pax Romana
Flavians
Julio-Claudians
third-century crisis

Virgil
Tacitus
Jesus of Nazareth
Paul of Tarsus
Christianity
rabbinic Judaism

AUGUSTUS AND THE PRINCIPATE, 31 B.C.–A.D. 68

 N 31 B.C. Gaius Julius Caesar Octavianus (63 B.C.–A.D. 14), or Octavian, as Augustus was then known, stood at the top of the Roman world. His forces had defeated those of Mark Antony and Cleopatra at the Battle of Actium in northwestern Greece, whereupon his two chief enemies committed suicide. Few could have predicted the vision and statesmanship that Octavian now displayed. He spent the next forty-five years healing the wounds of a century of revolution. He did nothing less than lay the foundations of the prosperous two centuries enjoyed by the empire under the Roman peace (see Map 6.1).

■ The Political Settlement

Octavian was both an astute politician and a lucky one. He was lucky in the length and violence of the civil wars. After Actium, most of his enemies were dead, so establishing the one-man rule that he claimed was necessary

to restore stability was relatively easy. He was also lucky to live to be nearly 80—he had plenty of time to consolidate his rule. He was a cagey man and a sharp judge of others. A careful planner who loved to gamble with dice, Octavian never took chances in the game of power. Octavian learned the lesson of Caesar's greatest mistake. He understood that the Roman elite, however weakened, was still strong enough to oppose a ruler who flaunted monarchial power. To avoid a second Ides of March, therefore, Octavian was infinitely diplomatic.

Rather than call himself Dictator, Octavian took the title of *Princeps*° ("First Citizen"), an old title of respect in the senate. From *princeps* comes *Principate*,° a term often used to describe the constitutional monarchy of the "Early Empire," the name that historians have given to the period from 31 B.C. to A.D. 192. Four years after Actium, in 27 B.C. the senate granted Octavian the honorific title *augustus*, symbolizing the augmentation, or increase, of Octavian's authority. He was also known as *Caesar* and *divi filius* ("son of a god"), which tied him to Julius Caesar. Another name, *imperator* ("commander" and, later, "emperor"), recalled the military might that Augustus (as we shall henceforth call him) could call on if needed.

---

pax Romana (PAHKS ro-MAHN-uh)

princeps (PRIN-keps)   **Principate** (PRIN-sih-pate)

In 27 B.C. Augustus proclaimed "the transfer of the state to the free disposal of the senate and the people"—that is, the restoration of the Republic. Remembering similar claims by Sulla and Caesar, few Romans were likely to believe this, and few would have wanted the Republic restored in any case. They no doubt appreciated their ruler's tact, however. (See the box "Reading Sources: Augustus: The Official Story.")

Two strokes of genius marked the new regime. First, Augustus held power without monopolizing public offices. He held the civil authority of the tribunate without being a tribune and the military authority of provincial generals without holding a specific command. Ambitious Romans could still attain public office while deferring to Augustus's power. Second, the new government divided the provinces between Augustus and the senate. To check any new would-be Caesar, Augustus kept for himself the frontier provinces, with the main concentration of armies, as well as grain-rich Egypt (which had been annexed as a Roman province after Actium). The local commanders were loyal equestrians who owed their success to Augustus. Most of the other provinces continued to be ruled as before by senators serving as governors.

Augustus wanted advice without dissent. He used the senate, or rather a committee of senators and magistrates, as a sounding board; the group evolved into a permanent advisory body. Ordinary senate meetings, however, what with informers and secret agents, lost their old freedom of speech. The popular assemblies fared even worse, as their powers were limited and eventually transferred to the senate. Nor would unruly crowds be tolerated. Augustus established the city of Rome's first police force and also stationed there his own personal guard. Called the praetorians°, or Praetorian Guard, the name used for a Roman general's bodyguard, the guard would play a crucial role in future imperial politics.

More important for the public good, Augustus established the first civil service, consisting of a series of prefectures—or departments—supervising, for example, the city watch, the grain supply, the water supply, the building of roads and bridges, tax collection, and the provisioning of the armies. Equestrians and freedmen were prominent in these prefectures and in provincial government, so they enthusiastically supported the Principate.

Although one may speak loosely of "imperial bureaucracy," neither Augustus nor his successors ever established a tight administrative grip on their far-flung empire. As in all ancient empires, Roman government tended to be decentralized and limited. In an age in which few public officials received a salary, bribes were winked at.

CHRONOLOGY

31 B.C.	Octavian defeats Antony and Cleopatra at Actium
27 B.C.	Augustus establishes Principate
27 B.C.–A.D. 68	Julio-Claudian dynasty
19 B.C.	Death of Virgil
ca. A.D. 27–30	Ministry of Jesus
ca. 67	Death of Paul of Tarsus
69–96	Flavian dynasty
70	Temple in Jerusalem destroyed
79	Eruption of Vesuvius
96–180	The "Five Good Emperors"
ca. 117	Death of Tacitus
193–235	Severan dynasty
ca. 200	Mishnah and New Testament each completed
212	Almost all free inhabitants of empire awarded Roman citizenship
235–284	Period of military anarchy

■ The Economic and Social Settlement

The old Roman ruling class made its peace with Augustus, but some never forgave him for ending their ancient privileges. The conservative historian Tacitus° (ca. A.D. 55–117) looked back wistfully to the Late Republic as a golden era of freedom, eloquence, and "the old sound morality." (See the box "Reading Sources: Augustus: A Skeptical View.") Even Tacitus, however, was forced to admit that most people in the Roman world welcomed and admired the Principate. The reason is simple: Augustus and his successors brought peace and prosperity after a century of disasters under the Late Republic.

The Augustan period enjoyed affluence, especially in Italy; the other provinces caught up with Italy by the second century A.D. Agriculture flourished with the end of civil war. Italian industries became leaders in exports. Italian glass bowls and windowpanes, iron arms and tools, fancy silver eating utensils and candlesticks, and

---

praetorians (pre-TOR-ee-unz)

Tacitus (TASS-ih-tus)

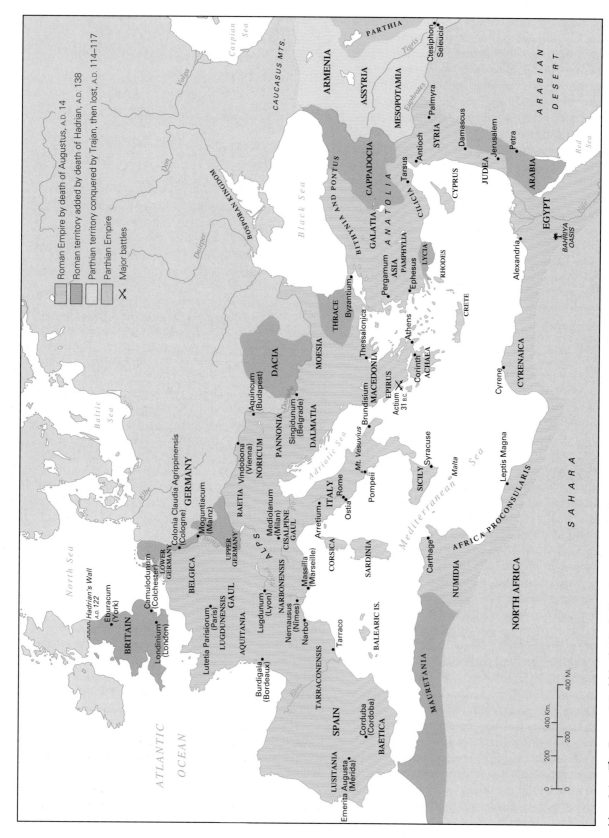

Map 6.1   The Roman World in the Early Empire   Many modern cities are built on the sites of Roman foundations, evidence of the immense extent of the Roman Empire at its height.

Roman Empire by death of Augustus, A.D. 14

Roman territory added by death of Hadrian, A.D. 138

Parthian territory conquered by Trajan, then lost, A.D. 114–117

Parthian Empire

X   Major battles

PARTHIA

ARMENIA

ASSYRIA

MESOPOTAMIA

Tigris

Ctesiphon
Seleucia

Palmyra

Damascus

SYRIA

Antioch

Jerusalem

JUDEA

Petra

ARABIA

ARABIAN DESERT

Red Sea

EGYPT

Alexandria

BAHRIYA OASIS

Nile

Euphrates

CAPPADOCIA

GALATIA

ANATOLIA

BITHYNIA AND PONTUS

Tarsus

CILICIA

PAMPHYLIA

LYCIA

ASIA

Pergamum

Ephesus

RHODES

CYPRUS

CRETE

Caspian Sea

Volga

Don

CAUCASUS MTS.

BOSPORAN KINGDOM

Dnieper

Black Sea

THRACE

Byzantium

MOESIA

DACIA

Aquincum (Budapest)

Danube

Singidunum (Belgrade)

PANNONIA

DALMATIA

NORICUM

Vindobona (Vienna)

RAETIA

GERMANY

Colonia Claudia Agrippinensis (Cologne)

Moguntiacum (Mainz)

UPPER GERMANY

LOWER GERMANY

BELGICA

Thessalonica

MACEDONIA

EPIRUS

Actium 31 B.C.

Athens

Corinth

ACHAEA

Adriatic Sea

Brundisium

CYRENAICA

Cyrene

Leptis Magna

SAHARA

AFRICA PROCONSULARIS

Mediterranean Sea

Malta

Carthage

NUMIDIA

NORTH AFRICA

MAURETANIA

SICILY

Syracuse

SARDINIA

CORSICA

ITALY

Rome

Ostia

Pompeii

Mt. Vesuvius

Arretium

Mediolanum (Milan)

CISALPINE GAUL

Po

ALPS

Rhine

Danube

NARBONENSIS

Nemausus (Nîmes)

Narbo

Massilia (Marseille)

LUGDUNENSIS

GAUL

Lugdunum (Lyon)

Lutetia Parisiorum (Paris)

AQUITANIA

Burdigala (Bordeaux)

TARRACONENSIS

Tarraco

BALEARIC IS.

SPAIN

Corduba (Cordoba)

BAETICA

LUSITANIA

Emerita Augusta (Mérida)

Ebro

Elbe

BRITAIN

Hadrian's Wall A.D. 122

Eburacum (York)

Camulodunum (Colchester)

Londinium (London)

North Sea

Baltic Sea

ATLANTIC OCEAN

400 Mi.

400 Km.

200

200

0

0

❧ R E A D I N G   S O U R C E S

Augustus: The Official Story

Not long before his death in A.D. 14, the emperor Augustus arranged for the display in Rome of two bronze tablets containing a record of his achievements. Copies of "the achievements of the Divine Augustus, by which he brought the world under the empire of the Roman people, and of the expenses which he bore for the state and people of Rome" were displayed around the empire. A complete copy survived in the Roman city of Ancyra in Anatolia (modern Ankara, Turkey).

1. At the age of nineteen on my own responsibility and at my own expense I raised an army, with which I successfully championed the liberty of the republic when it was oppressed by the tyranny of a faction. . . .

3. I undertook many civil and foreign wars by land and sea throughout the world, and as victor I spared the lives of all citizens who asked for mercy. 2. [*sic*] When foreign peoples could safely be pardoned I preferred to preserve rather than eliminate them. 3. The Roman citizens who took the soldier's oath of obedience to me numbered about 500,000. I settled rather more than 300,000 of these in colonies or sent them back to their home towns after a period of service; to all these I assigned lands or gave money as rewards for their military service. . . .

20. I restored the Capitol and the theatre of Pompey, both works at great expense without inscribing my name on either. 2. I restored the channels of the aqueducts, which in several places were falling into disrepair through age, and I brought water from a new spring into the aqueduct called Marcia, doubling the supply. . . . 4. In my sixth consulship I restored eighty-two temples of the gods in the city on the authority of the senate, neglecting none that required restoration at the time. . . .

26. I extended the territory of all those provinces of the Roman people on whose borders lay peoples not subject to our government. . . .

27. I added Egypt to the empire of the Roman people. . . .

28. . . . I compelled the Parthians to restore to me the spoils and standards of three Roman armies and to ask as suppliants for the friendship of the Roman people. Those standards I deposited in the innermost shrine of the temple of Mars the Avenger. . . .

35. In my thirteenth consulship the senate, the equestrian order and the whole people of Rome gave me the title of Father of my Country, and resolved that this should be inscribed in the porch of my house and in the Curia Julia and in the Forum Augustum below the chariot which had been set there in my honor by decree of the senate. 2. At the time of writing I am in my seventy-sixth year.

Source: P. A. Brunt and J. M. Moore, eds., *Res Gestae Divi Augusti: The Achievements of the Divine Augustus* (New York: Oxford University Press, 1967), pp. 19–37.

---

bronze statues and pots circulated from Britain to central Asia.

The perennial problem of the Late Republic had been land-hunger, which drove peasants into the arms of ambitious generals. Augustus kept his troops happy by compensating 300,000 loyal veterans with land, money, or both, often in new overseas colonies. At first he paid out these rewards from his own private sources; after A.D. 6, he made the rich pay via new taxes. In other words, Augustus made the elite part of a property transfer that they had resisted since the time of the Gracchi. Yet it was only a partial transfer, limited to soldiers and their families. The result kept the peace, but many nonsoldiers in Italy remained poor, as of course did the huge numbers of slaves.

As for the renegade commanders who had bedeviled the Late Republic, Augustus cut their potential power base by reducing the size of the army, gradually cutting

🕮 READING SOURCES

Augustus: A Skeptical View

Tacitus, a member of the senatorial elite of the Early Empire, looked back longingly to the freedom of the Roman Republic. His Annals *offer a scathing view of the early emperors, beginning with Augustus, whose reign he discusses briefly.*

Famous writers have recorded Rome's early glories and disasters. The Augustan Age, too, had its distinguished historians. But then the rising tide of flattery exercised a deterrent effect. The reigns of Tiberius, Gaius, Claudius, and Nero were described during their lifetimes in fictitious terms, for fear of the consequences; whereas the accounts written after their deaths were influenced by still raging animosities. So I have decided to say a little about Augustus, with special attention to his last period, and then go on to the reign of Tiberius and what followed. I shall write without indignation or partisanship: in my case the customary incentives to these are lacking.

The violent deaths of Brutus and Cassius left no Republican forces in the field. Defeat came to Sextus Pompeius in Sicily, Lepidus was dropped, Antony killed. So even the Caesarian party had no leader left except the "Caesar" himself, Octavian. He gave up the title of Triumvir emphasizing instead his position as consul; and the powers of a tribune, he proclaimed, were good enough for him—powers for the protection of ordinary people.

He seduced the army with bonuses, and his cheap food policy was successful bait for civilians. Indeed, he attracted everybody's goodwill by the enjoyable gift of peace. Then he gradually pushed ahead and absorbed the functions of the senate, the officials, and even the law. Opposition did not exist. War or judicial murder had disposed of all men of spirit. Upper-class survivors found that slavish obedience was the way to succeed, both politically and financially. They had profited from revolution, and so now they liked the security of the existing arrangement better than the dangerous uncertainties of the old regime. Besides, the new order was popular in the provinces. There, government by Senate and People was looked upon skeptically as a matter of sparring dignitaries and extortionate officials. The legal system had provided no remedy against these, since it was wholly incapacitated by violence, favoritism, and—most of all—bribery.

Source: Tacitus, *The Annals of Imperial Rome,* rev. ed., trans. Michael Grant (Harmondsworth, England: Penguin, 1988), p. 32.

---

the number of legions from over sixty to twenty-eight. The total size of the army, including light infantry and cavalry, was about 300,000. This reduction lightened Rome's tax burden but left Augustus with little room to expand the empire. In A.D. 9 Rome lost three legions to a native revolt against Rome's plan to extend its rule in Germany as far east as the Elbe River. Short of manpower, Augustus had to accept the Rhine River as Rome's new German frontier (see Map 6.1).

Imperial defense remained a major issue. Strong Roman armies were a necessity along the hostile European frontier. On the friendlier border in western Asia and northern Africa, Augustus and his immediate successors set up client kingdoms, such as Judea and Armenia, to protect Roman territory. As for Parthia, Augustus compromised. He won no new territory but did achieve the symbolic victory of a return of the legionary standards lost by Crassus at Carrhae in 53 B.C.

Back in Rome the urban poor, many of them freedmen, enjoyed a more efficient system of free grain distribution under Augustus and a large increase in games and public entertainment—the imperial policy of "bread and circuses" designed to content the masses. Augustus also set up a major public works program, which provided jobs for the poor. He prided himself on having found Rome "a city of brick" and having left it "a city of marble."

To promote his ideology of renewal, Augustus sponsored social legislation embodying the old Republican virtues. He passed a series of laws encouraging marriage and childbearing and discouraging promiscuity and adultery. Such legislation was so flagrantly disobeyed that in 2 B.C. Augustus felt compelled to make an example of his own daughter, Julia (39 B.C.–A.D. 14), his only child, whose adulteries were the talk of Rome. As punishment she was banished to a barren islet.

Augustus's era marks the beginning of the classical period of Roman jurisprudence, during which the professionalism that had begun to mark Roman law in the Late Republic became a permanent fact. It was probably Augustus who established the practice, followed by later

Augustus of Prima Porta   Named for the place where it was found, this statue (early first century A.D.) depicts an idealized and heroic Augustus. Scenes of victory, peace, and prosperity—symbols of the Principate—decorate his breastplate. Riding a dolphin, the Cupid at Augustus's feet recalls the Julian family's claim of descent from the goddess Venus. *(Alinari/Art Resource, NY)*

emperors, of granting a few distinguished jurists the exclusive right to issue legal opinions "on behalf of the princeps." He ensured, therefore, that experts guided the administration of justice. The first law school was opened in Rome under Augustus. Roman jurists, many of them provincials, adapted Roman law to the practices of the provinces. Although various provincial legal systems remained in use, the international system of Roman law was also used widely in the provinces.

In religion, too, Augustus was a legislator and reformer. He restored once-neglected cults and temples in order to appear as Rome's savior. He would probably have approved when, after his death, he was deified, just as Julius Caesar had been. Even while he was still alive, Augustus was worshiped in the provinces as a god—in both the East, where the cult of Roma and Augustus grew in popularity, and the West, where centers of emperor-worship were established at the sites of Lyon and Cologne (see Map 6.1). The imperial cult, an important part of state propaganda until the empire became Christian in the fourth century A.D., was well underway.

Deification, whether formal or informal, was a heady brew, but Augustus deserved it more than most. He not only ended the Late Republican era of civil wars but established the Roman Empire on a completely new footing. Republican freedom was gone, but the emperor and bureaucrats brought stability. The peace of the Augustan Principate would last, with few interruptions, for two hundred years. Few people in history have created order so successfully.

■ The Culture of the Augustan Age

Like *Periclean,* the adjective *Augustan°* has come to signify an era of literary and artistic flowering. In both periods strong elements of classicism shaped the arts—that is, an attempt to project fundamental, heroic, and idealized values, the values that the self-confident rulers of each epoch wished to promote. Both prose and poetry flourished in Augustus's empire. The emperor and his close adviser Maecenas° (d. 8 B.C.) were patrons of a number of important poets, chief among them Virgil° (70–19 B.C.) and Horace (65–8 B.C.). The historian Livy° (59 B.C.–A.D. 17), who wrote his history of Rome from the founding of the city to 9 B.C. under Augustus, also elicited the princeps's interest in his work. All three men contributed in their writings to the Augustan renewal and rededication of Rome.

Augustan (aw-GUS-tin)   **Maecenas** (my-SEE-nus)
Virgil (VER-jill)   **Livy** (LIV-ee)

Virgil Writing the Aeneid   This Roman mosaic from second- or third-century A.D. Tunisia shows Virgil seated, holding a copy of the *Aeneid*. He is flanked by two Muses, mythical sources of inspiration.   *(C. M. Dixon)*

In many ways, Virgil speaks for his contemporaries. In the *Eclogues,* poems that, following an Alexandrian model (see page 122), have rustic settings, Virgil describes the miseries of the civil wars and the blessings of peace under Augustus. "A god created this peace for us; for he will always be a god to me," as one character says. In the Fourth Eclogue, Virgil speaks of the birth of a child to usher in a restored Golden Age. At the church Council of Nicaea in A.D. 325 (see page 213), and later, this poem was given a Christian interpretation. In the *Georgics,* Virgil describes the glories of Italian agriculture, which, thanks to Augustus, could be practiced peacefully again.

Virgil's masterpiece is an epic poem, the *Aeneid*°, "the story of Aeneas," the legendary Trojan founder of Rome, or at least of the Latin town from which Rome's founders eventually came. Legend also makes Aeneas the ancestor of Augustus. Thus the *Aeneid* indirectly celebrates Augustus, often considered Rome's second founder. The poem explores the pain and burden as well as the glory of empire.

If Virgil's work has the grandeur of marble, Horace's poems—*Odes, Epodes, Satires, Epistles,* and *Ars Poetica* (*Art of Poetry*)—are more like finely cut gems. They tend to be polished, complex, and detached. Like Virgil, Horace explores the themes of war and peace and praises Augustus. "With Caesar [Augustus] holding the lands, I shall fear neither turmoil nor violent death," declares one of the *Odes.* Both Horace and Virgil successfully adapted Greek models and, in the process, created something new. Few writers have had a greater influence on the later Western literary tradition.

Only 35 of the original 142 books of Livy's ambitious history have survived. Livy is both a master storyteller and a superb ironist. His anecdotes of Roman history are vivid and told in a grand rhetorical style. Livy is our major source for the Roman monarchy and Early Republic, although his account of early Rome is long on myth and short on fact. Nevertheless, Livy is not merely an entertaining stylist but a profound thinker on the meaning of history. He embroiders the facts and engages in frank, subjective judgments intended to inspire both patriotism and reflection on the ironies of history.

Another patron of writers in Augustus's circle was Messalla, himself an orator as well as a statesman. Love poetry was his special interest. Among the poets Messalla supported were Ovid, best known for works on love and mythology; Tibullus, an eligist; and his ward, Sulpicia. Although little survives of Sulpicia's work, more of her work exists than of any other Roman woman. She describes her passion for one Cerinthus: "a worthy man . . . at last a love . . . of such a kind that my shame, Gossip, would be greater if I kept it covered than if I laid it bare."[1]

Augustus and his entourage were also great patrons of the arts and of architecture, which they considered propaganda tools. They sponsored many major building projects throughout the empire, especially in Rome, which gained temples, a new Forum of Augustus, the Theater of Marcellus, the Baths of Agrippa, the Pantheon, and the Mausoleum of Augustus.

■ The Julio-Claudians

Augustus and his successors presented the imperial household to the world as the ideal family, the very model of social order. Behind the walls of the palace, however, dwelt a troubled and sordid reality.

Augustus had only one child, Julia, from his first marriage, which ended in divorce. In 38 B.C. Augustus took as his second wife Livia° (58 B.C.–A.D. 29), who divorced her husband to marry Augustus even though she was pregnant with their second son. She did not bear Augustus children. Seeking a male successor, Augustus used Julia as a pawn in a game of dynastic marriage, divorce, and re-

---

Aeneid (ee-NEE-id)

Livia (LIV-ee-uh)

Julio-Claudian Cameo   Known as the Grand Camée de France, this superb gem depicts the imperial family in its glory. The central scene shows Tiberius, Livia, and, among others, the child Caligula (extreme left). The deified Augustus hovers above them while barbarian captives are below.   *(Giraudon/Art Resource, NY)*

marriage, but to no avail. Julia's first two husbands both predeceased her, as did two sons, each of whom Augustus had adopted. (In Rome it was common for a man without a birth son to adopt a son.) In the end, Augustus was forced to choose as successor, and adopt, a man he disliked, Tiberius° (42 B.C.– A.D. 37), Livia's elder son.

Livia was among the most powerful women of Roman history. One of Augustus's main advisers, she developed a reputation for intrigue, aimed, so gossip had it, at securing the succession for Tiberius. Livia's enemies accused her of poisoning many people, including Julia's husbands and sons; her own grandson, Germanicus (a brilliant general whose popularity threatened Tiberius's); and even Augustus himself, who died in bed after a short illness in A.D. 14.

From A.D. 14 to 68, Rome was ruled by other emperors from Augustus's family. The dynasty, known as the Julio-Claudians, consisted of Augustus's stepson Tiberius, great-grandson Caligula, grandnephew Claudius, and great-great-grandson Nero. For many elite Romans, this era was one of decadence and scandal and oppression of the old nobility. Ordinary people, however, generally enjoyed the benefits of stable, effective, and peaceful government.

The reign of Tiberius (r. 14–37) was remembered with trepidation by the elite for its treason trials and murders. The senate chafed as it steadily lost power to the princeps. The Roman masses grumbled because Tiberius cut back on games and building projects. But despite his shortcomings, Tiberius was a skilled and prudent administrator. He wisely drew back from war on the borders, reduced taxes and spending, and promoted honesty among provincial governors.

His successor, his nephew Gaius (r. 37–41), nicknamed Caligula° ("Baby Boots," after the boots he had worn as a little boy in his father's army camp), humiliated the senate and tried to have himself declared a living god. He made scandal into an art form. For example,

---

Tiberius (ty-BEER-ee-us)

Caligula (ca-LIG-yoo-luh)

he appointed his favorite horse not only high priest of a new cult in honor of Caligula the god but also a member of the senate. Caligula raised taxes and trumped up charges of treason in order to confiscate property. He wanted to have his statue erected in the Temple at Jerusalem. He would have had his way, but he was assassinated first, the victim of a high-level Roman conspiracy. After his death the senate debated restoring the Republic, but it was not to be.

Caligula's uncle, Claudius, was proclaimed emperor by the Praetorian Guard, which left the senate little choice but to support him. Physically handicapped, Claudius (r. 41–54) was often the butt of jokes, but he was a man of substance: a historian, politician, and priest and someone fully versed in the cunning ways of his family. An activist emperor, he expanded the imperial offices with their powerful freedmen; oversaw the construction of an artificial harbor at Rome's silt-clogged port of Ostia; and conquered Britain, where Roman arms had not intervened since Julius Caesar's forays in 55–54 B.C.

Claudius's death may have been the result of poisoning by his wife, who was also his niece, Agrippina° the Younger (A.D. 15–59); in any case, her son by a previous marriage, Nero, became emperor (r. 54–68). As princeps, Nero's scandalous behavior rivaled Caligula's, and his treason trials outdid Tiberius's. A great fire in 64 destroyed half of Rome. Nero mounted an extravagant rebuilding program afterward, although he was accused of having started the fire so that he could become famous as a builder. Nero found a scapegoat for the fire in the members of a small and relatively new religious sect, the Christians, whom he persecuted. Yet most ordinary Romans received good government from Nero, and they rewarded him with support. He was unpopular with the senatorial elite, however, and more serious, he failed to pay all his troops promptly. Confronted with a major revolt in 68, Nero committed suicide.

The next year, 69, witnessed Rome's first civil war in about a century. Three men each claimed the imperial purple after Nero. Finally, a fourth, Vespasian° (Titus Flavius Vespasianus, r. 69–79), commander of the army quelling revolt in the province of Judea, was able to make his claim stick. Peace was restored, but not the rule of Augustus's family. Vespasian founded a new dynasty, the Flavians° (r. 69–96), which was followed in turn by the Nervo-Trajanic (r. 96–138) and Antonine° (r. 138–192) dynasties. The ultimate tribute to Augustus may be that his regime was stable enough to survive the extinction of his family.

THE ROMAN PEACE AND ITS COLLAPSE, A.D. 69–284

MUCH about Rome in the second century A.D. appears attractive today. Within the multiethnic empire, opportunities for inhabitants to become part of the elite were increasing. The central government was on its way to granting Roman citizenship to nearly every free person in the empire, a process completed in the year 212. The emperors emphasized sharing prosperity and spreading it through the provinces. Italy was no longer the tyrant of the Mediterranean, but merely first among equals. To be sure, rebellions were crushed, but few people rebelled. This period, known as *pax Romana* or "the Roman peace," seems particularly golden in contrast with what followed: the disastrous and disordered third century A.D., in which the empire came close to collapse but survived because of a radical and rigid transformation.

■ The Flavians and the "Good Emperors"

The Flavian dynasty of Vespasian (r. 69–79) and his sons Titus (r. 79–81) and Domitian (r. 81–96) provided good government, and their successors built on their achievements. Unlike the Julio-Claudians, Vespasian hailed not from the old Roman nobility but from an Italian propertied family. A man of rough-and-ready character, Vespasian is supposed to have replied when Titus complained that a new latrine tax was beneath the dignity of the Roman government, "Son, money has no smell." Unlike his father and brother, Domitian reverted to frequent treason trials and persecution of the aristocracy, which earned him assassination in 96, although the empire as a whole enjoyed peace and sound administration under his reign.

The so-called Five Good Emperors are Nerva (r. 96–98), Trajan° (r. 98–117), Hadrian° (r. 117–138), and the first two Antonines, Antoninus Pius (r. 138–161) and Marcus Aurelius° (r. 161–180). They are in several ways examples of the principle of merit. Trajan, a Roman citizen born in Spain, was Rome's first emperor from outside Italy. Hadrian and Marcus Aurelius also came from Spain, and Antoninus Pius from Gaul. Each of the Five Good Emperors except Marcus Aurelius adopted the most competent person, rather than the closest blood relative, as his son and successor, thus elevating duty over sentiment. Marcus Aurelius, a deeply committed

---

Agrippina (a-grip-PIE-nuh)   **Vespasian** (ves-PAY-zhun)
Flavians (FLAY-vee-unz)   **Antonine** (AN-toe-nine)

Trajan (TRAY-jun)   **Hadrian** (HAY-dree-un)
Marcus Aurelius (MAR-kus o-REEL-ee-us)

Stoic, gave full vent to his sense of duty in his *Meditations,* which he wrote in Greek while living in a tent on the Danube frontier, where he fought long and hard against German raids. Antoninus was surnamed "Pius" (Dutiful) because he was devoted to his country, the gods, and his adoptive father, Hadrian.

The Five Good Emperors made humaneness and generosity the themes of their reigns. Trajan, for example, founded a program of financial aid for the poor children of Italy. They also went to great lengths to care for the provinces. These emperors not only commonly received petitions from cities, associations, and individuals in far-off provinces but answered them. Yet humaneness does not mean softness. Hadrian, for instance, ordered a revolt in Judea (A.D. 132–135) suppressed with great brutality.

Like the Julio-Claudians, the Five Good Emperors advertised their wives to the world as exemplars of traditional modesty, self-effacement, and domesticity. In fact, they were often worldly, educated, and influential. Trajan's wife, Plotina, for example (d. A.D. 121 or 123), acted as patron of the Epicurean school at Athens, whose philosophy she claimed to follow. She advised her husband on provincial administration as well as dynastic matchmaking. Hadrian's wife, Sabina, traveled in her husband's entourage to Egypt (A.D. 130), where her aristocratic Greek friend, Julia Balbilla, commemorated the trip by writing Greek poetry, which she had inscribed alongside other tourists' writings on the leg of one of two statues of Amenhotep III at Thebes, referred to in classical times as the "colossi of Memnon."

A darker side of the second-century empire was the problem of border defense. Augustus and the Julio-Claudians had established client kingdoms where possible, to avoid the expense and political dangers of raising armies. The emperors of the day tended to be more aggressive on the borders than were Augustus and the Julio-Claudians. They moved from client kingdoms to a new border policy of stationary frontier defense. Expensive fortification systems of walls, watchtowers, and trenches were built along the perimeter of the empire's border and manned with guards. A prominent example is Hadrian's Wall, which separated Roman Britain from the enemy tribes to the north. Stretching 80 miles, the wall required fifteen thousand defense troops.

The most ambitious frontier policy was that of Trajan, who crossed the Danube to carve out the new province of Dacia (modern Romania) and who used an excuse to invade Parthian Mesopotamia. He won battles as far away as the Persian Gulf, but he lost the war. As soon as his army left, Mesopotamia rose in revolt, followed by Germany. Trajan's reign marked the empire's greatest geographic extent, but Trajan had overextended Rome's resources. When he died, his successor, Hadrian, had to abandon Trajan's province of Mesopotamia (see Map 6.1).

■ Prosperity and Romanization in the Provinces

Compared with a modern economy, the Roman economy was underdeveloped. Most people worked in agriculture, employed primitive technology, and lived at a subsistence level. Even so, the Roman Empire experienced modest economic growth during the first two centuries A.D. The chief beneficiaries were the wealthy few, but ordinary people shared in the economic expansion as well. In addition to stability and peace, several other factors encouraged economic development. The western provinces witnessed the opening of new lands to agriculture, where improved techniques were applied. The growth of cities increased agricultural demand. Changes in Roman law aided commerce by making it easier to employ middlemen in business transactions. Travel and communications were relatively easy and inexpensive.

Trade boomed, as a recent archaeological discovery in the Italian city of Pisa° recalls. Nine Roman ships were found in the site of the ancient harbor here in 1999: they are merchant ships, both coastal freighters and small harbor craft. One of the ships was filled with amphoras (storage jars), still stacked in neat rows and filled with wine and sand. Both come from the region of the Bay of Naples, whose sand was used for concrete that could set under water. The finds, which seem to date from the mid-second century A.D., offer a vivid picture of trade up and down the west coast of Italy. When the cargo was unloaded at Pisa, the ships probably picked up the local grain and marble, which was shipped in turn to Rome.

Rome was an economic magnet, but so, to a lesser extent, were all cities, and the second century A.D. was a great age of city life. New cities were founded far from the Mediterranean. They began as veterans' colonies, market towns, and even army camps, and some grew into cities of permanent importance in European history: Cologne (Colonia Claudia Agrippinensis), Paris (Lutetia Parisiorum), Lyon (Lugdunum), London (Londinium), Mérida (Emerita Augusta), Vienna (Vindobona), and Budapest (Aquincum).

Whether old or new, cities attracted a large elite population. The Principate was not a domain of country gentry, but rather one in which ambitious people wanted to live in great cities, in emulation of the greatest

---

Pisa (PEE-zuh)

Double Portrait, Pompeii This wall painting from a house joined to a bakery depicts a married couple, possibly the wealthy baker P. Paquius Proculus and his wife. The portraiture is realistic. The couple carry symbols of education: she holds wax tablets and a stylus (pen), while he grasps a sealed scroll. *(Scala/Art Resource, NY)*

city of the empire, Rome, which was by Augustus's day a city of perhaps a million people. In cities men competed for positions as magistrates, in imitation of the two consuls, or for seats on the local town council, often called a *curia°*, like the senate in Rome; town councilors were called *decurions°* and known collectively as the *curial order.* Decurions further played one-upmanship in sponsoring public buildings in the Roman style, one man endowing a new forum, another a triumphal arch, a third a library, a fourth an amphitheater, and so on. From Ephesus in Anatolia to Colchester in Britain, from Mainz in Germany to Leptis Magna in Libya, a Roman could find familiar government institutions, architecture, and street plans. At Zeugma on the Euphrates River, for example, a city of seventy thousand people, aristocrats on Rome's eastern frontier lived in Italian-style villas, decorated with classical frescoes and mosaics and adorned with bronze statues of the Greco-Roman gods.

---

curia (KYOO-ree-uh)   decurion (day-KYOO-ree-un)

Unlike men, women did not usually hold magistracies, but wealthy women of the empire could and did lavish money on public benefactions. Women endowed temples and synagogues, amphitheaters and monumental gateways, games and ceremonies. They were rewarded with wreaths, front-row seats, statues, priesthoods, and inscriptions honoring them as "most distinguished lady," "patron," and even as "father of the city," to cite an extraordinary case from Roman Egypt.

The buildings were visible examples of Romanization, although the Romans did not use the term. If they had, it would have had a limited meaning because the emperors neither would nor could impose a lock-step cultural uniformity on their subjects. The empire was too big and ancient technology too primitive for that. The total population of the empire consisted of between 50 and 100 million people, most of whom lived in the countryside. The small and largely urbanized Roman administration had little direct contact with most people. So, for example, only a minority of the inhabitants of the empire spoke Latin; in the East, Greek was the more common language of administration. Millions of people spoke neither Greek nor Latin. Celtic, Germanic, Punic, Berber, Coptic, Aramaic, and Syriac were other common languages in Roman domains. In short, the empire lacked the unity of a modern nation-state.

What, then, besides buildings and language might Romanization entail? One index has already been suggested: the participation of provincials in the central government, even as emperor. By around A.D. 200, for example, about 15 percent of the known Roman equestrians and senators came from North Africa. By this time, the senate was no longer dominated by Italians but was representative of the empire as a whole.

Participation in government implies another index of Romanization, the extension of Roman citizenship, outside Italy, to magistrates, decurions, or even whole cities. Citizens took Roman names reflecting the emperor or promagistrate who had enfranchised them. Thus the provinces were full of Julii, Claudii, and Flavii, among others.

The spread of Roman customs is another measure of Romanization. For example, the gladiatorial shows that Romans loved became popular from Antioch to England. These combats advertised both Roman culture and Roman brutality. (See the feature "Weighing the Evidence: Gladiators" on pages 200–201.)

By the same token, native customs might be adopted by Romans. Consider the case of Egypt where, in the late 1990s, archaeologists discovered a vast Roman-era cemetery about 230 miles southwest of Cairo, in the Bahriya Oasis, Roman Egypt's wine country. The population was Romanized here. Yet the cemetery, with its dozens of gilded mummies from the first and second centuries A.D., shows the persistence of mummification processes of the pharaohs.

Another ambiguous symbol of Romanization is found in A.D. 212. In a law known as the *Constitutio Antoniana*, the emperor Caracalla (r. 211–217) rendered nearly all of the free inhabitants of the empire Roman citizens. On the one hand, the law is a historical landmark. Near-universal Roman citizenship was a kind of halfway point between ancient empire and modern mass democracy. On the other hand, the *Constitutio Antoniana* was something of a gimmick. It was probably less an instrument of unification than of taxation, for citizens had a heavier tax burden than noncitizens.

The Roman army, by contrast, did promote Romanization. In antiquity as today, military service offered education and social mobility. Only citizens could join the legions; non-Romans served as auxiliaries. They received Roman citizenship after completing their regular term of service, twenty-five years. And with good reason

because, for example, a Syrian or Gallic peasant who served in the Roman military would experience a way of life with old and deep roots in central Italy.

Non-Italians had, and took, the opportunity to rise high in the army or government. This was all to Rome's credit. Yet as Italians became a minority in the Roman army, and as ever larger numbers of frontier peoples were recruited, it became conceivable that someday the army might abandon its loyalty to Rome.

◼ Roman Law on Class and Marriage

Roman law is one of the ancient world's most influential and enduring legacies. Logical, practical, orderly, and—within the limits of a society of slaves and masters—relatively fair, Roman law influences today the legal system in most Western countries and in many non-Western countries. The law governing Roman citizens was called *ius civile,* or "civil law." Originally this term covered a very broad range of legal matters, but in the empire its meaning was narrowed to private matters. Criminal law became a separate category.

Theater in Roman Spain   This splendid structure at Mérida (ancient Augusta Emerita) was originally built in 24 B.C. and later reconstructed.   *(Vanni/Art Resource, NY)*

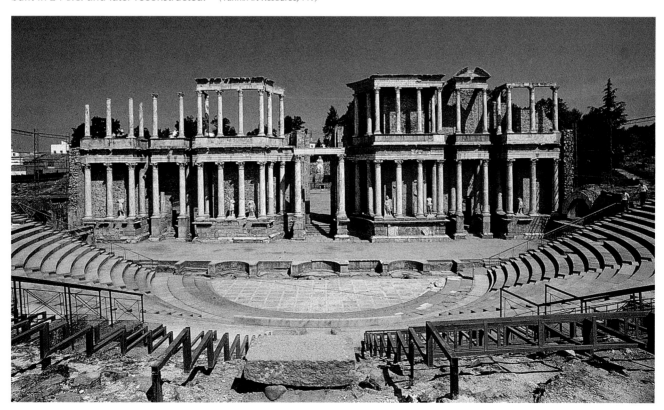

The law helped Rome administer its empire. Roman law was not universal, and noncitizens continued to use their own laws for local matters, but the governors used Roman law to run their provinces, so local elites had to become familiar with it. Like so many Roman customs, the law was both hierarchical and flexible. Let us consider two areas in which the law affected daily life: class and marriage.

The law reflected Roman society's ingrained social inequality. Traditional special classes such as senators and equestrians survived, to be joined by the new distinction between citizens and noncitizens. Another important division cut across the citizen-alien distinction, that between *honestiores* (in general, the curial order) and *humiliores* (everyone else). Privileges previously inherent in citizenship, such as exemption from flogging by officials, now tended to be based on this new distinction, enshrined in private and criminal law.

The most basic legal distinction was that between free and slave—and the empire contained millions of slaves. A third category, ex-slaves or freedmen, also became increasingly important. Freedmen technically owed service to their former masters, who became their patrons, and most freedmen were humble. A few, however, grew rich in commerce or wielded enough power in imperial administration to lord it over even Roman aristocrats. The result was strong elite hostility to freedmen, which is often reflected in Roman literature. Witness the stereotype of the vulgar freedman, embodied in Trimalchio in the *Satyricon*°, a novel by Petronius (first century A.D.). Trimalchio had more estates than he could remember and so much money that his wife counted it by the bushel-load.

As regards marriage, in principle, Roman family law was strict and severe. In practice, it often proved pragmatic and even humane. Consider three cases: elite marriages, slave marriages, and soldiers' marriages.

As in the Late Republic, so in the Early Empire most Roman women married without legally becoming members of their husband's family—or their children's. This gave women a degree of freedom from their husbands but it left elite women, who owned property, with a problem: technically that property was controlled by their fathers or brothers. Yet society recognized a woman's wish to leave her property to her children, and imperial law increasingly made it possible for her to do so—although the conservative Romans waited until the sixth century A.D. before abolishing completely the rights of greedy uncles. Another case is a mother's right to have a say in

her children's choice of marriage partner. This maternal prerogative became accepted social practice even though Roman law gives women no such right.

Roman slaves married and had children, but they had to do so in the face of both legal and practical obstacles. Roman law gave slaves no right to marry, and it made slave children the property of the owner of the slave mother. Owners could and did break up slave families by sale. Even if a slave was freed, the law expressed far more concern with the continuing obligations of freedmen to their former masters than with the rights of slave families. Yet during the Early Empire cracks appeared in the wall of law that allowed slave families to slip through. (See the box "Reading Sources: Slaves with the Right Stuff.")

For example, although the law insisted a slave be age 30 before being freed, it made an exception for an owner who wished to free a female slave younger than 30 in order to marry her. To take another example, the law conceded that slave children owed devotion and loyalty (*pietas*) to their slave parents.

Career soldiers from at least the time of Augustus on could not marry, probably on the grounds of military discipline. Yet soldiers often cohabited anyhow, often with noncitizen women in the area where they served, and frequently children were the result. Not until the reign of Septimius Severus° (r. 193–211) were soldiers permitted to marry formally, and that only after twenty-five years of service. Yet not only had commanders permitted cohabitation for two centuries, but the law made concessions now and then. For example, the Flavians gave soldiers a degree of freedom to make wills, which could allow them to leave property to illegitimate children. Various emperors gave groups of soldiers the privilege, on discharge, to legalize a marriage with a noncitizen, which was not permitted ordinary Romans.[2]

■ The Culture of the Roman Peace

In Latin poetry the century or so after the death of Augustus is often referred to as the "Silver Age," a term sometimes applied to prose as well. The implication is that this period, though productive, fell short of the golden Augustan era. It might be fairer to say that the self-confidence of the Augustan writers did not last. As the permanence of monarchy became clear, many in the elite looked back to the Republic with nostalgia and bitterness. Silver Age writing often takes refuge in satire or

Satyricon (suh-TEER-uh-con)

Severus (SEH-ver-us)

Slaves with the Right Stuff

In his book On Agriculture, *Columella (first century A.D.) reveals Roman attitudes toward slaves, who he suggests need to be hardened for farmwork after the corruption of city life. He thinks of female slaves as breeding machines and as a restraining influence on male slaves. He opposes cruelty but not chains, if needed.*

A landowner must be concerned about what responsibility it is best to give each slave and what sort of work to assign to each. I advise that you not appoint a foreman from that type of slave who is physically attractive, and certainly not from the type who has been employed in the city, where all skills are directed toward increasing pleasure. This lazy and sleepy type of slave is accustomed to having a lot of time on his hands, to lounging around [waiting for his master at] the Campus Martius [playing fields], the Circus Maximus [race track], the theaters, the gambling dens, the snack bars, and the brothels, and he is always dreaming of these same foolish pleasures. If a city slave continues to daydream when he has been transferred to a farm, the landowner suffers the loss not just of the slave but actually of his whole estate. You should therefore choose someone who has been hardened to farm work from infancy, and who has been tested by experience. . . .

The foreman should be given a female companion both to keep him in bounds and also to assist him in certain matters. . . . He should not be acquainted with the city or the weekly market, except in regard to matters of buying and selling produce, which is his duty. . . .

. . . The foreman should not only be skilled in agricultural operations, but also be endowed with such strength and virtue of mind (at least as far as his slave's personality permits) that he may oversee men neither with laxity nor with cruelty. . . . There is no better method of maintaining control over even the most worthless of men than demanding hard labor. . . . After their exhausting toil, they will turn their attention to rest and sleep rather than fun and games. . . .

It should be an established custom for the landowner to inspect the slaves chained in the prison, to examine whether they are securely chained, whether their quarters are safe and well guarded, whether the foreman has put anyone in chains or released anyone from chains without his master's knowledge. . . .

A diligent master investigates the quality of his slaves' food and drink by tasting it himself. He examines their clothing, hand-coverings, and foot-coverings. He should even grant them the opportunity of registering complaints against those who have harmed them either through cruelty or dishonesty. . . . I have given exemption from work and sometimes even freedom to very fertile female slaves when they have borne many children, since bearing a certain number of offspring ought to be rewarded. For a woman who has three sons, exemption from work is the reward; for a woman who has more, freedom.

Source: Jo-Ann Shelton, *As the Romans Did: A Sourcebook in Social History,* 2d ed. (New York: Oxford University Press, 1998), p. 169.

 For additional information on this topic, go to http://college.hmco.com.

---

rhetorical flourish. Writing under Trajan, for example, the historian Tacitus pours scorn on the Julio-Claudians and Flavians. Other Silver Age writers indulged in flattery and obsequiousness toward the emperor.

The Silver Age was an era of interest in antiquities and in compiling handbooks and encyclopedias, an era of self-consciousness and literary criticism. In the first two centuries A.D., Roman writers came from an ever greater diversity of backgrounds and wrote for an ever wider audience, as prosperity and educational opportunities increased. Consider Lucian (ca. A.D. 115–185), an essayist and satirist. A native of Syria who probably spoke Aramaic before learning Greek, he served as an administrator in Roman Egypt.

Many writers of the era pursued public careers, which offered access to patronage. Tacitus, for instance, rose as high as proconsul of the province of Asia. Prominent literary families emerged, such as that of Pliny° the Elder (A.D. 23–79), an encyclopedic author on natural science, geography, history, and art; and his nephew, Pliny the Younger (ca. A.D. 62–ca. 113), orator and letter writer. The most notable literary family is that of Seneca° the Elder (ca. 55 B.C.–A.D. 40), a historian and scholar of rhetoric; his son, Seneca the Younger (ca. 4 B.C.– A.D. 65); and Seneca the Younger's nephew, the epic poet Lucan (A.D. 39–65).

The family came from Cordoba in Spain. The younger Seneca moved at an early age to Rome, where he became a successful lawyer and wealthy investor. He was well connected enough to be banished in A.D. 41 for alleged adultery with a sister of Caligula. Recalled in 49, he became tutor to the young Nero. When Nero became emperor in 54, Seneca became one of his chief advisers and helped bring good government to the empire. Seneca eventually fell out of favor, however, and was forced first into retirement and then, in A.D. 65, into suicide. He had been the major literary figure of his age, a jack-of-all-trades: playwright, essayist, pamphleteer, student of science, and noted Stoic philosopher.

A literary career was safer under the Five Good Emperors. Consider Tacitus and his contemporary, the poet Juvenal° (ca. A.D. 55–130). Juvenal's *Satires* are bitter and brilliant poems offering social commentary. He lamented the past, when poverty and war had supposedly kept Romans chaste and virtuous. Amid "the woes of long peace," luxury and foreign ways had corrupted Rome, in his opinion. Critics often blame society's troubles on marginal groups. Juvenal, for example, launches harsh attacks on women and foreigners. Tacitus, too, is sometimes scornful of women.

Yet if he is biased on matters of gender, Tacitus was far from ethnocentric. Few historians have expressed graver doubts about the value of their country's alleged success. For example, Tacitus highlighted the simple virtues of the German tribes, so different from the sophisticated decadence of contemporary Rome. Nostalgia for the Republic pervades his two greatest works, *The Histories,* which covers the civil wars of A.D. 69, and *The Annals* (only parts of which survive), chronicling the emperors from Tiberius through Nero. A masterpiece of irony and pithiness, Tacitus's style makes an unforgettable impression on the reader. (See the box on page 178.)

Plutarch° (ca. A.D. 50–120), whose *Parallel Lives of Noble Greeks and Romans* later captured the imagination of Shakespeare, is probably the best-known pagan Greek writer of the first two centuries A.D. Like Livy, Plutarch emphasized the moral and political lessons of history. A careful scholar, Plutarch found his true calling in rhetorical craftsmanship—polished speeches and carefully chosen anecdotes. As in Rome, rhetoric was the basis of much of Greek literary culture in this period.

Another star of Greek culture in this period was the physician Galen° of Pergamum (A.D. 129–?199). In his many writings, Galen was to medicine what Aristotle had been to philosophy: a brilliant systematizer and an original thinker. He excelled in anatomy and physiology, and proved that the arteries as well as the veins carry blood. He was destined to have a dominant influence on European medicine in the Middle Ages.

■ The Crisis of the Third Century, A.D. 235–284

Leaving the relative calm of the second century A.D. behind, the third-century Roman Empire descended into an ever widening spiral of crisis. Barbarian invasions, domestic economic woes, plague, assassinations, brigandage, urban decline: the list of Rome's problems is dramatic. The empire went "from a kingdom of gold to one of iron and rust," as Dio Cassius put it, summing up Roman history after the death of Marcus Aurelius in A.D. 180, when the seeds of crisis were sown.

Stability first began to slip away during the reign of the last of the Antonines, Marcus Aurelius's birth-son, Commodus° (r. 180–192), a man with Nero's taste for decadence and penchant for terrorizing the senatorial elite. His predictable assassination led to civil war, after which Septimius Severus, commander of the Danube armies, emerged as the unchallenged emperor (r. 193–211); he founded the Severan dynasty, which survived until 235.

Severan reformers attempted to re-establish the empire on a firmer footing, but they only brought the day of crisis nearer. The main theme of Septimius's reign was the transfer of power—from the senate to the army and from Italy to the provinces. To extend the Roman frontier in North Africa and western Asia, Septimius expanded the army and improved the pay and conditions of service. These measures might have been necessary, but Septimius went too far by indulging in war with Parthia (197–199)—unnecessary war, because the crumbling Parthian kingdom was too weak to threaten Rome. What

---

Pliny (PLIH-nee) **Seneca** (SEH-neh-kuh)
Juvenal (JOO-veh-nal)

Plutarch (PLOO-tark) **Galen** (GAY-len)
Commodus (KOM-uh-dus)

Hadrian's Wall   Built in A.D. 122–126, this extensive structure protected Roman England from raids by the tribes of Scotland. It represents the strategy of stationary frontier defense.
(Roy Rainford/Robert Harding Picture Library)

the war *did* accomplish, however, was to inspire the enemy's rejuvenation under a new Eastern dynasty, the Sassanids°.

The Sassanid Persians spearheaded increased pressure on Rome's frontiers. The Sassanids overran Rome's eastern provinces and captured the emperor Valerian himself in 260. (See the box "Global Encounters: Syria Between Rome and Persia.") The caravan city of Palmyra (in Syria) took advantage of Rome's weakness to establish independence; its most famous leader was the queen Zenobia. Meanwhile, two Germanic tribes, the Franks and the Goths, hammered the empire from the northwest and northeast.

Fending off invasions at opposite fronts stretched Rome to the breaking point. To pay for defense, the emperors devalued the currency, but the result was massive inflation. As if this were not bad enough, a plague broke out in Egypt in midcentury and raged through the empire for fifteen years, compounding Rome's military manpower problems.

Assassinations and civil wars shook the stability of the government. Between 235—when the last Severan emperor, Severus Alexander, was murdered—and 284, twenty men were emperor, however briefly in some cases. Civilians suffered in the resulting disorder.

Yet the empire rebounded, which is a tribute to Roman resilience as well as a sign of the disunity and lack of staying power among the empire's enemies. Recovery began during the reign of Gallienus (r. 253–268), who ended the Frankish threat and nearly polished off the Goths. By 275, Aurelian (r. 270–275) had defeated the Goths and reconquered the eastern provinces, including Palmyra. Gallienus excluded senators from high military commands and replaced them with professionals. Moreover, he began a new, more modest policy of border defense. The Romans now conceded much of the frontier to the enemy and shifted to a defensive mode: fortified cities near the frontier served as bases from which to prevent deeper enemy penetration into Roman territory.

Sassanid (SASS-uh-nid)

⊕ GLOBAL ENCOUNTERS

Syria Between Rome and Persia

Rome and Persia fought three great battles in western Asia in A.D. 244, 252, and 260, all resounding victories for Persia under King Shapur I (r. ca. 241–272). In the first selection Shapur celebrates his success in an inscription carved in rock near Persepolis. The second selection provides a Greek view of what Syria's inhabitants endured when Shapur "burned, ruined and pillaged" in A.D. 252. It comes from the Thirteenth Sibylline Oracle, *a verse commentary on contemporary events, purporting to be ancient prophecy.*

The Persian Inscription

I, the Mazda worshipping lord Shapur, king of kings of Iran and non-Iran, whose lineage is from the Gods. . . .

When at first we had become established in the empire, Gordian Caesar raised in all of the Roman Empire a force from the Goth and German realms and marched on Babylonia against the Empire of Iran and against us. On the border of Babylonia at Misikhe, a great "frontal" battle occurred. Gordian Caesar was killed and the Roman force was destroyed. And the Romans made Philip Caesar. Then Philip Caesar came to us for terms, and to ransom their lives, gave us 500,000 denars, and became tributary to us. . . .

And Caesar lied again and did wrong to Armenia. Then we attacked the Roman Empire and annihilated at Barbalissos a Roman force of 60,000 and Syria and the environs of Syria we burned, ruined and pillaged all. In this one campaign we conquered of the Roman Empire fortresses and towns . . . a total of 37 towns with surroundings.

In the third campaign when we attacked Carrhae and Urhai [Edessa] and were besieging Carrhae and Edessa Valerian Caesar marched against us. He had with him a force of 70,000. . . .

And beyond Carrhae and Edessa we had a great battle with Valerian Caesar. We made prisoner ourselves with our own hands Valerian Caesar and the others, chiefs of that army, the praetorian prefect, senators; we made all prisoners and deported them to Persis.

And Syria, Cilicia and Cappadocia we burned, ruined and pillaged. . . .

And men of the Roman Empire, of non-Iranians, we deported. We settled them in the Empire of Iran. . . .

We searched out for conquest many other lands, and we acquired fame for heroism, which we have not engraved here, except for the preceding. We ordered it written so that whoever comes after us may know this fame, heroism, and power of us.

The Sibylline Oracle

. . . the evil Persians . . .
. . . the Persians, arrogant men . . .
. . . the arrow-shooting Persians . . .

Now for you, wretched Syria, I have lately been piteously lamenting; a blow will befall you from the arrow-shooting men, terrible, which you never thought would come to you. The fugitive of Rome will come, waving a great spear; crossing the Euphrates with many myriads, he will burn you, he will dispose all things evilly. Alas, Antioch, they will never call you a city when you have fallen under the spear in your folly; he will leave you entirely ruined and naked, houseless, uninhabited; anyone seeing you will suddenly break out weeping. . . .

Alas . . . they will leave ruin as far as the borders of Asia, stripping the cities, taking the statues of all and razing the temples down to the all-nourishing earth.

Sources: Inscription: Richard N. Frye, trans., in his *History of Ancient Iran* (Munich: C. H. Beck'sche Verlagsbuchhandlung, 1984), pp. 371–372. Oracle: D. S. Potter, trans., in his *Prophecy and History in the Crisis of the Roman Empire* (Oxford: Clarendon Press, 1990), p. 175.

They also concentrated mobile armies at strategic points in the rear, moving them where needed.

Gallienus's reforms pointed the way to imperial reorganization, but they remained to be completed by the two great reforming emperors at the end of the third century and the beginning of the fourth: Diocletian (r. 284–305) and Constantine (r. 306–337), subjects of the next chapter. When their work was done, the new Roman Empire of Late Antiquity might have been barely recognizable to a citizen of the Principate.

EARLY CHRISTIANITY

 NCREASING contact between Rome and its western provinces served to plant Roman cities, Roman law, and the Latin language (or its derivatives) in western Europe. As Rome in turn owed much to other Mediterranean peoples, it may be said that the Roman Empire was a vessel that transported ancient Mediterranean civilization to northern and western Europe. No feature of that civilization was to have a greater historical impact than the religion born in Tiberius's reign: Christianity.

Christianity began in the provincial backwater of Palestine among the Jews, whose language, Aramaic, was understood by few in Rome. It immediately spread to speakers of the two main languages of the empire, Greek and Latin, and the new movement addressed the common spiritual needs of the Roman world. By the reign of Diocletian, Christians had grown from Jesus's twelve original followers to perhaps millions, despite government persecution (see Map 6.2). In the fourth century A.D., Christianity unexpectedly became the official religion of the entire Roman Empire, replacing polytheism—one of the most momentous changes in Mediterranean history. We turn to that change in the next chapter; here we consider the career of Jesus and the early spread of the Christian Gospel (literally, "Good Tidings").

■ Jesus of Nazareth

Christianity begins with Jesus. For all its historical importance, Jesus's life is poorly documented. The main source of information about it is the New Testament books of Matthew, Mark, Luke, and John. Jesus left no writings of his own. Early Christians, however, wrote a great deal. Between the second and fourth centuries A.D., Christians settled on a holy book consisting of both the Hebrew Bible, called the "Old Testament" by Christians, and a collection of writings about Jesus and his followers, called the "New Testament." The account of the Gospel According to Mark, probably the earliest Gospel, was most likely written about forty years after Jesus's crucifixion; several of the letters written by Paul of Tarsus (see page 194) date from the 40s A.D.; the earliest non-Christian sources are later in date and are scanty.

No personality has generated as much discussion among Western scholars as has Jesus. Many would distinguish the Jesus of theology, the object of faith, from the Jesus of history, the figure who really lived in first-century Palestine. Recent work argues that the historical Jesus must be understood within the Judaism of his day. He was a product of the popular culture of the Palestinian countryside, a culture that was peasant and oral. Much of what the Gospels have to say about Jesus, some argue, must be rejected as later invention. These are controversial points, but many scholars would agree with one thing: we must be careful to avoid anachronism. By A.D. 200, two new religions had emerged, orthodox Christianity and rabbinic Judaism. Both groups claimed to be the rightful heir of the biblical covenant. They engendered new perspectives that have colored the way Christians and Jews envisage the past before 200. The following account of Jesus seeks a middle ground among today's schools of interpretation.

Jesus was born a Jew. A speaker of Aramaic, he may have also known at least some Greek, widely spoken by both Jews and non-Jews in the several Hellenized cities of Palestine. To his followers, Jesus was Christ—"the anointed one" (from Greek *Christos*), the man anointed with oil and thus marked as the king of Israel. They considered him, that is, the Messiah (from the Hebrew for "anointed one") foretold in the Hebrew Bible who would redeem the children of Israel and initiate the kingdom of heaven. The dynamism and popularity of his teachings led to a clash with Jewish and Roman authorities in Jerusalem, the capital city of Judea, and to his crucifixion. His mission began, however, in a corner of the Jewish world, in the northern region of Galilee°, where he lived in the town of Nazareth° (see inset, Map 6.2).

Jesus was probably born not long before the death in 4 B.C. of Herod, the Roman-installed client-king of Judea. (The date of 1 A.D. for Jesus's birth, a mistaken calculation of Late Antiquity, does not accord with the data of the New Testament.) At around age 30, Jesus was baptized by the mysterious preacher John the Baptist; soon afterward Herod Antipas, the Romans' client-king of

---

Galilee (GAL-uh-lee)   **Nazareth** (NAZ-uh-reth)

Map 6.2   The Expansion of Christianity to A.D. 200   After its origin in Palestine, early Christianity found its main centers in the Greek-speaking cities of the Roman East. Missionaries such as Paul also brought the new faith to the Latin-speaking West, as well as to Ethiopia and Mesopotamia.

Galilee, ordered the execution of John. John had preached that God's kingdom was about to arrive, a time of universal perfection and an end of misery. In preparation, sinful humankind needed to repent. Just how much influence John had on Jesus is a matter of debate, as is the question of John's relationship to the religious community of the Essenes°. Debate may be appropriate, for Judaism in the first century A.D. was in a state of creative disagreement. This era endorsed no one normative Judaism, but rather a variety of Judaisms.

The Essenes lived apart from society in pursuit of a new covenant with God. The community at Qumran° in the Judean desert, whose history is documented in the

Dead Sea Scrolls, ancient texts discovered in 1947, was probably Essene. The tenets of Qumran included frugality, sharing, participating in a sacred communal meal, and avoiding oath-taking. Adherents anticipated the coming of the Messiah and an end of days in which God would punish the wicked. Although Essene doctrine has much in common with early Christianity, early Christians did not withdraw from the world as the Essenes did, but faced it.

There are both similarities and differences between Jesus's teaching and contemporary doctrines of Palestinian Judaism. The most popular group among Palestinian Jews, the Pharisees°, focused on the spiritual needs of

Essenes (ES-seenz)   **Qumran** (koom-RAHN)

Pharisees (FAIR-uh-seez)

The Good Shepherd   This ceiling painting comes from a Christian catacomb in Rome dating before A.D. 284. The pastoral image, common in the early church, recalls Christ's ministry. It symbolizes both his beneficence and his sacrifice, as well as his closeness to ordinary people.
(Scala/Art Resource, NY)

ordinary folk (see page 132). Pharisees believed that law was central to Judaism but argued that it could be interpreted flexibly, in light of the oral tradition that had grown up alongside the written text of the Hebrew Bible. The Pharisees emphasized charity toward the poor. They spoke in parables, vivid allegories that made their teaching accessible.

Jesus argued similarly. Like the Pharisees, moreover, he strongly criticized the pillar of the Jewish establishment, the Sadducees°, the priests and wealthy men who saw the Jerusalem Temple and its rites as the heart of Judaism. Like the Pharisees, Jesus rejected the growing movement of the Zealots°, advocates of revolt against Roman rule, although there were Zealots among his followers. Yet Jesus was neither a Pharisee nor an Essene.

His teaching went further than the Pharisees in rejecting the need to follow the letter of biblical law. Inward purity became the key principle, as reflected in Jesus's statement to his disciples (that is, close followers): "Whoever does not accept the kingdom of God like a child will never enter it" (Mark 10:15). Only an adult could become expert in biblical law, but it is probably easier for a child than for an adult to attain spiritual innocence.

Jesus argued that the kingdom of God, which John the Baptist had said was coming soon, was actually already beginning to arrive. Jesus, moreover, said that he himself, acting through the direct order of God, could forgive sins. He emphasized the notion of God as a loving and forgiving father. Jesus often spoke in parables and announced himself through miracles, particularly faith healing. He welcomed marginalized groups, including prostitutes and lepers.

Sadducees (SAD-yoo-seez)   **Zealot** (ZELL-ot)

Jesus's teaching is typified in the Sermon on the Mount, addressed to his many followers in Galilee. He praised the poor and the humble and scorned the pursuit of wealth instead of righteousness. He called for generosity and forgiveness, recalling the traditional Jewish Golden Rule—to treat others as one would like to be treated. He said that prayer, fasting, and acts of charity should be conducted in private, not in public, in order to emphasize purity of motive. He called on his followers to endure persecution in order to spread his teachings: "You are light for all the world," he told them.

Jesus spoke with conviction and persuasiveness—with "authority," as his followers said. In Galilee they greeted him as king. For some this was a purely spiritual designation; others planned an overthrow of Roman rule, although Jesus rejected that course of action. In any case, his teachings won him hostility from some Pharisees, who considered blasphemous his claim to be able to forgive sins, and from Sadducees stung by his criticisms. Neither group accepted Jesus as the Messiah. It should be emphasized, nevertheless, that most of Jesus's followers were Jewish.

Jesus challenged central authority by going to Jerusalem and teaching and healing in the Temple under the eyes of the priests whom he criticized. Nor did he confine his opposition to words: he drove merchants and money-changers away from the Temple precincts by overturning their tables and perhaps even threatening them with a whip. Jesus attracted large crowds of followers, at least some of whom were armed. Sadducee authorities feared trouble, and so did the overlords of Judea, the Romans. The governor, Pilate (Pontius Pilatus), had already endured vehement Jewish objections to the display in Jerusalem of an imperial medallion and of an inscription that seems to have asserted Augustus's divinity. Pilate had no need of further uproar. Temple police and Roman soldiers were called on to arrest Jesus quietly.

Jesus's subsequent trial and execution have always been controversial. The New Testament emphasizes the role of the Jewish leadership and the Jerusalem mob in Jesus's death. Written after the First Jewish Revolt (A.D. 66–77), however, the Gospels may reflect anti-Jewish sentiment in the empire. Crucifixion, the method used to execute Jesus, was a Roman penalty (the traditional Jewish method was stoning), and Jesus was executed by Romans, not Jews. Jesus probably appeared in informal and hurried proceedings before both the Jewish Council and Pilate. He suffered slow death by crucifixion on Golgotha (Calvary) Hill just outside the city. It was a spring Friday, on the eve of the Passover festival, around A.D. 30.

■ Paul of Tarsus

According to the Gospel writers, Jesus died on a Friday and rose from the dead on Sunday, an event commemorated by Christians at Easter. He is said to have then spent forty days on earth, cheering and commissioning his disciples in Galilee and working miracles, before finally ascending to heaven. Heartened, the disciples returned to Jerusalem and spread Jesus's teachings. They preached in synagogues, private households, and even the Temple, and to Greek-speaking as well as Palestinian Jews. Their movement spread in the thirties and forties A.D. throughout Palestine and into Syria. In Jerusalem Christians were known as Nazarenes—that is, followers of Jesus of Nazareth; it was at Antioch that they were first called "men of Christ" (*christianoi*).

The leaders of the movement were known as apostles, from the Greek *apostolos*, "one who is sent" and who enjoys the authority of the sender. The apostles, that is, believed that Jesus had sent them and given them authority. The apostles included Jesus's twelve original followers or disciples. The most prominent disciple was Peter, a Galilean fisherman whom Jesus endowed with particular authority. After the crucifixion, Peter became a miracle-worker and leading apostle. According to a reliable tradition, he went to Rome, whose church he headed and where he died as a martyr in A.D. 64.

It was not clear at first that Christians would form a new religion separate from Judaism. Although Sadducees and Jewish civil officials were hostile, Christians found much support among Pharisees. Some Christians, however, contemplated a radical break; among them no one was more important than Paul of Tarsus (d. A.D. 67?).

Only Jesus himself played a greater role than Paul in the foundation of Christianity. A remarkable figure, Paul embodied three different and interlocking worlds. Born with the name of Saul, he was a Jew of the Diaspora from the southern Anatolian city of Tarsus. A learned Pharisee, Paul was a native speaker of Aramaic and knew Hebrew and Greek. His father was one of the few Jews to attain Roman citizenship, a privilege that Paul inherited. Paul's heritage speaks volumes about the variety of the Roman peace, and his religious odyssey speaks volumes more (see Map 6.2).

At first Paul joined in the persecution of the Christians, whom he considered blasphemous. Around A.D. 36, however, he claimed to see a blinding light on the road to Damascus, a vision of Jesus that convinced him to change from persecutor to believer. It was a complete turnaround, a *conversio* ("conversion"), to use the

Latin word that would grow so important in years to come. Saul changed his name to Paul and became a Christian.

He also changed what being a Christian meant. The key to Paul's faith was not so much Jesus's life, although that was a model for Christian ethics, as it was Jesus's death and resurrection. Jesus's fate, Paul wrote, offered all humanity the hope of resurrection, redemption, and salvation. Paul retained his belief in Jewish morality and ethics but not in the rules of Jewish law. Following the law, no matter how carefully, would not lead to salvation; only faith in Jesus as Messiah would.

Such doctrines bespoke a break with Judaism, as did Paul's attitudes toward converts. Hellenistic Judaism had long reached out to Gentiles. Some became Jews. Others, scattered throughout the cities of the Roman Empire, were known as "God-fearers"—that is, they accepted the moral teachings of Judaism but refrained from following strict dietary laws, circumcision, and other Jewish rituals. Seneca the Younger, writing in the sixties, complains about the spread of Judaism: "The customs of this accursed race have gained such influence that they are now received throughout the world."[3]

The Jerusalem church baptized converts and considered them Jews, but Paul considered them not Jews but converts in Christ. For Pauline Christians, circumcision, dietary laws, and strict observance of the Sabbath were irrelevant. From the late forties to the early sixties A.D., Paul tirelessly undertook missionary journeys through the cities of the Roman East and to Rome itself. He aimed to convert Gentiles, and so he did; but many of his followers were Hellenized Jews and "God-fearers." (See the box "Reading Sources: Christian Community and Christian Relationships.")

Paul started Christianity on the road to complete separation from Judaism. Events over the next century widened the division. First, while Pauline churches prospered, departing ever more from Jewish customs, the Jerusalem church was decimated. Jewish authorities persecuted its leaders, and after Rome's suppression of the First Jewish Revolt and destruction of the Jerusalem Temple in A.D. 70, the rank and file of Palestinian Jews rallied to the Pharisees. Second, Jews and Christians competing for converts emphasized their respective differences. Third, although many Jews made their peace with Rome in A.D. 70, enough Jewish-Roman hostility remained to lead to uprisings in the Diaspora in 115 and to the Second Jewish Revolt in 132–135. Both were suppressed mercilessly by Rome, and Judaism became ever more stigmatized among Gentiles.

Bereft of the Temple at Jerusalem, Judaism nonetheless continued to prosper as a religion. Indeed, Jewish missionary activities continued, although they did not keep pace with the number of converts gained by Christianity. More striking is the emergence of the rabbis (the religious leaders of the Pharisees) as the mentors of Judaism. Popular among Jews, the rabbis also attracted the Romans because most rabbis opposed revolt. After both A.D. 70 and 135, the Romans made the rabbis responsible for Jewish self-government in Palestine. The rabbis left their mark on history, however, not in administration but in an intellectual movement. Continuing in the tradition of the Pharisees, the rabbis amplified the oral law; that is, they wrote interpretations of the Hebrew Bible that clarified the practice of Judaism. They developed the notion of the "dual Torah," elevating the oral law to equal authority with the written law of the Hebrew Bible. The notion legitimized the rabbis' enterprise, which made it possible for Judaism to evolve flexibly. The basic text of rabbinic Judaism is the Mishnah° (ca. A.D. 200), a study of Jewish law. In rabbinic Judaism lies the basis of the medieval and modern forms of the Jewish religion.[4]

■ Expansion, Divergence, Persecution

Although Jesus's mission was mainly in the countryside, early Christianity quickly became primarily an urban movement. Through missionary activity and word of mouth, the religion slowly spread. It was concentrated in the Greek-speaking East, but by the second century A.D. Christian communities dotted North Africa and Gaul and, beyond Roman boundaries, appeared in Parthian Iraq and in Ethiopia (see Map 6.2).

By around A.D. 200, an orthodox (Greek for "right-thinking") Christianity had emerged. Rooted in Judaism, it was nonetheless a distinct and separate religion that found most of its supporters among Gentiles. A simple "rule of faith," emphasizing belief in one God and the mission of his son, Jesus, as savior, united Christians from one end of the empire to the other. Christianity attracted both rich and poor, male and female; its primary appeal was to ordinary, moderately prosperous city folk. Believers could take comfort from the prospect of salvation in the next world and in a caring community in the here-and-now. Christians emphasized charity and help for the needy, qualities all too often absent in Greco-Roman society. A Christian writer justly described a

---

Mishnah (MISH-nuh)

❧ READING SOURCES

Christian Community and Christian Relationships

Traditionally considered a letter of Paul to the church of Ephesus, the New Testament book of Ephesians is perhaps rather the work of a Pauline Christian in about A.D. 100. As in undisputed letters of Paul, the text emphasizes the union of Jew and Gentile in the new Christian community: a community of spiritual equality but physical hierarchy by age, class, and gender.

Remember then your former condition, Gentiles as you are by birth, "the uncircumcised" as you are called by those who call themselves "the circumcised" because of a physical rite. You were at that time separate from Christ, excluded from the community of Israel, strangers to God's covenants and the promise that goes with them. Yours was a world without hope and without God. Once you were far off, but now in union with Christ Jesus you have been brought near through the shedding of Christ's blood. For he is himself our peace. Gentiles and Jews, he has made the two one, and in his own body of flesh and blood has broken down the barrier of enmity which separated them; for he annulled the law with its rules and regulations, so as to create out of the two a single new humanity in himself, thereby making peace. This was his purpose, to reconcile the two in a single body to God through the cross, by which he killed the enmity. So he came and proclaimed the good news: peace to you who were far off, and peace to those who were near; for through him we both alike have access to the Father in the one Spirit. Be subject to one another out of reverence for Christ.

Wives, be subject to your husband as though to the Lord; for the man is the head of the woman, just as Christ is the head of the church. Christ is, indeed, the saviour of the body; but just as the church is subject to Christ, so must women be subject to their husbands in everything.

Husbands, love your wives, as Christ loved the church and gave himself up for it, to consecrate and cleanse it by water and word, so that he might present the church to himself all glorious, with no stain or wrinkle or anything of the sort, but holy and without blemish. In the same way men ought to love their wives, as they love their own bodies. In loving his wife a man loves himself. For no one ever hated his own body . . . the husband must love his wife as his very self, and the wife must show reverence for her husband.

Children, obey your parents; for it is only right that you should. . . .

Fathers, do not goad your children to resentment, but bring them up in the discipline and instruction of the Lord.

Slaves, give single-minded obedience to your earthly masters with fear and trembling, as if to Christ. Give cheerful service, as slaves of the Lord rather than of men. You know that whatever good anyone may do, slave or free, will be repaid by the Lord.

Masters, treat your slaves in the same spirit: give up using threats, and remember that you both have the same Master in heaven; there is no favouritism with him.

Source: The Letter of Paul to the Ephesians 2:11–17, 5:21–6:9, in *The Oxford Study Bible: Revised English Bible with the Apocrypha* (New York: Oxford University Press, 1992).

pagan's amazed comment on Christian behavior: "Look how they love each other." Most early Christians expected Christ's return—and the inauguration of the heavenly kingdom—to be imminent.

Early churches were simple and relatively informal congregations that gathered for regular meetings. The liturgy, or service, consisted of readings from the Scriptures (the Old and New Testaments), teaching, praying, and singing hymns. Baptism was used to initiate converts. The Lord's Supper, a communal meal in memory of Jesus, was a major ritual. The most important parts of the meal were the breaking and distribution of bread at the beginning and the passing of a cup of wine at the end; these recalled the body and blood of Christ. As organizational structures emerged (see pages 212–213), churches in different cities were in frequent contact with one another, discussing common concerns and coordinating doctrine and practice.

Just as Jewish women were not rabbis, so early Christian women did not hold the priesthood. Jewish women, however, did hold office in the synagogue, and Christian women likewise served as deaconesses. Both endowed buildings and institutions. For example, consider the Italian Jewish woman Caelia Paterna, an officeholder honored by her congregation as "mother of the synagogue of the people of Brescia." Or the two Christian deaconesses, both slaves, whom Pliny the Younger had tortured during his governorship of the Anatolian province of Bithynia (ca. A.D. 110) in an attempt to extract information about the worrisome new cult. Deaconesses played an active part in church charities and counseling and now and then preached sermons.

As Christianity spread, its troubles with the authorities deepened. For one thing, Christians met in small groups, a kind of assembly that conservative Romans had long suspected as a potential source of sedition. More troubling, however, was Christians' refusal to make sacrifices to the emperor. The Romans expected all subjects to make such sacrifices as a sign of patriotism. The only exception was the Jews, who were permitted to forgo the imperial cult because their ancestral religion prohibited them from worshiping idols. The Christians, however, were a new group, and Romans distrusted novelty.

As a result, the emperors considered Christianity at best a nuisance and at worst a threat. Christians were tested from time to time by being asked to sacrifice to the emperor; those who failed to do so might be executed, sometimes in the arena. More often, however, Romans tacitly tolerated Christians as long as they kept their religion private. Christians could not proselytize in public places, put up inscriptions or monuments, or build churches. Christianity thus spread under severe restrictions, but spread it did, particularly in the cities of the East. The willingness of martyrs to die for the faith made a strong impression on potential converts. Although the number of Christians in the empire is not known, it is clear that by the late third century they were, although a minority, a significant and growing one.

■ Mystery Religions

Roman policy toward Christianity by no means reflected an attempt to impose a single, unified religion on the empire. As polytheists, Romans were usually willing to admit new gods to their pantheon, as long as their worshipers took part in the patriotic emperor cult. Roman conservatism, moreover, engendered respect for other peoples' traditional faiths. Although from time to time during Roman history the authorities had tried to expel these faiths from the city of Rome itself, the spread of new religions during the first three centuries A.D. proved irresistible. Besides Christianity and Judaism, the most important were Greek mystery cults, the cults of Isis and Mithras, and Manichaeism. These religions displayed a tendency toward syncretism, often borrowing rites, doctrines, and symbols from one another.

Greek mystery cults included cults of Dionysus, the god of wine, and of Demeter, goddess of grain, who was worshiped at annual ceremonies at Eleusis, a town outside Athens. The "mystery" consisted of secret rites revealed only to initiates. In the case of Demeter, the rites apparently had something to do with the promise of eternal life.

The cult of Isis° derived from the ancient Egyptian cult of Isis (see page 26), her brother and husband, Osiris, and their son, Horus. Its central theme, too, was eternal life, through the promise of resurrection achieved by moral behavior in this life. Isis, the "Goddess of Ten Thousand Names," was portrayed as a loving mother caring for her son; elements of Isis were later syncretized in the cult of the Virgin Mary. Followers of Isis marched in colorful and at times terrifying parades through the streets of Roman cities, flagellating themselves as a sign of penitence.

Although men joined in the worship of Isis, the cult appealed particularly to women. The goddess's popularity crossed class lines; devotees ranged from slaves to one Julia Felix, whose estate at Pompeii included a garden shrine to Isis and Egyptian statuettes. By contrast with the followers of Isis, men, especially soldiers, dominated the worship of Mithras°. Mithras, a heroic Persian god of light and truth, also promised eternal life. His worshipers believed that Mithras had captured and killed a sacred bull whose blood and body were the source of life. Accordingly, Mithraism focused on bull sacrifice carried out in a vaulted, cavelike temple called a *Mithraeum.* Initiates were baptized with bull blood and participated in various other rituals, among them a

---

Isis (EYE-sis)   **Mithras** (MYTH-rus)

Mithraeum   This sculpted relief comes from an underground sanctuary along the Rhine frontier. It shows the hero-god Mithras sacrificing a bull, the central symbol of Mithraism. Actual bull sacrifices were carried out in temples known as Mithraea.   *(Hildesheim Museum/Richard Erdoes)*

sacramental meal. Their moral code advised imitating the life of their hero.

Manichaeism° also originated in Persia, but later, in the third century A.D. The founder, the Persian priest Mani, was martyred by conservative religious authorities. Mani is said to have traveled to India. His cult recognized not only Jesus but Zoroaster and Buddha as

Manichaeism (MAN-ih-kee-izm)

prophets. The main tenet of Manichaeism was philosophical dualism, which emphasized the universal struggle between good (Light) and evil (Darkness). According to believers, the world had been corrupted by Darkness, but eventually the Light would return. In the meantime, good Manichaeans were to attempt to lead pure lives. Manichaeism was a powerful religious force for two centuries; the great theologian Augustine flirted with it before becoming a Christian.

SUMMARY

 B ETWEEN the first century B.C. and the third century A.D., the Romans changed from a people who had come to destroy into a people who had come to fulfill. At the beginning of this period, the conquered provinces were oppressed by greedy bureaucrats and tax collectors, and Rome's imperial victories had nearly ruined the Italian peasantry. The Republic had collapsed under the weight of political maneuvering, judicial murders, gang skirmishes, and civil war.

A shrewd and sickly outsider, Octavian, confounded expectations by creating a new empire that would enjoy two centuries of stability; as Augustus, he served as its first emperor. Augustus reconciled the senatorial class by sharing a degree of power, but he guaranteed peace by keeping most of the armies in his own hand. He wisely reduced military spending and compromised with Rome's enemies to stabilize the frontiers. He solved the problem of rebellious soldiers by raising taxes to provide farms for veterans. Perhaps most important, he began a new policy toward the provinces, which were slowly raised to equality with Italy. In short, Augustus initiated the prosperous Roman peace, an era lasting until the third century A.D. To survive the crises of that century, it was necessary for Rome to maintain a bigger army supported by higher taxes collected by a larger bureaucracy, requirements that would shake the social, political, and cultural foundations of the empire, as Chapter 7 discusses.

Literature and the arts flourished in the peaceful period of the Early Empire. In the provinces, the Roman peace made possible an era of architectural and literary flowering. It was a prosperous era but not for everyone, as slavery remained widespread. Rome was a multi-ethnic empire whose inhabitants increasingly mixed with one another and exchanged ideas. None of these exchanges was more momentous than the emergence of several new religions, one of which would become in Late Antiquity the main religion of the Roman world: Christianity. Without the pax Romana of the Caesars, the Christian Gospel could not have been spread.

■ Notes

1. Mary R. Lefkowitz and Maureen B. Fant, trans., in their *Women's Life in Greece & Rome: A Source Book in Translation,* 2d ed. (Baltimore: Johns Hopkins University Press, 1992), p. 9.
2. This discussion of marriage and law owes much to Susanne Dixon, *The Roman Family* (Baltimore: Johns Hopkins University Press, 1992), pp. 36–60.
3. Seneca, *De Superstitione,* trans. Menachem Stern, in *Greek and Latin Authors on Jews and Judaism,* vol. 1 (Jerusalem: Israel Academy of Sciences and Humanities, 1976), p. 431.
4. On these points, see Lawrence H. Schiffman, *From Text to Tradition: A History of Second Temple and Rabbinic Judaism* (Hoboken, N.J.: Ktav Publishing House, 1991), pp. 1–16.

■ Suggested Reading

Cohen, Shaye J. D. *From the Maccabees to the Mishnah.* 1987. An excellent synthesis of work that sites the origins of both Christianity and rabbinic Judaism in the turbulent Jewish history of this era.

Earl, D. C. *The Age of Augustus.* 1968. A beautifully illustrated introduction to government, society, and religion.

Fantham, Elaine, Helene Peet Foley, Natalie Boymel Kampen, Sarah B. Pomeroy, and H. A. Shapiro. *Women in the Classical World: Image and Text.* 1994. Chapters 10–13 provide an excellent introduction to the social and cultural history of women in the Roman Empire.

Frend, W. H. C. *The Rise of Christianity.* 1984. A thorough and detailed account from the first century B.C. to the sixth century A.D., emphasizing religion in its social context.

Garnsey, Peter, and Richard Saller. *The Roman Empire: Economy, Society, and Culture.* 1987. A thematic rather than chronological introduction by two distinguished social historians.

Luttwak, E. N. *The Grand Strategy of the Roman Empire from the First Century A.D. to the Third.* 1976. A perceptive overview by a nonspecialist of the evolution of strategies of imperial defense from Augustus to the Late Empire.

Wells, Colin. *The Roman Empire.* 2d ed. 1995. A sweeping, lively, and thoughtful overview of the subject from 44 B.C. to A.D. 235.

 For a searchable list of additional readings for this chapter, go to http://college.hmco.com.

Gladiators

Historians and novelists write about them, film makers portray them, revolutionaries salute them, and a few years ago television athletes claimed to be American updates of them. They are gladiators, literally men who carried a *gladius*, or sword. They fought to the death as entertainment, and they enraptured the Roman Empire.

Gladiators took part in so-called games or combat before large crowds. Armed with various specialized weapons, they fought each other and sometimes wild animals. Some unfortunates were thrust into fights with no weapons at all. The audience, seated in rank order, ranged from slaves to senators to the emperor himself. There was nothing tame about what they had come to see. Consider the word *arena*, referring to the site of the games. It literally means "sand," which is what covered the floor, and soaked up the blood.

Our fascination with the gladiator is nothing compared to the Romans'. Everybody in Rome talked about gladiators. At Pompeii, graffiti celebrated a star of the arena whom "all the girls sigh for." Jokes poked fun at gladiators, philosophers pondered their meaning, and literature is full of references.

Gladiatorial images decorated art around the empire, from mosaics to household lamps. Look at this mosaic from a Roman villa in Germany, one of several mosaic panels on the floor of the building's entrance hall, depicting scenes from the arena. The illustration shows a *retiarius*, or net-and-trident bearer, fighting a better-armed *secutor*, literally "pursuer," under the watchful eyes of a *lanista*, or trainer. As was typical, the retiarius wears no armor except for a shoulder-piece protecting his left side. To defend himself against the dagger wielded by the secutor (in the mosaic, hidden behind the shield), the retiarius had to be fit enough to be able to keep moving. The difference between various types of gladiators would have been as obvious to a Roman as the difference between a catcher and a pitcher is to a baseball fan today.

As for the amphitheaters where gladiatorial combats took place, they were as common in Italy and the Roman Empire as skyscrapers are in a modern city. Look, for example, at this photograph of the amphitheater in the city of El Djem in modern Tunisia (the Roman province of Africa). Built of high-quality local stone in the third century A.D., the structure was meant to have sixty-four arches but it was never completed. The openings in the floor permitted animals to be released into the arena. A large amphitheater like this one held at least thirty thousand spectators and the largest amphitheater of all, the Flavian Amphitheater—or Colosseum—at Rome, seated around fifty thousand. Amphitheaters were less common in the East, but the fans there too were loyal so the games went on—in theaters.

Most gladiators were condemned criminals, prisoners of war, or slaves bought for the purpose. The most famous slave gladiator was Spartacus, a Thracian. Along with seventy-seven other gladiators in the Italian city of Capua, Spartacus instigated a slave rebellion that attracted thousands and shook Italy for two years (73–71 B.C.).

Yet some gladiators were free men who volunteered for a limited term of service. Once even the emperor Commodus (r. 180–192) served, to the disgust of other Roman nobles, who found the arena fascinating but low-class. The gladiator was part warrior, part athlete, part showman, and part butcher. Yet there was something of the pagan priest in the gladiator too, for his was a solemn profession. Every gladiator took an oath to endure being burned, bound, beaten, and killed by the sword. They began each combat by greeting the official in charge (in Rome, the emperor): "We who are about to die salute you."

Students of the Romans find it hard to believe that they adored such a murderous sport, in which dozens and occasionally hundreds of men might die in a single day, to the roar of the crowds. Yet perhaps the arena makes us uncomfortable not so much because it is foreign but because it is familiar. Although we no longer flock to games in which men kill each other, we do go in droves to blood sports such as boxing, and we pack hockey rinks to watch men regularly give each other concussions. Modern people no longer kill animals in the arena for sport, but we hunt, fish, go on big-game safaris, watch cock-fights, and, in Spain, kill bulls and occasionally get killed by them.

Besides, perhaps our discomfort reflects our instinctive understanding of the symbolism of the arena. The games were brutal, but so was the empire. Rome had brought peace to three continents, but it had done so by

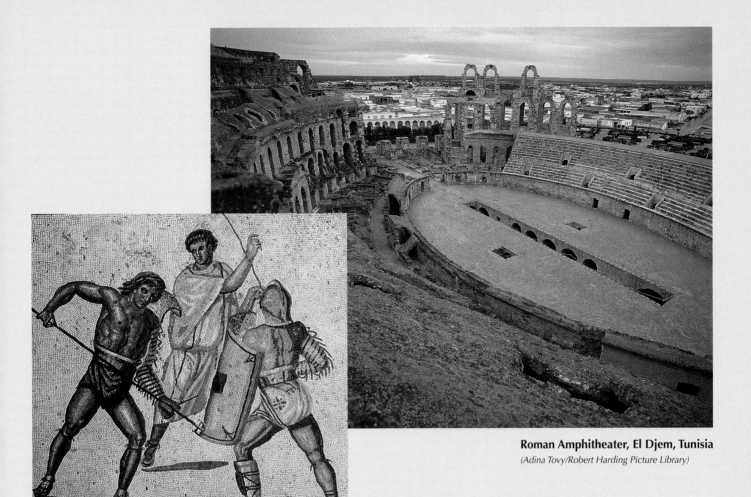

Roman Amphitheater, El Djem, Tunisia
(Adina Tovy/Robert Harding Picture Library)

Gladiator Mosaic, Nennig, Germany
(Bildarchiv Preussischer Kulturbesitz)

brandishing a sword, and it kept the peace by its readiness to fight. The arena kept Romans tough and warlike, or so an intellectual could argue, as does Pliny the Younger, who says that gladiatorial games

> inspired a glory in wounds and a contempt of death, since the love of praise and desire for victory could be seen, even in the bodies of slaves and criminals.
> (*Panegyric* 33)

Arguably the arena also contributed to public order. This was no small achievement since the imperial army could not police a population of 50–100 million, and few places had even the elementary police force that the city of Rome did. The violence that bloodied the amphitheater stepped into the breach by reminding criminals—or those defined as criminals—what punishment awaited them. Rob or kill and you might end up in the arena. Refuse to worship the emperor and you might be fed to the lions, as Christians were from time to time. Rebel against Rome and you might find yourself on a chaingang building a new amphitheater, as tradition says thirty thousand prisoners of the Jewish Revolt (A.D. 66–70) did. The result was the Colosseum.*

Occasionally pagan as well as Christian writers condemned gladiatorial games. Seneca the Younger (ca. 4 B.C.–A.D. 65), for example, criticized them for inciting greed, aggression, and cruelty. Yet gladiators and their games were not abolished until around A.D. 400. And not until A.D. 681 did the Byzantines abolish the feeding of criminals to wild beasts. So popular was Rome's theater of power.

 For additional information on this topic, go to http://college.hmco.com.

---

*The preceding two paragraphs lean heavily on the fine discussion in Colin Wells, *The Roman Empire*, 2d ed. (Cambridge, Mass.: Harvard University Press, 1995), pp. 248–255.

CHAPTER 7

The World of Late Antiquity 284–ca. 600

CONSTANTINE the Great (r. 306–337) erected a huge basilica in Rome that featured his own monumental statue. The surviving head from this statue, itself more than 8 feet tall, is depicted on the left. Statues of earlier Roman emperors tended to be life-size or a bit larger, but Constantine's statue defies all human scale. His expressionless face did not meet the gaze of his subjects. He cared, it seems, nothing for them. His immense size proclaims imperial majesty in the abstract, not the visible presence of a human ruler.

The scale of Constantine's statue is proportionate to this emperor's place in Roman history. Calling himself "the restorer of the Roman Empire," Constantine struggled to solve some of the pressing problems that, as we saw in Chapter 6, were afflicting the empire. He instituted military reforms that paved the way for a massive militarization of public life in the Roman world. He contracted treaties with various barbarian peoples that, in the long run, allowed them to incorporate themselves into, and finally radically transform, the Roman Empire itself. He ended the persecution of Christianity and became a Christian himself, the first emperor to do so. But in granting privileges to the Christian church, he intertwined the Roman regime and the emerging Catholic Church. When Constantine died, the Roman Empire was stronger than it had been for generations. But it was also very different.

The reigns of Constantine and his immediate predecessor, Diocletian (r. 284–305), inaugurate a period that scholars now label "Late Antiquity." For many years educated people, often taking their lead from the elegant and influential *Decline and Fall of the Roman Empire* by the British historian Edward Gibbon (1737–1794), believed

Rebuilding the Roman Empire, 284–395

The Catholic Church and the Roman Empire, 313–604

The Rise of Germanic Kingdoms in the West, ca. 370–530

The Roman Empire in the East, 395–565

Society and Culture in Late Antiquity

Colossal statue of Constantine.
(Scala/Art Resource, NY)

that, beset by insurmountable problems, the Roman Empire "fell" in the fifth century. With that fall, such a view insisted, the glories of classical civilization gave way to the gloom of the "Dark Ages." Today, on the contrary, specialists in the period from roughly 300 to 600 see vigor and achievement. They emphasize continuity and coherence over calamity and collapse. No one denies that the Roman world in 600 was different from the Roman world of 300. But recent scholarship stresses how the Romans themselves created a stable framework for change. No catastrophic time, place, or event marked the "fall of Rome."

From the time of its founding, the Roman Empire had suffered from various structural problems. In particular, the Roman world was vast geographically and diverse in its human and material resources. Changes were inevitable in such a world. This chapter identifies the most important changes that took place while the Roman Empire was evolving into its medieval European, Byzantine, and Muslim successors.

QUESTIONS TO CONSIDER

- What were the most important reforms of Diocletian, Constantine, and their successors, and what roles did those reforms play in saving and in transforming the empire?

- Who were the "barbarians," and what kinds of relations did Romans and barbarians have in Late Antiquity?

- How and why did a Catholic Church emerge in Late Antiquity?

- How did women and men, elites and ordinary people, urban dwellers and farmers, experience continuity and change in Late Antiquity?

TERMS TO KNOW

tetrarchy	barbarian kingship
Edict of Milan	Visigoths
Arianism	Justinian
Council of Nicaea	Hagia Sophia
papacy	Saint Augustine
Monophysitism	Vulgate Bible
monasticism	

REBUILDING THE ROMAN EMPIRE, 284–395

THE third-century Roman Empire had lurched from crisis to crisis. Decisive action was needed if Rome were to survive. The chronic civil wars had to be brought to an end. The army needed to be reformed and expanded to meet new threats on the frontiers. And the economy had to be stabilized to bring in the revenue the government needed for administrative and military reforms. Rome was fortunate in raising up two rulers, Diocletian° and Constantine, with more than fifty years of rule between them, who understood the empire's problems and legislated energetically to address them. Although these rulers thought of themselves as traditional Romans, they actually initiated a far-reaching transformation of the Roman Empire.

■ The Reforms of Diocletian (r. 284–305)

The son of a poor Dalmatian farmer, Diocletian rose through the ranks of the army until he attained a key position in the emperor's elite guards. When the emperor was murdered, the soldiers elevated Diocletian to the imperial office.

In about 293 Diocletian devised a regime that historians call the "tetrarchy°," or rule by four (see Map 7.1). He intended to address both the political instability of the Roman regime and the awesome size and complexity of the empire. First Diocletian decided to divide the empire into eastern and western halves and then selected an imperial colleague for himself. Ruling from Nicomedia, and retaining the position of senior emperor, Diocletian took charge of the wealthy and militarily threatened eastern half of the empire. Diocletian and his colleague each selected a subordinate official who would eventually succeed to the imperial office. The ad-

---

Diocletian (dy-oh-KLEE-shun)

tetrarchy (teh-TRAR-kee)

vantage of the tetrarchy was that it yielded four men of imperial rank who could lead armies and make decisions in political and administrative matters. Diocletian hoped that the tetrarchy would provide orderly succession to the imperial office and promote experienced, respected men.

Historians call the regime instituted by Augustus the "Principate" because the emperors pretended to be the "first citizen" and heir of the republican magistrates even though their real power depended on control of the army. Diocletian abandoned all pretense of being a magistrate. Scholars call his regime the "Dominate" from the Latin *Dominus,* meaning "lord and master." Diocletian adopted Eastern, especially Persian, habits, such as wearing gorgeous clothes and a jeweled diadem, sitting on an elevated throne, rarely appearing in public and then only amid awe-inspiring ceremony, and requiring those who approached to prostrate themselves before him. Diocletian succeeded in enhancing the prestige of the imperial office but did so at the price of making the emperor more remote from his subjects.

Given its size and problems, the Roman Empire was dramatically *under*governed. The empire had some fifty provinces, which varied greatly in size, population, wealth, strategic importance, and degree of Romanization, but the imperial administration was made up largely of aristocratic amateurs and numbered only a few hundred men when Diocletian ascended the throne. Rome had traditionally asked for relatively little from its empire—primarily taxes, military recruits, and loyalty. Local authorities generally did the tax collecting and military recruiting, with little interference from imperial agents.

Diocletian increased the number of officials and doubled the number of provinces by dividing old, large provinces into smaller ones. He then organized groups of provinces into thirteen dioceses and joined the dioceses into four prefectures. Diocletian subordinated each prefecture to a tetrarch and equipped each prefecture with a force of military, legal, financial, and secretarial officials headed by a praetorian prefect. By 350 the number of officers from the provincial to the prefectorial level had risen from a few hundred to thirty-five or forty thousand. Diocletian wished to fill the bureaucracy with trained administrators instead of with wealthy senators and equestrians who viewed government service as a means of enriching themselves and advancing the interests of their families.

Diocletian also attended to Rome's military problems. His major initiative was an attempt to double the size of the army from about 300,000 to 600,000 men, although the final total ended up being only around 450,000. Diocletian also built new forts along the fron-

CHRONOLOGY

284–337	Reforms of Diocletian and Constantine
300–400	Origins and spread of Christian monasticism
325–553	First five ecumenical councils of the Christian church
325–360	Foundation and development of Constantinople
379–395	Reign of Theodosius I, last emperor of a united empire
350s–ca. 600	Age of the Church Fathers
370s–530s	Beginnings of the Germanic kingdoms inside the Roman Empire
410	Visigoths sack Rome
412–418	Visigoths settle in Gaul
430	Vandals begin conquest of North Africa
450–600	Anglo-Saxons settle in Britain
476	Last Roman emperor in the West deposed
481–511	Clovis founds Frankish kingdom
493	Beginning of Ostrogothic kingdom in Italy
408–450	Reign of Theodosius II; consolidation of eastern Roman Empire
440–604	Development of the Roman papacy
527–565	Reign of Justinian I

tiers and improved the roads that supplied frontier defenders. He began the systematic incorporation of barbarians into the army, a step that led to a blurring of the distinction between Romans and barbarians. Military service had long been attractive to people in the empire because it provided Roman citizenship as well as a secure income. After 212, almost every free man in the empire enjoyed automatic citizenship. As a result, mainly noncitizen barbarians living along the frontiers, whose only hope of citizenship was military service, found the army attractive. For a while the army tended to Romanize the barbarians, but as the proportion of barbarian soldiers and officers grew, the culture and ethos of the army began to change.

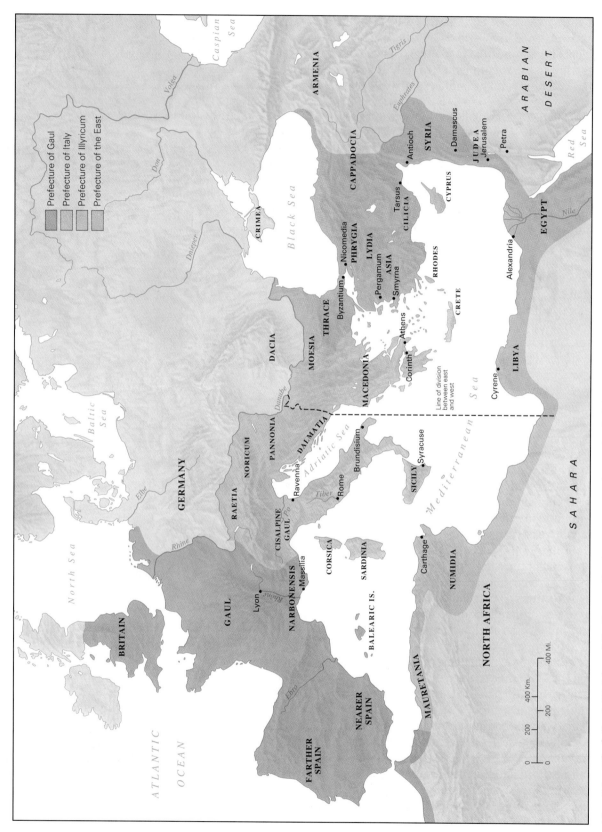

Map labels (on figure):

Caspian Sea · Volga · ARMENIA · Tigris · ARABIAN DESERT · Don · CAPPADOCIA · Euphrates · SYRIA · Damascus · Antioch · JUDEA · Jerusalem · Petra · Red Sea · CRIMEA · Dnieper · Black Sea · CYPRUS · Tarsus · CILICIA · EGYPT · Nile · Nicomedia · PHRYGIA · LYDIA · Pergamum · ASIA · Smyrna · RHODES · Alexandria · Byzantium · CRETE · THRACE · Athens · Mediterranean Sea · LIBYA · DACIA · MOESIA · MACEDONIA · Corinth · Cyrene · Baltic Sea · Line of division between east and west · PANNONIA · DALMATIA · Adriatic Sea · SICILY · Syracuse · GERMANY · NORICUM · Ravenna · Rome · Brundisium · Elbe · RAETIA · CISALPINE GAUL · Po · Tiber · Rhine · CORSICA · SARDINIA · Carthage · NUMIDIA · NARBONENSIS · Massilia · BALEARIC IS. · NORTH AFRICA · SAHARA · GAUL · Lyon · Rhône · BRITAIN · MAURETANIA · NEARER SPAIN · FARTHER SPAIN · Ebro · ATLANTIC OCEAN · North Sea

Legend:
Prefecture of Gaul
Prefecture of Italy
Prefecture of Illyricum
Prefecture of the East

Scale: 400 Mi. · 400 Km. · 200 · 0

Map 7.1 Diocletian's Division of the Roman Empire, 286 Diocletian divided the empire into eastern and western halves; each half was divided into two prefectures. Thus, four regions, rulers, and bureaucratic administrations replaced the ineffective rule of one man.

Diocletian's reforms were expensive and required a predictable income. Thus, Diocletian attempted to regularize the tax system in the empire. The government conducted a census to identify all taxpayers and assessed the productive value of land. To address the mounting inflation of the third century, Diocletian issued in 302 the Edict of Maximum Prices, which froze the costs of goods. Since senators successfully defended their long-standing exemptions from taxes, and the taxation of business ventures remained low, virtually the whole cost of the Roman system continued to fall on agriculture, in particular on small farmers. Diocletian's reform of the tax structure brought in more revenue, but it also caused hardships. A rising tax burden threatened those who were most vulnerable. And with more officials handling vastly greater sums of money, corruption ran rampant. Most people never saw the emperor, but they saw too much of his tax-gouging local minions. (See the box "Reading Sources: A Contemporary View of Diocletian's Reforms.")

The rationale behind Diocletian's reforms is easy to understand; their results were less easy to anticipate. The actions were costly in three unintended respects: moral, social, and economic. The emperors had always been military dictators, but Diocletian removed all pretense that they served at the behest of the Roman people. His frankness may have enhanced the aura of the imperial office, but it also loosened the ties between

Tetrarchy   Ideal and reality are both evident in this sculpture of the tetrarchy. The rulers, depicted equal in size, embrace one another but also bare their weapons—to one another and to the world.
(Scala/Art Resource, NY)

🕮 READING SOURCES

A Contemporary View of Diocletian's Reforms

Historians usually praise Diocletian's reforms, but this passage, from a bitterly hostile Christian writer who hated Diocletian as a persecutor, may actually give the view of the ordinary person.

While Diocletian, who was the inventor of wicked deeds and the contriver of evil, was ruining everything, he could not keep his hands even from God. This man, through both avarice and cowardice, overturned the whole world. For he made three men sharers in his rule; the world was divided into four parts, and armies were multiplied, each of the rulers striving to have a far larger number of soldiers than the emperors had had when the state was ruled by single emperors. The number of those receiving pay from the state was so much larger than the number of those paying taxes that, because of the enormous size of the assessments, the resources of the tenant farmers were exhausted, fields were abandoned, and cultivated areas were transformed into wildernesses. And to fill everything with fear, provinces were cut into bits; many governors and more minor offices lay like incubi [evil spirits] over each region and every municipality, likewise many procurators of revenues, administrators, and deputy prefects. Very few civil cases came before all of these, but only condemnations and frequent confiscations, and there were not merely frequent but perpetual exactions of innumerable things, and in the process of exaction intolerable wrongs.

Whatever was imposed to maintain the soldiery might have endured, but Diocletian, with insatiable avarice, would never permit the treasury to be diminished. . . . When by various iniquities he brought about enormously high prices, he attempted to legislate the price of commodities. Thus much blood was spilled, and nothing appeared on the market, and prices soared still higher. . . . In addition he had a certain endless passion for building, and made no small exactions from the provinces for maintaining laborers and artisans and for supplying wagons and whatever else was necessary for the construction of public works. Here basilicas, there a circus, here a mint, there a shop for making weapons, here a house for his wife, there one for his daughter.

Source: Lactantius, *On the Deaths of the Persecutors*, vii, in *Roman Civilization. Sourcebook II: The Empire*, Naphtali Lewis and Meyer Reinhold, ed. and trans. (New York: Harper and Row, 1966), pp. 458–459.

the ruler and his subjects. By reducing the official duties of the senatorial order, Diocletian alienated an influential group of about two thousand leading citizens. The enlarged imperial administration necessarily impinged on the autonomy of cities and their local leaders, for three centuries the key components of the imperial system. Finally, the expanded administration and army cost dearly in real cash. That cash had to be extracted from an empire that was in serious economic distress.

■ The Reforms of Constantine (r. 306–337)

Diocletian's careful plans for the imperial succession collapsed almost immediately after his voluntary retirement in 305. When Diocletian's western colleague (Constantius

I) died in 306, his troops reverted to the hereditary principle and declared his son, Constantine, emperor. From 306 to 313 as many as six men claimed to be emperor somewhere in the empire. From 313 to 324, Constantine shared rule with one man, and from 324 to 337 he ruled alone over a reunited empire, although he made his sons subordinates in various parts of the empire. This compromise between the hereditary and tetrarchal systems persisted for the next two centuries.

Constantine had entered the imperial court as a young man in 293, when his father was made co-emperor, and he later served with him in Britain and Gaul. He knew the system well and maintained the administrative structure that Diocletian had introduced. Constantine continued the eastward shift of power by creating a second imperial capital in the east. He selected an old Greek city, Byzantium°, and renamed it after himself, "Constantine's polis" or Constantinople (modern Istanbul). Byzantium's location more than its size, wealth, or fame recommended it. The city straddled military roads between the eastern and western halves of the empire, overlooked crucial trade lanes to and from the Black Sea region, and was well sited to respond to threats along both the Balkan and the eastern frontiers (see Map 7.1).

In financial affairs, too, Constantine's work echoed his predecessor's. He issued a new gold *solidus*, the principal money of account in the Roman Empire. This coin promoted monetary stability in the Mediterranean world for nearly a thousand years. Unfortunately, both a stable currency and Diocletian's price controls braked but could not stop the headlong rush of inflation.

In military affairs, Constantine believed that Rome's frontiers stretched too far to be held securely by garrisons so he expanded the use of mobile field armies. These armies, recruited largely (as under Diocletian) from barbarians living along or beyond the frontiers, were stationed well inside the borderlands so that they could be mobilized and moved quickly to any threatened point. They were given their own command structures, under officers whom the Romans called "Masters of the Soldiers." The praetorian prefects were deprived of their military responsibilities and became exclusively civilian officials. The separation of civilian and military command made sense administratively and politically because it meant that no individual could combine the command of an army with the authority of a government post.

Scholars have long debated the strategic and political wisdom of Constantine's arrangements. Moving experienced troops away from the frontiers may have invited rather than deterred attacks. Recruiting barbarians into the field armies and leaving frontier defenses to barbarian auxiliaries may have created divided loyalties and conflicts of interest. Most Roman provincials had not lived near soldiers. Now the soldiers and the veterans of the field armies became daily companions. One certain result of the reforms of Diocletian and Constantine was the militarization of Roman society—the transformation of the Roman Empire into a vast armed camp. The financial resources of that empire were now largely devoted to maintaining an expensive military establishment that was socially diverse and potentially politically volatile.

Byzantium (bizz-AN-tee-um)

Diocletian and Constantine responded with imagination to the third-century crisis. They created a new kind of rulership. The statue of Constantine with which this chapter begins is an indicator of the late antique imperial ideology. Constantine's size in stone serves to emphasize a distance that the viewer cannot articulate but cannot help feeling. The huge statue does not so much depict Constantine as proclaim emperorship. The majesty of Constantine and his long, productive reign, in conjunction with Diocletian's success and longevity, stands in stark contrast to the troubles of the third century. But we may ask, as contemporaries did, whether order was purchased at too high a price in terms of personal freedom.

■ The Fourth-Century Empire: A Fragile Stability

Diocletian and Constantine considered themselves to be Roman traditionalists, but their wide-ranging reforms had actually introduced deep changes in the Roman system. When Constantine died in 337, the Roman Empire was more peaceful and stable than it had been throughout the crisis-ridden third century. But Rome's rulers were now more despotic; Rome's government was bigger, more intrusive, and more expensive; and Rome's military was larger and increasingly barbarian in composition. The open question in 337 was whether Rome would revert to the chaos of the third century or continue along the path marked out by the reforms of Diocletian and Constantine.

Succession to the imperial office remained a troubling issue despite the introduction of the tetrarchy. Constantine had employed a combination of the tetrarchal and dynastic systems. He had three subordinates, all of them his sons. They did not base their activities in the four prefectures, and they succeeded him jointly when he died. Constantine's sons had no heirs of their own, and when the last of them died in 361, the army turned to Julian (331–363), a nephew of Constantine. Julian was a great leader and a man who looked out for his troops. Nevertheless, people were trying to find a legitimate heir to Constantine, not merely a general who would reward the army. (See Table 7.1 for the succession of emperors in the eastern and western empires.)

Julian ruled for only two years before he was killed fighting in Mesopotamia. Because Julian had no heirs, the army controlled the succession. The choice fell on Valentinian (r. 364–375) and his brother, Valens (r. 364–378). Valentinian ruled in the west, his brother in the east. Valentinian established a dynasty that ruled the Roman world for ninety-one years (364–455). In 378, when

Table 7.1
Roman Emperors from Diocletian to Justinian, 284–565

East	West
Diocletian (284–305)	Maximian (285–305, 307–310)
	Constantius I (293–306)
Galerius (293–311)	
	Constantine I (306–337)
Maximinus (305–313)	Severus (306–307)
	Maxentius (307–312)
Licinius (308–324)	
Licincianus (317–323)	
	Crispus (317–325)
Constantius II (324–361)	Constantine II (317–340)
	Constans (333–350)
	Dalmatius (335–337)
Gallus (350–354)	
	Julian (355–363)
Julian (361–363)	Jovian (363–364)
Valens (364–378)	Valentinian I (364–375)
	Gratian (375–383)
	Maximus (383–387)
Theodosius I (379–395)	Valentinian II (383–392)
	Theodosius I (392–395)
Arcadius (395–408)	Honorius (395–423)
Theodosius II (408–450)	John (423–425)
Marcian (450–457)	Valentinian III (425–455)
Leo I (457–474)	Petronius Maximus (455)
	Avitus (455–456)
	Majorian (457–461)
	Libius Severus (461–465)
	Anthemius (465–472)
	Olybrius (472)
	Glycerius (473)
Leo II (474)	Julius Nepos (473–480)
Zeno (474–491)	Romulus Augustulus (475–476)
Anastasius (491–518)	
Justin I (518–527)	
Justinian I (527–565)	

Valens was killed in battle, Valentinian's sons sent their brother-in-law, Theodosius° I (r. 379–395), who had risen through the military ranks in Spain, to the east to restore order.

Until his own death in 395, Theodosius was the most powerful man in the Roman world, and, after his last brother-in-law died in 392, sole ruler. He enjoyed the confidence of the people and the army—the former because he was exceptionally competent and honest and the latter because he was an old military man and a superb general. He divided the empire between his two sons without dynastic or military challenge. His branch of the family lived on until the deaths of Theodosius II in the east in 450 and of Valentinian III in the west in 455. Later rulers of the dynasty sometimes ruled alone, sometimes with chosen colleagues or subordinates. Dynastic and tetrarchal systems were thus blended effectively.

Following the reforms of Diocletian and Constantine, the army was supposed to protect the empire, not play a role in Roman politics. Events proved otherwise. In the 340s the Romans faced a renewed threat in the east from Persia, where an ambitious king sought to revive the glories of his ancestors. The Romans did not take this Persian threat lightly, for they knew that in the Persians they faced an old and formidable foe. In the west, Rome faced one serious challenge from the Visigoths (discussed below). These military provocations inevitably enhanced the role of the army in public life and elevated military concerns over civilian ones. The presence of new threats contributed to the army's prominence in selecting emperors.

The fourth century did not witness the kind of intensive and sustained administrative reforms that characterized the reigns of Diocletian and Constantine. But emperors did introduce many modest measures, some of which had outcomes very different from those intended by their implementers. One example may stand for many.

During his reign, Valentinian I, a soldier raised to the imperial office by the army, wanted to make military careers more attractive and soldiers' lives more comfortable. To achieve these ends, Valentinian proposed to provide soldiers with plots of land and seed grain. He aimed to supplement soldiers' pay, to tie them more securely to a particular region, and to make them more loyal to him. This creative idea complemented earlier military reforms.

Nonetheless, Valentinian's program angered the senators, who were still rich and influential. They agitated

---

Theodosius (thee-oh-DOE-zhus)

Missorium of Theodosius I   Dating from 388, this commemorative plate depicts Theodosius investing an official (the figure just below and to the left of the emperor) with his office. Pictured, too, are Theodosius's imperial colleagues and his Germanic retainers. The overall scene is Classical but the figures are expressionless and eternal (compare Constantine on page 202).   *(Scala/Art Resource, NY)*

against the reform because, they said, the emperor was spending too much time worrying about the army, and he was depriving them of lands they desired. The senators also complained that the new program was expensive, and they were absolutely right. To pay for land and seed, Valentinian had to raise taxes.

Higher taxes were especially unpopular in the cities, where the burden of collecting them fell on the *decurions,* the main local officials who composed the town councils. From the time of Valentinian in the late fourth century, evidence points to a steady decline in loyalty to Rome among these provincial urban elites. Part of Rome's success under the Principate had been directly tied to the regime's ability to win over local elites all over the empire. Now, a military reform whose rationale was clear and defensible actually provoked suspicion and disloyalty among senators and decurions.

When Theodosius died in 395, the Roman world still seemed reasonably secure. The families of Constantine and Valentinian had produced effective rulers. Scattered threats clouded the frontiers, but for the moment conditions appeared stable. Programs of institutional and economic reform continued apace, generally along the lines marked out by Diocletian and Constantine.

In the late fourth century, the empire may have numbered some 50 or 60 million inhabitants. Of these, not more than 5 to 10 million lived in towns. Because Roman government was based on towns, the actual capacity of the Roman administration to keep track of, tax, coerce, and Romanize the population as a whole was limited. Nevertheless, as the Roman Empire became an increasingly militarized state, its towns were being dominated by central authorities as never before, and its rural population was being pressed hard by tax policies necessitated by larger civil and military structures. The reforms of Diocletian and Constantine continued to provide the framework within which these changes took place.

THE CATHOLIC CHURCH AND THE ROMAN EMPIRE, 313–604

 WHILE Rome's rulers were trying to stabilize the state during the fourth century, the empire was experiencing a dynamic process of religious change. The formerly small and persecuted communities of Christians were achieving majority status in the Roman world and building an impressive organizational structure. The Christianization of the empire's population (see Map 7.2), first in towns and then in the countryside, along with the emergence of the Catholic Church were two of the greatest transformations of the ancient world. Still, these changes took place slowly, and with different results in different areas.

■ The Legalization of Christianity

Since the first century, Christianity had been making steady progress throughout the Roman world, and by 300, Christians were living in every province. The Roman Empire was rich in varieties of religious experience, but no pagan cult combined compelling teachings with a sophisticated institutional foundation.

The earliest Christian communities were urban and had three kinds of officials, whose customary titles in English are *bishop, priest,* and *deacon.* Deacons were clearly subordinate to the other two. They were responsible for charitable works and for arranging meetings. Bishops and priests presided at celebrations—most prominently the Eucharist (or Holy Communion as it came to be called)—preached, and taught. Distinctions between bishops and priests developed over time. Depending on

Map 7.2   The Spread of Christianity to A.D. 600   From its beginnings in Palestine (see Map 6.2 on page 192), Christianity, while still illegal, spread mainly in heavily urbanized regions. After Constantine legalized Christianity, the faith spread into every corner of the Roman world.

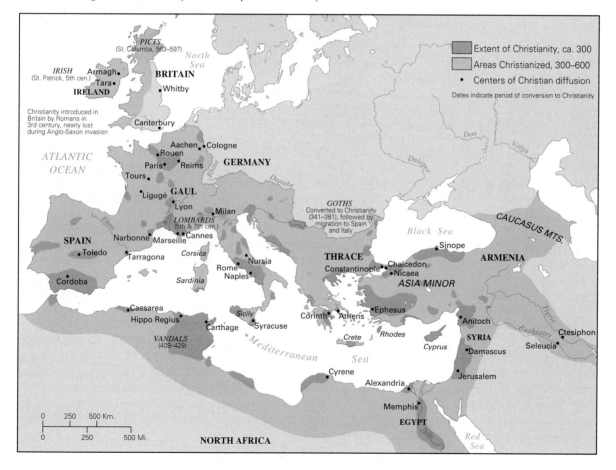

their relative size, towns would have many independent Christian groups, each headed by a priest. By about 200, as a sign of unity and authority, the eldest priest came to be called "overseer," the literal meaning of *bishop.* As more people converted, as the church acquired property, and as doctrinal quarrels began to cause divisions among the faithful, bishops began to be influential local officials. By the late fourth century, the bishops in the major cities of the empire were called *metropolitan bishops,* or sometimes *archbishops,* and they had responsibility for territories often called *dioceses.* In essence, the church was adapting to its own purposes the administrative geography of the Roman Empire.

Diocletian will always be remembered for undertaking the last persecution of Christianity, between 303 and 305. Why did he do it? He was a man of conventional Roman piety, and he was truly convinced that the presence of Christians in the army offended his ancestral gods. The persecution was harsh and well planned. Diocletian ordered churches to be closed and the Scriptures seized. His decrees demanded the arrest of the clergy and required citizens to make sacrifices at a temple. Since Diocletian's agents had trouble enforcing his decrees, it is difficult to gauge the effect of the persecution. It certainly did not eradicate Christianity, and it may even have strengthened the faith by making heroes of its victims, the martyrs whose blood, according to a contemporary, was "the seed of the church."

Unlike Diocletian, Constantine sought to promote the unity of the empire by embracing, not attacking, Christianity. No full explanation has ever been found for the source or depth of Constantine's Christianity. Constantine's mother, Helena, was a Christian. She surely exposed her son to the new faith, but the young Constantine was raised at the court of Diocletian, where he received a traditional pagan upbringing. In 312, while marching toward Rome to fight one of his rivals for the imperial office, Constantine believed that he saw in the sky a cross accompanied by the words, "In this sign you shall conquer." Persuaded, Constantine put chi-rho monograms (the first two letters of *Christos,* "Christ" in Greek) on his soldiers' uniforms and defeated his rival Maxentius at the Milvian Bridge near Rome. Constantine attributed his victory to the God of the Christians. In 313 Constantine and his eastern colleague issued the Edict of Milan, which made Christianity a legal religion in the empire. In the years ahead, Constantine did more than just treat Christianity as the equal of all other religions. He promoted the Christian church, granting it tax immunities and relieving the clergy of military service. He

chi-rho

provided money to replace the books and buildings that had been destroyed in persecutions. He and his mother sponsored vast church-building projects in Rome, Constantinople, and Jerusalem.

Constantine soon discovered that his support of the church drew him into heated disputes over doctrine and heresy. *Heresy* comes from a Greek word meaning "to choose." Heretics are persons who choose teachings or practices that religious or state authorities deem wrong. The first and most widespread heresy arose over the central mystery of Christianity itself: the deity (or "godness") of Jesus Christ.

Christian belief holds that there is one God who exists as three distinct but equal persons: Father, Son, and Holy Spirit. But around 320 a priest of Alexandria, Arius° (ca. 250–336), began teaching that Jesus was the "first born of all creation." Christians had long been stung by the charge that their monotheism was a sham, that they really worshiped three gods. Arianism, as the faith of Arius and his followers is called, preserved monotheism by making Jesus slightly subordinate to the Father. Arianism won many adherents.

Constantine was scandalized by disagreements over Christian teachings and distressed by riotous quarrels among competing Christian factions. Constantine dealt with religious controversies by summoning individual theologians to guide him and by assembling church councils to debate controversies and reach solutions. In 325 at Nicaea°, near Constantinople (see Map 7.2), the emperor convened a council of more than three hundred bishops, the largest council by far that had met up to that date. This was the first of many "ecumenical"—or all-world—councils in church history. The Council of Nicaea condemned Arius and his teaching. The bishops issued a creed, a statement of beliefs, one of whose central tenets maintained that Christ was "one in being with the Father," co-equal, and co-eternal.

By the middle of the fifth century that creed took definitive shape as the "Nicene Creed," which is still recited regularly in many Christian churches. With the Council of Nicaea we can see the first clear evidence that people were striving for a *catholic* form of Christianity. This Greek word means "universal." Strictly speaking, catholic Christianity would be the one form professed by all believers. A fifth-century writer said the catholic faith was the one believed "everywhere, all the time, by everyone."

Religious unity remained elusive, however. The Council of Nicaea's attempt to eliminate Arianism was

---

Arius (AIR-ee-us)   **Nicaea** (ny-SEE-uh)

unsuccessful in the short term. Constantius II (r. 337–361), Constantine's son and successor in the eastern half of the empire, was an avowed Arian, as were some later emperors. For more than forty years, Rome's rulers occasionally embraced a faith that had been declared heretical. It was during this time that the Visigothic priest Ulfilas entered the empire, was converted to Arian Christianity, and returned to spread this faith among his people. Arian Christianity spread widely among the barbarian peoples living along the empire's frontiers. By the time those people began to enter the empire in significant numbers (see pages 219–224), catholic Christianity had triumphed over Arianism, leaving the barbarians as heretics.

One emperor, Constantine's nephew, Julian, called "the Apostate" by his Christian opponents, made a last-ditch attempt to restore paganism during his short reign (361–363). He did not resort to persecution but forbade Christians to hold most government or military positions or to teach in any school. Christianity had only been legalized in 313 but by the 360s it was too well entrenched to be barred from the public sphere, and Julian's pagan revival died with him.

■ The Institutional Development of the Catholic Church, ca. 300–600

The Catholic Church was hierarchically organized under bishops and usually aligned with the imperial government. Whereas individual Christian communities had developed hierarchical structures under their own bishops in the second and third centuries, the growing authority of the bishops of Rome within the church as a whole is the most striking organizational process of the fourth and fifth centuries. But the steadily growing importance of bishops everywhere was a marked feature of the age. Beginning when Constantine called the Council of Nicaea and granted privileges to the church, the Catholic Church's entanglement with the Roman state grew more intense, just as its involvement with the lives of ordinary people expanded dramatically.

From its earliest days the Christian community had espoused the doctrine of *apostolic succession*. In other words, just as Jesus had charged his apostles with continuing his earthly ministry, that ministry was passed on to succeeding generations of Christian bishops and priests through the ceremony of ordination. When one or more bishops laid their hands on the head of a new priest or bishop, they were continuing an unbroken line of clerics that reached back through the apostles to Jesus himself. The bishops of Rome coupled this general notion of apostolic succession with a particular emphasis on the original primacy of Peter, in tradition the leader of the apostles and the first bishop of Rome. The theory of "Petrine Primacy" held that just as Peter had been the leader of the apostles so the successors to Peter, the bishops of Rome, continued to be the leaders of the church as a whole. By the late fourth century the bishop of Rome was usually addressed as "papa," or *pope* in English.

The Roman world continued to experience religious controversies in the years after Nicaea. Attempts to resolve these controversies strengthened the ecumenical council as a regular organ of church government, increased the power of the papacy, and drew emperors more deeply into the public life of the church. What were the religious controversies? We have already met Arianism, and we have seen that despite its condemnation at Nicaea, this heresy persisted. Arianism was the major "Trinitarian" heresy of Late Antiquity. Trinitarian theology tries to explain the relationships among the Father, Son, and Holy Spirit, the three persons of the Trinity. In the fourth century these disputes gave way to "Christological" controversies. Christology is the branch of theology that addresses itself to the relationship between the divine and human natures in Jesus Christ.

In 380 Emperor Theodosius I (r. 379–395), in the hope of imposing religious unity on the battling groups of Christians, issued a decree requiring all Christians to believe as the bishops of Rome. This was essential, Theodosius said, because Peter had transmitted the unblemished faith directly to Rome and Peter's successors had preserved it there. The bishops of Rome took an ambivalent view of Theodosius's actions. On the one hand, they were glad to have the emperor's support. On the other hand, they did not wish for their authority or teaching to rest on imperial decrees. Theodosius's decree reflects the growing power of the bishops of Rome and demonstrates the degree to which the state and the church were becoming intertwined.

The decree itself failed to achieve the unity Theodosius desired. Accordingly in 381 he summoned another ecumenical council in Constantinople. This council again condemned Arianism, which thereafter declined in significance within the empire although it remained vigorous among the barbarian peoples living along Rome's frontiers.

In the fifth century Monophysitism—literally "one-nature-ism"—emerged. Theologians were struggling to find a way to talk about the divine and human natures in Christ. Some emphasized one nature, some the other. Logically either proponent could have been called a

Santa Maria Maggiore   Imagine away the altar canopy and some of the decoration, and this church in Rome is a splendid example of a fifth-century basilica. Note its elegant, harmonious design. Secular buildings of the same time were no longer being built on this scale.   *(Alinari/Art Resource, NY)*

Monophysite°, but true Monophysites stressed the divine over the human nature of Christ. In 451 the eastern emperor Marcian called a new council at Chalcedon° to deal with the issue of Monophysitism. Like his predecessors, the emperor sought unity, and he was willing to let the theologians define the doctrines. At Chalcedon the theologians condemned the Monophysites and pronounced that Jesus Christ was true God and true man—that he had two authentic natures.

Pope Leo I (440–461) had sent representatives to the council bearing his doctrinal formulation. Leo insisted that as the bishop of Rome he had full authority to make decisions in doctrinal controversies. Marcian skillfully

steered Leo's "Tome" to acceptance by the council, but to appease many eastern bishops, who felt that too much authority was being claimed by the pope, the emperor also encouraged the council to assert that the bishop of Constantinople (or patriarch, as he was often called) was second in eminence and power to the bishop of Rome. Leo, the greatest exponent, although not the originator, of the "Petrine theory" of papal primacy, objected strenuously to Chalcedon's procedures. He disliked the prominent role of the emperor, complained that eastern bishops had no right to challenge his doctrinal authority, and particularly opposed the elevation of Constantinople's status. Indeed, Leo said, Rome's position derived from its Petrine succession and not from imperial or conciliar decrees.

Monophysite (muh-NAH-fizz-ite)   **Chalcedon** (KAL-seh-dun)

A generation later Pope Gelasius° I (r. 492–496) sent a sharply worded letter to Emperor Anastasius (r. 491–518), who had intervened in a quarrel between the Catholics and the still numerous monophysites. Gelasius protested the emperor's intervention. He told the emperor that the world was governed by the "power" of kings and by the "authority" of priests. Ordinarily, the pope said, the jurisdictions of kings and priests are distinct. In a controversy between them, however, priestly authority must have precedence because priests are concerned with the salvation of immortal souls whereas kings rule only mortal bodies. Gelasius was telling the emperor to stay out of theology, but he was implying much more. His opposition of the words *power*—meaning mere police power, the application of brute force—and *authority*—legitimacy, superior right—was of great importance. Gelasius elevated the church, with the pope at its head, above the whole secular regime with the emperor at its head. Despite his lofty claims, Gelasius had no means of coercing emperors. Moreover, many clergy in the eastern Mediterranean refused to accept the idea that the pope had supreme authority in either doctrine or church government.

The pontificate of Pope Gregory I "the Great" (r. 590–604) exemplifies the position of the papacy as Late Antiquity drew to a close. Gregory was the scion of an old senatorial family. He had risen through several important positions in the Roman administration but then decided to abandon public life, sell off his family's property, and pursue a life of spiritual retreat. Soon, however, the Roman people elected him pope. His reputation for holiness was important to his election but so too were his impeccable social credentials and wide political connections. Rome was threatened by the Lombards (a barbarian group who had entered Italy in the 560s), the local economy was in a shambles, and relations with the imperial government had been strained. Gregory did not wish to be elected pope, but given his conventional Roman sense of duty and obligation, he had little choice but to accept the office. Immediately he undertook dangerous diplomatic measures to ward off the Lombard threat. He also tried hard to improve relations with the emperor. And he put the local economy on reasonably sound footing. He reorganized the vast patrimonies of the church to place their products and revenues at the disposal of the Romans. In the absence of effective imperial administration in and around Rome, Gregory also began to attend to urban services and amenities: streets, aqueducts, baths.

By 600, then, the bishops of Rome—the popes—viewed themselves as the heads of a universal, a catholic, church. Many members of the clergy disputed that view. Some simply disagreed with specific papal teachings. Others claimed that Jesus had given his authority equally to all the apostles and not uniquely to Peter, and thus to Peter's successors. Emperors, too, rejected papal overreaching. After all, they had always claimed for themselves authority in all aspects of their subjects' lives, religious affairs included. By 600, however, there were no longer emperors in the West and the eastern rulers had few means of controlling the bishops of Rome. For their part, the bishops of Rome were gradually focusing their efforts on the western regions of the old Roman world.

The rise of the pope in the church as a whole was paralleled by the rise of bishops throughout the empire. By the last years of the fourth century, various ranking members of the social elite were everywhere entering the clergy and rising to its highest offices. This capture of the elite was the final, decisive factor in the triumph of Christianity.

The clergy was an outlet for the talents and ambitions of the elite. For some time, senators had been excluded from military offices and reduced in civilian influence, and decurions were growing dissatisfied with public service. The *episcopal* office (that is, the office of bishop) was desirable to prominent men for many reasons. It was prestigious. Bishops wore distinctive clothing when officiating and were addressed by special titles—traditional Roman marks of respect. They had opportunities to control patronage in the way that prominent Romans always had done. They could intervene on behalf of individuals at the imperial court. They came to control vast wealth, as the generosity of pious Christians put more resources at their disposal. Communities elected their own bishops, and by the middle of the fifth century the dominant person in most towns was the bishop, not a civilian official. The bishops, however, were the same persons, from the same families, who had once dominated local society through civic service. The overall affect of these social changes was dramatic in the long run, but it happened very gradually.

The change from a secular to an ecclesiastical elite in Roman cities even led to alterations of the topography of the cities themselves. The elite usually financed local building projects, such as temples, basilicas, forums, and amphitheaters. Such benefactions declined sharply during the third century because of the uncertainty of the times. The fourth century at first saw little building on private initiative, but then came the construction of Christian cathedrals (a bishop's church, from *cathedra*,

---

Gelasius (jul-LAY-zee-us)

the chair or seat of the bishop's authority), episcopal residences, baptisteries, and local parish churches. Such buildings as a rule were not placed in the old city centers, which had associations with the pagan past. Instead, they were placed away from town centers and on the edges of populated districts. In the future, these Christian centers served as poles around which ancient towns were reconfigured. The Roman elites built to show pride in their cities and to promote themselves. This did not change in Late Antiquity, but this time the elites were bishops or rich Christians, and the buildings were religious.

■ The Rise of Christian Monasticism

For some men and women the call of the Gospel was radical. They yearned to escape the world and everything that might come between them and God. To do so, many of them embraced a new way of life—monasticism. Christian monks and nuns developed a theology and an institution that were among the most creative and long-lived achievements of Late Antiquity.

The practice of rigorous self-denial (*askesis*) was common to several religious and philosophical sects in antiquity—for example, the Pythagoreans and the Stoics—and was well known among the Jews in the time of Christ, as the Essenes show (see page 192). Ascetics believed that if they could conquer the desires of the body, they could commune with the supernatural beings who were greater and purer than humans encumbered by lust for food, drink, knowledge, sex, and adventure. Sometimes ascetic practices were adopted by tightly knit groups, sometimes by heroic solitaries.

The founder of Christian monasticism was a young Egyptian layman, Anthony (d. 356). At 19, Anthony gave away all his possessions and took up in the Egyptian desert a life of prayer and renunciation. His spiritual quest became famous, and many disciples flocked to him. Finally, he decided to organize these seekers into a very loose community: the followers remained in solitude except for worship and meals. Anthony's form of monasticism is called *eremitic,* from the Greek *heremos* for "desert," hence the word *hermit.*

Pachomius° (290–346) created a more communal form of monastic life. A former Roman soldier, he was baptized a Christian in 313 and retired to the Egyptian desert, where he studied with a hermit. Eventually Pachomius founded a community of ascetics, which before long had grown to thousands of members. Perhaps be-

cause of his military background, or because his religious instincts favored order and unity, Pachomius wrote the first Rule, or code for daily living, for a monastic community. He organized most aspects of his community by designing a common life based on routines of private prayer, group worship, and work. By the time of his death Pachomius led nine male and two female communities. Pachomius's pattern of monasticism is called *cenobitic°*, from the Greek for "common life." People living this common life were called *monks,* and the place where they lived this orderly life was called a *monastery.* The head of the community was designated *abbot,* a word meaning "father." In later times the term *abbess,* meaning "mother," was coined for the woman who led a female community, and those communities of nuns came to be called convents.

Monasticism spread from Egypt by means of texts such as the *Life of Anthony* (a late antique "best-seller"), collections of the wise sayings of famous desert abbots, and books written by persons who went to Egypt seeking a more perfect life—among whom were several prominent women. (See the box "Reading Sources: Melania the Younger: The Appeal of Monasticism to Women.") One attraction of monasticism among the devout was that it seemed to be a purer form of Christian life, uncorrupted by the wealth, power, and controversy of the hierarchical church. Many pious women embraced monasticism at least partly because they could not be ordained priests. Positions in monasteries, including that of abbess, provided responsible roles for talented women. Monasticism gave women a chance to choose a kind of family life different from the one available in households dominated by fathers and husbands.

Eremitic monasticism was prominent in Palestine and Syria and eventually throughout the Greek-speaking world. Eastern monasticism produced a great legislator in Basil (330–379), whose Rule was the most influential in the Orthodox Church (for this term, see page 231). Generally these monks assembled only for weekly worship and otherwise ate, prayed, and worked alone.

Eremitic monasticism arrived in the West in the person of Martin of Tours (336–397). Like Pachomius, Martin was a pagan Roman soldier who, after his military service, embraced both Christianity and asceticism. Even though he was elected bishop of Tours, Martin kept to his rigid life of denial. Martin's form of monasticism influenced many in the western regions of the Roman world but struck especially deep roots in Ireland. There

---

Pachomius (pack-OH-mee-us)

cenobitic (sen-oh-BIT-ik)

ஒ READING SOURCES

Melania the Younger: The Appeal of Monasticism to Women

The appeal of monasticism was great for men and women, rich and poor, as the career of Melania (383–438) shows. She came from a wealthy Roman family but renounced her possessions and traveled widely in Italy, North Africa, Egypt, and Palestine, visiting holy men and women. These selected passages from her biography provide glimpses of her life.

Melania was foremost among the Romans of senatorial rank. Wounded by divine love, she had from earliest youth yearned for Christ, and longed for bodily chastity. Her parents, because they were illustrious members of the Roman senate and expected that through her they would have a succession of the family line, forcibly united her in marriage . . . when she was fourteen and her husband, seventeen. [After having two children, Melania persuaded her husband to join her in renouncing the world.] She bridled nature and delivered herself to death daily, demonstrating to everyone that woman is not surpassed by man in anything that pertains to virtue, if her decision is strong. She was by nature a gifted writer and wrote without mistakes in notebooks. She decided for herself how much she should write every day, and how much she should read in the canonical books and in the collections of homilies. Then she would go through the Lives of the fathers as if she were eating dessert. The blessed woman read the Old and New Testaments three or four times a year. The most holy fathers [Egyptian abbots] received her as if she were a man. In truth, she had been detached from the female nature, and had acquired a masculine disposition, or rather, a heavenly one.

Source: Elizabeth A. Clark, ed. and trans., *The Life of Melania the Younger*, cc. 1, 12, 23, 26, 39, *Studies in Women and Religion*, vol. 14 (New York: Edwin Mellen Press, 1984), pp. 27–28, 35, 46, 53–54.

the whole organization of the church was based on monasteries. At Kildare the abbess Brigid (d. 523) had more authority than the local bishop.

In the West cenobitic monasticism became the dominant pattern. Benedict of Nursia (480–545) abandoned his legal studies and a potential government career to pursue a life of solitary prayer in a mountain cave east of Rome. Benedict's piety attracted a crowd of followers, and in about 520 he established a monastery at Monte Cassino, 80 miles south of Rome. The Rule he drafted for his new community is marked by shrewd insights into the human personality. It emphasizes the bond of mutual love among the monks and obedience to the abbot. The Rule assigns the abbot wide powers but exhorts him to exercise them gently. The Rule allows monks a reasonable diet and decent, though modest, clothing. Although providing for discipline and punishment, the Rule prefers loving correction. In later centuries Benedict's Rule dominated monastic life.

Eremitic or cenobitic, East or West, monasticism was a conscious alternative and an explicit challenge to the civic world of classical antiquity. Monks and nuns did not seek to give their lives meaning by serving the state or urban communities. They went into remote places to serve God and one another. They sought not to acquire but to abandon. Spiritual wisdom was more important to them than secular learning, and they yearned for acknowledgment of their holiness not recognition of their social status.

At the dawn of Late Antiquity, the church was persecuted and struggling. By the end of the period, the church was rich and powerful, its leaders were prominent and prestigious, and in the monasteries at least, its spiritual fervor deep. This change was gradual but fundamental.

THE RISE OF GERMANIC KINGDOMS IN THE WEST, CA. 370–530

THE years from the 370s to the 530s were decisive in the history of the Roman Empire in the west. When this period opened, the dynasty of Valentinian was firmly in control. When it closed, the western provinces of the empire had become a number of Germanic kingdoms, most of which maintained some formal relationship with the eastern Roman Empire. Roman encounters with the barbarians took many different forms ranging from violent conflict to peaceful accommodation. The key point to understand is that although the barbarians supplanted Roman rule in the West, they did so slowly and often with Roman permission and assistance.

■ Invasions and Migrations

Few images of the ancient world are more fixed in the popular imagination than the overrunning of the Roman Empire by hordes of barbarians who ushered in a dark age. The Romans inherited the word *barbarian* from the Greeks, who had divided the world between those who spoke Greek and those who did not. Barbarians were literally babblers, foreigners who spoke an unknown language. After the Romans granted citizenship to virtually everyone in the empire in 212, they adopted a Greek-style differentiation between Romans and barbarians. Technically, the latter were merely foreigners, but in practice Romans thought barbarians inferior to themselves.

Individual groups of barbarians did invade the empire in various places at different times, but there was never a single, coordinated barbarian invasion of the Roman world that had well-formulated objectives. The Romans and barbarians did not face one another as declared enemies. Indeed, peaceful encounters outnumbered violent confrontations in the history of Romano-barbarian relations. The Romans had long traded with the barbarian peoples, carried out complicated diplomacy with them, and recruited them into their armies. Barbarian veterans were settled in most provinces of the empire.

If we cannot label one grand movement as "the barbarian invasions," we must also avoid the idea that the barbarians were naturally nomadic and migratory. Holding this view would tempt us to see the entry of the barbarians into the empire as one stage in a long process of human movement. Archaeological evidence collected to date makes it clear that the barbarians were settled agriculturalists. They lived in villages, farmed the surrounding country, and raised livestock. If barbarians moved

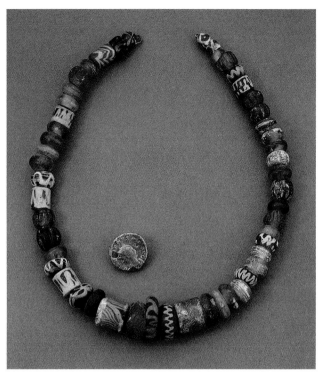

Frankish Woman's Necklace   This sixth-century "choker" necklace consists of brightly colored beads of glass, amber, amethyst, and rock crystal. The Franks were accomplished glassmakers, and this necklace provides some insight into women's taste.   *(Staatliche Museen zu Berlin, Museum für Vor- und Frühgeschichte/Bildarchiv Preussischer Kulturbesitz. Photo: Klaus Goken)*

from one place to another, their movement must be explained with reference to specific developments and cannot be attributed to migratory habits.

Who were the barbarians? Linguists classify them as belonging to the Germanic branches of the Indo-European family of languages. The Germanic peoples can be differentiated from the Celts and Slavs with whom they shared much of central and eastern Europe, but apart from some minor linguistic variations, it is difficult to distinguish one Germanic group from another. What are we to make of the profusion of names offered to us by our sources: Franks, Saxons, Vandals, Visigoths, Ostrogoths, Lombards, Burgundians? The Romans referred to the Germanic peoples as tribes, but that does not mean that they were actually groups of related people. Every Germanic "tribe" was a confederation, and these confederations formed, dissolved, and re-formed many times. For example, the Visigoths who crossed the Danube in 376 included Visigoths proper and more than a half-dozen other peoples. The confederations were formed either by powerful leaders who coerced less powerful people to join them or by groups of villages that banded together to protect themselves from aggressive neighbors. As a tribe was forming, its constituent peoples would intermarry and adopt the language, law, and lifestyle of the dominant group.

■ Incorporating the Barbarians

The transformation of the western Roman Empire began as a result of an unexpected set of events involving the Huns, nomadic warriors from the central Asian steppes. After plundering the frontiers of Persia and China for centuries, they turned west in search of booty and tribute. In 374 or 375 they fell on the Ostrogoths, who lived near the Black Sea, and frightened the Visigoths, who requested permission to cross the Danube and enter the empire.

Recent years had been difficult for the empire. Julian had fallen in battle with the Persians in 363, and dynastic quarrels were disturbing the West. The Romans thus delayed responding to the Visigoth request. Fearful of the Huns, the Visigoths crossed the Danube on their own and then asked if they might settle in the Balkans. Reluctantly, Valens° (r. 364–378) acceded but postponed permanent arrangements. While the central government considered how to deal with the Visigoths, local authorities sold them food at exorbitant prices and even traded dog meat for Gothic children, who were then enslaved. When the Visigoths revolted, Valens foolishly marched north to meet them with a small force. The Visigoths defeated his army and killed him at Adrianople in 378.

The history of the Visigoths thus presents an instructive example of Romano-Germanic relations. They had served as auxiliary troops entrusted with defending a stretch of the Danube frontier for a long time when they requested permission to enter the empire in 376. They did not cross the border as part of a massive invasion but because they were themselves sorely threatened. In 382 Theodosius, whom we have met several times already, marched east to pacify the situation. He agreed to grant the Visigoths what they had been demanding: land to settle on and a Roman military title—that is, official status—for their king. A spokesman for Theodosius explained the emperor's motives: "Which is better: To fill Thrace with corpses or with farmers? To fill it with graves or with people? To travel through wilderness or cultivated land? To count those who have perished or those who are ploughing?" For decades, barbarians had been settling inside the Roman frontiers, and they had served loyally in the army. Beginning in the fourth century, most

high military officers in the Roman world were barbarians. The only peculiarity about the Visigoths' situation was that never before had the Romans admitted a whole people.

For about thirty years the Visigoths struggled to improve the terms of their settlements in the Balkans. Alaric°, the Visigothic king after 395, grew tired of unfulfilled promises and forced matters by attacking Italy. In 410 the Visigoths sacked Rome. The taking of the city for the first time in eight hundred years shocked the entire Roman world, and has loomed large for centuries in people's ideas about the "fall" of the Roman Empire. Actually, it was a ploy by Alaric to improve the terms of his already official status. Alaric died in 410 and his brother led the Visigoths north into southern Gaul. For good measure, the new Visigothic king captured the western emperor's sister, Galla Placidia, and forced her to marry him. However objectionable this act must seem, the Visigoths viewed it as a further demonstration of their loyalty to Rome and their determination to effect a satisfactory new treaty.

In 418 the Roman government gave in. A new treaty permitted the Visigoths to settle in southern Gaul, with Toulouse as their base of operations. They were assigned the task of protecting the area from marauding bands of brigands. In return for their service, the Visigoths were given land allotments and a portion of Roman tax receipts as pay.

The Visigoths' treaty with Rome made theirs the first Germanic kingdom on Roman soil. From 418 to 451 the Visigoths' king, Theodoric I, served Rome loyally and earned the respect of the Gallo-Roman aristocrats among whom he ruled. Between 466 and 484, the Visigothic kingdom in Gaul reached its high point and continued to receive official recognition from Roman rulers. Southern Gaul, one of Rome's oldest provinces, gradually passed from the hands of the Roman bureaucracy and the local nobility into the control of the Visigoths. Nevertheless, from Constantine's first treaty with the Visigoths through the continuing recognition by the Romans of Visigothic kings, it was Roman policy more than Visigothic policy that determined the accommodation of this first Germanic kingdom within the framework of the western Roman Empire.

While they were dealing with the Visigoths, the Roman authorities realized that the Huns, who had settled in the Danube basin after driving the Visigoths into the empire, were a serious menace. They raided the Balkans, preyed on trade routes that crossed the region, and demanded tribute from the eastern emperor. In 434 the

---

Valens (VAY-lenz)   **Alaric** (AL-uh-rik)

Two Views of the Huns

The dread and disgust inspired by the Huns is well captured in the first passage, from the Roman historian Ammianus Marcellinus, while the second passage, from a surviving fragment of the history of Priscus, shows the Huns in quite a different light.

(a)

From the moment of their birth they make deep gashes in their children's cheeks, so that when in due course hair appears its growth is checked by the wrinkled scars; as they grow older this gives them the unlovely appearance of beardless eunuchs. They have squat bodies, strong limbs, and thick necks, and are so prodigiously ugly and bent that they might be two-legged animals. Their shape, however disagreeable, is human. They have no use for seasoned food, but live on the roots of wild plants and the half-raw flesh of any animal, which they warm a little by placing it between their thighs and the backs of their horses. They have no buildings to shelter them. They wear garments of linen or of the skins of field-mice stitched together. Once they have put their necks into some dingy shirt they never take it off or change it until it rots and falls to pieces. They have round caps of fur on their heads, and protect their hairy legs with goatskins. They are ill-fitted to fight on foot, and remain glued to their horses, hardy but ugly beasts, on which they sometimes sit like women to perform their everyday business and they even bow forward over their beasts' narrow necks to enjoy a deep and dreamy sleep.

(b)

[The Roman ambassadors] came upon a very large village in which the dwelling of Attila was said to be more notable than those elsewhere. It had been fitted together with highly polished timbers and encircled

with a wooden palisade, conceived not for safety but for beauty. Next to the king's dwelling that of Onegisus [chief minister to Attila] was outstanding, and it also had a circuit of timbers but was not embellished with towers in the same way as Attila's. Not far from the enclosure was a large bath. . . . Maidens came to meet Attila as he entered this village, advancing before him in rows under fine white linen cloths stretched out to such a length that under each cloth, which was held up by the hands of the women along either side, seven or even more girls walked. There were many such formations of women under the linen cloths, and they sang Scythian songs. When he [Attila] came near the house of Onegisus, the wife of Onegisus came out with a host of servants, some bearing dainties and others wine, greeted him and asked him to partake of the food which she had brought for him with friendly hospitality. To gratify the wife of his intimate friend, he ate sitting on his horse, the barbarians accompanying him having raised the silver platter up to him. Having also tasted the wine, he went on to the palace, which was higher than the other houses and situated on a high place.

Sources: Excerpt (a): Ammianus Marcellinus, *The Later Roman Empire (A.D. 354–378)*, ed. and trans. Walter Hamilton (Harmondsworth, England: Penguin, 1986), 31.2, pp. 411–412. Excerpt (b): Priscus, Fragment 8, in C. D. Gordon, *The Age of Attila: Fifth-Century Byzantium and the Barbarians* (Ann Arbor: University of Michigan Press, 1961), pp. 84–85.

fearsome warrior Attila murdered his brother and became sole ruler of the Huns. In return for a huge imperial subsidy, he agreed to cease raiding in the Balkans. At the same time, a Roman general in Gaul concluded an alliance with the Huns in an attempt to use them to check the expansion of the Burgundians, an allied people who lived in the central Rhineland.

Together Attila and the Romans routed the Burgundians, but Attila realized the weakness of the Roman position in the west. He attacked Gaul in 451 and was stopped only by a combined effort of Romans, Visigoths, Burgundians, and Franks. Attila turned to Italy in 452, even approaching Rome, where Pope Leo I, not the emperor, convinced, or bribed, him to withdraw. Attila died in 454, and before another year was out, the short-lived Hunnic kingdom, largely Attila's personal creation, had vanished. (See the box "Global Encounters: Two Views of the Huns.")

■ More Kingdoms: The End of Direct Roman Rule in the West

To meet threats in Gaul and elsewhere, the Romans had begun pulling troops out of Britain in the fourth century and abandoned the island to its own defense in 410. Thereafter, raiding parties from Scotland and Ireland, as well as seaborne attackers—called "Saxons" by contemporaries because some of them came from Saxony in northern Germany—ravaged Britain. The British continually appealed to the military authorities in Gaul for aid, but to no avail. Between 450 and 600, much of southern and eastern Britain was taken over by diverse peoples whom we call the "Anglo-Saxons." The newcomers jostled for position with the Celtic Britons, who were increasingly confined to the north and west of the island. Gradually several small kingdoms emerged. Although Britain retained contacts with Gaul, the island had virtually no Roman political or institutional inheritance.

Valentinian III (r. 425–455) was born in 419 and became emperor of the West as a 6-year-old. Even when he came of age, his court was weakened by factional strife, and his regime was dominated by military men. After Valentinian the western empire saw a succession of nonentities, the last of whom was deposed by Odoacer°, a Germanic general, in 476. Ruling in Italy, Odoacer simply sent the imperial regalia to Constantinople and declared that the West no longer needed an emperor. This is all that happened in 476, the traditional date for the "fall" of the Roman Empire.

After the vast coalition defeated the Huns in Gaul in 451, the remaining Roman authorities in the Paris region discovered that the Visigoths were expanding north of the Loire River into central Gaul. To check this advance, the Roman commander in Paris forged an alliance with the Franks. The Franks, long Roman allies, had been expanding their settlements from the mouth of the Rhine southward across modern Holland and Belgium since the third century.

The fortunes of the Frankish kingdom, indeed of all of Gaul, rested with Clovis. He became king of one group of Franks in 481 and spent the years until his death in 511 subjecting all the other bands of Franks to his rule. He gained the allegiance of the Frankish people by leading them to constant military victories that brought territorial gains, plunder, and tribute. The greatest of Clovis's successes came in 507, when he defeated the Visigoths and drove them over the Pyrenees into Spain.

Clovis was popular, not only with the Franks but also with the Gallo-Roman population, for three reasons. First, Clovis and the Romans had common enemies: Germanic tribes still living beyond the Rhine and pirates who raided the coast of Gaul. Second, whereas most of the Germanic peoples were Arian Christians, the majority of the Franks passed directly from paganism to Catholicism. Thus, Clovis and the Gallo-Romans had a shared faith that permitted Clovis to portray his war against the Visigoths as a kind of crusade against heresy. Third, Clovis eagerly sought from Constantinople formal recognition and titles, appeared publicly in the dress of a Roman official, and practiced such imperial rituals as distributing gold coins while riding through crowds. The Frankish kingdom under Clovis's family—called "Merovingian°" from the name of one of his semilegendary ancestors—became the most successful of all the Germanic realms.

Several early Germanic kingdoms were short-lived. The Burgundian kingdom that had once prompted the Romans to ally with the Huns was swallowed up by the Franks in the 530s. The Vandals, who crossed the Rhine in 406 and headed for Spain, crossed to North Africa in 429 (see Map 7.3). They were ardent Arians who persecuted the Catholic population. They refused imperial offers of a treaty on terms similar to those accepted by other Germanic peoples. And they constantly plundered the islands of the western Mediterranean and the Italian coast, even sacking Rome in 455. Roman forces from Constantinople eliminated the Vandals in 534.

The Ostrogoths, allies who had been living in Pannonia since the 370s as subjects of the Huns, began to pose a threat to the eastern empire after Attila's death. In 493 the emperor decided to send them to Italy to remove Odoacer, who had earned the displeasure of the Roman administration by laying hands on the sentimentally significant land of Italy—and doing so on his own initiative instead of the emperor's directive. The government at Constantinople was familiar with the Ostrogoths' king, Theodoric, because he had been a hostage there for several years. The emperor also wished to remove the Ostrogoths from the Danube basin. Sending Theodoric to Italy seemed like a way to solve two problems simultaneously.

Theodoric ousted Odoacer quickly enough and set up his capital in Ravenna°, the swamp-surrounded and virtually impregnable city that had sheltered the imperial administration for much of the fifth century after the

---

Odoacer (OH-doe-ace-er)

Merovingian (mehr-oh-VIN-jun)   **Ravenna** (rah-VEN-nuh)

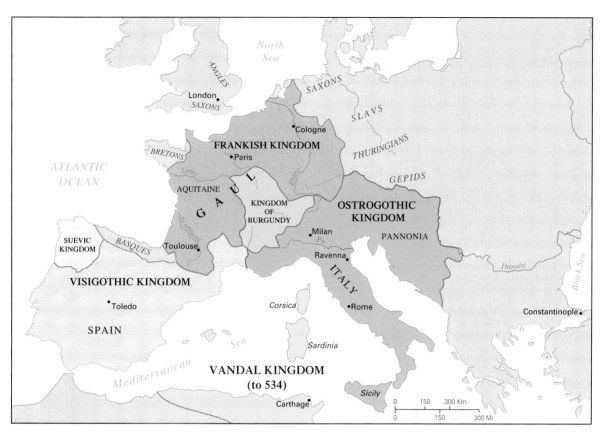

Map 7.3   The Germanic Kingdoms, ca. 530   By 530 the western provinces of the Roman Empire (compare Map 6.1 on page 176) had evolved into Germanic kingdoms. Just as Roman provincial boundaries had changed numerous times, the existence and extent of Germanic kingdoms were also impermanent.

Visigothic attack had exposed the weakness of Rome's defenses. Through the force of his personality, and by a series of marriage alliances, Theodoric became the dominant ruler in western Europe. In Italy he promoted peace, stability, and good government. Still, Theodoric had two strikes against him. One, he and his people were Arians. Two, although the population of Italy was accustomed to having an imperial court dominated by barbarians and to having Germanic military men in Gaul as the real powers in the state, they had never been directly ruled by a barbarian, and some of them could not accept Theodoric. By the 520s Theodoric grew increasingly suspicious and dictatorial. After he died in 526, the government in Constantinople launched an attack on Italy that put an end to the Ostrogothic kingdom but also devastated Italy in twenty years of brutal warfare.

By the 530s the western Roman Empire had vanished, the conclusion of a process initiated by the entry of the Visigoths into the Balkans in 376. Of all the peoples who had contested for a share of Rome's legacy, only the Franks in Gaul, the Visigoths in Spain, and the Anglo-Saxons in Britain had created durable political entities. Most of two prefectures with their several dozen provinces had turned into a small number of kingdoms (see Map 7.3).

Why did the Roman government perish in the West? Beginning with Diocletian, Rome's best rulers were resident in and concerned mainly about the East. The Visigoths and other peoples were settled in their own kingdoms on Roman soil instead of being enrolled in and dispersed among Roman army units. Also during Diocletian's rule, the army was increasingly Germanized, and Germanic military men gained high offices in the state. Those leaders often dominated imperial courts and negotiated the series of treaties that submitted former provinces to barbarian peoples. Provincial elites had long

Amalasuntha, Daughter of Theodoric   This ivory plaque (ca. 530) depicts Amalasuntha in the way that Roman consuls and emperors had long been depicted on their assumption of office. Since the late fifth century, empresses had been depicted this way, too. Amalasuntha projects an image of legitimacy. Compare her appearance with that of Theodora on page 227. *(Kunsthistorisches Museum, Vienna)*

been accustomed to having prominent Germans in their midst. The new situation was not unusual to them. Churchmen readily embraced the Catholic Franks and tolerated Arians, such as the Visigoths, when they promoted peace and good government without abusing the Catholic population.

■ Old and New in the West

The Germanic kingdoms had a great deal in common with one another and very much resembled the late Roman Empire, which had been their common tutor. Each realm was led by a king who usually appeared in two distinct guises. To his people, the king was the military leader. The essential bond of unity among each Germanic people was loyalty to the leader, who repaid his followers in booty, tribute, land, legal protection, and military security. To the Romans, the king appeared as an ally and magistrate. Almost all Germanic kings bore Roman titles such as *consul* or *patrician,* and in these officially conferred titles resided the authority necessary to govern Roman populations. The kings also succeeded to a long line of Germanic Masters of the Soldiers, the title of the highest military officers in a prefecture. Each monarchy was led by a dynasty—for example, the Merovingians among the Franks—that was pre-eminent in wealth and possessed a sacral aura not unlike that of the Roman emperors.

The most common local officials were counts, a combined civilian-military position that made its first appearance in the fifth century. Initially a direct representative of the emperor, a count had financial, judicial, and military responsibilities. Local notables, usually great landowners, initially resented counts but gradually aspired to the office. Kings were careful to promote important locals, both Romans and their own people, to the office of count.

Local administration remained based in cities and towns. Taxes continued to be paid to royal governments throughout the sixth century. Provincial populations did not find this policy odd or unjust. Their taxes had always gone primarily to pay for the Roman military establishment, and the monarchies were the heirs of that establishment. Latin persisted as the language of administration. Until the end of Late Antiquity, notaries continued to draw up wills, records of land transactions, and legal documents of all kinds. Law codes issued by the Germanic kingdoms were largely adaptations of Roman provincial law. In other words, the legal conditions under which most people lived changed little. In sum, people's daily lives changed surprisingly little as a result of the replacement of Roman provinces by Germanic kingdoms.

THE ROMAN EMPIRE IN THE EAST, 395–565

HE creation of the tetrarchy at the end of the third century had separated the eastern and western halves of the Roman Empire administratively. In theory there was only one empire, ruled by one senior emperor, but in practice the eastern and western courts followed different policies in many areas, notably in their relations with the Germanic peoples. Fundamental cultural differences also distinguished East from West. The East was more populous, more heavily urbanized, and more prosperous. The eastern Mediterranean was Greek in culture and livelier intellectually than the West. From Diocletian in the third century to Justinian in the sixth, the eastern Roman Empire evolved slowly along the path marked out by its first great reformers. Moreover, the eastern empire survived as the western empire was being parceled out into kingdoms.

■ Constantinople and Its Rulers

Constantius II (r. 337–361), Constantine's son and his successor in the East, began making Constantinople a truly imperial city. He gave "New Rome" its own senate and urban magistrates, placing the city on an equal constitutional footing with Rome. Constantinople did not have an ancient aristocracy, so Constantius had to create a senatorial order. This he did by recruiting some Romans and promoting prominent and cultivated persons from cities in the eastern half of the empire, thereby forging bonds between the capital and its hinterland. Constantius and his successors also built palaces, public buildings, and churches to give the city a truly imperial character (see Map 7.4).

With the exception of the founder, the ablest members of the dynasty of Valentinian ruled in the East. The greatest of these was Theodosius II (r. 408–450), who enjoyed the longest imperial reign in Roman history. Through skillful diplomacy and the occasional application of force, he managed to keep the eastern empire free of serious Germanic incursions and the Persians at bay in Mesopotamia. To protect his capital on the landward side, he built massive walls whose ruins are impressive even today. Along with his wife and his sister, he promoted learning in the city and both added and beautified important buildings. Theodosius and his family made the new capital a real intellectual center.

Theodosius's greatest achievement was his law code of 438. The most comprehensive collection of Roman law yet produced, this code brought together all Roman laws issued since Constantine and arranged them in systematic fashion. The principal Germanic kingdoms were established just after the Theodosian code was issued. From this text, and from the Roman institutional structures that employed it, the barbarians were taught the rule of law and regulations for the conduct of daily affairs.

■ Emperor Justinian (r. 527–565)

After Theodosius II died in 450, the eastern empire endured seventy-seven years of rule by military men who lacked the culture, vision, or administrative capacity of their predecessors. But they preserved the empire and kept its government functioning. It was from these rough soldiers that Justinian emerged to become the greatest ruler of Late Antiquity, one of the greatest of all Rome's emperors. (See the feature "Weighing the Evidence: The Ravenna Mosaics" on pages 236–237.)

Justinian was born in an Illyrian village (Croatia, today), entered the army, and secured high office under his illiterate uncle Justin, who had likewise risen from the peasantry to the imperial office (518–527). Despite growing up in rural military camps, Justinian showed a wide range of interests and abilities. He surrounded himself with remarkable people and gave them considerable latitude. He flouted convention by marrying the actress Theodora (d. 548). A woman of intelligence, imagination, and great courage, Theodora was one of Justinian's key advisers. Justinian identified and promoted such previously obscure figures as the gifted general Belisarius°, the administrative genius John the Cappadocian, and the greatest legal mind of the age, Tribonian°. He entrusted two mathematicians, Anthemius° of Tralles and Isidore of Miletus, with the task of designing the church of Hagia Sophia, which remains his principal monument.

Almost immediately on assuming the throne, Justinian put John the Cappadocian to work reforming an administration that had been little altered in two centuries despite vast changes in the scope of the empire. John worked particularly to secure tighter control of provincial administrators, to ensure a steady flow of tax revenue, and to eliminate official corruption. Tribonian and

Belisarius (bel-uh–SAR-ee-us)   **Tribonian** (tree-BONE-ee-un)
Anthemius (an-THEE-mee-us)

Map 7.4   Constantinople in Late Antiquity   Protected by the sea, the Golden Horn, and its massive landward walls, Constantine's new city was an impregnable fortress for a thousand years. Note how the city was equipped with palaces, forums, wide thoroughfares, and other urban amenities.   *(Source: The Cambridge Illustrated History of THE MIDDLE AGES, edited by Robert Fossier, translated by Janet Sondheimer. Copyright © 1989. Used by permission of Cambridge University Press.)*

a commission were assigned the task of producing the first comprehensive collection of Roman law since that of Theodosius II in 438. Between 529 and 533, Justinian's code was issued in three parts. The *Code* was a systematically organized collection of all imperial legislation. The *Digest* was a collection of the writings of the classical Roman jurists, the legal philosophers of the Early Empire. The *Institutes* was a textbook for law students. (See the box "Reading Sources: Basic Principles of Roman Law.") Justinian's code is the most influential legal collection in human history. It summarized a thousand years of legal

work, remained valid in the eastern empire until 1453, and has subsequently influenced almost every legal system in the modern world.

Not long after undertaking his legal and administrative reforms, Justinian launched an ambitious attempt to reunite the empire by reconquering its lost western provinces. Belisarius retook Africa from the Vandals and Italy from the Ostrogoths. Justinian also landed an army in Spain to attempt to wrest Iberia from the Visigoths. However, he never had the resources to carry out this daunting task successfully.

Justinian's ability to sustain major campaigns in the west was limited by the need to ward off constant threats in the east. The empire faced new enemies—Bulgars and Slavs—in the Balkans and a resurgent old foe—the Persians in Mesopotamia. Costly treaties and humiliating subsidies bought a string of cease-fires but no definitive settlements in these areas. The emperor's campaigns were so expensive that his administrative reforms wound up looking like contrivances to make more money for the emperor to waste. In 532 violent mobs coursed through the streets of Constantinople demanding the dismissal of John the Cappadocian and other imperial agents. Justinian almost fled but Theodora persuaded him to put down the riot. In 542 the Mediterranean world was visited by the most devastating plague in centuries, one more blow to the empire.

Justinian's religious policy also met with sharp opposition. A genuinely pious man, Justinian legislated frequently on behalf of the church and, along with Theodora, practiced generous charitable benefactions. Still, by both personal conviction and a sense of official duty, Justinian desired religious unity. Justinian was mildly Monophysite, and his wife was enthusiastically so. Justinian tried again and again to find a compromise that would bring all parties together. His church council of 553 assembled amid high hopes, but his proposed doctrinal compromises alienated the clergy in Syria, Egypt, and Rome.

To create a monument equal to his lofty vision of the empire, Justinian sought out Anthemius and Isidore. He charged the two great mathematicians to design a church that would represent the place where heaven and earth touched. Regular meetings in this place of the emperor, the patriarch, and the people gave repeated symbolic confirmation of the proper ordering of the state. There is no evidence that Justinian dictated the form of

Theodora   This magnificent sixth-century mosaic from Ravenna (it is one of a pair; see page 237) depicts Empress Theodora in all her power and majesty.   *(Scala/Art Resource, NY)*

Basic Principles of Roman Law

Roman law is distinguished not only by its particular rules but also by its approach to the subject of law as a whole. These words are from the beginning of Justinian's Institutes, *his lawbook for students.*

Justice is an unswerving and perpetual determination to acknowledge all men's rights. Learning in the law entails knowledge of God and man, and mastery of the difference between justice and injustice. . . . The commandments of the law are these: live honorably; harm nobody; give everyone his due. There are two aspects to the subject: public and private. Public law is concerned with the organization of the Roman state, while private is about the well-being of individuals. [Private law] has three parts, in that it is derived from the law of nature, of all peoples, or of the state. The law of nature is the law instilled by nature in all creatures. It is not merely for mankind but for all creatures of the sky, earth and sea. From it comes intercourse between male and female, which we call marriage; also the bearing and bringing up of children. Observation shows that other animals also acknowledge its force. The law of all peoples and the law of the state are distinguished as follows. All peoples with laws and customs apply law which is partly theirs alone and partly shared by all mankind. The law which each people makes for itself is special to its own state. It is called "state law," the law peculiar to that state. But the law which natural reason makes for all mankind is applied the same everywhere. It is called the "law of all peoples" because it is common to every nation. The law of the Roman people is also partly its own and partly common to all mankind. . . . The name of a particular state, Athens for example, is used to identify its state law. Similarly we refer to the law of the Roman people as the Roman state law. By contrast, the law of all peoples is common to all mankind. The reality of the human condition led the peoples of the world to introduce certain institutions. Wars broke out. People were captured and made slaves contrary to the law of nature. By the law of nature all men were initially born free. Nearly all the contracts come from this law of all peoples: sale, hire, partnership, deposit, loan, and many others. Next, our law is either written or unwritten. . . . Written law includes acts, plebeian statutes, resolutions of the senate, imperial pronouncements, magistrates' edicts, and answers given by jurists. . . . Law comes into being without writing when a rule is approved by use. Long-standing custom founded on the consent of those who follow it is just like legislation. . . . The law of nature, which is observed uniformly by all peoples, is sanctioned by divine providence and lasts forever, strong and unchangeable. The law which each state establishes for itself is often changed either by tacit consent of the people or by later legislation.

Source: Peter Birks and Grant McLeod, ed. and trans., *Justinian's Institutes*, 1.1–2 (Ithaca, N.Y.: Cornell University Press, 1987), pp. 37–39.

 For additional information on this topic, go to http://college.hmco.com.

his church—the church of Hagia Sophia° ("Holy Wisdom")—but the fact that he did not turn to any of the city's regular builders suggests that he was not looking for a traditional basilica.

Hagia Sophia was the largest Christian church ever built. The building begins with a square just over 100 feet on a side, 70 feet above which are four great arches. Two of the arches are solid and form the nave walls of the church; the other two give way to semicircular continuations of the nave. Above the main square is a dome that seems to float on the blaze of light that pours through its windows. The inside is a riot of color achieved by marble fittings in almost every imaginable hue and by the mysterious play of light and shadow. The effect of the whole is disorienting. Space in most basilicas is ordered, controlled, elegant. Space in Hagia Sophia is horizontal and vertical, straight and curved, square and round. The inside is by turns dark and light, purple and green, red and

---

Hagia Sophia (AYE-yuh so-FEE-yuh)

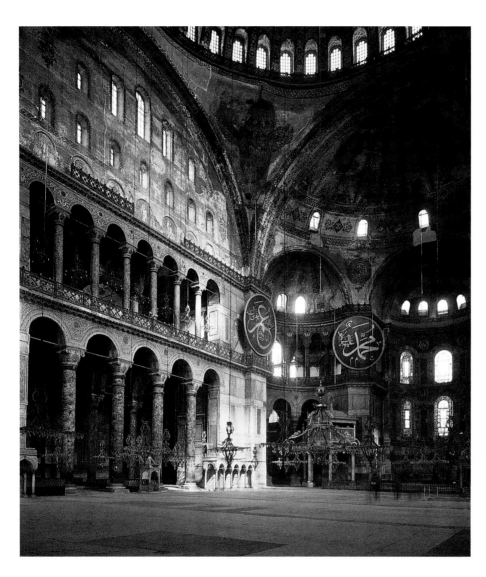

Hagia Sophia   This interior view of Hagia Sophia conveys some sense of the dazzling complexity of this greatest of all late antique buildings. Compare it to Santa Maria Maggiore (page 215).
(Giraudon/Art Resource, NY)

blue. It is indeed as if one has entered a realm that is anchored to this world but that gives access to another one. When Justinian first saw his church in its completed state, he said, "Solomon, I have outdone thee."

It is appropriate that in assessing his great church Justinian should have looked backward to Solomon, the Hebrew king who built Jerusalem's Temple. In almost all respects Justinian was a traditional, backward-looking ruler. His concern for the administrative minutiae of his empire would have made perfect sense to Diocletian. His combination of military and diplomatic initiatives would have been appreciated by Theodosius I, whose namesake, Theodosius II, would have admired Justinian's legal code. In his religious policies, especially in his quest for unity, Justinian drew from a deep well of imperial precedent. Even in his attempt to restore direct rule in Rome's former western provinces, Justinian showed himself a traditionalist.

SOCIETY AND CULTURE IN LATE ANTIQUITY

DURING these centuries of the ascendancy of the eastern Roman Empire, and the splintering of the western, the daily lives of men and women of every social class changed relatively little in terms of power relationships and economic opportunities. Nevertheless, provincial elites, members of the clergy, and barbarians gained unprecedented influence. Ordinary farmers, the overwhelming majority of the population, experienced changes in their legal status but not in their material well-being. Secular intellectual life lost most of its vitality, but a vibrant Christian culture flourished in the writings of the Church Fathers. Christianity added yet another element to the diversity that always characterized the Roman world.

◼ Social Hierarchies and Realities

Roman society had long been hierarchical, and from Republican times Rome had been governed by a hereditary class. Although the members of this class affected a style of life that set them apart, they were never a closed caste. First, they did not reproduce themselves very effectively. About two-thirds of the Roman aristocracy was replaced every century—a typical pattern in premodern societies. This turnover created significant opportunities for social mobility. Second, just as the empire had been born in a social transformation that brought the Italian aristocracy into the Roman governing class, so Late Antiquity was characterized by a transformation that brought provincial elites and barbarians into the framework of power. Paradoxically, social change was always masked as social continuity because when new men reached the top, they tried to embrace the culture and values of those whom they had replaced.

Three ideals guided the lives of elite men: *otium, amicitia,* and *officium. Otium,* leisure, meant that the only life worth living was one of withdrawal in which the finer things of life—literature, especially—could be cultivated. *Amicitia,* friendship, implied several things. It could mean the kinds of literary contacts that the thousands of surviving letters from Late Antiquity reveal. Friendship could also mean patronage. The doorstep of every noble household was crowded every morning with hangers-on who awaited their small offerings and any commands as to how they might do their patron's will. *Officium,* duty, was the sense of civic obligation that Roman rulers communicated to the provincial upper classes.

Aristocrats governed in both public and private ways, which are almost impossible to differentiate. Though gradually excluded from key military and administrative posts, nobles did not lose their influence. They used their wealth to win or reward followers, bribe officials, and buy verdicts. In towns decurions controlled local market privileges, building trades, police forces, fire brigades, and charitable associations. Their public and private means of persuasion and intimidation were immense. In the West, in the growing absence of an imperial administration, Roman public power did not so much "decline and fall" as find itself privatized and localized. Patronage and clientage in Roman society had a benevolent dimension, but they also revealed the raw realities of power.

In Roman society power was everything and those who lacked power were considered "poor," regardless of their financial status. On this reckoning, much of the urban population was poor because they lacked access to the official means of coercion and security that the nota- bles enjoyed. Merchants, artisans, teachers, and others were always vulnerable because their social, political, or economic positions could change at a moment's notice. They lacked the influence to protect themselves.

Most citizens of the late antique world can be classed as farmers, but this categorization is misleading because it lumps together the greatest landowners and the poorest peasants. Late Antiquity saw a trend in the countryside that continued into the Middle Ages: freedom and slavery declined simultaneously. Many small, independent farmers, probably people who had long been the clients of local grandees, handed over their possessions—*commended* them is the technical term— and received back the use of them in return for annual rents in money or in kind. They became *coloni,* tenants. Their patrons promised to protect them from lawsuits or from severe economic hardship. More and more, these coloni were bound to their places of residence and forced to perform services or pay fees that marked their status as less than fully free. At the same time, many landlords who could no longer afford to house, feed, and equip slaves gave them their freedom and elevated them to the status of coloni. Probably the day-to-day lives of the great mass of the rural population changed very little, and their position at the bottom of the social hierarchy did not alter.

Women's lives are not as well known to us as men's. "Nature produced women for this very purpose," says a Roman legal text, "that they might bear children and this is their greatest desire." Ancient philosophy held that women were intellectually inferior to men; science said they were physically weaker; and law maintained that they were naturally dependent. In the Roman world women could not enter professions, and they had limited rights in legal matters. Christianity offered women opposing models. There was Eve, the eternal temptress through whom sin had fallen on humanity, and then there was Mary, the virginal Mother of God. The Bible also presented readers with powerful, active women, such as Deborah and Ruth, and loyal, steadfast ones, such as Jesus's female disciples. Amid this varied popular and learned opinion, we can still detect some possibilities for independent and influential activity on the part of women.

Girls usually did not choose their marriage partners. Betrothals could take place as early as age 7 and lawful marriages at 12. Most marriages took place when the girl was around 16; husbands were several years older. A daughter could reject her father's choice only if the intended man was unworthy in status and behavior. Women could inherit property from their fathers and retained some control over their marital dowries. Divorce was possible but only in restricted cases. A divorced woman who had lost the financial security provided by her husband and father was at a distinct disadvantage legally and economically unless she had great wealth.

Christianity brought some interesting changes in marriage practices. Since the new faith prized virginity and celibacy, women now had the option of declining marriage. The church at Antioch supported three thousand virgins and widows. Christian writers tried to attract women to the celibate life by emphasizing that housework was drudgery. Christianity required both men and women to be faithful in marriage, whereas Roman custom had permitted men, but not women, to have lovers, prostitutes, and concubines. Christianity increased the number of days when men and women had to abstain from sex. Ancient cultures often prohibited sexual intercourse during menstruation and pregnancy but Christianity added Sundays and many feast days as forbidden times. Further, Christianity disapproved of divorce, which may have accorded women greater financial and social security, although at the cost of staying with abusive or unloved husbands.

Traditionally, women were not permitted to teach in the ancient world, though we do hear of women teachers such as Hypatia of Alexandria (355–415), renowned for her knowledge of philosophy and mathematics. Some Christian women, such as Melania (see page 218), were formidably learned. Until at least the sixth century the Christian church had deaconesses who had important responsibilities in the instruction of women and girls. Medical knowledge was often the preserve of women, particularly in areas such as childbirth, sexual problems, and "female complaints."

Christianity also affected daily life. Churchmen were concerned that women not be seen as sex objects. They told women to clothe their flesh, veil their hair, and use jewelry and cosmetics in moderation. Pious women no longer used public baths and latrines. Male or female, Christians thought and lived in distinctive new ways. All Christians were sinners, and so all were equal in God's eyes and equally in need of God's grace. Neither birth nor wealth nor status was supposed to matter in this democracy of sin. Theological equality did not, however, translate into social equality.

The church also introduced some new status distinctions. Holiness became a badge of honor, and holy men and women became Late Antiquity's greatest celebrities. After their death they were venerated as saints. Sanctuaries were dedicated to them, and people made pilgrimages to their tombs to pray and seek healing from physical and spiritual ailments. Miracle stories became popular. Thus, in some ways Christianity produced a society the likes of which the ancient world had never known, a society in which the living and the dead jockeyed for a place in a hierarchy that was at once earthly and celestial. But in other ways, Christianity reoriented traditional Roman patron-client relations so that client sinners in this world were linked to sanctified patrons in heaven.

■ The Quest for a Catholic Tradition

As a practical matter, the Catholic Church had been striving for doctrinal universality since the Council of Nicaea. It is no accident that the Catholic Church grew up in a Roman world steeped in ideas of universality. The most deeply held tenet of Roman ideology was that Rome's mission was to civilize the world and bend it to Roman ways.

One intriguing development in Late Antiquity is the emergence of several Christian communities claiming fidelity to a universal—a catholic—tradition. The Latin Christian church in the West was staunchly Nicene and Chalcedonian and took its bearings from Latin church writers. In the eastern Mediterranean, writers tended to use the word *Orthodox,* which means "right believing" but also carries clear implications of catholicism, that is, of universality. The Orthodox Church centered primarily on the emperors and patriarchs, used Greek, and followed Greek Christian writers. The Coptic Church in Egypt was Monophysite, followed the teachings of the patriarchs of Alexandria, and used the Coptic language. The Jacobite Church, a mildly Monophysite, Syriac-speaking group, was originally strong in Syria, from where it spread to Mesopotamia and beyond. Each of these churches produced a literature, an art, and a way of life that marked its members as a distinct community. These traditions did not reflect the emergence of something new in Late Antiquity so much as a Christian reinterpretation of very old cultures and ideals. Each of these traditions exists today.

Christianity drew much from the pagan and Jewish environments within which it grew, but its fundamental inspiration was the collection of writings called in modern times the Bible. In antiquity this material was called *ta hagia biblia* or *sacra biblia,* meaning "the holy books." It was understood to be a collection of sacred writings, and the individual items in that collection had different meanings. From the second century, Christian writers began trying to define a canon, a definitive list of genuine Old and New Testament scriptures. It was widely recognized that without an official, standardized set of Christian writings, there could be no uniformity of Christian belief. This process of determining authentic

Sarcophagus of Junius Bassus   Junius Bassus, prefect of Rome, died in 359 and was laid to rest in this splendid sarcophagus (from the Greek "body eater"!). Three points are important: First, as members of the Roman elite became Christian, they could afford to employ the finest craftsmen. Second, as Christianity became legal, it could search for artistic expression. Third, these Old and New Testament scenes proclaim Christ's divinity but, in an age of intense theological quarrels, glide over his humanity.   *(Hirmer Verlag Munchen)*

Scripture was not completed until the middle of the fifth century.

While the search was underway for an authoritative list of books, it was also necessary to try to get uniform versions of the books that were being pronounced canonical. The Greek East used the Greek version of the Old Testament and the Greek New Testament. But that version was unsuitable in the West, where Latin was the principal tongue. Late in the fourth century, Pope Damasus° commissioned Jerome (331–420), a man who had renounced his wealth for a life of monasticism and scholarship, to prepare a Latin version based on a new translation of the Hebrew Scriptures and Greek New Testament. Jerome's version was called the "Vulgate" because it was the Bible for the "people" (*vulgus*) who knew Latin.

Once a scriptural canon had been identified, there was also a need for a creedal statement that would set down precisely what Christians believed. The councils of Nicaea and Constantinople defined the nature of the Trinity, and Chalcedon formulated the relationship between the human and divine natures of Christ. There were also debates about the nature of the priesthood, the structure and authority of the church, and the problem of human free will. Practical questions came up, too. How could Christians fulfill the moral demands of their faith while living in a world whose values were often at odds with church teachings?

Answers to these kinds of questions were provided by a group of Greek and Latin writers who are called the "Church Fathers" and whose era is called "patristic" (from *patres*, the Latin word for "fathers"). In versatility and sheer output they have few rivals at any time. Their intellectual breadth was matched by their elegant style and trenchant reasoning.

Many Christian writers addressed the problems of moral living in the world. In his treatise *On Duties*, Ambrose of Milan (339–397) attempted to Christianize the public ethos that Cicero had spelled out many years before in his book of the same name. Cicero talked of citizens' obligations to one another and to the law and the need for those in power to be above reproach in the conduct of their personal lives. Ambrose reinterpreted these obligations as duties that Christians owed to one another because of their common worship of God.

Pope Gregory I wrote *The Pastoral Rule* to reformulate Cicero's and Ambrose's ideas in ways that made them relevant to society's Christian leaders, the clergy. John Chrysostom° (347–407), a patriarch of Constantinople and one of the most popular and gifted preachers of Late Antiquity (his name means "golden tongued"), bitterly castigated the immorality of the imperial court and aristocracy: by setting a bad example, they endangered the souls of their subjects.

Damasus (DAM-uh-sus)

Chrysostom (KRIH-sus-tum)

■ Saint Augustine and the Christian Tradition

The most influential Christian thinker after Saint Paul was Augustine of Hippo (354–430). Augustine was born in North Africa to a pagan father and a Christian mother. His family was of modest means but, at great sacrifice, they arranged for him to receive the best education available. He embarked on a career as a professor of rhetoric. Once he had established himself, he moved on to Rome and then to Milan, which in the fourth century was the unofficial western capital. Augustine fell under the spell of Ambrose and embraced the Christianity that his mother, Monica, had been urging on him throughout his life. Later Augustine chronicled his quest for truth and spiritual fulfillment in his *Confessions,* a classic of Western literature. (See the box "Reading Sources: The Moment of Augustine's Spiritual Awakening.") In 395 Augustine became a bishop and until his death served the North African community at Hippo, and the wider Christian world, with a torrent of writings.

Not a systematic thinker, Augustine never set out to provide a comprehensive exposition of the whole of Christian doctrine. Instead he responded to problems as they arose, crucial among which were the relationship between God and humans, the nature of the church, and the overall plan of God's creation.

In the early fifth century some people believed that they could achieve salvation by the unaided operation of their own will. Augustine responded that although God did indeed endow humankind with free will, Adam and Eve had abused their will to rebel against God. Ever since that first act of rebellion, a taint, called by theologians "original sin," predisposed all humans to continual rebellion, or sin, against God. Only divine grace can overcome sin, and only by calling on God can people receive grace. Here was a decisive break with the classical idea of humanity as good in itself and capable of self-improvement, perhaps even perfection, in this world. According to Augustine, all people were sinners, in need of God's redemption.

Some North African heretics taught that sacraments celebrated by unworthy priests were invalid. Augustine believed that the efficacy of the church's sacraments—those ritual celebrations that were considered to be channels for the communication of grace, of God's special aid and comfort to the faithful—did not depend on the personal merit of the minister. A priest or a bishop acted in God's place and through divine grace. Therefore, faith in God was paramount. The church was thus a community of acknowledged sinners led by the clergy in a quest for eternal salvation. To Augustine, God alone was perfect. Clergy, rulers, churches: these were all hu-

man institutions, all more or less good in particular circumstances.

To many adherents of the traditional Roman religion, the sack of Rome by the Visigoths in 410 was repayment for Rome's abandonment of its traditional gods. To refute them, Augustine wrote the most brilliant and difficult of all his works, *The City of God.* This book is a theology of history. Augustine sees time not as cyclical, the traditional classical view, but as linear. Since the creation of the world, a plan has been in operation—God's plan—and that plan will govern all human activity until the end of time. History is the struggle between those who call on divine grace, who are redeemed, who are citizens of the City of God, and those who keep to the ways of the world, who persist in sin, who live in the earthly city. One may observe the unfolding of the divine plan by seeing how much of the earthly city has been redeemed at any given time.

Even though the Roman Empire was officially Christian, Augustine refused to identify his City of God with it. Nor would he say that the church and the City of God were identical. What he did say was that the sack of Rome was a great irrelevance because many kingdoms and empires had come and gone and would continue to do so, but only the kingdom of God was eternal and, in the long run, important. To a Roman people whose most cherished belief held that the world would last exactly as long as Rome's dominion, Augustine's dismissal of Rome's destiny sounded the death knell of the classical world-view.

Augustine also addressed the problem of education. He regarded salvation as the goal of life but realized that people had to carry on with their ordinary occupations. He also knew that almost the entire educational establishment was pagan in design and content. Education was confined mainly to the elite, who sought schooling partly to orient themselves within their cultural tradition and partly to gain employment, often in the imperial or urban service. This education had three mainstays. Latin or Greek grammar—rarely both—was the first. Augustine, for instance, knew little Greek, and by the sixth century few people in the East knew Latin. The second was rhetoric, once the art of public speaking but now, increasingly, literary criticism. The third was dialectic, or the art of right reasoning. In Late Antiquity public schools were fast disappearing as the need for them slipped away. But the church still needed educated persons, so it provided schools in cathedrals and monasteries.

In a treatise entitled *On Christian Doctrine,* Augustine expressed some ideas about education that proved influential for a millennium. He argued that everything a person needs to know to achieve salvation is contained

The Moment of Augustine's Spiritual Awakening

In this passage Augustine relates the moment of his conversion and abandonment of his former life. Notice the roles of God, books, his old friend Alypius, and his devoted mother, Monica.

So that I might pour out all these tears and speak the words that came with them I rose up from Alypius and went further away that I might not be embarrassed even by his presence. This was how I felt and he realized it. No doubt I had said something or other, and he could feel the weight of my tears in the sound of my voice. And so I rose to my feet, and he, in a state of utter amazement, remained in the place where we had been sitting. I flung myself down on the ground somehow under a fig tree and gave free rein to my tears; they streamed and flooded from my eyes. . . . And in my misery I would exclaim: "How long, how long this 'tomorrow and tomorrow'? Why not now? Why not finish this very hour with my uncleanness?"

So I spoke, weeping in the bitter contrition of my heart. Suddenly a voice reaches my ears from a nearby house. It is the voice of a boy or a girl (I don't know which) and in a kind of singsong the words are constantly repeated: "Take it and read it. Take it and read it." At once my face changed and I began to think carefully of whether the singing of words like these came into any kind of game which children play, and I could not remember that I had ever heard anything like it before. I checked the force of my tears and rose to my feet, being quite certain that I must interpret this as a divine command to me to open the book and to read the first passage which I should come upon. For I had heard this about Anthony: He had happened to come in when the Gospel was being read, and as though the words read were spoken directly to himself, he had received the admonition: "Go, sell your possessions, and give to the poor. You will then have treasure in heaven. After-

ward, come back and follow me" [Matthew 19:21]. And by such an oracle he had been converted to you.

So I went eagerly back to the place where Alypius was sitting, since it was there that I had left the book of the Apostle [Paul] when I rose to my feet. I snatched up the book, opened it, and read in silence the passage on which my eyes first fell: "Not in carousing and drunkenness, not in sexual excess and lust, not in quarreling and jealousy. Rather, put on the Lord Jesus Christ and make no provisions for the desires of the flesh" [Romans 13:13–14]. I had no wish to read further; there was no need to. For immediately I had reached the end of this sentence, it was as though my heart was filled with a light of confidence and all the shadows of my doubt were swept away.

Before shutting the book I put my finger or some other marker in the place and told Alypius what had happened. By now my face was perfectly calm. Alypius in his turn told me what had been going on in himself. He asked me to see that passage which I had read. . . . He was strengthened by the admonition. . . . The next thing we do is go inside and tell my mother. How happy she is! We describe to her how it all took place, and there is no limit to her joy and triumph . . . for she saw that with regard to me you had given her so much more than she used to ask for when she wept so pitifully before you. . . . I was now standing on that rule of faith just as you had shown me to her in a vision so many years before.

Source: St. Augustine, *The Confessions of St. Augustine,* trans. Rex Warner (New York: Mentor, 1963), pp. 182–183.

in the Bible. But the Bible, written in learned language, is full of difficult images and allusions. How is an ordinary person to learn what he or she needs to know in order to master this great book of life? Only by getting some schooling, and that education would inevitably be in the classical languages and literatures. To express his attitude toward that schooling, Augustine used the image of "spoiling the Egyptians," borrowed from the account of

the Hebrews' Exodus from Egypt, when they took with them whatever they could use. Augustine's attitude toward classical learning was that it was useful only to the extent that it equipped individuals to read the Bible, to understand it, and to seek salvation. Classical culture had no intrinsic merit. It might give pleasure, but it was equally likely to be a distraction or a temptation to immorality.

The Italian writer Cassiodorus° (ca. 485–580) gave this Augustinian interpretation of the classical heritage its definitive statement in his treatise *On Divine and Human Readings*. After the fall of the Ostrogothic kingdom, whose king Theodoric he had served loyally, Cassiodorus retired and set up a school of Christian studies. His treatise served as a kind of annotated bibliography and curriculum of the major writings on school subjects such as grammar, rhetoric, and dialectic, and on biblical commentary. For centuries, schools organized on Augustine's and Cassiodorus's model did an estimable job of preparing the clergy to carry out their functions.

SUMMARY

HEN the late antique period opened, Rome's vast and diverse empire was beset with innumerable political, military, and economic problems. The classical culture that had evolved over centuries in the Mediterranean, world seemed to have lost much of its vigor and appeal. But energetic rulers such as Diocletian and Constantine undertook a half-century of intense military, economic, and administrative reform that put the empire on firm footings while simultaneously changing forever the basic nature of the Roman state.

By 600 a Roman Empire still survived, but it was confined to the eastern Mediterranean, where it would persist for another millennium. In the West, Rome's former provinces had evolved into a series of barbarian kingdoms. Each of those kingdoms retained significant features of the governmental systems of the provinces in which they arose. Whether in the East or in the West, military men led a world whose culture was less civilian than in early imperial times. But the militarization of public life in Late Antiquity preserved the eastern empire and created a stable framework for the transition from empire to kingdoms in the West.

In 300, barbarians were a worrisome threat along the northern frontiers of the empire. By 600, barbarians had created, from Britain to Spain, a succession of kingdoms the most successful of which owed great debts to Rome. The barbarians did not appear suddenly in Late Antiquity. Rome knew these people, had traded, fought, and allied with them for centuries. The barbarians did not come to destroy Rome but to join it, to benefit from it, to learn its ways. The creation of the barbarian kingdoms was in many ways one of Rome's most creative political acts.

In 300 the Christian church was suffering persecution. By 600 the church spanned the old Roman world. A hierarchy of sophisticated leaders ably governed the church. Christianity had absorbed what it could of ancient culture, and the church had adapted Roman institutions. Prominent families had once governed Roman towns and provinces through urban institutions. The bishops and patriarchs who governed late antique towns via their church offices often came from those same families, or families just like them. The Church Fathers addressed some of the most fundamental problems of human existence in correct, sometimes elegant and moving, Greek and Latin.

The late antique world was fully embroiled in a process of evolution. That evolution would go on. In the West, kingdoms would appear and disappear, but the basic political structure of the European Middle Ages would be the kingdom. The eastern Roman Empire would shed more and more of its Roman heritage and turn into a regime we call "Byzantine." But the Byzantines themselves always insisted that they were Romans. The lands of North Africa and the Middle East that had long but tenuous relations with Rome would produce a new political order under the followers of the prophet Muhammad. But that world too would owe much to its Roman predecessor while also inheriting some of that world's old and deep divisions. In 600 the basic building blocks of the West were in place: Greco-Roman culture and institutions, Judeo-Christian religious beliefs, and barbarian peoples. In the world we call "medieval" those building blocks would be assembled in new configurations.

■ Suggested Reading

Bowersock, G. W., P. Brown, and O. Grabar, eds., *Late Antiquity: A Guide to the Post-Classical World*. 1999. Although basically an encyclopedia, this masterful volume contains long entries on all the major topics and up-to-date essays on big themes.

Brown, Peter. *The World of Late Antiquity.* 1971. A sprightly and beautifully illustrated interpretation of cultural crosscurrents by the most gifted interpreter of Late Antiquity.

Cameron, Averil. *The Mediterranean World in Late Antiquity, A.D. 395–600.* 1993. A superb and readable survey of all the major problems and interpretations.

Clark, Gillian. *Women in Late Antiquity: Pagan and Christian Lifestyles.* 1993. A first-ever attempt to capture the lives of late antique women in all respects.

Markus, Robert. *The End of Ancient Christianity.* 1990. This stimulating and beautifully written book explores the changing meanings of sacred and secular in the period from 400 to 600.

 For a searchable list of additional readings for this chapter, go to http://college.hmco.com.

Cassiodorus (cass-ee-oh-DOR-us)

The Ravenna Mosaics

Propaganda. The word has unsavory connotations. It suggests that someone is trying to convince someone else to do or to believe what is wrong. Actually, the word means only "things to be propagated," a message to be gotten out. The message itself may be good or bad, true or false.

When we think of propaganda, we must consider both the message and the medium in which it is conveyed. In antiquity, governments had several means of getting their messages out. Almost all the means were public, visible, striking.

Mosaics are among the most spectacular art forms of Late Antiquity, and in the churches of Ravenna they attained the summit of their propagandistic power. A mosaic is a picture formed by the intricate arrangement of thousands of tiny bits (called *tesserae*) of glass, stone, or metal. An artist created a rough sketch of the intended picture and then laid out the tesserae to conform to the sketch. Next the artist applied wet plaster to a small section of the surface, usually a wall or a floor, that was to receive the picture and then embedded that section's tesserae into the plaster. This process was repeated until the whole mosaic was completed. The result was a durable art form of great beauty and visual interest. In the picture on the opposite page you can see the tesserae and even some of the sparkle produced by the effect of sunlight and candlelight reflecting off the mosaic.

Mosaics were sometimes placed in private homes by the very wealthy, but more often they were put in conspicuous public places. Churches commonly received them in Late Antiquity. As more of society became Christian, aristocrats in particular were happy to spend lavishly to adorn their places of worship with beautiful decorations. Masses of people saw those decorations, reflected on who had financed them, and pondered the meaning of the image itself.

The greatest patron of all was the emperor. By putting up any work of art, the emperor proclaimed his power and influence. His reach was vast even if he never left Constantinople. Nothing shows this better than the Ravenna mosaics erected by Justinian.

Let us recall the situation. The Arian Ostrogoths had taken over Italy in 493. Ruling from Ravenna, they claimed to be imperial allies and representatives. Down to 535 there were always strains between Ravenna and Constantinople, and in that year Justinian launched the twenty-year-long Gothic War. During and after the war churches were erected as symbols of the imperial restoration.

The mosaic pictured here is located on the left-hand side of the apse, above and behind the altar, in the church of San Vitale in Ravenna. Its central figure is the emperor Justinian. Immediately opposite it is another mosaic (partially reproduced on page 227) focusing on Empress Theodora. San Vitale was a monument to the defeat of the Arian Goths. Any worshiper who raised his or her eyes from the altar saw immediately both Justinian and Theodora. These images made a powerful statement in a city that had been ruled by a Gothic king for thirty-three years. Justinian was leaving no doubt about who was now in charge. Consider, too, the prominence accorded to Theodora. Justinian really did view her as a partner in his rule.

That the emperor and empress were in charge is indicated in several distinct ways. They are slightly larger and are standing in front of their attendants. They are not quite like the other humans shown in the mosaic. They wear crowns and rich purple—that is to say, imperial—garments. They present gifts: he a gold paten holding the eucharistic bread and she a golden chalice containing the eucharistic wine. Thus the emperor and empress are represented as the donors of the church and as the guarantors of authentic worship.

Justinian tried throughout his reign to promote *homonoia* ("concord"). He tried to reconcile many political and religious factions. Notice the figure to Justinian's left (your right), over whose bald head you can read "MAXIMIANUS." This man was the archbishop of Ravenna, a close ally of the emperor and the person responsible both for eradicating Arianism and for reconciling Arians. His prominent position next to the emperor, and the fact that he alone is named, assured everyone of the correct doctrinal position. And in case anyone needed a further reminder, Maximianus holds in his hand the cross of Christ: there would be no more Arian subordination of the second person of the Trinity to the first.

We may note one more piece of propaganda. Look at the man standing to the left of Justinian and slightly behind him—between Justinian and Maximianus. This is Julianus Argentarius, a wealthy layman who was in all things the emperor's agent in Ravenna. He helped to finance and oversaw the construction of not only San Vitale but also several other churches in Ravenna. His presence signifies *homonoia*, the traditional concord between the emperor and the elite throughout the empire. Relations between the court and the Italian elite had been very strained under the Ostrogoths. Julianus's presence signaled that all was well once again. Vanity played a role too. Julianus paid for the art, so he had himself included in it.

The church of San Vitale was itself a propaganda statement. Theodoric was buried in a grand octagonal tomb. Justinian's builders chose an octagonal form for San Vitale. This church, too, is a sepulchre—a shrine for the remains of Saint Vitalis, an early Ravenna Christian who was martyred for the true faith.

In a world without the modern mass media, the media of antiquity served well to broadcast messages to people who understood their real and symbolic language. Recall the image on a Hellenistic coin (page 134). Look again at the statue of the tetrarchs (page 207) and the massive statue of Constantine (page 202). Cassiodorus once said that Rome was "a forest of statues." Every one of them was a propaganda statement.

 For additional information on this topic, go to http://college.hmco.com.

Justinian and His Courtiers, Apse Mosaic, San Vitale, Ravenna *(Scala/Art Resource, NY)*

CHAPTER 8

Early Medieval Civilizations 600–900

A N empty throne: grand, majestic, imperial perhaps, and a little mysterious. The photo to the left is of Charlemagne's throne, modeled on that of King Solomon and placed in a setting rich with Roman architectural reminiscences. The West had known no emperors since 476, but on Christmas Day in 800, Pope Leo III placed a crown on the head of Charles, the king of the Franks. A contemporary called Charles "the Father of Europe," and in truth the last decades of the eighth century and the first decades of the ninth witnessed the birth of something new in the lands that had once been Rome's western provinces. Charles did not rule from Rome, however. After his coronation he trekked far to the north to his palace and chapel, where this throne sits—to Aachen°, a small town near the modern border between Holland and Germany.

A time traveler transported to the Mediterranean world of 600 would almost certainly have predicted only two heirs to Rome: the eastern empire and the kingdoms of the barbarian West. It is extremely unlikely that our intrepid wanderer would have foreseen one of the most dramatic developments in the history of Western civilization: the rise of the Arabs and their Islamic faith. In this chapter, three areas and histories, not just two, engage our attention: the Islamic East, the Byzantine Empire, and the Latin West. For each, the seventh century was an era of dramatic change, the eighth century an era of reform and consolidation, and the ninth century a time of upheaval. A new imperial tradition developed in all three areas. Muslims, Orthodox, and Catholics all believed themselves to be chosen by God, and their rulers defined themselves as God's earthly agents. In all

Aachen (AH-ken)

The throne of Charlemagne, Aachen Palace chapel.
(Erich Lessing/Art Resource, NY)

three realms the interaction of local traditions with the Roman past produced new forms of central government that would prove influential for centuries. Commercial ties began to transform the Mediterranean world into a community of peoples who needed to balance mutual interests with bitter rivalries.

The period from 600 to 900 is commonly called the "early Middle Ages." What does this term mean? In the seventeenth century a Dutch scholar wrote of the *Medii Aevi*, the "Middle Times" that lay between antiquity and the dawning modern world. The name stuck. As a label for the post-Roman world, "Middle Ages" (whose adjectival form is "medieval") has become traditional. The fact that we no longer talk of an abrupt and catastrophic "fall" of the Roman Empire means that we no longer use the word *medieval* in negative ways.

QUESTIONS TO CONSIDER

■ What were the most important factors in the rise of the Arab peoples and of the Islamic faith?

■ Why did a distinctive civilization that can be called "Byzantine" emerge?

■ In what ways were the Frankish and Anglo-Saxon kingdoms successful?

■ What were the chief similarities among the early medieval civilizations? the chief differences?

TERMS TO KNOW

Muhammad	Papal States
Five Pillars of Islam	Charlemagne
Quran	vassal
caliphate	Carolingian Renaissance
Orthodoxy	manor
iconoclasm	

THE ISLAMIC EAST

 NCIENT writers took little notice of the Arabs, who inhabited much of the area from the Arabian peninsula to the Euphrates River. Around 600 the prophet Muhammad (570–632) appeared among them preaching a faith old in its basic elements but new in its formulation. With unprecedented spiritual and military fervor, converts to that new faith conquered territories from Spain to the frontiers of China. Slowly, they built an imperial system with a coherent government and ideology. At the same time, cultural elites began forging a new civilization out of the ethnic, religious, and historical diversity of that vast realm.

■ Arabia Before Muhammad

The Arab world in the early seventh century was large and turbulent. Long dominated by the Roman and Persian Empires, the region had no stable, large-scale political entities. People belonged to close-knit clans, or extended families, that in varying associations formed tribes. In theory, tribes were groups of people tracing descent from a known ancestor; in reality—and in this

Arab and Germanic peoples were alike—tribes were complex groups of relatives, allies, and political or economic clients.

As complex as its political situation was the region's ethnic and religious composition. The Roman world was overwhelmingly Christian, though there were many kinds of Christians. The Persian realm was officially Zoroastrian, but it had Jewish, Christian, Manichaean, and Buddhist minorities. The Arabs themselves were generally pagans, but Arabia had Jewish and Christian minorities.

The Arab East was also economically intricate and fragile. Bedouins° (Arabs who were nomadic pastoralists) provided for their own needs from their herds of sheep and goats, from small-scale trading in towns, and from regular raids on one another and on caravans. Some farmers worked the land, but in many areas soils were too poor and rain was too infrequent to support agriculture. Cities supported traders who carried luxury goods, such as spices, incense, and perfumes, from the Indian Ocean region and southern Arabia along caravan routes to the cities of the eastern Mediterranean. These traders formed the economic and political elite of Arabia, and they led the tribes. Mecca, dominated by the

---

bedouins (BED-oo-inz)

powerful tribe of the Quraysh°, was the foremost city of Arabia, but competition among cities and tribes was fierce.

A solution to the competition among tribes and towns for control of trade routes was the institution of *harams*°, or sanctuaries—places where contending parties could settle disputes peacefully. Mecca was one of the chief harams in Arabia, and its founding was attributed to the Israelite patriarch Abraham and one of his sons, Ishmael. The focus of the sanctuary was the black stone shrine known as the Kaaba°, founded by Abraham, according to Arab tradition. For centuries people from all over Arabia had made pilgrimages to Mecca, to the Kaaba, supposedly following Abraham's example.

■ The Prophet and His Faith

Muhammad was born in 570 to a respectable though not wealthy or powerful clan of the Quraysh tribe. His father died before he was born, his mother shortly afterward, leaving Muhammad under the care of his grandparents and an uncle. Like many young Meccans, he entered the caravan trade. By the time he was 20, Muhammad held such a reputation for competence and moral uprightness that he became financial adviser to a wealthy Quraysh widow, Khadija° (555–619). Although older than Muhammad, she became his wife in 595, and they had a loving marriage until her death.

From his youth Muhammad was a man of spiritual insight. In 610 he received the first of many revelations that commanded him to teach all people a new faith that called for an unquestioned belief in one god, Allah, and a deep commitment to social justice for believers. Muhammad began teaching in Mecca, but he converted few people outside his own circle—his wife was his first convert. Some Meccans were envious of Muhammad. Others feared that his new faith and new god might call into question the legitimacy of the shrines in Mecca and jeopardize the traditional pilgrimages to the Kaaba and the trade that accompanied them. By 619, Muhammad's well-connected wife and uncle were dead, and his position was precarious.

At this juncture citizens from Medina, a smaller trading community wracked by dissension among pagan Arabs, Jews, and followers of Muhammad, asked Muhammad to establish a haram there. In the summer of 622, small groups of Muhammad's disciples made their way to Medina, and in September Muhammad joined them. His journey from Mecca to Medina, the

hijra°, marks the beginning of a new era, symbolized to this day in the Arab world by a calendar that dates "In the year of the Hijra."

Although Muhammad was fully in control in Medina, Mecca remained the focus of his attention. In addition to his sentimental attachment to Mecca, its political and economic importance were critical to his emerging desire to convert all of Arabia. His followers began attacking Meccan caravans and battled with the Meccans several times in the 620s. In 630 Muhammad and many

Quraysh (KOOR-aysh)   harams (HAR-ahmz)
Kaaba (KAH-bah)   Khadija (KAH-dee-ah)

hijra (HEEZH-rah)

CHRONOLOGY

570–632	Life of Muhammad
597	Pope Gregory I sends missionaries to England
610–641	Reign of Heraclius in Byzantium
622	Hijra
632–733	Muslim conquests
661–750	Umayyad caliphate
664	Council of Whitby
711–716	Muslim conquest of Spain
750	Founding of Abbasid caliphate
751	Lombard conquest of Ravenna
755–774	Frankish conquest of Lombards
755–756	Foundation of Papal States
717–802	Isaurian dynasty at Byzantium
726–787, 815–842	Byzantine iconoclasm
757–796	Reign of Offa of Mercia
768–814	Reign of Charlemagne
786–809	Reign of Harun al-Rashid
800	Imperial coronation of Charlemagne
780s–860s	Carolingian Renaissance
843	Treaty of Verdun creates three Frankish kingdoms
867–886	Reign of Basil I

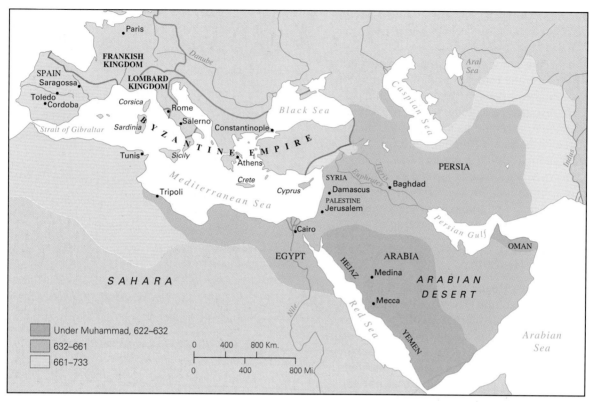

Map 8.1   Arab Conquests to 733   This map vividly illustrates the spectacular gains by the Arabs in the time of Muhammad, under the first caliphs, and under the Umayyads. Later, slow, steady gains in Africa, central Asia, and India expanded the empire even farther. Muslim conquest did not at first mean widespread conversion to Islam; Egypt, for example, was not majority Muslim before the tenth century.

of his followers returned to Mecca in triumph. Muhammad left the Quraysh in control, and he retained the Kaaba as a focus of piety. After making local arrangements, he returned to Medina and set about winning over the bedouins of the Arabian desert. When Muhammad died in 632, he had converted most of Arabia (see Map 8.1).

To what, exactly, had Muhammad and his followers converted? At the most basic level, people were asked to surrender completely to Allah, the one true God—that is, they were asked to make *al-Islam*, "the surrender." Those who surrendered became *Muslims* and joined the *umma muslima*°, a completely new kind of community in which membership depended only on belief in Allah and acceptance of Muhammad as Allah's prophet. No longer were one's duties confined to a particular clan, tribe, or town. All members of the umma were understood to have personal and communal responsibility for all other

members. Because of the experience of the hijra, Islam was a religion of exile, of separation from the ordinary world, and of reliance on God.

The basic teachings of Islam are traditionally described as "Five Pillars": (1) the profession of faith, "There is no God but Allah and Muhammad is His Prophet"; (2) individual prayer five times daily, plus group prayers at noon on Friday in a *mosque*, a Muslim house of prayer; (3) the sunup-to-sundown fast for one month per year; (4) the donation of generous alms to the poor; and (5) pilgrimage to Mecca at least once in a person's lifetime. These pillars are still the central requirements of Islam.

In the early decades the pillars sustained a faith that stressed strict monotheism and practices that affirmed Islam and built up a sense of community. At certain times of the day all Muslims everywhere bowed in prayer, with their heads facing toward Mecca. Everyone paid alms, creating thereby a feeling of solidarity among all members of the umma. Mecca itself and the experi-

umma muslima (OO-mah MOOSE-lee-mah)

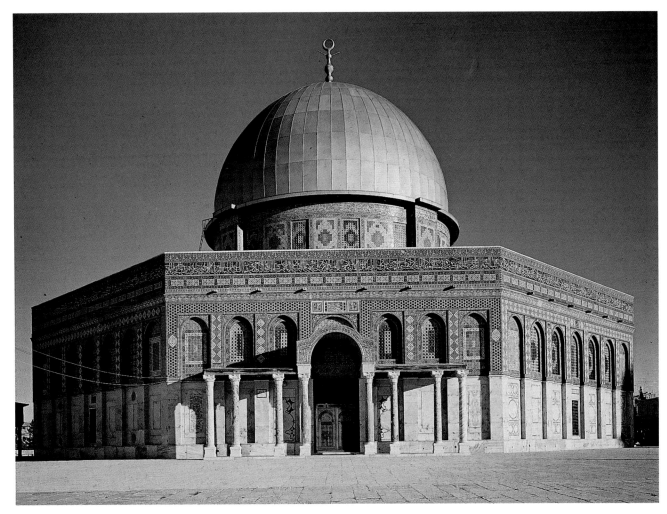

Dome of the Rock   This magnificent mosque in Jerusalem (built in 691–692) is the third holiest shrine of Islam—after the Kaaba in Mecca and the prophet's mosque in Medina. Muslims believe that Muhammad ascended to heaven from this spot.   *(Michael Holford)*

ence of pilgrimage were central to all Muslims. Originally there was no elaborate theology, intricate doctrinal mysteries, creed, or clergy. Men called *imams* led the Friday prayers in the mosque and usually offered sermons that applied Muslim teaching to the issues of the day, but Islam involved no ordained priesthood as in Judaism or Christianity and no hierarchy as in the Christian churches.

Muhammad communicated God's teaching to his followers, always insisting that he was transmitting a direct, verbal revelation and not offering his own interpretations. That revelation came in the form of "recitations" that make up the *Quran*°, the scriptures of Islam. Not

Quran (koo-RAHN)

long after Muhammad's death his closest followers arranged the recitations into 114 *Suras*, or chapters. The Quran contains legal and wisdom literature like the Hebrew Scriptures and moral teaching like the Christian New Testament. It also prescribes regulations for diet and for personal conduct. For example, the Quran forbids alcohol and gambling, censures luxury and ostentation, and imposes strict sexual restraints on both men and women. (See the box "Reading Sources: The Message of the Quran.")

Initially the Quran was interpreted rather freely within the umma, doubtless because there was no clergy to impose a uniform interpretation. After the prophet's death, some people felt the need for an authoritative teaching—as early Christians had felt the need for a

The Message of the Quran

The Quran consists of 114 Suras, literally the "steps" by which one rises to knowledge of Allah; we might say chapters. The Quran in its earliest versions was also equipped with a running commentary. The first four extracts below illustrate the simplicity and elegance of Muslim prayer and the absolute transcendance of Allah. The last two extracts demonstrate the profound sense of religious continuity that marked Muhammad's teaching.

Sura 1

In the name of Allah, Most Gracious, Most Merciful. / Praise be to Allah, the Cherisher and Sustainer of worlds; / Most Gracious, Most Merciful. / Master of the Day of Judgment. / Thee do we worship and Thine aid we seek. Show us the straight way, the way of those on whom Thou hast bestowed Thy grace, Thou whose portion is not wrath, and who do not go astray.

Sura 4.171

O People of the Book! Commit no excesses in your religion, nor say of Allah anything but truth. Christ Jesus the son of Mary was a messenger of Allah . . . so believe in Allah and in his messengers. Say not "Trinity" . . . for Allah is One God. Glory be to Him for He is exalted above having a son. To him belong all things in the heavens and on earth.

Sura 3.84

Say ye: We believe in Allah, and the revelation given to us, and to Abraham, Ismail, Isaac, Jacob and the descendants (children of Jacob), and that given to Moses and to Jesus and that given to all prophets from their Lord, but we make no difference between one and another of them, and we bow to Allah.

Sura 2.87

We gave Moses the book and followed him up with a succession of messengers; We gave Jesus the son of Mary clear signs and strengthened him with the Holy Spirit.

Sura 48

If the People of the Book rely upon Abraham, let them study his history. His posterity included both Israel and Ismail. Abraham was a righteous man of Allah, a Muslim, and so were his children. Abraham and Ismail built the Kaaba as the house of Allah and purified it, to be a centre of worship for all the world: For Allah is the God of all peoples.

Sura 56

God's truth is continuous, and His prophets from Adam, through Noah and Abraham, down to the last of the prophets, Muhammad, form one brotherhood. Of Imran father of Moses and Aaron sprang a woman, who devoted her unborn offspring to Allah. That child was Mary the mother of Jesus. Her cousin was the wife of the priest Zakariya, who took charge of Mary. To Zakariya, in his old age, was born a son Yahya, amid prodigies: Yahya was the herald of Jesus the son of Mary and was known as John the Baptist.

Source: The Meaning of the Holy Qur'an, New edition with revised translation, commentary, and newly compiled comprehensive index by Abdullah Yusuf Ali (Beltsville, Md.: Amana Publications, 1998), pp.14, 40, 51, 55–56, 134–35.

canon of Christian scripture and teaching—and their efforts resulted in the collections called the *sunna,* which means roughly the "good practice"—that is, the words and customs of Muhammad himself. Crucial in the development of the sunna were the *hadith,* the "sayings" of the prophet, the comments he sometimes made about how God's revelation was to be understood and applied. Extant compilations of the sunna date from the ninth century, and scholars are not sure what portion of them derives authentically from the age of the prophet.

■ The Arab Conquests

Muhammad's death brought a crisis. Who or what was to succeed him? In 632 the Meccan elite chose Abu Bakr as *caliph*°, or "successor to the prophet." Abu Bakr was elderly, an early convert to Islam, and a former secretary to Muhammad. He and his three successors down to 661 (Umar, Uthman, and Ali) were all Meccans, relatives of the prophet by marriage, and early converts. Islamic tradition calls them the "Rightly Guided Caliphs."

Abu Bakr left his successor, Umar, a united Arabia (see Map 8.1), no small feat in that fractious world. Umar began the lightning conquests by the Arabs of much of the Roman and Persian Empires. He initiated the policy of granting choice positions in the expanding caliphate, the Arab empire, to old converts and of ranking them according to precedence in conversion. As the old elite divided up the new provinces of the caliphate, some of them became *emirs* (governors), and others became lower administrators. Arab administrators then collected from all conquered people personal taxes and land taxes. Converts to Islam paid only land taxes. Arab settlers paid no taxes and received salaries from the taxes paid by others.

Umar was murdered by a slave in 644, leaving his successor, Uthman, a huge empire to administer. A great centralizer, Uthman chose emirs, regulated the finances of the provinces, and authorized the preparation of the definitive text of the Quran. In attempting to preserve the advantages of the old Meccan elite, Uthman alienated many people, particularly in Egypt, Syria, and Iraq, who had benefited from conquest and who guarded jealously their newfound local wealth and power. Uthman was murdered in 656 and replaced by Ali, Muhammad's son-in-law, whose goal was to create a truly Islamic government by emphasizing the religious side of the caliph's office as the leader of the umma. Ali was in turn killed by a disillusioned follower in 661. Years later some Muslims looked back to Ali as the true model for the caliph. These Muslims formed the *Shi'a*, the "Party of Ali."

When Ali was killed, the caliphate passed to Mu'awiya°, a Meccan who was the governor of Syria and commander of the finest army in the Arab world. That army ensured Mu'awiya's position. From 661 to 750 the Umayyads°, as Mu'awiya's family is called, built many of the caliphate's institutions.

Umayyads instituted greater centralization. This involved the introduction of a unified coinage, the Ara-bization of the administration—granting all key positions to Arabs—and taking tight control of provincial government and taxation. The Umayyads moved the capital of the caliphate to Damascus in their own power base of Syria, more centrally located than the old towns of Mecca and Medina and closer to the militarily active zones in eastern Iran and along the Byzantine frontier in Syria. In addition, the Umayyads presided over the final territorial expansion of the caliphate (see Map 8.1). To the west, the caliph's forces took North Africa and Spain and conducted raids deep into Gaul. In the east, though stymied by unsuccessful sieges against Constantinople, campaigns moved the frontier against the Byzantine Empire into the mountains of southern Anatolia and, farther east, established nominal authority as far as the Indus River valley.

Rome's empire expanded for 350 years, but the caliphate reached its zenith in scarcely 100. How can we account for the astonishingly rapid creation of such a vast empire? External factors were important. Byzantium and Persia had financially and militarily weakened themselves in a series of wars that ended just as the caliphate of Umar commenced. Moreover, the Byzantine and Persian states were exceedingly diverse, and the Arab armies dismantled them piecemeal. Both old empires, but especially the Byzantine, had deep religious divisions. Coptic Egypt and Jacobite Syria, for example, willingly yielded to the Arabs, who demanded taxes and submission but otherwise left them alone. The Byzantines and Persians tended to depend on static frontier garrisons and large armies that could not be quickly mobilized and moved long distances. The Arabs rarely risked great pitched battles. They preferred a gradually expanding military frontier gained by numerous lightning strikes.

Internal factors were more significant, however. For centuries, raiding and plundering had been a way of life in Arabia, but because Islam forbade Muslims from raiding other Muslims, a new outlet for traditional violence was needed. The prophet himself had believed firmly in the need to expand the faith, and his successors shared that belief. Muslim ideology divided the world into the "House of Islam" and the "House of War." In the House of Islam, the justice of Allah reigned supreme. In the House of War, *jihad*, holy war, was the rule. Christians and Jews, as fellow "Peoples of the Book"—sharers in a scriptural tradition reaching back to Abraham—were spared the choice of conversion or death, but "infidels" were expected to submit and convert. The Arab conquests were carefully planned and directed to channel violence out of Arabia, to populate much of western Asia with loyal Muslims, and to reward members of the umma.

---

caliph (KAY-lif)   **Mu'awiya** (MOO-ah-wee-uh)
Umayyads (OO-my-ahdz)

■ The Abbasid Revolution

Despite their military and administrative successes, the Umayyads were not popular. Many resented their bureaucratic centralization. Such resentment was acute in areas heavily populated by recent converts, who had always disliked the old Arabian elites, and in frontier provinces, where Arab immigrants along with local converts desired autonomy. The secular nature of Umayyad rule also offended those pious Muslims who expected a high standard of personal morality from their rulers. The opposition came to a head in a series of rebellions that culminated in the naming of a rival caliph, Abu'l Abbas, in 749. In 750 he defeated his Umayyad opponent.

The Abbasids° reigned until the thirteenth century. Initially, especially in the caliphate of Harun al-Rashid° (r. 786–809), they brought the Islamic world its first golden age. Harun's reign was marked by political stability, economic prosperity, and cultural achievements. Abbasid successes are attributable to political acumen and ideological restructuring.

With their frontier origins, the Abbasids were sympathetic to the caliphate's provincial populations. Thus, they created a more international regime. Non-Arabs and recent converts felt toward Islam, the prophet, and the prophet's family a loyalty that they would not grant to the old Arabian potentates who had led and initially benefited from the Arab conquests. The Abbasid polity was based on the idea of the fundamental equality of all believers, old or new, Arab or not.

Members of the Abbasid family received some key government posts, as did Iranians and other non-Arabs. Most importantly, however, local persons got more choice positions than Meccan or Syrian aristocrats. The capital of the caliphate was moved from Syria to Iraq, but to avoid favoring any existing group or region, the Abbasids built a new city, Baghdad, which they called "the navel of the universe." By addressing regional and ethnic sensitivities in an effective way, they were able to maintain, even extend, the centralized state of the Umayyad period.

The daily business of governing was usually in the hands of the *wazir,* who headed the administration, advised the caliph, and often exercised a powerful formative influence on the caliph's children and heirs. The first caliphs chose administrators from loyal Arabs and from experienced Christian subjects. Under the Umayyads the regime was Arabized. Then under Harun al-Rashid the government became international, professional, and hereditary. The chief agency of government was the treasury, which had separate branches dealing with the Muslim alms, with the land and poll taxes paid by subjects, and with the land taxes paid by converts. Alone among early medieval governments, the caliphate could draw up annual budgets. Alongside the treasury in exerting power was a prestigious group of palace servants. They did not hold major offices, but their informal influence on the caliph and his family was great. The army was another prominent body within the state.

The central government had several links to the provinces. In addition to controlling the army and provincial governorships, the caliph employed a network of regular envoys and spies. The court, especially under the Abbasids, drew able young men from all over into the service of the caliph and created hopes among provincial elites that they too might be chosen. In every district and city there were judges, *qadi°,* to oversee the application of Islamic law. Qadi were under the authority of the caliph.

The death of Harun in 809 sparked a century of problems. Intense family rivalries touched both the succession to the caliphate and the possession of key provincial positions. The bureaucracy became an increasingly influential pressure group, and the palace servants began to foment intrigues. The army became more and more a professional body comprising non-Arabs, especially Turks, hired from the frontiers and beyond because Arabs, enjoying their salaries, declined to serve. The parallel with the Germanization of the late Roman army is striking. The army, the bureaucracy, and the courtiers all had different and conflicting interests and did not hesitate to press their own advantages. Religious divisions persisted, even intensified. Many felt the Abbasids had not gone far enough in erecting a truly Islamic regime, but some felt that the caliphs had gone too far in claiming both the political and religious authority of the prophet. Whole regions took advantage of Abbasid leniency in granting local autonomy and began to fall away. After the early tenth century the Abbasid caliphs had little effective power.

■ The Emergence of Islamic Culture

Two currents are apparent in the culture of the Islamic East. One is the elaboration of religious thought; the other is the assimilation of multiple cultural heritages. Both were influenced by the spread of Islam that mixed Greek, North African, Iranian, Turkish, and even Hindu elements into a culture already rich with Arab, Christian, and Jewish ingredients.

Abbasids (uh-BASS-idz)
Harun al-Rashid (hah-ROON al-rah-SHEED)

qadi (KAH-dee)

Muslims assembled for prayer in mosques, the often beautiful buildings usually modeled on the original mosque in Medina. The worshipers—with men and women in separate areas—arrayed themselves in parallel rows and were led in prayer by an imam. In time the imams started offering interpretations of the Quran, and collections of these interpretations began to circulate. Similarly, Muslim judges began to issue opinions on how the Quran and sunna might be applied to the daily lives of believers. Teachers in mosque schools were also influential. Together these authority figures, collectively the *ulama*, developed a body of religious thought. Lacking elaborate theology and creeds, Islamic religious thought pertains to practice and allegiance more than ideas. The point is less to *know* Islam than to *live* it.

The late ninth and early tenth centuries saw the emergence of a religious split in the Islamic world that persists to this day. The opposing groups were Shi'ite and Sunni Muslims. Shi'ites believed that caliphs should be chosen only according to strict standards of moral and spiritual worthiness. Further, they insisted that the only way to ensure such worthiness was to choose caliphs from the line of Ali, the fifth caliph, husband of Muhammad's daughter Fatima and, in 661, a victim of assassination. Moreover, they believed that the whole ulama should measure up to Shi'ite standards. Sunni Muslims, always the vast majority, proclaimed that only they adhered to the sunna, the "good practice" of Muhammad himself. Sunnis accept the legitimacy of the whole line of Umayyad and Abbasid caliphs and the teachings of the ulama.

In 832 an Abbasid caliph endowed the "House of Wisdom," an academy for scholars in Baghdad (compare Charlemagne's palace school, pages 262–264), and from this point on Muslim scholars had the leisure and wherewithal to begin tackling the corpus of Greek thought, especially the scientific writers. The earliest Arab scholars sought mainly to master the learning of the past. Greek, Persian, and Indian works were collected and translated, manuscripts were copied, and libraries were built. Muslims showed little interest in the *literary* heritage of antiquity, the ancient legacy that was so important and controversial to Christian scholars.

So we may ask: Was the Islamic caliphate part of the West or not? Was it brother, or cousin, to the emerging Byzantine and Latin worlds? From the vantage point of 900, the answer we might give to those questions—"largely Western"—differs from the answer we might give today—"largely Eastern." In later chapters we will see how the Islamic world became less western and more eastern.

THE BYZANTINE EMPIRE

THE century after Justinian's death in 565 was difficult for the eastern Roman Empire. Attacks by Persians, Bulgars, and Muslims, riots and rebellions, plagues and famines, and some weak rulers put the empire in a perilous position. Two fundamental changes transformed the eastern Roman Empire into a new civilization that we call "Byzantine°," from Byzantium, the ancient Greek name for the capital city, Constantinople. In external affairs, the empire experienced a sharp geographic contraction until it stabilized into the shape it would hold into the thirteenth century. In internal affairs, the empire changed both its basic administrative structures and its cultural orientation.

■ External Changes

In 600 the empire still laid claim, along the southern and eastern shores of the Mediterranean, to most of the lands that Rome had ruled for centuries. But in the east the empire had been suffering recurrent losses to Persia. In 610 Heraclius°, a gifted ruler, ascended the throne. Between 622 and 629 Heraclius campaigned brilliantly and recovered almost everything that had been lost. But he faced a cruel irony. When the Arab expansion began under Umar, Heraclius's empire was militarily and financially exhausted. As the seventh century wore on, Arabs captured Syria and Palestine, Mesopotamia, and began a centuries-long push into Anatolia. Eventually they even threatened the capital, Constantinople.

In the Balkans Heraclius and his successors fought constant battles, with mixed results. They checked the advance of the Slavic peoples, who had been expanding southward for some years. The Slavic advance was partly generated by social and political forces among the Slavs themselves and partly a result of pressure from the Avars and Bulgars. These peoples, who were related to the Huns, had begun penetrating into the Danube basin in the late sixth century. The empire tried hard, with varying success, to check their forward march.

Where the West was concerned, Heraclius and his successors were powerless to stop the Arab advance in North Africa and Spain. In Italy, imperial control was confined to a few outposts around Rome, Ravenna, and Sicily. Generally, Italy was too far away and strategically insignificant to attract much attention from the imperial government.

Byzantine (BIZZ-un-teen)   **Heraclius** (her-ACK-lee-us)

Greek Fire   Invented in the seventh century by Callimachus, a Syrian engineer, Greek fire was a mixture formed from petroleum, sulfur, saltpeter, and lime that ignited on contact with water. It was first used to repel the Muslim siege of Constantinople in 678.   *(Institut Amatller d'Art Hispanic)*

By around 700 the empire was assuming the basic geographic shape it would hold for centuries. In contrast to the vast lands once ruled by Rome, the empire was now confined to the eastern Balkans and to western Anatolia. Then in 717 Leo III "the Isaurian°" (Leo was actually Syrian but later legends made him a resident of Isauria in Anatolia) became emperor in a moment of acute crisis. Arab armies had seized much of Anatolia and had laid siege to Constantinople itself. The city would surely have fallen had it not been for the "Greek fire" that made it impossible for the attacking navy to operate beneath the seaward walls. Leo repulsed the attack and then ruled successfully until 741. He was followed by his able and charismatic son, Constantine V (r. 741–775). Constantine held the line in Anatolia and enjoyed decades of military success along the Balkan frontier.

In Italy alone Isaurian policy was unsuccessful. When Justinian reconquered Italy from the Ostrogoths (see page 226), his armies devastated the region and left it poor and weak. Into the gap stepped the Lombards, who gradually built a kingdom in the north of Italy—Lombardy still bears their name—and set up a series of duchies in the center and south of Italy. The Byzantines prudently dedicated their resources to holding their Balkan and Anatolian frontiers, but this strategy left their subjects in Italy clamoring for aid. Eventually the popes put themselves at the head of a movement in Italy that turned to the Franks for protection. In 755 and 756 the Frankish king marched to Italy, defeated the Lombards, and donated the territories he seized from them to the pope. On the one hand, this inaugurated the "Papal States," the ever-changing set of lands in Italy whose current remnant is Vatican City. On the other hand, this military encounter put an end to effective Byzantine control in Italy, except for the areas around Naples and Sicily. In 827 Muslims seized Sicily, and in the ensuing decades they subjected southern Italy to continuous raids and occasional conquests.

Constantine V's promising son, Leo IV (r. 775–780), survived him only briefly. He left a 6-year-old heir, Constantine VI, and a remarkable widow, Irene, as regent for her son. Irene was a skilled politician, but under her the army grew restive because she preferred to make treaties, sometimes on unfavorable terms, than to send troops into the field. She did not trust the military's loyalty. Moreover, Irene had to contend with a foolish son who spent his time trysting with ladies of the court rather than attending to his official duties. In 797 Irene had him blinded, ironically in the very palace chamber where she had given birth to him. This was not a barbaric

---

Isaurian (eye-SOAR-ee-un)

Muslim and Byzantine "Diplomacy"?

This excerpt from an Arabic chronicle reveals something of the attitudes of Muslims and Byzantines toward each other and of their frontier relations. Notice the mistakes and misunderstandings.

A woman [Irene] came to rule over the Romans because at that time she was the only one of their royal house who remained. She wrote to the Caliphs with respect and deference and showered them with gifts. When her son [Constantine VI] grew up and came to the throne in her place, he brought trouble and disorder and provoked [Harun] al-Rashid. The empress, who knew al-Rashid and feared his power, was afraid lest the kingdom of the Romans pass away and their country be ruined. She therefore overcame her son by cunning and put out his eyes so that the kingdom was taken from him and returned to her. But the people disapproved of this and hated her for it. Therefore Nicephorus [emperor, 802–811] rose against her. . . . He wrote to al-Rashid, "From Nicephorus, the king of the Romans, to al-Rashid,

the king of the Arabs" as follows: "That woman put you in the place of kings and put herself in the place of a commoner. I put you in a different place and am preparing to invade your lands and attack your cities unless you repay me what that woman paid you. Farewell." Al-Rashid replied, "In the name of God, the Merciful, the Compassionate, from the servant of God, Harun, Commander of the faithful, to Nicephorus, dog of the Romans" as follows: "I have understood your letter, and I have your answer. You will see it with your eye, not hear it." Then he sent an army against the land of the Romans.

Source: Abu'l-Faraj al-Isfahani, *Al-Aghani,* in Bernard Lewis, ed., *Islam from the Prophet Muhammad to the Conquest of Constantinople,* vol. 1 (New York: Harper & Row, 1974), pp. 27–28.

---

act in the Byzantine way of thinking. By mutilating Constantine VI, she merely rendered him unfit to rule—Roman ideology held that only a physically perfect person could reign; the alternative would have been to murder him. In any case, Irene's credibility sank to nothing, and in 802 she was deposed by a wily old soldier, Nicephorus° (r. 802–811).

Whether in some ideal situation Nicephorus might have been successful is impossible to say. His problems came from two fearsome foes. In Anatolia he faced the redoubtable and aggressive Harun al-Rashid, and in the Balkans he contended with the clever Bulgarian Khan Krum° (r. ca. 803–814). Nicephorus got a break when Harun died in 809, but he fell in battle with Krum, who gruesomely made a drinking cup out of his skull. The Isaurian reputation for invincibility died on that battlefield. (See the box "Global Encounters: Muslim and Byzantine 'Diplomacy'?")

For two generations Byzantium suffered through short reigns, usurpations, political unrest, and military reverses. In 867 a rough soldier, Basil I (r. 867–886), seized the throne and, like Heraclius and Leo III before him, reversed the fortunes of the state. He established a new dynasty, the "Macedonian," and for the first time in years won important military victories. Faced as they were by worthy foes in both Anatolia and the Balkans, the Byzantines, the heirs of the Romans, might have vanished from history. But capable leaders emerged just often enough, especially in the eighth century, to preserve a state that, even in a vastly reduced shape, carried the Roman legacy into the future.

■ Internal Changes

Even as its territory was shrinking, Byzantium undertook military and administrative reforms, revised its laws, and refocused its culture, particularly its religious practices. In the early Middle Ages a distinctive "Byzantium" emerged in place of Rome.

Nicephorus (nye-SEFF-for-us)
Krum (KROOM)

250

Map 8.2 The Byzantine Empire in the Eighth and Ninth Centuries After suffering tremendous territorial losses to the barbarians and Arabs, the Byzantine Empire transformed its military, institutional, and cultural structures to create a regime that lasted until it was conquered by Crusaders in 1204. This map shows the *themes*, Byzantium's major institutional innovation.

Leo and Constantine, the Isaurians, are reminiscent of Diocletian and Constantine, or of Justinian. They energetically brought to completion military reforms that had been pursued half-heartedly since the late sixth century. These reforms amounted to a major administrative change. For centuries, Rome had recruited, trained, and paid professional troops out of tax revenues; they even used tax revenues to settle barbarian soldiers in their midst. Leo and Constantine put the finishing touches on a new "theme" system.

Men from frontier regions were now recruited and settled on farms in military districts called *themes.* All themes, whether land-based army ones or sea-based naval ones, were under the command of a leader who was simultaneously the civil and military chief of his theme. The farmer-soldiers did not pay tax on their farms but discharged their obligation to the state by personal service. Some standing troops were retained, mainly around the capital, but henceforth the thematic armies (see Map 8.2) formed the backbone of the Roman system.

The new system was less of a drain on the state treasury than the old one. Lower tax revenues were needed and, correspondingly, fewer bureaucrats to collect the money. The empire was smaller than in the past and needed a different kind of army: smaller squadrons concentrated near the threatened frontier regions in Anatolia and the Balkans rather than large armies that were expensive to maintain and cumbersome to transport over long distances.

The Isaurians undertook other reforms too. Leo issued the *Ecloga°*, the first major revision and updating of Roman law since Justinian's. Issuing a law code was a matter of pride and a clear representation of power and authority. But the *Ecloga* was "a selection of laws," an abridgment whose purpose was to provide a simplified code adapted to the empire's new circumstances.

Leo and Constantine also instituted far-reaching reforms in imperial administration, which had changed little in centuries. Roman bureaucracy had consisted of a few large departments headed by officials with immense responsibilities and power. The revised Byzantine system was characterized by a profusion of departments under officers who had little real power or sway. The emperor neutralized the bureaucrats by drawing them from all social classes, paying them well, giving them pompous titles and lots of public recognition, all the while dividing their responsibilities, curbing their influence, and making them dependent on himself. The

Ecloga (ECK-low-guh)

Byzantine government was never a breeding ground for factional squabbles as in the caliphate.

Byzantine culture came to be increasingly defined by the church. The massive Arab conquests that stripped Byzantium of so much territory also removed the ancient patriarchates of Alexandria, Jerusalem, and Antioch from effective contact with Constantinople. Often in the past the empire had been disturbed by severe theological quarrels generated by the differing views held in the several patriarchates. These disputes had been disruptive, but they had also prompted a great deal of learned religious writing. Now, deprived of this stimulus, Byzantium turned inward.

Inside the smaller Byzantine Empire, monasticism gradually assumed a more prominent place in religious life. So many members of elite families sought to become monks that the Isaurians actually tried to limit entry into the religious life. Byzantine monks tended to be deeply learned, intensely critical of the patriarchs of Constantinople—whom they regarded as worldly and political—and opposed to imperial interference in the church. In Theodore of Studion (759–826) Byzantine monasticism found its greatest reformer and legislator since Basil, four centuries earlier.

In 726 Emperor Leo III embarked on a bold new religious policy: iconoclasm. For centuries a beautiful and inspiring religious art had been emerging that troubled the emperor. Leo, a man of simple but fervent piety, believed that the presence of religious images, called "icons," in churches and public places was offensive to God. Moreover, Leo was convinced that the military disasters suffered by the empire in recent years were attributable to divine displeasure at the violation of the Mosaic prohibition of "graven images." Accordingly, he and his son banned religious images. They and some of their more enthusiastic followers even destroyed a few of them. Hence they were called "iconoclasts," which means "image breakers." Iconoclasm was officially proclaimed by a church council in 754, repudiated by another council in 787, proclaimed again in 815, and then definitively rejected in 843.

Although it might seem like an odd and local dispute, iconoclasm had several important consequences in its own time and reveals important aspects of emerging Byzantium to the modern observer. Iconoclasm was categorically rejected as heretical by the popes. This difference drove a sharp wedge between Eastern and Western Catholics. The debates over iconoclasm finally sharpened Byzantine thinking on the role and function of art in religious life. To this day, the icon plays a more prominent role in religious devotion in the East than in the West.

Moreover, the battle over iconoclasm evoked some of the most sophisticated Greek religious writing since Late Antiquity. Writers such as John of Damascus (675–749) and Theodore of Studion wrote learned treatises in defense of religious art that drew on Greek patristic writing and on ancient Greek philosophy in ways that sharply differentiated Byzantine and Western religious thought.

Saint Peter   A rare pre-iconoclastic icon from Mt. Sinai: Peter is depicted as a late antique magistrate—wise and distinguished—not as a simple fisherman. The medallions depict Christ in the center, Mary on the right, and John the Evangelist on the left. In a late antique depiction of a consul, the images would have had the emperor in the center, the empress on the right, and the co-consul on the left.
(Alexandria-Michigan-Princeton Archeological Expedition to Mount Sinai/Roger Wood/Corbis)

As the Byzantines turned more and more deeply into their own traditions, they exposed other differences between themselves and the West. Some of these were important such as the dispute over the so-called *filioque*. In the East, people taught and believed that the Holy Spirit proceeded "from the Father." In the West, people said that the Holy Spirit proceeded "from the Father *and from the Son*" (*filioque* in Latin). Greek monks shaved the front of their heads whereas Western monks shaved a circlet on the top. The Greek Church used leavened (with yeast) bread in worship whereas the Western church used unleavened bread. Taken together these differences amounted to a sharpening of the divide between Christian groups whom we may now label "Orthodox" and "Roman Catholic." Neither group wished to see a division in the Christian world, but physical separation and independent cultural evolution were producing two different traditions based, paradoxically, on a single late antique Christianity.

With its new geographic shape and its Orthodox faith, Byzantium was at once something old and something new. In official Byzantine ideology, the Roman Empire had always been one and inseparable. It is interesting to ask how familiar Augustus Caesar would have found the empire of Constantine V. With its indebtedness to classical and Christian traditions, there can be no question that Byzantium was a part of the West. But in its comparatively modest size, its constantly threatened frontiers, and its Orthodox traditions, Byzantium was going to have a somewhat different future than the portions of the West situated inside Rome's former western provinces. It is worth noting too that, as in the Muslim world, so also in Byzantium, the seventh and ninth centuries were acutely tumultuous whereas the eighth was marked by consolidation and achievement.

CATHOLIC KINGDOMS IN THE WEST

IN the Latin West, too, the seventh century was marked by challenges, the eighth century by innovation and accomplishment, and the ninth century by new threats and in some areas near collapse. The social and political heritages of both the Germanic and the Roman past interacted with Christianity and the church to produce the third early medieval civilization: Catholic Europe. Crucial to these developments were the evangelization of the countryside, the growth of an ecclesiastical hierarchy, the shift of papal interests away from the Mediterranean world toward western Europe, and the evolving relationship between royal governments and the Catholic Church.

■ The Struggles of Visigothic Spain

After their defeat at Clovis's hand in 507, the Visigoths were never able to re-establish dynastic continuity. As a result, Spain witnessed rebellions and usurpations more frequently than any other area in the West. In addition to internal struggles, Spain faced external threats from the Franks, the Ostrogoths in Italy, the Byzantines, and finally the Muslims.

The accomplishments of the Visigothic king Leovigild° (r. 568–586) seem remarkable given the state of Spain on his accession. He nearly unified the country, and he established a capital (Toledo) and a seat of government—which the Visigoths had been lacking since they lost Toulouse in 507. Leovigild was a good general and a charismatic leader who understood the value of enhancing the royal office. He wore royal vestments, sat on a throne, and issued coins with his own image and name. Leovigild's greatest problem was the Arianism of the Visigothic minority in the midst of the Catholic population. An Arian himself, he tried hard to convert Catholics to Arianism but failed. In 589, under King Reccared (r. 586–601), the Visigoths officially embraced Roman Catholicism.

The conversion of the Visigoths permitted close cooperation between the church and the monarchy and placed the resources of the church at the disposal of the king as he attempted to unite and govern the country. The career of Archbishop Isidore of Seville (560–636) is a prime indicator of those resources. He came from an old Hispano-Roman family, received a fine education, and wrote histories, biblical commentaries, and a learned encyclopedia. By the mid-seventh century, economic prosperity, a high degree of assimilation between Goths and Hispano-Romans, and a brilliant culture marked the high point of Visigothic Spain. The succession problem, however, was never overcome, and a stable central government was beyond reach.

In 711, Muslims from North Africa invaded Spain. Within five years Berbers (native North Africans and recent converts to Islam who were led by Arabs) completed the conquest of much of the Iberian Peninsula, except for the northwest. In 716 the caliph at Damascus introduced an emir who ruled from Cordoba. The emirate of Cordoba struggled to make good its authority over all of Spain but failed to do so. Christians in the rugged mountains of the northwest—the region called Asturias°—could not be dislodged, and the Muslims' part of Spain—known as al-Andalus°—was plagued by the same divisions as the Islamic East: Arab factions against other Arab factions, Arabs against non-Arab Muslims, and Muslims against non-Muslims. Secure in mountainous Asturias (see Map 8.3 on page 259), Christian kings built a capital at Oviedo and, in the ninth century, launched attacks against al-Andalus. For six hundred years this conflict between Christians and Muslims was the chief dynamic of Spanish history.

■ Italy and the Papal States

In 600 the Italian political scene was crowded. Several Germanic groups, several Byzantine outposts, and the popes were all contending for power. By the late eighth century, the Franks dominated northern Italy, the popes had created a state in the center, and the Byzantines clung to Naples and Sicily, much of which they lost to Muslims in the ninth century.

As we have seen, the Lombards conquered most of the Italian peninsula after the Gothic Wars. Neither numerous nor united, the Lombards were also Arians. Although the Lombard kings converted to Catholicism by 680, formed a strong government, and issued the most sophisticated Germanic law code, they always faced a dilemma. The kings had not systematically organized the conquest of Italy. From their capital at Pavia, they dominated the Po Valley, but other Lombards settled elsewhere and created independent duchies. Kings were weakened because they did not control the duchies and because between Lombardy and the duchies lay Rome and Ravenna, which were nominally Byzantine.

The strongest Lombard king of the eighth century, Aistulf° (r. 749–757), decided to risk the consequences of attacking Ravenna and Rome. He conquered the former but caused the pope to turn to Pippin III, the king of the Franks, for aid and protection. Pippin came to Italy, defeated Aistulf, and forced him to give to the pope all the lands he had taken from Rome and from Ravenna. A few years later Aistulf's successor reopened hostilities in central Italy. In 774 Charlemagne, Pippin's son and successor, defeated the Lombards, deposed their king, and took the Lombard crown for himself.

The Franks guaranteed to the popes undisputed possession of a substantial territory in central Italy. This first papal state was the culmination of three processes. First, as Roman imperial power declined in Late Antiquity, bishops often became the effective leaders of their towns. This position brought them power and prestige but also burdens. The popes found themselves responsible for

---

Leovigild (lee-OH-vuh-gild)   **Asturias** (ahs-TOUR-ee-ahs)
al-Andalus (al-AHN-dah-loose)

Aistulf (ICE-tulf)

A Mother Hen and Seven Chicks   This delightfully frivolous object may have been a gift from Pope Gregory I to the Lombard queen Theudelinda. It helps us to appreciate the aesthetic tastes of the barbarians. *(Cathedral Treasure, Monza/Scala/Art Resource, NY)*

Rome's food and water supply, the upkeep of its public buildings, and local charitable services. To pay for these functions, the popes began to organize the efficient bureaucratic administration of the patrimonies, the lands of the Roman church.

Second, the popes took the lead in protecting many people in central Italy, whether they lived on the patrimonies or not: preserving their purses from Byzantine taxes and their souls from heresy. This effort, too, forged bonds between the popes and the Italians. Third, eighth-century Rome spawned a justification for papal temporal rule. According to the *Donation of Constantine,* a document written in Rome (probably in the 760s), when Constantine departed Rome for the East in the 320s, he allegedly gave to the pope the authority to rule Rome and the whole West. In reality, no pope ever made such grandiose claims, and no concrete claims were ever based on the *Donation.* But the existence of the document signals a crucial progression from protection to direct rule. From the beginning, however, the Papal States were vulnerable and required a protector.

■ The Fate of the British Isles

Britain was less thoroughly Romanized, more quickly abandoned by the Romans, and more deeply influenced by Germanic peoples than any other locality in the West. Around 600 the small Anglo-Saxon kingdoms created in the sixth century took the first steps toward converting to Christianity, transforming Britain into England, and joining England inseparably to the European world (see Map 8.3). And another history was unfolding in the

British Isles, that of the Celtic peoples in the north and west of Britain itself and in Ireland.

The Celts—Britain's inhabitants before the Romans invaded in the first century—were related to peoples who lived in a broad band from Anatolia to Ireland and Spain. The Anglo-Saxons confined the British Celts to the western regions of Cornwall and Wales and to the northern area of Scotland. Ireland, seemingly beyond reach, had almost no Roman or Anglo-Saxon imprint.

The period between 600 and 900 saw only the faint beginnings of consolidation in the Celtic realms where the development of the Catholic Church preceded large-scale political organization. Each Celtic region produced an elaborate mythology connected with heroic missionaries who supposedly brought the Christian faith in Late Antiquity. The best-known stories swirl around Ireland's Saint Patrick (390?–461?). The son of a Roman official in the north of Britain, Patrick was captured by pirates, enslaved in Ireland, freed, and eventually made a priest; he then returned to Ireland as a missionary. From his base at Armagh°, Ireland's first bishopric, Patrick and his successors spread Christianity, and a vigorous monasticism, throughout the island. Historical too is the Irish aristocrat Columba (521–597) who, after his family lost a great battle, migrated in 563 to the isle of Iona off the coast of Scotland. From his monastery on Iona, Columba and his successors began the evangelization of the native Picts in Scotland.

Among the most successful Anglo-Saxon kingdoms were Wessex, Northumbria, and Mercia. Each had a rea-

---

Armagh (ARR-mah)

The Prophet Ezra from the Codex Amiatinus
This huge manuscript (13.3 inches by 19.7 inches; 1,033 folios) was written at Wearmouth, England, and shows an adaptation of Mediterranean styles. In tradition Ezra was the prophet who helped the Jews recover their law and heritage after the exile. The seventh- or eighth-century manuscript, or codex, makes the point that biblical law had come to England. *(Scala/Art Resource, NY)*

sonably large population and territory and opportunities for expansion. Wessex, for example, spread south and west into Devon, Cornwall, and Wales; Northumbria, which stretched along the North Sea coast, spread west to the Irish Sea and north into lowland Scotland (see Map 8.3). These kingdoms had ambitious rulers whose wars provided booty, land, and glory for old followers and new recruits. English kings quickly adopted symbolic aspects of rule to legitimize their authority and enhance their prestige. Archaeologists have found fine scepters and coins bearing early kings' names. The kings of Northumbria presided in a magnificent wooden hall and their movements were preceded and announced by banners.

Relations with the church were important also. Two issues proved crucial: the conversion to Christianity and the development of an ecclesiastical hierarchy. In 597 Pope Gregory I sent a small band of missionaries under a Roman monk named Augustine (d. 604) to King Aethelbert of Kent, whose Christian wife, Bertha, had prepared the ground for the newcomers. From their base of operations at Canterbury in southeastern England, Augustine and his successors had limited success spreading Christianity, but a new field of influence was opened to them when Aethelbert's daughter married a king of Northumbria and took missionaries to her new home. Monks from Iona, as noted, were already introducing Christianity into central and lowland Scotland. When later Northumbrian kings turned to Iona for missionaries and bishops, Roman and Celtic Christianity came face to face in Northumbria.

Two English Holy Women: Hilda and Leoba

These passages reveal some of the opportunities available to high-born women who embraced the religious life. Hilda, abbess of Whitby, was of royal descent and involved herself in many of the great events of her day. Leoba, of noble birth, joined a significant monastery in Wessex but later, and quite unusually, migrated to the continent where she joined forces with the famous missionary Boniface.

[Hilda] led her life in two equal parts, the first thirty-three years devoted to secular occupations and the second even more nobly devoted to the Lord in monastic life. She was indeed nobly born, the daughter of Hereric, a nephew of King Edwin. . . . When, having abandoned her secular garb, she decided to serve God alone, she went away to the land of the East Angles, whose king was a relative, from where she aimed to travel to Gaul and live as an exile for the Lord's sake where her sister Hereswith, mother of king Aldwith of the East Angles, was already living. But Bishop Aidan called her home and gave her land for a monastery. . . . Later she undertook to found a monastery at Whitby . . . and there she taught righteousness, mercy, purity, and other virtues, but above all peace and charity. . . . So great was her discretion that not only common people but even kings and princes used to come and ask her advice. . . . Those who submitted to her leadership had to study the scriptures . . . and five men from this monastery became bishops.

[Leoba's] mother consecrated her and handed her to Mother Tetta (abbess of Wimbourne and sister of an English king) to be taught the sacred sciences. . . . The girl, therefore, grew up and was taught with such care by the abbess and all the nuns that she had no interests other than the monastery and the pursuit of sacred knowledge. She took no pleasure in aimless jests and wasted no time on girlish romances but, fired by the love of Christ, fixed her mind always on reading or hearing the Word of God. Whatever she heard or read she committed to memory, and put all that she learned into practice. . . . Boniface sent messengers to Tetta asking him to send Leoba . . . for Leoba's reputation for learning and holiness had spread far and wide and her praise was on everyone's lips. . . . When she came, the man of God [Boniface] received her with the deepest reverence, holding her in great affection, not so much because she was related to him on his mother's side as because he knew that by her holiness and wisdom she would confer many benefits by her word and example. . . . He gave her the monastery at a place called Bischofsheim, where there was a large community of nuns. These were trained according to her principles in the discipline of monastic life and made such progress in her teaching that many of them became superiors of others, so that there was hardly a convent of nuns in that part that did not have one of her disciples as abbess.

Sources: (Hilda): Venerabilis Baedae, *Historiam Ecclesiasticam Gentis Anglorum,* 4.21, ed. Charles Plummer (Oxford: Oxford University Press, 1896), pp. 252–254 (translated and adapted by T. Noble); (Leoba): Thomas F. X. Noble and Thomas Head, eds., *Soldiers of Christ: Saints and Saints' Lives from Late Antiquity and the Early Middle Ages* (University Park: Pennsylvania State University Press, 1995), pp. 264–266.

The Christianity brought from Ireland did not differ in fundamental ways from the Roman Christianity imported at Canterbury. Indeed, the Irish were Roman Catholics. But Ireland had been isolated from the centers of Christian life since Late Antiquity, and its church had developed a number of distinctive local customs. For example, the two traditions used different calendars and thus celebrated Easter—the commemoration of the resurrection of Jesus Christ and the central celebration of the Christian year—on different days. In 664 a Northumbrian king called a church council at the monastery of Whitby, whose abbess was the former royal princess Hilda (614–680), a champion of Celtic customs. (See the box "Reading Sources: Two English Holy Women: Hilda and Leoba.") At Whitby, Roman and Irish representatives debated their positions. The king, choosing the universal over the particular, decided for Rome.

In 668 the pope sent to England a new archbishop of Canterbury, Theodore (r. 668–690). He was a Syrian monk who had traveled widely in the East, lived for a time in Rome, gained great experience in church administration, and acquired a reputation for both learning and discretion. The church in England was in an administrative shambles. Working tirelessly, Theodore built up a typical Roman ecclesiastical structure, introduced authoritative Roman canon law for the church, and promoted Christian education. Theodore laid the foundations for a unified English church that contributed to the eventual political unification of England.

Ecclesiastical peace led to the flourishing of monastic life. Monasteries played two important roles in this period. First, they led the way in bringing Christianity to ordinary people. Despite early gains among kings and nobles, Christianity had barely begun to penetrate the countryside. Second, monks maintained international connections, ranging from Ireland to Rome, that attached England to the major intellectual currents of the day and enabled the English to make their own contributions.

After Theodore's school at Canterbury, the most important early center of learning was in Northumbria. There English, Irish, Frankish, and Roman currents flowed together in the monasteries of Lindisfarne, Wearmouth, and Jarrow, and in the cathedral school of York. British schools produced some of the most beautiful illuminated manuscripts—books whose texts are adorned with gorgeous paintings—of the early Middle Ages.

The greatest product of this intellectual tradition was Bede (673–735). When he was 7, his parents placed him in the monastery at Wearmouth. He soon transferred to neighboring Jarrow and spent the rest of his life there. Bede was a teacher of genius, an erudite scholar, and a superb Latin stylist. His *Ecclesiastical History of the English People,* the most important source for English history from the fifth century to the eighth, did much to identify the Anglo-Saxons as a single English people. His biblical commentaries remained influential all over Europe for centuries. His studies of temporal reckoning popularized the use of A.D. dating, which replaced a bewildering array of local systems.

The career of King Offa of Mercia° (r. 757–796) shows the trends in early Britain. His ancestors were pagans, but he was a patron of the church, convener of councils, and recipient of papal envoys. He dominated all of Britain and was the first to call himself "King of the English." He issued a law code, reformed Mercia's institutions, and signed England's first international trade agreement—with Charlemagne.

After Offa's death, Viking raiders (see page 265) destroyed whatever unity had been achieved. For two

Mercia (MUR-sha)

generations, local rulers struggled just to survive, and in 865 a Viking army launched a conquest of the whole country. In 871 Alfred the Great (r. 871–899) ascended the throne of Wessex, won a series of military victories, rallied the English, and began the slow reconquest of northern and eastern England from the Vikings. Alfred promoted intellectual recovery, church reform, and political stability. After a half-century of chaos, Alfred revived the centralizing and unifying work of his eighth-century predecessors and laid the foundations for the English state of the tenth and eleventh centuries.

Britain's integration into the wider world is revealed by a seventh-century ship burial unearthed near Sutton Hoo (in East Anglia) in 1939. The ship, either a grave for or a memorial to an unknown king, had been hauled up onto the land, filled with treasures, and buried. The array of goods found at Sutton Hoo is astonishing. The hull contained Byzantine silver, represented by spoons and a large dish; Frankish gold, in the form of dozens of coins, jewelry, and personal adornments from many places; and pots, beakers, and other domestic items of varied provenance. The artistic decorations on these items demonstrate influences ranging from the Mediterranean to the Rhineland, Scandinavia, and Ireland.

THE CAROLINGIAN EMPIRE

 LOVIS and the Franks created the most effective of the early Germanic kingdoms. During the seventh century that kingdom, too, experienced difficulties but did not disappear. Just as Roman aristocrats had borne the ancient heritage into the Middle Ages, so now a Frankish family, called "Carolingian" from the name of its greatest member, Charlemagne, assembled the talent and resources of the Frankish realm in a new way. Charlemagne reformed his government and church, patronized learning, and resurrected the western empire. Early medieval civilization reached its culmination in the work of Charlemagne and his dynasty.

■ The Rise of the Carolingian Family, 600–768

When Clovis died in 511, he divided his realm among his sons, and thereafter several kingdoms coexisted. The Merovingian royal families feuded constantly, sought to expand at one another's expense, and drew local aristocracies into their battles. Trade and intellectual life declined, and some regions that had been conquered in the sixth century slipped away.

Nevertheless, the *idea* of a single kingdom of the Franks persisted. Kings and aristocrats in the small kingdoms competed for leadership of the realm as a whole. The flourishing culture of late antique Gaul was largely gone, but a creative Christian monastic culture was growing up in all parts of the Frankish kingdom. Monks began accomplishing the difficult task of converting the countryside to Christianity. The seventh century, in other words, was a time when the late antique regime was slowly changing into the medieval regime.

Central to this development was the rise to prominence of the Carolingians. The family appeared in history just after 600 and thereafter monopolized the office of mayor of the palace (sort of a prime minister) to the king in Austrasia° (the easternmost kingdom; see Map 8.3). The Carolingians were the boldest and wealthiest family in Austrasia, perhaps in the Frankish world. Within two generations they unified the Frankish realm and increased their own power.

The Carolingians used several methods to accomplish their ends. They formed alliances with powerful noble families in many regions. They waged war against the enemies of the Franks to restore the territorial integrity of the kingdom. Charles Martel (d. 741), Charlemagne's grandfather, led the Frankish forces that put an end to Arab raiding in Gaul, defeating a large force near Poitiers in 733. With booty from their wars, tribute from conquered peoples, spoils taken from recalcitrant opponents, and even lands seized from the church, the Carolingians attracted and rewarded more and more followers until no one was a match for them. The Carolingians also allied themselves very early with leading churchmen, both episcopal and monastic. They aided missionaries in the work of converting central Germany, thereby expanding Frankish influence in that area.

For years the Carolingians were content with the office of mayor of the palace. Then in 749, Pippin III (son of Charles Martel) decided to send envoys to the pope to ask whether it was right that the person who had all the power in the land of the Franks was not the king. The pope responded that this situation ran counter to the divine plan. Accordingly, in 751, the last Merovingian king was deposed, and Pippin was elected in his place (r. 751–768). Pippin had prepared his usurpation very carefully with his Frankish supporters, but he appealed to the pope to make it appear that he had become king with divine approval and not by crude seizure. Hard-pressed by the Lombards in Italy, the pope probably gave Pippin the answer he wanted primarily to enlist him as an ally.

Map 8.3 The Carolingian World   The territory over which Charlemagne exerted direct or indirect control was vast. The areas beyond the Rhine and Danube, never part of the Roman Empire, became under the Carolingians a permanent part of Western civilization. The Treaty of Verdun (see inset), signed by Charlemagne's grandsons in 843, was the first and most important of many divisions of the Carolingian Empire that eventually led to the emergence of France and Germany.

Three years later the pope visited the Frankish kingdom, where he crowned and anointed Pippin and his sons, including Charlemagne. (The practice of anointing the head of a ruler with holy oil, which renders the recipient sacred, dates back to the kings of Israel. The head and hands of Catholic bishops were also anointed. The anointing of rulers and churchmen persisted throughout the Middle Ages and into the modern world.) The pope also forbade the Franks ever to choose a king from a family other than the Carolingians and received from their new favorites a promise of aid in Italy.

■ The Empire of Charlemagne, 768–814

Charlemagne (Carolus Magnus, "Charles the Great" in Latin) was a huge man, and his stature has grown in European history and legend. (See the box "Reading Sources: A Contemporary Portrait of Charlemagne.") Like all great leaders, Charlemagne (r. 768–814) was complex. He spoke and read Frankish, Latin, and some Greek but never learned to write. He promoted Christian morality but perpetrated unspeakable brutalities on his enemies and enjoyed several concubines. Many battles were fought in his name, but he rarely accompanied his armies and fought no campaigns that are remembered for strategic brilliance. Determination and organization were the hallmarks of his forty-six-year reign.

It took until the mid-780s for Charlemagne to assess and understand his world (see Map 8.3). His first major achievement was the articulation of a new ruling ideology in the Latin West. In capitularies°—royal executive orders—of 789, Charlemagne required all males to swear an oath of allegiance to him, and he compared himself to a biblical king in his responsibility to admonish, to teach, and to set an example for his people. He referred to the people of his realm as a "New Israel," a new chosen people. Interestingly, this chosen people was not exclusively Frankish. No distinctions were to be made among Franks or Bavarians or Saxons. Everyone was to be equal

---

Austrasia (aw-STRAY-zhuh)

capitularies (kuh-PITCH-u-lar-eez)

0   150   300 Km.

0   150   300 Mi.

- Asturias Kingdom
- Frankish Kingdom, 768
- Areas conquered by Charlemagne
- Tributary peoples
- Byzantine territories

TREATY OF VERDUN, 843

KINGDOM OF LOUIS THE GERMAN

TRIBUTARY PEOPLES

Aachen

Paris   Verdun

Strasbourg

KINGDOM OF CHARLES THE BALD

KINGDOM OF LOTHAIR

PAPAL STATES

Rome

0   200   400 Km.

0   200   400 Mi.

SCOTLAND

Iona

Armagh

Jarrow

IRELAND   Dublin

NORTHUMBRIA

York

MERCIA

WALES

EAST ANGLIA

CORNWALL   WESSEX   ESSEX

Canterbury

DEVON   SUSSEX   KENT

DANISH MARCH

SAXONY 804

Utrecht

FLANDERS

Aachen

AUSTRASIA

Fulda

Mainz

Rouen

Echternach

Rhine

Paris

BRITTANY

NEUSTRIA   Orléans

BAVARIA 788

ALEMANNIA

TRIBUTARY

Tours

Poitiers

SLAVIC

Danube

BURGUNDY

AQUITAINE   Lyon

PEOPLES

Bordeaux

VENETIA

Milan

GASCONY

Venice

ISTRIA

Rhône

Pavia

Oviedo

Aniane

LOMBARDY   Ravenna

DALMATIA

ASTURIAS   Roncesvalles

Ebro

Marseille   Lérins

PAPAL STATES

SPANISH MARCH 811

DUCHY OF SPOLETO

UMAYYAD SPAIN

Barcelona

CORSICA

Spoleto

Toledo

Rome

Monte Cassino

DUCHY OF BENEVENTO

Salerno

SARDINIA

Cordoba

BALEARIC IS.

BYZANTINE EMPIRE

SICILY

A Contemporary Portrait of Charlemagne

Here is Einhard's description of Charlemagne. Einhard selected suitable passages from Lives of the Caesars, *by the first-century Roman historian Suetonius, to build up a picture of Charlemagne that accords well with what is otherwise known about him.*

He loved foreigners and took great pains in receiving them, so much so that their vast numbers seemed an unwelcome burden not only for his palace but even for his kingdom. On account of his magnanimity he was scarcely troubled by this burden for the praise of his liberality and of his good name more than compensated for this considerable inconvenience. His body was full and strong, very tall but not more than was fitting, for his height was seven times the length of his feet. His head was round and his eyes, large and piercing. His nose was longer than normal, his white hair was beautiful, and his expression was happy, even joyful. The power and dignity of his form were very great when he was sitting or standing. His neck was short and thick and his belly stuck out a bit, but the overall fineness of his form veiled these features, indeed his step was firm and all his bearing was manly. His voice was clear but too high for so great a body. His health was good until fevers struck him in the last four years of his life, and at the end he was lame in one foot. Even then he acted more on his own than on the advice of his doctors, whom he practically considered to be enemies because they tried to convince him to give up the roasted foods to which he was accustomed and to live on boiled dishes. He always exerted himself vigorously in riding and hunting which came naturally to him—indeed you cannot find any race on earth that equals the Franks in this activity. He loved the hot-steam baths at Aachen (they were his reason for

his constructing his palace there) and he exercised in the water when he could. No one could beat him in swimming. . . . Sometimes he invited his sons, nobles, and as many as a hundred men into the baths with him. . . . He dressed in the Frankish style. Next to his body he put on a linen shirt and drawers, then hose and a tunic with a silk border. He wore shoes and strips of cloth wound around his legs. In winter he protected his chest and shoulders with a jacket of otter or ermine. He wrapped himself in a blue cloak and wore a sword with hilt and belt of gold and silver. On festive days or to receive ambassadors, he wore a jeweled sword. The clothes of other peoples, however beautiful, he hated and would never endure to put them on except at Rome, once when Pope Hadrian asked him to and again when his successor Leo requested it at Rome. Then he dressed in a long tunic and a heavy cloak and wore shoes made in the Roman style. On feast days he wore clothing woven with gold, jeweled shoes, a golden brooch to fasten his cloak, and crown with gold and gems. On other days his clothing hardly differed from that of the ordinary people. He was temperate in eating and drinking, particularly in drinking, for he hated drunkenness in anyone and especially in himself or in his own men.

Source: Eginhard [Einhard], *Vie de Charlemagne*, 4th ed., ed. Louis Halphen (Paris: Société d'Edition [Les Belles Lettres], 1967), cc. 21–23, pp. 64–70 (translated and adapted by T. Noble).

in allegiance to the king and in membership in a sort of Augustinian City of God.

Einhard (ca. 770–840), Charlemagne's friend and biographer, reports that Augustine's *City of God* (see page 233) was the king's favorite book. The king understood it to mean that two opposing domains contended for power on earth: a City of God consisting of all right-thinking Christians—the "New Israel"—and a City of

Man consisting of pagans, heretics, and infidels. This idea is similar to the Islamic umma (see page 242). To Charlemagne and his advisers, it was obvious that as God was the sole legitimate ruler in heaven, Charlemagne was the sole legitimate and divinely appointed ruler on earth.

Modern readers may think that Charlemagne had crossed a boundary between church and state. It is crucial to understand that to Charlemagne, as to his Muslim and Byzantine contemporaries, no such boundary existed. Church (or religion) and state were complementary attributes of a polity whose end was personal salvation, not military security or personal fulfillment. Charlemagne's ideological legacy was twofold. On the one hand, it created possibilities for bitter struggles later in the Middle Ages between secular rulers and ecclesiastical powers about the leadership of Christian society. On the other hand, it made it hard to define the state and its essential purposes in other than religious terms.

The most disputed event in the reign of Charlemagne was his imperial coronation in Rome on Christmas in 800. It is important to separate how this event happened from what it meant to the participants. In April 799, some disgruntled papal bureaucrats and their supporters attacked Pope Leo III (r. 795–816) in an attempt to depose him. Leo was saved by an ally of Charlemagne and then traveled all the way to Saxony, where the king was camped with his army. Charlemagne agreed to restore the pope to Rome and, as his ally and protector, to investigate those who had attacked him. No real offenses could be proved against the pope, who appeared publicly in Rome to swear that he had done nothing wrong. Everything was handled to avoid any hint that the pope had been put on trial. When Charlemagne went to Saint Peter's Basilica on Christmas Day, he prayed before the main altar. As he rose from prayer, Pope Leo placed a crown on his head, and the assembled Romans acclaimed him as emperor.

Debate over this coronation arises from a remark of Einhard, who said that if Charlemagne had known what was going to happen, he would not have gone to church that day, even though it was Christmas. Einhard's point was not that Charlemagne did not wish to be emperor. For at least fifteen years, prominent people at the Carolingian court had been addressing Charlemagne in imperial terms in letters, treatises, and poems. Moreover, some were saying that because of Irene's usurpation, the imperial throne was vacant—implying that a woman could not truly rule. What Einhard did mean was that Charlemagne saw himself as a Frankish and Christian emperor, not as a *Roman* emperor. The imperial office dignified his position as leader of the Frankish "Israel." Charlemagne did not wish to be beholden to the pope or to the Romans.

Charlemagne's policies did not change after his coronation. He continued his program of legal and ecclesiastical reform and put the finishing touches on some military and diplomatic campaigns. In 806 he divided his empire among his three legitimate sons; but then two of them died, so in 813 he made Louis his sole heir and successor. Charlemagne outlived most of the friends and companions of his youth and middle age. He outlived four wives and many of his children. Old and alone, ill and lame, he died in early 814.

Charlemagne's legacy was great. He brought together the lands that would become France, Germany, the Low Countries, and northern Italy and endowed them with a common ideology, government, and culture. He provided a model that Europeans would look back to for centuries as a kind of golden age. His vast supra-regional and supra-ethnic entity, gradually called "Christendom," drew deeply on the universalizing ideals of its Roman, Christian, and Jewish antecedents but was, nevertheless, original. With its Roman, Germanic, and Christian foundations, the Carolingian Empire represented the final stage in the evolution of the Roman Empire in the West.

■ Carolingian Government

Charlemagne accomplished much through the sheer force of his personality and his boundless energy. But he also reformed and created institutional structures. These helped him to carry out his tasks, guaranteed a measure of permanence to his reforms, and created government patterns that lasted in many parts of Europe until the twelfth century.

The king (or emperor—the offices differed little in practical importance) was the heart of the system. In theory, the king ruled by God's grace and did not have to answer for his conduct to any person. In reality, the king necessarily sought consensus through a variety of means. The king controlled vast lands, which gave him great wealth of his own and also the means to reward loyal followers. By controlling appointments to key positions, the king required men to come to him for power, wealth, and prestige.

The Eastern contemporaries of the Carolingians relied on large numbers of carefully trained, paid civil servants. In contrast, the Carolingians employed a limited number of men who were tied to them by bonds of familial and personal allegiance. The Carolingian court included several ceremonial officers and a domestic staff, all desirable positions. For example, the constable, an officer in charge of transporting the royal entourage, was usually a great aristocrat; the real work of the office was carried out by underlings. The treasurer was the keeper of the king's bedchamber, where the royal treasure chest was kept. Several chaplains, whose primary duty was to see to the spiritual needs of the court, kept official records. The queen controlled the domestic staff and the stewards who managed the royal estates.

Local government was mainly entrusted to counts. About six hundred counts, and several times that number of minor officials, managed the empire. As in Merovingian times, the counts were administrative, judicial, and military officials. Most came from prominent families, and the office increased the wealth and importance of its holders. Counts had to promulgate and enforce royal orders and preside in regular sessions of local courts. They got one-third of the fines, so the zealous pursuit of justice was in their interest.

The royal court and the localities were linked in several ways. Under Charlemagne and his successors it became usual for all major officers, whether secular (counts and their subordinates) or ecclesiastical (bishops, abbots), to be *vassals* of the king. Vassals solemnly pledged loyalty and service to the king. Vassalage drew on both Roman and Germanic customs. Patron-client ties had always been socially and politically important among the Romans, and the allegiance of warriors to a chief was a key Germanic bond. But by connecting personal loyalty with public office, Charlemagne created something essentially new. Only a few thousand men, a tiny fraction of the total population, were vassals at any time. They constituted the political and social elite.

Another connection between the king and his local agents was the assembly that met in various places once or twice a year. In theory, all free men could attend these gatherings, which sometimes had separate secular and ecclesiastical sessions, to advise the king on matters of great importance, such as war and peace or legal reforms. In practice only the vassals had the means or the interest to ensure their presence. Most of the great Carolingian reforms were formulated in these assemblies by cooperation between the king and his most important subjects. The assemblies served to defuse dissension, but the king also brought his power to bear locally by traveling widely. The monarchy possessed estates all over the heartlands of the kingdom, and the royal entourage often moved from one place to another. Monasteries and cathedrals provided hospitality to the king. As the royal party traveled about the realm, they were able to check on local conditions and to compel local officials to comply with royal wishes.

In 788 Charlemagne began to build a palace at Aachen, and in the last twenty years of his life he usually resided there (see Map 8.3). The later Carolingian rulers all tended to have fixed residences, as did the Byzantines and the Abbasids. In adopting fixed residences and elaborate court rituals, the Carolingians may have been returning to Roman precedents or copying their contemporaries to appear as sophisticated as they. Elegant courts and intricate rituals project an aura of grandeur that enhances people's respect for their rulers. It is no accident that a key innovation of Charlemagne's reign coincided with his permanent residence in Aachen. In the late 780s he began to send out pairs of roving inspectors, *missi dominici*°, envoys of the lord king. Their function was to see that royal orders were being observed, that counts were dispensing justice honestly, and that persons of power were not oppressing the powerless.

■ The Carolingian Renaissance

Charlemagne's reforms culminated in a revival of learning that scholars have named the "Carolingian Renaissance" (from *renaissance*, French for "rebirth"). Charlemagne's fundamental ideas are revealed by the constant use in contemporary sources of words such as *rebirth, renewal, reform,* and *restoration.* Charlemagne, his advisers, and his successors looked back for inspiration to Christian and papal Rome, to Saint Peter and Constantine, and to the Church Fathers. To them, the rebirth of Western society as a "New Israel" was equivalent to the theological rebirth of an individual in baptism. The Carolingians were the driving force behind intellectual growth in their era, and in all areas they subordinated learning to their ideological program.

To accomplish his objectives, Charlemagne required every cathedral and monastery to establish a school. To set up and run those schools, he summoned to his court many of the most able and influential intellectual figures of the day, among them Franks, such as his biographer Einhard, grammar teachers from Italy, and Visigothic theologians from the Spanish border. His most famous recruit was the Anglo-Saxon Alcuin° (735–804), the most learned man of his day and the heir of Bede and of the brilliant culture of Northumbria.

Much of the work of Alcuin and his associates was devoted to producing textbooks and to teaching elementary knowledge. Charlemagne was convinced that people needed to be taught the basic truths of Christianity if he were to accomplish his task of leading them to salvation. A massive effort was thus undertaken to copy manuscripts of the Bible and the writings of the Latin Church Fathers. These books, the essential resources for the whole program, needed to be disseminated as widely as possible. The process of copying was facilitated by a new script, Caroline minuscule. (See the feature "Weighing the Evidence: The Manuscript Book" on pages 272–273.)

---

missi dominici (MISS-ee doe-MEE-nee-kee)
Alcuin (AL-kwin)

Model of Charlemagne's Palace at Aachen   In the foreground is the octagonal chapel and throne room of Charlemagne's palace at Aachen. It is joined by galleries to the residential quarters in the background. Construction was begun in 788. The models for these buildings were found in Rome and Ravenna.   *(Römische-Germanisches Zentralmuseum)*

It is significant that Charlemagne could attract Alcuin from York, the most renowned school in the West, to head his palace school, just then forming. Alcuin recognized that Charlemagne could place more resources at his disposal than anyone else, and had the will to do so. Alcuin also saw the long-term benefits that would come from his work. Alcuin's pupils spread out in the next generation to create a network of schools that went right on multiplying across the ninth century. That is a powerful legacy. And Alcuin did more than just teach. He wrote learned works and poetry and was for twenty years Charlemagne's most trusted adviser.

With his plan, personnel, and schools in place, Charlemagne took many concrete steps. He secured from Rome a copy of the then-authoritative canon law of the church. In 789, after some years of study by his court scholars, this law was issued for his whole kingdom. In about 786, Charlemagne got from the pope a sacramentary, a service book for worship in cathedral churches, and, again after a period of examination, this was imposed throughout the kingdom. Charlemagne sought an authoritative copy of the *Rule of St. Benedict*, and after study and commentary, this Rule was imposed on all monasteries in the kingdom.

Secular reforms mirrored religious ones. Orders regularized the management of all royal estates. Charlemagne attempted to update local law codes and to make them as uniform as possible. Not since Rome had governments possessed either the interest in or the means to promote such centralization. It is striking that in the eighth century the caliphate, the Byzantine Empire, and the Carolingian Empire were engaged in similar centralizing activities.

Maiestas Domini (The Lord in Majesty)   An ivory book cover from Charlemagne's court or a closely associated workshop, this image shows the enthroned Christ trampling beasts and encircled by scenes from his life. The image is an excellent Carolingian adaption of late antique themes and styles. *(Stiftsbibliothek, St. Gallen)*

Versatility was a hallmark of Carolingian learning. Various scholars excelled at poetry, history, and biography. Biblical studies and theology attracted a lot of attention. One figure who personifies the Carolingian Renaissance is the Visigoth Theodulf°. He came to court in about 790 and served thereafter as a missus, royal adviser, abbot of several monasteries, and bishop of Orléans. He issued important legislation for his diocese. He was the foremost Old Testament expert of his day and the only one who knew Hebrew. He wrote the official Frankish response to Byzantine iconoclasm. He also composed theological treatises, many letters, and dozens of poems. At Germigny° he designed a church that is a masterpiece of early Carolingian architecture.

Carolingian art is a crowning glory of the age. The manuscripts decorated under Charlemagne's patronage and then, for three generations, under the patronage of his descendants and of prominent churchmen show versatility, respect but not awe for the past, and innovation. Several distinct currents inspired and informed Carolingian art. Most prominent were the animal and geometric decorative motifs of Irish and Anglo-Saxon art; the elegance, formality, and sense of composition of classical art; basic elements of style from Byzantine painting; actual scenes from papal Rome; and the mysteries of Christian theology. Every element was borrowed, but the finished product was new.

Architecture shows the same trends. Charlemagne's palace complex at Aachen has parallels in imperial Constantinople, papal Rome, and Ostrogothic Ravenna. Workers and building materials were fetched from all over the empire. From 768 to 855, 27 cathedrals were built along with 417 monasteries and 100 royal residences. For basic buildings the Carolingians adapted the basilica. The classical basilica was a horizontal building, but the Carolingians, by altering the western end and façade, added the dimension of verticality. In Romanesque and Gothic architecture this innovation would have a long career (see pages 346–349).

■ The Fragmentation of Charlemagne's Empire, 814–887

The Carolingian Empire itself did not outlive the ninth century. Rome's empire lasted much longer, as did Byzantium's and Islam's. All of these realms were fatally weakened by similar problems, but those problems arose more quickly and acutely in the Carolingian world than elsewhere. By the end of the ninth century small political entities had replaced the unified Carolingian Empire.

Size and ethnic complexity contributed to the disintegration of the Carolingian Empire. The empire included many small regions—Saxony, Bavaria, Brittany, and Lombardy, for example—that had their own resident elites, linguistic traditions, and distinctive cultures, which had existed before the Carolingians came on the scene and persist to this day. The Merovingian and Carolingian periods were basically a unifying intrusion into a history characterized by regional diversity. The Carolingians

Theodulf (THEE-oh-dulf)

Germigny (JHER-mee-nee)

made heroic efforts to build a common culture and to forge bonds of unity, but the obstacles were insuperable.

Another key issue in the breakup of the Carolingian Empire was political and dynastic. The Carolingians regularly tried to create subkingdoms for all their legitimate sons while preserving the imperial title for one of them. This was a creative attempt to concede limited autonomy to particular regions by means of local kingships—for instance in Bavaria, Italy, and Aquitaine—while preserving the "Augustinian" unity of the empire as a whole. Unfortunately, younger sons rarely yielded to their older brothers, and the bonds of loyalty among cousins, nephews, and grandchildren grew slender. Frequent divisions of the empire, or of segments of it, placed local nobilities in the difficult position of changing their allegiance frequently and of jeopardizing their offices and landholdings.

In the Treaty of Verdun in 843 (see the Map 8.3 inset) the three grandsons of Charlemagne—Charles the Bald, Louis the German, and Lothair—divided the empire into three realms: the West Frankish, the East Frankish, and the Middle Kingdoms. After fierce battles among the brothers, each appointed forty members to a study commission that traversed the whole empire to identify royal properties, fortifications, monasteries, and cathedrals so that an equitable division could be made of these valuable resources. Each brother needed adequate resources to solidify his rule and to attract or hold followers. The lines drawn on the map at Verdun did not last even for a generation.

Slowly large West Frankish and East Frankish Kingdoms emerged, swallowing the Middle Kingdom, and created a framework for the future France and Germany. But they had to compete with many smaller entities. Some of these, in Italy, in the Rhineland, and in southern France, were old and distinctive regions that recaptured their former independence. Other areas were essentially new creations, born in the absence of firm Carolingian control. Newcomers also appeared on the scene, most prominently Scandinavian and Slavic principalities.

Before the ninth century, Scandinavia had known only small-scale political units under local chieftains and their trusted followers. Economic and political pressure from the Carolingians gradually began to push both Denmark and Norway in the direction of greater political consolidation. A single Danish monarchy has a continuous history from the late ninth century, and Norway's monarchy dates from the early tenth.

To the east of the Carolingian Empire lay a vast swath of Slavic lands. The Carolingians fought, allied, and traded with these peoples for decades. Charlemagne destroyed the Avar khanate in the Danube basin in campaigns between 788 and 804. By the middle of the ninth century, the princes of Great Moravia dominated the region and played a complicated diplomatic game between the East Frankish rulers and the Byzantine emperors. To the east of the Moravians, the Bulgarians profited from the Avar and then the Carolingian collapse to expand their kingdom. For two centuries the Bulgarians dominated eastern Europe and threatened Byzantium.

The most durable consequence of this political restructuring along the eastern frontier of the Frankish world was religious. In 863, on an invitation from Moravia and in hopes of countering the Franks, the Byzantine emperor sent the missionaries Cyril° (826–869) and Methodius° (805–884) into eastern Europe. The emperor hoped to erect an Orthodox union of his own realm, the southern Slavs, and the newly converted Bulgarians. Likewise he was seeking a diplomatic bulwark between the Bulgarians in the east and the Franks in the west. Unfortunately for Byzantium, Cyril and Methodius agreed with the pope to introduce Roman Catholic Christianity in return for the pope's permission to use the Slavonic language in worship. Cyril and Methodius were formidable linguists who created a religious literature in "Church Slavonic" that went far toward creating a new cultural realm in central Europe.

Finally, a new wave of attacks and invasions contributed decisively to the fragmentation of the Carolingian Empire. In the middle decades of the ninth century, Muslims, Vikings, and Magyars wreaked havoc on the Franks.

Based in North Africa and the islands of the western Mediterranean, Muslims attacked Italy and southern France. The Byzantines lost Sicily to raiders from North Africa in 827 and found themselves seriously challenged in southern Italy. In the 840s, Muslims raided the city of Rome. These same brigands preyed on trade in the western Mediterranean and even set up camps in the Alps to rob traders passing back and forth over the mountains.

"From the fury of the Northmen, O Lord, deliver us," was a plaintive cry heard often in ninth-century Europe. Those Northmen were Vikings, mainly Danes and Norwegians, seeking booty, glory, and political opportunity. Most Viking bands were formed by leaders who had lost out in the dawning institutional consolidation of the northern world. Some were opportunists who sought to profit from the weakness of Carolingian, Anglo-Saxon, and Irish rule. In the mid-ninth century, Vikings began settling and initiated their own state-building activities in Ireland, England, northwestern France ("Normandy"—the region of the Northmen), and Rus (early "Russia").

Cyril (SEER-ul)   **Methodius** (meth-oh-DEE-us)

Magyars, relatives of the Huns and Avars who had preceded them into eastern Europe, were accomplished horsemen whose lightning raids, beginning in 889, hit Italy, Germany, and even France. East Frankish Carolingians tried to use the Magyars as mercenaries against the troublesome Moravians. In the end, the Magyars destroyed the incipient Moravian state and raided with impunity.

All of these attacks were unpredictable and caused local regions to fall back on their own resources rather than look to the central government. Commerce was disrupted everywhere. Schools, based in ecclesiastical institutions, suffered severe decline. The raids represented a thousand pinpricks, not a single, deadly sword stroke. Yet their collective effect amounted to despair and disruption on a massive scale.

Even though the Carolingian Empire itself disintegrated, the idea of Europe as "Christendom," as a single political-cultural entity, persisted. The Latin Christian culture promoted by Carolingian schools and rulers set the tone for intellectual life until the twelfth century. Likewise, Carolingian governing structures were inherited and adapted by all of the successor states that emerged in the ninth and tenth centuries. In these respects the Carolingian experience paralleled the Roman, and the Islamic and Byzantine, too: A potent, centralizing regime disappeared but left a profound imprint on its heirs. For hundreds of years, Western civilization would be played out inside the lands that had been Charlemagne's empire and between those lands and their Byzantine and Muslim neighbors.

EARLY MEDIEVAL ECONOMIES AND SOCIETIES

THE economic and social history of the early Middle Ages provides additional evidence of the similarities among the three early medieval civilizations, while also revealing differences. Overall, the world remained rural, society was hierarchical, and women were excluded from public power. Although broad political frameworks changed, the lives of most people changed rather little.

■ Trade and Commerce

In the simplest terms, trade is a mechanism for exchanging goods from one person or group to another. There are many such exchange mechanisms. The Roman government, for example, moved large amounts of goods from the center of the empire to the frontiers to supply its armies. Roman, Byzantine, and Islamic governments raised taxes in one place, bought goods in another, and then consumed their purchases someplace else. Tribute and plunder were also effective exchange mechanisms, as were diplomatic gifts: a caliph, for example, sent Charlemagne an elephant.

The commonest exchanges were intensely local, but several major trading networks operated during the early Middle Ages. In the East, Mesopotamia was linked by rivers to the Persian Gulf, East Africa, and southern Asia, by land and sea to Byzantium, and by land and rivers to the Black Sea region, Slavic Europe, and the Baltic. Byzantines traded mainly by sea. The whole Mediterranean was open to them, and from the Black Sea they received the products of the Danube basin. The Muslim world was fundamentally a land empire that had relatively poor roads and primitive wheeled vehicles, so transport considerations were crucial: a caravan of some five hundred camels could move only one-fourth to one-half the cargo of a normal Byzantine ship.

The West had many trade routes. The Rhône-Saône river system carried goods, as did the land routes through the Alpine passes. The North and Baltic Seas were the hubs of a network that linked the British Isles, the whole of the Frankish north—by means of its rivers— the Rhineland, Slavic Europe, Byzantium, and the Muslim world. The Danube was also a major highway. The major trade networks intersected at many points. Despite religious and ideological differences, Rome's three heirs regularly traded with one another.

Food and other bulk goods never traveled very far because the cost was prohibitive. Most towns were supplied with foodstuffs by their immediate hinterlands, so the goods that traveled long distances were portable and valuable. Cotton and raw silk were transported to the Mediterranean, where they were made into cloth in, respectively, Egypt and Byzantium. Paper and pottery were transported around the caliphate. Asian spices and perfumes were avidly sought everywhere. The Byzantines traded in silk cloth, fine ivories, delicate products of the gold- and silversmiths' art, slaves, and naval stores. Byzantium, with its large fleet, usually controlled the Black and Mediterranean Seas. Reduced in prosperity, the empire could no longer dictate trade terms to subject peoples and competed badly with the Muslims. Trade in the west was partly in high-value luxury goods but mainly in ordinary items such as plain pottery, raw wool, wool cloth, millstones, weapons, and slaves.

■ Town and Countryside

To think of the ancient world is to think of cities. But to think of the medieval world is to envision forests and fields. Actually, from 80 to 90 percent of people in antiquity lived in rural settings, and in the early Middle Ages the percentage was not much higher. What changed was the place occupied by towns in the totality of human life. Fewer government functions were based in towns, cultural life was less bound to the urban environment, and trade in luxuries, which depended on towns, declined.

Towns in the West lost Roman governmental significance but often survived as focal points of royal or, more often, ecclesiastical administration. A cathedral church required a large corps of administrators. Western towns were everywhere attracting *burgs*, new settlements of merchants, just outside their centers. Because Vikings frequently raided these burgs, their existence was precarious. Few Western towns were impressive in size or population. Rome may have numbered a million people in the time of Augustus, but only about 30,000 lived there in 800. Paris had perhaps 20,000 inhabitants at that time. These were the largest cities by far in Catholic Europe.

In the Byzantine East, apart from Constantinople, the empire had a more rural aspect after the Muslims took control of the heavily urbanized regions of Syria, Egypt, and parts of Anatolia in the seventh century. The weakening of the caliphate in the second half of the ninth century was a spur to renewed urban growth in the Byzantine Empire. In provincial cities, population growth and urban reconstruction depended heavily on military conditions: cities threatened by Arabs or Bulgarians declined.

The Arabs were great city-builders. Baghdad—four times larger in area than Constantinople, with a million residents to the latter's 400,000—was created from scratch. The most magnificent city in the West was Cordoba, the capital of Muslim Spain. Its population may have reached 400,000, and its great mosque, begun in 785, held 5,500 worshipers, more than any Latin church except Saint Peter's. The city had 900 baths, 1,600 mosques (Rome had about 200 churches), 60,000 mansions, and perhaps 100,000 shops. Its libraries held thousands of books when the largest Carolingian book collections numbered a few hundred.

Agriculture nevertheless remained the most important element in the economy and in the daily lives of most people in all three realms. Farming meant primarily the production of cereal grains, which provided diet

IAN | FEBR | MAR
APR | MAI | IUN
IUL | AUG | SEPT
OCT | NOUB | DECEMB

Labors of the Months From a ninth-century West Frankish manuscript, this picture illustrates the labors of the various months of the year. How many of them can you figure out? How do these compare with farm labors where you live?
(Österreichische Nationalbibliothek)

staples such as bread, porridge, and beer. Regions tended to specialize in the crops that grew most abundantly in local circumstances. For example, olives and grapes were common in the Mediterranean area whereas cereals predominated around the Black Sea and in central Gaul. Animal husbandry was always a major part of the rural regime. English sheep provided wool and meat. In Frankish and Byzantine regions pigs, which were cheap to raise, supplied meat, but for religious reasons pork was almost absent in the Muslim East—Islam adopted the Jewish prohibition against it.

A key development in the Frankish West was the appearance of a bipartite estate, sometimes called a "manor." On a bipartite estate, one part of the land was set aside as a reserve (or *demesne*°), and the rest was di-

vided into tenancies. The reserve, consuming from one quarter to one half of the total territory of the estate, was exploited directly for the benefit of the landlord. The tenancies were generally worked by the peasants for their own support. The bipartite estate provided the aristocrats with a livelihood while freeing them for military and government service.

Estates were run in different ways. A landlord might hire laborers to farm his reserve, paying them with money exacted as fees from his tenants. Or he might require the tenants to work a certain number of days per week or weeks per year in his fields. The produce of the estate might be gathered into barns and consumed locally or hauled to local markets. The reserve might be a separate part of the estate, a proportion of common fields, or a percentage of the harvest. The tenants might have individual farms or work in common fields. Al-

---

demesne (duh-MEEN)

though the manor is one of the most familiar aspects of European life throughout the Middle Ages, large estates with dependent tenants were also evolving in the Byzantine and Islamic worlds.

■ Social Patterns

Most of the surviving medieval records were written by elite members of society and reveal little about the middle and lower orders of society. Nevertheless, certain similarities are evident in the social structures of all levels in all three societies. The elites tended to be large landholders, to control dependent populations, and to have access to government offices. There were regional differences, too. Scholars ranked higher in Byzantium and the caliphate than in the West; and churchmen, especially bishops, were powerful in Christian societies but had no counterparts in Muslim ones. Literature, surely reflecting social realities, portrays the cultivated Muslim gentleman in the Abbasid period. This social type, marked by learning, good manners, and a taste for finery, does not appear in Byzantium or in the West until the twelfth century.

The middling classes show some disparities among the regions. Merchants, for example, often rose through the social ranks to become great aristocrats in Muslim societies. Islamic society often evinced great mobility, because of its restless, expanding nature and because Islamic ideology rejected distinctions in the umma. In Byzantium, traditional Roman prejudices against merchants and moneymaking activities persisted. Thus, rich merchants whose wealth gave them private influence frequently lacked public power and recognition. In the West, merchants were neither numerous nor powerful in the Carolingian period. In some towns, moreover, commerce was in the hands of Jews, always outsiders in a militantly Christian society. (See the box "Reading Sources: The Status of Carolingian Jews.")

Merchants were not the only people occupying the middle rungs of the social ladder. All three societies, in fact, possessed both central elites and provincial elites. Service at the Carolingian, Byzantine, or Abbasid court counted for more than service in a provincial outpost. It was one thing to be abbot of a great monastery and quite a different thing to preside over a poor, tiny house. The thematic generals in Byzantium were lofty personages; their subordinates held inferior positions. The vassals of a Carolingian king formed a real aristocracy; but vassals' vassals were of decidedly lower rank.

Degrees of freedom and local economic and political conditions shaped the lives of peasants. In all three societies some farmers were personally free and owed no

cash or labor services to anyone but the central government. In areas such as Abbasid Iraq, ordinary free farmers led a comfortable life. In the Frankish world, most peasants existed outside the dawning manorial system. They were free, and if they lived in areas of good land and political security, such as the Paris basin, their lives most likely were congenial. Byzantine peasants, though free, often lived in areas of military danger, and in some parts of the Balkans they eked a living from poor soils. Highly taxed and perpetually endangered, their freedom may have been small compensation for their economic and personal insecurity. All peasants were alike in their subjection to political forces over which they had no control.

At the bottom of the social scale everywhere were slaves. Christianity did not object to slavery itself but forbade the enslavement of Christians. Islam likewise prohibited Muslims from enslaving other Muslims. Slaves therefore tended to be commonest in still-pagan societies—Scandinavia, for example—or in frontier regions where neighboring pagans could be captured and sold. There were more slaves in the Muslim world than in Byzantium, which had, in turn, more than the West.

Women were bound to the same social hierarchies as men. Predictably enough, women had few formal, public roles to play. Their influence, however great, tended to function in the private sphere, rarely revealed to us by sources that stem from the public realm of powerful men. Aristocratic women had opportunities and power that were denied ordinary women. Irene ruled at Byzantium as empress. Frankish and Anglo-Saxon queens were formidable figures in the life of their realms. Carolingian queens managed the landed patrimony of the dynasty, dozens of huge estates with tens of thousands of dependents. A lack of evidence and the rigorous exclusion of women from public life in the Islamic world means that virtually no Muslim women emerge as distinct personalities in the early Middle Ages.

The conversion of England to Christianity was fostered by women. Most convents of nuns had aristocratic abbesses who presided over complex enterprises and, often, schools. In the Frankish world aristocratic women secured some learning, and one, Dhuoda, wrote in 841 a manual of advice for her son that conveys biblical and patristic teachings as well as practical wisdom. The Frankish convent at Chelles was a renowned center for the copying of manuscripts. Some Anglo-Saxon nuns owned ships and invested in commercial activities to support their convents. Almost all aspects of the cloth industry were in women's hands.

One example of the problems in the evidence concerning women relates to church roles. Women could not hold priestly office; and although deaconesses

The Status of Carolingian Jews

In 826 or 827 Archbishop Agobard of Lyon wrote this protest to Emperor Louis the Pious because the emperor had issued legislation favorable to the Jewish minority in general and to Jewish merchants in particular. Agobard's anti-Semitism is probably typical for the period and serves to indicate the precarious position of the Jews in the militantly Christian Frankish empire.

I commit myself to your goodness and patience as I inform you of what is ruinous to pass over in silence. There came Gerric and Frederick who were preceded by Evrard, your missi [envoys] in fact, yet not doing your will completely but rather acting on behalf of another. They showed themselves to be terrible to the Christians and mild to the Jews, especially in Lyon, where they set up a persecuting faction against the Church and they goaded the church to many groans, sighs, and tears.

When the Jews first arrived, they gave me a message in your name and another one to the man who rules the district of Lyon in place of the count; [this message] ordered him to offer aid to the Jews against me. We absolutely did not believe that such messages as these issued from your judgment, although they were read out in your sacred name and sealed with your ring. The Jews began to rage with a certain odious insolence, threatening that we would be afflicted with every sort of injury by the agents whom they had obtained to take vengeance upon Christians. After them, Evrard arrived and repeated the same thing and said that your majesty was truly angry with me because of the Jews. Then the aforementioned agents arrived, holding in their hands a tax code and a capitulary of sanctions which we do not believe exists by your command. Consequently, certain of our priests whom they threatened by name, did not dare to show their faces. We suffered these things from the Jews' supporters and for no other reason but that we preached to Christians that they should not sell Christian slaves to them; that they should not allow these Jews to sell Christians to Spain nor to possess them as paid domestics lest Christian women celebrate the Sabbath with them, work on Sundays, eat with them during Lent, and their paid servants eat meat on these days; and that no Christian should buy meats sacrificed and butchered by Jews and sell them to other Christians; and that they should not drink their wine or other things like this. . . .

. . . It is absolutely necessary that your pious solicitude know how the Christian faith is being harmed by the Jews in certain ways. For when they lie to simple Christians and boast that they are dear to you because of the patriarchs; that they enter and leave your sight with honor; that most excellent people desire their prayers and blessings and confess that they wished they had the same author of the law as the Jews; when they say that your counselors are aroused against us for their sake, because we forbid Christians from drinking their wine; when, in trying to claim this, they boast that they have received from Christians many, many pounds of silver from the sale of wine and cannot find out, after running through the canons, why Christians should abstain from their food and drink; when they produce commands signed with golden seals in your name and containing words which, in our opinion, are not true; when they show people women's clothes as if they were sent to their wives by your kinsmen or matrons of the palaces; when they expound upon the glory of their forefathers; when they are permitted, contrary to the law, to build new synagogues— [when all this occurs] it even reaches the point when naive Christians say that the Jews preach to them better than our priests. And this was particularly true when the aforementioned agents ordered that the markets that usually occur on Saturdays should be moved lest [the Jews'] Sabbatism be impeded, and they let [the Jews] choose on which days they had to go to market from then on, claiming that this suited the utility of the Christians because of the Sunday vacation.

Source: Translated by W. L. North from *Agobardi Lugdunensis Opera Omnia,* Opusculum XI, ed. L. Van Acker, Corpus Christianorum. *Continuatio Mediaevalis* 52 (Turnholt: Brepols, 1981), pp. 191–195.

 For additional information on this topic, go to http://college.hmco.com.

served at Hagia Sophia in the sixth century, they disappeared soon after and had long before vanished in the West. Religious power could come from personal sanctity as well as holding office. One study of some 2,200 saints from the early Middle Ages finds only about 300 females. It was hard for women to gain recognition as saints. And if a woman became a saint, her holiness was inevitably described either as "manly"—an extreme ascetic was praised for having the strength and courage of a man—or as beautiful, virginal, and domestic, in other words, with female stereotypes.

The domestic sphere is another difficult realm to enter. The Quran permitted a man up to four wives, if he could care for them and would treat them equitably. A Muslim woman, however, was given her dowry outright, and multiple marriages may have meant that relatively more Muslim women could gain a measure of security. In Byzantium and the West, families rarely arranged marriages for more than one or two daughters. Others remained single or entered convents. Women at all social levels tended to pass from the tutelage of their fathers to that of their husbands. In antiquity a suitor usually paid a fee, a "bride price," to his prospective wife's father and then endowed his wife with "bridewealth," money or possessions of her own. Gradually this practice changed to a system whereby a bride's father paid a dowry to her future husband. Thus, a wife who was cast aside could be left impoverished, for in most places the law did not permit her to inherit land if she had brothers. Females were such valuable property in the marriage market that rape was an offense not against a girl but against her father. A man could divorce, even kill, his wife for adultery, witchcraft, or grave robbing, and then marry again. A woman could usually gain a divorce only for adultery, and she could not remarry. For the vast majority of women, daily life was hedged about with legal limitations and personal indignities.

SUMMARY

 WE have traced three parallel histories in the development of early medieval civilizations. The first one is chronological. In the Arab, Byzantine, and Latin worlds, the seventh century was an age of rapid, dynamic change, the eighth century a time of consolidation and reform, and the ninth century a period of renewed challenges.

The second history is political, religious, and ideological. Three different peoples built large imperial states. Each state fashioned a central government that focused on a powerful leader who was seen as a specially

chosen agent of God. Each state erected a system of rule that tied a government capital to its outlying regions. In the Muslim and Byzantine worlds, that system was highly bureaucratic; in the Carolingian Empire, the system was more amateur and personal. A religion—Islam, Orthodoxy, or Roman Catholicism—provided the glue that held each society together and defined the mission of its government. The cultural life of each area was inspired mainly by an attempt to integrate a powerful religious message with older intellectual traditions.

The third history concerns the fate of these imperial realms. In the Islamic and Latin worlds, large states broke down to leave many smaller heirs. In each instance, changes in the caliber of leadership, unpredictable foreign attacks, and the sheer diversity of the polity pulled the large state apart. The Byzantine Empire, much smaller than the Roman Empire had been, managed to defend its territory, but that territory was greatly reduced from former times.

We began this chapter by imagining what Rome's legacy might be. Islam and the caliphate emerged as surprising elements, while Byzantium and the Carolingian worlds followed more predictable courses. In the next chapter, we ask what happened after about 900. This time the surprising element will be found in the West. Although battered in 900, western Europe was on the verge of an astonishing period of growth and development.

■ Suggested Reading

Brown, Peter. *The Rise of Western Christendom*. 2d ed. 2000. A verbal feast, this book presents a stimulating assessment of the place of Christianity in the rise of Western culture.

Collins, Roger. *Charlemagne*. 1997. The first new biography of Charlemagne in a generation, this one is brief and readable.

Denny, Frederick M. *An Introduction to Islam*. 2d ed. 1994. By far the most accessible, readable account of the Islamic faith; the book covers all periods but is helpful for the early centuries.

Kennedy, Hugh. *The Prophet and the Age of the Caliphates: The Islamic Near East from the Sixth to the Eleventh Century*. 1986. Detailed but readable, this is the best modern introduction to the emergence and spread of Islam.

Riché, Pierre. *Daily Life in the World of Charlemagne*. Translated by Jo Ann McNamara. 1978. A highly readable account of how people lived—from diet, wardrobe, and dwellings, to their customary beliefs and superstitions.

Whittow, Mark. *The Making of Orthodox Byzantium, 600–1025*. 1996. Lively, readable, controversial, engaging, this book challenges standard views.

 For a searchable list of additional readings for this chapter, go to http://college.hmco.com.

The Manuscript Book

How long do you think it would take you to copy this whole textbook by hand? We know that it took about a year for two skilled monastic scribes to copy a Bible. Every medieval book was literally a manuscript (from *manuscriptum*, "written by hand"). Manuscripts contain important texts but are also revealing artifacts in their own right.

Codicology and paleography are the primary manuscript sciences. Codicology, the study of books as physical objects, investigates the materials and techniques used to make them. Paleography, the study of handwriting, seeks to read texts and to date and localize surviving books.

Depicted here is a folio (a page) of the Dagulf Psalter, named for the Carolingian scribe who wrote it in 795 on Charlemagne's orders as a gift for Pope Hadrian I (r. 772–795). The rich and powerful often used books as gifts. A psalter is a collection of the 150 biblical psalms and other canticles (songs or prayers derived from the Bible and used for worship). Can you make out the Latin words INCIPIUNT CANTICI, at the very top of the page? They mean "Here begin the canticles." The text is the Canticle of the Prophet Isaiah (Isaiah 12:1–6). Its title is CANTICUM ESAIE PROP[H].

Cathedrals and monasteries usually had *scriptoria*, "writing offices," where scribes and illuminators worked with bookmakers to produce manuscripts. Manuscripts were made from parchment, animal skin. According to an old legend, in the second century B.C. the Egyptians cut off the supply of papyrus to the kingdom of Pergamum forcing the Pergamenes to use animal hides to make writing material. Be that as it may, the English word *parchment* derives from the Latin name for this writing material: *pergamenum*. By the sixth century A.D., parchment had supplanted papyrus as the primary writing material in most of Europe.

Parchment was made by soaking an animal's hide in a caustic lye solution for three to six weeks to remove fat, hair, and blemishes. The hide was then scraped vigorously, washed, rubbed smooth with ashes or pumice, and then stretched on a frame to dry. The finest parchments, called *vellum*, were made from the hides of calves, lambs, or kids. It was almost white in color and nearly translucent. Most parchments were not so fine.

When the parchment was dry, the bookmaker cut and lined it—notice how straight and even the lines are in the picture. Then he took four sheets, or folios, of parchment, laid them down together, and folded them, placing the fold at the left, to form a booklet of sixteen pages called a quire (see the drawing). Because the two sides of a piece of parchment differ in color (the "hair side," or outside, is usually darker than the "flesh side," or inside) the quires were arranged so that hair sides faced hair sides and flesh sides faced flesh sides. A manuscript consisted of many quires sewn together. The smallest surviving manuscript is 2 inches by 3 inches; the largest is about 36 by 19. The larger the pages, the more costly was the book. One huge Bible produced in Bede's Northumbria required the hides of five hundred sheep.

The first page of the first quire was numbered 1^r and 1^v, or 1 recto and 1 verso, meaning 1 "right side" and 1 "turned side." The second sheet was numbered 2^r and 2^v. Today, book pages are numbered 1, 2, 3, and so on, and books always start with an odd-numbered page on the right side—an inheritance from medieval manuscripts.

Scribes and illuminators received the prepared quires. Scribes wrote text onto the parchment. Illuminators added beautiful pictures or designs. You have on pages 248, 255, 268, 278, 287, 300, 303, and 329 examples of the magnificent illuminations that were painted into medieval books. Most books, however, had no such images at all.

Now you are ready to learn some paleography. We have already deciphered the first two lines of the folio shown here. These lines are written in a "display script." For visual appeal and to facilitate reference, scribes often used different handwritings, colors, or both to highlight first letters, first words, or first lines. Books, including the one you are reading, maintain this tradition. The huge writing—can you make out CONFITE?—marks the beginning of Isaiah's text. It continues, on line four, with *bor tibi dne qnm ira*. Line five carries on with *tus es mihi.conversus*. Look at line six: *est furor tuus&consolatusesme*. Can you make out the letters yourself? These words mean, "I will confess to you, O Lord, for you were angry with me but you turned your anger away and brought me consolation."

Several things bear notice here. First, the main script is Caroline minuscule, the new script that accompanied

The Dagulf Psalter *(Österreichische Nationalbibliothek)*

A Quire

Charlemagne's educational reforms. Because of its clarity, it is the basis for many modern typefaces. Compare the letters in the picture with the ones you are reading.

Second, notice the frequent recourse to abbreviation. Writing was time- and space-consuming, prompting the development of elaborate systems of abbreviation. Can you see, in line four, the letters *dne* with a strike over them, and then the letters *qnm*, also with a strike? In this case the words expand to *domine* and *quoniam*. Look at line two, where you see *propʰ*, shorthand for *Prophetae*, ("Prophet"). Also notice the ampersands in lines six, eight, nine, and ten. They stand for *et*, Latin for "and." Note too how the last words in line six run together.

Third, in antiquity, texts had neither breaks between words nor punctuation. As non–Latin-speakers learned to write the language, however, they usually put breaks between the words to facilitate understanding. You can see that most of this text has breaks, except in line six. In lines one, eight, and ten, you can also see a rather curious symbol: "; . It is a full stop, or period.

What else might you learn from a manuscript? Handwriting and systems of abbreviation are distinctive, and specialists use them to date and localize manuscripts. Because parchment was prepared in different ways, some manuscripts can be dated or placed by an analysis of their parchment. Inks differed in chemistry and in appearance and thus help to date and localize books as well. Styles of illumination and forms of images can also be localized or traced from one scriptorium to another. By knowing when, where, and by whom books were written or illuminated, historians can reconstruct the life and work of intellectual centers that were scattered long ago.

It is estimated that a medieval manuscript without illuminations was worth one year's wages for an ordinary working person. Would you spend a year's wages on a book?

CHAPTER 9

THE picture to the left represents one small section of the Bayeux Tapestry, a narrative account—in words and illustrations—of the conquest of England in 1066 by Duke William of Normandy. This scene is an apt introduction to the central theme of this chapter: expansion.

This section of the 230-foot-long tapestry depicts William setting sail for England. William had already gained greater authority in the duchy of Normandy than any duke before him. Now he was about to press his claim to the throne of England. He gathered soldiers from all over western France and boldly crossed the English Channel. Leaving nothing to chance, he transported horses too, as you can see in the picture.

One group of Normans conquered England while another seized control of southern Italy. Still other Normans played a decisive role in the period's most prominent manifestation of expansion: the Crusades. Meanwhile, certain Scandinavians settled Iceland and Greenland to the west while others founded the first state on Russian soil. Spanish Christians pushed back the Muslims in Iberia. From the Baltic to the Balkans, Slavic rulers founded new states and pressed hard against their neighbors. German rulers crossed the Alps into Italy, French kings reached the Pyrenees, and English monarchs pushed into Wales, Scotland, and Ireland. Seldom has Europe's political geography expanded so dramatically as during the High Middle Ages.

Between 900 and 1300, Europe's population began one of its longest periods of sustained growth. People brought more land under cultivation, introduced new crops, and made agriculture more efficient. Villages, towns, and cities grew in number and size. Trade expanded in every material and in every direction.

The Expansion of Europe in the High Middle Ages 900–1300

Economic Expansion

The Heirs of the Carolingian Empire: Germany, Italy, and France

The British Isles

The Growth of New States

The Crusades, 1095–1291

Bayeux Tapestry (ca. 1077), depicting the fleet of William the Conqueror of Normandy sailing to England in 1066.   (Michael Holford)

Europe witnessed the re-emergence of centralizing monarchies in France, England, and Spain. Some new realms, for example, Denmark and Hungary, built strong central governments. And an explosion of new states occurred along the frontiers of the old Carolingian Empire.

The "West" began taking on a more *western European* character. The Crusades complicated relations between Christian Europeans and Muslims, and both the Crusades and increasing religious differences alienated western Europe from Byzantium, and Roman Catholics from Orthodox believers. The center of Western civilization became more and more anchored to northwestern Europe. And that same western Europe was expanding to influence lands in Scandinavia and the Slavic world that had played no role at all in the West's classical, Mediterranean phase. The High Middle Ages repeatedly posed the question: Where is the West?

QUESTIONS TO CONSIDER

- What were the main causes of the economic, political, and military expansion of Europe during the High Middle Ages?
- What basic problems confronted rulers who wished to expand the power and influence of central governments?
- How did the Catholic Church both help and hinder political development?
- What basic factors contributed to the rise, persistence, and eventual decline of the crusading movement?

TERMS TO KNOW

guilds
lay investiture
communes
Papal Monarchy
feudal revolution

Magna Carta
Parliament
Reconquista
Crusades

ECONOMIC EXPANSION

THE economic expansion of Europe is manifest in many kinds of evidence that are more often qualitative than quantitative. Medieval people did not keep the kinds of records of births, deaths, population, or business activity that modern states routinely accumulate. Literary anecdotes can be revealing of course, but they are no substitute for hard data. After about 1000, every available indicator points to a growing population and an expanding scale and sophistication of economic activity.

■ The Growing Population

The population of Europe began rising slowly in the Carolingian period and may have doubled between 1000 and 1200. Scattered bits of evidence suggest that the total population of western Europe grew from around 30 million in 1000 to 55 or 60 million in 1200. In the thirteenth century, population growth gradually slowed.

In a few regions where family size can be estimated, fertile marriages were producing on the average 3.5 children in the tenth century and from 6 to 7 in the twelfth. All families continued to experience the loss of children. Three queens—those of William "the Conqueror," John of England, and Louis VIII of France—lost, respectively, 4 of 10, 6 of 14, and 7 of 12 children. The key change is that more babies were being born. People were also living longer than their forebears. Studies of aristocrats, high clergy, and soldiers show that a surprising 40 percent of them were over 40 years old. Male life expectancy was surely longer than female because of the dangers of childbirth, always the great killer of women in the pre-modern world. The general trend is clear: more babies being born, more infants living into adulthood, more adults living longer.

Everywhere in Europe, new land was brought into cultivation. More than half of the French documents relating to land in the twelfth century mention *assarting*, the bringing of previously untilled land under the plow. Literary texts often tell about knights wandering in a dense forest and suddenly entering a meadow. Those meadows did not get there by nature or accident. Thousands of acres of forest were felled. Marshes were reclaimed from the sea. Some 380,000 acres were drained along the western coast of France and probably twice that amount in both Flanders and England. This activity is inexplicable without assuming a growing number of mouths to feed.

Agriculture benefited from a warmer and drier climate through this whole period. Not a single vegetable blight was recorded. Food was more abundant and also more nutritious. Animals were increasingly reared for their meat, and higher meat consumption meant more protein in the diet. Beans and other legumes, also rich in protein, were more widely cultivated. Fine grains such as wheat replaced poorer cereals, ryes and spelts, in many areas. People of every class and region were almost certainly eating better and living longer and healthier lives.

■ Technological Gains

The eleventh century was a decisive period in the spread of new technologies in Europe. Innovations occurred in agriculture, transportation, mining, and manufacturing. Agricultural changes came first as a rising population created an increased demand for food that could be met only by new practices. In the Carolingian period, the return on seed—the amount of seed realized for each seed sown—is estimated at about 3 or 4 to 1. By the late twelfth century, this ratio had risen in many areas to 8 or 10 to 1. Given the combination of more land under cultivation and more yield per acre, the overall gains in the food supply were enormous.

The increases can be accounted for in several ways. Horses were more frequently used as draft animals. They were more expensive to acquire than oxen but no more costly to feed, and they did, in a day, a third or half again as much work. For much less "fuel," horses could haul loads farther and faster than oxen. Thus, fewer people could, with horses, cultivate more land than their predecessors managed with oxen. In addition, they could cultivate the land more frequently and increase yields because more seed would fall on more finely plowed soil. The dissemination of the horse collar made possible the expanded use of horses—older forms of harness suitable for the low-slung, broad-shouldered ox would have choked a horse.

Plows too were improved. The light wooden scratch plow used by the Romans was satisfactory for the thin soils of the Mediterranean region but barely disturbed the heavy soils of northern Europe. The invention of a heavy wheeled plow with an iron coulter (or plowshare)

CHRONOLOGY	
862	Founding of Kiev
870–930	Settlement of Iceland
962	Imperial coronation of Otto I
987	Accession of Hugh Capet in France
988	Kievan Rus accept Orthodox Christianity
1016	Conquest of England by Cnut
1066	Norman Conquest of England
1072–1085	Pontificate of Gregory VII
1077	Henry IV at Canossa
1078	Decree against lay investiture
1085	Spanish reconquest of Toledo
1086	*Domesday Book*
1095–1099	First Crusade
1122	Concordat of Worms
1171	Henry II of England invades Ireland
1176	Battle of Legnano
1198–1216	Pontificate of Innocent III
1202–1204	French drive English out of Normandy
1203	Fourth Crusade
1212	Battles of Bouvines and Las Navas de Tolosa
1215	Magna Carta
1250–1272	Germany's "Great Interregnum"
1265	First Parliament in England
1295	Model Parliament
1294–1303	Quarrel between Boniface VIII and Philip IV

and a moldboard was a real breakthrough. The iron plowshare cut deep furrows, and then the moldboard turned and aerated the soil. This heavy plow allowed farmers to exploit good soils more fully without exhausting the ground too rapidly. This plow seems to have been introduced into Carolingian Europe from the Slavic world, but it was not widely adopted before the eleventh century.

Wider adoption of nitrogen-fixing crops, such as peas and some kinds of beans, retarded soil exhaustion and also put more protein in the diet. Leaving land fallow was another means of avoiding soil exhaustion. In the early Middle Ages this meant setting aside about half of the arable land every year (the two-field system) or working the land intensively for a few years and then moving on. By the twelfth century three-field schemes of crop rotation were common.

Under the three-field system, two-thirds of the arable land saw nearly constant use. The amount of an estate under cultivation rose from 50 to 67 percent. Crop rotation brought other benefits as well. Horses ate oats, but (except in a few places such as Scotland) medieval

Heavy Wheeled Plow   The improved plow, the horse collar, and the cooperative labors of many peasants in preparing the fields led to an agricultural boom in the European countryside. *(Bibliothèque Nationale de France)*

people generally did not. If farmers wished to use horses, they had to dedicate some of their land to growing oats. A three-field rotation allowed some flexibility. Finally, the alternation of winter crops (wheat and rye), spring crops (oats, barley, and legumes), and fallow ensured against a single season of unusually harsh weather.

Surplus produce was intended mainly for the growing towns. To supply that market, improvements in transportation were necessary. Kings often passed laws to secure the safety of highways, and popes three times (in 1097, 1132, and 1179) threatened highwaymen—robbers who preyed on travelers—with excommunication. Landlords required their dependents to maintain roads and bridges. Many stone bridges were constructed in France between 1130 and 1170 because wooden bridges were so vulnerable to fire. Indeed, fire destroyed the bridge at Angers (in western France) five times between 1032 and 1167.

Transport improved not only because of safer roads but also thanks to better vehicles. Documents and pictures in manuscripts agree that the old two-wheeled cart, drawn by oxen, began giving way to the sturdy four-wheeled, horse-drawn wagon. Because greater quantities of foodstuffs could be moved farther and faster, urban communities could be supplied from larger areas. This was a crucial factor in enabling cities to grow and in providing urban residents with a predictable and diverse range of foods.

Evidence from several parts of Europe points to the years after 925 as the beginning of real growth in the mining industry. Notable improvements occurred in both the quarrying of stone and the extraction of metals. Mines were not deep because people lacked the means to keep the shafts and galleries free of water. Still, the exploitation of surface and near-surface veins of ore—principally iron but also tin and silver—intensified, to supply the increased demand for plowshares, tools, weapons, construction fittings, and coins. Stone quarrying, the commonest form of mining in the Middle Ages, benefited directly from more efficient stone saws and indirectly from improvements in transport. Better techniques in stone cutting, construction, and conveyance help to explain, for example, the increase in the number of England's stone religious buildings from sixty to nearly five hundred in the century after 1050.

■ Forms of Enterprise

Agricultural specialization became common. People began to cultivate intensively those crops that were best suited to local conditions. The area around Toulouse, for example, concentrated on herbs from which blue and yellow dyes were made. The central regions of France focused on cereal grains, while the Bordeaux and Burgundy regions emphasized the grapes that produced wine. Northern Germany specialized in cattle raising; northern England favored sheep.

Agricultural specialization helps to explain the growth in trade that is discernible everywhere (see Map 9.1). For certain commodities, local trade continued to flourish. Italian wines and olive oil, for example, were not produced for far-off markets; they tended to move from countryside to town within a region. The same was true of French or English grains. However, French wines were much prized throughout Europe, especially in England; and certain products, such as English wool and Flemish cloth, were carried far and wide. Salt fish from the Baltic found its way all over the continent. Lumber was routinely traded across the Mediterranean to the wood-poor Muslim world. Spain was a source of warhorses. Southern Europe supplied the northern demand for spices, oranges, raisins, figs, almonds, and other exotic foodstuffs. Caen, in Normandy, sent shiploads of its beautifully colored and textured stone to England for the construction of churches and monasteries. Rising population, higher productivity, and greater prosperity added up to a larger volume of goods moving farther and more frequently.

The lumber industry reveals many facets of medieval economic activity. Before the twelfth century, wood was the main building material, and even later it yielded to stone mainly for the church and aristocracy. But wood could be used for more than construction. For example, the Venetian shipyards needed about twenty oaks, twenty towering pines, and fifty or so beeches to make a ship. In the early twelfth century the Venetians were making about ten vessels a year, twice the number they had been building two centuries earlier. Whether for ships or for homes, the demand for wood grew steadily. In England, to take another example, about 500 cords (a cord is a stack measuring 128 cubic feet) of wood, nearly ten acres' worth, were needed to smelt one ton of silver. Under King Ethelred II (r. 978–1016), moneyers coined thirty tons of silver, consuming in the process some 15,000 cords of wood.

Wood exemplifies the expansion and interconnectedness of the medieval economy and society. Forests were essential to daily life, providing the wood for houses, fences, and fuel in villages and towns. Animals, especially pigs, were grazed at the edges of the forest to permit as much land as possible to be dedicated to food crops. Wild animals were hunted in the forest. For aristocrats hunting was as much for sport as for food. For poorer rural people, however, wild game made up a significant part of

Map 9.1 **European Resources and Trade Routes, ca. 1100** In an age of expansion, some products were consumed locally, but many others were transported over longer and longer distances. Commercial connections expanded too, creating several interlocking networks.

Legend:
— Major routes of trade and commerce
Grain-growing region
Wine-producing region
Coal Primary product

Labels on map:
Volga, Novgorod, Furs, Pskov, Furs, Reval, Wax, Riga, Furs, Smolensk, Kiev, Divna, Dnieter, Tana, Caffa, Black Sea, Varna, Constantinople, Phocea, Alum, Ephesus, Beirut, Acre, Jerusalem, Famagusta, CYPRUS, Candia, CRETE, Stockholm, Copper, Iron, Visby, Baltic Sea, Danzig, Lübeck, Magdeburg, Frankfurt an der Oder, Prague, Oder, Elbe, Silver, Tin, Iron, Nuremberg, Augsburg, Salt, Vienna, Danube, Cracow, L'vov, CARPATHIAN MTS., Bergen, North Sea, Copper, Iron, Iron, Frankfurt am Main, Salt, Besançon, Rhine, Utrecht, Bruges, Lille Coal, Ypres, Woad, Paris, Seine, Loire, Dijon, Lyon, ALPS, Po, Milan, Pavia, Parma, Genoa, Marseilles, Arles, Salt, Rhône, Padua, Venice, Woad, Bologna, Florence, Lucca, Siena, Ancona, Orvieto, Rome, Naples, Barletta, Ragusa (Dubrovnik), Hull, Chester, Salt, Boston, Wool, Ipswich, London, Wool, Bristol, Southampton, Dublin, ATLANTIC OCEAN, Tours, Salt, Albi, Toulouse, Bordeaux, Garonne, Bayonne, Iron, PYRENEES, Barcelona, Palma, Valencia, Murcia, Málaga, Almeria, Cadiz, Lisbon, Salt, Honein, Bougie, Bone, Tunis, SARDINIA, Cagliari, CORSICA, SICILY, Syracuse, Mediterranean Sea

Scale: 0 150 300 Mi. / 0 150 300 Km.

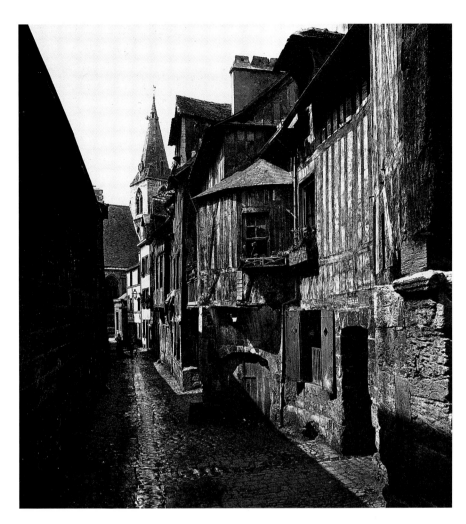

Twelfth-Century Timbered House, Rouen, France The house at the center of this picture was destroyed in World War II after holding its place for nearly eight hundred years. It shows one of the many uses of timber, and its narrow street gives an authentic feel of a medieval town. *(Roger-Viollet)*

the regular diet. The forest was also a plentiful source of fruits, nuts, and honey. If the peasants in a given place decided to cut a stand of timber to process the king's silver, or to build a wooden stockade around their village, or to dispatch masts to Venice, they had to wrestle with serious consequences. After the trees were gone, where would they hunt, or graze their animals, or gather their berries?

■ The Roles of Cities and Towns

All over Europe, towns grew impressively in size and importance. Table 9.1 shows the growth of three Italian cities. Such growth also occurred in cities in Flanders, such as Bruges and Ghent, and in Paris, London, and other cities that were becoming national capitals. Ghent expanded its city walls five times between 1160 and 1300, a sure sign of growth even in the absence of population figures. Similar forces were operating in the countryside, too. In 1100 about 11 fortified villages surrounded Florence, but by 1200 the city was ringed by 205.

Table 9.1
Population Increases in Italian Cities, 1200–1300

City	1200	1300	Percentage of increase
Florence	15,000	96,000	+640%
Siena	19,000	52,000	+274%
Pisa	20,000	38,000	+190%

Source: Adapted from Malcolm Barber, *The Two Cities: Medieval Europe,* 1050–1320 (London: Routledge, 1992), p. 270.

For the first time since late antiquity, cities were becoming centers for many activities. Governments, which required larger staffs of trained personnel, settled in towns. The towns of Italy and Flanders, though not national capitals, ruled over extensive hinterlands. Schools and eventually universities (see pages 341–342) were urban institutions. Mercantile, industrial, and legal organizations were located in towns. Ecclesiastical organization was always urban based. Towns began to compete with royal and aristocratic courts as literary centers, and cathedrals, the great buildings of the age, were exclusively urban.

One distinctive urban phenomenon was the rise of guilds. In 1200, for example, Paris had one guild of merchants and four or five craft or trade associations. By 1270 the city had 101 craft or trade guilds, and by 1292 the number had risen to 130.

The guilds had many functions. Their main purpose was economic: to regulate standards of production, to fix prices, and to control membership in their respective trades. But as towns grew larger and more impersonal, these associations of people engaged in similar occupations fostered a sense of belonging, a feeling of community. Members tended to live in the same areas and to worship together in a parish church. Growing wealth in general, coupled with fierce local pride, produced building competitions whose results are still visible in the huge neighborhood churches that survive in most European towns. The guilds indulged in elaborate festivals and celebrations, which sometimes turned into drunken debauches despite being held to honor saints. The guilds were also mutual assurance societies. That is, they assisted colleagues who fell on hard times, saw to the funeral expenses of members, and provided for widows and orphans.

The guilds had a damaging impact on women. As more economic activity came under the umbrella of the guild structures, women were more systematically excluded from guild membership. Usually women could become guild members only as wives or widows. They could not open economic enterprises of their own, although they were workers in many trades. Despite a growing, diversifying economy, women were increasingly denied opportunities, although later centuries would find women establishing their own guilds.

■ Commercial Growth and Innovation

Towns were focal points in commercial networks. The basic trade routes and networks had existed since Carolingian times, but a novelty of the twelfth century was the emergence of the Champagne fairs as a meeting point for the commerce of north and south. Since the early Middle Ages, a few locations hosted permanent fairs, and many places sponsored occasional fairs. By the middle of the twelfth century, however, the spices, silks, and dyes of the Mediterranean, the wool of England, the furs and linens of Germany, and the leather products of

Spain began to be sold in a series of six fairs held in the Champagne region of France from spring to autumn.

At any time of year, travel was difficult and costly. Few dared to venture across the Alps in the winter, and the northern seas, especially the passage around Denmark, were treacherous in cold weather. Even in the relatively calm Mediterranean, the Venetians refused to send out their trading fleet between November and March. Overland trade was impeded by snow, rain, mud, and highwaymen. Governments tried to restrain robbers, but no one could change the weather. After the road between Pisa and Florence was paved in 1286, it was passable most of the time, but paved roads were few. All these hazards made overland trade extraordinarily expensive, often multiplying the cost of goods tenfold. No wonder transport by water was preferred wherever possible.

Seaborne trade expanded. The stern rudder, better sails, the compass (in use by 1180), and better navigational charts facilitated sea travel, as did the growing use of larger ships. An Italian fleet sailed to Flanders in 1277, and within a few years the old overland trade routes, and with them the Champagne fairs, began a decline that was not reversed until the invention of the railroad in the nineteenth century. (See the box "Reading Sources: Two Views of Medieval Markets.")

■ Changing Economic Attitudes

As medieval society generated more wealth and populations concentrated in cities, people who were relatively well-off became more conscious of those who were less fortunate. Moralists began to argue that the poor were a special gift of God to the rich, who could redeem their own souls by generous charitable benefactions. Most towns established schemes of poor relief. But the numbers of poor people grew so rapidly, particularly in large towns, that helping seemed hopeless, and some gave up trying. Hospitals, for example, began to refuse abandoned babies for fear that they would be deluged with them.

Efforts to alleviate the condition of the poor constituted one ethical concern of medieval thinkers, but two issues attracted even more attention. First, theologians and lawyers alike discussed the "just price," the price at which goods should be bought and sold. Christian teaching had long held that it was immoral to hoard food during a famine or knowingly to sell a damaged item. But what was the correct price in ordinary circumstances? A theological view, often dismissed as unrealistic, held that items could be sold for only the cost of the materials in

❧ R E A D I N G   S O U R C E S

Two Views of Medieval Markets

Europe's expanding commerce induced rulers to foster conditions favorable to trade but provoked serious concerns in the minds of moralists. In the first of these documents Germany's emperor Frederick Barbarossa (1152–1190) takes steps to promote a fair at Aachen; in the second, the distinguished theologian Humbert of Romans (1194–1277) criticizes and satirizes the new economy.

Frederick Promotes

Since the royal palace of Aachen excels all provinces and cities in dignity and honor . . . it is fitting and reasonable that we . . . should fortify that same place with lavish gifts of liberty and privileges as if with walls and towers. We have therefore decreed that there should be held twice a year the solemn and universal fairs of Aachen. And this we have done on the advice of the merchants. . . . We have given this liberty to all merchants, that they may be quit and free of toll throughout the year at these fairs in this royal place, and they may buy and sell goods freely just as they wish. No merchant nor any other person may take a merchant to court for payment of debt during these fairs, nor take him there for any business that was conducted before the fairs began. . . . And all people coming to, or staying at, or going from the fairs shall have peace for their persons and goods. And lest the frequent changing of coins, which are sometimes light and sometimes heavy, redound to the hurt of so glorious a place . . . we have ordered money to be struck there of the same purity, weight, and form, and in the same quantity, and to be kept to the same standard. . . . Whoever out of boldness decides to oppose our decree, or by temerity to break it, shall be in our mercy and will pay a hundred pounds of gold to our court.

Humbert Protests

Though markets and fairs are terms often used indiscriminately, there is a difference between them, for fairs deal with larger things, occasionally, and to them come men from afar. But markets are for lesser things, the daily necessities of life, and they are held weekly and only people near at hand come. Hence markets are usually morally worse than fairs. They are held on feast days and men thereby miss the divine office and sermon . . . sometimes too they are held in graveyards and other holy places. Frequently you will hear men swearing there "By God I will not give you so much for it," or "By God I will not take a smaller price." . . . Sometimes the lord is defrauded of market dues, which is perfidy and disloyalty . . . sometimes quarrels happen and violent disputes . . . drinking is occasioned. . . . Thus the legend runs of a man who, entering an abbey, found many devils in the cloister but in the market place found only one. This filled him with wonder. But it was told to him that in the cloister all is arranged to help souls to God, so many devils are required to lead monks astray, but in the market place, since each man is a devil to himself, only one other demon suffices.

Source: Roy C. Cave and Herbert H. Coulson, *A Source Book for Medieval Economic History* (New York: Bruce, 1936), pp. 120–121, 113 (slightly adapted).

them and the labor absolutely necessary to produce them. A commercial view, often dismissed as immoral, insisted that a fair price was whatever the market would bear, regardless of costs or consequences. A working consensus held that a just price was one arrived at by bargaining between free and knowledgeable parties.

The other ethical issue concerned usury, the lending of money at interest. Christian writers were always hostile to commercial enterprise, and they had plenty of biblical warrant for their view. Psalm 15 warned that no one can be blameless "who lends his money at usury." Luke's Gospel admonished Christians to "give without expecting to be repaid in full." Luke actually forbade the profit that makes most commercial enterprises possible. In the twelfth century, churchmen began to be much more assiduous in their condemnations of usury, a practice that had been winked at for centuries.

Prohibitions against usury in twelfth-century Europe (a society in full economic expansion) produced some remarkably inventive ways to get around the prohibitions. One person might agree to sell another person an item at a certain price and then buy it back on a fixed date at a higher price. Exchange rates between currencies could be manipulated to mask usurious transactions. Gradually thinkers began to defend usury on the grounds that a person who lent money incurred a risk and deserved to be compensated for that risk.

Investment demands credit, and credit requires some payback for the lender. Even in the face of deep hostility, credit mechanisms spread in thirteenth-century Europe. They were held up to minute scrutiny by theologians and popular preachers and were found to be evidence of man's sinfulness, acquisitiveness, greed. But all these practices persisted, fueled by the expansion of the European economy, and began putting individual profit alongside community interest at the heart of social and economic thought.

THE HEIRS OF THE CAROLINGIAN EMPIRE: GERMANY, ITALY, AND FRANCE

THE scope of political and institutional life expanded everywhere between 900 and 1300. In 900 the Carolingian Empire was collapsing. By 1300 France had emerged as a large, stable kingdom, and Italy had turned into several reasonably coherent regional entities. One might have predicted these post-Carolingian outcomes from the pre-Carolingian experience of these two areas. The most surprising political development within the old Carolingian lands, indeed within Europe as a whole, was Germany's rise to a premier position in the tenth century and then its long, slow decline. The states that evolved out of the Carolingian Empire faced common challenges: the achievement of territorial integrity; the growing responsibility of the central government; complicated political relations among kings, aristocrats, and churchmen; and the elaboration of new ideas about the state and its responsibilities.

■ Germany and the Empire, 911–1272

From the ninth century to the present, no state in Europe has been less stable territorially and politically than Germany and the German Empire. Time after time the Germans confronted new possibilities and challenges. An investigation of four questions in particular will help us comprehend German history after the Carolingians. First, what role did dynastic instability play in German history? Second, exactly where and what is Germany, and what constituted its empire? Third, what rules governed political development in the German lands? Fourth, how did the German rulers regulate relations with the leaders of the church?

When the Treaty of Verdun (see page 265) assigned an East Frankish kingdom to Louis the German in 843, it created something essentially new. Frankish rulers had long claimed authority over some of the lands that eventually became Germany, but before 843 no kingdom had ever existed in the territories east of the Rhine River (see Map 9.2). The Carolingians tried hard to impose common institutions on the diverse regions running from Saxony in the north to Bavaria in the south but they faced immense difficulties in doing so. The lands had no tradition of common or unified rule. There was no single "German" people; Saxons thought of themselves as Saxon, for example, not as German. Roman culture had barely penetrated into German lands, and Christian culture was recent and fragile. "Germany" had—has—no natural frontiers. Germany was, finally, the most thoroughly rural area of the Carolingian world.

After the last East Frankish Carolingian died in 911, the dukes—or leaders—of Germany's major regions chose one of their number as king. In 919 they did so again, their choice this time falling on Duke Henry of Saxony. Henry and his successors, each of whom was named Otto, ruled capably until 1002 when Otto III died without an heir. This time the German dukes turned to a distantly related family, the Salians. The Salian family died out in the middle of the twelfth century and was replaced by the Staufer, who ruled until 1250. Then, after twenty-two years without a recognized ruler, the Germans elected a member of the Habsburg family. Although not always Germany's rulers, this family was a powerful force in German politics until the twentieth century. This record of frequent dynastic change might be compared with the situation in France, where one family reigned from 987 to 1328, followed by another branch of the same family until 1598.

Who were these dukes, and why were they so influential? German romantic tradition regarded them as the

Map 9.2   Germany and Its Duchies, ca. 1000–1200
The chief political dynamic in Germany was a contest for power between the kings and the dukes. The duchies emerged in the ninth and tenth centuries and outlived one dynasty of kings after another.

heroic leaders of distinct ethnic communities, the so-called Tribal Duchies. In fact, the dukes were the descendants of local potentates introduced by the Carolingians. Between about 750 and 900, many dukes held authority over large territories that were often threatened militarily by neighboring Slavic peoples. By the middle of the tenth century five main duchies constituted the basis for German political life: Saxony, Franconia, Lorraine, Swabia, and Bavaria. The dukes were wealthy and powerful. They often controlled the bishops and abbots in their duchies. In most cases, they had managed to make vassals out of the lower ranks of the aristocracy in their territories. Although their ancestors had owed their offices to the Carolingians and were usually their vassals, the dukes of the tenth and later centuries rarely were beholden to the currently reigning dynasty. And they were extremely jealous of their independence.

Rulers of Medieval Germany

Saxons
  Henry I (919–936)
  Otto I (936–973)
  Otto II (973–983)
  Otto III (983–1002)
  Henry II (1002–1024)
Salians
  Conrad II (1024–1039)
  Henry III (1039–1056)
  Henry IV (1056–1106)
  Henry V (1106–1125)
Staufer
  Conrad III (1138–1152)
  Frederick Barbarossa (1152–1190)
  Henry VI (1190–1197)
  Frederick II (1212–1250)

One royal dynasty after another devised various stratagems to control the dukes. Kings sometimes married into ducal families, or tried to introduce their own relatives into a duchy if the reigning ducal family died out. Force and intimidation were not unusual. Frederick Barbarossa (1152–1190), the first great Staufer, patiently worked to get the dukes to recognize his overlordship even though he was powerless to demand payments or services from them. His plan was slowly to build up the idea that the king was the highest lord in the land (a plan that his French and English contemporaries used effectively). In the thirteenth century Frederick II (1212–1250) so despaired of governing Germany that he conceded the "Statute in Favor of the Princes," which lodged royal power in ducal hands in return for a vague acknowledgment of his overlordship. The kings themselves were dukes and their areas of truly effective control were usually limited to one duchy. The Saxons were based in the north, the Salians in the center, and the Staufer and Habsburgs in the south. The German monarchy thus had a very limited territorial base and, compared with their Carolingian predecessors or their French and English contemporaries, they possessed unimpressive governmental institutions.

If Germany was a collection of duchies over which the kings had little control, Germany's kings were not without means of enhancing their authority. The Saxons were especially capable military leaders. They fended off the Vikings, pressed deep into the Slavic lands lying to the east, and won a great victory over the Magyars at the Battle of Lechfeld in 955. The Saxons had been elected at a time of acute military crisis and knew how to take advantage of the honor afforded by constant victories. But after the tenth century military successes were few.

In 962 Otto I was crowned emperor in Rome by the pope, thus reviving the Carolingian imperial office. The imperial title conferred two benefits on the German kings. It gave them immense prestige and power that owed nothing to the dukes, and it raised the possibility of securing huge material resources in Italy where, as emperors, they did not have to share power the way they did in Germany. In 1158 Frederick Barbarossa summoned representatives of the major northern and central Italian cities to demand full recognition of his regalian, or ruler's, rights. These included military service; control of roads, ports, and waterways, tolls, minting, fines, vacant fiefs, and confiscated properties; appointment of magistrates; construction of palaces; and control of mines, fisheries, and saltworks. No king had these kinds of rights inside Germany.

Germany's involvement with Italy and the imperial title has occasioned no end of controversy. To some, royal involvement in Italy signals a failure to deal imaginatively with Germany itself. To others, the quest for prestige, power, and money in Italy was actually a creative solution to the monarchy's relative impotence in Germany. Nevertheless, the struggle for control of Italy brought Germany's rulers two unforeseen consequences. First, since the imperial title had to be obtained in Rome from the pope, the papacy was handed an unprecedented opportunity to meddle in German politics. That opportunity evolved from an initial request for protection, through periodic demands for political concessions, to a claim that the pope actually had the right to decide whether a particular individual was morally fit to be crowned emperor.

Second, some feared that Italy itself would become the prime object of the German ruler's attention. This actually happened with the Staufer. Frederick I (Barbarossa, or "Red Beard"), who had negotiated for regalian rights south of the Alps, tried hard to impose his will on Italy only to have a group of Italian cities ally against him in the Lombard League and then inflict a humiliating defeat on him at Legnano° in 1176. Shortly thereafter, his grandson Frederick II was born in Sicily. His father had married a Sicilian heiress and then died suddenly leaving a widow who knew nothing of Germany and an infant son who grew up in the sunny south and neither liked nor knew much about Germany itself. Frederick tried creatively to build effective institutions in

---

Legnano (len-YAN-oh)

Italy but incurred the wrath of the Italians and of the popes, neither of whom wanted a powerful rival in their own back yard.

The Italian entanglement was not the only reason for German rulers' struggles with the church. The Saxon dynasty inherited from the Carolingians the idea that the king was God's specially chosen agent on earth and that the higher clergy were the king's natural helpers in governing the realm. Even though the kings could not control the dukes they could sometimes wrest the naming of bishops and abbots all over Germany from ducal hands. Control of the church was partly a matter of practical politics and partly a matter of royal ideology.

In the middle of the eleventh century, a group of ardent church reformers appeared in Rome. Committed to improving the moral and intellectual caliber of the clergy all over Europe, they targeted the chief impediment to reform: the control of church appointments by laymen—"lay investiture," as they called it. German kings,

or emperors, of course regarded themselves as much more than mere laymen. Just as Charlemagne had reigned supreme in the Carolingian "City of God," so these German rulers stood, in their own view, nearest to God in a great hierarchy; the clergy occupied the rungs beneath them in human society. To the reformers, the proper organization of society was just the opposite: the clergy, with the pope at its head, stood nearest to God, with secular monarchs subordinate to the church. In the eleventh century, these reformers challenged royal supremacy.

When Henry III died in 1056, he left a 6-year-old heir, and in the next decade Germany collapsed into anarchy. When Henry IV (1066–1106) came of age, he faced opposition on all sides, controlled no duchies, was not yet emperor, and had lost much of his father's control of the church. When he tried to make church appointments in the traditional way, he encountered the fierce opposition of the new reformers in the person of Pope Gregory

Henry IV, Duchess Matilda of Tuscany, and Abbot Hugh of Cluny The embattled Henry IV here implores Matilda, a tremendously wealthy landowner and ally of Pope Gregory VII, to intercede with the pope. The powerful abbot of Cluny looks over the scene protectively. Written documents do not portray women's power as vividly as this image does. *(Vatican Library, Rome)*

READING SOURCES

The Issues in the Investiture Controversy

These two documents illustrate the range of issues involved in the conflict between the emperor Henry IV and Pope Gregory VII. The first excerpt is from a long letter written by Henry in 1076. The second is a decree issued by Gregory in 1078.

Henry Denounces the Pope

Henry, king not by usurpation but by the holy ordination of God, to Hildebrand, not now pope but false monk:

Such greeting as this you have merited through your disturbances, for there is no rank in the church on which you have brought, not honor but disgrace, not blessing but curse. To mention only a few notable cases, you have dared to assail the holy rulers of the church, archbishops, bishops, and priests, and you have trodden them underfoot like slaves ignorant of what their master is doing; . . . you have regarded them as knowing nothing, yourself as knowing all things. . . .

We have endured all this in our anxiety to save the honor of the apostolic see, but you have mistaken our humility for fear and have ventured to attack the royal power conferred on us by God, and threatened to divest us of it. As if we had received our kingdom from you! As if the kingdom and empire were in your hands, not God's! For our Lord Jesus Christ did call us to the kingdom. . . . You have assailed me who, though unworthy of anointing, have nevertheless been anointed to the kingdom and who, according to the traditions of the holy fathers, are subject to the judgment of God alone. . . . The true pope Peter exclaims "Fear God, honor the king."

But you, who do not fear God, dishonor me, His appointed one. . . .

You, therefore, damned by this curse and by the judgment of all our bishops and ourselves, come down and relinquish the apostolic chair which you have usurped. I, Henry, king by the grace of God, together with all our bishops, say to you: "Come down, come down, to be damned throughout all eternity."

Gregory Strikes Back

[Gregory VII] Inasmuch as we have learned that, contrary to the ordinances of the holy fathers, the investiture of churches is, in many places, performed by lay persons, and that from this cause many disturbances arise in the church by which the Christian religion is degraded, we decree that no one of the clergy shall receive the investiture of a bishopric, abbey, or church from the hand of an emperor, or king, or of any layperson, male or female. If anyone shall presume to do so, let him know that such investiture is void by apostolic authority, and that he himself shall lie under excommunication until fitting satisfaction shall have been made.

Source: James Harvey Robinson, *Readings in European History,* vol. 1 (Boston: Ginn, 1904), pp. 279–281, 275 (slightly adapted).

VII (1073–1085). Gregory was brilliant, proud, and inflexible—and determined to bend Henry to his will. Their battles inaugurated the so-called investiture controversy, which lingered on until 1122 when both of the original foes were long dead. (See the box "Reading Sources: The Issues in the Investiture Controversy.") Control of church offices was one key issue, but just as important was a contest over authority in the Christian world. Everyone agreed that all legitimate authority came from God. They disagreed, however, over who on

earth was primarily responsible for exercising authority in God's name. Finally the Concordat of Worms° stipulated that episcopal (bishopric) elections should be free and conducted according to church law. Only after a man had been duly elected bishop could a king, or emperor, invest him with the symbols and offices of secular authority. The Concordat was a blow to the German political system as it had existed for centuries and yet

---

Worms (VORM)

another destabilizing factor in medieval Germany. In the middle of the twelfth century, Frederick Barbarossa spoke of his "Holy Roman Empire." He meant that his power came, on the one hand, from God himself and, on the other, from the Romans via Charlemagne. Theory and reality did not match, however, and the papacy was able to thwart virtually every political initiative by the German rulers.

Even so, Germany was not without great rulers. Otto III was universally acclaimed as "the Great." Barbarossa was intelligent, handsome, athletic, chivalrous. Frederick II maintained a brilliant court and instituted governmental reforms in Italy that were ahead of their time. Yet rulership itself failed in Germany. One wonders: Might a long-lived dynasty have made a difference? Was the Italian venture a mistake? Given that France, England, and other states had difficult but not disastrous relations with the papacy, might Germany's have been handled differently? With its promise, undoubted achievements, yet ultimate failure, Germany is the political mystery of medieval Europe.

■ The Varying Fortunes of Italy

The history of Italy has always been played out in three regions: north, central, and south. The Carolingians and the Germans after them laid a heavy hand on northern Italy. In the center of the peninsula the Papal States was the key player. Outsiders always dominated the south, but their identities changed often.

As we have seen, German attempts to impose their authority on northern Italy met with limited success. One key obstacle to German rule was the communal movement (see Map 9.3), the most dynamic element on the Italian scene. Two conditions help to explain the rise of communes. The first relates to economic expansion. In the early eleventh century Italian towns began to rid the Mediterranean of Muslim pirates. By 1100 Italian merchants could trade anywhere in the Mediterranean world with confidence.

The second contributing factor relates to political developments in Italian towns. The Carolingians governed towns through resident counts, and German emperors tried to maintain this system. The powers of the counts tended to be weak, however, so the Germans also relied on bishops, who were, in Italy as in Germany, key props to the system of imperial rule. But bishops and counts were not alone in holding urban power. Since the late tenth century both bishops and counts had been granting fiefs to local men in order to strengthen their own authority and to procure defenses for the towns.

Gradually these men, whose lands made them wealthy in the expanding economy, moved into the towns and, in turn, gave fiefs to other men in the countryside. These lords were wealthy and jealous of their power.

Communes were sworn associations of the local nobility—these landed lords—and their vassals. Commune members swore to uphold one another's rights and called themselves the *popolo,* the "people," although the people as a whole had nothing to do with the early communes. The commune accorded a high degree of participation to its members in choosing leaders and in coming together in an assembly that voted on matters of common concern. The leaders of the early communes were usually called *consuls*—a deliberate attempt to evoke the Roman past. Usually elected for a single year, the consuls varied in number from four to twenty in different cities. The consuls proposed matters to an assembly for ratification. By the 1140s every significant city in northern and central Italy had a commune.

The communes did not necessarily originate as attempts to make cities independent. Frequently, however, as communal governments became more established and confident, that is what they did. One by one, cities either refused to recognize papal or imperial overlordship or else renegotiated the terms under which they would acknowledge the rule of their historic masters. The working out of this ongoing relationship was a major development in the history of the Italian cities in the twelfth century.

Although each Italian commune constituted an entity unto itself, a fairly coherent evolution is evident. By the late twelfth century, the consular communes were still governed by oligarchies of men whose wealth and power came from land, trade, and industry. Guild interests, however, gained in prominence at the expense of the landed groups among whom the communal movement had arisen, and ordinary workers began to clamor for participation. The communes were becoming increasingly volatile and violent.

One solution to this potential crisis was the introduction of the *podestà°,* a sort of city manager chosen by the local oligarchy. The podestà often came from the outside, served for a set period (usually six months or a year), and underwent a careful scrutiny at the conclusion of his term. He was expected to be competent not only at ordinary administration but also at military leadership, so that he could police the city as well as defend it. He brought with him a group of seasoned officials as subordinates. Normally, he could not be a property

podestà (poe-des-TAH)

Map 9.3   The Communal Movement in Italy   Beginning in the late eleventh century, many towns in northern Italy, some in the central regions, and a very few in the south erected communal forms of government. This distribution reflects the relative wealth of north and south and the power of the popes in the center. North of the Alps only Flanders and northern France experienced comparable communal movements.

owner in the town, marry into local society, or dine privately with any citizen. By the middle of the thirteenth century, some podestàs were becoming virtual professional administrators. One man, for example, was elected sixteen times in nine cities over a period of thirty-four years, four times in Bologna alone.

The Italian commune was a radical political experiment. Everywhere else in medieval Europe, power was thought to radiate downward—from God, the clergy, the emperor, the king. In a commune, power radiated upward from the popolo to its leaders. For several centuries, the Italian city was arguably the most creative institution in the Western world. When Frederick Barbarossa tried to introduce tight imperial control, the future of northern and central Italy hung in the balance. But his defeat at the hands of the Lombard League at

Legnano in 1176 left the Italian cities free to continue their distinctive political evolution.

Although some communes emerged in central Italy—even, briefly, in Rome in the 1150s—the key power in this region was the papacy, and the main political entity the Papal States. In the political turmoil of the tenth and eleventh centuries, the papacy lost a great deal of territory. Throughout the twelfth and thirteenth centuries, therefore, a basic objective of papal policy was to recover lost lands and rights. This quest to restore the territorial basis for its power and income helps explain why the popes so resolutely opposed German imperial influence in Italy.

The most striking development pertaining to the papacy is the expansion of its institutions. Gradually there emerged what historians have long called the "Papal Monarchy." This term is meant to characterize a church whose power was increasingly centralized in the hands of the popes. In Rome, the pope presided over the *curia,* the papal court. The College of Cardinals, potentially fifty-three in number, formed a kind of senate for the church. They elected the popes (by majority after 1059 and by a two-thirds majority after 1179), served as key advisers, headed the growing financial and judicial branches of the papal government, and often served as legates. Legates were papal envoys, some of whom were sent to particular people or places provisionally, to communicate a message or to conduct an investigation, and some of whom were more like resident ambassadors who represented the pope on a continuing basis. Lateran Councils met often and gathered the clergy from all over Europe to legislate for the church as a whole. The hierarchical structure of the church became more visible as ecclesiastical business tended to accumulate in Rome.

High medieval popes also reserved to themselves certain jurisdictional and coercive prerogatives. Only popes could officially canonize a saint, a powerful reservation of rights against local communities. Popes could excommunicate persons, that is, exclude them from the sacraments of the church and the community of Christians. This was a form of social death in that excommunicated persons could not eat, converse, or socialize with others. Popes could lay a territory under interdict. This decree forbade all religious services except baptisms and burials and was designed to bring maximum pressure to bear on a particular individual. Finally, popes could invoke the inquisition. Despite horror stories about the inquisition, this was a judicial mechanism fully rooted in Roman law and widely used in the medieval West. Basically, an inquisition involved churchmen taking sworn testimony in an attempt to discover heresy.

Important Popes During the High Middle Ages
Gregory VII (1073–1085)
Urban II (1088–1099)
Innocent III (1198–1216)
Boniface VIII (1294–1303)

Who were the popes? What were they like? Most of them had been cardinals with years, if not decades, of experience in the government of the church. Many of the twelfth- and thirteenth-century popes were lawyers, which may explain, in part, their dedication to institutional and legal reforms. Not a single pope from this period has been canonized as a saint. One Englishman was elected; the rest were Roman, Italian, or French. Most were noblemen.

Institutions were important, but personalities mattered, too. Innocent III (r. 1198–1216), for example, was the most powerful man ever to hold the papal office. He came from a minor Italian noble family, received early training in theology and law, and entered the papal administration while in his twenties. His entire life was dedicated to promoting the legal prerogatives of the papacy and the moral improvement of Christian society. As a young man Innocent wrote *On the Contempt of the World,* in which he expressed his hope for a life of peace and contemplation. As an older man he hurled legal thunderbolts at the greatest public figures of the day.

Finally, the south: From the ninth century, the region south of Rome was contested among Byzantines, North African Muslims, and local potentates. In 1026 Norman pilgrims bound for the Holy Land landed in southern Italy, where local people invited them to enlist in the fight against the Muslims. By the 1040s the original Normans had been joined by many more who were seeking land and adventure. Initially opposed to the Normans, the papacy later allied with their leader as a counterweight against the Germans.

From his capital at Palermo, Roger II "the Great" (r. 1130–1154) ruled a complex state that blended Byzantine, Lombard, and Norman structures. In Italy, as in England (see page 297), the Normans showed a genius for adaptation. Perched advantageously at the juncture of the Latin, Greek, and Arab worlds, the Norman court was more advanced in finance and bureaucratic administration than any of its European contemporaries. No one forgot for a moment, however, that the Normans were primarily great warriors. A chronicler said of the Normans, "They delight in arms and horses."

Coronation of Roger II of Sicily, 1130   Roger's coronation by Jesus Christ makes a powerful ideological statement: he owes his office to no earthly power. The cultural crosscurrents of Sicily are visible: Roger is depicted more like a Byzantine emperor than a Western king, and the inscriptions above his head ("Rogerios Rex") and above Christ's ("JesuS CHristos") are in Greek, not Latin.   *(Scala/Art Resource, NY)*

When the male Norman line died out, its heiress, Constance, married Henry VI of Germany (Barbarossa's son) and gave birth to Frederick II. For two generations the papacy struggled to break German control of southern Italy. Once the popes had defeated Frederick II, they decided to look for more pliant allies in the south. They invited a succession of French and Spanish princes to assume the crown thus touching off long-standing rivalries in the area. A profusion of outsiders always dominated southern Italy.

■ Capetian France, 987–1314

When the Treaty of Verdun created the West Frankish Kingdom, no one knew what the future France might be like. The twentieth-century French leader Charles de Gaulle once quipped, "It is impossible to govern a country with 325 kinds of cheese." He was referring to France's tremendous diversity, not its dairy industry. During the late ninth century and much of the tenth, the area suffered cruelly from constant waves of Viking attacks and from repeated failures of the Carolingian family to produce adult heirs to the throne. Chroniclers often quoted the lament of King Solomon: "Woe to thee, O land, whose king is a child." At the end of the tenth century, however, the Carolingians were replaced by the Capetians°, the family of Hugh Capet (r. 987–996). Thereafter the French monarchy steadily enhanced its position. That is the first issue we address. Then, bearing in mind de Gaulle's joke, we explore how a large—France is today about the size of Texas—but very complex group of territories was assembled into a kingdom. Finally we look at the nature of government in medieval France.

The Capetian kings of France were remarkably successful in capitalizing on their resources and opportunities. Of utmost significance is the fact that one family ruled for over three centuries. Contrast this with Germany's experience. Very early, the reigning Capetian kings began during their own lifetimes to have their sons crowned as successors. This meant that when the old king died, a new king was already in place and the nobility could not meddle in the succession. Robert I (r. 996–1030) displayed the "royal touch," a ceremony in which the king was believed to be able to cure people of scrofula (a common respiratory ailment) by touching them. No French nobleman, no matter how powerful, ever laid claim to such miraculous powers. Capetian kings had an elevated sense of the grandeur of the royal office. Louis VII (r. 1137–1180) began to make elegant tours of the country to put himself, his office, and his sparkling entourage on display. In Louis IX (r. 1226–1270) the Capetian family produced a saint of the Catholic Church—Saint Louis.

In addition to its religious and ideological resources, Capetian kingship also had some valuable practical bases. If the kings did not control directly much of France in the tenth and eleventh centuries, they nevertheless controlled the old, rich, prestigious, and centrally located city of Paris. The kings promoted the shrine of St.

Capetians (kuh-PEE-shunz)

The Capetian Kings of France
Hugh Capet (987–996)
Robert II (996–1031)
Henry I (1031–1060)
Philip I (1060–1108)
Louis VI (1108–1137)
Louis VII (1137–1180)
Philip II (1180–1223)
Louis VIII (1223–1226)
Louis IX (1226–1270)
Philip III (1270–1285)
Philip IV (1285–1314)

Denis, the legendary first bishop of Paris, as a kind of "national" shrine for France. The kings were also keen to attract to their court the most powerful men of the realm and to get those men to swear oaths of allegiance to the Crown. Slowly but surely the Capetians turned this ceremonial obedience into effective subjection. This is certainly what Frederick Barbarossa was aiming at in Germany. The kings also controlled about two dozen bishoprics and some fifty monasteries in northern France. This power base gave the king unrivaled opportunities to extend his influence and, in turn, to build up a cadre of loyal and articulate supporters. Although French kings provoked a few battles with the papacy, France experienced no investiture controversy.

The French kingdom, understood as the territory ruled more or less directly and effectively by the king, expanded dramatically from 900 to 1300. Internal politics and foreign wars contributed to this result. The Capetian family were heirs of the dukes of Paris. This meant that they controlled no more than Paris and its immediate region. In reality they contested for control of this region with a number of ambitious and aggressive families. In the early twelfth century Louis VI (r. 1108–1137) systematically ground down all his local opponents and made his area—the Ile de France—one of the best-governed regions in all of France.

But military successes were even more important than local political ones. The background to French military success is complicated. In the late eleventh and early twelfth centuries, one family of French magnates, the counts of Anjou° (see Map 9.4), acquired control over

a good deal of western France by marriage, diplomacy, and intimidation. Then Geoffrey of Anjou married the heiress of the duchy of Normandy whose father, William the Conqueror, we will meet later. A bit later Geoffrey's son and heir married Duchess Eleanor of Aquitaine, the recently divorced wife of Louis VII of France. In 1154 Henry of Anjou, as a result of incredibly complicated political and matrimonial alliances, became King Henry II of England. But he still retained control of about 60 percent of France.

For several generations the kings of France hammered away at this "Angevin° Empire." Henry of Anjou's four sons were viciously jealous of one another, and French kings exploited their rivalries to weaken Angevin authority in western and southwestern France. When one of Henry's sons, King John of England, absconded with the fiancée of a vassal of Philip II, the king of France, Philip summoned him to court to answer for his conduct. Of course, John refused to appear, and war ensued between 1202 and 1204. Philip won a resounding victory and a substantial portion of western France fell into his hands. Several times in the thirteenth century the kings of England and France came to blows over their competing claims to French territory. Each time the French won, including a major victory over an allied English and German army at Bouvines° in 1214.

Southeastern France was gained by wars of a different kind. In the last decades of the twelfth century, several cities in the southeast became hotbeds of the Albigensian° heresy—an important religious movement (see Chapter 10). Some Catholic locals and many churchmen urged the kings to undertake military action against the heretics. The French kings were prudent and bided their time until they had the resources to deal with this turbulent region. Under Louis VIII and Louis IX, the French monarchy finally extended its authority to France's Mediterranean coast.

The chief political dynamic in France was the contest for power between the kings and the territorial princes (see Map 9.4). Who were the territorial princes? In fact, they were rather like the German dukes. That is, they were locally powerful magnates, most of whose ancestors had been officials appointed by the Carolingians. But whereas Germany comprised five major duchies, France had a dozen or more territorial principalities. Obviously the Carolingians had elevated more than just a dozen local officers. In the tumultuous

---

Anjou (ahn-JHOU)

Angevin (AN-juh-vin)   Bouvines (BOO-veen)
Albigensian (al-buh-JEN-see-un)

Map 9.4   French Territorial Principalities, ca. 1200   As the Carolingian West Frankish Kingdom (see Map 8.3, page 259) broke down and feudal bonds proliferated, many territories arose under counts and dukes. Their struggles to impose control locally and to fight off royal supervision animated French history.

circumstances of the tenth and eleventh centuries, some individuals and families had been remarkably successful in building castles, reducing the local population to subjection, and gathering into their own hands the powers that the Carolingian kings had once

exercised in their localities. (See the feature "Weighing the Evidence: The Medieval Castle" on pages 314–315.) The fate of the French monarchy depended on the ability of the kings to cooperate with and finally to supersede these potentates.

Ironically, the territorial princes also faced localized rivalries for power and influence. Countless individuals also built castles, brutally subjected local peasants, and became lords. Sometimes these individuals were the vassals of the territorial princes—say the dukes of Normandy or the counts of Anjou—and sometimes they had vassals of their own. In the increasing absence of effective royal public authority, these lords wielded power for which they rarely answered to anyone. In the Carolingian world the number of vassals was small, their fidelity reasonably solid, and their services reliable. By 1100 the number of vassals was immense, their fidelity was constantly shifting, and they tended to provide only local military service. Scholars call this shift from effective Carolingian government to myriad local lordships a "feudal revolution."

For the kings of France to recreate central government, they had to overcome the disruptive tendencies of this revolution and then rebuild consolidated institutions. In the twelfth and thirteenth centuries the Capetians patiently and consistently followed a few basic policies to increase their ability to govern. They circumvented the local lords as much as possible. When they won military victories, the kings did not dole out the seized lands to lords as new fiefs but instead kept them in their own hands, or in the hands of family members as *appanages*. What is more, the kings introduced into these lands local officials, called bailiffs or provosts, who were of modest social background, had no personal ties to their assigned regions, often had some schooling in law, and were intensely loyal to the kings. By the time of Saint Louis, officials called *enqueteurs*° were sent around the country to inspect the work of bailiffs and provosts. Such roles had been unheard of since the Carolingian *missi dominici*. Louis also began to issue *ordonnances*, what we might call executive orders, that were binding on all the land under the king's control. These precepts are reminiscent of Carolingian capitularies.

If in 1000 France was a land of innumerable tiny lordships, then by 1300 it was the best-governed kingdom in Europe. Indicative of France's position is the outcome of two battles between King Philip IV (r. 1285–1314) and Pope Boniface VIII (r. 1294–1303). First Philip attempted to tax the French clergy, and then he sought to bring a bishop before his court. Boniface angrily objected to Philip's intervention in ecclesiastical affairs. But things had changed drastically since the fateful con-

frontation between Henry IV and Gregory VII. Boniface had to back down.

Welsh humorist Walter Map (1140–1209) provides this assessment of France in his day:

> The emperor of Byzantium and the king of Sicily may boast about their gold and silken cloth, but they have no men who can do more than talk, men incapable of war. The Roman emperor or, as they say, the emperor of the Germans, has men apt in arms and warlike horses, but no gold, silk or any other wealth. . . . The king of England lacks nothing and possesses everything, men, horses, gold, silk, jewels, fruits and wild beasts. And we in France have nothing except bread, wine and joy.[1]

Walter comically underestimates the resources of the French. In 1300 theirs was the largest, richest, and best-governed kingdom in Europe. French culture and language were increasingly dominant. Considering France's situation in 900, and compared with Germany's in 1300, these were impressive achievements.

THE BRITISH ISLES

I N the British Isles, expansion had three dimensions: the tremendous growth of the English government; England's relentless push into the Celtic world; and the emergence of states in the Celtic world itself. England, about the size of Alabama, is smaller than France or Germany and more homogeneous in population, culture, and language than either of them, or than Italy. Building effective governance in England was therefore a somewhat easier task than it was elsewhere. Nevertheless, England faced some acute dynastic, military, and political crises. Moreover, England shared an island with two Celtic neighbors, Wales and Scotland, whose inhabitants were close kin to the people of England's neighboring island, Ireland (see Map 9.5). For better or worse, the fates of the English and Celtic inhabitants of the British Isles are inseparable.

■ England: Wars and Families, 871–1307

Ironies abound in England. Dynastic instability was as prevalent in England as in Germany but without the disastrous consequences. Military victories helped the French to grow, and most of those victories came at the

---

enqueteurs (on-KEH-turs)

expense of the English. But losses did not severely weaken England or its kings.

Alfred (see page 257) rallied the English against the Vikings, and his descendants ruled England for more than a century. They gradually rolled back the frontier of the "Danelaw," the areas of eastern and northern England controlled by Viking settlers (mainly Danes, hence the name). Late in the tenth century, however, English leadership failed in the face of a severe threat from a new generation of Vikings. These were powerful, ambitious men who had contested unsuccessfully for the kingship in Denmark and Norway. One of them, Swein Forkbeard, conquered England in 1014, but he survived his conquest by only two years. He was replaced by his son Cnut, who ruled from 1016 to 1035, and then by Cnut's sons, who ruled until 1042.

Cnut was no wild and woolly barbarian. He was simultaneously king of Denmark and England, and for a time of Norway too. He was a gifted ruler who maintained what was best in English institutions. He wed his daughter to Emperor Henry III and himself married Emma, the widow of the last English king. He was cultured, Christian, and an acquaintance of the pope.

When Cnut's sons died without heirs, the English nobles called over from Normandy Edward, called "the Confessor," the son of the last English king. Edward had grown up in Normandy, was unusually pious, and had taken a vow of chastity. Because he was not going to have an heir, claimants to the English throne began jockeying for position. Edward seems to have promised his throne to William, the duke of Normandy. Most of the English nobles preferred Harold of Wessex, one of their number. In Norway, Harald Hardrada prepared to make a claim as Cnut's rightful heir.

When Edward died, the English elected Harold, and immediately he learned that Hardrada had invaded. He marched to meet the Norse challenger and won an impressive victory at Stamford Bridge only to learn that William had meanwhile landed in the south. Foolishly, Harold rushed south to meet William without resting or

Map 9.5   Northern and Eastern Europe, ca. 1200   Apart from Germany, the core states of Europe emerged inside the former Roman frontiers or right alongside them. After 900 an arc of new states emerged from the Celtic realms and Iceland in the west, to Scandinavia in the north, to the western, southern, and eastern Slavs in eastern Europe.

Important Kings of England

Alfred (871–899)
Ethelred II (978–1016)
Cnut (1016–1035)
Edward the Confessor (1042–1066)
Harold of Wessex (1066)
William I (the Conquerer) (1066–1089)
William II (1089–1100)
Henry I (1100–1135)
Stephen I (1135–1154)
Henry II (1154–1189)
Richard I (1189–1199)
John (1199–1216)
Henry III (1216–1272)
Edward I (1272–1307)

reinforcing his troops. At Hastings, William defeated Harold and England was his for the taking.

With a brutal pacification campaign from 1066 to 1071, William assured himself control of most of the country. William was succeeded by two of his sons in turn, William II (1089–1100) and Henry I (1100–1135). Henry's only son drowned in a shipwreck, and the English nobles would accept neither his daughter Matilda as their queen nor her husband Geoffrey of Anjou as their king. Owing to William's conquest and settlement, most of the English elite were in fact Normans, and the Normans and Angevins were old, bitter foes. Consequently, the English turned in 1135 to a French prince, Stephen of Blois, who was a grandson of William the Conqueror through a daughter.

Stephen then died childless in 1154 and bequeathed his kingdom to Henry of Anjou—Henry II of England, the son of Geoffrey and Matilda. Henry's family, the Angevins, ruled England for centuries. But Henry was as much a French prince as an English king. From his father, mother, and wife (Eleanor of Aquitaine; see page 293), he had inherited a large part of France and was much preoccupied with his continental realm. He constantly battled with his sons for control of these vast French holdings without ever imposing on them common law or institutions. One of Henry's sons, John, was defeated by Philip II, inducing contemporaries to mock him as John "Lackland" and John "Softsword." Gradually the Angevins learned to focus their attention on England, although they never gave up their interests in France.

■ The Government of England

Alfred and his successors built strong central, and centralizing, institutions. All free men in the realm owed allegiance to the king and could in principle be called to the militia, the *fyrd*°. The great men of the realm attended meetings of the royal council, the *witan*°, which was partly a court of law and partly a deliberative, consultative body. The king could issue writs, executive orders rather like Carolingian capitularies. Danegeld—literally "money for the Danes"—was originally collected solely in times of danger and then slowly transformed into a regular tax. All of England was divided into shires, and each shire had a royally appointed officer the shire-reeve (or sheriff).

No other rulers in Europe had so effective a system so early, and it is no surprise that neither Cnut nor William the Conqueror desired to dismantle or replace the old English institutions. But William had won England by conquest, and he did introduce some changes. He turned most of the estates in England into fiefs and distributed them among some 180 of his most loyal followers. Each of these vassals held his fief in return for a fixed quota of soldiers for the royal army. To raise the approximately five thousand soldiers required by William, each of his vassals had to create vassals of his own. The technical name for this process of vassals creating vassals is *subinfeudation*. In 1087 William exacted the Salisbury Oath, which established the principle of liege homage°, according to which the king was the final lord of all vassals. To avoid creating compact territorial principalities on the French model, William scattered his vassals' holdings around the kingdom. Finally, to learn as much as he could about his new kingdom, and about the fiefs he had assigned to his followers, William conducted a massive survey of England that resulted in 1086 in the *Domesday Book,* named for the day of judgment against which there was no appeal. No comparable survey of any state was accomplished until the American census of 1790.

In the twelfth century English kings pursued four broad policies. They refined the financial machinery of the English government, the Exchequer, named for the checkerboard table on which the accounts were reckoned. They vastly improved the judicial institutions. Henry I began to send itinerant justices around the realm. He brought the royal court with its swift, fair, and competent justice within the reach of most people, and

---

fyrd (FEERD)   **witan** (WHIT-un)
liege homage (LEEGE AHM-idge)

he made royal justice more attractive than the justice available in local lords' courts. Henry II expanded the work of the courts and created an extensive system of writs. These documents, available to almost anyone, had the effect of transferring cases into the royal courts. This expansion of the work of the royal courts led to the emergence of a common law in England—a law common to all people, courts, and cases.

Henry II used the sworn inquest to learn about his realm. He conducted an inquest of knights' service to find out what service vassals owed to which people. He conducted an inquest of sheriffs to learn how the sheriffs were performing their jobs. On discovering that some were shirking their responsibilities, Henry replaced them. This action is the context for the Robin Hood stories about the cruel sheriff of Nottingham and the kind king who looks out for the people. Finally, the Norman and Angevin kings employed in their government "men raised from the dust," as one aristocratic contemporary contemptuously called them. These were men from the middling ranks of society, perhaps with some training in law, who were loyal to the king and advanced his interests against the aristocrats who were intensely jealous of their own rights and privileges.

The rising power of the king and his agents provoked the struggles of thirteenth-century England. Barons, a general name for the upper ranks of English society, were increasingly upset that an expanding royal government limited their influence. In 1215 a large group of disgruntled barons forced King John to sign the Magna Carta, the "Great Charter" (so called because it was written on an unusually large sheet of parchment). This document was a pact between the king and his social elite requiring the king to respect the rights of feudal lords, not abuse his judicial powers, and consult his "natural" advisers, that is, the barons. (See the box "Reading Sources: Selections from Magna Carta.")

John tried to wiggle out of the Magna Carta provisions, but he died in 1216 leaving only a minor heir, and the barons exacted many concessions from the regency government. When Henry III came of age, he struggled to win a limited application of Magna Carta. The barons, on the contrary, wanted a voice in devising royal policy, especially military policy in light of recent defeats (that is, Normandy and Bouvines). They also wished to have some say in naming the king's closest advisers and in controlling the work of the king's agents, especially judges.

Several times in the thirteenth century contemporaries called meetings of the royal court *parliaments*. This was a French word meaning, roughly, "talking together." The genuine ancestors of England's historic Parliament met in 1265 and 1295. Initially these meetings had no fixed rights or procedures, no set group of attendees, and no defined role. The kings viewed them as rubber stamps, clever political devices to win support for royal policies. The barons viewed them as opportunities to play a real role in a government that had been marginalizing them. In retrospect we can see that the English were groping to find a way to build consultation into their system.

England's relations with the church fell somewhere between Germany's and France's in both intensity and outcome. Anglo-Saxon kings generally enjoyed cordial relations with the church on a traditional Carolingian model. William the Conqueror controlled the church with an iron hand but introduced reforms and reformers who were acceptable to Rome. Perhaps Gregory VII left William alone because he did not wish to fight on too many fronts simultaneously. Archbishop Anselm of Canterbury and Henry I had a quarrel that lasted several years but finally mended their differences in a settlement that anticipated the terms of the Concordat of Worms.

England's most famous clashes with the church came in the reigns of Henry II and John. Henry was always anxious to extend the influence of his courts. In 1164 he decided that "criminous clerks," or members of the clergy who had committed a crime, should be judged in royal courts. The archbishop of Canterbury, Thomas Becket (ca. 1118–1170), protested that clerics could be tried only in church courts. He fled the country and Henry suffered widespread criticism, so a reconciliation was patched together and Becket returned to England. Unfortunately a band of overly zealous knights murdered Becket, believing that they were doing the king's bidding. In fact, the crime so outraged the church and the public that Henry had to back down on criminous clerks.

John's case was a little different. He had run afoul of the church several times for illegally seizing church revenues. Then he got into a row with Pope Innocent III because he refused to admit to England the pope's candidate for the archbishopric of Canterbury. Finally, however, John submitted because Innocent had laid England under interdict, and the king needed the pope's support for his planned war against Philip II of France. True to his nickname "Softsword," John lost at Bouvines and thus ended his quarrel with Rome. If no English king ever cowed a pope into submission, at least no English king suffered the humiliations of an investiture controversy. English government did not depend so heavily on the church that it was vulnerable to a challenge to its authority in ecclesiastical affairs.

🙈 READING SOURCES

Selections from Magna Carta

When the English barons forced King John to sign the Magna Carta in 1215, they had very practical grievances and concrete priorities. The following selections from the charter's sixty-three articles are representative of the kinds of issues involved in the barons' dispute with the king. Note the absence of flowery rhetoric and grandiose statements of philosophical principles.

1. Know that we in the first place have granted to God and by this our present charter have confirmed, for us and for our heirs in perpetuity, that the English church shall be free, and shall have its rights undiminished and its liberties unimpaired.

2. If any of our earls or barons, or others holding of us in chief by knight service shall die, and at his death his heir be of full age and owe relief [a payment for an heir to succeed to a fief], he shall have his inheritance on payment of the ancient relief. . . .

4. The guardian of the land of such an heir who is under age shall not take from the land more than the reasonable revenues, customary dues and services, and that without destruction or waste of men or goods.

7. After her husband's death, a widow shall have her marriage portion and her inheritance at once and without any hindrance; nor shall she pay anything for her dower, her marriage portion, or her inheritance which she and her husband held on the day of her husband's death; and she may stay in her husband's house forty days after his death, within which period her dower shall be assigned to her.

8. No widow shall be compelled to marry so long as she wishes to live without a husband, provided that she gives security that she will not marry without our consent if she holds of us, or without the consent of the lord of whom she holds, if she holds of another.

12. No scutage [tax] or aid is to be levied in our realm except by the common counsel of our realm, unless it is for the ransom of our person, the knighting of our eldest son, or the first marriage of our eldest daughter.

16. No man shall be compelled to perform more service for a knight's fee or any other free tenement than is due from it.

38. Henceforth no bailiff shall put anyone on trial by his own unsupported allegation, without bringing credible witnesses to the charge.

39. No free man shall be taken or imprisoned or disseised [dispossessed] or outlawed or exiled or in any way ruined, nor will we go or send against him, except by the lawful judgment of his peers or by the law of the land.

Source: J. C. Holt, *Magna Carta* (Cambridge: Cambridge University Press, 1969), pp. 317, 319, 321, 323, 327.

 For additional information on this topic, go to http://college.hmco.com.

■ The Celtic Realms

When the Romans appeared on the scene, Celtic peoples could be found in virtually every region from Ireland to Anatolia. Most Celts were absorbed by more numerous and powerful Germanic and Slavic peoples. It was in the British Isles that the most durable and distinctive Celtic regions evolved into Ireland, Wales, and Scotland. Two essential dynamics characterized each of these regions. First, tiny political entities gradually turned into larger kingdoms. Second, relations between England and the Celtic realms were everywhere decisive in the historical development of the latter (see Map 9.5).

In each of the Celtic realms the movement toward greater unity was opened by the efforts of powerful, ambitious leaders to subjugate numerous well-entrenched

Howell the Good   This picture of Howell, from a manuscript of his laws, depicts him wearing a crown, holding a scepter, and sitting on a tufted throne that looks like a palace. These are key symbols of rule.   *(The National Library of Wales)*

local potentates, many of whom had expanded their power during the period of Viking invasions. In Ireland, Brian Boru (r. 976–1014) became the first ruler to exercise real authority over most of the island. In Wales, Rhodri the Great (d. 898) and Howell the Good (d. 950) were the first rulers to gain at least nominal authority over the whole of the land. Although disunity is a continuous theme of Scottish history, the centuries after the reign of Kenneth MacAlpin (r. 843–858) give evidence for the slow creation of a national tradition.

The course of development in the Celtic lands was disrupted by the English in the eleventh and especially in the twelfth century. The Norman Conquest of England brought adventurers to the frontiers of Wales and Scot-

land. Sometimes these continental knights advanced with the support of William the Conqueror and his sons, but more often they looked to wild frontier regions for opportunities to escape tight control. In Wales some Normans allied with various local princes who resented the growing power of the Welsh kings. Prince Grufydd ap Cynan° (d. 1137) then turned to King Henry I in 1114 and promised allegiance if Henry would aid him in his quest to establish his authority throughout Wales. From that time forward the actual power of Welsh rulers varied greatly, and English kings usually claimed some author-

---

Grufydd ap Cynan (GRIFF-ith op KY-nun)

ity over the region. Scottish kings managed to enlist a good many Norman knights into their service, but this recruitment effort angered the English kings and clouded the lines of allegiance in Northumbria, where many of those knights had been sent in the first place. Civil disturbances in Ireland induced King Rory O'Connor to turn to King Henry II of England for mercenaries to help him establish his power. But by 1171 Henry had invaded Ireland himself and inaugurated the complicated English involvement in the affairs of Ireland that persists to this day.

Edward I of England intervened repeatedly in the Celtic world. In 1277 he invaded Wales with the intention of totally subduing the Welsh. He built immense castles whose ruins are impressive today. Edward also made his son the Prince of Wales—still the title of the heir to the British throne. Between 1100 and 1260, England and Scotland went to war four times, and Edward resolved to put an end to this struggle by annexing Scotland. The Scots, however, rallied to the standard of Robert Bruce (r. 1306–1328), a dashing knight who was, ironically, of Norman extraction. Robert managed to free Scotland for centuries.

THE GROWTH OF NEW STATES

THE proliferation of new states constitutes one of the most remarkable examples of expansion in high medieval Europe. In Spain, Christian rulers waged a steady war of reconquest against the Islamic caliphate of Cordoba that led to the emergence of the kingdoms of Portugal, Castile, and Aragon. In Scandinavia, mighty leaders built durable kingdoms in Denmark, Norway, and Sweden. Local potentates created a band of new Slavic states running from the Baltic to the Balkans, from Poland to Bulgaria. To the east of those Slavic realms, around the city of Kiev, the Scandinavian Rus founded the first state on Russian soil. Between 900 and 1300, the geographic range of Europe's political entities more than doubled.

■ Reconquista and Kingdom Building in Spain

Historians perceive two driving forces in the rich and colorful history of medieval Spain. One is the bloody experience of several centuries of war along an expanding frontier. The other is the constant interplay within the Iberian Peninsula of three vibrant cultures: Christian,

Jewish, and Muslim. We describe the first of these forces in this chapter and the second in the next.

The emirate of Cordoba (see page 253) began breaking up after 1002, and the weakness of the tiny successor realms afforded an unprecedented opportunity to the Christians living in the north of the peninsula. King Sancho I (r. 1000–1035) of Navarre launched an offensive against the Muslims. This war, carried on intermittently until the fifteenth century, came to be called the *Reconquista°*, the Reconquest.

Before he died, Sancho divided his realm among his sons; thus, the kingdoms of Aragon and Castile arose alongside Navarre. Alfonso I (r. 1065–1109) of Castile really advanced the Reconquista. In 1085 his forces captured the Muslim stronghold and old Visigothic capital of Toledo, an important moral and strategic victory. Alfonso's military successes owed much to the dashing warrior Rodrigo Díaz de Vivar, known as "El Cid" ("the Lord," from the Arabic *sayyid*). Rodrigo, a gifted but slightly unscrupulous mercenary, fought for both Muslims and Christians. The Reconquista was moving on three fronts (see Map 9.6). In the east, the emerging kingdom of Aragon-Catalonia advanced along the Mediterranean coast. In the center, León-Castile pressed hard against al-Andalus. In the west, the nascent kingdom of Portugal became a factor in Iberian politics. Rodrigo's successes, and the reconquest of Toledo, led the retreating Muslims to summon aid in the 1150s from militant North African Muslims. The Christian advance temporarily stopped.

In the early thirteenth century Pope Innocent III stirred up crusading zeal and lent encouragement to clerics and nobles in Spain who wished to reopen hostilities against the Muslims. In 1212 a combined Castilian-Aragonese army won a decisive victory at Las Navas de Tolosa, south of Toledo. The victory of Las Navas de Tolosa was a great turning point in Spanish history. The outcome of the Reconquista, which did not conclude until the fifteenth century, was never again in doubt.

Twelfth-century Spanish kings, especially in Castile, imposed hereditary rule and exacted oaths of allegiance from their free subjects. The kings tried to force powerful nobles to become their vassals. They were more successful on the military frontier than back in their homelands because in the war zones nobles could be assigned new fiefs carved out of recent conquests. Kings

Reconquista (ray-con-KEE-stuh)

Map 9.6   The Christian Reconquista of Muslim Spain   From slow beginnings in the ninth century to the epochal Battle of Las Navas de Tolosa (1212), the Christians in Spain pushed back the Muslim frontier and built durable states behind it. *(Source: David Nicholas, The Evolution of the Medieval World. Copyright © 1992. Used by permission of Longman Group UK.)*

profited from the Reconquista to enhance their status and power.

In the thirteenth century Spain produced kings of genius, especially James I of Aragon (r. 1213–1276) and Ferdinand III (r. 1217–1252) and Alfonso X (r. 1252–1284) of Castile. These rulers were pious men, genuinely inspired by the ideal of the Crusades (discussed below), zealous in the promotion of the church. They were also hard-headed rulers. James turned Aragon-Catalonia into the greatest naval power of the western Mediterranean and a formidable economic power, too. Ferdinand and Alfonso derived great prestige from their successful wars. Those wars also provided a flow of booty and a supply of lands to reward the Castilian nobles who spent

their energy on the frontier rather than on attacking the king. These kings built strong central governments. Increasingly they used professional officers in key government posts and dispatched roving officials from the court to check on local rulers. Alfonso issued a major law book for the whole of Castile. These laws were based on Roman law and emphasized royal power. The Cortes, a representative assembly made up primarily of urban notables, began forging an alliance between the king and the towns. Iberia was not united in the thirteenth century, but it had evolved into four coherent blocks: a small and impotent Muslim region in Valencia and Granada, and three vibrant kingdoms centered on Portugal, Castile, and Aragon.

Alfonso X "the Wise"   The Spanish king, depicted here in a thirteenth-century manuscript from Spain, is judging his Muslim and Christian subjects. Alfonso's reputation for impartiality was important in his culturally diverse realm.   *(Biblioteca Nacional, Madrid)*

■ Scandinavia

Europe's expanding map saw new states in Scandinavia, the Roman name for the lands that became Denmark, Norway, and Sweden. Although the faint beginnings of political consolidation in Denmark can be traced to the Carolingian period, actual development of the states of Scandinavia dates from the tenth and eleventh centuries. Overseas expansion played one key role in northern political development. Another was the slow achievement of political unity by kings who had to overcome powerful local interests (see Map 9.5).

The sea, not the land, is the great fact of Scandinavian history. Norway has more than 1,000 miles of coastline, and no point in Denmark is more than 35 miles from the sea. Scandinavia did not offer opportunities for large, land-based kingdoms or empires, but the sea provided Scandinavians with a wide scope for activities.

More than any other people of the north, the Vikings capitalized on the sea as a highway. Vikings were raiders, of course, but also settlers. Much of northeastern England, the Danelaw, was settled by Northmen. In 911 the Norwegian Rollo and his followers settled what became Normandy in northern France. Between 870 and 930 many Norwegians and some Danes settled Iceland and a little later established bases in Greenland. In 862 a Swedish force, accustomed to raiding and trading along

The Jelling Stone King Harald Bluetooth of Denmark (d. ca. 984) erected this stone with its runic inscription as a memorial to his parents. It reads, "King Harald had this monument made for his father Gorm and his mother Thyri: This was the Harald who won for himself all Denmark and Norway, and made the Danes Christian." *(National Museum, Copenhagen)*

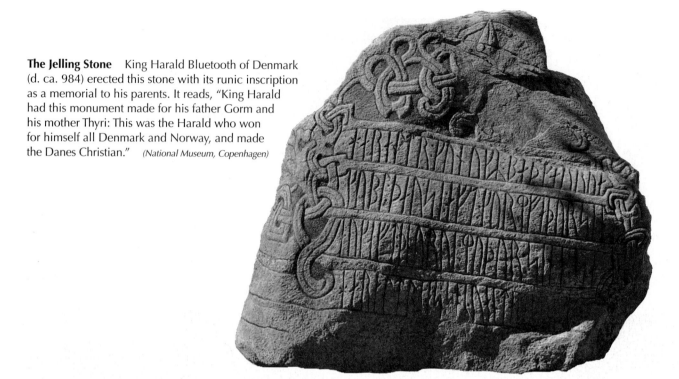

the rivers of later Russia, established a base at Novgorod. Raiders, traders, and settlers, the Scandinavians fostered the expansion of Europe.

Because the sea made exit from Scandinavia so easy, and because the whole region had absolutely no tradition of unified government, kings had a hard time establishing their power. Essentially kings were war-leaders with loyal bands of followers. Territorial states were thus built up as powerful leaders persuaded or forced more and more men to join them. Denmark's was the first of the northern monarchies to emerge in the early tenth century. Norway's monarchy arose a little later in the tenth century, but for much of the eleventh century Norway was under Danish control. As the Danes fell more and more under German influence in the eleventh century, Norway managed to break free. Sweden's monarchy was the last to emerge in the northern world; it was not fully stable until the twelfth century, but by 1300, it had become the most powerful.

Christianity came rather late to Scandinavia, with the first missionaries entering the region in the ninth century and widespread conversion ensuing in the eleventh. Norway's King Olaf (r. 1016–1028), affectionately remembered as Saint Olaf, was the first northern king who actively promoted Christianization. Scandinavian kings viewed the church as a useful adjunct to their power. They cooperated in creating bishoprics on the assumption that members of the high clergy would be educated, talented allies in the process of building central governments. Ironically, the church was a stabilizing force in Scandinavia during the very years when the investiture controversy wreaked havoc in Germany.

■ The Slavic World

In eastern Europe, between the rivers Elbe and Dnieper° lived numerous peoples customarily called Slavs. Their languages were once much alike but differentiated over time. Partly because of language differences and partly because of the areas in which these people settled, scholars divide them into western, southern, and eastern Slavs. These peoples were never conquered by the Romans, assimilated few influences from the classical world, and received Christianity later than western Europe. Still, as states began emerging in eastern Europe, they exhibited many of the same problems that older and more westerly states had encountered: shifting frontiers, clashes between ambitious rulers and powerful nobles, and outside military and cultural influences (see Map 9.5).

Dnieper (NEE-per)

Twelfth-Century Polish Castle   This reconstruction of a castle shows it to have been a combination of earthworks and wooden stockades. Such castles, common in western Europe in the tenth and eleventh centuries, afforded protection to people from a wide area and permanent dwellings to a few.   *(CAF Warsaw/Sovfoto)*

The first west Slavic state was Great Moravia, created in the 830s by capable dukes while the Carolingian Empire was experiencing civil wars. As we saw in Chapter 8 (page 265), the Moravian leaders invited the missionaries Cyril and Methodius to their realm, thereby beginning the establishment of Christianity in eastern Europe. Moravia's early promise was cut short in 906 by the Magyars. Also in the late ninth century the Přemysl° dynasty forged a kingdom in Bohemia that lasted through the Middle Ages although for long periods it was under German domination.

The greatest of the west Slavic states was Poland. In the 960s and 970s Duke Mieszko° (d. 992) unified a substantial territory and received Christianity from Rome. The first action created the Polish state, and the second anchored Poland firmly within the orbit of the Latin West. Mieszko's descendants, the Piast dynasty of kings, ruled until Boleslav III divided the kingdom among his three sons in 1138. For more than two centuries Polish development was retarded as weak rulers contested for power with local magnates, who themselves were successfully subordinating both peasants and men of middling status.

Přemysl (PURR-em-ih-sill)

Mieszko (mee-ESH-koe)

The creation of a Hungarian state played a decisive role in dividing the western and southern Slavs. The Magyars were disruptive raiders from the 880s until their defeat by Otto I in 955. After that disaster, the Magyars concentrated on building a state within the Danube basin, the home base from which they had launched their raids. Magyars, who were related to the Huns and Avars, blended with local Slavs. King, later Saint, Stephen (r. 997–1038), who received Christianity from Rome, was the real founder of Hungary. Like Poland, then, Hungary was attached to the Latin West. Stephen's family, the Arpads, ruled in Hungary for centuries. They built ruling centers at Buda and Esztergom, created an impressive

Virgin of Vladimir   The holiest icon of Russia, once the miraculous protector of the city of Vladimir and later of Moscow, this image was painted in Constantinople in 1131. Rus, and later Russian, icons tended to follow Byzantine traditions very closely.   *(Scala/Art Resource, NY)*

territorial organization, and promoted the growth of the church. They also expanded in almost every direction.

The southern Slavs built a band of states that extended across the Balkans. The first, reaching back to the seventh century, was Bulgaria. The Bulgars were a Turkic people who first led and then merged into the local Slavic population. The first Bulgarian state lasted until the early eleventh century when the Byzantines, who had suffered many defeats at Bulgarian hands, destroyed it. By the late twelfth century, when Byzantium itself had weakened, a new Bulgarian state emerged, but its rulers never had the firm control that their predecessors had wielded. Under Khan Boris (r. 852–879), Bulgaria made the momentous decision to accept Orthodox Christianity from Constantinople instead of Roman Catholicism, despite the pope's best efforts.

To the west of Bulgaria lay Serbia, a region dominated until the fourteenth century by Bulgaria and Byzantium. Perhaps because of constant outside threats, Serbia made little progress toward internal unity. The region accepted Orthodox Christianity. To the west of Serbia lay Croatia, a land formed when two originally independent areas, Dalmatia on the Adriatic coast and Croatia itself, were joined together in the early tenth century. Through much of the tenth and eleventh centuries, Croatia managed to preserve itself and evade the clutches of Hungary, Byzantium, and Venice. By 1107, however, Croatia was incorporated by Hungary as a more or less autonomous region. Croatia, owing to Italian and Hungarian influence, became Roman Catholic.

The creation of the major east Slavic state is shrouded in mystery and legend. It seems that in 862 a Swedish Viking named Rurik and his followers, called Varangians, established or seized a trading camp at Novgorod. A few years later Oleg (r. 879–912) took over Kiev and made it his base of operations. Thus was founded Kievan Rus, a state that, like Hungary and Bulgaria, began with an outside, elite leadership over a local Slavic majority. Kievan Rus lasted until the Mongols destroyed it in 1240.

Kiev was ruled by grand dukes who pursued four basic policies. They created a vast trading network that linked Germany, Scandinavia, Byzantium, and the caliphate. They shared power with regional nobles who built up several important towns of their own. They received Orthodox Christianity from Constantinople in 988. And, finally, they struggled to defend Kiev, indeed the Rus territory as a whole, from wave after wave of invaders from the eastern steppes.

Eventually, Kievan Rus was destroyed by the Mongols. These were a loose coalition of pastoral nomads

William of Rubruck Reports on the Mongols

Mongol attacks deep into eastern Europe prompted the papacy to send missionaries to convert the Mongols to Catholicism, in hopes of using them in a grand crusade against the Muslims. Here are extracts from the report of William of Rubruck, who visited the khan Baatu, the grandson of Jenghiz Khan and the founder of the Golden Horde, between 1253 and 1255. Rubruck was particularly struck by domestic arrangements.

The dwelling in which they sleep has as its base a circle of interlaced sticks, and is made of the same material; these sticks converge into a little circle at the top and from this a neck juts up like a chimney; they cover it with white felt . . . the felt around the top they decorate with lovely and varied paintings. Before the doorway they also hang felt worked in multicolored designs. . . . The married women make for themselves really beautiful carts. . . . A wealthy Mongol may well have a hundred such carts with chests. Baatu has twenty-six wives and each of these has a large house . . . belonging to each house a good two hundred carts. When they pitch their houses the wife places her dwelling at the extreme west end and after her the others according to their rank, so that the last wife will be at the far east end, and there will be the space of a stone's throw between the establishment of one wife and another. . . . The camp of a rich Mongol will look like a large town and yet there will be very few men in it. One woman will drive twenty or thirty carts, for the country is flat. They tie together the carts, which are drawn by oxen or camels, one after the other, and the woman will sit on the front one driving the ox. . . . When they have pitched their houses with the door facing south, they arrange the master's couch at the northern end. The women's place is always on the east side . . . and the men's place is on the west side. On entering the house the men would by no means hang up their quivers in the women's section. Over the head of the master there is always an idol like a doll or little image of felt which they call the master's brother, and a similar one over the head of the mistress, and this they call the mistress's brother. . . . In the winter they make an excellent drink from rice, millet, wheat, and honey . . . in the summer they do not bother about anything but *cosmos* [fermented mare's milk]. *Cosmos* is always to be found inside the house before the entrance door, and near it stands a musician with his instruments. Our lutes and viols I did not see but many other instruments that are not known among us. When the master begins to drink, then one of his attendants cries out in a loud voice "Ha!" and the musician strikes his instrument. When it is a big feast they are holding they all clap their hands and also dance to the sound of the instrument, the men before the master and the women before the mistress. . . . Then they drink all around, the men and the women, and sometimes they vie with each other in drinking in a really disgusting and gluttonous manner. . . .

Source: Christopher Dawson, ed., *The Mongol Mission* (New York: Sheed and Ward, 1953), pp. 93–98, 103–104, passim.

from Mongolia (lands lying east of the Caspian Sea and north of China) and Turkic soldiers. The charismatic leader Jenghiz Khan (1154–1227) turned the Mongols into an invincible fighting force. He and his successors built an empire stretching from China to eastern Europe. In 1221 the Mongols began their attacks on the Rus and in 1240 Kiev fell.

Jenghiz Khan's empire was divided into several khanates on his death, with the Rus dominated by the Golden Horde, so called because of the splendid golden tent from which they ruled. The Mongols accorded subject people considerable autonomy, but they demanded heavy taxes and occasionally carried out brutal raids to remind everyone who was in control. Through their domination of trade, the Mongols weakened the urbanization and commerce built up by the Kievan Rus. (See the box "Global Encounters: William of Rubruck Reports on the Mongols.")

When Charlemagne was crowned emperor in 800, only Bulgaria existed as a state in the vast lands of eastern Europe. But the overriding trends of the era inexorably swept into that region. Three centuries later those lands were home to several small states and also to some impressively large and successful ones. The Slavic world was thoroughly pagan in 800 and largely Christian by 1200. State building and Christianization in eastern Europe represent two significant examples of European expansion in the High Middle Ages.

THE CRUSADES, 1095–1291

N 1096 an army of Christian knights who called themselves pilgrims left Europe to liberate the Holy Land from the Muslim "infidel." (This was the first of many Crusades, so called because the warriors were *crucesignati*, "signed by the cross.") By the late eleventh century, Europe was a fortress that had marshaled its resources for an attack on the world around it. Europe's expanding population, economic dynamism, political consolidation, and buoyant optimism made possible not only the First Crusade, but many more over two centuries.

■ The Background: East and West

With the accession in 867 of the Macedonian dynasty in the person of Basil I, the Byzantine Empire experienced a period of vigorous, successful rule that lasted until 1025. Although the Macedonians fostered striking cultural achievements, carried out significant administrative reforms, and established the kind of tight control of the church that had been so elusive in the iconoclastic era (see page 251), they were primarily great soldiers. Along the Balkan frontier the Macedonian rulers kept both the Bulgarians and Kievan Rus at bay while also neutralizing many smaller Slavic principalities. Basil II (r. 976–1025), called "the Bulgar Slayer," wore down Bulgaria in a series of relentless campaigns. In the west, the Macedonians maintained an effective diplomacy with Venice that permitted lucrative commercial opportunities in the Adriatic. In the east, the Macedonian rulers profited from the gradual dissolution of the Abbasid caliphate by expanding their frontier in Anatolia.

By contrast, throughout the ninth and tenth centuries the ability of the caliphs in Baghdad to control their vast empire declined precipitously. Egypt and North Africa escaped Baghdad's control almost completely, and religious strife between Sunni and Shi'ite Muslims further destabilized the Islamic state.

After Basil II's death in 1025, Byzantium suffered a long period of short reigns and abrupt changes in policy. Great aristocratic families in Anatolia slipped from imperial control. In the capital, factional squabbling swirled around the imperial court, and in the person of Patriarch Michael Cerularius (r. 1043–1058) the church sought to break out from two centuries of domination. When in 1054 Cerularius and Pope Leo IX quarreled so bitterly over ecclesiastical customs that they excommunicated each other, the traditionally cooperative papal-Byzantine religious diplomacy gave way to a deep schism between the Roman and Orthodox Churches that still exists. Religious tensions were complicated when the staunchly anti-Byzantine Normans began creating their kingdom in southern Italy.

It was in these divisive circumstances that the Seljuk Turks appeared on the eastern frontier of Anatolia. Bands of Turks, peoples from central Asia, had been serving the caliphs as mercenaries since the ninth century. With new leaders at their head, and with both the caliphate and the empire distracted, the Turks broke into Anatolia with a vengeance. In 1071 at Manzikert a skirmish between Byzantine and Turkish soldiers turned into a rout in which Byzantium lost an army, an emperor, and the Macedonian reputation for military prowess.

Ever since the emergence of the Turkish threat in the early eleventh century, the Byzantines had been seeking mercenary help. The imperial defeat at Manzikert made their search more urgent and led to appeals to the West. Some troops were rounded up but not enough, so in 1095 Emperor Alexius Comnenus (r. 1081–1118) sent envoys to ask Pope Urban II to support a plea for mercenary help against the Turks.

To most in western Europe, the Turkish threat to Byzantium mattered little. What *did* alarm Westerners was Turkish attacks on pilgrims to Jerusalem. The popes saw in the plight of the Byzantines and of Western pilgrims some opportunities to manifest their leadership of the church. The papacy also wanted very much to heal the Roman-Orthodox rift. The popes therefore placed a high value on aiding the Byzantines.

Moreover, a crusade was perfectly consonant with the ethos of the knights of western Europe. Knights were born and trained to fight. The literature of the age glorified war and warriors. But churchmen had for some years been advancing an ideal of Christian knighthood that stressed fighting God's enemies. In the late tenth century there arose, first in France and then in many other places, peace movements called the "Peace of

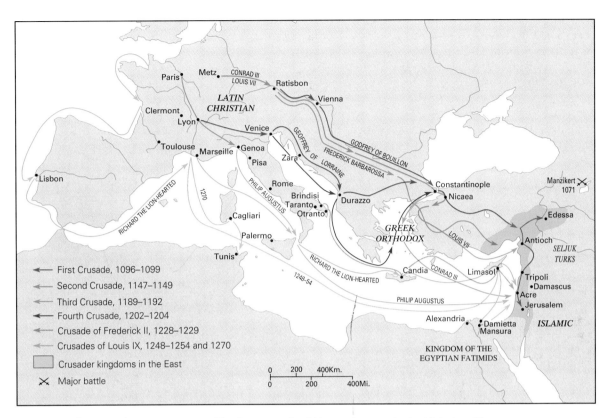

Map 9.7   The Crusades, 1095–1270   The long-standing Western interest in the Holy Land is vividly illustrated by the Crusades. Note the numerous routes taken, lands traversed, destinations attained, and points of cultural encounter.

God" or the "Truce of God." These movements sought to prevent war in certain seasons, such as around Christmas and Easter, and on certain days of the week, chiefly Sundays. Peace movements also attempted to outlaw fighting near churches, protect noncombatants, and soften the treatment of enemies and captives. Together the movements induced knights to fight non-Christians outside Europe.

■ The "Pilgrimage" to Jerusalem

Pope Urban II received Alexius's envoys in 1095 and then left Italy for France. He was actually a fugitive because Henry IV controlled Rome. In November at Clermont, Urban delivered a rousing speech to a vast Christian assembly. He ignored the eastern emperor's appeal for aid and instead promised salvation to soldiers who would enlist in a great struggle to free the Holy Land. The crowd acclaimed his words with a shout of "God wills it!"

By 1096 four large armies, which eventually swelled to perhaps a hundred thousand men—mostly French

knights with a smattering of troops from other parts of Europe—assembled under the leadership of the pope's legate. The forces were to rendezvous at Constantinople, where they seem to have expected a cordial imperial welcome and all necessary assistance. Alexius, however, took a rather different view. A ragtag band of ordinary people preceding the Crusaders had torn through the Balkans like a plague of locusts. Then, the crusading armies themselves sorely taxed the imperial authorities, who spent a lot of time and money arranging their passage from the frontier of Hungary to the gates of Constantinople. Finally, Alexius wanted mercenaries to fend off Turks in Anatolia, not armed pilgrims intent on liberating Palestine (see Map 9.7).

After receiving nominal promises of loyalty and the return or donation of any lands captured, Alexius moved the Crusaders into Anatolia. Almost immediately the Latin army defeated a Turkish force, thus earning a valuable, though short-lived, reputation for invincibility. The troops then entered Syria and laid siege to Antioch, which did not fall until 1098. At this point, rivalries

☙ READING SOURCES

An Arab Perspective on the First Crusade

The Muslim historian Ibn al-Athir (1160–1233) provides several interesting perspectives on the First Crusade in his work The Perfect History. *The Baldwin with whom this account opens is not historical; or perhaps he is a composite of the many Baldwins then active in the West. Nevertheless, al-Athir's depiction of the crudeness of Roger of Sicily is interesting as are his incidental revelations of Christian-Muslim cooperation and of divisions in the Islamic world.*

Baldwin, their king, assembled a great army and sent word to Roger [of Sicily] saying: "I have assembled a great army and now I am on my way to you, to use your bases for my conquest of the African coast. Thus you and I shall become neighbors." Roger called together his companions and consulted them about these proposals. "This will be a fine thing for them and for us!" they declared, "for by this means these lands will be converted to the Faith." At this Roger raised one leg and farted loudly, and swore that it was of more use than their advice. "Why?" "Because if this army comes here it will need quantities of provisions and fleets of ships to transport it to Africa, as well as reinforcements from my own troops. Then, if the Franks succeed in conquering this territory they will take it over and will need provisioning from Sicily. This will cost me my annual profit from the harvest. If they fail they will return here and be an embarrassment to me here in my own domain. As well as this Tamim [the emir of Tunisia in North Africa] will say that I have broken faith with him and violated our treaty, and friendly relations and communications between us will be disrupted. As far as we are concerned, Africa is always there. When we are strong enough we will take it."

He summoned Baldwin's messenger and said to him: "If you have decided to make war on the Muslims your best course will be to free Jerusalem from their rule and thereby win great honour. I am bound by certain treaties and promises of allegiance with the rulers of Africa." So the Franks made ready to attack Syria.

Another story is that the Fatimids [local rulers] of Egypt were afraid when they saw the Seljuqids extending their empire through Syria as far as Gaza, until they reached the Egyptian border and Atziz [a general] invaded Egypt itself. They therefore sent to invite the Franks to invade Syria and so to protect Egypt from the Muslims [the Fatimids, although militantly Muslim, were regarded as heretics by other Muslims]. But God knows best.

Source: Francesco Gabrieli, *Arab Historians of the Crusades* (Berkeley: University of California Press, 1969), pp. 3–4.

among the Crusaders came into the open. One force went to the frontier of Armenia and carved out a principality. One of the ubiquitous Normans kept Antioch for himself. The main army pressed on to Jerusalem and, after a short but fierce siege, conquered it in July 1099. A Muslim historian described the scene:

> In the Masjid [Mosque] al-Aqsa the Franks slaughtered more than 70,000 people, among them a large number of Imams and Muslim scholars, devout and ascetic men who had left their homelands to live lives of pious

seclusion in the Holy Place. The Franks stripped the Dome of the Rock [the Mosque of Umar, near the al-Aqsa mosque, pictured on page 243] of more than forty silver candelabra, each of them weighing 3,600 drams [almost 40 pounds], and a great silver lamp weighing forty-four Syrian pounds, as well as a hundred and fifty smaller candelabra and more than twenty gold ones, and a great deal more booty.[2]

Godfrey of Bouillon, leader of the troops that had "liberated" Jerusalem, was named "Advocate of the Holy Sepulcher" and became ruler of the Christians in the East. He lived only a short time, however, and was replaced by his brother, Baldwin, as king of Jerusalem in 1100.

Judged on its own terms, the First Crusade was a success. The Holy Land was retaken from the infidel, and the pilgrim routes were passable once more. Entirely uncertain, however, were the prospects of the crusader states, the future course of Western relations with Byzantium, and the reaction of the Islamic world once it recovered from its initial shock. (See the box "Reading Sources: An Arab Perspective on the First Crusade.")

■ **The Later Crusades**

Crusading was intended to protect the Holy Land and keep open the pilgrim routes to Jerusalem. The creation of the small crusader states in the hostile environment of Syria and Palestine made continued crusading almost inevitable. In 1144 the tiny crusader state at Edessa on the Armenian frontier fell to a Muslim army. Although the news saddened Europeans, it took immense efforts by the papacy and other religious leaders to launch another crusade. Finally Conrad III of Germany and Louis VII of France agreed to lead it, but because neither would willingly submit to the other's authority, the Second Crusade accomplished little. Its one achievement was an accident. In 1147 an army of English, French, and Flemish soldiers who were proceeding to the Holy Land by sea put in on the Iberian coast and captured Lisbon. This opened a new front in the Reconquista and laid the foundations for the later kingdom of Portugal (see Map 9.7).

The papacy called for the Third Crusade when Saladin° (1138–1193), a powerful local leader typical of the disintegrating Abbasid caliphate, recaptured Jerusalem in 1187. It is a measure of the force of the crusading ideal that the greatest crowned heads of the day—Frederick Barbarossa, Philip II, and Richard the Lionheart—answered the call. It must be said, however, that only Frederick did so enthusiastically. Frederick died en route in 1190, while Philip returned home in 1191 and Richard in 1192. Because neither Richard nor Philip would stay in Palestine to fight Saladin, this crusade merely won access to Jerusalem for pilgrims.

Disappointed with the results of the Third Crusade, Innocent III began calling for another crusade immediately on his election in 1198. Popular preachers summoned an army, once again largely French, and the pope and the Fourth Crusade's military leaders engaged the

Venetians to construct a fleet of war and transport ships. In less than eighteen months they produced 50 galleys and 450 transports, a tribute to the awesome capabilities of the Venetian shipyards.

Ships, however, were expensive, and the Venetians drove hard bargains. When too few Crusaders and too little money appeared, the Venetians suggested that the Crusaders could discharge some of their debt by recapturing from the Hungarians the formerly Venetian port of Zara on the Dalmatian coast. This idea outraged the pope, but he could do little about it. Then into the camp of the Crusaders came a pretender to the Byzantine throne, who promised that if the Crusaders would help him to claim his patrimony, he would contribute to the cost of the Crusade. The Venetians urged the indebted Crusaders to accept this offer, and, to the horror of Innocent III, the Fourth Crusade turned to Constantinople.

Once in Constantinople, the Crusaders learned that their new ally had few friends in the Byzantine capital, but the venture hardly collapsed. The Venetians saw an opportunity to expand business opportunities in the East, and the soldiers welcomed a chance to plunder the Mediterranean's greatest city and to avenge what they regarded as a century of Byzantine perfidy. Thus, the Fourth Crusade captured not Jerusalem but Constantinople. Until 1261, the Eastern and Western churches were reunited under papal leadership, and substantial tracts of the Balkans fell to Western knights under a "Latin emperor" of Constantinople.

In later decades, popes began to take a more active role in planning crusades. No pope wanted to lose control of a crusade as Innocent had done, and all popes saw that the liberation of Jerusalem required a solid base of operations in the eastern Mediterranean. Egypt was the objective of the Fifth Crusade (1218–1221) and of the Sixth (1248–1250). Despite a few victories, the Crusaders could not win a secure base. No further crusades to the East were organized in the thirteenth century. In 1291 Acre, the last Crusader stronghold, fell and the original crusading era ended.

During the crusading period, the Holy Land was not the sole object of Crusaders' attentions. In about 1140 the pope preached a crusade against the Normans in southern Italy, and several popes in the thirteenth century, fearful of imperial encroachment, preached crusades against the Staufer dynasty in Italy. In 1147 the papacy authorized a crusade in the Baltic that opened nearly four centuries of German expansion into the pagan Slavic lands to the east of Saxony. In 1208 Innocent III proclaimed a crusade against the Albigensians in southwestern France.

Saladin (sah-lah-DEEN)

Why did the Crusades end? There are several reasons. By the late thirteenth century, more violence was being directed inward against heretics and political foes of the papacy than outward against the alleged enemies of Christendom itself. As rulers became more sophisticated and controlled more territory, they had less interest in the intangible benefits of crusading such as prestige. Whereas the cities of Italy once needed to open up Mediterranean ports, now they wished to secure comparative advantage over one another. The Christian ideals of poverty, charity, and service were incompatible with warfare. Literary images provide another insight into the decline of the Crusades. After 1300, we are less likely to read about a Christian knight fighting honorably for God and king than about a gentleman of manners seeking the favor of a fair lady.

A balance sheet for the crusading movement as a whole reveals more losses than gains. The Crusades exported many violent men from Europe, but it is not clear that Europe became a less violent place. As might be expected, the Crusades devastated relations between Christian Europe and the Muslim world. The Fourth Crusade mortally wounded Byzantium and worsened the already tense standoff between the Catholic and Orthodox Churches. Crusading zeal was directed deliberately against heretics and coincidentally against Jews. The Crusades did not create anti-Semitism, but they aggravated it. Some women, particularly in France, from which the majority of all Crusaders came, may have enjoyed momentary benefits in terms of control of land, wealth, and people while their husbands were away. But the long-term trend in feudal society was disadvantageous to women, and the Crusades did not change that. Finally, the Crusades may have done as much to disrupt Mediterranean trade as to promote it. Italian urban rivalries took the place of Latin-Muslim-Byzantine ones. That a single new product, the apricot, entered Europe in the crusading era seems small reward for such huge effort.

SUMMARY

ETWEEN 900 and 1300 Western civilization experienced a long period of dramatic, sustained expansion. In the early Middle Ages, Rome's three heirs—western Europe, Byzantium, and the Islamic caliphate—were poised in a rough equilibrium. By the High Middle Ages, western Europe had seized the upper hand thanks to a strong economy, political centralization, and Europe's first concerted attempt to reverse the tide of Islamic conquests.

Several factors contributed to Europe's economic growth. The population rose steadily. People everywhere brought new land under cultivation, adopted better agricultural techniques, and improved transportation systems. Greater efficiencies in agriculture promoted urban growth, as some people were freed from farming to undertake commercial and artisanal pursuits. Never before had Europe's economy grown so rapidly.

Governments expanded their power in most parts of Europe. Rulers in England, France, and Spain drew on both precedent and the innovative spirit of the present to create effective centralized institutions. In the Celtic, Scandinavian, and Slavic worlds, dynamic new states emerged. In Italy, durable urban governments dotted the landscape while the Roman church expanded its governing structures and the popes assumed a leading position in European society. A German kingdom arose where none had existed before, became briefly the greatest state in Europe, and then collapsed under the weight of innumerable problems.

European rulers faced a variety of problems in enlarging or consolidating their states. England, Spain, and Hungary all expanded at the expense of their neighbors. England, again, as well as France, Denmark, and Norway, expanded by extending control over local magnates. England, France, Hungary, and Spain developed the strongest governmental institutions.

Several states failed to consolidate their power. The German emperors were challenged by local rulers and buffeted by the investiture controversy. Their dream of a unified German state faded away. Poland could not survive dynastic divisions and a Mongol attack. The largest European state, Kievan Rus, was wiped from the map by an expansionary power from the East, the Mongols.

Europe's economic dynamism, increasing political stability, military might, and militant Christianity came together to produce the Crusades. Around 900, Europe was suffering attacks from Vikings, Muslims, and Magyars. Vikings and Magyars were incorporated into Europe, but from 1100 to 1300 Europe retaliated against the Muslim world. The Crusades embittered relations between Latin Christians, on the one hand, and Orthodox Christians and Muslims, on the other. But the crusading movement stands for the history student as perhaps the key indicator of the expansive nature of late medieval Europe.

Europeans of the High Middle Ages did more than just plant fields, pass laws, and fight wars. They lived in increasingly complex social structures, broadened their range of religious experiences, invented two new architectural styles, created a novel intellectual institution (the university), and wrote literary masterpieces. To all these creative—and expanding—realms of human endeavor we will turn in the next chapter.

■ Notes

1. Walter Map, *De nugis curialum*, 5.5, in John H. Mundy, *Europe in the High Middle Ages* (London: Longman, 1973), p. 387.
2. From the *Gesta Francorum*, trans. August C. Krey, in *The First Crusade* (Princeton, N.J.: Princeton University Press, 1921), p. 257 (slightly adapted).

■ Suggested Reading

Bartlett, Robert. *The Making of Europe: Conquest, Colonization and Cultural Change, 950–1350*. 1993. An engaging account of the expansion and "Europeanization" of Europe.

Bisson, Thomas, ed. *Cultures of Power: Lordship, Status, and Process in Twelfth-Century Europe*. 1995. The thirteen sparkling essays in this book cover much of Europe and attempt to explain how power was actually wielded in a society in which states were just emerging.

Bloch, Marc. *Feudal Society*. Translated by L. A. Manyon. 2 vols. 1964. This best-known book by one of this century's greatest historians seeks to explain the total history of the post-Carolingian world in terms of the ideals and practices of feudalism.

Reynolds, Susan. *Fiefs and Vassals*. 1994. Brilliant, controversial, and difficult, this massive book challenges many long-standing ideas about feudalism.

———. *Kingdoms and Communities in Western Europe, 900–1300*. 2d ed. 1997. After exploring the kinds of legal notions that guided medieval community building, this lively book turns to communities themselves, ranging from the parish to the kingdoms.

Riley-Smith, Jonathan, ed. *The Oxford Illustrated History of the Crusades*. 1997. A set of essays with lavish illustrations that explores almost every aspect of the Crusades and the world that produced them.

 For a searchable list of additional readings for this chapter, go to http://college.hmco.com.

The Medieval Castle

Storybook castles, in the manner of Disneyland, figure prominently in almost everyone's idea of the Middle Ages. The reality was different. Medieval castles were generally small, stark, and uncomfortable, not beautiful and romantic.

Castles represent a stage in the history of both dwellings and fortifications. Initially, castles were private, residential, and military. A consideration of these three elements will place the castle in historical context and illustrate what historians learn from the impressive ruins that dot the landscape of Europe and the crusader states.

The first medieval castles were constructed in the tenth century. The French word *château* (from the Latin *castellum*) means "great house," signifying the castle's residential purpose. Powerful aristocrats erected castles not just as their principal dwellings but also as a base for securing and extending their social and political influence. From his castle a lord could dominate the surrounding region. The castle also sheltered the lord's immediate dependents temporarily in the event of an attack and his military retainers more or less permanently.

A few castles were built exclusively for military purposes. In 1110 Crusaders captured a strategic plateau rising 2,000 feet above the main road from inner Syria to the Mediterranean. Between 1142 and 1205 Crusaders continually expanded the fortifications of the castle pictured here, the "Krak des Chevaliers" (from Syriac *karka*, meaning "fortress," and the Old French word for "horsemen"). This castle fell to Muslim attackers in 1271. The techniques of fortification developed in the crusader East influenced castle building in Europe.

The privately built castles of the tenth, eleventh, and twelfth centuries reflected the extreme localization of power in Europe at that time. As European governments grew stronger in the twelfth century, they began to monopolize the construction of castles and suppressed private castles as military entities. For example, Cerreg Cennen°, on the opposite page, was built by a Welsh prince, Lord Rhys° (d. 1197), and then seized from his descendants by Edward I around 1300. From the fourteenth century on, as in Roman times, fortresses served

essentially public and military purposes, and resident garrisons were their primary occupants.

Castles took many forms. From 900 to 1200 the "motte and bailey" castle was the most common. A lord commanded his dependents to dig a circular ditch and heap the dirt into a mound (the motte). The ditch, together with a wooden palisade—a fencelike wall—was the bailey. A wooden tower was often built atop the mound. Some castles included an elaborate series of mounds, ditches, and wooden walls—look at the picture of the Polish motte and bailey castle on page 305—but usually these structures were quite simple.

As siege techniques improved (catapults could hurl projectiles weighing 600 pounds), the wooden building of the bailey began to be replaced by stone. By 1150 or 1200, stone towers (*donjons*, from the Latin *dominium* for "lordship") were only the inner portion—the "keep"—of a more complicated structure of walls, towers, and gates. It was not unusual for walls to be 75 or 100 feet high. Because of the growing power of bombarding engines, castle walls often had to be made thicker. Towers built at 40- or 50-foot intervals projected beyond the walls so that defenders armed with bows and arrows could fire at attackers along the length of a castle wall. Look at the spacing of the towers in the castles pictured here. At Krak des Chevaliers we see one of the earliest examples of a double ring of walls. Two walls made it more difficult for attackers to take the keep and permitted defenders to battle invaders from inside both the inner and the outer walls.

To allow people to enter and leave, castles had gate towers, usually with two gates, one on the outside and one on the inside. Intricate systems of winches, cranks, and counterweights regulated the raising and lowering of the gates. Speedy operation was essential. Some castles had small "sally-ports" from which soldiers could make a rapid dash to attack a besieging enemy.

When possible, lords sited their castles on the edges of cliffs because fewer sides were open to assault and a garrison of modest size could defend the remaining walls. Cerreg Cennen stands 300 feet above a gorge, as you can see from the left side of the picture. Krak too sits on an impressive natural site. To walls and natural defenses were sometimes added ditches, as at Krak.

Cerreg Cennen (CARE-reg KEN-nen)   **Rhys** (REES)

Krak des Chevaliers, Syria, ca. 1200
(Michael Jenner/Robert Harding Picture Library)

Cerreg Cennen Castle, Wales, Late Twelfth Century
(Michael Holford)

Much can be learned from the number of castles in a particular area. The presence of numerous small castles across the countryside suggests an extreme decentralization of power in that place and time. Remains of several hundred castles have been found in France alone; and England in 1100 boasted a castle every 10 miles. Conversely, areas with only a few large, strategically sited castles were likely subject to greater central control. Careful mapping of the known locations of castles can tell historians a great deal about the structure of social and political relationships.

Castles both contributed and responded to developments in military technology, such as more powerful catapults. Stone castles proliferated as Europe grew wealthier and as quarrying technology improved. Castles grew larger as monarchies rather than private individuals built them. Like cathedrals, massive state-funded castles tended to be built by professionals rather than by local laborers.

Both fortifications and magnificent dwellings have existed in Western civilization for millennia. From about 900 to 1200 the castle met the needs of a politically dominant warrior aristocracy for a private residence with military significance. In later centuries, the castle, as a château, retained its private and residential nature but lost much of its military character to garrisoned fortresses in the service of kings and princes.

 For additional information on this topic, go to http://college.hmco.com.

CHAPTER 10

Medieval Civilization at Its Height
900–1300

LOOKING down the nave of Chartres Cathedral, built between 1192 and 1220, produces a number of somewhat contradictory sensations. The size and verticality, the play of light and dark, the amazing array of shapes, corners, and angles, all are a bit mysterious. They were meant to be. At the same time, there is a logically ordered geometric elegance to the building that is plain to see. And this was intended too.

The cathedral at Chartres aptly symbolizes the range of historical currents dominant in high medieval Europe. We saw in Chapter 9 that Europe was expanding economically, politically, and militarily. Like its greater context, this building is very large; the cathedrals built in the burgeoning cities of the twelfth and thirteenth centuries were larger than any that had been built since Justinian erected Hagia Sophia. The bishops of Chartres expended most of their considerable income—Chartres lies in France's richest grain-growing region—for some twenty years to build this church. Literally dozens of these great buildings were going up at the same time all over Europe, providing employment for thousands of ordinary workers and numerous master craftsmen. Nobles and townsfolk donated windows and other fixtures to the building, making the building itself an expression of the period's more complex society.

Chartres Cathedral is an excellent example of the Gothic style in architecture, medieval Europe's supreme architectural achievement, Gothic being one of two major stylistic innovations in this period. The other was Romanesque, a style that had reached the summit of its beauty and power in the early twelfth century just as Gothic was about to appear. This change in architectural styles parallels others in the High Middle Ages. The Carolingian focus on grammar, on the

The Traditional Orders of Society

Social and Religious Movements, ca. 1100–1300

Latin Culture: From Schools to Universities

The Vernacular Achievement

Nave of Chartres Cathedral, looking east.
(Éditions Gaud)

most basic literary skills, gave way to an interest in logic. Intellectual problems that had in the past been solved by appeals to scriptural or patristic authority were now addressed by human reason. This produced a new style of intellectual endeavor called "Scholasticism." Monasteries and cathedrals housed schools in the Carolingian world, but by the thirteenth century the university had emerged as a higher kind of cultural institution.

Latin remained the dominant language of scholars, but almost everywhere the vernacular spoken languages were becoming graceful and effective tools for written communication. Religious themes were still foremost in writings of all kinds, but adventures, romances, and other works dedicated to secular themes were gaining in prominence. The Christian tradition still undergirded intellectual life, but that tradition was now spurred on to new heights of insight and expression by encounters with long-lost Greek texts and with the writings of Jewish and Muslim intellectuals. Look where you will, cultural life was richer and more complex than ever before.

The previous chapter concentrated on the economic foundations of society and on the ways in which people organized themselves politically. This chapter begins by introducing the increasingly complex social structures within which people lived and then turns to a study of what those people thought, said, and built.

QUESTIONS TO CONSIDER

■ Into what principal social groups were the people of high medieval Europe organized?

■ What role did logic play in spurring intellectual development and in contributing to the growth of Scholasticism?

■ Why did some spiritual movements result in heresy while others ended in new religious orders?

■ What cultural achievements mark the High Middle Ages as a period of crowning achievement?

TERMS TO KNOW

Cluny (Cluniacs)	canon law
Bernard of Clairvaux	Thomas Aquinas
Hildegard of Bingen	summa
chivalry	Romanesque
Dominic	Gothic
Francis of Assisi	

THE TRADITIONAL ORDERS OF SOCIETY

A FTER centuries of various experiments with ordering social relations after the end of the Roman Empire in the West, a new social order had evolved by 900 that was distinctively medieval. Alfred the Great (r. 871–899) of England once said that a kingdom needed "men of prayer, men of war, and men of work." In the tenth century two French bishops wrote lengthy works exploring this same theme. This three-way division reveals the way the elite looked at the world. It provided neat places for the clergy, warrior-aristocrats, and peasants. The clergy and the nobility agreed that they were superior to the "workers," but fierce controversies raged over whether ultimate leadership in society belonged to the "pray-ers" or to the "fighters."

By the time this tripartite view of society was fully established in the West, it had begun to fit social realities less well. It excluded townspeople, who were becoming ever more important. Town residents worked for a living, of course, but only farmers were considered "workers." Alfred and the bishops did not speak about women, and they consciously excluded minorities, chiefly Jews. To form a full picture of Europe's increasingly intricate social relations, we begin with contemporary theoretical pronouncements and then look for the people whom the theoreticians neglected.

■ Those Who Pray: The Clergy

As the church promoted its own vision of the tripartite ordering of society, it assigned primacy to the "pray-ers," to its own leaders. Within the clergy, however, sharp disagreements arose over whether the leading "pray-ers" were the monks in the monasteries or the bishops in their cathedrals. Whereas in the Carolingian world, the clergy served occasionally as an avenue of upward social mobility for talented outsiders, in the High Middle Ages church offices were usually reserved to the younger sons of the nobility. The church was always hierarchical in organization and outlook so the increasingly aristocratic character of the church's leadership tended to reinforce those old tendencies.

In the aftermath of the Carolingian collapse, a great spiritual reform swept Europe. It began in 910 when Duke William of Aquitaine founded the monastery of Cluny° in Burgundy on lands that he donated (see Map 9.4, page 294). At a time when powerful local families dominated almost all monasteries, Cluny was a rarity because it was free of all lay and episcopal control and because it was under the direct authority of the pope. Cluny's abbots were among the greatest European statesmen of their day and became influential advisers to popes, French kings, German emperors, and aristocratic families.

In the tradition of the Carolingian monastic reforms, Cluny placed great emphasis on liturgical prayer. The monks spent long hours in solemn devotions and did little manual work. Because Cluniac prayer was thought to be especially efficacious, nobles all over Europe donated land to Cluny and placed local monasteries under Cluniac control. Many independent monasteries also appealed to Cluny for spiritual reform. By the twelfth century, hundreds of monasteries had joined in a Cluniac order. Individual houses were under the authority of the abbot of Cluny, and their priors had to attend an annual assembly. Although the majority of houses reformed by Cluny were male, many convents of nuns also adopted Cluniac practices.

Cluny promoted two powerful ideas. One was that the role of the church was to pray for the world, not to be implicated deeply in it. The other was that freedom from lay control was essential if churches were to concentrate on their spiritual tasks.

The same spiritual forces that motivated the Cluniacs inspired Bishop Adalbero of Metz in 933 to promote the restoration of Benedictine practices in the dilapi-

CHRONOLOGY	
ca. 900	*Beowulf*
910	Foundation of Cluny
940–1003	Gerbert of Aurillac
960–1028	Fulbert of Chartres
d. 970	Roswitha of Gandersheim
1000–1088	Berengar of Tours
ca. 1033–1109	Anselm of Canterbury
ca. 1050–1150	Emergence of the Romanesque
1079–1142	Peter Abelard
1184	Waldensians declared heretics
1090–1153	Bernard of Clairvaux
1098	Foundation of Cîteaux
1098–1179	Hildegard of Bingen
ca. 1100	*Song of Roland*
1135–1183	Chrétien de Troyes
1170–1221	Dominic
ca. 1177–1213	Mary of Oignies
1181–1226	Francis of Assisi
1194–1253	Clare of Assisi
1208	Albigensian Crusade launched
1210–1280	Mechtild of Magdeburg
1225–1274	Thomas Aquinas
1265–1321	Dante Alighieri

dated Lorraine monastery of Gorze°. Customs at Gorze resembled those at Cluny, and they spread widely in Lorraine, Germany, and England. The Gorze reform was well received by kings and nobles; its aim was not so much to withdraw from the world as to improve it. Monks from the Gorze and Cluniac traditions bitterly condemned clerical immorality and inappropriate lay interference in the church. They preached against clerical marriage and simony, the buying and selling of church offices.

Cluny (CLUE-nee)

Gorze (GORTZ-eh)

Reconstruction of Cluny A view of the monastic complex at Cluny in the early twelfth century. Note the basilica (the largest church in Europe until the sixteenth century), the cloister (to the left, actually south, of the basilica, with its dormitory in the foreground and refectory opposite the basilica), and the workshops. *(Based on a drawing from* Cluny des Églises et la Maison du Chef d'Ordre, *by R. J. Conant. Courtesy, Medieval Academy of America)*

Reformers in the more ascetic eremitic tradition (see page 217) desired more profound changes. They criticized the monastery at Cluny, saying that it had become too opulent and successful, and the monastery at Gorze because it seemed too immersed in worldly affairs. A desire to build new communities according to their vision of the apostolic church, featuring a life of poverty, self-denial, and seclusion, captivated the ascetics. Thus, the eleventh and early twelfth centuries saw a proliferation of both male and female experiments in eremitic monasticism. Other Europeans believed that the apostolic calling demanded not only an austere regimen of personal renunciation but also an active life of Christian ministry. Cathedral clergy, called canons, in particular, adapted the rule of Saint Augustine so that they could live a communal life and also carry out priestly duties.

The greatest critics of the Cluniac tradition, and the real monastic elite of the early twelfth century, were the Cistercians. In 1098 Abbot Robert left his Burgundian monastery of Molesme° because he believed it had abandoned the strict teachings of Saint Benedict. He founded a new monastery at Cîteaux° in Burgundy. This

---

Molesme (MOE-lem) **Cîteaux** (SEE-toe)

house was to follow the Benedictine Rule literally and to refuse all secular entanglements: lands, rents, and servile dependents. So rigorous and poor was the community that it struggled until a charismatic young Burgundian nobleman named Bernard (1090–1153) joined in 1112. Three years later Bernard left to found a daughter house at Clairvaux, of which he remained abbot for the rest of his life. Through his writing, preaching, and personal example, Bernard dominated the religious life of Europe in his lifetime. By the end of the twelfth century there were about 500 Cistercian (from the Latin for *Cîteaux*) monasteries in Europe, and Bernard's own Clairvaux had 700 monks. Initially the Cistercians wished to be an order of adult men. They successfully avoided admitting young boys, but by 1200 they had authorized about 100 convents of Cistercian nuns.

And it was not just the Cistercians and the traditional Benedictines who attracted women. The twelfth century saw many new communities of women from England to eastern Europe. The age's growing prosperity and population contributed both potential nuns and healthy endowments, but the key factor was that women were responding to the spiritual forces of the age in the same way men were.

With the monastic clergy gaining so much in prestige and visibility, the episcopal clergy countered with its own view of society. Surely, the bishops agreed, spiritual, moral, and intellectual improvement were desirable. Likewise, it was time to end the grossest examples of lay interference in the church. But precisely because so many bishops came from great families and were so well connected, they were less inclined to be rigid about the line of demarcation between lay and clerical responsibilities. In Germany, for example, the king's chapel recruited young noblemen to train them as clerics and to inculcate in them the policies and ethos of the court. Many of these chaplains were appointed to bishoprics and then advanced the king's interests in their new ecclesiastical areas of authority. They were often men of spiritual depth and resented what they regarded as monastic carping about their worldliness. By the middle of the twelfth century, bishops, and finally popes, too, had imposed on the church a view that monks belonged in their monasteries and that bishops should lead society.

It was always the special responsibility of the clergy to look after the moral order of society. In the turbulent world of gentlemen-warriors, the church had its own ideas about what a perfect "fighter" should do. The English bishop and scholar John of Salisbury (d. 1180), reflecting on knighthood in the twelfth century, concluded that it existed "to protect the church, to attack infidelity, to reverence the priesthood, to protect the poor, to keep the peace, to shed one's blood and, if necessary, to lay down one's life for one's brethren."

Turning large numbers of violent young men into servants of the church was a tall order for the clergy, and they had only limited success. One strategy that worked was the creation of military orders. The Palestine-based Knights of St. John, or Hospitallers, and Knights of the Temple, or Templars, are the major examples, but others existed in Spain and Germany. The Hospitallers started near Jerusalem as a foundation under Benedictine auspices dedicated to charitable works and care of the sick. They evolved into a monastic order using a version of the Rule of Saint Benedict and devoted themselves to the defense of pilgrims to the Holy Land. The Templars were men living under religious rule and sworn to protect the small states created by the Crusaders (see pages 309–311). These military orders measured up very well to the clergy's idea of what a perfect knight should be.

The clergy could also regulate disputes in society. For example, when a community was divided by a difficult conflict that demanded resolution, it might turn to the *ordeal*—a judicial procedure that sought divine judgment by subjecting the accused to a physically painful or dangerous test. An accused person might walk a certain distance carrying hot iron or plunge a hand into a boiling cauldron to pluck out a pebble. The resulting wounds would be bandaged for a set time and then examined. If they were healing, the person was considered innocent; if festering, guilty. The clergy officiated at ordeals until the papacy forbade their participation in 1215.

Clergymen were also the conservators of the shrines where people gained special access to the holiness of the saints. The clergy wrote and preached about the miracles of the saints, and stories circulated through the church about relics, or artifacts associated with these martyrs. The shrines where relics were preserved attracted pilgrims seeking healing from illness, injury, or misfortune. The clergy thus played unique roles in forming and nurturing communities in the world and in interceding for this world with God in the next.

■ Those Who Fight: The Nobility

In recent years scholars have spilled a sea of ink trying to define the medieval nobility. The matter is important because even though the nobility constituted only a small minority of the total population, nobles were and expected to be the ruling class. To appreciate their crucial role, we need to consider the shape of the nobility and the nobles' lifestyle and ethos.

The Knight at Prayer   This stained glass window from Chartres depicts the church's idealized conception of one of God's warriors: his sword and pious disposition combat the enemies of religion.
(Sonia Halliday Photographs)

In English the word *noble* can be either an adjective or a noun. More commonly, it is an adjective, as in a "noble sentiment" or a "noble deed." Before the twelfth century, the Latin *nobilis* was almost exclusively an adjective. The word pertained to certain desirable personal qualities. Then, gradually, the word became a noun and pertained to a certain kind of person.

What kind of a person? In the ideal case, a noble was a well-born, cultivated, office-holding soldier. In the earlier Middle Ages, many men held offices without necessarily being considered noble. Virtually all free men were expected to be soldiers, but few of them ranked as nobles. It was in the century or so following the feudal revolution (see page 295) that these distinct elements were fused into a single social order.

In a world in which lords were everywhere extending their power, military prowess became more valuable. At the same time, the need for horses and for more expensive arms and armor made it almost impossible for ordinary freemen to be soldiers. Likewise, ambitious lords who wished to expand their influence, and who were often, in an expanding economy, more prosperous than their forebears, were looking for ways to use their resources to gain followers. These trends came together as lords granted to their followers either military gear or lands, which would generate the income necessary to obtain arms and horses. We call those followers "vassals" and the lands they obtained "fiefs°." Vassalage became a widespread institution all over Europe and fief-holding became a normal accompaniment to vassalage. By contrast vassalage was unusual in the Carolingian world and rarely connected with fief-holding (see page 262).

These vassals, often called knights by contemporary sources, obviously could not claim high birth or venerable ancestry. Nor were they initially officeholders appointed by kings or emperors. Moreover, they were not wealthy and could not sustain the kind of lavish lifestyle that one might expect from nobles. Across the eleventh and twelfth centuries, knights saw their status change, in part because they aped the behavior of the nobles who themselves accepted the necessity of military ability.

All over Europe, especially where royal power was ineffective, both knights and nobles secured tighter control of peasant labor. This process provided knights and nobles with the money to build castles and to acquire fine possessions. As governments expanded their competence, these nobles and knights often held high offices, or if they did not, they pressured kings to concede such offices to them. Lords also tended to gather their lands into coherent blocks and to name themselves after the castles they built on their lands. Families also began to produce genealogies tracing their ancestry to relatives in the distant past, and to kings if at all possible. At the same time, families began to practice primogeniture— that is, reserving their lands, castles, and titles to the *primus genitus*, or "first-born" son.

This allotment of the choicest inheritances to a shrinking group turned loose a large number of younger sons. Many of them entered the clergy, a tendency that helps to explain the rising aristocratic character of the church. It should be emphasized right away, however, that this was not a punishment. Sons were not "dumped" on the church. Clerical careers were prestigious and relatively comfortable. But more numerous than clerics were the young men who were without an estate and who lacked the means to secure a bride and to form a family of their own. It was from these men that vast crusading armies were recruited. These were also the men who traipsed about Europe looking for fame and fortune, or failing that, a lord to serve. Many of these "young" men were 30 or 40 years old. They were called young because they had not yet established themselves.

So, by 1200 the nobility was a group identified by the profession of arms, the holding of office, a consciousness of family traditions, and an elevated lifestyle. A specific ethos—chivalry—belonged to the nobility. Today, chivalry is often thought of as either an elaborate code of conduct regulating relations between the sexes or the value system behind the literary image of dashing knights in shining armor saving damsels in distress from fire-breathing dragons. Actually, its very name derives from *cheval,* French for "horse," the classic conveyance of a knight, a *caballarius* in Latin. Chivalry began as the code of conduct for mounted warriors.

Chivalry highly esteemed certain masculine, militant qualities. Military prowess was the greatest of chivalric virtues. A knight who was not a great warrior was useless. Literature of the time exalts the knight who slays fearsome beasts or the hero who single-handedly overwhelms impossible numbers of the enemy. Open-handed generosity was another key virtue. The truly noble person engaged in sumptuous display to manifest his power, to show concern for his dependents, and to enlarge his entourage. Medieval literature is full of rich banquets and stunning presents. In Anglo-Saxon England the king was called "the giver of rings." Knights were obsessed with their honor, their reputations. They sought glory, the better to win a lord or a bride or, if a lord already, to attract followers.

Chivalry also involved loyalty, the glue that held feudal society together. But we must take into account statements such as the following one by a twelfth-century English historian, William of Malmesbury: "They [knights] are faithful to their lords, but swift to break faith. A breath of ill fortune and they are plotting treachery, a bag of money and their mind is changed." Knights, especially the "young," were loyal to their lords when they could be, but fundamentally they were loyal to themselves.

What role was left to noblewomen in a world of chivalry and lordship? By the late eleventh century three developments adversely affected the position of aristocratic women. First, the elaboration of the chivalric ethos defined most key social and political roles as military and "manly" and thereby excluded women. By the middle of the twelfth century it was rare for a woman to hold a castle and unheard-of for one to ride to arms. Second, the consolidation of lineages by aristocratic families accompanied a moral campaign by the church to promote monogamous, unbreakable marriages. This situation subordinated women's freedom in the marriage market to the dynastic and patrimonial demands of great families. Third, the spread of lordship, with its intricate network of personal and proprietary relationships based on military service, tended to deprive women of independent rights over land.

But every rule has its exceptions. As noble families married off fewer of their daughters to noblemen, "extra"

---

fiefs (FEEFS)

daughters account in part for the dramatic increase in the number and size of convents. Convents of aristocratic nuns were places where women could be highly educated and almost entirely in control of their own affairs. Matilda, daughter of the German empress Adelaide, was abbess of Quedlinburg, mistress of vast estates in northern Germany, and a dominant figure in German politics. But knights looking for brides would often marry the younger daughters of noblemen because, if they could establish a household, then any children born of that marriage could lay claim to the noble lineage of their maternal grandfathers.

Less predictably, Gaita, wife of a Norman prince in Italy, fought in helmet and armor alongside her husband, as did Duchess Agnes of Burgundy. And let us reflect on the career of Adela of Blois (ca. 1067–1137). She was a daughter of William the Conqueror, the wife of a powerful French count, and the mother of King Stephen I of England (see page 297). In addition to regularly accompanying her husband as he administered his county, Adela founded monasteries, promoted religious reform, hosted Pope Paschal II, helped to reconcile her brother Henry I with the archbishop of Canterbury (thus averting an English investiture controversy), issued formal legal judgments, held fairs, and skillfully negotiated the aristocratic politics of western France after her husband's death. Adela may be unusual because we know so much about her. In other words, noblewomen in high medieval society may often have led interesting, active lives.

■ Those Who Work: The Peasants

The peasants were the "workers" in the tripartite model. An extremely diverse segment of society, "peasants" ranged from slaves to free persons of some means. Except in frontier zones, where victims were available and religious scruples diminished, slaves declined dramatically in numbers during the tenth and eleventh centuries (as illustrated by the shift in meaning of the classical Latin *servus* from "slave" to "serf"). Serfs, persons bound to the soil, everywhere constituted the majority of the peasants, although their legal and social statuses differed considerably from place to place. In the twelfth century serfdom was disappearing in France even as its terms were hardening in central and eastern Europe. Serfdom was a mixture of economic, legal, and personal statuses. The serf could be flogged in public, could be set upon by dogs, was excluded from many judicial proceedings, required approval to contract a marriage, and was denied the right to bear arms.

The tenth and eleventh centuries were decisive in the reshaping of rural society. As lordships of all kinds and sizes formed in the countryside, they drew communities of people. Castles were critical. Powerful men generally sited their castles in close proximity to wood, water, and iron. Sometimes a monastery, rural church, or graveyard also attracted a castle or else grew up near one and helped to anchor a site. (See the feature "Weighing the Evidence: The Medieval Castle" in Chapter 9 on pages 314–315.)

People from a fairly wide area settled in the vicinity of the castle. Many, originally free, commended themselves to the local lord by handing over their properties and receiving them back in return for rents or personal services. Other people fell into dependent status through military or economic misfortune. What eventually emerged was the manor, an institution best described as a powerful lord controlling the lives of an often large number of dependents. He required payments and services from them and regulated their ordinary disputes. His control was simultaneously public and private.

A minor castellan, or lord of a castle, might control only a small manor and would probably be the vassal of a great lord. A powerful landed lord, on the other hand, would generally control many manors and would often give some of them to retainers as fiefs. In other words, the reorganization of the countryside affected the nobility and the peasantry and created parallel sets of vertical bonds of association: Feudal lords and vassals entered into political bonds; lords and peasants entered into economic bonds.

The structure of individual manors, and the dues owed by peasants, varied tremendously across Europe. Certain trends were fairly consistent, however. As the economy expanded, as trade brought more and different products into Europe, and as a more consciously aristocratic lifestyle spread, the nobility began to want disposable cash. Thus, in many places corvées° (labor services) were commuted into cash payments. Peasants were required to pay rent from their own holdings instead of working on the lord's lands. But lords still needed provisions, so they sometimes split peasant payments into cash and kind. Old forms of service could be wholly retained, involving many days per year of work on the lord's demesne, the portion of the manor the lord reserved for his own benefit. In such cases, the lord could still extract money from his peasants by requiring them to use his mill and oven and then charging them gristing and kilning fees.

---

corvées (KOR-vays)

The Furnishings of a Welsh Household

This passage from the laws of Howell the Good concerns the distribution of household property in case of divorce. The aim was to achieve a nearly even split. Notice the kinds of objects a house might hold and who got what.

The husband shall have all the pigs, the wife the sheep. The husband shall have all the horses and mares, the oxen and cows, bullocks and heifers; the wife shall have the goats. . . . All the vessels for milk, except one pail, are the wife's; all the dishes, except one meat dish, are the husband's. One cart and yoke are the wife's. All the jars and drinking vessels are the husband's. Of the bedding, the husband shall have all the bedclothes which are beneath, the wife those which are above. The husband shall have the cauldron, the pillow, the winnowing sheet, the coulter, the wood axe, the gimlet [hole-borer], the flog, all the sickles except one, and the gridiron. The wife shall have the pan and the tripod, the broadaxe and the sieve, the ploughshare, the flax and the seed of the flax, and the precious things except gold and sil-

ver. If there are any of these (gold or silver) they are to be divided in two equal parts. The products of the loom shall be divided in two equal parts, both linens and woolens. The husband shall have the barn and the grain and whatever is above or in the ground, and the hens and the geese and one cat. The wife shall have the meat that is salted and the cheese that is fresh . . . and the vessel of butter . . . and the ham . . . and as much of the flour as she can carry. Each of them shall have his or her personal clothing, except the cloaks, which shall be divided.

Source: Ian F. Fletcher, ed. and trans., *Latin Redaction A of the Law of Hywel* (Aberystwyth, Wales: Center for Advanced Welsh and Celtic Studies, 1986), pp. 58–59.

The trend everywhere, however, was for labor services to diminish. In one region in northern France, twelfth-century peasants owed only three corvées of two days' each per year for harvesting and haymaking. Elsewhere, peasants might still be required to haul crops to market or to keep roads, bridges, and buildings in repair. On many estates where the menfolk had been largely freed from corvées, the women might still have to work in the lord's house washing laundry, sewing, plucking fowl, cooking, minding dogs, and tending to other household chores.

In the expanding economy of the eleventh and twelfth centuries, the peasants grew more prosperous, and their lords constantly sought new ways to extract the fruits of that prosperity. Peasants thus began to band together to demand that "customs" be observed. These customs were more-or-less formal agreements spelling out the terms under which work and fees would be arranged. In general, life improved for the peasants in terms of both legal status and living conditions.

The European village was a key product of the tenth and eleventh centuries. People who originally gathered together around a castle for security and livelihood began to form a durable human community. Their church

and graveyard helped to reinforce the community by tying together the living and the dead and by giving the village a sense of memory and continuity. Peasants generally worked only 250 to 270 days per year so they had a good deal of time for festivals and celebrations. Births, baptisms, betrothals, and deaths provided opportunities for the community to come together and affirm its mutual ties. Market days and sessions of the lord's court also assembled the village. Villagers needed to cooperate in many of the operations of daily life. They shared tools, plow teams, and wagons. They performed their corvées together. The peasants experienced much less social differentiation than the nobility, and so less tension.

The status of women in peasant society tended to be, in legal theory and in daily reality, the same as that of men at a time when the status of aristocratic women was fragile. Marriage contracts from northern Italy show that brides often entered marriages with a complement of valuable tools. This suggests that peasant women retained some control over their own personal property and also reminds us that the huge gains in rural productivity are almost certainly attributable in part to the work and ingenuity of women. (See the box "Reading Sources: The Furnishings of a Welsh Household.")

■ Those Left Out: Townspeople and Jews

The tripartite model excluded two important groups of people. The first neglected group consisted of the increasingly numerous citizens of Europe's growing towns. Obviously people in towns worked; but the prejudices of the aristocracy were rural, so the only "workers" deemed necessary to the smooth functioning of the social order were farmers. In the second group were Europe's principal religious minority, the Jews. Jews could be found almost everywhere although they constituted only about 1 percent of the population as a whole and, outside of Rome and parts of Spain, formed no single community numbering more than 1,500 to 2,000.

The central factor in the growth of towns was the rise in the productivity and profitability of medieval agriculture. For the first time in history, a regular and substantial farm surplus could support an urban population that did not produce its own food. Increased local exchange,

coupled with the relentless growth of a money economy, meant there were fortunes to be made and cash to be spent. Some of that cash was spent on luxury and exotic products that increasingly became the objects of far-flung commercial networks. A good part of the cash was spent by rural nobles, who earned it from rents, booty, and the profits of the private exercise of public power. When those nobles moved into towns, they created opportunities for merchants, craftsmen, day laborers, domestic servants, and professional people such as notaries and lawyers. This was particularly true in Europe's most heavily urbanized regions: Flanders, southern France, and northern Italy. The key point is that the growth of the medieval city and of its human community began in the medieval countryside.

Town society was hierarchical, but its structures were new, ill defined, and flexible. Rich men built up bands of followers who supported them in urban politics, protected their neighborhoods, and occasionally

San Gimignano   The towers of this Tuscan city reveal the concentrated and competitive nature of power in the Italian communes. Most of these towers date from around 1300.   *(Scala/Art Resource, NY)*

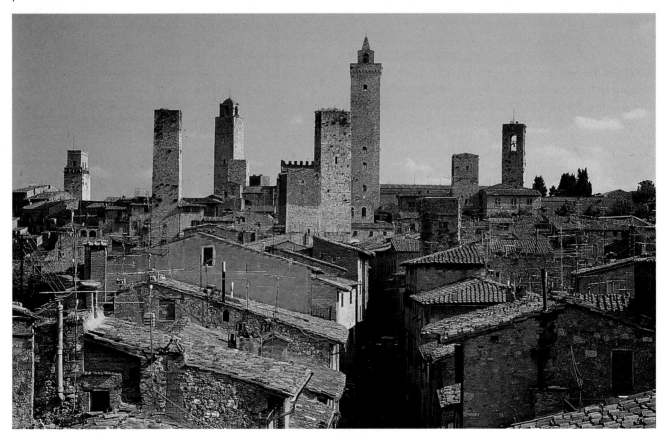

raided the houses of their enemies in the next neighbor-hood. Relatives, friends, neighbors, people from a common rural district, or those engaged in similar trades tended to worship together in particular churches, observe certain festivals, and look after one another's families.

In the rapidly changing world of the tenth and eleventh centuries, towns provided numerous opportunities for women. In urban industries such as cloth making, tanning, laundering, and brewing, women sometimes managed and even owned enterprises. Apart, perhaps, from finance and the law, distinctions between male and female roles were not as sharp in towns as in rural areas.

If urban men and all women stood in an ambiguous relationship to the ideals of the male, rural, aristocratic elite, we can hardly imagine what it must have been like for Jews. Jewish communities had existed in most European towns since antiquity. Then, because the Byzantine and Islamic worlds vacillated between persecution and toleration, many Jews migrated to western Europe, with the largest numbers settling in northern France and the German Rhineland. The Jewish community in England formed only around 1100. Paris had northern Europe's largest Jewish community, perhaps 2,000 people in the twelfth century. Many cities had Jewish populations numbering 200 to 300, but groups of 40 or 50 were common. Although some Jews in Italy, Spain, and Germany owned farms and vineyards, most Jews settled in cities, where they could live and worship in community with other Jews. Urban clusters also provided strength in numbers for people who could at any moment fall victim to persecution and whose power was not based on land-holding.

Three of the most important developments in high medieval Europe were disastrous for the Jews. First, the growth of the European economy with its attendant urban and commercial expansion brought countless Christians into the practice of trade, an occupation dominated by Jews since Late Antiquity. As Jews were excluded from commercial opportunities, they were more and more confined to moneylending. Jews had been moneylenders before the economic surge of the High Middle Ages, and they were never alone in this practice. But the expanding economy made financial operations more widespread than ever before. Given that, as we saw in Chapter 9, Christian moralists considered handling money to be the devil's own work, the visibility of Jews as moneylenders brought them much criticism.

The second phenomenon that adversely affected Jews was the reform of the church. With so much attention being paid to the proper Christian life and the cor-

rect organization of the church, it was inevitable that more attention would be directed to the one prominent group in Western society that was not Christian.

Third, the Crusades unleashed vicious attacks on the Jews. As crusading armies headed east in 1096, they visited unspeakable massacres on the Jewish communities of several German towns. This awful process was repeated on the eve of the Second Crusade in 1146–1147 and again just before the third in 1190. Popular frenzy identified the Jews as Christ-killers and equated them with Muslims as the enemies of Christianity. In fact, and despite grotesque and groundless stories about Jews kidnapping and ritually killing Christian children, Jews everywhere wished to live in peace with their Christian neighbors and to be left alone to observe their distinctive religious, dietary, and social customs.

The Jews were not without sympathetic champions, however. From the time of Gregory I (r. 590–604), the papacy urged peaceful coexistence and prayers for Jewish conversion. In the twelfth and thirteenth centuries, popes forcefully reminded Christians that while converting Jews was highly desirable, Jews were to be tolerated and left in peace. The Carolingians had protected the Jews, and some kings in succeeding centuries repeated or even expanded upon Carolingian legislation. Spanish Jews were taken under royal protection in reconquered areas in 1053, and Henry IV took German Jews under his protection in 1084. In England and France Jews enjoyed royal protection until the late twelfth century. Jews frequently served as royal advisers in Spain and were often entrusted with sensitive diplomatic missions elsewhere.

Despite such policies, Jews were vulnerable to attack at almost any time from people who simply disliked them or who owed them money. But in 1181 Philip II of France, always on the lookout for income, had his henchmen arrest Jews and confiscate their possessions. In 1182 he expelled them from the royal demesne. Across the thirteenth century French kings accorded the Jews less and less protection and often abused them financially. In 1306 Philip IV expelled the Jews from France after confiscating their goods. In England the story is much the same. The impecunious Henry II laid crushing taxes on the Jews in 1171. In 1189 in London and in 1190 in York, massive riots stirred by false rumors raged against the Jewish populations. In 1290 Edward I seized Jewish possessions and expelled them from the country. Royal protection of German Jews was reasonably effective until the death of Frederick II in 1250, after which time local princes often repudiated debts to Jewish lenders and appropriated Jewish property.

Social and Religious Movements, ca. 1100–1300

WELFTH- and thirteenth-century Europe witnessed several social movements unlike any that had occurred before. Spurred by increasingly intrusive governments, economic dislocation, and spiritual turmoil, they involved large numbers of people; cut across lines of gender, wealth, status, and occupation; and appeared in many places. Most of these movements had cohesive beliefs, even ideologies, and well-determined goals. They are the first large-scale social movements in European history.

■ Heretics and Dissidents

The canon lawyer Gratian (see page 335) defined *heresy* as a situation in which "each man chooses for himself the teaching he believes to be the better one"; that is, he ignores official doctrines. For Gratian and his like-minded contemporaries, faith was not an individual matter. Unity of belief was crucial in a Catholic ("universal") Christian Europe. In the twelfth century, the church reacted ever more strictly to challenges to its teachings or to its exclusive right to teach. The effort by the church to define its law, theology, and bureaucratic procedures with greater precision drew lines more sharply than ever before between what was and was not acceptable.

Heretics did not see themselves as secessionists from the true church. Quite the contrary, they saw themselves as its only representatives. Church teachings always encountered a degree of popular skepticism. Not everyone believed, for example, that Jesus was born of a virgin or that he was true God and true man. But such doubts had not previously led to mass defections. Before the middle of the twelfth century, challenges to the church came from men—as far as we can tell the ringleaders were all men—who saw themselves as inspired reformers.

Tanchelm° of Antwerp preached between 1100 and 1115 in the Netherlands. He scandalized the mainstream by calling churches brothels and clerics whores. He rejected the sacraments and the payment of tithes. Although Tanchelm was radical and pugnacious, his ideas constituted a fairly coherent program of criticism. Like many others, he was concerned about the immorality and wealth of the church. But Tanchelm and his follow-

ers went even further. The heretic distributed his nail and hair clippings as relics of a sort, and in a bizarre public ceremony he "married" a statue of the Virgin Mary. Across the twelfth century church orthodoxy was challenged by others whose influence seems to have been local. What is interesting is how numerous, and similar, they all were.

Coherent movements of much larger proportions emerged later in the century. In 1173 Waldo, a rich merchant of Lyon, decided to sell all his property, give the proceeds to the poor, and embrace a life of poverty and preaching. Waldo was motivated by the same quest for the apostolic life that had animated the eremitical movement of the eleventh century. But there was a difference: he was a layman. Waldo attracted many followers (known as Waldensians), and in 1179 Pope Alexander III (r. 1159–1181) scrutinized him closely, found his beliefs to be essentially correct, and approved his vow of poverty. But the pope commanded Waldo to preach only when invited to do so by bishops. The bishops, jealous about their own power, extended no such invitations.

Waldo and his "Poor Men of Lyon" went right on preaching and in 1184 were formally declared heretics. Until this point it was not their ideas so much as their appropriation of a clerical duty, preaching, that had set the church against them. From this time on, however, the Waldensians became more radical in their attacks. In about 1204 one group of Waldensians was reconciled to the Catholic Church; but the majority, who had spread all over southern France and Italy, into Germany, and as far away as Poland, remained estranged. Waldensian communities exist to this day.

The most serious of the popular heretical movements was Catharism (from the Greek *katharos*, meaning "pure"). Because there were numerous Cathars near the southern French town of Albi, the whole movement is sometimes called "Albigensian." In fact, Cathars could be found all over Europe, although they did cluster in northern Italy and southern France. Cathars were the religious descendants of Mani (see page 198), a third-century Persian who taught an extreme dualism that featured polarities in almost all things: good-evil, love-hate, flesh-spirit. Extreme Cathars abstained from flesh in all ways: they were vegetarians and renounced sexual intercourse so as not to produce offspring—that is, more flesh. Probably radiating from Bulgaria, Cathar ideas had spread widely in the West by the 1140s. Catharism attracted many converts when Nicetas, the Cathar bishop of Constantinople, visited northern Italy and southern France between 1166 and 1176. People of every station joined the new church, which, in its own view, was the only true church.

Tanchelm (TANK-elm)

The Expulsion of the Albigensians from Carcassone in 1209
This picture from a fourteenth-century manuscript depicts the grim realities of the Albigensian Crusade launched in 1208. But the Cathars of Carcassone fared less badly than those of Beziers, who were massacred.

(British Library)

The Catholic Church sent isolated preachers against the Cathars, but with little success. In 1198 and 1203, Pope Innocent III organized systematic preaching tours in southern France, but these too lacked solid results, and in 1208 the pope's legate was murdered by a supporter of the count of Toulouse, who was sympathetic to the Cathars. The killing led to the launching of the Albigensian Crusade, a loosely structured military action that lasted into the 1260s. Although the crusade itself was largely over by the 1220s, violence against Albigensians sputtered for decades: a massacre in 1244, and inquisitorial campaigns in 1246 and again in 1256–1257. Isolated resisters struggled on into the fourteenth century.

Albigensians denounced the clergy of their day as rich and corrupt. These teachings attracted urban dwellers who resented the wealth and pretensions of the clergy—the same people who followed Waldo. Nobles may have been drawn to the movement because it gave them opportunities to take possession of extensive tracts of church lands, something the investiture controversy had denied them. In addition, embracing Catharism may have been a way for nobles to resist the increasing encroachment of the government of far-off Paris. The Albigensians also attracted many women. Unlike the Catholic Church, which denied clerical, preaching, and teaching offices to women, the heretical sects tended to permit women to hold leading roles.

The Albigensians, like the Waldensians, were driven by the same spiritual zeal and desire for ecclesiastical reform that moved many of their contemporaries. They differed from other would-be reformers in that they did not seek to reform the Catholic Church from within but departed from it or insisted that they alone represented it. Thus these heretical movements marked the first serious challenge to the ideology of a uniformly Catholic Christendom since Late Antiquity. (See the box "Reading Sources: Pronouncements of the Fourth Lateran Council on Heresy.")

❧ READING SOURCES

Pronouncements of the Fourth Lateran Council on Heresy

By 1215 the papacy had become alarmed at the number and strength of the heretical movements in Europe, and it began to take strong measures to counter the dissidents.

3. Convicted heretics shall be handed over for due punishment to their secular superiors, or the latter's agents. If they are clerks [members of the clergy], they shall first be degraded [lose their clerical rank]. The goods of the layman thus convicted shall be confiscated; those of the clergy shall be applied to the churches from which they drew their stipends. . . . If a temporal lord neglects to fulfil the demand of the church that he purge his land of the contamination of heresy, he shall be excommunicated by the metropolitan and other bishops of the province. If he fails to make amends within a year, it shall be reported to the Supreme Pontiff, who shall pronounce his vassals absolved from fealty to him and offer his land to Catholics. . . . Catholics who assume the cross and devote themselves to the extermination of heretics shall enjoy the same indulgence and privilege as those who go to the Holy Land. . . .

7. Further we add that every archbishop and bishop, in person or by his archdeacon or other suitable and trustworthy persons, shall visit each of his parishes, in which there are said to be heretics, at least once a year. And he shall compel three or more men of good reputation, or even, if need be, the whole neighborhood, to swear that, if any of them knows of any heretics or of any who frequent secret conventicles or who practise manners and customs different from those common amongst Christians, he will report them to the bishop; and, unless they clear themselves of the accusation, or if they relapse into their former mischief, they shall receive the canonical punishment.

Source: Henry Bettenson, *Documents of the Christian Church*, 2d ed. (London: Oxford University Press, 1963), p. 133.

■ Reform from Within: The Mendicant Orders

Traditional monastic orders continued to win adherents, but their interpretation of the apostolic life meant ascetic withdrawal from the world, not pastoral work and preaching. Laymen who wished both to embrace poverty and to preach fell under the suspicion of the ecclesiastical authorities. Early in the thirteenth century a new movement arose, the mendicants (literally, beggars). Mendicants were men who aimed to preach, to be poor, and to create formal but noncloistered religious orders. Though similar to the heretics in many ways, they submitted willingly to ecclesiastical authority.

The mendicant phenomenon began when Francis of Assisi° (1181–1226), the son of a rich Italian merchant, decided to renounce the wealth and status that were his

Assisi (uh-SEE-zee)

birthright. He carried out his renunciation in a most public display before the bishop of Assisi in 1206. Francis had gradually grown tired of a life of ease and luxury, but he also experienced a blinding moment of spiritual insight when, by chance, his eyes fell on the passage in the Scriptures in which Christ commanded the rich young ruler, "Go, sell all you have, and follow me." Francis stripped himself naked so "that naked he might follow the naked Christ."

For a few years Francis wandered about Italy begging for his meager sustenance, repairing churches, caring for the sick, and preaching repentance to all who would listen. By 1210 he had attracted many followers, and together they set out to see Innocent III to win approval. After considering the matter for a while, Innocent decided to approve the new order of friars (that is "brothers," from the Latin *fratres*) as long as they would accept monastic tonsure—a ritual haircut signifying

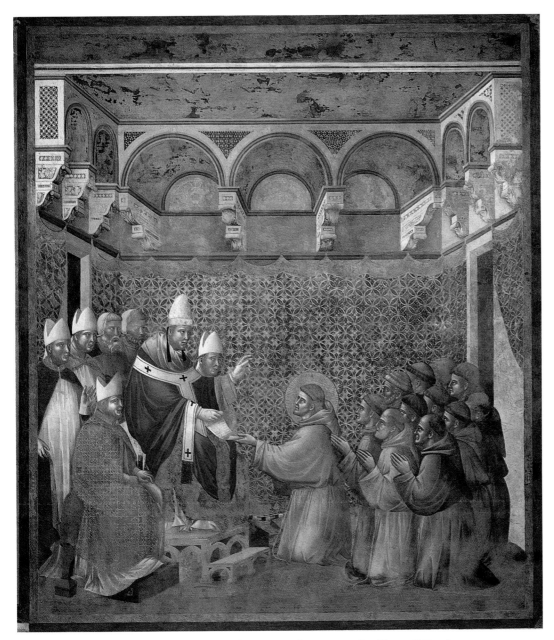

The Confirmation of the Rule of Saint Francis, 1223   This painting by Giotto di Bondone (1265–1337) depicts Pope Honorius III confirming the much-revised version of Francis's rule, first approved by Innocent III in 1210. Giotto, one of the greatest medieval painters, pioneered the use of geometric perspective.   *(Scala/Art Resource, NY)*

submission—profess obedience to the pope, and swear obedience to Francis. The pope was genuinely won over by Francis himself, but he also sensed that by permitting the formation of the Franciscan order, he could create a legitimate and controllable repository for the explosive spiritual forces of the age.

Francis prepared a simple Rule based on his understanding of the scriptural ideals of poverty, preaching, and service. Alarmed by the vagueness of the first Rule and by the extraordinary influx of new members, the papal curia in 1223 prevailed on Francis to submit a revision that stressed order, a hierarchy of officials, and a novitiate—a regularized period of training for new members. Somewhat disappointed by this regulated formality, Francis withdrew more and more from the world and lived reclusively in the hills near Assisi.

After Francis died, the issues of property, power, education, and ordination provoked deep controversies within his order. Usually called "Franciscan," Francis's order is technically the "Friars Minor." The movement had begun among laymen, but over time more Franciscan brothers became ordained priests. Franciscans established schools in most great cities, and by the middle of the thirteenth century some of Europe's greatest intellects were Franciscans. This prominence, like the sacramental power of ordination, was a kind of wealth that Francis had wished to avoid. The real issue of wealth, however, turned on the possession of property. Francis had aimed for both personal and corporate poverty. In the 1230s papal legislation had alleviated strict poverty by permitting the order to acquire property to support its work. Nevertheless, the issue of property continued to spark controversy among the Franciscans.

Of the nine or ten mendicant orders that developed, the other major one was the Dominican, a product of very different experiences than the Franciscan. Its founder, Dominic de Guzman (1170–1221), was the son of a Spanish nobleman. He became a priest and later a cathedral canon. While traveling, he saw firsthand the Albigensian heresy in southern France, and in 1206 he went to Rome to seek permission to preach against the heretics. The Albigensian Crusade began in 1208, but Dominic's methods were those of persuasion, not coercion.

Albigensian criticisms of the ignorance, indifference, and personal failings of the clergy could never be applied to Dominic and his fellow preachers. Dominic and his followers were supported enthusiastically by the bishop of Toulouse, who saw how useful these zealous preachers of unblemished lives could be. In 1215 Dominic, with his bishop's assistance, attempted to form a new order, but by that time Rome had forbidden the creation of new orders for fear of heresy or uncontrollable diversity. Thus, Dominic's "Order of Preachers" (the proper name for the "Dominicans") adopted the Rule of Saint Augustine, which many communities of cathedral canons had been using since the eleventh century.

In 1217 Dominic presided at the first general meeting of the order. The Dominicans decided to disperse, some going to Paris, some (including Dominic) to Rome, some to other cities in Europe. Henceforth, the order saw its mission as serving the whole church. Dominican schools were set up all over Europe, and the order acquired a reputation for learning and scholarship. The Dominicans were voluntarily poor, but the order was never rent by a controversy over property as the Franciscans were. Dominic's was a vision of personal, not corporate, poverty. Likewise, as a preaching order, the Dominicans had to be learned and ordained. Franciscan misgivings on these issues did not touch them.

Both the Franciscan and Dominican orders reflected a widespread desire to emulate the apostolic life of the early church by poverty and preaching. Both submitted to legitimate authority. Francis's religious vision of charity and service was the product of a heartfelt need for repentance and renewal. This concern for the soul caused Franciscans often to serve as missionaries. Dominic set out to save the church from its enemies. He desired preachers who were sufficiently learned that they could combat the errors of heretics. Both men saw the need for exemplary lives. Francis was a more charismatic figure than Dominic, and his apostolate to the urban poor was more compelling. By 1300 Franciscan houses outnumbered Dominican by 3 to 1. The mendicants were the greatest spiritual force in high medieval Europe.

■ Communities of Women

The religious forces that attracted men drew women as well. Traditional orders, however, tended to be hostile to women. Cluniacs and Cistercians struggled to keep women out of their ranks. The wandering preachers of the twelfth century, without exception, acquired women as followers, but the usual results were either segregation of the women in cloisters or condemnation of the whole movement.

In 1212 Francis attracted the aristocrat Clare of Assisi (1194–1253), who was fleeing from an arranged marriage. She wanted to live the friars' life of poverty and preaching, and Francis wanted to assist her. Aware that the sight of women begging or preaching would be shocking, in 1215 he gave Clare and his other female followers their own rule. Clare became abbess of the first community of the "Poor Clares." Although cloistered and forbidden to preach, the Clares lived lives of exemplary austerity and attracted many adherents.

Beguines° were communities of women who lived together, devoted themselves to charitable works, but did not take vows as nuns. The Beguine movement grew from the work in Nivelles, near Liège°, of Mary of Oignies° (ca. 1177–1213). She was drawn to the ideals of voluntary

---

Beguines (BAY-geenz)   **Liège** (lee-EZHE)
Oignies (OWN-yeese)

poverty and service to others. So strong was the pull that she renounced her marriage, gave away all her goods, worked for a while in a leper colony, and thought of preaching against the Cathars. Instead she formed a community.

Groups of Beguines appeared all over the Low Countries, western Germany, and northern France. This was the first exclusively women's movement in the history of Christianity. Beguines sometimes vowed poverty and sometimes did not. They sometimes cloistered themselves into communities and sometimes taught and served the poor and outcast. They neither challenged the officials and teachings of the church nor demanded a right to preach. As laywomen, they did not give rise to scandal as noncloistered nuns would have. They were content to have power over their own lives and communities but not seek a voice in the wider world around them. (See the box "Reading Sources: New Orders for Women: Clares and Beguines.")

Thirteenth-century Europe knew more female than male mystics, and female mysticism tended to focus on Jesus, especially on His presence in the Eucharist. This is

The Parting of Mary from the Apostles   Duccio di Buoninsegna lived from the middle of the thirteenth century to 1318 or 1319. He did his finest work in Siena, including a huge altarpiece, one of whose panels depicts the touching scene of Mary taking leave of the apostles just before her death. Note the clever way Duccio has arranged the figures, and how he balances Saint Paul, standing in the doorway, with Mary, reclining on the bed.   *(Scala/Art Resource, NY)*

❧ READING SOURCES

New Orders for Women: Clares and Beguines

These excerpts, from the prologue to Clare's Rule and from a document detailing the origins of the Beguines, illustrate the initiative of women in the new religious orders. Observe too how the women's submission to authority relieved them from suspicion of heresy or insubordination.

Clare's Rule

Clare, the unworthy servant of Christ and the little plant of the most blessed Francis, promises obedience and reverence to the Lord Pope Innocent [III] and his canonically elected successors, and to the Roman Church. And, just as at the beginning of her conversion, together with her sisters she promised obedience to the Blessed Francis, so now she promises his successors to observe that same obedience inviolably, and the other sisters shall always be obliged to obey the successors of Blessed Francis and Sister Clare and other canonically elected abbesses who succeed her.

The Beguines

Those ladies of good memory, Joanna and her sister Margaret, successive countesses of Flanders and Hainault, noticed that the region was greatly abounding in women for whom, because of their own position or that of their friends, suitable marriages were not possible, and they saw that the daughters of re-spectable men, both nobles and commoners, wished to live chastely, but could not easily enter a monastery because of the great number of these girls and the poverty of their parents, and that respectable and noble but impoverished damsels had to go begging or shamefully support themselves or seek support from their friends, unless some solution could be found. Then by divine inspiration, as it is piously believed, having first obtained the advice and consent of respectable men of the diocese and elsewhere, in various parts of Flanders they set up certain spacious places which are called Beguinages, in which the aforesaid women, girls, and damsels were received, so that living in common therein, they might preserve their chastity, with or without taking vows, and where they might support and clothe themselves by suitable work, without shaming themselves or their friends.

Source: Emilie Amt, *Women's Lives in Medieval Europe* (New York: Routledge, 1993), pp. 236, 264.

---

the first religious devotion that can be shown to have been more common to women than to men. Most of the mystics were either nuns or Beguines. As the clergy was defining its own prerogatives more tightly, and excluding women more absolutely from the exercise of formal public power, female communities provided a different locus for women's activity.

Women who spent their lives in community with other women reveal, in their writings, none of the sense of moral and intellectual inferiority that was routinely attributed to women by men and often by women themselves. Women who were in direct spiritual communion with God acquired, as teachers, mediators, and counselors in their communities, power that they simply could not have had outside those settings.

LATIN CULTURE: FROM SCHOOLS TO UNIVERSITIES

THE dynamism so evident in the economic, social, and political life of Europe is just as apparent in cultural life. As in the late antique and Carolingian periods, courts and churches were the greatest patrons of artists and authors. But in this age of expansion the number and geographic spread of such patrons increased dramatically. By 1150 the church comprised 50 percent more bishoprics and about three times as many monasteries as it had in 900. In 1300 monarchies reigned in many places—Scandinavia and the Slavic world, for example—where none had existed in

900. In addition to an increase in the sheer amount of cultural activity, the years between 900 and 1300 also witnessed innovations. Logic replaced grammar at the heart of the school curriculum. Latin letters remained ascendant, but literature in many vernacular (native) languages began to appear in quantity and quality. Romanesque art and architecture were fresh and original interpretations of their Carolingian ancestors. Europe's incipient urbanization produced the first stirrings of a distinctively urban culture. In one of those cities, Paris, a new kind of academic institution emerged—the university—which was arguably the period's greatest legacy to the modern world.

■ The Carolingian Legacy

Cultural life depends on both creative geniuses and generous patrons. Political dislocation and constant attacks in the ninth and tenth centuries initially deprived schools and masters of the Carolingian patronage that they had enjoyed for a century or more. The Carolingians left firm enough foundations in a few centers for intellectual life to continue, but the scale of activity between 900 and 1050 was smaller than before. Three examples serve to capture the spirit of the age that set the stage for the High Middle Ages.

Gerbert of Aurillac° (940–1003) was the most distinguished intellect of his age. He left his home in Aquitaine to study in Spain and Italy before settling in Reims, in northern France, where he was a teacher and then briefly a bishop. He attracted the attention of the emperor Otto III and spent some time at the German court, earning appointments as abbot of Bobbio, bishop of Ravenna, and, finally, pope. Gerbert followed Carolingian tradition in being a collector of manuscripts and critic of texts, but he departed from older traditions in his interest in mathematics and in his study of logic, the formal rules of reasoning that, in the Western tradition, trace back over many thinkers to Aristotle (see pages 97–98).

Fulbert of Chartres° (960–1028), Gerbert's finest pupil, elevated the cathedral school of Chartres to the paramount place in academic Europe. Fulbert wrote letters in elegant Latin and composed fine poems. He carried on his master's literary interests more than his scientific ones, and well into the twelfth century Chartres remained a major center of literary studies.

Another figure of interest is the aristocratic German nun Roswitha of Gandersheim (d. 970). She wrote poems on saints and martyrs, as well as a story about a priest who sold his soul to the devil. In her mature years, Roswitha wrote Latin plays in rhymed verse based on the Roman writer Terence. In these plays she refashioned tales from Roman and biblical history to convey moral truths.

■ The Study of Law

Law was a field of major innovation. The increasing sophistication of urban life demanded a better understanding of law. The growing responsibilities of the church called for orderly rules, and the church's frequent quarrels with secular rulers demanded careful delineations of rights and responsibilities. Governments issued more laws and regulations than at any time since antiquity.

In about 1012, Burchard, bishop of Worms, produced a collection of canon law that was influential for more than a century and heightened reformers' awareness of the law of the church. By midcentury, scholars studying canon law in Italy and France helped to promote the papal view of reform. In Bologna (see map 10.1), Irnerius° (d. ca. 1130), a transplanted German and protégé of Emperor Henry V, began teaching Roman law from the law code of Justinian (see page 226). This legal work culminated in the publication in 1140 of the *Decretum* of the Bolognese monk Gratian°. The most comprehensive and systematic book of canon law yet written, Gratian's work remained authoritative for centuries.

Throughout the twelfth century, canon lawyers studied and wrote commentaries on Gratian's *Decretum*. These legists are called "decretists." Gratian had systematically collected earlier papal decretals, official pronouncements, but popes continued to issue them. Several collections of these new decretals were prepared in the thirteenth century, and the scholars who studied these later decrees are called "decretalists." The church thus produced a vast corpus of law and of legal commentary.

Law was by no means confined to the church. England was precocious in creating a common law, a single law applied uniformly in its courts. But English law was based on the careful accumulation of legal decisions—or precedents—and not on the routine application of the provisions of a law code. Of law codes elsewhere, there were many. Alfonso X of Castile issued the *Siete Partidas*, a comprehensive law code largely reliant on Roman law. Prince Iaroslav (d. 1054) is reputed to have issued the first version of the laws of the Kievan Rus (see Map 9.5 on page 296). Iaroslav's laws were written in Old Russian but

---

Gerbert of Aurillac (DJAIR-bear of OR-ee-ak)
Fulbert of Chartres (FULL-bear of SHART)

Irnerius (ear-NAIR-ee-us)   Gratian (GRAY-shun)

336

Map 10.1 Europe, ca. 1230 By the early thirteenth century the European states that would exist into modern times were clearly visible, although each would continue to undergo changes. To gain a sense of the evolution of Europe, compare this map with Maps 6.1, 7.3, and 8.3.

they drew heavily on the laws and legal traditions of neighboring peoples. Byzantine law was revised under the Macedonian dynasty.

■ Greek, Arab, and Jewish Contributions

Norman and German settlement in southern Italy and Sicily, the Reconquista in Spain, the Crusades, and the creation of Italian communities in many Mediterranean cities brought European thinkers face to face with the intellectual traditions of classical Greece, Islam, and medieval Judaism. Between 1100 and 1270 almost the whole corpus of Aristotle's writings, virtually unknown in the West for a millennium, became available. Arab commentaries on Aristotle, as well as Jewish philosophical and theological works, began to circulate. The presence of all these texts and currents of thought was decisive in expanding the range and raising the level of Western thought.

Prior to about 1100 only a few of Aristotle's writings had been available in the West, primarily some of his early writings on logic. Gradually scholars recovered Aristotle's full treatment of logic, then his scientific writings, and finally his studies of ethics and politics. Aristotle's books posed a number of problems for Christian scholars. If knowledge is a good thing, and good things are gifts of God, how did a pagan get so smart? Is it possible that faith is unnecessary to knowledge? What relationship exists between faith and reason? Aristotle taught that the universe was eternal and mechanistic. His thought left no room for creation or for the continuing role of a Creator. For Christian thinkers Aristotle asked questions that demanded answers: Were the Scriptures true? Did God create the world as Genesis said? Did God continue to intervene in this world?

Between 750 and 900, mainly in Iran, a group of Arabic-speaking Christians began translating into Arabic the Greek texts of Aristotle as well as the more than fifteen thousand pages of commentary on Aristotle that had been produced between about A.D. 100 and 600. These translators were Monophysite Christians chased out of Syria by Emperor Heraclius when he conquered the area from the Persians (see page 247). This flood of material inspired generations of Arab scholars to tackle the thought of the man often called simply "The Philosopher."

Two major Arab thinkers were particularly influenced by the vast Aristotelian corpus. Ibn-Sina (980–1037), called Avicenna° in the West, was drawn to the fundamental problem of how to understand the relationship between objects that exist in the world and the knowledge of those objects that is formed and held in the human mind. (See the box "Global Encounters: The Making of an Arab Scholar.") Ibn Rushd (1126–1198), called Averroes°, wrote no fewer than thirty-eight commentaries on the works of Aristotle, and at least fifteen of these were translated into Latin in the thirteenth century. Among many contributions, Averroes particularly tried to clarify the relationship between truths acquired through the exercise of reason and truths that depended on divine revelation. Although his exact meaning remains controversial, his contemporaries and many later scholars understood him to teach the "double truth." Truths about the natural world were more or less accessible to everyone depending on a person's intellectual ability. Revealed truths, however, were available only to the most enlightened.

Spain and northern France were both important centers of Jewish thought. In Spain some Jewish thinkers also grappled with Aristotle. Solomon ibn Gebirol (1021–1070), called Avicebron°, wrote *The Fountain of Life*, a treatise that attempted to reconcile Aristotle with the Jewish faith by finding a role for God in communicating knowledge to every human mind. The greatest of all medieval Jewish thinkers, Moses ben Maimon (1135–1204), called Maimonides°, wrote *A Guide for the Perplexed*. The perplexed he had in mind were those who had trouble reconciling the seemingly opposed claims of reason and faith. Maimonides taught a doctrine very close to Averroes's double truth.

Solomon ben Isaac (1040–1105), called Rashi, was educated in Jewish schools in the Rhineland and then set up his own school in Troyes°. He became the most learned biblical and Talmudic scholar of his time, indeed one of the wisest ever. The Talmud was a detailed and erudite commentary on the scriptural studies of the ancient rabbis. It existed in two collections made in the fifth century, one in Palestine and one in Babylon. Later in the twelfth century Rashi's grandsons carried on his work and earned great fame on their own. Christian scholars who wished to know the exact meaning of passages in the Bible sometimes consulted them.

From Persia to Spain to France, then, countless thinkers were engaged in serious reflection on the mechanics of knowing, the nature of reality, the relationship between reason and faith, and the meaning and significance of revelation. In the years just around 1100, Latin Christian scholars began to encounter this torrent of thought and writing.

Avicenna (ah-vih-SENN-uh)

Averroes (uh-VERR-oh-eese)   Avicebron (uh-VIH-sih-bron)
Maimonides (my-MON-uh-deez)   Troyes (TWAH)

The Making of an Arab Scholar

These excerpts from the engaging life of Avicenna reveal not only his remarkable intellectual attainments but also his ongoing encounter with Greek thought. Avicenna was deeply influenced by Aristotle, and, in turn, his writings influenced Jewish and Christian writers who were also coming to grips with the greatest of Greek philosophers. His writings on medicine were authoritative until the seventeenth century.

My father was from Balkh and moved from there to Bukhārā [now Turkmenistan] . . . where I was given teachers of the Quran and polite letters [literature, especially poetry]. By the time I was ten years old I had mastered the Quran and so much of polite letters as to provoke wonderment. My father decided to send me to a certain grocer who knew Indian arithmetic so that I could learn it from him. Then Abu Abdallah al-Natili, who claimed to be a philosopher, came to Bukhārā. My father lodged him in our house in the hope that I would learn something from him. Before he came I was studying jurisprudence . . . and I was one of the best pupils. Then, under the guidance of al-Natili, I began to study the *Isagogue* [a commentary on some of Aristotle's works]. Thus I learned from him the broad principles of logic, but he knew nothing of the subtleties. Then I began to read books and study commentaries on my own until I mastered logic. I also read the geometry of Euclid. Then I passed on to the *Almagest* [Ptolemy's second-century astronomical treatise]. Eventually I busied myself with the study of the [treatises] and other commentaries on physics and metaphysics [subjects treated at great length by Aristotle and by Avicenna's Arab predecessors, especially al-Farabi], and the doors of knowledge opened before me. Then I took up medicine and began to read books written on this subject. Medicine is not one of the difficult sciences, and in a very short time I undoubtedly excelled in it, so that physicians of merit studied under me. At the same time I carried on debates and controversies in jurisprudence. At this point I was sixteen years old.

I resumed the study of logic and all parts of philosophy. During this time I never slept a whole night through and I did nothing but study all day long.

Whenever I was puzzled by a problem . . . I would go to the mosque, pray, and ask the Creator of All to reveal to me that which was hidden from me and to make easy for me that which was difficult. Then at night I would return home, put a lamp in front of me, and set to work reading and writing.

I returned to the study of divine science. I read the book called *Metaphysics* [by Aristotle], but could not understand it, the aim of its author remaining obscure for me. I read the book forty times, until I knew it by heart, but I still could not understand its meaning or its purpose. Then one afternoon I happened to be in the market of the booksellers, and a crier was holding a volume in his hand and shouting the price. I bought it and found that it was Abu'l Nasr al-Farabi's book explaining the meaning of the *Metaphysics*. I returned to my house and made haste to read it. Immediately the purposes of this book became clear to me because I already knew it by heart. I was very happy at this, and the next day I gave much alms to the poor in thanksgiving to Almighty God.

In my neighborhood there lived a man who asked me to write him an encyclopedic work on all the sciences. I compiled the *Majmū* for him and named it after him. In it I dealt with all sciences other than mathematics. I was then twenty-one years old.

Source: Bernard Lewis, ed., *Islam: From the Prophet Muhammad to the Capture of Constantinople*, 2 vols. (New York: Harper and Row, 1974), vol. 2, pp. 177–181.

 For additional information on this topic, go to http://college.hmco.com.

■ The Development of Western Theology

Carolingian schools had focused on grammar, that is, on the basic foundations of language. Gradually logic supplanted grammar at the center of both intellectual interests and school curricula. Problems inside Europe initiated this shift, but soon the external influences we just described increased its scope. Eventually the wider application of logic produced a new intellectual style and also evoked bitter criticisms.

Berengar (ca. 1000–1088), master of the school of Tours, wrote a treatise that denied Christ's presence in the Eucharist—the communion bread and wine received by Catholics and Orthodox in the celebration of the mass. This position was heretical. Ordinarily, churchmen would have refuted Berengar simply by quoting various passages from the Scriptures or from the writings of the Church Fathers along with conciliar pronouncements about the consecrated elements. The evidence, however, was ambiguous. Berengar's claim was finally proved false, at least to the satisfaction of his opponents, by Lanfranc, archbishop of Canterbury during the reign of William the Conqueror. Lanfranc used Aristotelian logical argumentation to dispose of Berengar's heretical arguments.

Anselm (ca. 1033–1109), Lanfranc's successor as archbishop of Canterbury, developed an ingenious logical proof for the existence of God. The French theologian and philosopher Peter Abelard (1079–1142) used logic to reconcile apparent contradictions in the Scriptures and in the writings of the Church Fathers. We must not suppose that Anselm and Abelard were skeptics. Anselm's motto was "Faith seeking understanding." For him logic was the servant of divine truth. He would have agreed completely with Abelard's assessment that "Faith has no merit with God when it is not the testimony of divine truth that leads us to it, but the evidence of human reason."

For conservatives such as Bernard of Clairvaux (1090–1153) and Hildegard of Bingen (1098–1179), however, faith and immediate divine inspiration were primary. To them, logical approaches to divine truth were the height of arrogance. Hildegard, well educated, gifted musically, knowledgeable in medical matters, was perhaps the most profound psychological thinker of her age. More than anyone before her, Hildegard opened up for discussion the feminine aspects of divinity. She, like Bernard, believed that God was to be found deep within the human spirit, not in books full of academic wrangling. (See the box "Reading Sources: The Making of a Saint and Scholar: Hildegard of Bingen.")

The future lay with Anselm and Abelard, however. Anselm was the most gifted Christian thinker since Augustine. He wrote distinguished works on logic, and his theological treatise *Why God Became Man* (ca. 1100) served for three hundred years as the definitive philosophical and theological explanation of the incarnation of Christ, the central mystery of the Christian faith.

Peter Abelard was a more colorful figure. He argued rudely and violently with all his teachers, though in the end he was probably more intelligent than any of them. He rose to a keener understanding of Aristotle than anyone in centuries, and he developed a sharper sense of both the power and the limitations of language than anyone since the Greeks. He concerned himself with ethics, too, and was one of the first writers to see intention as more important than simple action.

Abelard seduced and then secretly married Heloise, one of his pupils and the daughter of an influential Paris churchman. Heloise's relatives castrated Abelard for his refusal to live openly with his wife. Abelard then arranged for Heloise to enter a convent, and he joined a monastic community, where he continued writing and teaching. The two carried on a voluminous correspondence that reveals Heloise as a first-rate philosophical thinker and one of her age's most knowledgeable connoisseurs of classical literature. Some of Abelard's more imaginative ideas earned him formal ecclesiastical condemnations in 1121 and 1140. He popularized the schools of Paris, however, and attracted to them promising scholars from all over Europe.

Abelard and several of his contemporaries engaged in one of the first widespread intellectual debates in Western history, the quarrel over "universals." *Universal* is the philosophical name for a concept that applies to more than one seemingly related object. The dispute over universals went to the heart of people's understanding of reality, their sense of the limitations of human reason, and their awareness of problems of language.

To illustrate: May we agree that you are reading a book right now? May we further agree that the book you are reading is not identical to any other book on your bookshelf? And may we go one step further and agree that no book on your bookshelf is exactly like any other book on that shelf? So, why do we call all of these objects books? "Book" is here the universal that we are trying to understand.

A medieval "realist," whose thought may be traced back to Plato, would say that there is a concept, let us call it "bookness," that exists in our minds before we ever encounter any particular object that we label a book. Just as no book is ever identical to any other, so too no specific

➤ READING SOURCES

The Making of a Saint and Scholar: Hildegard of Bingen

Although she was a great scholar, Hildegard's biographers stressed her native intelligence and divine inspiration more than her formal education.

When Henry IV was the king of the Holy Roman Empire, there lived in Rhenish Franconia a maiden lady well known because of her aristocratic background as well as her holiness. Her name was Hildegard. Although her parents were involved in the cares of the world and were richly blessed with temporal goods, they were thankful for the gifts of their creator, and they consecrated their daughter to the service of God. Even in her early years the young lady showed signs of virginity since she appeared to withhold consent to desires of the flesh. When she was hardly able to utter her first words, she made those around her understand through her words and signs that she was conscious of an exceptional gift of visions.

When she was eight years old, she entered the monastery on the mountain of St. Disibod in order to be buried with Christ and to rise with him to immortality. She was under the care of the pious, consecrated Jutta. It was this lady who carefully trained her in the virtues of humility and chastity, and superbly trained her in learning and singing the sacred songs of David. Except for simple instruction in the psalms, she received no other schooling, either in reading or in music. Still, she left behind not a small, but rather a significant legacy of writings. It is worthwhile to explain this by using her own words:

"When I was twenty-four years and seven months old, I saw an extremely strong, sparkling, fiery light coming from the open heavens. It pierced my brain, my heart, and my breast through and through like a flame which did not burn; however, it warmed me. It heated me up very much like the sun warms an object on which it is pouring its rays. And suddenly I had an insight into the meaning and interpretation of the psalter, the Gospel, and the other Catholic writings of the Old and New Testaments, but not into the meaning, the sentence structure and the hyphenation; also I had no understanding of events and times."

Source: Gottfried and Theodoric, *The Life of the Holy Hildegard*, 1.1, trans. James McGrath (Collegeville, Minn.: Liturgical Press, 1995), pp. 35–36.

book is a perfect representation of that concept "bookness." The concept is fully real, and all representations of it in the world are mere hints, suggestions of a more perfect reality.

A medieval "nominalist," on the contrary, would say that "book" is merely a name (*nomen* in Latin, whence nominalism) that we apply to objects that we deem to bear sufficient similarity to one another that they can be adequately captured by one name. But only each particular book is fully real.

Problems aplenty surround the quarrel over universals: Is reality purely an intellectual proposition, or is reality a quality of existence in the world? How does the mind acquire knowledge of the universal? How does the mind know to which objects to apply the universal? What specific differences exist between objects to which the same name is applied?

With the emergence of the problem of universals, we enter fully into a new intellectual approach that has long been called "Scholasticism." This word has come to have many different meanings, but at the most basic level it describes a movement that attempted to show that Christian theology is inherently rational, that faith and reason need not be contradictory or antithetical. Scholasticism also implies a certain systematization of thought. Gratian's attempt to organize all of canon law rationally and systematically was a Scholastic exercise. Twelfth-century biblical scholars tried to produce a single, systematic commentary on the Bible. In 1160 Peter Lombard produced the *Four Books of Sentences*, a comprehensive treatment of all of Christian theology.

Thomas Aquinas (1225–1274) was the greatest of the Scholastics, the most sensitive to Greek and Arab thought, and the most prolific of medieval philosophers.

A Dominican friar, Thomas was educated at Naples, Cologne, and Paris. Apart from brief service at the papal court, he spent the years after 1252 teaching and writing in Paris. His two most famous works are the *Summa Contra Gentiles* and the *Summa Theologiae*. A *summa* was an encyclopedic compendium of carefully arrayed knowledge on a particular subject. One might think of Gratian's and Peter Lombard's works as precursors to the great summas of the thirteenth century. Thomas's first summa addressed natural truth—that is, the kinds of things that any person could know through the operation of reason. His second summa was a summation of the revealed truths of the Christian faith.

Thomas's works are distinctive for two reasons. First, no one before him had so rigorously followed the dialectical method of reasoning through a whole field of knowledge, not just a particular problem. For thousands of pages, Thomas poses a question, suggests answers, confronts the answers with objections, refutes the objections, and then draws a conclusion. Then he repeats the process. Second, Thomas carefully distinguished between two kinds of truths. On the one hand were *natural truths,* truths (even theological ones) that anyone can know (or so Thomas thought)—for example, that God exists. On the other hand were *revealed truths,* truths that can be known (if not understood) only through faith in God's revelation—for example, the Trinity or the incarnation of Christ. Thomas maintained that natural and revealed truths simply could not contradict one another because God was ultimately the source of both. If natural truth—for example, Aristotle's contention that the world is eternal—appeared to contradict a revealed truth, then Aristotle was wrong. Thomas was accused by some contemporaries of applying reason too widely, and after his death some of his ideas were condemned by the church. But he actually steered a middle path between intellectual extremes. In this respect Thomas was like Maimonides and Averroes.

■ The University

In the early decades of the twelfth century, students gathered wherever famous teachers might be found. Such teachers—figures like Peter Abelard—clustered in a few centers, and the students congregated there as well. The last decades of the twelfth century saw a swarm of masters and students in Paris. Like members of secular guilds (see page 282), the masters organized. The University of Paris was the result of their efforts. By 1300 universities had formed elsewhere in France, as well as in Italy, England, and western Germany.

Several forces drove masters to organize. They wanted to negotiate with the bishop's chancellor, the traditional head of all schools in an episcopal city. They wanted to regulate the curriculum that students followed and to prescribe the requirements for entry into their own ranks. They also desired to set the fees to be charged for instruction. By 1209 the bishop of Paris, the pope, and the king of France had granted formal recognition to the university.

In Bologna, the university developed a little differently. Here the students came primarily to study law, after already acquiring a basic education. These law students were usually older and more affluent than students elsewhere, and foreign to Bologna. Consequently, in Bologna the university arose from a guild of students who united to set standards in fees and studies and to protect themselves against unscrupulous masters.

Universities were known for certain specializations: Paris for arts and theology, Bologna for law, Salerno in Italy and Montpellier in France for medicine, Oxford for mathematical and scientific subjects. Still, the basic course of study was similar. At Paris, a young scholar came to the city, found lodgings where he could, and attempted to find a master who would guide him through the arts curriculum. These boys might be in their early teens or several years older, depending on their earlier educations and financial resources. The arts course, which was the prerequisite to all higher faculties, usually lasted from four to six years. The bachelor's degree was a license to teach, but a bachelor who wished to teach in a university needed to go on for a master's degree. The master's degree required at least eight years of study (including the baccalaureate years), which culminated in a public oral examination. Some masters went on to become doctors in theology, law, or medicine. A doctorate required ten to fifteen years of study. Medieval academicians were immensely learned.

Student life was difficult. In many ways, students were always foreigners. Although their presence in a town enhanced its prestige, townspeople exploited them by charging exorbitant prices for food and rent. Students' own behavior was not always above reproach. There was surely some truth in the frequently lodged charge that students were noisy, quarrelsome, given to drinking, and excessively fond of prostitutes. England's Oxford and Cambridge were unique in always providing residential colleges for students; Paris got one later and the mendicants often established houses of study. Typically, though, students were on their own.

Students had to work very hard. The arts curriculum demanded a thorough acquaintance with all the famous texts of grammar, logic, and rhetoric. Higher studies added more Aristotle, particularly his philosophical writings. In theology, the students had to master the Scriptures, the principal biblical commentaries from patristic times to the present, and the *Four Books of Sentences.* In medicine, the ancient writings of Galen and Hippocrates were supplemented by Arab texts as well as by observation and experimentation.

The basic method of teaching provides yet another definition of Scholasticism; that is, the method of studying in the schools. The teacher started by reciting a short piece of a set text, carried on with the presentation and discussion of many authoritative commentaries on that text, and concluded with his own explanations. The teacher then presented another passage of the set text and repeated the whole process. This education focused on standard books and accepted opinions and required students to remember large amounts of material. The curriculum nevertheless produced thinkers of prodigious originality.

In principle, universities were open to free men, but in practice they were restricted to those who had the means to attend them. Women were not accepted at universities, either as students or as teachers. It was generally thought, by men, that learning made women insubordinate. Lacking the required education, women were denied entry into the learned professions of theology, law, and medicine, despite the fact that many rural and some urban medical practitioners were women. Nevertheless, women commonly possessed and transmitted knowledge of both folk remedies and scientific medicine. Trotula of Salerno, who probably lived in the twelfth century, wrote a knowledgeable treatise, *On the Diseases of Women.* Documents from medieval Naples record the names of twenty-four women surgeons between 1273 and 1410. How these women were educated is utterly unknown.

THE VERNACULAR ACHIEVEMENT

 MAJOR achievement of high medieval civilization, from Iceland to Kievan Rus, was the appearance of rich literatures in native tongues. Vernacular, from the Latin *vernaculus* meaning "home-born" or "domestic," is the name for the languages other than Latin, say, English or French. Although Latin remained the language of the clerical elite, writers of vernacular prose and poetry produced some of the greatest works in Western literature.

■ Literatures and Languages

The number of people who could speak, read, or write Latin was always a minority in western Europe, just as native Greek-speakers were a minority in Byzantium. As Latin, beginning in Late Antiquity, slowly evolved into the Romance (from Roman) languages, people who used what eventually became French, Italian, and Spanish had some advantages over the peoples in Celtic, Germanic, or Slavic lands, where the languages bore no obvious relationship to Latin. Persons who spoke Old French in their towns and villages would have had an easier time learning Latin than people who spoke Irish or Polish. Nevertheless, vernacular literatures began to appear at roughly the same time all over Europe, between about 800 and 1000.

Of course, many writers continued to use Latin for several centuries. University scholars continued to compose their learned treatises in the ancient tongue, but now often in a style that was less ornate than before. Most law books and public documents were still in Latin, but in a "vulgar" Latin that was reasonably close to the vernacular in areas where Romance languages were spoken. Technical manuals, on farming and animal husbandry, on warfare and armaments, or on law and government, were prepared in Latin, too, but again in a style that was far more accessible than that of their ancient models. Popular literature—poetry, history and biography, and romance and adventure—was still often written in Latin. Some of this material was serious, but some breathed a light and carefree spirit. The anonymous German known as the Archpoet (d. 1165) wrote poems about drinking and womanizing. These lines are typical of his work:

> In the public house to die
> Is my resolution;
> Let wine to my lips be nigh
> At life's dissolution:
> That will make the angels cry,
> With glad elocution
> "Grant this drunkard, God on high,
> Grace and Absolution!"[1]

No less insouciant were the authors of biting satires such as the anonymous *The Gospel According to the Silver Marks,* which parodied the wealth and greed of the papal curia. But after 1200 this fresh spirit was largely confined to writings in the vernacular. For after that year Latin was rarely used as the language for serious, original literary compositions. (See the feature "Information Technology: Paper.")

The literary masterpieces of the High Middle Ages are almost entirely written in vernacular languages. The epic poem *Beowulf* is the first classic of English literature. We do not know who wrote it or when it was written. Scholars formerly assigned it to the eighth century, but they now usually place it later, in the ninth or possibly in the tenth century. The story focuses on three great battles fought by the hero, Beowulf°. The first two are against the monster Grendel and Grendel's mother, who have been harrying the kingdom of an old ally of Beowulf's family; the third is against a dragon. *Beowulf* is a poem of adventure and heroism, of loyalty and treachery. It treats lordship, friendship, and kinship. Themes of good and evil resound throughout. The poem is barely Christian but nevertheless deeply moral. It speaks, in a mature, vigorous, and moving language, to and for the heart of a warrior society.

Beowulf is the best-known Anglo-Saxon work but by no means the only one. One of the Viking attacks that led to the undoing of Ethelred II was commemorated in *The Battle of Maldon.* Several volumes of elegiac and lyric poetry, mostly on religious themes, also survive. And Anglo-Saxon writers produced chronicles, legal materials and charters, and at least one large collection of homilies.

Some fragments of poetry in Old French survive from the ninth century, but the great *chansons de gestes* ("songs of deeds," or celebrations of the great) appeared in the eleventh century. Undoubtedly they were transmitted orally for a long time before they were written down. The best is the *Song of Roland,* written around 1100. In 778 as Charlemagne's army was returning from Spain, Basques raided the baggage train and killed Count Roland. By 1100 this obscure event, long kept alive in oral traditions, had been transformed into a heroic struggle between Charlemagne and his retinue and an army of countless thousands of "paynim," who are crude caricatures of Muslims.

Like *Beowulf, Roland* is a story about loyalty and treachery, about bravery in the face of insuperable odds, about the kindness and generosity of leaders. They take us into a man's chivalric world. Females are all but absent. The two works do not show us personal hopes, fears, or motivations. Everything that we think should be private is made public. What pours forth is the communal ethos and the dominant values of the elite, male social group. Although *Beowulf* is lightly clothed in Christianity, *Roland* is thickly vested in the faith.

The heroic epic tradition that *Beowulf* and the *Song of Roland* represent did not disappear as the Middle Ages unfolded, but literary energies were applied in new directions. Southern France, in the middle and last decades of the twelfth century, added something new to Western literature: the love lyrics of the troubadours. This poetry, composed by both men and women, profoundly influenced an age and created the literary movement that has long been called "courtly love." Chivalry was initially a code for men interacting with other men. In the world of courtly love, chivalry became an elaborate set of rules governing relations between men and women.

Courtly love had several sources. The classical poet Ovid (43 B.C.–?A.D. 17), who wrote *The Art of Love,* a manual of seduction, was one. Another was the lyrical poetry of Muslim Spain. Ironically, feudal values such as loyalty and service played a critical role as men became, in effect, love vassals. Platonic ideas made some contribution, too, particularly the notion that any love in this world could be only a pale imitation of real love. The courtly poets sung of *fin'amours,* a pure love in contrast to the mere lust of the masses. A lover cherished an unattainable lady. He would do anything for the merest display of pleasure or gratitude on her part, as we see in these lines from Bernart de Ventadorn, court poet of the counts of Toulouse in the late twelfth century:

> Down there, around Ventadorn, all my friends
> have lost me, because my lady does not love me;
> and so, it is right that I never go back there again,
> because always she is wild and morose with me.
> Now here is why the face she shows me is gloomy and
>   full of anger:
> because my pleasure is in loving her and I have settled
>   down to it.
> She is resentful and complains for no other reason.[2]

Male troubadours placed women on pedestals and, in ballads, worshiped them from afar. Women troubadours took a different line. Women's poems were more realistic, more human, more emotionally satisfying. Castellozza° (b. ca. 1200), the southern French wife of a Crusader, idealized not at all when she wrote these lines:

> Friend, if you had shown consideration,
> meekness, candor and humanity,
> I'd have loved you without hesitation,
> but you were mean and sly and villainous.

Beowulf (BAY-oh-wolf)

Castellozza (KAHS-teh-lohtz-eh)

Paper

Today paper is so common, so plentiful, that we scarcely give it a moment's notice. The words you are reading right now are printed on paper. Chances are, you have paper of several kinds, sizes, thicknesses, and colors around your desk. But paper was not always so familiar. In Europe, paper was not widely used before 1300 and did not supplant parchment as a writing material until about 1600. Where, then, did paper come from? What is it, exactly, and how is it made? Why is it important?

The Chinese invented paper, probably in the second century B.C. For two or three centuries, however, the Chinese did not discern paper's possibilities as a writing material. Instead, they used it as a wrapping material, for personal hygiene—rather like a tissue—and for clothing. By A.D. 100 the Chinese had adopted paper as their preferred writing material. For centuries thereafter they kept the papermaking process a closely guarded secret.

Legend has it that in 751 the Arabs learned the art of papermaking from some Chinese prisoners of war in Samarkand and carried the knowledge westward into the caliphate. Until perhaps 1200 the Arabs kept the secret from contemporary Christians, largely because they were able to sell paper in Mediterranean ports at hugely profitable prices. The oldest surviving Western paper document is the 1102 will of Adelaide of Sicily, the widow of King Roger I. Gradually, Christians in Sicily and Spain, places with intense Muslim-Christian contacts, learned how to make paper. By the thirteenth century there were a number of papermaking centers in Italy, southern France, and Spain. By 1500 the paper industry was flourishing all over Europe.

Paper takes its name from papyrus, the writing material common in antiquity but largely replaced by parchment (see page 272) in the early Middle Ages. Paper and papyrus are, however, utterly different. Papyrus was made from the inner bark of the papyrus plant, whereas the Chinese originally made paper from pulpy plants such as flax or hemp. Gradually the Chinese learned to make paper from rags, discarded textiles. The Arabs learned how to make rag paper and communicated this knowledge, not quite willingly, to the Christian West. Today most paper is made from wood pulp.

A papermaker would put rags and water in a cauldron and repeatedly stir and beat the contents, sometimes over heat, until a thick, gooey film formed on the surface. The papermaker then would take a square or rectangular metal frame with tiny perforations in it and drag it through the thick mixture. When he pulled out the frame, it would have a thin coating of the fluid, known as the "deckel." After the deckel was dry, he peeled it off the frames and placed it on a sheet of felt. Another felt cloth was then placed on top of the deckel, followed by another deckel, another felt, and so forth, until the pile was perhaps a foot high. Using a mechanical press, the papermaker removed excess moisture from the pile of deckels and felts. He then hung up the deckels—now paper—to dry. Finally he "sized" the sheets, coating them with animal glue so that they would accept ink without smudging.

And she did not assign the active role exclusively to the man:

> Handsome friend, as a lover true
> I loved you, for you pleased me,
> But now I see I was a fool,
> for I've barely seen you since.[3]

Count William IX of Poitou° (1071–1127) was among the first of the troubadours, and his daughter, Eleanor of Aquitaine, brought the conventions of this poetry and point of view to the French and Angevin courts. She and her daughters were the greatest literary patrons of the late twelfth century. The wives of kings and nobles who were frequently away from home maintained stunning courts and cultivated vernacular literature.

The courtly literature of northern France owed much to the troubadour tradition of the south but broke new ground in both forms and content. The romance and the lay were the chief new forms. Both drew on classical literature, the heroic Germanic past, and the Arthurian legends of the Celtic world to create stories of love and adventure. The romance usually develops a complex narrative involving several major characters

---

Poitou (PWAH-too)

Paper's historical importance may be considered from several points of view. Paper provides an exceptionally good example of a technology that the West learned from other people, and it illustrates how technologies can travel long distances. The wider use of paper promoted business firms dedicated to selling notebooks, tablets, and fine single sheets. Written documents ranging from personal letters to public records became more numerous once a cheaper writing material became more readily available. One scholar suggests that alphabetization became widespread only after the existence of paper made the arranging of disposable slips feasible. When printing (about which you will learn in Chapter 12; see page 414) was introduced into Europe, the possibility arose of quickly making multiple copies of a given book or document. Parchment was too expensive for this purpose. Thus the more rapid dissemination of books and ideas that marks the transition from the medieval to the modern world was facilitated by the fortunate conjunction of paper and printing.

Woodcut by Jost Amman, the Oldest Illustration of Papermaking   Note the vat, frame, and press. The printer's assistant ("devil") is carrying away deckels to dry.   *(From Jules Heller,* Papermaking *[New York: Watson-Guptill Publications, 1978]. Reproduced with permission.)*

over a long time. The lay is brief and focuses on a single incident. The most famous twelfth-century writer of romance was Chrétien de Troyes (1135–1183), the court writer of Marie of Champagne, a daughter of Eleanor of Aquitaine. The greatest writer of lays was Marie de France, who wrote at the Angevin court in the 1170s.

The romances and lays explore the contradictions and tensions in a variety of human relationships. Loyalty and honor make frequent appearances. Lancelot, a paragon of knightly virtue, desperately loves his lord Arthur's wife, Guinevere. What is he to do? How can he be loyal to his lord, to his love, and to himself? What will he do when a single course of action brings both honor and dishonor?

In the epics, speeches are made to swords, to horses, or sometimes to no one in particular; the points being made are universalized. In the romances, credible human beings struggle to resolve powerful and conflicting emotional and moral dilemmas.

Slavic literatures began with the missionaries Cyril and Methodius (page 265), who developed both a language, Church Slavonic, and a script, Glagolitic. The Glagolitic script was modified into the Cyrillic, which was adopted by all the Slavic peoples who embraced Orthodoxy and remains in use today. The earliest writing in the Slavic languages was religious: biblical translations, saints' lives, and selections from the Church Fathers.

Among the Kievan Rus, in the twelfth century, historical writings and imaginative literature, such as the *Tale of Igor*, made their appearance. The latter work, a semilegendary account of Prince Igor and his many battles, is reminiscent of the *chansons des gestes*.

The Scandinavians who settled Iceland produced a diverse literature. They created law books, detailed accounts of their settlements, and a mighty saga tradition. *Saga* means "things said," and it is almost certainly the case that the greatest sagas were oral tales long before they were written down between about 1150 and 1350. Sagas fall into two categories: Historical sagas blend fact and fiction to praise the deeds of the great heroes of the Viking age. Family sagas mix history and myth to relate the stories of the great families who settled Iceland.

France led the way in the production of vernacular literature, but French models did not inspire slavish imitation. This is seen most clearly in the work of the master of all vernacular writers, Dante Alighieri° (1265–1321). Dante began as a poet in *la dolce stil nuova*, "the sweet new style" that came from France and captivated Italians. But he moved beyond it in many ways. Dante was a man of extraordinarily wide learning and reading. He served Florence in public capacities and became an exile amid political strife. He wrote a long treatise in defense of the empire—or, really, against the secular rule of the church. But he is best known for one of the masterpieces of world literature, *The Divine Comedy*.

The secret of the *Comedy*'s success is not easy to grasp. It is a long and difficult poem, but it is also humorous, instructive, and moving. In an exquisitely beautiful Italian, Dante took the most advanced theology and philosophy of his time, the richest poetic traditions, a huge hoard of stories, many contemporary events, and a lot of common sense and wove them into an allegorical presentation of the journey of the whole human race and of the individual lives of all people.

Accompanied by the Roman poet Virgil (see page 180), Dante travels through Hell and Purgatory, commenting along the way on the condition of the people he meets. Then, because Virgil is a pagan and only Dante's true love can accompany Dante into paradise, Beatrice, the love of Dante's youth, joins him for a visit to Heaven. The poet's central metaphor is love; the love he feels for Beatrice symbolizes the love God feels for the world. Dante canvasses humanity from the pits of Hell, which he reserved for traitors, to the summit of Paradise, where a man inspired by pure love might, despite his sinfulness, dare to look into the face of God.

Although the romances and lays were by no means the exclusive preserve of the elite, very little is known about popular literature. Two exceptions are the mystery play and women's devotional writing. Mystery plays made their first appearance in the eleventh century. The liturgy of the church, which formally re-enacted the life of Christ, was confined to the clergy. But this limitation did not prevent troupes of actors from staging, on church porches or village greens, scenes from the life of Christ in simple, direct language. By the twelfth and thirteenth centuries, guilds in many towns sponsored the production of plays commemorating the Christian mysteries. Such plays served as both a form of popular entertainment and a device for teaching elementary Christian ideas. The female religious movements of the age gave rise to prose and verse works in various vernaculars. Mechtild of Magdeburg (1210–1280), a German Beguine, wrote *The Flowering Light of Divinity*, a mystical, allegorical account of the marriage between God and a spiritual woman. The vernaculars opened avenues of expression to women, who were normally denied Latin learning.

■ Innovations in Architecture

Romanesque, "in the Roman style," is a term coined in the nineteenth century to characterize the architecture and, to a lesser extent, the painting of the period between the waning of Carolingian art and the full emergence of Gothic art in the late twelfth century. Today scholars view the Romanesque style as transitional between Carolingian and Gothic.

At several places in Ottonian Germany, a return of political stability led to the construction of churches. Ducal dynasties and women of the imperial family were among the most generous patrons. Pride in their Carolingian inheritance and their new imperial dignity led the Germans to a distinctive architectural style marked by very thick walls, alternating piers and columns in the nave, and galleries. As this architectural style spread all over Europe in the eleventh century, it produced true Romanesque, a style that differed from Roman and Carolingian styles mainly in the greater internal height and space made possible by vaulting (see Figure 10.1). To the rectangular elegance of the classical basilica and the height of the Carolingian westworks (see page 264), Romanesque builders added a refined verticality.

Among the distinctive features of Romanesque churches were their wall paintings and frescoes, their sculpture, reliquaries, pulpits, and baptisteries—in short, their exuberant decoration and ornament. Europe's growing wealth and sophistication, and the pride of the church's aristocratic patrons, are very much in ev-

---

Dante Alighieri (DAHN-tay ah-lih-GYAIR-ee)

idence. Especially in the south of France, the façades of Romanesque churches provided space for sculpture. The tympanum above the doors, a space seen by all who entered, was a favored location. Large-scale sculpture had made a comeback after its almost total absence in the early Middle Ages.

It is surely no coincidence that Gothic art and architecture emerged just as the West was absorbing the rediscovery of Euclid's mathematical writings and applying the intensely ordered logic of Aristotle to everything from legal problems to theological mysteries. One of the most familiar images of the Middle Ages is the inspiringly beautiful Gothic cathedral. It is thus ironic that the word *Gothic* first appeared in the sixteenth century as a term of derision for what was then regarded as an outmoded style so ugly that only the horrible conquerors of Rome, the Goths, could have been responsible for it. The name stuck, but today it simply identifies a period in

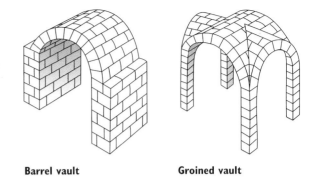

Barrel vault   **Groined vault**

Figure 10.1   The Structure of Romanesque Architecture
The basic structural element of Romanesque architecture was the barrel vault, which, when two were joined at right angles, formed a groin vault. These vaults produced great height and strength but gave buildings a massive, fortresslike appearance. *(Source: Anne Shaver-Crandell,* The Middle Ages. *Copyright © 1982 Cambridge University Press. Reprinted with permission of Cambridge University Press.)*

Saint Sernin, Toulouse   This fortresslike church (ca. 1080–1120) was paid for by the offerings of pilgrims on their way to shrines in Spain. Its massive walls and numerous colonnades are typical of Romanesque architecture. The form of the building suggests the cross of Christ. For the interior of a Romanesque church (Vezelay) see page 348.   *(Jean Dieuzaid, Toulouse)*

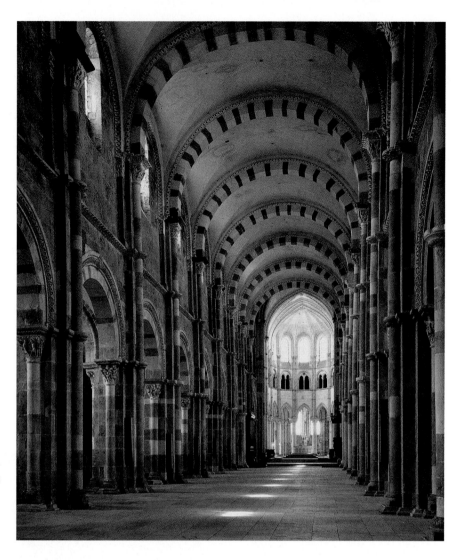

Nave of Vezelay, 1104–1132 The basilica of Sainte-Madeleine is a crowning achievement of French Romanesque architecture, featuring height and a sense of airy spaciousness. Compare this nave with the Gothic nave of Chartres on page 316. *(Éditions Gaud)*

European architecture, sculpture, and painting that began in the middle of the twelfth century and that in some places lasted until the early sixteenth century.

Gothic is a French invention. It was Abbot Suger° (1085–1151) of St.-Denis, a monastery outside Paris, who, in rebuilding his basilica beginning in 1135, consciously sought a new style. He desired to achieve effects of lightness, almost weightlessness, in the stonework of his church and to admit large amounts of light to create a dazzling and mysterious aura on the inside. The Bible often uses images of light to refer to God, and Suger wished to give expression to those images in the house of God for which he was responsible.

Suger produced something startlingly original by combining a number of elements that had long been in use—three in particular: A *pointed arch* is more elegant than a round one; and it permits the joining of two arches of identical height but different widths, which, in turn, permits complex shapes and sizes. The *ribbed vault* is lighter and more graceful than the barrel and groin vaults characteristic of Romanesque architecture; it also exerts less stress and facilitates experimentation with shapes (see Figure 10.2). Finally, *point support*—basically, the support of structural elements at only certain points—permitted the replacement of heavy, stress-bearing walls with curtains of stained glass. The points of support might be massive internal piers or intricate skeletal frameworks, called *buttresses*, on the outside of the church.

These three elements—pointed arch, ribbed vault, and point support—produce a building that is characterized by verticality and translucency. Everything seems to spring upward, and stone surfaces appear so frequently punctured by light as almost to disappear altogether. The desired, and achieved, effect is one of harmony, order, and mathematical precision.

Suger (SOO-jhay)

The Gothic style soon spread in central and northern France. The cathedral of Notre-Dame of Paris was built beginning in the 1150s, and the royal portal at Chartres Cathedral was reconstructed after 1145. Gothic churches could be huge. The interior of Notre-Dame, for example, is 493 feet long and 107 feet high. To avoid a sense of sheer mass, Gothic builders used triple or quadruple elevations inside the buildings and took advantage of point support to pierce the walls at frequent intervals with stained glass windows. Exterior surfaces were broken up with windows, sculptures, colonnades, and towers. No opportunity was missed to create visual interest and complexity. (See the feature "Weighing the Evidence: Stained Glass" on pages 350–351.)

The thirteenth century was the most mature period for French Gothic architecture and also the time when Gothic spread most widely throughout Europe. Its popularity may be attributed to the superiority of French masons and stonecutters and also to the tremendous prestige of French culture. By 1300 distinctive Gothic traditions shaped the urban landscape in almost all parts of Europe from Iceland to Poland.

Figure 10.2   The Structure of Gothic Architecture
The adoption of pointed arches, an import from the Islamic world, let Gothic builders join structures of identical heights but different widths (something that barrel and groin vaulting could not do; see Figure 10.1 on page 347). The resulting structures were high, light, airy, and visually interesting.
(Source: Anne Shaver-Crandell, The Middle Ages. *Copyright © 1982 Cambridge University Press. Reprinted with permission of Cambridge University Press.)*

Exterior of Notre-Dame, Paris   This most famous of cathedrals (1163–1220) shows all the classic elements of the Gothic style: highly decorated western end, cross shape formed by the nave and transept, flying buttresses to support the walls and roof, and side walls that seem like curtains of glass.   *(Altitude, Paris)*

(continued on page 352)

Stained Glass

To walk into one of Europe's great churches is to enter a realm of mystery and beauty produced by the play of light—the brilliant light of the morning sun, the softer glow of the evening sun, the muted tones of a cloudy day—on thousands of square feet of colored glass. This mystery and beauty were created intentionally in Europe in the High Middle Ages. But the magnificent surviving medieval windows are not important solely for their beauty. Their images provide unique and crucial insights into religious and secular life.

Pictured here are two thirteenth-century cathedral windows. The one from Canterbury depicts that city's great bishop and martyr, Thomas Becket. A large window at Chartres depicts Saint Lubin, a sixth-century bishop of the city who was the patron saint of the town's inn and tavern keepers, and Noah, according to the Bible the first planter of grape vines. Here we see barrels of wine being hauled to market, in a window donated by the vintners guild.

Many of Canterbury's windows represent aspects of the life of the murdered archbishop. The one pictured here shows Thomas as a bishop, not as a martyr. He is wearing a mitre, the traditional headgear of a bishop. He also wears a *pallium*, a white wool band sent to a new archbishop by the pope. Becket's vestments are green, the commonest liturgical color of the religious year (others were white, purple, and red). This window, then, would have served to remind people of their beloved bishop as he was in life, not martyrdom.

In Chartres, wine was important to the church because of its use in Mass, and it was also a staple of the local economy. Accordingly, the vintners are portrayed in twenty-three of this window's forty-one panels. By comparison, most guilds are depicted only once in the windows they donated. These windows remind us, as they reminded contemporaries, of how these magnificent buildings fitted into the daily life of their communities. Religious devotions and secular preoccupations blended in one spot.

Glass is made by heating silica, found naturally in sand, flint, and quartz, to a very high temperature and then fusing the molten silicate with a borate or phosphate often obtained from ashes produced by burning natural substances. Colored glass was made by adding metal oxides to the molten mixture. Iron oxide produced red, copper oxide produced green, and cobalt, blue.

Such glass, called "pot" glass, tended to be opaque, obviously unsuitable for windows. To achieve greater translucency, glassmakers made "flashed" glass by fusing at low temperature a layer of colored liquid to the surface of a panel of clear glass. Although fine glass vessels were made in a number of places, notably in Venice and the Rhineland, the large sheets of colored glass used for church windows were commonly manufactured in Lorraine and Normandy.

To make a stained glass window, a master glazier first drew a cartoon—a sort of rough draft—on a flat board, or perhaps on a piece of parchment. He then cut pieces of colored glass into various irregular shapes according to his design. To produce facial features, folds in garments, or other details, the glazier painted the inner sides of the colored glass pieces with dark-colored paints and then fired them at low temperatures to produce an enamel-like effect. You can see this patina on Thomas's face. Once the glazier had all his pieces cut and placed, he joined them together by means of lead strips that were **H** shaped. If you look closely, you can see the pieces of glass, lead stripping, and painted details in the images on these pages. The whole picture was then fitted into a metal frame and mounted in a window opening.

Documents first mention the use of glass in church windows in the sixth century. The oldest surviving fragments of stained glass date from the ninth century, and the oldest complete windows from around 1100. With large Romanesque, and even more with the huge Gothic churches, came opportunities to use more and more glass. First the greater height of Romanesque buildings meant that tall windows could be placed high up in the nave walls. Then the structural innovations of Gothic architecture that removed stress, and hence stone, from the walls permitted them to become vast expanses of glass. Chartres Cathedral has 176 windows. Many high medieval churches had windows more than 50 feet high.

So far we have looked at *how* medieval Europeans created stained glass and incorporated it into their greatest churches. But *why* did they undertake such time-consuming and costly decoration? Suger, the scholarly twelfth-century abbot of St.-Denis outside Paris who rebuilt his basilica in the Gothic style, spoke of the spiritual force of his new glass windows:

**Canterbury, Thirteenth-Century Window:
Thomas Becket** *(Sonia Halliday Photographs)*

**Chartres, Thirteenth-Century Window:
Story of Saint Lubin** *(© Clive Hicks)*

When . . . the loveliness of the many-colored gems has called me away from external cares . . . then it seems to me that I see myself dwelling in some strange region of the universe which neither exists entirely in the slime of the earth nor entirely in the purity of heaven; and that, by the grace of God, I can be transported from this inferior to that higher world.*

In the Greek philosophers, the Bible, and the Church Fathers, light always represents one way of imagining the unimaginable reality of God. For Suger and his contemporaries, the luminous effect of stained glass suggested the very presence of God.

Earthquakes, fires, and wars have destroyed most of the glass that was installed in the Middle Ages. Today's

visitor to Europe views more-or-less valid nineteenth-century reconstructions except at Canterbury in England and Chartres in France, where almost all of the original glass survives. Usually, medieval churches were laid out on an east-west axis. The western façade was normally pierced by tall "lancet" windows and by a single "rose" window (look at the front of Notre-Dame on page 349). These typically portrayed scenes from the life of Christ and/or the Virgin Mary. The northern aisle windows usually contained Old Testament scenes, the southern windows New Testament scenes.

Stained glass played a key role, alongside sculpture, preaching, and churchyard dramas, in communicating the faith to ordinary people. Seldom has a teaching tool been so beautiful! Scholars also speak of stained glass as "painting with glass." Indeed, the art form most like stained glass is painting, especially the painting of illuminations on the pages of manuscripts.

---

* Suger, *De rebus in administratione sua gestis*, ed. E. Panofsky, 2d ed. (Princeton, 1979), pp. 63–65.

SUMMARY

COMPARISONS between the Europe of 900 and 1300 are instructive both as reminders of what had happened and as suggestions of what was to come. In 900 Carolingian Europe was being attacked on every side. By 1300 Europe was vastly larger than in Carolingian times; not only was its geography greater, so also had it expanded in economic, political, military, and cultural terms.

Europe's traditional social orders—the "Three Estates" as they would later be called—came fully into view after 900. Described by contemporaries as pray-ers, fighters, and workers, these orders accounted for some but not all of the major groups. The clergy was more numerous and more diverse in structure than ever before. Women played important roles as nuns, writers, and reformers. The nobility was more tightly organized into lineages, and an aristocratic ethos, chivalry, characterized noble lifestyles. Some peasants gained in personal freedom, some lost; some grew more prosperous and comfortable, some lived in want and misery. The townsfolk of an expanding Europe constituted a growing and increasingly important group that was never a part of the society of rural gentlemen-warriors. Minorities, chiefly Jews, enjoyed some new opportunities in the High Middle Ages but also suffered attacks and prejudice.

Large-scale social movements appeared for the first time in Western history. These movements were generally religious. Sometimes they were motivated by desires to reform the church, and sometimes they arose from a longing for the primitive, pristine days of Christianity. A few of the movements, the Waldensians and Albigensians, for example, would end up as heresies. Other groups, the mendicants above all others, managed to accommodate themselves to the church and thus lent it their energy and insight. For the first time, women played important roles in the new religious movements.

As Europe expanded, Latin Christendom encountered long-lost classical learning as well as Arab and Jewish thought. The cultural life of the traditional intellectual centers—monastic and cathedral schools—was immeasurably enriched by these cultural meetings and mixings. Gradually European intellectual life was so stimulated that a new approach to scholarship—Scholasticism—and a new kind of institution—the university—ensued.

But while Latin remained the language of lecture hall and courtroom, vernacular languages took their place alongside the ancient tongue. Impressive literatures arose from Iceland to Rus in prose and verse. Tales of love and adventure predominated in vernacular literature, but inspiring moral and religious works appeared too. Women contributed in many languages. In addition to literature, the high medieval period saw first Romanesque and then Gothic architecture.

As the fourteenth century dawned, people all over Europe had reasons to be both hopeful and anxious. They were, in fact, at the start of one of the most turbulent and creative periods in Western history, a period when crisis after crisis would afflict the expanded Europe and the spectacular achievements of the High Middle Ages.

■ Notes

1. John Addington Symonds, *Wine, Women and Song: Medieval Latin Students' Songs* (reprint, New York: Cooper Square, 1966), p. 69.
2. Frederick Goldin, *Lyrics of the Troubadours and Trouvères: An Anthology and a History* (New York: Doubleday, 1973), p. 135.
3. Meg Bogin, *The Women Troubadours* (New York: Norton, 1976), p. 69.

■ Suggested Reading

Bony, Jean. *French Gothic Architecture of the Twelfth and Thirteenth Centuries.* 1983. Huge, clearly presented, and magnificently illustrated, this is a browser's book as well as a sustained essay by a master of his subject.

Bouchard, Constance B. S*trong of Body, Brave and Noble: Chivalry and Society in Medieval France.* 1998. A superb summation of the social and cultural history of the medieval aristocracy.

Bynum, Caroline Walker. *Jesus as Mother: Studies in the Spirituality of the High Middle Ages.* 1982. A collection of sparkling essays by a major historian that makes the feminine in religious thought accessible, even central, to any discussion of medieval religion.

Colish, Marcia. *Medieval Foundations of the Western Intellectual Tradition.* 1997. The first original and comprehensive history of medieval thought in a generation.

Grundmann, Herbert. *Religious Movements in the Middle Ages.* 1995. Translated into English sixty years after its appearance in German, this book has lost none of its interest or explanatory power.

Jaeger, C. Stephen. *The Envy of Angels: Cathedral Schools and Social Ideals in Medieval Europe, 900–1200.* 1994. A work of vast learning and common sense on controversial topics.

Lambert, Malcolm. *Medieval Heresy: Popular Movements from the Gregorian Reform to the Reformation.* 2d ed. 1992. Brilliant and readable, this book is the best history of medieval heresy ever written and one of the best books on medieval religion generally.

Southern, R. W. *Scholastic Humanism and the Unification of Europe.* 1995. A truly brilliant overview of twelfth-century culture by its greatest twentieth-century student.

 For a searchable list of additional readings for this chapter, go to http://college.hmco.com.

Questa e lentrata et luscita della generale bicherna delchomuo
dj siena fatta altempo de savi huomini thomme di nostro ditu
ra chamarlengho per uno anno chominando adj p̄mo digienaio 1436.
et finito adj ultimo dj dicembre 1437. et dicheccho dj iognio misser baldassarre

CHAPTER 11

Crisis and Recovery in Late Medieval Europe 1300–1500

I N the fourteenth century, Europeans sang an old Franciscan hymn, "Day of Wrath, Day of Burning." Its verses described the fear and disorder that would accompany the end of the world and God's judgment of the saved and the damned. That hymn could well have been in the mind of the painter of the facing illustration. When countless Europeans, such as these poor souls beneath the winged angel of death, fell victim to epidemic disease, many people thought they knew why. The illustrator seems to believe it was God's judgment against sinners, including these gamblers sickened by the angel's plague-tipped arrows. The flood, fire, and pestilence that ravaged late medieval Europe were thought to be premonitions of the breakdown of the world and a time of judgment.

The late Middle Ages (ca. 1300–1500) are often described as a period of continued crisis and decline that put an end to the growth and expansion of the previous three centuries. In truth, however, the years of crisis in the fourteenth and early fifteenth centuries gave way to a dramatic economic, social, and political recovery in the fifteenth century. The cultural and intellectual changes that accompanied the crisis and recovery are the focus of Chapter 12, "The Renaissance."

Military, political, religious, economic, and social crises burdened Europe in the fourteenth and early fifteenth centuries. Between 1337 and 1453, France and England fought a war that touched most of the states of western Europe. The Hundred Years' War, as it has come to be known, was fought primarily over English claims to traditionally French lands. Problems were not confined to England and France. Aristocrats in many parts of Europe challenged the hereditary rights of their rulers. In the towns of Germany and Italy,

The Crisis of the Western Christian Church

War, Disorder, and Revolts in Western Europe, 1300–1450

Economy and Society

The Consolidation of the Late Medieval Governments, 1450–1500

Painted cover for a fifteenth-century government account book from Siena, Italy, showing symbols of death—arrows, a scythe, and a horse —to carry the angel of death from place to place. (Staatliche Museen zu Berlin, Preussischer Kulturbesitz Kunstgewerbemuseum. Photo: Mues-Funke)

patrician classes moved to reduce the influence of artisans and laborers in government, instituting oligarchies or even aristocratic dictatorships in place of more democratic governments.

Questions of power and representation also affected the Christian church as ecclesiastical claims to authority came under attack. Secular governments challenged church jurisdictions. Disputed papal elections led to the so-called Great Schism, a split between rival centers of control in Rome and Avignon (a city in what is now the south of France). In the aftermath of the crisis, the papacy was forced to redefine its place in both the religious life and the political life of Europe.

A series of economic and demographic shocks worsened these political and religious difficulties. Part of the problem was structural: the population of Europe had grown too large to be supported by the resources available. Famine and the return of the bubonic plague in 1348 sent the economy into long-term decline. In almost every aspect of political, religious, and social life, then, the fourteenth and early fifteenth centuries marked a pause in the growth and consolidation that had characterized the earlier medieval period.

Yet out of the crises, a number of significant changes would emerge. By 1500 the European population and economy were again climbing. England and France emerged strengthened by military and political conflicts. And the consolidation of the Spanish kingdoms, the Ottoman Empire, and the states of eastern Europe altered the political and social makeup of Europe. None of the transformations could have been predicted in 1300 as Europe entered a religious, political, and social whirlwind.

QUESTIONS TO CONSIDER

- How did the Great Schism change the church and the papacy?
- What forces worked to limit the power of rulers in the fourteenth and early fifteenth centuries?
- What was the impact of the Black Death?
- How did the political makeup of Europe in 1500 differ from that in 1300?

TERMS TO KNOW

Jan Hus	Golden Bull
Council of Constance	Black Death
Great Schism	Hanseatic League
Hundred Years' War	Spanish Inquisition
Joan of Arc	Sultan Mehmed II

THE CRISIS OF THE WESTERN CHRISTIAN CHURCH

EARLY in the fourteenth century, the Christian church endured a series of crises that instigated a debate about the nature of church government and the role of the church in society. First, the popes and their entourages abandoned their traditional residences in central Italy and moved to Avignon, an imperial enclave in the south of modern France. Then, in the wake of a disputed election, two and later three rivals claimed the papal throne. Simultaneously, the church hierarchy faced challenges from radical re-formers who wished to change it. At various times all the European powers became entangled in the problems of the church. By the mid-fifteenth century, the papacy realized that it needed a stronger, independent base. Papal recovery in the fifteenth century was predicated on political power in central Italy.

■ The Babylonian Captivity, 1309–1377

The Christian church was in turmoil as a result of an attack on Pope Boniface VIII (r. 1294–1303) by King Philip IV (r. 1285–1314) of France. The king attempted to kidnap Boniface, intending to try him for heresy because of the pope's challenges to the king's authority within his own kingdom. The outstanding issues revolved around the powers of the pope and the responsibilities of the clergy to political leaders. It was, in fact, largely because of tensions with the northern kingdoms that the French archbishop of Bordeaux° was elected Pope Clement V (r. 1305–1314). Clement chose to remain north of the Alps in order to seek an end to warfare between France and England and to protect, to the extent possible, the wealthy religious order of the Knights Templar (see page 321), which Philip was in the process of suppressing. Clement also hoped to prevent the king from carrying through his threatened posthumous heresy trial of Boniface. After the death of Boniface, it was clear that the governments of Europe had no intention of recognizing papal authority as absolute.

Clement's pontificate marked the beginning of the so-called Babylonian Captivity, a period during which the pope resided almost continuously outside of Italy. In 1309 Clement moved the papal court to Avignon, on the Rhône River in a region that was still part of the Holy Roman Empire—the name that by the fourteenth century was given to the medieval empire whose origin reached back to Charlemagne. His successor, Pope John XXII (r. 1316–1334), set the tone for the brilliant papal court. To celebrate the marriage of his grandniece in 1324, for example, he ordered a wedding feast during which the numerous guests consumed 4,012 loaves of bread, 8¾ oxen, 55¼ sheep, 8 pigs, 4 boars, and vast quantities of fish, capons, chickens, partridges, rabbits, ducks, and chickens. The repast was topped off with 300 pounds of cheese, 3,000 eggs, and assorted fruits. The guests washed down this feast with about 450 liters of wine.

The papacy and its new residence in Avignon became a major religious, diplomatic, and commercial center. The size of the court changed as dramatically as its venue: although the thirteenth-century papal administration required only two hundred or so officials, the bureaucracy in Avignon grew to about six hundred. It was not just the pope's immediate circle that expanded the population of Avignon. Artists, writers, lawyers, and merchants from across Europe were drawn to the new center of administration and hub of patronage. Kings, princes, towns, and ecclesiastical institutions needed representatives at the papal court. Papal administrators continued to intervene actively in local ecclesiastical affairs, and the pope's revenues from annates (generally a portion of the first year's revenues from an ecclesiastical office granted by papal letter), court fees, and provisioning charges continued to grow.

Bordeaux (bor-DOE)

CHRONOLOGY

1303	Pope Boniface VIII attacked at Anagni and dies
1305	Election of Pope Clement V
1309	Clement V moves papal court to Avignon; beginning of Babylonian Captivity
1337	Beginning of Hundred Years' War between England and France
1348–1351	The Black Death
1356	German emperor issues Golden Bull
1378	The Great Schism
1381	The English Rising
1397	Union of Kalmar unites Denmark, Norway, and Sweden
1410	Battle of Tannenberg
1414–1417	Council of Constance
1415	Battle of Agincourt
1420	Treaty of Troyes
1431	Execution of Joan of Arc
1438	Pragmatic Sanction of Bourges
1453	End of the Hundred Years' War Ottoman Turks conquer Constantinople
1469	Marriage of Ferdinand and Isabella unites kingdoms of Aragon and Castile
1480	Ivan III ends Tartar overlordship of Muscovy
1485	Tudor dynasty established in England
1492	Spanish conquest of Granada Jews expelled from Spanish lands Columbus commissioned to discover new lands
1494	Charles VIII invades Italy

🕮 READING SOURCES

Saint Catherine of Siena and the Avignon Papacy

Catherine Benincasa (1347–1380) joined the Dominican Order at age 16. Renowned for her piety and spirituality, she used her influence to pressure the popes to return to Rome and reform the church. This letter to Pope Gregory XI was probably dictated (Catherine was illiterate) in 1376.

My soul longs with inestimable love that God in His infinite mercy will take from you each passion and all tepidity of heart and will reform you into another man by rekindling in you an ardent and burning desire, for in no other way can you fulfill the will of God and the desires of all His servants. Alas, my sweetest Babbo [literally "Daddy"], pardon my presumption in what I have said and am saying—the sweet and primal Truth forces me. This is His will, Father; He demands this of you. He demands that you require justice in the multitude of iniquities committed by those nourished and sheltered in the garden of the Holy Church; He declares that beasts should not receive men's food. Because He has given you authority and because you have accepted it, you ought to use your virtue and power. If you do not wish to use it, it might be better for you to resign what you have accepted; it would give more honor to God and health to your soul.

In addition, His will demands that you make peace with all Tuscany where now you have strife. Receive all your wicked and rebellious sons whenever you can peacefully do so—but punish them as a father would an offending son. . . . [T]hat which appears impossible to you is possible to the sweet goodness of God who has ordained and willed that it be so. Beware, as you hold your life dear, that you are not negligent in this nor treat lightly the works of the Holy Spirit. . . . You can have peace by avoiding the perverse pomps and delights of the world and by preserving God's honor and the Holy Church's rights.

Source: Robert Coogan, *Babylon on the Rhone: A Translation of Letters by Dante, Petrarch, and Catherine of Siena on the Avignon Papacy* (Potomac, Md.: Studia Humanitatis, 1983), p. 115.

Not everyone approved of this situation. It was the Italian poet and philosopher Francesco Petrarch (1304–1374) who first referred to the Avignon move as a "Babylonian Captivity of the papacy." Recalling the account in the Hebrew Bible of the exile of the Israelites and New Testament images of Babylon as the center of sin and immorality, he complained of

> [an] unholy Babylon, Hell on Earth, a sink of iniquity, the cesspool of the world. There is neither faith, nor charity, nor religion, nor fear of God, nor shame, nor truth, nor holiness, albeit the residence . . . of the supreme pontiff should have made it a shrine and the very stronghold of religion.[1]

To Petrarch and others, the exile of the papacy epitomized all that was wrong with the church. Many people renowned for their piety, including women such as Saint Catherine of Siena and Saint Bridget of Sweden, appealed to the pope to return to simpler ways and to Rome, his episcopal city. (See the box "Reading Sources: Saint Catherine of Siena and the Avignon Papacy.")

■ The Great Schism, 1378–1417

In 1377 Pope Gregory XI (r. 1370–1378) bowed to critics' pressure and did return to Rome. He was shocked by what he found: churches and palaces in ruin and the city violent and dangerous. By the end of 1377 he had resolved to retreat to Avignon, but he died a few months later. In a tumultuous election during which the Roman populace entered the Vatican Palace and threatened to break into the conclave itself, the cardinals finally elected a compromise candidate acceptable to both the French cardinals and the Roman mob. Urban VI (r. 1378–1389)

Sixtus IV Appoints a Librarian
The pope's nephew, the future Pope Julius II, stands between the seated pope and a kneeling librarian. The influence of papal families was one of the excesses that reformers of the fifteenth and sixteenth centuries hoped to curb.   *(Scala/Art Resource, NY)*

may have been electable, but he was also violent, intemperate, and eager to reduce the privileges of the clerical hierarchy. In response the French cardinals questioned the legitimacy of the election, which they came to believe had been conducted under duress. Within months they deposed Urban and elected in his place a French cardinal who took the name Clement VII (r. 1378–1394). Urban responded by denouncing the cardinals and continuing to rule in Rome. The church now had two popes.

After some hesitation, Western Christians divided into two camps, initiating the Great Schism°, a period of almost forty years during which no one knew for sure who was the true pope. This was a deadly serious issue for all. The true pope had the right to appoint church

officials, decide important moral and legal issues, and allow or forbid taxation of the clergy by the state. Each side found ready supporters among the states of Europe; however, support for one pope or the other often had more to do with political rivalries than with religious convictions. The two sides largely mirrored the political tensions in Europe. France and those governments most closely allied with it tended to support Clement, who eventually resettled in Avignon. These included Burgundy, Savoy, Naples, Scotland, and Castile. The English, together with most Italian governments, the German Empire, Scandinavia, Hungary, Portugal, and Poland supported Urban, the pope in Rome.

The crisis gave impetus to new discussions about church government: Should the pope be considered the sole head of the church? Debates within the church

---

Schism (SKIZ-em)

followed lines of thought already expressed in the towns and kingdoms of Europe. Representative bodies—the English Parliament, the French Estates General, the Swedish Riksdag°—already claimed the right to act for the realm, and in the city-states of Italy ultimate authority was thought to reside in the body of citizens. Canon lawyers and theologians similarly argued that authority resided in the whole church, which had the right and duty to come together in council to correct and reform the church hierarchy. Even the most conservative of these "conciliarists" agreed that the "Universal Church" had the right to respond in periods of heresy or schism. More radical conciliarists argued that the pope as bishop of Rome was merely the first among equals in the church hierarchy and that he, like any other bishop, could be corrected by a gathering of his peers—that is, by an ecumenical council.

The rival popes found themselves under increased pressure to end the schism. The issue seemed on its way to resolution when the two parties agreed to meet in northern Italy in 1408. In the end, though, the meeting never took place, and in retrospect many doubted whether either party had been negotiating in good faith. In exasperation the cardinals, the main ecclesiastical supporters of the rival popes, called a general council in Pisa, which deposed both popes and elected a new one. Since the council lacked the power to force the rivals to accept deposition, the result was that three men now claimed to be the rightful successor of Saint Peter. Conciliarists, by themselves, could not mend the split in the church.

Resolution finally came when the Holy Roman emperor Sigismund (r. 1411–1437) forced the diplomatically isolated third papal claimant, John XXIII (r. 1410–1415), to call a general council of the church. The council, which met from 1414 to 1417 in the German imperial city of Constance, could never have succeeded without Sigismund's support. At one point he forced the council to remain in session even after Pope John had fled the city in an attempt to end deliberations.

■ Heresy and the Council of Constance, 1414–1418

Sigismund hoped a council could help him heal deep religious and civil divisions in Bohemia, the most important part of his family's traditional lands (see Map 11.3). Bohemia and its capital, Prague, were Czech-speaking.

Riksdag (RIX-dog)

But Prague was also the seat of the Luxemburg dynasty of German emperors and the site of the first university in the German world. Religious and theological questions quickly became embroiled in the competing claims of Czech and German factions. The preaching and teaching of Czech reformer Jan Hus (ca. 1370–1415) were at the center of the debate. As preacher in the Bethlehem Chapel in Prague from 1402 and eventually as rector of the university, Hus was the natural spokesman for the non-German townsmen in Prague and the Czech faction at the university. His criticisms of the church hierarchy, which in Prague was primarily German, fanned into flame the smoldering embers of Czech national feeling. It was Sigismund's hope that a council might clarify the orthodoxy of Hus's teachings and heal the rift within the church of Bohemia.

The council's response to the issue of heresy was based on the church's experience with heresy over the previous forty years, primarily the teachings of John Wyclif (1329–1384). In the 1370s Wyclif, an Oxford theologian and parish priest, began to criticize in increasingly angry terms the state of the clergy and the abuses of the church hierarchy. By 1387 his ideas had been declared heretical and his followers were hunted out. Wyclif's most dangerous criticism was his denial of the priest's indispensable position as an intermediary between God and believers. Wyclif believed that the church could be at once a divine institution and an earthly gathering of individuals. Thus, in his opinion, individual Christians need not unquestioningly obey the pronouncements of the church hierarchy. That special homage was due only to Scripture, insisted Wyclif, who sponsored the first translations of the Bible into English. He gathered about himself followers called Lollards, who emphasized Bible reading and popular piety; some even supported public preaching by women. According to one disciple, "Every true man and woman being in charity is a priest."[2] Because of their attacks on the ecclesiastical hierarchy, Lollards were popular among the nobility of England, and especially at the court of Richard II during the 1390s. In the first two decades of the fifteenth century, however, their influence waned.

Wyclif's influence continued on the Continent, in the circle of Jan Hus and the Czech reformers. While Hus disagreed with some of Wyclif's more radical ideas, he too attacked clerical power and privileges. By 1403 the German majority in the university had condemned Hus's teaching as Wycliffite, thus initiating almost a decade of struggle between Czechs and Germans, Hussites and Catholics. This was the impasse Sigismund hoped the

Council of Constance could settle. Accordingly he offered a suspicious Hus a safe conduct pass to attend the council. When Hus arrived, it became clear that the councilors and Hus himself were in no mood to compromise. The council reneged on the pledge of safe conduct and ordered Hus to recant his beliefs. He refused. The council condemned him as a heretic and burned him at the stake on July 6, 1415.

Far from ending Sigismund's problems with the Bohemians, the actions of the council provided the Czechs with a martyr and hero. The execution of Hus provoked a firestorm of revolution in Prague. Czech forces roundly defeated an imperial army sent in to restore order in Prague. The Hussite movement gathered strength and spread throughout Bohemia. Moderate Hussites continued Hus's campaign against clerical abuses and claimed the right to receive both the bread and the wine during the sacrament of communion. Radical Hussites argued that the true church was the community of spiritual men and women. They had no use for ecclesiastical hierarchy of any kind. The German emperors were unable to defeat a united Hussite movement. In 1433 a new church council and moderate Hussites negotiated an agreement that allowed the Hussites to continue some of their practices, including receiving both bread and wine at communion, while returning to the church. Radical Hussites refused the compromise, and the war dragged on until 1436. Bohemia remained a center of religious dissent, and the memory of Hus's execution at a church council would have a chilling effect on discussions of church reform during the Reformation in the sixteenth century.

Pope Martin Receiving the Crown from a Council
Delegates to the Council of Constance stated that even the pope had to accept the decrees of a council sitting for the whole church.   *(From* Chronik des Konstanzen Konzils, *1414–1418. Courtesy, Rosgartenmuseum, Constance)*

■ The Reunion and Reform of the Papacy, 1415–1513

To most of the delegates at the Council of Constance, the reunion and reform of the papacy were more important than the issue of heresy. And as we will see, the crisis of the schism brought in its aftermath a transformed Christian church.

After initially agreeing to abdicate if his rivals did the same, John changed his mind and fled from Constance. Sigismund recaptured him and returned him to the council, where he was deposed. Pope Gregory XII (r. 1406–1415), the Roman pope, realizing he had lost all his support, resigned—after himself calling the council, as a rightful pope should do. Benedict III (r. 1394–1417), the pope in Avignon, refused to resign and he too was deposed. Finally, in 1417, the council elected a Roman nobleman as Martin V (r. 1417–1431).

The council justified its actions in what was perhaps its most important decree, *Haec sancta synodus* ("This sacred synod"):

> This sacred synod of Constance . . . declares . . . that it has its power immediately from Christ, and that all men, of every rank and position, including even the pope himself are bound to obey it in those matters that pertain to the faith.[3]

Popes could no longer expect to remain unchallenged if they made claims of absolute dominion. And ecclesiastical rights and jurisdictions increasingly were matters for negotiation.

Critics agreed that the pope no longer behaved like the "Servant of the Servants of Christ" but instead acted like the "Lord of Lords." Cardinals claimed to represent the church at large as counterweights to papal abuse, but as the nobility of the church, they and other members of the hierarchy required the income from multiple offices to maintain their presence at the papal court. Both the cardinals and the popes viewed any reforms to the present system as potential threats to their ability to function. The council, however, recognized the need for further reforms. A second reform council met at Basel from 1431 to 1449, but with little success. The council again tried to reduce papal power, but this time it received little support from European governments.

Because of the continuing conciliarist threat, the papacy needed the support of the secular rulers of Europe. Thus the papacy was forced to accept compromises on the issues of reform, on ecclesiastical jurisdictions and immunities, and on papal revenues. Various governments argued that it was they, and not the pope, who should be responsible for ecclesiastical institutions and jurisdictions within their territories.

Lay rulers focused on several issues. They wanted church officials in their territories to belong to local families. They wanted ecclesiastical institutions to be subject to local laws and administration. And by the 1470s, it was clear that they wanted to have local prelates named as cardinal-protectors. These were not churchmen who could serve the church administration in Rome; rather they functioned as mediators between local government and the papacy. The most famous of these new political cardinals was Thomas Wolsey of England (ca. 1470–1530), who was an important supporter of King Henry VII and chancellor of England under Henry VIII.

The reunited papacy had to accept claims it would have staunchly opposed a century earlier. One of the most important of these was the Pragmatic Sanction of Bourges of 1438. The papacy was unable to protest when the French clergy, at the urging of the king, abolished papal rights to annates, limited appeals to the papal court, and reduced papal rights to appoint clergy within France without the approval of the local clergy or the Crown. Similar concessions diminished church authority throughout Europe. Perhaps the most momentous was a bull issued in 1478 by Pope Sixtus IV (r. 1471–1484) that allowed Ferdinand and Isabella of Aragon and Castile to institute a church court, the Spanish Inquisition, under their own auspices (see page 387).

With reduced revenues from legal fees, annates, and appointments, the popes of the fifteenth century were forced to derive more and more of their revenue and influence from the Papal States in central Italy. By 1430, the Papal States accounted for about half of the annual income of the papacy. Papal interests increasingly centered on protecting the papacy's influence as a secular ruler of a large territory. Thus, the papacy had to deal with many of the same jurisdictional, diplomatic, and military challenges that faced other medieval governments.

WAR, DISORDER, AND REVOLTS IN WESTERN EUROPE, 1300–1450

 LAWYER who served King Philip IV of France (r. 1285–1314) observed that "everything within the limits of his kingdom belongs to the lord king, especially protection, high justice and dominion."[4] Royal officials in England and France generally believed that "liberties"—that is, individual rights to local jurisdictions—originated with the king. These ideas were the result of several centuries of centralization of political power in royal hands. At almost the same time, however, an English noble challenged royal claims on his lands, saying, "Here, my lords, is my warrant," as he brandished a rusty longsword. "My ancestors came with William the Bastard [that is, with William the Conqueror in 1066] and conquered their lands with the sword, and by the sword I will defend them against anyone who tries to usurp them."[5] The views of the royal lawyer and the feisty earl exemplify the central tension over power in the late Middle Ages. A series of political, dynastic, and military crises in the fourteenth and early fifteenth centuries made clear that many believed it was time to rein in royal claims.

■ England, France, and the Hundred Years' War, 1337–1453

In the twelfth and thirteenth centuries centralization of royal power in England and France had proceeded almost without interruption. In the fourteenth century, matters changed in both countries. Questions of the nature of royal power, common responsibility, and hereditary rights to rule challenged the power of the English and French monarchs.

In England fears arising from the growing power of the English crown and the weakness of a gullible king brought issues to a head during the reign of Edward II (r. 1307–1327). By the early fourteenth century, resident justices of the peace (JPs) were replacing the expensive and inefficient eyre system of traveling justices. In theory, the JPs were royal officials doing the king's bidding.

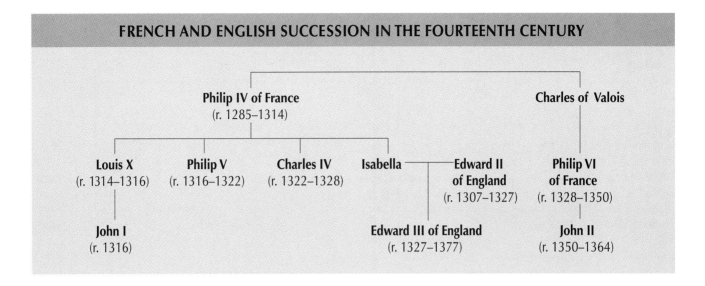

FRENCH AND ENGLISH SUCCESSION IN THE FOURTEENTH CENTURY

In reality, these unpaid local officials were modestly well-to-do gentry who were often clients of local magnates. Justices were known to use their offices to carry out local vendettas and feuds and to protect the interests of the wealthy and powerful.

The barons, the titled lords of England, were interested in controlling more than just local justices. Fearing that Edward II would continue many of the centralizing policies of his father, the barons passed reform ordinances in 1311 limiting the king's right to wage war, leave the realm, grant lands or castles, or appoint chief justices and chancellors without the approval of Parliament, which they dominated. Special taxes or subsidies were to be paid to the public Exchequer rather than into the king's private treasury. Some of these ordinances were later voided, but the tradition of parliamentary consent remained a key principle of English constitutional history. In spite of Parliament's potential power to limit royal acts, kings needed Parliament because it alone had the power to vote new taxes and generally did so when funds were necessary for the defense of the realm—a common occurrence during these centuries. Thus, English kings willingly supported the establishment of a parliamentary tradition since Parliament generally gave them the financial support they needed.

The baronial influence grew because Edward II was a weak and naive king, easily influenced by court favorites. After a humiliating defeat at the hands of the Scots at the Battle of Bannockburn (1314), his position steadily deteriorated until he was deposed in 1327 by a coalition of barons led by his wife, Queen Isabella. After a short regency, their son, Edward III (r. 1327–1377), as-

sumed the throne. He was a cautious king, ever aware of the violence and rebelliousness of the baronage.

A continuing succession crisis during the early fourteenth century made clear the limits of French kingship. In 1328 the direct Capetian line, which had sired the kings of France since the election of Hugh Capet in 987, finally died out. The last Capetians did produce daughters, but by the fourteenth century many argued that according to custom the French crown should pass through the male line only. Thus, the French nobility selected as king Philip of Valois (Philip VI; r. 1328–1350), a cousin of the last king through the male line. He was chosen in preference to the daughters of the last kings and, more significantly, in preference to King Edward III of England, whose mother was the daughter of the late king Philip IV.

Controversy over succession was just one of the disputes between the French and English. An even longer-standing issue was the status of lands within France that belonged to the English kings. In 1340, climaxing a century of tensions over English possessions in France, Edward III of England formally claimed the title "King of France."

The Hundred Years' War was a series of short raids and expeditions punctuated by a few major battles and marked off by truces or ineffective treaties. The relative strengths of the two kingdoms dictated the sporadic nature of the struggle. With a population of about 16 million, France was far richer and more populous than England. On at least one occasion the French managed to field an army of over 50,000; at most the English mustered only 32,000. These armies were easily the largest

1337
(before the Battle of Crécy)

■ English holdings

□ French holdings

— Extent of English holdings
after Treaty of Paris, 1259

1360
(after the Battle of Poitiers)

■ English holdings

□ French holdings

✕ Major battles

ca. 1429
(after the siege of Orléans)

■ English holdings

□ French holdings

□ Burgundian lands allied
with England to 1435

✕ Major battle

1453
(end of war)

■ English holdings

□ French holdings

□ Burgundian lands reconciled
with France after 1435

✕ Last battle

Map 11.1   England and France in the Hundred Years' War
The succession of maps depicts both why hit-and-run tactics worked for the English early in the war and why the English were ultimately unable to defeat the French and take control of all of France.

ever assembled by a medieval European kingdom. In almost every engagement the English were outnumbered. The most successful English strategy was to avoid pitched battles and engage in a series of quick, profitable raids during which they stole what they could, destroyed what they could not steal, and captured enemy knights to hold for ransom.

Initially, the war was characterized by a rapid series of English assaults and victories (see Map 11.1). The few pitched battles, Crécy (1346) and Poitiers (1356), occurred when the English found themselves trapped and unable to avoid the French. In these cases the English gathered their forces in careful defensive positions and took advantage of an individualistic French chivalric ethos according to which, in the words of one knight, "Who does the most is worth the most." The key to the English defensive position was use of longbowmen to attack the French knights as they labored up a hill in a vain attempt to reach the English lines. The longbow was developed in Wales, and the English perfected their use of it in numerous border wars with the Scots. Arrows from the longbow had more penetrating power than a bolt from a crossbow. And as significant, a longbow could be fired much more rapidly.

In the confusion and unrest following the French disaster at Poitiers in 1356, Étienne Marcel, provost (director) of the merchants of Paris, mobilized a protest movement designed to reduce royal and aristocratic power. This revolution seemed too radical to conservative townsmen in the provinces. Marcel's only allies were bands of rebellious countrymen roaming the region around Paris. The rural movement, or *jacquerie*° (the name comes from *jacque*, French for the "jacket" typically worn by peasants), began in response to long-standing economic and political grievances in the countryside that had been worsened by warfare. The rebels and eventually Marcel himself were isolated and then defeated by aristocratic armies.

England was soon rocked by unrest as well. The Rising of 1381 is often called the Peasants' Revolt despite

the fact that townsfolk as well as peasants participated. Already, England seethed with unrest as a result of plague (see page 371) and landlord claims for traditional dues. But the final straw was a poll tax to pay for the war: commoners responded with violent protests. The heart of the uprising was a revolt by rural peasants and artisans in the southeast, primarily in Kent and Essex. Popular armies led by Wat Tyler (d. 1381), who may have had some military experience, converged on London in June 1381. Tyler was murdered during a dramatic meeting with Richard II outside London, and a reaction against the rebels quickly ensued. (See the box "Reading Sources: The Rising of 1381.")

The rest of Richard's reign was anything but tranquil. Recognizing the dangers of noble influence, Richard II tried to insulate himself from the peers of the realm by choosing advisers from the lesser nobility and the middle classes as well as from the peerage. The result was increasing tensions with the peers and charges that Richard's rule was tyrannical. Simmering discontent boiled over, and leaders of the peers captured and forced Richard to abdicate in 1399. Parliament then elected as king Henry IV (r. 1399–1413), the first ruler from the house of Lancaster. Richard himself died in prison under mysterious circumstances in 1400.

Ever mindful of the situation that brought him to power, Henry IV was quite successful, placating both the masses and the magnates. He avoided war taxes and was careful not to alienate the nobles. The effect was that Lancastrian caution brought a truce to the French and English hostilities.

A fateful shift in relations occurred in the early fifteenth century. King Charles VI (r. 1380–1422) of France suffered bouts of insanity throughout his long reign, which made effective French government almost impossible. With the aid of the dukes of Burgundy, the English king Henry V (r. 1413–1422) renewed his family's claim to the French throne. At Agincourt in 1415, the English (led by Henry himself) again enticed a larger French army into attacking a fortified English position, and again a hail of arrows from English longbows shattered the advance. With Burgundian aid, Henry gained control over Normandy, Paris, and much of northern France. By the terms of the Treaty of Troyes (1420), Charles VI's son (the future Charles VII) was declared illegitimate and disinherited; Henry married Catherine, the daughter of Charles VI; and he was declared the legitimate heir to the French throne. A final English victory seemed assured, but both Charles VI and Henry V died in 1422, leaving Henry's infant son, Henry VI (r. 1422–1461), to inherit both thrones.

---

jacquerie (jack-eh-REE)

The Rising of 1381

The author of this chronicle—probably the most complete account of the English peasant revolt of 1381—seems to have been an eyewitness to the dramatic events in London. Like most literate people, the chronicler seems more comfortable with the attitudes and opinions of civil officials and landlords than with the concerns of the "rabble."

Wherefore the commons rose against [the royal] commissioner sent to investigate [rebellious acts in the region] and came before him to tell him that he was a traitor to the king and the kingdom and was maliciously proposing to undo them by the use of false inquests taken before him. Accordingly they made him swear on the Bible that never again would he hold such sessions nor act as a justice in such inquests. They proposed to kill all the lawyers, jurors and royal servants they could find. . . .

[The rebels came to London, where they executed several royal servants. They, and possibly their leader, Wat Tyler, forced the king to agree to allow them to deal "with all the traitors against him."] And they required that henceforth no man should be a serf nor make homage or any type of service to any lord, but should give four pence for an acre of land. They asked also that no one should serve any man except at his own will and by means of a regular covenant. . . .

[In a confused melée during a meeting with King Richard, Tyler was stabbed.] Wat spurred his horse, crying to the commons to avenge him, and the horse carried him some four score [eighty] paces and then he fell to the ground half dead. And when the commons saw him fall, and did not know for certain how it happened, they began to bend their bows and to shoot. Therefore the king himself spurred his horse, and rode out to them, commanding them that they should all come before him at the field of St. John of Clerkenwell [a few hundred yards from where Tyler was wounded].

Afterwards, when the king had reached the open fields, he made the commons array themselves on the west side. . . . [The mayor of London had Wat Tyler] carried out to the middle of Smithfield [a market area on the edge of town]. . . and had him beheaded. . . . And so ended his wretched life. But the mayor had his head set on a pole and carried before him to the king, who still remained on the field. . . . And when the commons saw that their chieftain, Wat Tyler, was dead in such a manner, they fell to the ground there among the corn, like beaten men, imploring the king for mercy for their misdeeds. And the king benevolently granted them mercy.

Source: The Anonimalle Chronicle, in R. B. Dobson, The Peasant's Revolt of 1381 (New York: St. Martin's Press, 1970), pp. 123, 125, 128, 161, 166–167.

The kings' deaths ushered in the final stage of the Hundred Years' War, the French reconquest, from 1422 to 1453. In 1428, military and political power seemed firmly in the hands of the English and the great aristocrats. Yet in a stunning series of events, the French were able to reverse the situation.

In 1429, with the aid of the mysterious Joan of Arc (d. 1431), the French king—Charles VII—was able to raise the English siege of Orléans° and begin the reconquest of the north of France. Joan was the daughter of prosperous peasants from an area of Burgundy that had suffered under the English and their Burgundian allies. Like many late medieval mystics, she reported regular visions of divine revelation. Her "voices" told her to go to the king and assist him in driving out the English. Dressed as a man, she was Charles's most charismatic and feared military leader. With Joan's aid, the king was crowned in the cathedral at Reims, the traditional site of French coronations. Joan was captured during an audacious attack on Paris itself and eventually she fell into

Orléans (or-lay-OHN)

The Battle at Agincourt   The English victory at Agincourt marked the high point of English influence in France. Once again, English archers defeated a larger, mounted force.
(The Granger Collection, New York)

English hands. Because of her "unnatural dress" and her claim to divine guidance, she was condemned and burned as a heretic in 1431. A heretic only to the English and their supporters, Joan almost instantly became a symbol of French resistance. Pope Calixtus III reversed the condemnation in 1456, and in 1920 she was canonized. (See the box "Reading Sources: The Inquisition of Joan of Arc.") The heretic became Saint Joan, patron of France.

Despite Joan's capture, the French advance continued. By 1450 the English had lost all their major centers except Calais°. In 1453 the French armies captured the fortress of Castillon-sur-Dordogne° in what was to be the last battle of the war (see Map 11.1). There was no treaty, only a cessation of hostilities.

Calais (Ca-lay)
Castillon-sur-Dordogne (kas-ti-YON sir dor-DON-ya)

The war touched almost every aspect of life in western Europe: political, religious, economic, and social. It ranged beyond the borders of France as Scotland, Castile, Aragon, and German principalities were at various times drawn into the struggle. French and English support for rival popes prevented early settlement of the Great Schism in the papacy (see pages 358–361). Further, the war caused a general rise in the level of violence in society. As Henry V casually observed, "War without fire is as bland as sausages without mustard."[6] And because of the highly profitable lightning raids, the war was never bland. Soldiers regularly stole or ransomed all the booty they could take. What they could not carry, they burned. During periods of truce many soldiers simply ranged through France pillaging small towns and ravaging the countryside. Others went in search of work as mercenaries especially in Germany, Poland, and Italy. Truces in France did not necessarily mean peace in Europe.

❧ READING SOURCES

The Inquisition of Joan of Arc

An important question at the trial of Joan of Arc was whether her acts had any authoritative value: Did the voices she heard originate with God or the Devil? The judges wanted to demonstrate to their own satisfaction that Joan was one of "the sowers of deceitful inventions" of which the Gospels warned. They fully expected that external signs could reveal hidden truths.

The following memorandum is a summation of the commission's case against the maid.

You said that you wore and still wear man's dress at God's command and to His good pleasure, for you had instruction from God to wear this dress, and so you put on a short tunic, jerkin, and hose with many points. You even wear your hair cut above the ears, without keeping about you anything to denote your sex, save what nature has given you. . . . The clergy declare that you blaspheme against God, despising Him and His sacraments, that you transgress divine law, Holy Scripture and the canons of the Church, that you think evil and err from the faith, that you are full of vain boasting, that you are given to idolatry and worship of yourself and your clothes, according to the customs of the heathen.

You have declared that you know well that God loves certain living persons better than you, and that you learned this by revelation from St. Catherine and St. Margaret; also that those saints speak French, not English, as they are not on the side of the English. And since you knew that your voices were for your king, you began to dislike the Burgundians.

Such matters the clergy pronounce to be a rash and presumptuous assertion, a superstitious divination, a blasphemy uttered against St. Catherine and St. Margaret, and a transgression of the commandment to love our neighbors.

And you have said . . . that you know that all the deeds of which you have been accused in your trial were wrought according to the command of God and that it was impossible for you to do otherwise. . . . Wherefore the clergy declare you to be schismatic, an unbeliever in the unity and authority of the Church, apostate and obstinately erring from the faith. . . . [The inquisitor admonished her,] "You have believed in apparitions lightly, instead of turning to God in devout prayer to grant you certainty; and you have not consulted prelates or learned ecclesiastics to enlighten yourself: although, considering your condition and the simplicity of your knowledge, you ought to have done so."

Source: The Trial of Jeanne d'Arc, trans. W. P. Barrett (New York: Gotham House, 1932), pp. 331–338.

 For additional information on this topic, go to http://college.hmco.com.

■ Italy

Compared with France and England, fourteenth- and fifteenth-century Italy was a land of cities. In northern Europe a town of over 20,000 or 30,000 people was unusual; only Paris and London boasted more than 100,000 people in the fourteenth century. Yet at one time or another in the late Middle Ages, Milan, Venice, Florence, and Naples all had populations near or exceeding 100,000, and countless other Italian towns boasted populations of well over 30,000. Unlike northern European states with their kings or emperors, however, the Italian peninsula lacked a unifying force. The centers of power were in Italy's flourishing cities. Political life revolved around the twin issues of who should dominate city governments and how could cities learn to coexist peacefully.

By the late thirteenth century, political power in most Italian towns was divided among three major groups. First was the old urban nobility that could trace its wealth back to grants of property and rights from kings, emperors, and bishops in the tenth and eleventh centuries. A second was made up of merchant families who had grown wealthy in the twelfth and thirteenth centuries as Italians led the European economic expansion into the Mediterranean. Challenging these entrenched urban groups were modest artisans and merchants who had organized trade, neighborhood, or militia groups and referred to themselves as the *popolo*, that is, "the people." Both within these groups and between them, competition for political power and social influence was fierce. "War and hatred have so multiplied among the Italians," observed one Florentine, "that in every town there is a division and enmity between two parties of citizens." Townsmen gathered themselves together in factions based on wealth, family, profession, neighborhood, and even systems of clientage that reached back into the villages from which many of the townsmen had come.

Riven with factions, townsmen would often turn control of their governments over to a *signor°*, that is, a "lord," or "tyrant," often a local noble with a private army. Once firmly in power, a tyrant often allowed the town's government to continue to function as it had, requiring only that *he* now should control all major political appointments. The process might seem democratic, but it represented a profound shift in power. In 1264, for example, Obizzo d'Este° took control of the town of Ferrara when a carefully managed assembly of the people proclaimed him to be "Governor and Ruler and General and Permanent Lord of the City of Ferrara." The rise of the Este lords seemed peaceful, but the transformation was clearer in Mantua. "[Pinamonte Bonacolsi (d. 1293)] usurped the lordship of his city and expelled his fellow-citizens and occupied their property," according to a chronicler. "And he was feared like the devil."[7] In the case of Milan, the noble Visconti° used support from the Emperor Henry VII (r. 1308–1313) to drive their opponents out of the city. Eventually granted Milan and its territories as a duchy, the Viscontis and later their Sforza successors made marriage alliances with the French crown and created a splendid court culture. In a series of wars between the 1370s and 1450s, the dukes of Milan expanded their political control throughout most of Lombardy, Liguria, and, temporarily, Tuscany. The Visconti maintained control of the city and much of the region of Lombardy until the last scion of the family died in 1447.

The great republics of Venice and Florence escaped domination by signori, but only by undertaking significant constitutional change. In both republics political life had been disrupted by the arrival of immigrants and by the demands of recently enriched merchants and speculators for a voice in government. In 1297, reacting to increased competition for influence, the Venetian government enacted what would come to be known as the Closing of the Grand Council. The act enlarged to about eleven hundred the number of families eligible for public office, but its ultimate effect was to freeze out subsequent arrivals from ever rising to elite status. The Venetian patriciate became a closed urban nobility. Political, factional, and economic tensions were hidden beneath a veneer of serenity as Venetians developed a myth of public-spirited patricians who governed in the interests of all the peoples, leaving others free to enrich themselves in trade and manufacture.

In Florence the arguments over citizenship and the right of civic participation disrupted public life. Violent wealthy families, immigrants, and artisans of modest backgrounds were cut off from civic participation. A series of reforms culminating in the Ordinances of Justice of 1293–1295 restricted political participation in Florence to members in good standing of certain merchant and artisan guilds. Members of violence-prone families were defined as "Magnate" (literally, "the powerful") and disqualified from holding public office. The reforms guaranteed that political power remained concentrated in the hands of the great families, whose wealth was based primarily on banking and mercantile investments. These families used their political influence and economic power to dominate Florentine life.

There were short-lived attempts to reform the system and extend the rights of political participation to include the more modest artisans and laborers. The most dramatic was in 1378 when the Ciompi°, unskilled workers in Florence's woolen industry, led a popular revolution hoping to expand participation in government and limit the authority of the guild masters over semiskilled artisans and day laborers. They created new guilds to represent the laborers who previously had had no voice in government. Barely six weeks after the Ciompi insurrection, however, wealthy conservatives began a reaction suppressing, exiling, or executing the leaders of the movement and eventually suppressing the new guilds. Political and economic power was now even more firmly in the grip of the patricians.

Following a crisis in 1434 brought on by war and high taxes, virtual control of Florentine politics fell into the hands of Cosimo de' Medici, the wealthiest banker in the city. From 1434 to 1494, Cosimo; his son, Piero; his grandson, Lorenzo; and Lorenzo's son dominated the government in Florence. Although the Medicis were

---

signor (sin-YOUR)   **Obizzo d'Este** (oh-BITZ-oh duh-ES-tay)
Visconti (vis-KON-tee)

Ciompi (CHOMP-ee)

The Journey of the Magi   The story of the journey of the Magi to Bethlehem to find the baby Jesus seemed a perfect image of the power and wisdom of rulers. This painting (a detail) of the Magi was commissioned for the private chapel of Cosimo de' Medici, the de facto ruler of Florence.   *(Palazzo Medici Riccardi, Florence/Scala/Art Resource, NY)*

tions among the great cities of Milan, Venice, Florence, Rome, and Naples were stabilized by the Peace of Lodi and the creation of the Italian League in 1454. In response to endemic warfare in Italy and the looming threat of the Ottoman Turks in the eastern Mediterranean (see page 381), the five powers agreed to the creation of spheres of influence that would prevent any one of them from expanding at the expense of the others.

The limits of these territorial states of Italy became clear when King Charles VIII of France invaded Italy in 1494. Ludovico Sforza of Milan enticed the French king to assert his hereditary claim to the kingdom of Naples. The French invasion touched off a devastating series of wars called the Habsburg-Valois Wars. French claims were immediately challenged by the Spanish, who themselves made claims on southern Italy and much of Lombardy. The cost of prolonged warfare kept almost all governments in a state of crisis. Unrest brought on by the invasion even allowed Pope Alexander VI (r. 1492–1503) to attempt to create a state for his son, Cesare Borgia° (1475–1507), in central Italy.

In Florence the wars destroyed the old Medici-dominated regime and brought in a new republican government. Anti-Medici efforts were initially led by the popular Dominican preacher Girolamo Savonarola (1452–1498). In the constitutional debates after 1494, Savonarola argued that true political reform required a sweeping purge of the evils of society. Gangs of youth flocked to his cause, attacking prostitutes and homosexuals. Many of his followers held "bonfires of vanities," burning wigs, silks, and other luxuries. In 1498, when his followers had lost influence in the government, Savonarola himself was arrested, tortured, and executed.

In spite of republican reforms, new fortresses, and a citizen militia, the Florentine government was unable to defend itself from papal and imperial armies. In 1512 the Habsburg emperor restored Medici control of Florence. The Medicis later became dukes and then grand dukes of Tuscany. The grand duchy of Tuscany remained an independent, integrated, and well-governed state until the French Revolution of 1789. Venice also managed to maintain its republican form of government and its territorial state until the French Revolution; but, like the grand dukes of Tuscany, the governors of Venice were no longer able to act independently of the larger European powers.

The Habsburg-Valois Wars continued for over a half-century, ending with the Treaty of Cateau-Cambrésis° in

always careful to pay homage to Florentine republican traditions, their control was virtually as complete as that of the lords of towns such as Ferrara or Milan.

Indeed, by the middle of the fifteenth century, little differentiated the republics—Florence and Venice—from the cities such as Milan or Mantua where lords held sway. Although Florentines maintained that they intervened to protect Florentine and Tuscan "liberty" when the Visconti of Milan threatened Tuscany and central Italy, their interests went beyond simple defense. Rela-

---

Borgia (BOR-zheh)
Cateau-Cambrésis (kah-toe kam-bray-SEE)

1559, which left the Spanish kings in control of Milan, Naples, Sardinia, and Sicily. Thus, war and the political integration of the fifteenth century destroyed the tiny city-republics and snuffed out any illusions among the remaining territorial states that they could act independently of foreign powers.

ECONOMY AND SOCIETY

FTER nearly three centuries of dramatic growth, Europe in 1300 was seriously over-populated, with estimates ranging from about 80 million to as high as 100 million. In some parts of Europe, populations would not again be this dense until the late eighteenth century! Opportunities dwindled because of overpopulation, famine, war, and epidemics. These shocks brought changes in trade and commerce. Lowered population, deflation, and transformed patterns of consumption also affected agriculture, which was still the foundation of the European economy. Recovery from these crises altered the structure and dynamics of families, the organization of work, and the culture in many parts of Europe.

■ The Plague and Demographic Crisis

People in many parts of Europe were living on the edge of disaster in 1300. Given the low level of agricultural technology and the limited amounts of land available for cultivation, it became increasingly difficult for the towns and countryside to feed and support the growing population. The nature of the problem varied from place to place. Evidence points to a crisis of both births (low birthrates) and deaths (from famine and illness).

Growing numbers of people competed for land to farm and for jobs. Farm sizes declined throughout Europe as parents tended to divide their land among their children. Rents for farmland increased as landlords found they could play one land-hungry farmer against another. Competition for jobs kept wages low, and when taxes were added to high rents and low wages, many peasants and artisans found it difficult to marry and raise families. Thus, because of reduced opportunities brought on by overpopulation, poor townsmen and peasants tended to marry late and have small families.

More dramatic than this crisis of births were the deadly famines that occurred in years of bad harvests. The great famine of 1315–1322 marks a turning point in the economic history of Europe. Wet and cold weather repeat-edly ruined crops in much of northern Europe. Food stocks were quickly exhausted, and mass starvation followed. People died so quickly, English chroniclers reported, that survivors could not keep up with the burials. At Ypres, in Flanders, 2,800 people (about 10 percent of the population) died in just six months. And shortages continued. Seven other severe famines were reported in the south of France or Italy during the fourteenth century.

If Europe's problem had merely been one of famine brought on by overpopulation, rapid recovery should have been possible. But because of the return of a deadly epidemic disease, the population did not recover. In 1348 the Black Death, or "the great Mortality" as contemporaries called it, struck Europe. The most likely cause is bubonic plague, which returned to western Europe for the first time in six hundred years. Genoese traders contracted the plague in Caffa on the Black Sea coast. Infected sailors carried the disease south into Egypt and west to Sicily and then on to Genoa and Venice. From there it followed established trade routes first into central Italy and later to the south of France, the Low Countries, England, and finally through the North and Baltic Seas into Germany and the Slavic lands to the east (see Map 11.2).

Mortality rates varied, but generally 60 percent or more of those infected died. In the initial infestation of 1348–1351, from 25 to 35 percent of Europe's population may have died. In some of Europe's larger cities, the proportion may have been as high as 60 percent. In Florence, the population probably declined by almost half, from about 90,000 to 50,000 or even less. (See the box "Reading Sources: The Black Death.") And the nearby town of Siena likely fared even worse, with a total mortality of 55 percent in the town and its suburbs.

Just as areas were rebounding from the initial outbreak, the plague returned again in 1363, and then for three centuries thereafter almost no generation could avoid it. Less is known about the plague in Muslim lands and in the eastern Mediterranean, but the situation seems to have been similar to the European experience. Because the plague tended to carry off the young, the almost generational return of the disease accounts for the depressed population levels found in many parts of Europe until the late fifteenth century and in western Asia until the late seventeenth or eighteenth century.

Lacking an understanding of either contagion or infection, fourteenth-century doctors depended on traditional theories inherited from the Greeks, especially the work of Galen°. In Galenic medicine, good health was a

Galen (GAY-len)

condition that depended on the proper balance of bodily and environmental forces; it could be upset by corrupt air, the movements of planets, and even violent shifts in emotions. Blind to the biological nature of the disease and its spread, Europeans were unable to treat the plague effectively. Yet in the fifteenth and sixteenth centuries, as the rhythms of the plague infestations became clearer, towns and, later, territorial governments perceived the contagious nature of the disease. Officials instituted increasingly effective quarantines and embargoes to restrict the movement of goods and people from areas where the plague was raging. This innovative effort at public health regulation that limited the movement of infected products probably explains the disappearance of plague from western Europe by the early eighteenth century.

Alongside medical theory, however, another class of explanations developed. Taking a lead from miracle stories in which Jesus linked illness and sin, many Christians considered "the great Mortality" a signal of the end times, or at least a sign of the severe judgment of God on a sinful world. Given that view, a traditional, and logical, religious response was to urge various moral reforms or penitential acts—charitable gifts, special prayers, holy processions. (See the feature "Weighing the Evidence: A Painting of the Plague" on pages 390–391.) Many Muslim theologians also concluded that "the plague is part of Allah's punishment." Women were often thought to be a source of moral pollution and hence one of the causes of God's wrath. In Muslim Egypt, women were ordered off the streets; in Christian Europe prostitutes were driven out of towns.

Map 11.2   The Progress of the Black Death   The Black Death did not advance evenly across Europe; rather, as is clear from the dates at which it struck various regions, it followed the main lines of trade and communication.

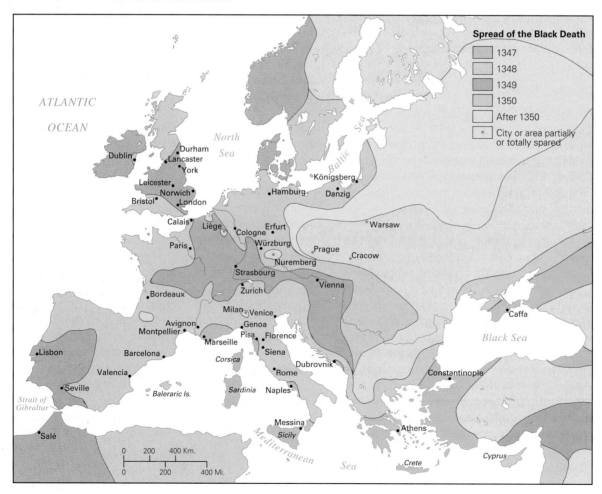

❧ READING SOURCES

The Black Death

The plague of 1348 in Florence dominates the histories of Florence written in the fourteenth century. Marchione di Coppo Stefani (1336–?) describes the impact of "the great Mortality" on the city of Florence itself as well as on the surrounding countryside.

In the year of the Lord 1348 there was a very great pestilence in the city and district of Florence. It was of such a fury and so tempestuous that in houses in which it took hold previously healthy servants who took care of the ill died of the same illness. Almost none of the ill survived past the fourth day. Neither physicians nor medicines were effective. Whether because these illnesses were previously unknown or because physicians had not previously studied them, there seemed to be no cure. There was such a fear that no one seemed to know what to do. When it took hold in a house it often happened that no one remained who had not died. . . . Child abandoned the father, husband the wife, wife the husband, one brother the other, one sister the other. In all the city there was nothing to do but to carry the dead to a burial. . . .

In the said year, when the mortality stopped, women and men in Florence were unmindful of [traditional modesty concerning] their dress. . . . The workers on the land in the countryside wanted rent contracts such that you could say that all they har-

vested would be theirs. And they learned to demand oxen from the landlord but at the landlord's risk [and liability for any harm done to the animal]. And then they helped others for pay by the job or by the day. And they also learned to deny [liability for] loans and [rental] payments. Concerning this serious ordinances were instituted; and [hiring] laborers became much more expensive. You could say that the farms were theirs; and they wanted the oxen, seed, loans quickly and on good terms. It was necessary to put a brake on weddings as well because when they gathered for the betrothal each party brought too many people in order to increase the pomp. And thus the wedding was made up of so many trappings. How many days were necessary and how many women took part in a woman's wedding. And they passed many other ordinances concerning [these issues].

Source: Marchione di Coppo Stefani, *Cronaca fiorentina, Rerum Italicarum Scriptores,* vol. 30, ed. Niccolo Rodolico (Città di Castello, 1927). Translation by Duane Osheim.

A movement of penitents called "flagellants" arose in Hungary and spread quickly into Germany and across France and the Low Countries. In an imitation of Christ's life and sufferings, they sought to atone in their own bodies for the sins of the world. Following an ancient Christian tradition, they ritually beat (flagellated) themselves between the shoulders with metal-tipped whips. Through their processions and sufferings, these pilgrims hoped to bring about a moral and religious transformation of society. The arrival of flagellants was often an occasion for an end of feuds and political violence within a community. In a quest for a purer, truly Christian society, the flagellants brought suspicion on all those who were not Christian or who were otherwise suspect.

Some parts of Europe witnessed murderous attacks on outsiders, especially lepers and Jews, who were suspected of spreading the contagion in an attempt to bring down Latin Christendom. These attacks probably have more to do with tensions and fears already existing in parts of Europe than with the provocations of the flagellants. Like many other anti-Semitic myths, the rumors of wells poisoned by Jews seemed to arise in the south of France and spread in their most virulent forms to German towns along the Rhine. In Strasbourg, attacks on Jews even preceded the arrival of plague. Except in a few districts, officials opposed attacks on Jews, lepers, and heretics. Doctors and churchmen often observed that Jews were unlikely culprits since plague claimed Jewish as well as Christian victims. After a few months of violence, the flagellants and the leaders of the religious riots were recognized as dangerous and driven from towns.

It was a commonplace among contemporary chroniclers that "so many did die that everyone thought it was the end of the world." Yet it was the very young, the elderly, and the poor—those least likely to pay taxes, own shops, or produce new children—who were the most common victims. Even in towns such as Florence, however, where mortality rates were extraordinarily high, recovery was rapid. Government offices were closed at most for only a few weeks; markets reopened as soon as the death rate began to decline. And within two years tax receipts were back at preplague levels. Below the surface, however, plague and population decline fueled the economic and social transformations of the late Middle Ages.

■ Trade and Agriculture

In the aftermath of plague, the economy of Europe changed in a number of profound ways. Disruptions brought on by population decline were accompanied by changes in the basic structure of economic life. In particular, Italy's domination of the European economy was challenged by the growth of trade and manufacturing in many other parts of Europe. Further, Italian bankers came to face competition from equally astute local bankers.

Discussions of the economy must begin with Italy because it was the key point of contact between Europe and the international economy. In 1300 Italian merchants sold woolens produced in Flanders and Italy to Arab traders in North Africa, who sold them along the African coast and as far south as the Niger Delta. The Italians used the gold that they collected in payment to buy spices and raw materials in Byzantium, Egypt, and even China. They resold these highly prized goods in the cities and at regional fairs of northern Europe. Italian traders also sold spices, silks, and other luxuries throughout Europe, from England to Poland.

Because of their expertise in moving bullion and goods and their ready sources of capital, Italian merchants, such as the Ricciardis of Lucca who flourished in England, were ideal bankers and financial advisers to the popes and European rulers, who appreciated sources of ready capital. In time of war, rulers tended to trade the rights to various revenues to Italian bankers, who had cash at hand. Merchants from Cremona, Genoa, Florence, and Siena forged commercial agreements with the kings of France, Aragon, and Castile, and with the papacy.

The most powerful bank in fifteenth-century Europe was the Medici bank of Florence. Founded in 1397 by Giovanni de' Medici° (1360–1429), the bank grew quickly because of its role as papal banker. Medici agents transferred papal revenues from all parts of Europe to Rome and managed papal alum mines, which provided an essential mineral to the growing cloth industry. Cosimo de' Medici° (1389–1464), Giovanni's son and successor, transformed the enterprise into a series of bilateral partnerships with easily controlled junior partners in other parts of Europe. In this way he avoided the problem of supervision and control that plagued other banks, whose partners were equal and free to speculate and invest as they wished.

The dramatic career of the Frenchman Jacques Coeur (1395?–1456) demonstrates that by the mid-fifteenth century, Italian merchants were not the only Europeans who understood international trade. After making a fortune trading in southern France, Coeur managed the French royal mint and became the financial adviser of King Charles VII (r. 1422–1461). He put the French monarchy back on a solid financial footing after the Hundred Years' War, becoming in the process the wealthiest individual in France. Not surprisingly, his wealth and influence earned him jealous enemies, who tried to bring him down with outrageous claims: he was accused of murdering the king's mistress, trading with Muslims, and stealing royal funds. In 1451 his property was confiscated, and he was jailed for a short time. He later led a papal expedition against the Turks in the Aegean, where he died.

By 1500 Italians faced increased competition from local merchants throughout Europe. From as early as the late thirteenth century, trade along the North and Baltic Seas in northern Europe was dominated by the Hanseatic League, an association of over a hundred trading cities centered on the German city of Lübeck. By the late fourteenth and early fifteenth centuries, the Hansa towns controlled grain shipments from eastern Europe to England and Scandinavia. The league's domination waned in the second half of the fifteenth century, however, as Dutch, English, and even south German merchants gained shares of the wool, grain, and fur trades. Towns in the eastern Baltic found that their interests no longer coincided with those of the towns in western Germany that made up the Hanseatic League. Wroclaw° (in

---

Giovanni de' Medici (joe-VAHN-nee day-MAY-di-chi)
Cosimo de' Medici (CAW-see-moe day-MAY-di-chi)
Wroclaw (VROT-swav)

The Feast of Saint John the Baptist   John the Baptist was the patron saint of Florence. Each year a procession in his honor included government officials, the great associations and guilds in the city, and representatives from surrounding villages.   *(Scala/Art Resource, NY)*

modern Poland) signaled the nature of the change when it resigned from the league in 1474 to expand trade connections with the south German towns.

In contrast to the Hanseatic League of towns, merchants in south Germany adopted Italian techniques of trade, manufacture, and finance to expand their influence throughout central Europe. German merchants regularly bought spices in the markets of Venice and distributed them in central and eastern Europe. By the fifteenth century, the townsmen of south Germany also produced linen and cotton cloth, which found ready markets in central and eastern Europe.

The Fugger° family of Augsburg in southern Germany, the most prosperous of the German commercial families, exemplifies the variety of activities undertaken by south German merchants. Hans Fugger (1348–1409) moved to Augsburg from a nearby village in the 1360s and quickly established himself as a weaver and wool merchant. By the 1470s, Hans's grandson, Jacob Fugger (1459–1525), was a dominant figure in the spice trade and also participated in a number of unusually large loans to a succession of German princes. The Fuggers

became leaders in the Tyrolean silver-mining industry, which expanded dramatically in the late fifteenth century. And in the early sixteenth century, they handled all transfers of money from Germany to the papacy. Jacob Fugger's wealth increased fourfold between 1470 and 1500. The Fuggers were indispensable allies of the German emperors. Jacob himself ensured the election of Charles V as Holy Roman emperor in 1519, making a series of loans that allowed Charles to buy the influence that he needed to win election.

As wealthy as the great merchants were, in most parts of Europe prosperity was still tied to agriculture and the production of food grains. In northern and western Europe, foodstuffs were produced on the manorial estates of great churchmen and nobles. These estates were worked by a combination of farmers paying rents, serfs who owed a variety of labor services, and day laborers who were hired during planting and harvesting. In the face of a decimated population, landlords and employers found themselves competing for the reduced number of laborers who had survived the plague. In 1351 the English crown issued the Statute of Laborers, which pegged wages and the prices of commodities at pre-plague levels. According to the statute, regulation was necessary because laborers "withdrew themselves from

---

Fugger (FOO-ger)

serving great men and others unless they have living [in food] and wages double or treble of what they were [before the plague]." This statute and similar ones passed in other parts of Europe were dead letters. So long as population levels remained low, landowners were unable to keep wages low and rents high.

Cloth manufacture, not agriculture, was the part of the European economy that changed most dramatically in the late Middle Ages. First in Flanders, then later in England, Germany, and the rest of Europe, production shifted from urban workshops to the countryside. Industries in rural areas tended to be free of controls on quality or techniques. Rural production, whether in Flanders, England, or Lombardy, became the most dynamic part of the industry.

Rural cloth production, especially in southwest Germany and parts of England, was organized through the putting-out system. Merchants who owned the raw wool contracted with various artisans in the city, suburbs, or countryside—wherever the work could be done most cheaply—to process the wool into cloth. Rural manufacture was least expensive because it could be done as occasional or part-time labor by farmers, their wives, or children during slack times of the day or season. Because production was likely to be finished in the countryside (beyond guild supervision), the merchant was free to move the cloth to wherever it could most easily and profitably be sold; guild masters had no control over price or quality.

Two other developments also changed the woolen trade of the fifteenth century: the rise of Spain as an exporter of unprocessed wool and the emergence of England, long recognized as a source of prime wool, as a significant producer of finished cloth. Spain was an ideal region for the pasturing of livestock. By the fifteenth century, highly prized Spanish wool from merino sheep was regularly exported to Italy, Flanders, and England. By 1500 over 3 million sheep grazed in Castile alone, and revenues from duties on wool formed the backbone of royal finance.

In England, in contrast, economic transformation was tied to cloth production. During the fifteenth century England reduced its export of its high-quality raw wool and began instead to export its own finished cloth. In 1350 the English exported just over 5,000 bolts of cloth. By the 1470s exports had risen to 63,000 bolts, and they doubled again by the 1520s. The growth of cloth exports contributed enormously to the expansion of London. During the fourteenth and fifteenth centuries, English commerce became increasingly controlled by London merchant-adventurers. Soon after 1500, over 80 percent of the cloth for export passed through the hands of the Londoners. This development, coupled with the rise of London as a center of administration and consumption, laid the foundation for the economic and demographic growth that would make London the largest and most prosperous city in western Europe by the eighteenth century.

All these patterns of economic change in the fifteenth century challenged customs and institutions by admitting new entrepreneurs into the marketplace. But Europe was still a conservative society in which social and political influence was more prized than economic wealth. Patricians in many European towns acted to dampen competition and preserve traditional values. Great banking families such as the Medicis of Florence tended to avoid competition and concentrations of capital. They did not try to drive their competitors out of business because the leaders of rival banks were their political and social peers. In northern Europe, governments in towns such as Leiden restricted the concentration of resources in the hands of the town's leading cloth merchants. Their aim was to ensure full employment for the town's laborers, political power for the guild masters, and social stability in the town.

Full employment was for men only, however. Opportunities for women declined significantly in the fifteenth century. Although men had controlled the guilds and most crafts in the thirteenth and early fourteenth centuries, women in England and many other parts of northern Europe had been actively involved in the local economy. Unlike southern Europe, where women had no public roles, some northern towns apparently allowed women's guilds to protect their members' activities as artisans and even peddlers. Because they often worked before marriage, townswomen in northern Europe tended to marry at a later age than did women in Italy. Many women earned their own marriage dowries. Since they had their own sources of income and often managed the shop of a deceased husband, women could be surprisingly independent. They were consequently under less pressure to remarry at the death of a spouse. Although their economic circumstances varied considerably, up to a quarter of the households in northern towns—for example, Bern or Zurich—were headed by women, almost all independent widows.

The fifteenth century brought new restrictions into women's lives. In England brewing ale had been a highly profitable part-time activity that women often combined with the running of a household. Ale was usually produced in small batches for household use and whatever went unconsumed would be sold. The introduction

Women at Work   Although guild records tended to ignore the contributions of women, many women worked in their husband's shop. In this miniature, a woman is selling jewelry. Widows often managed the shops they inherited.   *(Bibliothèque Nationale de France)*

of beer changed matters. Because hops were added during brewing as a preservative, beer was easier to produce, store, and transport in large batches. Beer brewing became a lucrative full-time trade, reducing the demand for the alewife's product and providing work for men as brewers. At the same time the rights of women to work in urban crafts and industries were reduced. Wealthy fathers became less inclined to allow wives and daughters to work outside the home. Guilds banned the use of female laborers in many trades and severely limited the rights of widows to supervise their spouses' shops. For reasons that are not entirely clear, journeymen—employees of guild masters who themselves hoped to become masters—objected to working alongside women. Their complaints may have come from workers who realized that their status as employees was permanent instead of a temporary stage before promotion to master. By the early sixteenth century, journeymen in Germany

considered it "dishonorable" for a woman, even the master's wife or daughter, to work in a shop.

Despite the narrowing of economic opportunities for women, the overall economic prospects of peasants and laborers improved. Lowered rents and increased wages in the wake of plague meant a higher standard of living for small farmers and laborers. Before the plague struck in 1348, most poor Europeans had subsisted on bread or grain-based gruel, consuming meat, fish, and cheese only a few times a week. A well-off peasant in England had lived on a daily ration of about two pounds of bread and a cup or two of oatmeal porridge washed down with three or four pints of ale. Poorer peasants generally drank water except on very special occasions. After the plague, laborers were more prosperous. Adults in parts of Germany may have consumed nearly a liter of wine and a third of a pound of meat along with a pound or more of bread each day. Elsewhere people could substitute an equivalent portion of beer, ale, or cider for the wine. Hard times for landlords were good times for peasants and day laborers.

Landlords in England responded to the shortage of labor by converting their lands to grazing in order to produce wool for the growing textile market. In parts of Italy, landlords invested in canals, irrigation, and new crops in order to increase profits. In eastern Germany and Poland, landlords were able to take advantage of political and social unrest to force tenants into semi-free servile status. This so-called second serfdom created an impoverished work force whose primary economic activity was in the lord's fields, establishing commercial grain farming. Increasingly in the second half of the century, grains cultivated in Poland and Prussia found their way to markets in England and the Low Countries. Europe east of the Elbe River became a major producer of grain, but at a heavy social cost.

The loss of perhaps a third of the urban population to the plague had serious consequences in the towns of Europe. Because of lower birthrates and higher death rates, late medieval towns needed a constant influx of immigrants in order to expand or even to maintain their populations. These immigrants did not find life in the cities to be easy, however. Citizenship in most towns was restricted to masters in the most important guilds, and local governments were in their hands, if not under their thumbs. In many towns, citizens constructed a system of taxation that worked to their own economic advantage and fell heavily on artisans and peasants living in territories controlled by the town. Unskilled laborers and members of craft guilds depended for their economic well-being on personal relationships with powerful citizens who controlled the government and the markets. Peace and order in towns and in the countryside required a delicate balance of the interests of the well-to-do and the more humble. When that balance was shattered by war, plague, and economic depression, the result was often a popular revolt, such as the jacquerie of 1356 in France, the Ciompi Revolution of 1378 in Florence, and the Rising of 1381 in England.

THE CONSOLIDATION OF THE LATE MEDIEVAL GOVERNMENTS, 1450–1500

 Y 1500 it seemed that the French royal lawyer's claim that all within the kingdom belonged to the king was finally accepted. With the exception of Italy and Germany, strong central governments recovered from the crises of war and civil unrest that

wracked the fourteenth and fifteenth centuries. The Hundred Years' War and the resulting disorganization in France and England seemed to strike at the heart of the monarchies. But through the foundation of standing armies and the careful consolidation of power in the royal court, both countries seemed stronger and more able to defend themselves in the second half of the century. And as the Italians learned in the wars following the French invasion of 1494, small regional powers were no match for the mighty monarchies.

■ France, England, and Scandinavia

In France recovery from a century of war was based on a consolidation of the monarchy's power. A key to French military successes had been the creation of a paid professional army, which replaced the feudal host and mercenary companies of the fourteenth century. Charles VII created Europe's first standing army, a cavalry of about eight thousand nobles under the direct control of royal commanders. Charles also expanded his judicial claims. He and his son, Louis XI (r. 1461–1483), created new provincial *parlements,* or law courts, at Toulouse°, Grenoble°, Bordeaux, and Dijon°. They also required that local laws and customs be registered and approved by the parlements.

A second key to maintaining royal influence was the rise of the French court as a political and financial center. Through careful appointments and judicious offers of annuities and honors, Charles VII and Louis XI drew the nobility to the royal court and made the nobles dependent on it. "The court," complained a frustrated noble, "is an assembly of people who, under the pretense of acting for the good of all, come together to diddle each other; for there's scarcely anyone who isn't engaged in buying and selling and exchanging . . . and sometimes for their money we sell them our . . . humanity."[8] One of Louis XI's advisers noted that Charles VII never had revenues greater than 18,000 francs in a single year but that Louis collected 4.7 million. By 1500 France had fully recovered from the crisis of war and was once again a strong and influential state.

The fate of the English monarchy was quite different. Henry VI (r. 1422–1461) turned out to be weak-willed, immature, and prone to bouts of insanity. The infirmity of Henry VI and the loss of virtually all French territories in 1453 led to factional battles known as the Wars of the Roses—the red rose symbolized Henry's house of Lancaster, the white the rival house of York.

Toulouse (too-LOOZ) **Grenoble** (greh-NO-bul)
Dijon (dee-ZHON)

Edward of York eventually deposed Henry and claimed the crown for himself as Edward IV (r. 1461–1483). He faced little opposition because few alternatives existed. English public life was again thrown into confusion, however, at the death of Edward IV. The late king's brother, Richard, duke of Gloucester, claimed the protectorship over the 13-year-old king, Edward V (r. April–June 1483), and his younger brother. He seized the boys, who were placed in the Tower of London and never seen again. Richard proclaimed himself king and was crowned Richard III (r. 1483–1485). He withstood early challenges to his authority but in 1485 was killed in the Battle of Bosworth Fields, near Coventry, by Henry Tudor, a leader of the Lancastrian faction. Henry married Elizabeth, the surviving child of Edward IV. Symbolically at least, the struggle between the rival claimants to the Crown appeared over.

Like his predecessor Edward IV, Henry VII (r. 1485–1509) recognized the importance of avoiding war and taxation. Like the French kings, he created a patronage network of local officials to secure allies for his dynasty. Royal power, however, was not based on a transformation of the institutions of government. Following Edward IV's example, Henry VII controlled local affairs through the traditional system of royal patronage. He also imitated Edward in emphasizing the dignity of the royal office. Though careful with his funds, he was willing to buy jewels and clothing if they added to the brilliance of his court. As one courtier summed up his reign, "His hospitality was splendidly generous. . . . He knew well how to maintain his majesty and all which pertains to kingship." Henry solidified ties with Scotland and Spain by marrying his daughter, Margaret Tudor, to James IV of Scotland and his sons, Arthur and (after Arthur's death) Henry, to Catherine of Aragon, daughter of the Spanish rulers Ferdinand and Isabella.

The English monarchy of the late fifteenth century departed little from previous governments. The success of Henry VII was based on several factors: the absence of powerful opponents; lowered taxation thanks to twenty-five years of peace; and the desire, shared by ruler and ruled alike, for an orderly realm built on the assured succession of a single dynasty.

In the fourteenth and fifteenth centuries, the Scandinavian kingdoms of Denmark, Sweden, and Norway lay open to economic and political influences from Germany. German merchants traded throughout the area and completely controlled access to the important port of Bergen in Norway. German nobles sought to influence northern political life, especially in Denmark. The Scandinavian aristocracy, however, especially in Denmark,

remained wary of German interests. Alert to outside pressures, Scandinavian elites tended to marry among themselves and forge alliances against the Germans.

Public authority varied greatly across Scandinavia. In Norway, Denmark, and Sweden, the power of the king was always mediated by the influence of the council, made up of the country's leading landowners. Power was based on ownership or control of lands and rents. All the Scandinavian countries were home to a significant class of free peasants, and they were traditionally represented in the Riksdag in Sweden and the Storting in Norway, popular assemblies that had the right to elect kings, authorize taxes, and make laws. Scandinavians spoke similar Germanic languages and were linked by close social and economic ties. Thus, it is not surprising that the crowns of the three kingdoms were joined during periods of crisis. In 1397 the dowager Queen Margaret of Denmark was able to unite the Scandinavian crowns by the Union of Kalmar, which would nominally endure until 1523.

■ Eastern Europe and Russia

Two phenomena had an especially profound effect on the governments of eastern Europe. One was the emergence of a newly important ruling dynasty. The other was the decline of Mongol, or Tartar, influence in the region. Since the thirteenth century, much of eastern Europe had been forced to acknowledge Tartar dominion and pay annual tribute. Now, the Tartar subjugation was challenged and finally ended.

As in much of Europe, political power was segmented and based on personal relationships between family members, communities, clients, and friends. Life in the east was further complicated by the mix of languages, cultures, and religions. In the fourteenth century Ashkenazi Jews migrating from Germany were added to the mix of Catholic and Orthodox Christian and Muslim communities. Like the other groups, the Ashkenazi in Poland, Lithuania, and certain Russian lands lived under their own leaders and followed their own laws.

This mix of cultures and religions played a role in the growth of new states. Under the pretext of converting their pagan neighbors to Christianity, the mostly German Teutonic knights sought to expand eastward against the kingdom of Poland and the Lithuanian state. They were thwarted, however, by a profound dynastic shift. In 1386 Duke Jagiello (r. 1377–1434) of Lithuania converted to Catholic Christianity and married Hedwig, the daughter and heir of King Louis of Poland (r. 1370–1382). The resulting dynastic union created a state with a population of perhaps 6 million that reached from the Baltic nearly to the Black Sea. Polish-Lithuanian power slowed and finally halted the German advance to the east. Most serious for the knights was their defeat in 1410 at Tannenberg in Prussia by a Polish-Lithuanian army led by Jagiello's cousin, Prince Vytautus of Lithuania. The Polish-Lithuanian union was only dynastic. The descendents of Jagiello, called Jagiellonians, had no hereditary right to rule in Poland, and the Lithuanians opposed any Polish administrative influence in their lands. Yet because of Jagiellonian power, the Poles continued to select them as kings. At various times, Jagiellonians also sat on the thrones of Bohemia and Hungary.

The fourteenth and fifteenth centuries represented a high point of Polish culture and influence. Polish nobles managed to win a number of important concessions, the most significant being freedom from arbitrary arrest and confinement. This civil right was secured in Poland well before the more famous English right of habeas corpus. It was during this period, and under the influence of the Polish kings, that Cracow emerged as the economic and cultural center of Poland. Cracow University was founded in 1364 in response to the foundation of Prague University by Emperor Charles IV in 1348. After the dynastic union of Poland and Lithuania, Polish language and culture increasingly influenced the Lithuanian nobility.

Lithuanian expansion was in part the result of a decline in Tartar power. The rise of Moscow, however, was even more directly related to Tartar decline. Since the Mongol invasions in the thirteenth century, various Russian towns and principalities had been part of a Tartar sphere of influence. This primarily meant payment of an annual tribute.

A key to the emergence of Moscow occurred when Ivan I (r. 1332–1341), Prince of Moscow, was named

Moscow The city's newly constructed walls allowed Muscovites to defeat the invading Lithuanian army in 1368, which was a key event in the growth of Muscovite power. *(Novosti)*

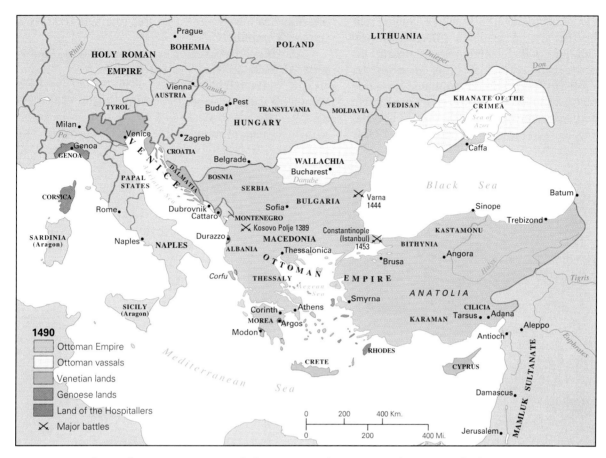

Map 11.3 Turkey and Eastern Europe With the conquest of Constantinople, Syria, and Palestine, the Ottoman Turks controlled the eastern Mediterranean and dominated Europe below the Danube River. The Holy Roman emperors, rulers of Italy, and kings of Spain had to be concerned about potential invasions by land or by sea.

Grand Prince and collector of tribute from the other Russian princes. Not for nothing was he called "the Moneybag." It was during this same period that the head of the Russian Orthodox Church was persuaded to make his home in Moscow. And in 1367, the princes began to rebuild the Kremlin walls in stone.

The decisive change for Moscow, however, was the reign of Ivan III (r. 1462–1505). By 1478, Ivan III, called "the Great," had seized the famed trading center of Novgorod. Two years later he was powerful enough to renounce Mongol overlordship and refuse further payments of tribute. And after marriage to an émigré Byzantine princess living in Rome, Ivan began to call himself "Tsar" (Russian for "Caesar"), implying that in the wake of the Muslim conquest of Constantinople, Moscow had become the new Rome.

■ The Ottoman Empire

The eastern Mediterranean area was a politically tumultuous area in the fourteenth century when the Ottoman Turks were first invited into the Balkans by the hard-pressed Byzantine emperor. Early in the fifteenth century, the Turks were only one, and perhaps not even the greatest, of the Balkan threats to the Byzantine Empire and the other Balkan states (see Map 11.3). Hungarians, Venetians, and Germans also competed for influence in this volatile area. Individuals and groups added to the turmoil by expediently switching their political allegiances and even their religions. In the 1420s, for example, as the Turks and the Hungarians fought for influence in Serbia, the Serbian king moved easily from alliance with one to alliance with the other. Elites often retained their political and economic influence by changing religion. The Christian aristocracy of late-fifteenth-century Bosnia, for example, was welcomed into Islam and instantly created a cohesive elite fighting force for the Turks. Conversely, as Turkish power in Albania grew, one noble, George Castriota (d. 1467), known by his Turkish name Skanderbeg, reconverted to Christianity and became a leading figure in the resistance to the Turks. Only after his death were the Turks able to integrate Albania into their empire.

An Ottoman victory over a Christian crusading army at Varna on the Black Sea coast in 1444 changed the dynamics and virtually sealed the fate of Constantinople. It was only a matter of time before the Turks took the city. When Mehmed II finally turned his attention to Constantinople in 1453, the siege of the city

The Siege of Constantinople The siege of Constantinople by the Turks required the attackers to isolate the city both by sea and by land. This miniature from the fifteenth century shows the Turkish camps, as well as the movements of Turkish boats, completing the isolation of the city. *(Bibliothèque Nationale de France)*

lasted only fifty-three days. Turkish artillery breached the walls before a Venetian navy or a Hungarian army could come to the city's defense. The destruction of the last vestiges of the Roman imperial tradition that reached back to the emperor Augustus sent shock waves through Christian Europe and brought forth calls for new crusades to liberate the East from the evils of Islam. It also stirred anti-Christian feelings among the Turks. The leader of the Ottoman army, Sultan Mehmed° II the Conqueror (r. 1451–1481), was acclaimed the greatest of all *ghazi*—that is, a crusading warrior who was, according to a Turkish poet, "the instrument of Allah, a servant of God, who purifies the earth from the filth of polytheism [i.e., the Christian Trinity]." The rise of the Ottoman Turks transformed eastern Europe and led to a profound clash between Christian and Muslim civilizations.

After the fall of Constantinople, the Turks worked to consolidate their new conquests. Through alliance and conquest, Ottoman hegemony extended through Syria and Palestine and by 1517 to Egypt. Even the Muslim powers of North Africa were nominally under Turkish control. To the west and north of Constantinople, the Ottoman advance was initially thwarted by Matthias Corvinus (r. 1458–1490), Hungary's greatest late medieval king. Matthias reduced the power of the Hungarian nobility, increased state revenues, and built a standing army to oppose the Ottomans. With his death, however, the Hungarian monarchy withered, and the Ottomans resumed their advance. In short order, they dominated Croatia, Bosnia, Dalmatia, Albania, eastern Hungary, Moldavia, Bulgaria, and Greece. Turkish strength was based on a number of factors. The first was the loyalty and efficiency of the sultan's crack troops, the Janissaries. These troops were young boys forcibly taken from the subject Christian populations, trained in Turkish language and customs, and converted to Islam. Although they functioned as special protectors of the Christian community from which they were drawn, they were separated from it by their new faith. Because the Turkish population viewed them as outsiders, they were particularly loyal to the sultan.

The situation of the Janissaries underlines a secondary explanation for Ottoman strength: the unusually tolerant attitudes of Mehmed, who saw himself not only as the greatest of the ghazi but also as emperor, heir to Byzantine and ancient imperial traditions. Immediately after the conquest of Constantinople, he repopulated the city with Greeks, Armenians, Jews, and Muslims.

Mehmed especially welcomed Sephardic Jews from Spain and Portugal to parts of his empire. Religious groups lived in separate districts centered on a church or synagogue, and each religious community retained the right to select its own leaders. (See the box "Global Encounters: A Disputation.") Mehmed made Constantinople the capital of the new Ottoman Empire. And by building mosques, hospitals, hostels, and bridges, he breathed new life into the city, which he referred to as Istanbul—that is, "the city." In the fifty years following the conquest, the population of the city grew an extraordinary 500 percent, from about 40,000 to over 200,000, making it the largest city in Europe, as it had been in Late Antiquity.

At a time when Christian Europe seemed less and less willing to tolerate non-Christian minorities, the Ottoman Empire's liberal attitude toward outsiders seemed striking. By Muslim law, Christians and Jews were supposed to be tolerated, and as long as they paid a special poll tax and accepted some Ottoman supervision, they were. Christian and Jewish leaders supervised the internal affairs of their respective communities. Muslims and non-Muslims belonged to the same trade associations and traveled throughout the empire. Mehmed had no qualms about making trade agreements with the Italian powers in an attempt to consolidate his power. And in Serbia, Bulgaria, Macedonia, and Albania, he left in place previous social and political institutions, requiring only loyalty to his new empire.

Mehmed had to tread carefully, though, because the Turks had a number of powerful enemies. Serious problems, for example, surfaced during the reign of Mehmed's son, Bayazid° (r. 1481–1512). Following Turkish tradition, Mehmed had not chosen a successor but let his sons fight for control. Normally, the successful claimant achieved the throne by doing away with his closest relatives. Bayazid's brother, Jem, however, fled into the protective custody of Christian powers, where he spent the rest of his life. In times of crisis, kings and popes would threaten to foment rebellion in Ottoman lands by releasing him. Bayazid also had to worry about the Mamluk Turks, who controlled Egypt and Syria, and the new Safavid dynasty in Persia. Although both were Muslim, they were willing to join with various Christian states to reduce the power of the Ottomans. Only in the second decade of the sixteenth century, after Bayazid's son, Selim (r. 1512–1520), had defeated the Persians and the Mamluks, were the Ottomans finally safe from attack from the east or south.

Mehmed (MEH-met)

Bayazid (bay-a-ZEED)

⊕ G L O B A L   E N C O U N T E R S

A Disputation

Konstantin Mihailovic, a Serb by birth, was captured by the Turks during the conquest of Constantinople in 1453. He later served with the Turks until he returned to the Christian forces in 1463. His description of a typical Turkish disputation, or debate, taking place in the presence of the sultan or other dignitary is an interesting example of how the Muslim, Jewish, and Christian peoples of the Balkans tried to understand one another.

The masters and scribes have among themselves this custom: they arrange their deliberations before the highest lord after the emperor. . . . And then they begin to argue one against the other, speaking mostly about the prophets. Some [of these Turkish scribes] recognize Our Lord Jesus Christ as a prophet, and others as an archprophet, alongside God the Creator of Heaven and earth. And also the Lord, from the time when the Mohammedan faith began, created eight hundred camels, like invisible spirits, which go around every night and gather evil *Busromane* [i.e., the Muslim, or the Chosen People of God] from our [Muslim] graves and carry them to *kaur* graves [the Kaury are "the Confused People," i.e., the Christians]; and then gather good kaury and carry them to our graves. And now the good kaury will stand with our Busroman council and the evil Busromane will stand with the kaur council on Judgment Day before God. For [a pious one] says . . . , "The Christians have a faith but have no works." Therefore Mohammed will lead the Busromane to Paradise and Jesus will order the Christians to hell. Moses will sorrow for the Jews that they have not been obedient to him. . . . He [one of the scribes] spoke in this way: "Elias and Enoch are both in body and soul in paradise; but before Judgment Day they must die. But Jesus both in body and in soul is in heaven. He is the only one who will not die a death but will be alive forever and ever. Mohammed both in body and soul was in heaven, but remained with us on earth." And then the masters began to dispute, one in one way and one in another, and there were many words among them. And having raised a cry one against another, they began to throw books at one another. [Then the official in charge of the disputation] . . . told them to cease this disputation and he ordered that food be brought them according to their custom and they gave them water to drink, since they do not drink wine. And then, having eaten their fill, they gave thanks to God, praying for the souls of the living and the dead and for those who fight against the kaury or Christians.

Source: Konstantin Mihailovic, *Memoirs of a Janissary*, translated by Benjamin Stolz; commentary and notes by Svat Soucek (Ann Arbor, Mich.: Joint Committee on Eastern Europe, American Council of Learned Societies; and the Department of Slavic Languages and Literatures, University of Michigan, 1975), pp. 25–27.

■ The Union of Crowns in Spain

While expanding across the Mediterranean, the Turks came in contact with the other new state of the fifteenth century, the newly unified kingdom of Spain. As in Poland-Lithuania, the Spanish monarchy was only a dynastic union. In 1469 Ferdinand, heir to the kingdom of Aragon and Catalonia, married Isabella, daughter of the king of Castile. Five years later Isabella became queen of Castile, and in 1479 Ferdinand took control of the kingdom of Aragon. This union of crowns eventually would lead to the creation of a united Spain, but true integration was still a distant dream in 1469.

The permanence of the union was remarkable because the two kingdoms were so different. Castile was a much larger and more populous state. It had taken the lead in the Reconquista, the fight begun in the eleventh century to reclaim Iberia from Muslim rule. As a result, economic power within Castile was divided among those groups most responsible for the Reconquista: military orders and nobles. The military orders of Calatrava, Santiago, and Alcantara were militias formed by men who had taken a religious vow similar to that taken by a monk, with an added commitment to fight against the enemies of Christianity. In the course of the Reconquista, the military orders assumed control of vast districts. Lay nobles who aided in the Reconquista also held large tracts of land, and proudly guarded their independence.

Castile's power stemmed from its agrarian wealth. During the Reconquista, Castilians took control of large regions and turned them into ranges for grazing merino sheep, producers of the prized merino wool exported to the markets of Flanders and Italy. To maximize the profits from wool production, the kings authorized the creation of the Mesta, a brotherhood of sheep producers. The pastoral economy grew to the point that by the early sixteenth century Castilians owned over 3 million sheep. Farmers who lived along the routes by which the vast flocks moved from mountains to the plains often lost their crops to the hungry animals. The agricultural economy was virtually extinguished in some areas.

Economic power in Castile lay with the nobility, but political power rested with the monarch. Because the nobility was largely exempt from taxation, nobles ignored the *cortes*°, the popular assembly, which could do little more than approve royal demands. The towns of Castile were important only as fortresses and staging points for militias rather than as centers of trade and commerce. No force was capable of opposing the will of the monarch. As John II of Castile (r. 1406–1454) explained

> All my vassals, subjects, and people, whatever their estate, . . . are, according to all divine, human, . . . and even natural law, compelled and bound . . . to my word and deed. . . . The king holds this position not from men but from God, whose place he holds in temporal matters.[9]

The kingdom of Aragon was dramatically different. The center of the kingdom was Barcelona, an important trading center in the Mediterranean. In the fourteenth and fifteenth centuries the kings of Aragon concentrated their efforts on expanding their influence in the Mediterranean, especially south of France and Italy. By the middle of the fifteenth century the Aragonese empire included the kingdom of Naples, Sicily, the Balearic° Islands, and Sardinia.

The power of the Aragonese king, in sharp contrast to the Castilian monarchy, was limited because the Crown was not unified. The ruler was king in Aragon and Navarre but only count in Catalonia. Aragon, Catalonia, and Valencia each maintained its own cortes. In each area the traditional nobility and the towns had a great deal more influence than did their counterparts in Castile. The power of the cortes is clear in the coronation oath taken by the Aragonese nobility: "We who are as good as you and together are more powerful than you, make you our king and lord, provided that you observe our laws and liberties, and if not, not."[10] The distinction with Castile could not be stronger.

Initially the union of the crowns of Aragon and Castile did little to unify the two monarchies. Nobles fought over disputed boundaries, and Castilian nobles felt exploited by Aragonese merchants. Trade duties and internal boundaries continued to be disputed. The two realms even lacked a treaty to allow for the extradition of criminals from one kingdom to the other. Castilians never accepted Ferdinand as more than their queen's consort. After the death of Isabella in 1504, he ruled in Castile only as regent for his infant grandson, Charles I (r. 1516–1556). "Spain" would not emerge in an institutional sense until the late sixteenth century.

Nonetheless, the reign of Isabella and Ferdinand marked a profound change in politics and society in the Iberian kingdoms. The monarchs visited all parts of their realm, reorganized municipal governments, took control of the powerful military orders, strengthened the power of royal law courts, and extended the international influence of the monarchies. Many of their actions were designed to advance the interests of Aragon in the Mediterranean. Ferdinand and Isabella married their daughter, Joanna, to Philip of Habsburg in 1496 to draw the Holy Roman Empire into the Italian wars brought on by the French invasion (see page 370). The marriage of their daughter, Catherine of Aragon, to Prince Arthur of England in 1501 was designed to obtain yet another ally against the French. Those two marriages would have momentous consequences for European history in the sixteenth century.

The reign of Ferdinand and Isabella is especially memorable because of the events of 1492. In January of that year, a crusading army conquered Granada, the last Muslim stronghold in Iberia. In March, Ferdinand and Isabella ordered the Jews of Castile and Aragon to convert or leave the kingdom within four months. In April, Isabella issued her commission authorizing Christopher Columbus "to discover and acquire islands and mainland in the Ocean Sea" (see pages 440–441).

---

cortes (cor-TEZ)   **Balearic** (ba-LEER-ik)

Ferdinand and Isabella Interrogating a Jew Jews in Spain and many other parts of Europe were considered to be under the specific jurisdiction of local rulers. Jews and their converso relatives turned to the king and queen in 1492 when Jews faced the order to convert or leave the kingdom.

(Museo de Zaragoza)

The conquest of Granada and the expulsion of the Jews represented a radical shift in the Spanish mentality. Until the beginning of the fifteenth century, Spain maintained a level of religious tolerance unusual in Christen-dom. In the fourteenth century, perhaps 2 percent of the population of Iberia was Jewish, and the Muslim population may have been as high as 50 percent. The various groups were inextricably mixed. The statutes of the Jewish community in Barcelona were written in Catalan, a Spanish dialect, rather than in Hebrew. *Maranos,* Jewish converts to Christianity, and *moriscos*, Muslim converts, mixed continuously with Christians and with members of their former religions. It was difficult at times to know which religion these converts, or *conversos,* actually practiced. One surprised northern visitor to Spain remarked that one noble's circle was filled with "Christians, Moors, and Jews and he lets them live in peace in their faith."

This tolerant mingling of Christians, Muslims, and Jews had periodically occasioned violence. All three communities, in fact, preferred clear boundaries between the groups. In 1391, however, a series of violent attacks had long-lasting and unfortunate effects on Iberian society. An attack on the Jews of Seville led to murders, forced conversions, and suppression of synagogues throughout Spain. In the wake of the assault, large portions of the urban Jewish population either converted to Christianity or moved into villages away from the large commercial cities. The Jewish population in Castile may have declined by a fourth. Although the anti-Jewish feelings were expressed in religious terms, the underlying cause was anger over the economic prominence of some Jewish or *converso* (recently converted Jewish-Christian) families. After 1391 anti-Jewish feeling increasingly became racial. As one rebel said, "The converso remains a Jew and therefore should be barred from public office."[11]

Hostility and suspicion toward Jews grew throughout the fifteenth century until Ferdinand and Isabella concluded that the only safe course was to order all Jews to accept baptism. Jews who would not convert would have to leave the kingdom within four months. The order was signed on March 31, 1492, and published in late April after an unsuccessful attempt by converso and Jewish leaders to dissuade the monarchs from implementing it.

Many Jews could not dispose of their possessions in the four months allowed and so chose to convert and remain. But it is estimated that about ten thousand Jews left Aragon and that even more left Castile. Many moved to Portugal and then to North Africa. Some went east to Istanbul or north to the Low Countries. A number of others moved to the colonies being established in the New World in the vain hope of avoiding the Inquisition. In 1504 the expulsion order was extended to include all Muslims.

The economic and social costs of the expulsion were profound. Not every Muslim or Jew was wealthy and cultured, but the exiles did include many doctors, bankers, and merchants. Spanish culture, long open to influences from Muslim and Jewish sources, became narrower and less willing to accept new ideas. After the expulsion, a chasm of distrust opened between the "Old Christians" and the "New," that is, newly converted. As early as the first decades of the fifteenth century, some religious orders had refused to accept "New Christians." They required that their members demonstrate *limpieza de sangre,* a purity of blood. By 1500 the same tests of blood purity became prerequisites for holding most religious and public offices. Thus, by the end of the fifteenth century, the Iberian kingdoms had created more powerful, unified governments, but at a terrible cost to the only portion of Christendom that had ever practiced religious tolerance.

Complaints that led to the expulsion arose from a variety of sources. The fact that many of the most important financiers and courtiers were Jews or conversos bred jealousies and tensions among the communities. The most conservative Christians desired a community free of non-Christian influences. All three religious communities favored distinct dress and identifying behaviors for each group. Christians seemed concerned that many of the conversos were likely to reconvert to Judaism, and the fear of reconversion, or "judaizing," led many to advocate the institution of the Spanish Inquisition.

Inquisitions were well known in many parts of Europe, but the Spanish Inquisition was unique because in 1478 Pope Sixtus IV placed the grand inquisitor under the direct control of the monarchs. Like most Christian rulers, Ferdinand and Isabella believed that uniform Christian orthodoxy was the only firm basis for a strong kingdom. Inquisitors attacked those aspects of converso tradition that seemed to make the conversos less than fully Christian. They were concerned that many conversos and maranos had converted falsely and were secretly continuing to follow Jewish or Muslim ritual. The "New Christians" tended to live near their Muslim or Jewish relatives, eat the foods enjoyed in their former communities, and observe holy days, such as Yom Kippur, the Jewish day of atonement. Over four thousand converso families fled from Andalusia in southern Spain following the arrival of an inquisitor in 1490.

Because its administration, finances, and appointments were in Spanish not papal hands, the Spanish Inquisition quickly became an important instrument for the expansion of state power. Many inquisitors used their offices to attack wealthy or politically important converso families not just to drive them from public life but also to fill the royal treasury, which was where the estates of those judged guilty wound up. "This inquisition is as much to take the conversos' estates as to exalt the faith," was the despairing conclusion of one conversa woman.[12]

■ The Limits of Consolidation: Germany

The issue of central versus local control played a key role in German affairs as well. The Holy Roman Empire of the late Middle Ages was dramatically different from the empire of the early thirteenth century. Emperors generally were unable to claim lands and preside over jurisdictions outside Germany. And within Germany, power shifted eastward. Imperial power had previously rested on lands and castles in southwestern Germany. These strongholds melted away as emperors willingly pawned and sold traditional crown lands in order to build up the holdings of their own families. Emperor Henry VII (r. 1308–1313) and his grandson, Charles IV (r. 1347–1378), for example, liquidated imperial lands west of the Rhine in order to secure the house of Luxemburg's claims to the crown of Bohemia and other lands in the east. The Habsburgs in Austria, the Wittelsbachs in Bavaria, and a host of lesser families staked out power bases in separate parts of the empire. As a result, Germany unraveled into a loose collection of territories. And more seriously, the power of each emperor depended almost entirely on the wealth and power of his dynastic lands.

The power of regional authorities in the empire was further cemented by the so-called Golden Bull of 1356, the most important constitutional document of late medieval German history. In it, Charles IV declared that henceforth the archbishops of Cologne, Mainz, and Trier plus the secular rulers of Bohemia, the Rhenish Palatinate, Saxony, and Brandenburg, would be the seven electors responsible for the choice of a new emperor. He further established that the rulers of these seven principalities should have full jurisdictional rights within their territories. The Golden Bull acknowledged the power of regional princes, but it did nothing to solve the inherent weakness of an electoral monarchy. Between 1273 and 1519, Germany elected fourteen emperors from six different dynasties, and only once, in 1378, did a son follow his father. The contrast between Germany and the monarchies of Iberia, France, and England is striking. By 1350 Germany had no hereditary monarchy, no common legal system, no common coinage, and no representative assembly. Political power rested in the hands of the territorial princes.

Territorial integration was least effective in what is now Switzerland, where a league of towns, provincial knights, and peasant villages successfully resisted a territorial prince. The Swiss Confederation began modestly enough in 1291 as a voluntary association to promote regional peace. By 1410 the confederation had conquered most of the traditionally Habsburg lands in the Swiss areas. By the 1470s the Swiss had invented the myth of William Tell, the fearless woodsman who refused to bow his head to a Habsburg official, as a justification for their independent and anti-aristocratic traditions. Although still citizens of the Holy Roman Empire, the Swiss maintained an independence similar to that of the princes. Their expansion culminated with the Battle of Nancy in Lorraine in 1477, when the Swiss infantry defeated a Burgundian army and killed Charles the Bold, the duke of Burgundy. From then on "Turning Swiss" became a battle cry for German towns and individuals who hoped to slow territorial centralization.

governments grew stronger as kings, princes, and town patricians used royal courts and patronage to extend their control. Military advances in the fifteenth century, such as the institution of standing armies, gave advantages to larger governments. This was as true in Hungary as it was in France.

Yet recovery among the traditional Western powers was largely overshadowed by the rise of Muscovite Russia and the Ottoman and Spanish Empires. These three emergent powers upset the political and diplomatic balance in Europe. It was they who would dominate politics and diplomacy in the next century.

In addition to their obvious political power, most of these states—from Spain to Scandinavia to Istanbul—became adept at using art, literature, and history to explain and magnify their courts and confirm their places in history and society. This was certainly true of the papacy and over the course of the fifteenth century; it became true of other governments as well. It is to the role of culture that we turn in the next chapter.

SUMMARY

EUROPE in 1500 was profoundly different from the Europe of two centuries earlier. The religious, political, and economic crises of the fourteenth and early fifteenth centuries seemed about to destroy the progress of the previous centuries. But the recovery of the second half of the fifteenth century was nearly as dramatic as the preceding disasters.

In the aftermath of schism and conciliar reform, the church also was transformed. Because of conciliar challenges to papal authority, popes had to deal much more carefully with the governments of Europe. They found themselves vulnerable to pressures from the other European powers. Recognizing that, in the end, popes could count on support only from those areas they controlled politically, the papacy became an Italian regional power.

The economy had grown more complex in the wake of plague and demographic change. New patterns of trade and banking and new manufacturing techniques spread throughout Europe. As important as simple recovery, the new economy was now more firmly rooted in northern Europe. Italian merchants and bankers faced stiff competition from local counterparts throughout Europe.

Recovery was equally dramatic for the kings of France and England, the princes and despots in Germany, and the rulers of eastern Europe. After the Hundred Years' War and challenges from aristocrats, townsmen, and peasants,

■ Notes

1. Quoted in Guillaume Mollat, *The Popes at Avignon, 1305–1378* (London: Thomas Nelson, 1963), p. 112.
2. Quoted in Mary Aston, *Lollards and Reformers: Images and Literacy in Late Medieval Religion* (Ronceverte, W.V.: Hambledon, 1984), p. 60.
3. Quoted in Francis Oakley, *The Western Church in the Later Middle Ages* (Ithaca, N.Y.: Cornell University Press, 1979), pp. 65–66.
4. Quoted in Charles T. Wood, *Joan of Arc and Richard III* (New York: Oxford University Press, 1988), pp. 56–57.
5. Quoted in Michael T. Clanchy, "Law, Government, and Society in Medieval England," *History* 59 (1974): 75.
6. A. Buchon, *Choix des Chroniques* (Paris, 1875), p. 565, as quoted in John Gillingham and J. C. Holt, eds., *War and Government in the Middle Ages* (Totowa, N.J.: Barnes & Noble, 1984), p. 85.
7. Salimbene de Adam, quoted in John Larner, *Italy in the Age of Dante and Petrarch, 1215–1380* (New York: Longman, 1980), p. 141.
8. Quoted in Peter Shervey Lewis, *Later Medieval France: The Polity* (New York: Macmillan, 1968), p. 15.
9. Quoted in Angus MacKay, *Spain in the Middle Ages: From Frontier to Empire, 1000–1500* (London: Macmillan, 1977), p. 137.
10. Ibid., p. 105.
11. Quoted in Angus MacKay, "Popular Movements and Pogroms, in Fifteenth-Century Spain," *Past & Present* 55 (1972): 52.
12. Haim Beinart, ed., *Records of the Trials of the Spanish Inquisition in Ciudad Real*, vol. 1, trans. Duane Osheim (Jerusalem: Israel Academy of Sciences and Humanities, 1974), p. 391.

■ Suggested Reading

Duffy, E. *Saints & Sinners: A History of the Popes.* 1997. An excellent introduction to the papacy by a leading historian. The sections on the late Middle Ages are clear and balanced.

Dyer, C. *Standards of Living in the Later Middle Ages: Social Change in England, c. 1200–1500.* 1989. An account that includes a sophisticated discussion of dietary changes in the wake of population decline and changed commodity prices in fifteenth-century England.

Guenée, B. *States and Rulers in Later Medieval Europe.* Translated by Juliet Vale. 1985. The best general introduction to the nature of government in the late Middle Ages. It introduces recent trends in historical research.

Herlihy, D. *The Black Death and the Transformation of the West.* 1997. This short, very readable book is an excellent introduction to the plague and its impact on Europe.

Inalcik, H. *The Ottoman Empire: The Classical Age, 1300–1600.* 1973. A general discussion of the growth of the Ottoman state by Turkey's best medieval historian.

Keen, Maurice H. *English Society in the Later Middle Ages, 1348–1500.* 1990. A recent general introduction to late medieval England that covers culture and religion as well as politics.

Nicholas, D. *The Transformation of Europe, 1300–1600.* 1999. A comprehensive survey of politics and society in Europe between 1300 and 1600; includes coverage of Scandinavia and the Slavic lands as well as northwestern Europe.

Oakley, Francis. *The Western Church in the Later Middle Ages.* 1979. The best general history of the church in the late Middle Ages. Oakley gives superior treatments of the Great Schism and conciliarism.

Warner, Marina. *Joan of Arc: The Image of Female Heroism.* 1981. An excellent and quite readable book that emphasizes the conflicting religious and political opinions about "the Maid."

 For a searchable list of additional readings for this chapter, go to http://college.hmco.com.

A Painting of the Plague

Writers who survived the coming of pestilential disease in 1348 described a world of terror in which things seemed changed forever. Look at this painting, *St. Sebastian Interceding for the Plague-Stricken,* created by the Flemish artist Josse Lieferinxe between 1497 and 1499. One dying man seems to be falling terrified to the ground while a female bystander in the background screams in alarm. Images of Christ, Saint Sebastian (pierced by arrows), a devil, and a priest seem to indicate that something terrifying and undreamed-of is happening. But what exactly was the terror, and what had changed?

The art of the later Middle Ages is an extremely valuable source for understanding social and religious values. As you look at *St. Sebastian Interceding for the Plague-Stricken*, the first step is to understand what men and women in the fourteenth and fifteenth centuries thought about death. After 1400, European Christians often depicted the universality of death in paintings showing the Dance of Death. The motif varies, but typically Death grasps the hands of men and women, rich and poor, noble and peasant, and leads them away. Deathbed scenes were another popular motif. In the late Middle Ages most people believed that at death the good and evil acts committed by an individual were tallied in the Book of Life and the person was either granted eternal life, first in Purgatory and then Paradise, or consigned to eternal suffering in Hell. Judgment scenes often depict the Virgin Mary or another saint pleading before God or contending with the Devil or demons over the souls of the dying.

It was essential for people to prepare for a good death. Individuals studied the *artes moriendi,* the arts of dying. A lingering, painful illness was often interpreted as an opportunity for penitential suffering that would benefit the soul. At the point of death, the dying person could confess and receive absolution for sins and the last sacraments of the church. From that moment on, he or she needed to maintain a calm faith, free from fear. Salvation and eternal life depended on avoiding further sin, especially the questioning of God's forgiveness and mercy. Death was a public event. Clergy, family, religious societies, even neighbors helped the dying person to avoid losing faith at the end. The person might pray,

"Virgin Mary, Mother of God, I have placed my hope in you. Free my soul from care, and from Hell, and bitter death."*

The concept of a good death is critical to understanding the European response to bubonic plague. To be sure, individuals rarely look forward to death, then or now. Numerous writers and chroniclers lamented the suddenness of death and the lack of priests to hear confession. (See the box "Reading Sources: The Black Death" on page 373.) Individuals who were healthy in the morning might be dead by nightfall. The suddenness, the lack of time to prepare for a good death, heightened the dread that accompanied the onset of the illness.

Medieval Christians turned to saints to represent them before God at the point of death and to stop the onslaught of the plague. Three patron saints were especially popular. The Virgin Mary was often shown using her cloak to shelter towns and individuals from arrows carrying pestilence. Saint Roch, himself a victim of plague, was thought to intercede and protect those who prayed in his name. And Saint Sebastian, an early Christian martyr slain with arrows (later understood as symbols of death by plague), was thought to be an especially effective patron during epidemics. In times of plague, people went on pilgrimages to local shrines dedicated to these or local saints, carried images of the saints in processions, and built churches and chapels in honor of the saints in thanks for deliverance from plague.

With these issues in mind, what do we see in Lieferinxe's painting? The painting portrays an outbreak of plague. We note first the body of the dead person, carefully shrouded. Ideally, the dead, like the corpse here, were taken to a church and given a Christian burial. But chroniclers often reported that so many died, and died so quickly, that no one could be found to bury them properly. In many towns the dead were gathered on carts and hauled to gaping common graves outside the town. We can see one such cart leaving the castle in the background. In a series of images, then, Lieferinxe shows what mattered most to people. In the foreground is the shrouded body attended by a priest and other clerics

*Quoted in Philippe Ariès, *The Hour of Our Death* (New York: Knopf, 1981), p. 108.

Lieferinxe: St. Sebastian
Interceding for the Plague-
Stricken (The *Walters Art
Museum, Baltimore*)

bearing a cross. This person experienced a good death. In contrast, the man who has fallen behind the body is suffering a bad death, one that caught him unaware. He is the object of the concern and grief of those near him. In the sky just above the castle walls, a white-robed angel and a horned, ax-wielding demon contend over the souls of the dead and dying. At the top of the painting, Christ listens to the prayers of Saint Sebastian. The painting thus portrays the impact and horror of plague and also the way Christians were expected to respond to it.

Returning to our original question, we can conclude that the terror of epidemic plague was not entirely like a modern panic. Medieval people saw the Black Death, its ghastly devastation—and its only possible solution or meaning—in terms of traditional religious values: the true terror was to be caught unaware.

 For additional information on this topic, go to http://college.hmco.com.

CHAPTER 12

The Renaissance

THE painting on the left, "The School of Athens" by Raphael, was commissioned for the Stanze°, the papal apartments in the Vatican. At the center Plato and Aristotle advance through a churchlike hall, surrounded by the great thinkers and writers of the ancient world. But Raphael portrayed more than just ancient wisdom. The figure of Plato is, in fact, a portrait of Leonardo da Vinci. A brooding Michelangelo leans on a marble block in the foreground. In a companion painting on the opposite wall, Raphael depicted a gathering of the greatest scholars of Christendom. In this way he brought together Christian and classical, writers and artists, and captured the entire cultural reform plan of the Renaissance.

The revival these paintings celebrate was a response to the religious, social, economic, and political crises discussed in the previous chapter. Italians, and later Europeans generally, found themselves drawn to imitate Roman literature, ethics, and politics. The ideas of the distant past seemed to offer more opportunity for moral and political reform than the theological ideas of the recent past.

Renaissance Italians wrote of themselves and their contemporaries as having "revived" arts, "rescued" painting, and "rediscovered" classical authors. They even coined the phrases "Dark Ages" and "Middle Ages" to describe the period that separated the Roman Empire from their own times. They believed that their society saw a new age, a rebirth of culture. And to this day we use the French translation of "rebirth," *renaissance,* to describe the period of intense creativity and change from 1300 to 1500, not just in Italy, but in all of Europe.

Stanze (STAN-zay)

Humanism and Culture in Italy, 1300–1500

The Arts in Italy, 1250–1550

The Spread of the Renaissance, 1350–1536

The Renaissance and Court Society

Raphael, *School of Athens* (detail). Raphael created this classical ruin by using the technique of linear perspective.
(Scala/Art Resource, NY)

This view comes to us primarily from the work of the nineteenth-century Swiss historian Jacob Burckhardt. In his book *The Civilization of the Renaissance in Italy* (1860), he argued that Italians were the first individuals to recognize the state as a moral structure free from the restraints of religious or philosophical traditions. Burckhardt believed that individuals were entirely free. Their success or failure depended on personal qualities of creative brilliance rather than on family status, religion, or guild membership. What Burckhardt thought he saw in Renaissance Italy were the first signs of the romantic individualism and nationalism that characterized the modern world.

In fact, as brilliant as Renaissance writers and artists were, they do not represent a radical shift from the ideas or values of previous medieval culture. As we have seen, there was no "Dark Age." Although the culture of Renaissance Europe was in many aspects new and innovative, it had close ties both to the ideas of the High Middle Ages and to traditional Christian values.

How, then, should we characterize the Renaissance in Europe? The Renaissance was an important cultural movement that aimed to reform and renew by imitating what the reformers believed were classical and early Christian traditions in art,

education, religion, and political life. Italians, and then other Europeans, came to believe that the social and moral values as well as the literature of classical Greece and Rome offered the best formula for changing their own society for the better. This enthusiasm for a past culture became the vehicle for changes in literature, education, and art that established cultural standards that were to hold for the next five hundred years.

QUESTIONS TO CONSIDER

- How did Europeans try to use classical values to reform their world?

- What was "new" about Renaissance art?

- In what ways did humanism outside Italy differ from Italian humanism?

- How did European rulers use Renaissance art and culture?

TERMS TO KNOW

humanism	linear perspective
civic humanism	Sistine Chapel
Petrarch	Gutenberg
On the Donation	Thomas More
of Constantine	Erasmus
Machiavelli	

HUMANISM AND CULTURE IN ITALY, 1300–1500

 TALIANS turned to models from classical antiquity in their attempts to deal with current issues of cultural, political, and educational reform. A group of scholars who came to be known as humanists began to argue the superiority of the literature, history, and politics of the past. As humanists discovered more about ancient culture, they were able to understand more clearly the historical context in which Roman and Greek writers and thinkers lived. And by the early sixteenth century, their debates on learning, civic

duty, and the classical legacy had led them to a new vision of the past and a new appreciation of the nature of politics.

■ The Emergence of Humanism

Humanism initially held greater appeal in Italy than elsewhere in Europe because the culture in central and northern Italy was significantly more secular and more urban than the culture of much of the rest of Europe. Members of the clergy were not likely to dominate government and education in Italy. Quite the reverse: Boards dominated by laymen had built and were administering the great urban churches of Italy. Religious hospitals and charities were often reorganized and centralized under government control. In 1300 four cities in Italy had populations of about 100,000 (Milan, Venice, Florence, and Naples), and countless others had populations of 40,000 or more. By contrast, London, which may have had a population of 100,000, was the only city in England with more than 40,000 inhabitants. Even the powerful Italian aristocracy tended to live at least part of the year in towns and conform to urban social and legal practices.

Differences between Italy and northern Europe are also apparent in the structure of local education. In northern Europe, education was organized to provide clergy for local churches. In the towns of Italy, education was much more likely to be supervised by town governments to provide training in accounting, arithmetic, and the composition of business letters. Public grammar masters taught these basics, and numerous private masters and individual tutors were prepared to teach all subjects. Giovanni Villani, a fourteenth-century merchant and historian, described Florence in 1338 as a city of about 100,000 people in which perhaps as many as 10,000 young girls and boys were completing elementary education and 1,000 were continuing their studies to prepare for careers in commerce. Compared with education in the towns of northern Europe, education in Villani's Florence seems broad-based and practical.

Logic and Scholastic philosophy (see page 340) dominated university education in northern Europe in the fourteenth and fifteenth centuries but had less influence in Italy, where education focused on the practical issues of town life rather than on theological speculation. Educated Italians of this period were interested in the *studia humanitatis*, which we now call humanism. By *humanism*, Italians meant rhetoric and literature—the arts of persuasion. Poetry, history, letter writing, and oratory based on standardized forms and aesthetic values consciously borrowed from ancient Greece and Rome were the center of intellectual life. In general, fourteenth-century Italians were suspicious of ideological or moral programs based on philosophical arguments or religious assumptions about human nature.

Italian towns were the focus of theorizing about towns as moral, religious, and political communities. Writers wanted to define the nature of the commune—the town government. Moralists often used "the common good" and "the good of the commune" as synonyms. By 1300 it was usual for towns to celebrate the feast days of their patron saints as major political as well as religious festivals. And town governments often supervised the construction and expansion of cathedrals, churches, and hospitals as signs of their wealth and prestige.

CHRONOLOGY

1304–1314	Giotto paints Arena Chapel in Padua
1345	Petrarch discovers Cicero's letters to Atticus
1348–1350	Boccaccio, *The Decameron*
1393–1400	Chaucer, *The Canterbury Tales*
1401	Ghiberti wins competition to cast baptistery doors, Florence
1405	Christine de Pizan, *The Book of the City of the Ladies*
1427	Unveiling of Masaccio's *Trinity*
1434	Van Eyck, *The Arnolfini Wedding*
1440	Valla, *On the Donation of Constantine*
1440s	Da Feltre establishes Villa Giocosa in Mantua
1450s	Gutenberg begins printing with movable metal type
1460	Gonzaga invites Mantegna to Mantua
1475	Pope Sixtus IV orders construction of Sistine Chapel
1494	Dürer begins first trip to Venice
1511	Michelangelo, *David* Erasmus, *The Praise of Folly*
1513	Machiavelli, *The Prince*
1516	More, *Utopia*
1527	Castiglione, *The Book of the Courtier*

Literature of the early fourteenth century tended to emphasize the culture of towns. The most famous and most innovative work of the fourteenth century, *The Decameron* by Giovanni Boccaccio° (1313–1375), pondered moral and ethical issues, but in the lively context of Italian town life. Boccaccio hoped the colorful and irreverent descriptions of contemporary Italians, which make his *Decameron* a classic of European literature, would also lead individuals to understand both the essence of

Giovanni Boccaccio (jo-VAH-nee bo-KAH-chi-o)

human nature and the folly of human desires. The plot involves a group of privileged young people who abandon friends and family during the plague of 1348 to go into the country, where on successive days they mix feasting, dancing, and song with one hundred tales of love, intrigue, and gaiety. With its mix of traditional and contemporary images, Boccaccio's book spawned numerous imitators in Italy and elsewhere. Many credit him with popularizing a new, secular spirit. But the point too often missed by Boccaccio's imitators was, as he himself said, that "to have compassion for those who suffer is a human quality which everyone should possess. . . ."

The majority of educated Italians in the early fourteenth century, such as Boccaccio, were not particularly captivated by thoughts of ancient Rome. Italian historians chose to write the histories of their hometowns. Most, including Giovanni Villani of Florence, were convinced that their towns could rival ancient Rome. Theirs was a practical world in which most intellectuals were men trained in notarial arts—the everyday skills of oratory, letter writing, and the recording of legal documents.

■ Early Humanism

The first Italians who looked back consciously to the literary and historical examples of ancient Rome were a group of northern Italian lawyers and notaries who imitated Roman authors. These practical men found Roman history and literature more stimulating and useful than medieval philosophy. Writers such as Albertino Mussato of Padua (1262–1329) adopted classical styles in their poetry and histories. Mussato used his play *The Ecerinis* (1315) to tell of the fall of Can Grande della Scala, the tyrannical ruler of Verona (d. 1329) and to warn his neighbors of the dangers of tyranny. From its earliest, the classical revival in Italy was tied to issues of moral and political reform.

This largely emotional fascination for the ancient world was transformed into a literary movement for reform by Francesco Petrarch (1304–1374), who popularized the idea of mixing classical moral and literary ideas with the concerns of the fourteenth century. Petrarch was the son of an exiled Florentine notary living at the papal court in Avignon. Repelled by the urban violence and wars he had experienced on his return to Italy, Petrarch was highly critical of his contemporaries: "I never liked this age," he once confessed. He criticized the "Babylonian Captivity" of the papacy in Avignon, as he named it (see page 358); he supported an attempt to resurrect a republican government in Rome; and he believed that imitation of the actions, values, and culture of the ancient Romans was the only way to reform his sorry world.

Petrarch believed that an age of darkness—he coined the expression "Dark Ages"—separated the Roman world from his own time and that the separation could be overcome only through a study and reconstruction of classical values: "Once the darkness has been broken, our descendants will perhaps be able to return to the pure, pristine radiance."[1] Petrarch's program, and in many respects the entire Renaissance, involved first of all a reconstruction of classical culture, then a careful study and imitation of the classical heritage, and finally a series of moral and cultural changes that went beyond the mere copying of ancient values and styles.

Petrarch labored throughout his life to reconstruct the history and literature of Rome. He learned to read and write classical Latin. While still in his twenties, he discovered, reorganized, and annotated fragments of Livy's *Roman History*, an important source for the history of Republican Rome. His work on Livy was merely the first step. In the 1330s he discovered a number of classical works, including orations and letters by Cicero, the great philosopher, statesman, and opponent of Julius Caesar (see page 166). Cicero's letters to his friend Atticus were filled with gossip, questions about politics in Rome, and complaints about his forced withdrawal from public life. They create the portrait of an individual who was much more complex than the austere philosopher of medieval legend.

Despite his role in heralding secular humanism, Petrarch was and remained a committed Christian. He recognized the tension between the Christian present and pagan antiquity. "My wishes fluctuate and my desires conflict, and in their struggle they tear me apart," he said.[2] Yet he prized the beauty and moral value of ancient learning. He wrote *The Lives of Illustrious Men*, biographies of men from antiquity whose thoughts and actions he deemed worthy of emulation. To spread humanistic values, he issued collections of his letters, written in classically inspired Latin, and his Italian poems. He believed that study and memorization of the writings of classical authors could lead to the internalization of the ideas and values expressed in those works, just as a honeybee drinks nectar to create honey. He argued that the ancient moral philosophers were superior to the Scholastic philosophers, whose work ended with the determination of truth, or correct responses. "The true moral philosophers and useful teachers of the virtues," he concluded, "are those whose first and last intention is to make hearer and reader good, those who do not merely teach what virtue and vice are but sow into our hearts love of the best . . . and hatred of the worst."[3] (See the box "Reading Sources: Petrarch Responds to His Critics.")

✒ READING SOURCES

Petrarch Responds to His Critics

Many traditional philosophers and theologians criticized humanists as "pagans" because of their lack of interest in logic and theology and their love of non-Christian writers. In this letter defending humanistic studies, Petrarch explains the value of Cicero's work to Christians.

[Cicero] points out the miraculously coherent structure and disposition of the body, sense and limbs, and finally reason and sedulous activity. . . . And all this he does merely to lead us to this conclusion: whatever we behold with our eyes or perceive with our intellect is made by God for the well-being of man and governed by divine providence and counsel. . . . [In response to his critics who argued for the superiority of philosophy he adds:] I have read all of Aristotle's moral books. . . . Sometimes I have become more learned through them when I went home, but not better, not so good as I ought to be; and I often complained to myself, occasionally to others too, that by no facts was the promise fulfilled which the philosopher makes at the beginning of the first book of his Ethics, namely, that "we learn this part of philosophy not with the purpose of gaining knowledge but of becoming better.". . . However, what is the use of knowing what virtue is if it is not loved when known? What is the use of knowing sin if it is not abhorred when it is known? However, everyone who has become thoroughly familiar with our Latin authors knows that they stamp and drive deep into the heart the sharpest and most ardent stings of speech by which those who stick to the ground [are] lifted up to the highest thoughts and to honest desire. . . .

Cicero, read with a pious and modest attitude, . . . was profitable to everybody, so far as eloquence is concerned, to many others as regards living. This was especially true in [Saint] Augustine's case. . . . I confess, I admire Cicero as much or even more than all whoever wrote a line in any nation. . . . If to admire Cicero means to be a Ciceronian, I am a Ciceronian. I admire him so much that I wonder at people who do not admire him. . . . However, when we come to think or speak of religion, that is, of supreme truth and true happiness, and of eternal salvation, then I am certainly not a Ciceronian, or a Platonist, but a Christian. I even feel sure that Cicero himself would have been a Christian if he had been able to see Christ and to comprehend His doctrine.

Source: Petrarch, "On His Own Ignorance and That of Many Others," in *The Renaissance Philosophy of Man,* ed. Ernst Cassirer, Paul Oskar Kristeller, and John H. Randall (Chicago: University of Chicago Press, 1948), pp. 86, 103, 104, 114, 115.

 For additional information on this topic, go to http://college.hmco.com.

■ Humanistic Studies

Petrarch's articulation of humanism inspired a broad-based transformation of Italian intellectual life that affected discussions of politics, education, literature, and philosophy. His style of historical and literary investigation of the past became the basis for a new appreciation of the present.

Petrarch's program of humanistic studies became especially popular with the wealthy oligarchy who dominated political life in Florence. The Florentine chancellor Coluccio Salutati° (1331–1406) and a generation of young intellectuals who formed his circle evolved an ideology of civic humanism. Civic humanists wrote letters, orations, and histories praising their city's classical virtues and history. In the process they gave a practical and public meaning to the Petrarchan program. Civic humanists argued, as had Cicero, that there was a moral and ethical value intrinsic to public life. In a letter to a friend, Salutati

Coluccio Salutati (ko-LOO-chi-o sal-you-TAH-tee)

Isabella d'Este As part of the program to revive ancient Roman practices, Italian rulers had medals struck containing their own images. This image of Isabella was meant to celebrate the woman herself and the fact that her husband held the imperial office of duke. *(Kunsthistorisches Museum, Vienna/ Erich Lessing/Art Resource, NY)*

wrote that public life is "something holy and holier than idleness in [religious] solitude." To another he added, "The active life you flee is to be followed both as an exercise in virtue and because of the necessity of brotherly love."[4]

More than Petrarch himself, civic humanists desired to create and inspire men of virtue who could take the lead in government and protect their fellow citizens from lawlessness and tyranny. In the early years of the fifteenth century, civic humanists applauded Florence for remaining a republic of free citizens rather than falling under the control of a lord, like the people of Milan, whose government was dominated by the Viscontis (see page 369). In his *Panegyric on the City of Florence* (ca. 1400), Leonardo Bruni (ca. 1370–1444) recalled the history of the Roman Republic and suggested that Florence could re-create the best qualities of the Roman state. To civic humanists, the study of Rome and its virtues was the key to the continued prosperity of Florence and similar Italian republics.

One of Petrarch's most enthusiastic followers was Guarino of Verona (1374–1460), who became the leading advocate of educational reform in Renaissance Italy. After spending five years in Constantinople learning Greek and collecting classical manuscripts, he became the most successful teacher and translator of Greek literature in Italy. Greek studies had been advanced by Manuel Chrysoloras (1350–1415), who, after his arrival from Constantinople in 1397, taught Greek for three years in Florence. Chrysoloras was later joined by other Greek intellectuals, especially after the fall of Constantinople to the Turks in 1453. Guarino built on this interest.

Guarino emphasized careful study of grammar and memorization of large bodies of classical history and poetry. He was convinced that through a profound understanding of Greek and Latin literature and a careful imitation of the style of the great authors, a person could come to exhibit the moral and ethical values for which Cicero, Seneca, and Plutarch were justly famous. Although it is unclear whether Guarino's style of education had such results, it did provide a thorough education in literature and oratory. In an age that admired the ability to speak and write persuasively, the new style of humanistic education pioneered by Guarino spread quickly throughout Europe. The elegy spoken at Guarino's funeral sums up Italian views of humanistic education as well as the contribution of Guarino himself: "No one was considered noble, as leading a blameless life, unless he had followed Guarino's courses."

Guarino's authority spread quickly. One of his early students, Vittorino da Feltre (1378–1446), was appointed tutor to the Gonzaga dukes of Mantua. Like Guarino, he emphasized close literary study and careful imitation of classical authors. But the school he founded, the Villa Giocosa°, was innovative because he advocated games and exercises as well as formal study. In addition, Vittorino required that bright young boys from poor families be included among the seventy affluent students normally resident in his school. Vittorino was so renowned that noblemen from across Italy sent their sons to be educated at the Villa Giocosa.

Humanistic education had its limits, however. Leonardo Bruni of Florence once composed a curriculum emphasizing literature and moral philosophy for a young woman to follow. But, he suggested, there was no reason to study rhetoric: "For why should the subtleties of . . . rhetorical conundrums consume the powers of a woman, who never sees the forum? . . . The contests of the forum, like those of warfare and battle, are the sphere of men."[5] To what extent did women participate in the cultural and artistic movements of the fourteenth and fifteenth centuries? Was the position of women better

Giocosa (jo-KO-sa)

than it had been previously? The current of misogyny—the assumption that women were intellectually and morally weaker than men—continued during the Renaissance, but it was not unopposed.

During the fifteenth century many women did learn to read and even to write. Religious women and wives of merchants read educational and spiritual literature. Some women needed to write in order to manage the economic and political interests of their families. Alessandra Macinghi-Strozzi° of Florence (1407–1471), for example, wrote numerous letters to her sons in exile describing her efforts to find spouses for her children and to influence the government to end their banishments.

Yet many men were suspicious of literate women. Just how suspicious is evident in the career of Isotta Nogarola (b. 1418) of Verona, one of a number of fifteenth- and sixteenth-century Italian women whose literary abilities equaled those of male humanists. Isotta quickly became known as a gifted writer, but men's response to her work was mixed. One anonymous critic suggested that it was unnatural for a woman to have such scholarly interests and accused her of equally unnatural sexual interests. Guarino of Verona himself wrote to her warning that if she was truly to be educated, she must put off female sensibilities and find "a man within the woman."[6]

The problem for humanistically educated women was that society provided no acceptable role for them. A noblewoman such as Isabella d'Este° (see page 420), wife of the duke of Mantua, might gather humanists and painters around her at court, but it was not generally believed that women themselves could create literary works of true merit. When women tried, they were usually rebuffed and urged to reject the values of civic humanism and to hold instead to traditional Christian virtues of rejection of the world. In other words, a woman who had literary or cultural interests was expected to enter a convent. That was a friend's advice to Isotta Nogarola. It was wrong, he said, "that a virgin should consider marriage, or even think about that liberty of lascivious morals."[7] Throughout the fifteenth and early sixteenth centuries, some women in Italy and elsewhere in Europe learned classical languages and philosophy, but they became rarer as time passed. The virtues of humanism were public virtues, and Europeans of the Renaissance remained uncomfortable with the idea that women might act directly and publicly. (See the box "Reading Sources: Cassandra Fedele Defends Liberal Arts for Women.")

Macinghi-Strozzi (ma-CHIN-ghee STRO-tzi)
d'Este (duh-ES-tay)

Women and Culture   This painting of Saint Barbara from the early fifteenth century shows a typical Flemish interior with a woman reading. It was not unusual for well-to-do women to read even if they could not write.   *(Museo de Prado/Institut Amatller d'Art Hispanic)*

READING SOURCES

Cassandra Fedele Defends Liberal Arts for Women

Cassandra Fedele (1465–1558) had learned Latin by age 12 and later learned Greek, rhetoric, and history. The Venetian senate praised her as an ornament of learning, but beyond being admired, there was no public role for an educated woman. In this oration delivered at the university, she adds her own plea for education for women.

Aware of the weakness of my sex and the paucity of my talent, blushing, I decided to honor and obey [those who have urged me to consider how women could profit from assiduous study] . . . in order that the common crowd may be ashamed of itself and stop being offensive to me, devoted as I am to the liberal arts. . . . What woman, I ask, has such force and ability of mind and speech that she could adequately meet the standard of the greatness of letters or your learned ears? Thus daunted by the difficulty of the task and conscious of my weakness, I might easily have shirked this opportunity to speak, if your well-known kindness and clemency had not urged me to it. For I am not unaware that you are not in the habit of demanding or expecting from anyone more than the nature of the subject itself allows, or the person's own strength can promise of them.

Even an ignorant man—not only a philosopher—sees and admits that man is rightly distinguished from a beast above all by [the capacity of] reason. For what else so greatly delights, enriches and honors both of them than the teaching and understanding of letters and the liberal arts? Moreover, simple men, ignorant of literature, even if they have by nature this potential seed of genius and reason, leave it alone and uncultivated throughout their whole lives, stifle it with neglect and sloth, and render themselves unfit for greatness. But learned men, filled with a rich knowledge of divine and human things, turn all their thoughts and motions of the mind toward the goal of reason and thus free the mind, [otherwise] subject to so many anxieties, from all infirmity. States and princes, moreover, who favor and cultivate these studies become much more humane, pleasing, and noble, and purely [through liberal studies] win for themselves a sweet reputation for humanity. For this reason the ancients rightfully judged all leaders deficient in letters, however skillful in military affairs, to be crude and ignorant. As for the utility of letters, enough said. Of these fruits I myself have tasted a little and [have esteemed myself in that enterprise] more than abject and hopeless; and armed with distaff and needle—woman's weapons—I march forth [to defend] the belief that even though the study of letters promises and offers no reward for women and no dignity, every woman ought to seek and embrace these studies for that pleasure and delight alone that [comes] from them.

Source: M. L. King and A. Rabil, *Her Immaculate Hand: Selected Works by and About the Women Humanists of Quattrocento Italy* (Binghamton, N.Y.: Center for Medieval and Early Renaissance Studies, State University of New York, 1983), pp. 74–77.

■ The Transformation of Humanism

The fascination with education based on ancient authorities was heightened by the discovery in 1416 in the Monastery of Saint Gall in Switzerland of a complete manuscript of Quintilian's *Institutes of Oratory*, a first-century treatise on the proper education for a young Roman patrician. The document was found by Poggio Bracciolini° (1380–1459), who had been part of the humanist circle in Florence. The discovery was hardly accidental. Like Petrarch himself, the humanists of the fifteenth century scoured Europe for ancient texts to read and study. In searching out the knowledge of the past, these fifteenth-century humanists made a series of

Poggio Bracciolini (PO-joe bra-chi-o-LEE-nee)

discoveries that changed their understanding of language, philosophy, and religion. Their desire to imitate led to a profound transformation of knowledge.

A Florentine antiquary, Niccolò Niccoli, coordinated and paid for much of this pursuit of "lost" manuscripts. A wealthy bachelor, Niccolò (1364–1437) spent the fortune he had inherited from his father by acquiring ancient statuary, reliefs, and, most of all, books. When he died, his collection of more than eight hundred volumes of Latin and Greek texts became the foundation of the humanist library housed in the Monastery of San Marco in Florence. Niccolò had specified that all his books "should be accessible to everyone," and humanists from across Italy and the rest of Europe came to Florence to study his literary treasures. Niccolò's library prompted Pope Nicholas V (r. 1447–1455) to begin the collection that is now the Apostolic Library of the Vatican in Rome. The Vatican library became a lending library, serving the humanist community in Rome. Similar collections were assembled in Venice, Milan, and Urbino. The Greek and Latin sources preserved in these libraries allowed humanists to study classical languages in a way not possible before.

The career of Lorenzo Valla (1407–1457) illustrates the transformation that took place in the fifteenth century as humanism swept Europe. Valla was born near Rome and received a traditional humanistic education in Greek and Latin studies. He spent the rest of his life at universities and courts lecturing on philosophy and literature. Valla's studies had led him to understand that languages change with time—that they, too, have a life and a history. In 1440 he published a work called *On the Donation of Constantine*. The *Donation of Constantine* purported to record the gift by the emperor Constantine (r. 311–337) of jurisdiction over Rome and the western half of the empire to the pope when the imperial capital was moved to Constantinople (see page 209). In the High and late Middle Ages, the papacy used the document to defend its right to political dominion in central Italy. The donation had long been criticized by legal theorists, who argued that Constantine had no right to make it. Valla went further and attacked the legitimacy of the document itself. Because of its language and form, he argued, it could not have been written at the time of Constantine:

> Through his [the writer's] babbling, he reveals his most impudent forgery himself. . . . Where he deals with the gifts he says "a diadem . . . made of pure gold and precious jewels." The ignoramus did not know that the diadem was made of cloth, probably silk. . . . He thinks it had to be made of gold, since nowadays kings usually wear a circle of gold set with jewels.[8]

Valla was correct. The *Donation* was an eighth-century forgery.

Valla later turned his attention to the New Testament. Jerome (331–420) had put together the Vulgate edition of the Bible in an attempt to create a single accepted Latin version of the Old and New Testaments (see page 232). In 1444 Valla published his *Annotations on the New Testament*. In this work he used his training in classical languages to correct Jerome's standard Latin text and to show numerous instances of mistranslations. His annotations on the New Testament were of critical importance to humanists outside Italy and were highly influential during the Protestant Reformation.

The transformation of humanism exemplified by Valla was fully expected by some Florentines. They anticipated that literary studies would lead eventually to philosophy. In 1456 a young Florentine began studying Greek with just such a change in mind. Supported by the Medici rulers of Florence, Marsilio Ficino° (1433–1499) began a daunting project: to translate the works of Plato into Latin and to interpret Plato in light of Christian doctrine and tradition.

Ficino believed that Platonism, like Christianity, demonstrated the dignity of humanity. He wrote that everything in creation was connected along a continuum ranging from the lowliest matter to the person of God. The human soul was located at the midpoint of this hierarchy and was a bridge between matter and God. True wisdom, and especially experience of the divine, could be gained only through contemplation and love. According to Ficino, logic and scientific observation did not lead to true understanding, for humans know logically only what they can define in human language; individuals can, however, love things, such as God, that they are not fully able to comprehend.

Ficino's belief in the dignity of man was shared by Giovanni Pico della Mirandola° (1463–1494), who proposed to debate with other philosophers nine hundred theses dealing with the nature of man, the origins of knowledge, and the uses of philosophy. Pico extended Ficino's idea of the hierarchy of being, arguing that humans surpassed even the angels in dignity. Angels held a fixed position in the hierarchy, just below God. In contrast, humans could move either up or down in the hierarchy, depending on the extent to which they embraced spiritual or worldly interests. Pico further believed that he had proved that all philosophies contain at least some

---

Ficino (fi-CHI-no)   **Giovanni Pico della Mirandola**
(joe-VAH-nee PIH-ko del-ah mi-RAHN-do-la)

truth. He was one of the first humanists to learn Hebrew and to argue that divine wisdom could be found in Jewish mystical literature. Along with others, he studied the Jewish Cabala, a collection of mystical and occult writings that humanists believed dated from the time of Moses. Pico's adoption of the Hebrew mystical writings was often controversial in the Jewish community as well as among Christians.

Pico's ideas were shared by other humanists, who contended that an original divine illumination—a "Pristine Theology," they called it—preceded even Plato and Aristotle. These humanists found theological truth in what they believed was ancient Egyptian, Greek, and Jewish magic. Ficino himself popularized the *Corpus Hermeticum* (the Hermetic collection), an amalgam of magical texts of the first century A.D. that was mistakenly thought to be the work of an Egyptian magician, Hermes Trismagistos. They assumed Hermes wrote during the age of Moses and Pythagoras. Like many neo-Platonic writings of the first century, Hermetic texts explained how the mind could influence and be influenced by the material and celestial worlds.

Along with exploring Hermetic magic, many humanists of the fifteenth and sixteenth centuries investigated astrology and alchemy. All three systems posit the existence of a direct, reciprocal connection between the cosmos and the natural world. In the late medieval and Renaissance world, astrological and alchemical theories seemed reasonable. By the late fifteenth century many humanists assumed that personality was profoundly affected by the stars and that the heavens were not silent regarding human affairs. It was not by accident that for a century or more after 1500, astrologers were official or unofficial members of most European courts.

Interest in alchemy was equally widespread though more controversial. Alchemists believed that everything was made of a primary material and that therefore it was possible to transmute one substance into another. The most popular variation, and the one most exploited by hucksters and frauds, was the belief that base metals could be turned into gold. The hopes of most alchemists, however, were more profound. They were convinced that they could unlock the explanation of the properties of the whole cosmos. On a personal and religious level as well as on a material level, practitioners hoped to make the impure pure. The interest in understanding and manipulating nature that lay at the heart of Hermetic magic, astrology, and alchemy was an important stimulus to scientific investigations and, ultimately, to the rise of modern scientific thought.

■ Humanism and Political Thought

The humanists' plan to rediscover classical sources meshed well with their political interests. "One can say," observed Leonardo Bruni, "that letters and the study of the Latin language went hand in hand with the condition of the Roman republic." Petrarch and the civic humanists believed that rulers, whether in a republic or a principality, should exhibit all the classical and Christian virtues of faith, hope, love, prudence, temperance, fortitude, and justice. A virtuous ruler would be loved as well as obeyed. The civic humanists viewed governments and laws as essentially unchanging and static. They believed that when change did occur, it most likely happened by chance—that is, because of fortune (the Roman goddess Fortuna). Humanists believed that the only protection against chance was true virtue, for the virtuous would never be dominated by fortune. Thus, beginning with Petrarch, humanists advised rulers to love their subjects, to be magnanimous with their possessions, and to maintain the rule of law. Humanistic tracts of the fourteenth and fifteenth centuries were full of classical and Christian examples of virtuous actions by moral rulers.

The French invasions of Italy in 1494 (see page 370) and the warfare that followed called into question many of the humanists' assumptions about the lessons and virtues of classical civilization. Francesco Guicciardini° (1483–1540), a Florentine patrician who had served in papal armies, suggested that, contrary to humanist hopes, history held no clear lessons. Unless the causes of separate events were identical down to the smallest detail, he said, the results could be radically different. An even more thorough critique was offered by Guicciardini's friend and fellow Florentine, Niccolò Machiavelli (1469–1527). In a series of writings Machiavelli developed what he believed was a new science of politics. He wrote *Discourses on Livy*, a treatise on military organization, a history of Florence, and even a Renaissance play entitled *The Mandrake Root*. He is best remembered, however, for *The Prince* (1513), a small tract numbering less than a hundred pages.

Machiavelli felt that his contemporaries paid too little heed to the lessons to be learned from history. Thus, in his discourses on Livy he comments on Roman government, the role of religion, and the nature of political virtue, emphasizing the sophisticated Roman analysis of political and military situations. A shortcoming more serious than ignorance of history, Machiavelli believed, was his contemporaries' ignorance of the true motivations for people's actions. His play *The Mandrake Root* is

---

Francesco Guicciardini (fran-CHES-ko gwih-char-DI-nee)

a comedy about the ruses used to seduce a young woman. In truth, however, none of the characters is fooled. All of them, from the wife to her husband, realize what is happening but use the seduction to their own advantage. In the play Machiavelli implicitly challenges the humanistic assumption that educated individuals will naturally choose virtue over vice. He explicitly criticizes these same assumptions in *The Prince*. Machiavelli holds the contrary view: that individuals are much more likely to respond to fear and that power rather than rhetoric makes for good government.

Machiavelli's use of the Italian word *virtù* led him to be vilified as amoral. Machiavelli deliberately chose a word that meant both "manliness" or "ability" and "virtue as a moral quality." Earlier humanists had restricted *virtù* to the second meaning, using the word to refer to upright qualities such as prudence, generosity, and love. Machiavelli tried to show that in some situations these "virtues" could have violent, even evil, consequences. If, for example, a prince was so magnanimous in giving away his wealth that he was forced to raise taxes, his subjects might come to hate him. Conversely, a prince who, through cruelty to the enemies of his state, brought peace and stability to his subjects might be obeyed and perhaps even loved by them. A virtuous ruler must be mindful of the goals to be achieved—that is what Machiavelli really meant by the phrase often translated as "the ends justify the means."

Machiavelli expected his readers to be aware of the ambiguous nature of virtue—whether understood as ability or as morality. "One will discover," he concludes, "that something which appears to be a virtue, if pursued, will end in his destruction; while some other thing which seems to be a vice, if pursued, will result in his safety and his well-being."[9]

Like Guicciardini, Machiavelli rejected earlier humanistic assumptions that one needed merely to imitate the great leaders of the past. Governing is a process that requires different skills at different times, he warned: "The man who adapts his course of action to the nature of the times will succeed and, likewise, the man who sets his course of action out of tune with the times will come to grief."[10] The abilities that enable a prince to gain power may not be the abilities that will allow him to maintain it.

With the writings of Machiavelli, humanistic ideas of intellectual, moral, and political reform came to maturation. Petrarch and the early humanists believed fully in the powers of classical wisdom to transform society. Machiavelli and his contemporaries admitted the importance of classical wisdom but also recognized the ambiguity of any simplistic application of classical learning to contemporary life.

Machiavelli   In this portrait Machiavelli is dressed as a government official. After being exiled from Florence by the Medici, he wrote to a friend that each night when he returned from the fields he dressed again in his curial robes and pondered the behavior of governments and princes. *(Scala/Art Resource, NY)*

THE ARTS IN ITALY, 1250–1550

TOWNSMEN and artists in Renaissance Italy shared the humanists' perception of the importance of classical antiquity. Filippo Villani (d. 1405), a wealthy Florentine from an important business family, wrote that artists had recently "reawakened a lifeless and almost extinct art." In the middle of the fifteenth century, the sculptor Lorenzo Ghiberti concluded that with the rise of Christianity "not only statues and paintings [were destroyed], but the books and commentaries and handbooks and rules on which men relied for their training." Italian writers and painters themselves believed that the recovery of past literary and artistic practices was essential if society was to recover from the "barbarism" that they believed characterized the recent past.

Giotto's Naturalism Later painters praised the naturalistic emotion of Giotto's painting. In this detail from the Arena Chapel, Giotto portrays the kiss of Judas, one of the most dramatic moments in Christian history. *(Scala/Art Resource, NY)*

The Renaissance of the arts is traditionally divided into three periods. In the early Renaissance, artists imitated nature; in the middle period, they rediscovered classical ideas of proportion; in the High Renaissance, artists were "superior to nature but also to the artists of the ancient world," according to the artist and architect Giorgio Vasari (1511–1574), who wrote a famous history of the eminent artists of his day.

■ The Artistic Renaissance

The first stirrings of the new styles can be found in the late thirteenth century. The greatest innovator of that era was Giotto° di Bondone of Florence (ca. 1266–1337). Although Giotto's background was modest, his fellow citizens, popes, and patrons throughout Italy quickly recognized his skill. He traveled as far south as Rome and

Giotto (JO-toe)

as far north as Padua painting churches and chapels. According to later artists and commentators, Giotto broke with the prevailing stiff, highly symbolic style and introduced lifelike portrayals of living persons. He produced paintings of dramatic situations, showing events located in specific times and places. The frescoes of the Arena Chapel in Padua (1304–1314), for example, recount episodes in the life of Christ. In a series of scenes leading from Christ's birth to his crucifixion, Giotto situates his actors in towns and countryside in what appears to be actual space. Even Michelangelo, the master of the High Renaissance, studied Giotto's painting. Giotto was in such demand throughout Italy that his native Florence gave him a public appointment so that he would be required by law to remain in the city.

Early in the fifteenth century, Florentine artists devised new ways to represent nature that surpassed even the innovations of Giotto. The revolutionary nature of these artistic developments is evident from the careers

Masaccio: The Trinity The Christian Trinity (three persons in one God) is represented by the Father behind the Son on the cross, with the Holy Spirit in the form of a dove in between. Using linear perspective, Masaccio seems to create depth in a flat wall. This painting was seen as revolutionary in the early fifteenth century.
(Erich Lessing/Art Resource, NY)

The Doors of Paradise Ghiberti worked on panels for the baptistery from 1403 to 1453. In his representations of scenes from the Old Testament he combined a love of ancient statuary with the new Florentine interest in linear perspective.
(Alinari/Art Resource, NY)

of Lorenzo Ghiberti (1378–1455), Filippo Brunelleschi° (1377–1446), and Masaccio° (born Tomasso di ser Giovanni di Mone, 1401–ca. 1428). Their sculpture, architecture, and painting began an ongoing series of experiments with the representation of space through linear perspective. Perspective is a system for representing three-dimensional objects on a two-dimensional plane. It is based on two observations: (1) As parallel lines recede into the distance, they seem to converge; and (2) a geometric relationship regulates the relative sizes of objects at various distances from the viewer. Painters of the Renaissance literally found themselves looking at their world from a new perspective.

In 1401 Ghiberti won a commission to design door panels for the baptistery of San Giovanni in Florence. He was to spend the rest of his life working on two sets of

bronze doors on which were recorded the stories of the New Testament (the north doors) and the Old Testament (the east doors). Ghiberti used the new techniques of linear perspective to create a sense of space into which he placed his classically inspired figures. Later in the sixteenth century Michelangelo remarked that the east doors were worthy to be the "Doors of Paradise," and so they have been known ever since.

Brunelleschi (broon-eh-LES-key) **Masaccio** (ma-SAH-cho)

In the competition for the baptistery commission, Ghiberti had beaten the young Filippo Brunelleschi, who, as a result, gave up sculpture for architecture and later left Florence to study in Rome. While in Rome he is said to have visited and measured surviving examples of classical architecture—the artistic equivalent of humanistic literary research. According to Vasari, he was capable of "visualizing Rome as it was before the fall." Brunelleschi's debt to Rome is evident in his masterpiece, Florence's foundling hospital. Built as a combination of hemispheres and cubes and resembling a Greek stoa or an arcaded Roman basilica, the long, low structure is an example of how profoundly different Renaissance architecture was from the towering Gothic of the Middle Ages.

In the first decade of the fifteenth century, many commentators believed that painting would never be as innovative as either sculpture or architecture. They knew of no classical models that had survived for imitation. Yet the possibilities in painting became apparent in 1427 with the unveiling of Masaccio's *Trinity* in the Florentine church of Santa Maria Novella. Masaccio built on revolutionary experiments in linear perspective to create a painting in which a flat wall seems to become a recessed chapel. The space created is filled with the images of Christ crucified, the Father, and the Holy Spirit.

In the middle years of the fifteenth century, artists came to terms with the innovations of the earlier period. In the second half of the fifteenth century, however, artists such as the Florentine Sandro Botticelli° (1445–1510) added a profound understanding of classical symbolism to the technical innovations of Masaccio and Brunelleschi. Botticelli's famous *Primavera* (*Spring*, 1478), painted for a member of the Medici family, is filled with neo-Platonic symbolism concerning truth, beauty, and the virtues of humanity. (See the feature "Weighing the Evidence: The Art of Renaissance Florence" on pages 426–427.)

The high point in the development of Renaissance art came at the beginning of the sixteenth century in the work of several masters throughout Italy. Artists in Venice learned perspective from the Florentines and added their own tradition of subtle coloring in oils. The works of Italian artists were admired well beyond the borders of Italy. Even Sultan Mehmed II of Constantinople valued Italian painters. (See the box "Global Encounters: Gentile Bellini Travels to Meet the Turkish Sultan.")

The work of two Florentines, Leonardo da Vinci (1452–1519) and Michelangelo Buonarroti (1475–1564),

Botticelli (bot-ti-CHEL-ee)

best exemplifies the sophisticated heights that art achieved early in the sixteenth century. Leonardo, the bastard son of a notary, was raised in the village of Vinci outside of Florence. Cut off from the humanistic milieu of the city, he desired above all else to prove that his artistry was the equal of his formally schooled social superiors. In his notebooks he confessed, "I am fully conscious that, not being a literary man, certain presumptuous persons will think they may reasonably blame me, alleging that I am not a man of letters."[11] But he defended his lack of classical education by arguing that all the best writing, like the best painting and invention, is based on the close observation of nature. Close observation and scientific analysis made Leonardo's work uniquely creative in all these fields. Leonardo is famous for his plans, sometimes prophetic, for bridges, airships, submarines, and fortresses. There seemed to be no branch of learning in which he was not interested. In painting he developed chiaroscuro, a technique for using light and dark in pictorial representation, and showed aerial perspective. He painted horizons as muted, shaded zones rather than with sharp lines. "I know," he said, "that the greater or less quantity of air that lies between the eye and the object makes the outlines of that object more or less distinct."[12] It was his analytical observation that made Leonardo so influential on his contemporaries.

Michelangelo, however, was widely hailed as the capstone of Renaissance art. In the words of a contemporary, "He alone has triumphed over ancient artists, modern artists and over Nature itself." In his career we can follow the rise of Renaissance artists from the ranks of mere craftsmen to honored creators, courtiers who were the equals of the humanists—in fact, Michelangelo shared Petrarch's concern for reform and renewal in Italian society. We can also discern the synthesis of the artistic and intellectual transformations of the Renaissance with a profound religious sensitivity.

The importance of Michelangelo's contribution is obvious in two of his most important works: the statue *David* in Florence and his commissions in the Sistine Chapel of the Vatican in Rome. From his youth Michelangelo had studied and imitated antique sculpture, to the point that some of his creations were thought by many actually to be antiquities. He used his understanding of classical art in *David* (1501). Citizens recalled David's defeat of the giant Goliath, saving Israel from almost certain conquest by the Philistines. *David* thus became a symbol of the youthful Florentine republic struggling to maintain its freedom against great odds. As Vasari noted, "just as David had protected his people and governed

Gentile Bellini Travels to Meet the Turkish Sultan

Giovanni and Gentile Bellini were two of the leading Renaissance artists in Venice. Their fame spread throughout the Mediterranean and resulted in this unusual cultural meeting in 1479. A portrait of the emperor Mehmed II by Gentile now hangs in the National Gallery in London.

Some portraits having been taken to Turkey to the Grand Turk [the sultan] by an ambassador, that emperor was so struck with astonishment that, although the Mohammedan laws prohibit pictures, he accepted them with great goodwill, praising the work without end, and what is more, requesting that the master himself be sent to him. But the senate, considering that Giovanni could ill support the hardships, resolved to send Gentile his brother, and he was conveyed safely in their galleys to Constantinople, where being presented to Mehmed [II], he was received with much kindness as an unusual visitor. He presented a beautiful picture to the prince, who admired it much, and could not persuade himself to believe that a mortal man had in him so much of the divinity as to be able to express the things of nature in such a lively manner. Gentile painted the Emperor Mehmed himself from life so well that it was considered a miracle, and the emperor, having seen many specimens of his art, asked Gentile if he had the courage to paint himself; and Gentile having answered "Yes," before many days were over he finished a life-like portrait by means of a mirror, and brought it to the monarch, whose astonishment was so great that he would have it a divine spirit dwelt in him. And had not this art been forbidden by the law

of the Turks, the emperor would never have let him go. But either from fear that people would murmur, or from some other cause, he sent for him one day, and having thanked him, and given him great praise, he bade him to ask whatever he would and it should be granted him without fail. Gentile modestly asked for nothing more than that he would graciously give him a letter of recommendation to the Senate and Lords of Venice. His request was granted in as fervent words as possible, and then, loaded with gifts and honors, and with the dignity of a cavalier, he was sent away. Among the other gifts was a chain of gold of two hundred and fifty crowns weight, worked in the Turkish manner. So, leaving Constantinople, he came safely to Venice, where he was received by his brother Giovanni and the whole city with joy, every one rejoicing in the honors which Mehmed had paid him. When the Doge and Lords [of Venice] saw the letters of the emperor, they ordered that a provision of two hundred crowns a year should be paid him all the rest of his life.

Source: Stories of the Italian Renaissance from Vasari, arranged and translated by E. L. Seeley (London and New York, 1908), pp. 135–137.

them justly, so whoever ruled Florence should vigorously defend the city and govern it with justice."[13]

Michelangelo was a committed republican and Florentine, but he spent much of his life working in Rome on a series of papal commissions. In 1508 he was called by Pope Julius II to work on the ceiling of the Sistine Chapel. Michelangelo spent four years decorating the ceiling with hundreds of figures and with nine scenes from the book of Genesis, including the famous *Creation of Adam.* In the late 1530s, at the request of Pope Clement VII, he

completed *The Last Judgment,* which covers the wall above the altar. In that painting the techniques of perspective and the conscious recognition of debts to classical culture recede into the background as the artist surrounds Christ in judgment with saints and sinners. In the hollow, hanging skin of flayed Saint Bartholomew we can detect a psychological self-portrait of an artist increasingly concerned with his own spiritual failings.

Michelangelo's self-portrait reminds us that the intellectual content of the artist's work is one of its most

The Sistine Chapel   Painted from 1508 to 1512, the ceiling of the Sistine Chapel is Michelangelo's most famous work. Powerfully summarizing Renaissance faith in the unity of Christian truth and pagan wisdom, Michelangelo illustrated God's giving life to Adam (among other biblical scenes), while around the ceiling's border he placed *sibyls,* classical symbols of knowledge. *(Vatican Museums. Photo: A. Bracchetti/P. Zigrossi)*

enduring traits. He was a Platonist who believed that the form and beauty of a statue were contained, buried, in the stone itself. The artist's job was to peel away excess material and reveal the beauty within. As he noted in one of his poems, sculpting was a process not unlike religious salvation:

> Just as by carving . . . we set
> Into hard mountain rock
> A living figure
> Which grows most where the stone is most removed;
> In like manner, some good works . . .
> Are concealed by the excess of my very flesh.[14]

■ Art and Patronage

The religious passion of Michelangelo's poetry indicates one of the reasons that art was so popular in Renaissance Italy. Art, like poetry, provided symbols and images through which Italians could reason about the most important issues of their communities. Italians willingly spent vast sums on art because of its ability to communicate social, political, and spiritual values.

Italy in the fourteenth and fifteenth centuries was unusually wealthy relative to the towns and principalities of northern Europe. Despite the population decline caused by plague and the accompanying economic dislocations, per person wealth in Italy remained quite high. Because of banking, international trade, and even service as mercenaries, Italians, and particularly Florentines, had money to spend on arts and luxuries. Thus, the Italians of the Renaissance, whether as public or private patrons, could afford to use consumption of art as a form of competition for social and political status. And it was not just the elite who could afford art. Surprisingly modest families bought small religious paintings, painted storage chests, and decorative arts. Thus the market for art steadily increased in the fourteenth and fifteenth centuries, as did the number of shops and studios in which artists could be trained.

Artists in the modern world are accustomed to standing outside society as critics of conventional ideas. In the late Middle Ages and Renaissance, artists were not alienated commentators. In 1300 most art was religious in subject, and public display was its purpose. Throughout Europe art fulfilled a devotional function. Painted crucifixes, altarpieces, and banners were often endowed as devotional or penitential objects. The Arena Chapel in Padua, with its frescoes by Giotto, was funded by a merchant anxious to pay for some of his sins.

In the late Middle Ages and Renaissance, numerous paintings and statues throughout Italy (and much of the rest of Europe) were revered for their miraculous powers. During plague, drought, and times of war, people had recourse to the sacred power of the saints represented in these works of art. (See the feature "Weighing the Evidence: A Painting of the Plague" in Chapter 11, pages 390–391.) The construction of the great churches of the period was often a community project that lasted for decades, even centuries. The city council of Siena, for example, voted to rebuild its Gothic cathedral of Saint Mary, saying that the blessed Virgin "was, is and will be in the future the head of this city" and that through veneration of her "Siena may be protected from harm." Accordingly, although the subject of art was clearly and primarily religious, the message was bound up in the civic values and ideas of the fourteenth and fifteenth centuries.

The first burst of artistic creativity in the fourteenth century was paid for by public institutions. Communal governments built and redecorated city halls to house government functionaries and to promote civic pride. Most towns placed a remarkable emphasis on the beauty of the work. Civic officials often named special commissions to consult with a variety of artists and architects before approving building projects. Governments, with an eye to the appearance of public areas, legislated the width of streets, height limits, and even the styles of dwelling façades.

The series of paintings called the *Good Government of Siena* illustrates the use of art to communicate political ideas. Painted in the first half of the fourteenth century by Ambrogio Lorenzetti° (ca. 1300–1348), *Good Government* combined allegorical representations of Wisdom and the cardinal virtues on one wall with realistic street scenes of a well-ordered Siena on an adjacent

wall. Across from the scenes of good government are its opposite, graphic representations of murder, rape, and general injustice and mayhem. In this ambitious work, with its specific scenes and unmistakable tone, the government broadcast a clear political message in realistic brushstrokes. The popular preacher San Bernardino of Siena (1380–1444) reinforced the point of Lorenzetti's painting: "To see Peace depicted is a delight and so it is a shame to see War painted on the other wall." And Bernardino's sermon reminded listeners of the conclusions they should draw: "Oh my brothers and fathers, love and embrace each other . . . give your aid to this toil which I have undertaken so gladly, to bring about love and peace among you."[15]

Public art in Florence was often organized and supported by various guild organizations. Guild membership was a prerequisite for citizenship, so guildsmen set the tone in politics as well as in the commercial life of the city. Most major guilds commissioned sculpture for the Chapel of Or San Michele, a famous shrine in the grain market (its painting of the Virgin was popularly thought to have wonder-working powers) and seat of the Guelf party, the city's most powerful political organization. Guilds took responsibility for building and maintaining other structures in the city as well. Guildsmen took pride in creating a beautiful environment, but as the cloth makers' decision to supervise the baptistery shows, the work reflected not only on the city and its patron saint but also on the power and influence of the guild itself.

The princes who ruled outside the republics of Italy often had similarly precise messages that they wished to communicate. Renaissance popes embarked on a quite specific ideological program in the late fifteenth century to assert their dual roles as spiritual leaders of Christendom and temporal lords of a central Italian state (see page 422). Rulers such as the Este dukes of Ferrara and the Sforza dukes of Milan constructed castles within their cities or hunting lodges and villas in the countryside and adorned them with pictures of the hunt or murals of knights in combat, scenes that emphasized their noble virtues and their natural right to rule.

By the mid-fifteenth century, patrons of artworks in Florence and most other regions of Italy were more and more likely to be wealthy individuals. Republics, in which all families were in principle equal, initially distrusted the pride and ambition implied by elaborate city palaces and rural villas. By the middle of the fifteenth century, however, such reserve was found in none but the most conservative republics, such as Venice or Lucca.

Ambrogio Lorenzetti (am-BROH-jo loh-ren-ZET-ee)

Palaces, gardens, and villas became the settings in which the wealthy could entertain their peers, receive clients, and debate the political issues of the day. The public rooms of these *palazzos* were decorated with portraits, gem collections, rare books, ceramics, and statuary. Many villas and palaces included private chapels. In the Medici palace in Florence, for example, the chapel is the setting for a painting of the Magi (the three Wise Men who came to worship the infant Jesus) in which the artist, Benozzo Gozzoli (1420–1498), used members of the Medici family as models for the portraits of the Wise Men and their entourage. The Magi, known to be wise and virtuous rulers, were an apt symbol for the family that had come to dominate the city.

Artists at princely courts were expected to work for the glory of their lord. Often the genre of choice was the portrait. One of the most successful portraitists of the sixteenth century was Sofonisba Anguissola° (1532–1625). Anguissola won renown as a prodigy because she was female and from a patrician family; one of her paintings was sent to Michelangelo, who forwarded it to the Medici in Florence. Since women would never be allowed to study anatomy, Anguissola concentrated her talents on portraits and detailed paintings of domestic life. Later she was called to the Spanish court, where the king, queen, and their daughter sat for her. She continued to paint after her marriage and return to Italy. Even in her nineties, she welcomed painters from all parts of Europe to visit and discuss techniques of portraiture.

THE SPREAD OF THE RENAISSANCE, 1350–1536

BY 1500, the Renaissance had spread from Italy to the rest of Europe. Well beyond the borders of the old Roman Empire, in Prague and Cracow, for example, one could find a renewed interest in classical ideas about art and literature. As information about the past and its relevance to contemporary life spread, however, the message was transformed in several important ways. Outside Italy, Rome and its history played a much less pivotal role. Humanists elsewhere in the West were interested more in religious than in political reform, and they responded to a number of im-

portant local interests. Yet the Renaissance notion of renewal based on a deep understanding and imitation of the past remained at the center of the movement. The nature of the transformation will be clearer if we begin by considering the nature of vernacular literatures before the emergence of Renaissance humanism.

■ Vernacular Literatures

The humanistic movement was not simply a continuation of practical and literary movements. The extent of its innovation will be clearer if we look briefly at the vernacular literatures (that is, written in native languages, rather than Latin) of the fourteenth and fifteenth centuries.

As in Italy, fourteenth-century writers were not immediately drawn to classical sources. Boccaccio's work, for example, influenced another vernacular writer, Geoffrey Chaucer (ca. 1343–1400), the son of a London burgher, who served as a diplomat, courtier, and Member of Parliament. In addition to the pervasive French influence, Chaucer read and studied Boccaccio. Chaucer's most well-known work, *The Canterbury Tales,* consists of stories told by a group of thirty pilgrims who left the London suburbs on a pilgrimage to the shrine of Saint Thomas Becket at Canterbury Cathedral. The narrators and the stories themselves describe a variety of moral and social types, creating an acute, sometimes bitter, portrait of English life. The Wife of Bath is typical of Chaucer's pilgrims: "She was a worthy woman all her life, husbands at the churchdoor she had five." After describing her own five marriages, she observes that marriage is a proper way to achieve moral perfection, but it can be so only if the woman is master.

Although Chaucer's characters present an ironic view of the good and evil that characterize society, Chaucer's contemporary, William Langland (ca. 1330–1400), takes a decidedly more serious view of the ills of English life. Whereas Boccaccio and Chaucer all told realistic tales about life as it truly seemed to be, Langland used the traditional allegorical language (that is, symbolic language in which a place or person represents an idea) of medieval Europe. In *Piers Plowman* Langland writes of people caught between the "Valley of Death" and the "Tower of Truth." He describes the seven deadly sins that threaten all of society and follows with an exhortation to do better. Both Chaucer and Langland expected that their audiences would immediately recognize commonly held ideas and values.

Despite the persistence of old forms of literature, new vernacular styles arose, although they still dealt

---

Anguissola (an-GWIS-so-lah)

with traditional values and ideas. Throughout Europe many writers directly addressed their cares and concerns. Letters like those of the Paston family in England or Alessandra Macinghi-Strozzi in Italy described day-to-day affairs of business, politics, and family life. Letters dictated and sent by Saint Catherine of Siena and Angela of Foligno offered advice to the troubled. Small books of moral or spiritual writings were especially popular among women readers in the fourteenth and fifteenth centuries, among them *The Mirror for Simple Souls* by Marguerite of Porete (d. 1310). Though Marguerite was ultimately executed as a heretic, her work continued to circulate anonymously. Her frank descriptions of love, including God's love for humans, inspired many other writers in the fourteenth and fifteenth centuries. Less erotic but equally riveting was the memoir of Margery Kempe, an alewife from England, who left her husband and family, dressed in white (symbolic of virginity), and joined other pilgrims on trips to Spain, Italy, and Jerusalem.

One of the most unusual of the new vernacular writers was Christine de Pizan (1369–1430), the daughter of an Italian physician at the court of Charles V of France. When the deaths of her father and husband left her with responsibility for her children and little money, she turned to writing. From 1389 until her death, she lived and wrote at the French court. She is perhaps best known for *The Book of the City of the Ladies* (1405). In it she added her own voice to what is known as the *querelle des femmes,* the "argument over women." Christine wrote to counter the prevalent opinions of women as inherently inferior to men and incapable of moral judgments. She argued that the problem was education: "If it were customary to send daughters to school like sons, and if they were then taught the natural sciences, they would learn as thoroughly and understand the subtleties of all the arts and sciences as well as sons." Christine described in her book an ideal city of ladies in which prudence, justice, and reason would protect women from ignorant male critics.

All these vernacular writings built on popular tales and sayings as well as on traditional moral and religious writings. Unlike the early humanists, the vernacular writers saw little need for new cultural and intellectual models.

◼ The Impact of Printing

The spread of humanism beyond Italy was aided greatly by the invention of printing. In the fifteenth century the desire to own and to read complete texts of classical works was widespread, but the number of copies was severely limited by the time and expense of hand copying, collating, and checking manuscripts. Poggio Bracciolini's letters are filled with complaints about the time and expense of reproducing the classical manuscripts he had discovered. One copy he had commissioned was so inaccurate and illegible as to be nearly unusable. Traveling to repositories and libraries was often easier than creating a personal library. It was rarely possible for someone who read a manuscript once to obtain a complete copy to compare with other works.

The invention of printing with movable lead type changed things dramatically. (See the feature "Information Technology: The Print Revolution" on pages 414–415.) Although block printing had long been known in China and was a popular way to produce playing cards and small woodcuts in Europe, only with the creation of movable type by Johann Gutenberg in the 1450s did printing become a practical way to produce books. Between 180 and 200 copies of the so-called Gutenberg Bible were printed in 1452–1453. It was followed shortly by editions of the Psalms. German printers spread their techniques rapidly. By 1470 printing had spread to Italy, the Low Countries, France, and England. It has been estimated that by 1500 a thousand presses were operating in 265 towns (see Map 12.1). The output of the early presses was extremely varied, ranging from small devotional books and other popular and profitable literature to complete editions of classical authors and their humanistic and theological texts.

Printing allowed for the creation of agreed-upon standard editions of works in law, theology, philosophy, and science. Scholars in different parts of the European world could feel fairly confident that they and their colleagues were analyzing identical texts. Similarly, producing accurate medical and herbal diagrams, maps, and even reproductions of art and architecture was easier. Multiple copies of texts also made possible the study of rare and esoteric literary, philosophical, and scientific works. An unexpected result of the print revolution was the rise of the printshop as a center of culture and communication. The printers Aldus Manutius (1450–1515) in Venice and Johannes Froben (d. 1527) in Basel were humanists. Both invited humanists to work in their shops editing their texts and correcting the proofs before printing. Printshops became a natural gathering place for clerics and laymen. Thus, they were natural sources of humanist ideas and later, in the sixteenth century, of Protestant religious programs.

Map 12.1   The Spread of Printing   Printing technology moved rapidly along major trade routes to the most populous and prosperous areas of Europe. The technology was rapidly adopted in peripheral areas as well as in highly literate centers such as the Low Countries, the Rhine Valley, and northern Italy.

■ Humanism Outside Italy

As the influence of the humanist movement extended beyond Italy, the interests of the humanists changed. Although a strong religious strain infused Italian humanism, public life lay at the center of Italian programs of education and reform. Outside Italy, however, moral and religious reform formed the heart of the movement. Northern humanists wanted to renew Christian life and reinvigorate the church. Critics of the church complained that the clergy were wealthy and ignorant and that the laity were uneducated and superstitious. To amend those failings, northern humanists were involved

in building educational institutions, in unearthing and publishing texts by Church Fathers, and in chronicling local customs and history. The works of the two best-known humanists, Thomas More and Desiderius Erasmus, present a sharp critique of contemporary behavior and, in the case of Erasmus, a call to a new sense of piety. The religious views of Erasmus were so influential that northern humanism has generally come to be known as "Christian humanism."

The intellectual environment of centers into which humanism spread from Italy had changed significantly since the thirteenth century. The universities of Paris and Oxford retained the status they had acquired earlier but found themselves competing with a host of new foundations. Like Paris, almost all had theological faculties dominated by Scholastically trained theologians. Nevertheless, the new foundations often had chairs of rhetoric, or "eloquence," which left considerable scope for those who advocated humanistic learning. These new universities, from Cracow (1367) to Uppsala in Sweden (1477), also reflected the increased national feeling in various regions of Europe. The earliest university in the lands of the German empire, the Charles University in Prague (1348), was founded at the request of Emperor Charles IV of Luxemburg, whose court was in Prague. The foundation of a new university at Poszony (1465) by Johannes Vitéz was part of a cultural flowering of the Hungarian court at Buda. A supporter of King Matthias Corvinus, Vitéz corresponded with Italian humanists, collected manuscripts, and tried to recruit humanist teachers to come to Buda. Vienna (1365), Aix (1409), Louvain (1425), and numerous other universities owed their foundations to the pride and ambition of local rulers.

Humanists on faculties of law in French universities used humanistic techniques of historical and linguistic study. Italian-trained French lawyers introduced what came to be called the "Gallican style" of jurisprudence. Because legal ideas, like language, changed over time, they argued that Roman law had to be studied as a historically created system and not as an abstract and unchanging structure. Humanists like Guillaume Budé (1468–1540) moved from the study of law to considerations of Roman coinage, religion, and economic life in order to better understand the formation of Roman law. The desire to understand the law led other humanist-legists to add the study of society in ancient Gaul to their work on Rome, and then to examine the law of other societies as well.

The new universities often became centers of linguistic studies. Humanistic interest in language inspired the foundation of "trilingual" colleges in Spain, France, and the Low Countries to foster serious study of Hebrew, Greek, and Latin. Like Italian humanists, other humanists believed that knowledge of languages would allow students to understand more clearly the truths of Christianity. Typical of this movement was the archbishop of Toledo, Francisco Jiménez de Cisneros (1436–1517), who founded the University of Alcalá in 1508 with chairs of Latin, Greek, and Hebrew. He began the publication of a vast new edition of the Bible, called the "Polyglot Bible" ("many tongue"; 1522) because it had parallel columns in Latin, Greek, and, where appropriate, Hebrew. Unlike Valla, Jiménez did not intend his translations to challenge the Vulgate, but merely clarify its meaning. The university and the Bible were part of an effort to complete the conversion of Muslims and Jews and to reform religious practices among the old Christians.

To these humanists, the discovery and publication of early Christian authors seemed critical to any reform within the church. Jacques Lefèvre d'Étaples° (1455–1536) of France was one of the most famous and influential of these humanistic editors of early Christian texts. After 1500 he concentrated on the edition of texts by the early Church Fathers. The true spirit of Christianity, he believed, would be most clear in the works and lives of those who had lived closest to the age of the apostles. Christian humanists inspired by Lefèvre became key players in the later Reformation movements in France. Lefèvre's faith in the value of classical languages was shared by John Colet (1467–1519) of England, founder of St. Paul's School in London. He instituted a thorough program of teaching Latin and Greek aimed at creating scholars who would have access to the earliest Christian writings.

Tensions between the humanists and the advocates of Scholastic methods broke out over the cultural and linguistic studies that formed the heart of the humanist program. Taking to heart the humanistic belief that all philosophies and religions, not just Christianity, contained universal moral and spiritual truths, Johannes Reuchlin° (1455–1522) of Württemberg embarked on a study of the Cabala. Johannes Pfefferkorn, a Dominican priest and recent convert from Judaism, attacked Reuchlin's use of Jewish traditions in the study of Christian theology. Sides were quickly drawn. The theological faculties of the German universities generally supported the Dominican. The humanists supported Reuchlin. In his own defense Reuchlin issued *The Letters of Illustrious Men*, a volume of correspondence he had received in support of his position. This work gave rise to one of the great satires of the Renaissance, *The Letters of Obscure Men* (1516), written by anonymous authors and purporting to be letters from various narrow-minded Scholastics in defense of the Dominican. Although the debate arose over the validity of Hebraic studies for Christian theology and not over humanistic ideas of reform or wisdom, it indicates the division between the humanists and much of the Scholastic community. Many initially misunderstood the early controversies of the Protestant Reformation as a continuation of the conflicts between humanists and Scholastic theologians over the uses of Hebrew learning.

Lefèvre d'Étaples (le-FEV-ra du-TAHP-le)
Reuchlin (RYE-klin)

The Print Revolution

For more than five thousand years, from the dawn of civilization in Mesopotamia and Egypt, people in the West wrote by hand. Imperial decrees, sacred scriptures, commercial transactions, private letters—all required the skills of a select group of scribes, clerks, or monks. In Korea and China, however, mechanical printing using carved wooden blocks had been introduced by A.D. 750. Moveable type, using characters made of baked clay, was invented in China in the eleventh century. But the Chinese continued to prefer block printing well into the modern period. Written Chinese consists of thousands of ideographic characters. The labor of creating, organizing, and setting so many different bits of type made it much simpler to cut individual pages from a single wooden block. European languages, which can be written with fewer than a hundred characters, were much better adapted to printing with movable, reusable type.

It appears that the Mongol armies brought examples of Chinese printing—the Venetian Marco Polo described seeing paper money during his travels—to western Asia and Europe at the end of the thirteenth century. In the early fourteenth century Europeans began using block printing techniques to produce religious images, short prayers, and even decks of playing cards. As with Chinese printing, European block printing was a slow and expensive process for printing large numbers of varied texts. The print revolution had to wait another century, until the innovations of the German goldsmith Johann Gutenberg (ca. 1399–1468).

Gutenberg drew on his knowledge of metallurgy to devise a lead-tin-copper alloy that could be cast into durable, reusable type. His crucial invention was a type mold consisting of a flat strip of metal—stamped in the same way a coin is minted, leaving the impression of a single letter—inserted in the bottom of a rectangular brass box held together by screws. Molten metal was poured into it, producing a single piece of type. An experienced type founder could produce up to six hundred pieces of type a day. No wooden-block carver could have approached that rate. To solve the remaining problems, Gutenberg adapted the screw press commonly used to produce linen, paper, and wine to make a printing press. He followed the example of Flemish painters by adding linseed oil to the ink to make it thick enough to adhere uniformly to the metal type.

In 1455 the Gutenberg Bible was published in Mainz, Germany—but not by Gutenberg. After years of costly experimentation, Gutenberg was forced to turn over his equipment and newly printed Bibles to his partner and creditor, the wealthy merchant and moneylender Johann Fust.

The new technology, which enabled printers to create a thousand or more copies in a single print run, was highly efficient. Simple printed school texts cost only a quarter of the price of hand-copied texts. The leading bookseller in the university town of Bologna managed to stock ten thousand copies of texts, treatises, and commentaries. By 1500 even street singers sold printed copies of their songs.

Gutenberg's invention was revolutionary because, for the first time, the same information and ideas were avail-

---

■ Thomas More and Desiderius Erasmus

The careers of two humanists in particular exemplify the strength of the humanistic movement outside Italy, and its limits: Sir Thomas More (1478–1535) of London and Desiderius Erasmus (1466–1536) of Rotterdam. Their careers developed along very different paths. More had been educated at St. Anthony's school in London and became a lawyer. A friend of John Colet, he translated Lucan and wrote a humanistic history of Richard III while pursuing his public career. He is most famous for his work *Utopia* (1516), the description of an ideal society located on the island of Utopia (literally, "nowhere") in the newly explored oceans. This powerful and contradictory work comprises two volumes. Book I is a debate over the moral value of public service between Morus, a well-intentioned but practical politician, and Hythloday, a widely traveled idealist. Morus tries to make the bureaucrat's argument about working for change from within the system. Hythloday rejects the argument out of hand. Thomas More himself seems to have been unsure at that time about the virtues of public service. He was of two minds, and the debate between Morus and Hythloday reflects his indecision. As part of his critique of justice and politics in Europe, Hythloday describes in Book II the commonwealth of Utopia, in which there is no private property but strict equality of possessions, and, as a result, harmony, tolerance, and little or no violence.

A French Printshop   The production of a book took many skills. This sixteenth-century illumination shows the entire process. On the left, one man works the press while a second prepares to ink a press. On the right we see the scholar with a manuscript (*rear*), a compositor selecting type as he checks the text in a book, and finally a second scholar checking the broadsides produced by the press.   *(Giraudon/Art Resource, NY)*

able throughout Europe at virtually the same time. The great Venetian printer Aldus Manutius (1450–1515) produced over 120,000 volumes, many in the new, smaller, easily portable "octavo" format—about 6 by 9 inches. Books from the Aldine Press and other humanistic publishers played a decisive role in spreading humanism to parts of Europe where manuscript books were difficult to acquire.

Moreover, book owning was no longer the exclusive preserve of scholars. This was all the more true because printers included on their lists works in vernacular languages, not just the ancient classics. Perhaps one half of the books produced by most publishers were small prayer books and short selections of Bible stories or saints' lives. The very popularity of printed vernacular texts affected language. William Caxton (1422–1492), for example, began printing books in English in 1472. His pioneering work helped standardize modern English, just as the publication of Martin Luther's German translation of the Bible in 1522 would standardize modern German. The advent of printing had other far-reaching consequences: it promoted the increase of literacy throughout Europe, and in the sixteenth century printed books and pamphlets would become a prime vehicle for Protestants and Catholics to spread religious ideas and protests.

By the eighteenth century, printed books had changed the nature of popular culture. Myths, folk songs, and popular histories were traditionally passed by word of mouth, often changing in the telling to fit the time and place. Once they appeared in print, they could no longer be performed and refashioned, only recited. Printing not only changed the way information was transmitted but also changed the information itself.

Since the publication of *Utopia*, debates have raged about whether More, or anyone, could ever really hope to live in such a society. Some scholars have questioned how seriously More took this work—he seems to have written the initial sections merely to amuse friends. Yet whatever More's intentions, Utopia's society of equality, cooperation, and acceptance continues to inspire social commentators.

Ironically, More himself, like his creation Morus, soon found himself trying to work for justice within precisely the sort of autocratic court that Hythloday criticized. Not long after the completion of *Utopia*, More entered the service of King Henry VIII (r. 1509–1547), eventually serving as chancellor of England. As a staunch Catholic and royal official, More never acted on utopian principles of peace and toleration. He was, in fact, responsible for the persecution of English Protestants in the years before the king's break with Rome (see page 479). More's opposition to Henry's divorce and repudiation of papal authority, and his refusal to acknowledge Henry as the head of the English church, led him to resign his offices. He was eventually imprisoned and beheaded. More's writing was a stinging critique of political values. He implied that society could be reformed, yet in the period after 1521, his humanism and his vision of Utopia had no influence on his own public life.

Unlike More, who was drawn to the power of king and pope, Erasmus always avoided working for authorities.

❧ READING SOURCES

A Pilgrimage for Religion's Sake

Desiderius Erasmus wrote numerous colloquies (short stories) as Latin exercises for young students. In this way, he hoped to reveal, in a humorous fashion, some of the contemporary customs that were long overdue for change. Here he describes a visit to the English pilgrimage shrine of Saint Thomas Becket at Canterbury.

My friend Gratian made a faux pas here. After a short prayer, he asked the keeper, "I say good father, is it true, as I have heard, that in his lifetime Thomas was most generous to the poor?" "Very true," the man replied, and began to rehearse the saint's many acts of kindness to them. Then Gratian: "I don't suppose his disposition changed in this matter, unless perhaps for the better." The custodian agreed. Gratian again: "Since then, the saint was so liberal towards the needy, although he was still poor himself and lacked money to provide for the necessities of life, don't you think he'd gladly consent now that he's so rich and needs nothing if some poor wretched woman with hungry children at home, or daughters in danger of losing their virtue because they have no money for dowries, or a husband sick in bed and penniless—if, after begging the saint's forgiveness, she carried off a bit of all this wealth to rescue her family as though

taking it from someone who wanted her to have it, either as a gift or a loan?" When the gatekeeper in charge of the gilded head made no reply to this, Gratian, who is impulsive, said, "For my part, I'm convinced the saint would even rejoice that in death, too, he would relieve the wants of the poor by his riches." At this the custodian frowned and pursed his lips, looking at us with Gorgon eyes, and I don't doubt he would have driven us from the church with insults and reproaches had he not been aware that we were recommended by the archbishop. I managed to placate the fellow by smooth talk, affirming that Gratian hadn't spoken seriously, but liked to joke, and at the same time I gave him some coins.

Source: Erasmus, *Ten Colloquies*, translated by Craig R. Thompson (London and New York: Macmillan, 1986), pp. 83–84.

Often called the "Prince of Humanists," he was easily the best-known humanist of the early sixteenth century. He was born the illegitimate son of a priest in the Low Countries. Forced by relatives into a monastery, he disliked the conservative piety and authoritarian discipline of traditional monastic life. Once allowed out of the monastery to serve as an episcopal secretary, he never returned. He lived and taught in France, England, Italy, and Switzerland. Of all the humanists, it was Erasmus who most benefited from the printing revolution. The printer Aldus Manutius invited him to live and work in Venice, and he spent the last productive years of his life at Johannes Froben's press in Basel. He left the city only when Protestant reformers took control of the city government.

Over a long career Erasmus brought out repeated editions of works designed to educate Christians. His *Adages*, first published in 1500, was a collection of proverbs from Greek and Roman sources. The work was

immensely popular, and Erasmus repeatedly issued expanded editions. He tried to present Greek and Roman wisdom that would illuminate everyday problems. *The Colloquies* was a collection of popular stories, designed as primers for students, that taught moral lessons even as they served as examples of good language. (See the box "Reading Sources: A Pilgrimage for Religion's Sake.") His ironic *Praise of Folly* (1511) was dedicated to Thomas More. An oration by Folly in praise of folly, it was satire of a type unknown since antiquity. Folly's catalog of vices includes everyone from the ignoramus to the scholar. But more seriously, Erasmus believed, as Saint Paul had said, that Christians must be "fools for Christ." In effect, human existence is folly. Erasmus's Folly first made an observation that Shakespeare would refine and make famous: "Now the whole life of mortal men, what is it but a sort of play in which . . . [each person] plays his own part until the director gives him his cue to leave the stage."[16]

Erasmus's greatest contributions to European intellectual life were his edition of and commentaries on the New Testament. His was a critical edition of the Greek text and a Latin translation independent of the fourth-century Latin Vulgate of Jerome. Unlike Jiménez, Erasmus corrected parts of the Vulgate. He rejected the authority of tradition, saying, "The sin of corruption is greater, and the need for careful revision by scholars is greater also, where the source of corruption was ignorance."[17] What was revolutionary in his edition was his commentary, which emphasized the literal and historical recounting of human experiences. Erasmus's Bible was the basis of later vernacular translations of Scripture during the Reformation.

Underlying Erasmus's scholarly output was what he called his "Philosophy of Christ." Erasmus was convinced that the true essence of Christianity was to be found in the life and actions of Christ. Reasonable, self-reliant, truly Christian people did not need superstitious rituals or magic. In his *Colloquies* he tells of a terrified priest who during a shipwreck promised everything to the Virgin Mary if only she would save him from drowning. But, Erasmus observed, it would have been more practical to start swimming!

Erasmus believed that a humanistic combination of classical and Christian wisdom could wipe away violence, superstition, and ignorance. Unlike More, Erasmus never abandoned the humanistic program. Yet his philosophy of Christ, based on faith in the goodness and educability of the individual, was swamped in the 1520s and 1530s by the sectarian claims of both Protestants and Catholics. Although Erasmus's New Testament was influential in the Reformation, his calls for reforms based on tolerance and reason were not.

■ Renaissance Art in the North

In the early fifteenth century, while Brunelleschi and Masaccio were revolutionizing the ways in which Italian artists viewed their world, artists north of the Alps, especially in Flanders, were making equally striking advances in the way they painted and sculpted. Artistic innovation in the North began with changes tied closely to the world of northern courts; only later did artists take up the styles of the Italian Renaissance. Northerners took Italian Renaissance art and fit it to a new environment.

Northern art of the late fourteenth and fifteenth centuries changed in two significant ways. In sculpture, the long, austere, unbroken vertical lines typical of Gothic sculpture gave way to a much more complex and emotional style. In painting, Flemish artists moved from ornate, vividly colored paintings to experiments with ways

to create a sense of depth. Artists strove to paint and sculpt works that more faithfully represented reality. The sculptures of Claus Sluter (1350–1406), carved for a family chapel of the Burgundian dukes at Champmol, captured a lifelike drama unlike the previous Gothic sculpture. Court painters such as Jan van Eyck (ca. 1390–1441) in miniatures, portraits, and altar paintings also moved away from a highly formalized style to a careful representation of specific places. In Van Eyck's portrait of the Italian banker and courtier Giovanni Arnolfini and his bride, the image of the painter is reflected in a small mirror behind the couple, and above the mirror is written, "Jan van Eyck was here, 1434." Whereas Italians of the early fifteenth century tried to recreate space through linear perspective, the Flemish used aerial perspective, softening colors and tones to give the illusion of depth.

Van Eyck: The Arnolfini Wedding   Careful observation of people and places was typical of the new art of both the north and the south. Van Eyck seems to have re-created this scene to the smallest detail. His own image appears in the mirror on the wall.   *(Reproduced by Courtesy of the Trustees, The National Gallery, London)*

Portrait of a Black Man Albrecht Dürer sketched this portrait in the early sixteenth century, most likely in a commercial center such as Venice or Nuremberg. By that time it was common to show one of the three Wise Men as black, but such depictions, unlike Dürer's drawing here, were rarely based on portrait studies. *(Graphische Sammlung, Albertina)*

The influence of Renaissance styles in the north of Europe dates from the reign of the French king Francis I (r. 1515–1547), when Italian artists in significant numbers traveled north. Francis invited Italian artists to his court—most notably Leonardo da Vinci, who spent his last years in France. The most influential of the Italian-style creations in France was doubtless Francis's château Fontainebleau, whose decorations contained mythologies, histories, and allegories of the kind found in the Italian courts. Throughout the sixteenth century, Italianate buildings and paintings sprang up throughout Europe.

Perhaps the most famous artist who traveled to Italy, learned Italian techniques, and then transformed them to suit the environment of northern Europe was Albrecht

Dürer of Nuremberg (1471–1528). Son of a well-known goldsmith, Dürer became a painter and toured France and Flanders learning the techniques popular in northern Europe. Then in 1494 he left Nuremberg on the first of two trips to Italy, during which he sketched Italian landscapes and studied the work of Italian artists, especially in Venice. What he learned in Italy, combined with the friendship of some of Germany's leading humanists, formed the basis of Dürer's works, which blended northern humanistic interests with the Italian techniques of composition and linear perspective. Dürer worked in charcoal, watercolors, and paints, but his influence was most widely spread through his numerous woodcuts covering classical and contemporary themes. His woodcut *Whore of Babylon*, prepared in the context of the debate over the reform of the church, is based on sketches of Venetian prostitutes completed during his first visit to Italy.

Numerous other artists and engravers traveled south to admire and learn from the great works of Italian artists. The engravings they produced and distributed back home made the southern innovations available to those who would never set foot in Italy. In fact, some now lost or destroyed creations are known only through the copies engraved by northern artists eager to absorb Italian techniques.

THE RENAISSANCE AND COURT SOCIETY

HE educational reforms of the humanists and the innovations in the arts between 1300 and 1550 provided an opportunity for rulers and popes alike to use culture to define and celebrate their authority. Art, literature, and politics merged in the brilliant life of the Renaissance Italian courts, both secular and papal. To understand fully the Renaissance and its importance in the history of Europe, we need to examine the uses of culture by governments, specifically investigating the transformation of European ideas about service at court during the fourteenth and fifteenth centuries. We will take as a model the politics and cultural life at one noble court: the court of the Gonzaga family of Mantua. We will also discuss the development of the idea of the Renaissance gentleman and courtier made famous by Baldassare Castiglione°, who was reared at the

Castiglione (ka-stil-ee-OH-nee)

Gonzaga court. Finally, we will see how the Renaissance papacy melded the secular and religious aspects of art, culture, and politics in its glittering court in Rome.

■ The Elaboration of the Court

The courts of northern Italy interested themselves in the cultural and artistic innovations of the Renaissance artists and humanists inspired by classical civilization, and they closely imitated many of the values and new styles that were developing in the courts of northern Europe, such as the court of Burgundy. Throughout Europe, attendance at court became increasingly important to members of the nobility as a source of revenue and influence. Kings and the great territorial lords were equally interested in drawing people to their courts as a way to influence and control the noble and the powerful.

Rulers in most parts of Europe instituted monarchical orders of knighthood to reward allies and followers. The most famous in the English-speaking world was the Order of the Garter, founded in 1349 by King Edward III. The orders were but one of the innovations in the organization of the court during the fourteenth and fifteenth centuries. The numbers of cooks, servants, huntsmen, musicians, and artists employed at court jumped dramatically in the late Middle Ages. In this expansion, the papal court itself was a model for the rest of Europe. The popes at Avignon in the fourteenth century already had households of nearly six hundred persons. If all the bureaucrats, merchants, local officials, and visitors who continually swarmed around the elaborate papal court were also counted, the number grew even larger.

Courts were becoming theaters built around a series of widely understood signs and images that the ruler could manipulate. Culture was meant to reflect the reputation of the ruler. On important political or personal occasions, rulers organized jousts or tournaments around themes drawn from mythology. The dukes of Milan indicated the relative status of courtiers by inviting them to participate in particular hunts or jousts. They similarly organized their courtiers during feasts or elaborate entries into the towns and cities of their realms.

The late fourteenth and fifteenth centuries were periods of growth in the political and bureaucratic power of European rulers. The increasingly elaborate and sumptuous courts were one of the tools that rulers used to create a unified culture and ideology. At the court of the Gonzagas in Mantua, one of the most widely known of the fifteenth-century courts, the manipulation of Renaissance culture for political purposes was most complete.

■ The Court of Mantua

The city of Mantua, with perhaps 25,000 inhabitants in 1500, was small next to Milan or Venice—the two cities with which it was most commonly allied. Located in a rich farming region along the Po River, Mantua did not have a large merchant or manufacturing class. Most Mantuans were involved in agriculture and regional trade in foodstuffs. The town had been a typical medieval Italian city-state until its government was overthrown by the noble Bonacolsi family in the thirteenth century. The Bonacolsis, in turn, were ousted in a palace coup in 1328 by their former comrades, the Gonzagas, who ruled the city until 1627.

The Gonzagas faced problems typical of many of the ruling families in northern Italy. The state they were creating was relatively small, their right to rule was not very widely recognized, and their control over the area was weak. The first step for the Gonzagas was to construct fortresses and fortified towns that could withstand foreign enemies. The second step was to gain recognition of their right to rule. In 1329 they were named imperial vicars, or representatives in the region. Later, in 1432, they bought the title "marquis" from Emperor Sigismund for the relatively low price of £12,000—equivalent to a year's pay for their courtiers. By 1500 they had exchanged that title for the more prestigious "duke."

Presiding over a strategic area between the Milanese and Venetian states, the Gonzagas maintained themselves through astute diplomatic connections with other Italian and European courts and through service as well-paid mercenaries in the Italian wars of the fifteenth and sixteenth centuries. Marquis Lodovico (d. 1478) served the Venetians, the Milanese, the Florentines, and even the far-off Neapolitans. With considerable understatement, Lodovico concluded, "We have worn armor for a long time."

The family's reputation was enhanced by Gianfrancesco° (d. 1444) and Lodovico, who brought the Renaissance and the new court style to Mantua. By 1500 as many as eight hundred or more nobles, cooks, maids, and horsemen may have gathered in the court. Critics called them idlers "who have no other function but to cater to the tastes of the Duke." It was under the tutelage of the Gonzagas that Vittorino da Feltre created his educational experiment in Villa Giocosa, which drew noble pupils from throughout Italy. It would be hard to overestimate the value for the Gonzagas of a school that attracted sons of the dukes of Urbino, Ferrara, and Milan

---

Gianfrancesco (jan-fran-CHES-ko)

and of numerous lesser nobles. The family also called many artists to Mantua. Lodovico invited Antonio Pisano, called Pisanello (ca. 1415–1456), probably the most famous court artist of the fifteenth century. Pisanello created a series of frescoes on Arthurian themes for the Gonzaga palace. In these frescoes Lodovico is portrayed as a hero of King Arthur's round table.

The Gonzagas are best known for their patronage of art with classical themes. Leon Battista Alberti redesigned the façade of the church of Sant'Andrea for the Gonzagas in the form of a Roman triumphal arch. The church, which long had been associated with the family, became a monument to the Gonzaga court just as the Arch of Constantine in Rome had celebrated imperial power a thousand years earlier. In the 1460s Lodovico summoned Andrea Mantegna (1441–1506) to his court. Trained in Padua and Venice, Mantegna was at that time the leading painter in northern Italy. His masterwork is the *Camera degli Sposi* (literally, "the room of the spouses"), completed in 1474. It features family portraits of Lodovico Gonzaga and his family framed in imitations of Roman imperial portrait medallions. One scene shows Lodovico welcoming his son, a newly appointed cardinal, back from Rome—proof to all of the new status of the Gonzagas.

The Gonzaga court, like most others, was both public and private. Finances for the city, appointments to public offices, and important political decisions were made by the men who dominated the court. On the other hand, as the prince's domestic setting, it was a place where women were expected to be seen and could exert their influence. Women were thus actively involved in creating the ideology of the court. Through the patronage of classical paintings, often with moral and political messages, wives of princes helped make the court better known and more widely accepted throughout Italy and Europe.

The arrival of Isabella d'Este (1494–1539) at court as the wife of Franceso Gonzaga marked the high point of the Renaissance in Mantua. Isabella had received a classical education at Ferrara and maintained an interest in art, architecture, and music all her life. As a patron of the arts, she knew what she wanted. (See the box "Reading Sources: Isabella d'Este Orders Art.") Isabella was also an accomplished musician, playing a variety of string and keyboard instruments. She and others of the Gonzaga family recruited Flemish and Italian musicians to their court. By the end of the sixteenth century, Mantua was one of the most important musical centers of Europe. One festival brought twelve thousand visitors to the city. Later, it would be in Mantua that Claudio Monteverdi

(1567–1643) wrote works that established the genre of opera.

In the fourteenth century Petrarch had complained that however enjoyable feasting in Mantua might be, the place was dusty, plagued by mosquitoes, and overrun with frogs. By the end of the fifteenth century, the Gonzagas had secured for themselves and their city a prominent place on the Italian, and the European, stage.

■ Castiglione and the European Gentleman

Renaissance ideas did not just spread in intellectual circles. They also were part of the transformation of the medieval knight into the early modern "gentleman." In 1528 Baldassare Castiglione (1478–1529) published *The Book of the Courtier*, a work in which he distilled what he had learned in his years at the various courts of Italy. Castiglione was born in Mantua, a distant relative to the ruling Gonzaga family. He grew up at court and was sent to the Sforza court in Milan to finish his education. During his career Castiglione met the greatest lights of the Renaissance. While he was in Rome, he became friends with Michelangelo and Raphael as well as with numerous humanistic writers. He died in Spain while on a mission for Pope Clement VII. When informed of his death, the emperor Charles V remarked, "One of the greatest knights in the world has died!" In his life and in his book, Castiglione summed up the great changes that had transformed the nature of late medieval chivalry.

The Book of the Courtier reports a series of fictional discussions at the court of Urbino held over the course of four nights in March 1507. Among the participants are the duchess of Urbino, Elizabeth Gonzaga; her lady-in-waiting; and a group of humanists, men of action, and courtiers. In four evenings, members of the circle try to describe the perfect gentleman of court. In the process they debate the nature of nobility, humor, women, and love.

It was in many respects a typical gathering at court, and its discourses reflect contemporary views of relations between men and women. The wives of princes were expected to be organizers of life at court, but still paragons of domestic virtues. The women organize the discussion, but the men discuss. Women direct and influence the talk by jokes and short interventions but cannot afford to dominate debate. "[Women] must be more circumspect, and more careful not to give occasion for evil being said of them . . . for a woman has not so many ways of defending herself against false calumnies as a man has."[18]

❧ READING SOURCES

Isabella d'Este Orders Art

Isabella d'Este, the marchioness of Mantua, created one of the foremost collections of Renaissance art in sixteenth-century Italy. In her quest to acquire representative works by the leading artists of the period, she has left an unparalleled collection of letters. In the following directive to Pietro Perugino, she describes what she expects from a painting she had commissioned from him.

Master Perugino, painter, [shall] make a painting on canvas 2½ braccia [5 feet] high and 3 braccia [6 feet] wide, and the said Pietro, the contractor, is obliged to paint on it a certain work of Lasciviousness and Modesty (in conflict) with these and many other embellishments, transmitted in this instruction to the said Pietro by the said Marchioness of Mantua, the copy of which is as follows:

Our poetic invention, which we greatly want to see painted by you, is the battle of Chastity against Lasciviousness, that is to say, Pallas [Athena] and Diana fighting vigorously against Venus and Cupid. And Pallas should seem almost to have vanquished Cupid, having broken his golden arrow and cast his silver bow underfoot; with one hand she is holding him by the bandage which the blind boy has before his eyes, and with the other she is lifting her lance and about to kill him. . . . And to give more expression and decoration to the picture, beside Pallas I want to have the olive tree sacred to her, with a shield leaning against it bearing the head of Medusa, and with the owl, the bird peculiar to Pallas, perched among the branches. And beside Venus I want her favorite tree, the myrtle, to be placed, but to enhance the beauty, a fount of water must be included, such as a river or the sea, where fauns, satyrs and more cupids will be seen, hastening to the help of Cupid, some swimming through the river, some flying, and some riding upon white swans, coming to join such an amorous battle. . . .

I am sending you all these details in a small drawing so that with both the written description and the drawing you will be able to consider my wishes in this matter. But if you think that perhaps there are too many figures in this for one picture, it is left to you to reduce them as you please, provided that you do not remove the principal basis, which consists of the four figures of Pallas, Diana, Venus and Cupid. If no inconvenience occurs I shall consider myself well satisfied; you are free to reduce them, but not to add anything else. Please be content with this arrangement.

Source: David S. Chambers, *Patrons and Artists in the Italian Renaissance* (London and New York: Macmillan, 1970), pp. 136–138.

The topics were not randomly chosen. Castiglione explained that he wished "to describe the form of courtiership most appropriate for a gentleman living at the courts of princes." Castiglione's popularity was based on his deliberate joining of humanistic ideas and traditional chivalric values. Although his topic was the court with all its trappings, Castiglione tells his readers that his models for the discussion are Greek and Latin dialogues, especially those of Cicero and Plato. As a Platonist, he believed that all truly noble gentlemen had an inborn quality of "grace." It had to be brought out, however, just as Michelangelo freed his figures from stone. Castiglione held that all moral and courtly virtues existed in tension with their opposites: "no magnanimity without pusillanimity." With numerous examples of good and bad in the world, wisdom could be revealed only through careful imitation, for like the classical authors favored by humanists, Castiglione advises, "He who lacks wisdom and knowledge will have nothing to say or do."[19]

But what struck Castiglione's readers was his advice about behavior. Francesco Guicciardini of

Florence once remarked, "When I was young, I used to scoff at knowing how to play, dance, and sing, and other such frivolities. . . . I have nevertheless seen from experience that these ornaments and accomplishments lend dignity and reputation even to men of good rank."[20] Guicciardini's comment underlines the value that readers found in Castiglione's work. Grace may be inbred, but it needed to be brought to the attention of those who controlled the court. Courtiers should first of all study the military arts. They had to fight, but only on occasions when their prowess would be noticed. Castiglione adds practical advice about how to dress, talk, and participate in music and dancing: never leap about wildly when dancing as peasants might, but dance only with an air of dignity and decorum. Castiglione further urges the courtier to be careful in dress: the French are "overdressed"; the Italians too quickly adopt the most recent and colorful styles. Reflecting political as well as social realities, Castiglione advises black or dark colors, which "reflect the sobriety of the Spaniards, since external appearances often bear witness to what is within."

The courtier always must take pains "to earn that universal regard which everyone covets." Too much imitation and obvious study, however, lead to affectation. Castiglione counseled courtiers to carry themselves with a certain diffidence or unstudied naturalness *(sprezzatura)*° covering their artifice. Accomplished courtiers will exhibit "that graceful and nonchalant spontaneity (as it is often called) . . . so that those who are watching them imagine that they couldn't and wouldn't even know how to make a mistake." Thus, Castiglione's courtier walked a fine line between clearly imitated and apparently natural grace.

Castiglione's book was an immediate success and widely followed even by those who claimed to have rejected it. By 1561 it was available in Spanish, French, and English translations. The reasons are not difficult to guess. It was critical for the courtier "to win for himself the mind and favour of the prince." And even those who disliked music, dancing, and light conversation learned Castiglione's arts "to open the way to the favour of princes." Many of the courtly arts that Castiglione preached had been traditional for centuries. Yet Castiglione's humanistic explanations and emphasis on form, control, and fashion had never seemed so essential as they did to the cultured gentlemen of the courts of the Renaissance and early modern Europe.

---

sprezzatura (spretz-ah-TU-ra)

■ The Renaissance Papacy

The issues of power and how it is displayed had religious as well as secular dimensions. After its fourteenth- and fifteenth-century struggles over jurisdiction, the Renaissance papacy found itself in need of a political and ideological counterweight to the centrifugal forces of conciliarism, reform, and local loyalties. Popes needed to defend their primacy within the church from conciliarists who had argued that all Christians, including the pope, were bound to obey the commands of general councils. The ideological focus of the revived papacy was Rome.

The first step in the creation of a new Rome was taken by Pope Nicholas V (r. 1446–1455), a cleric who had spent many years in the cultural environment of Renaissance Florence. Hoping to restore Rome and its church to their former glory, Nicholas and his successors patronized the arts, established a lively court culture, and sponsored numerous building projects. Nicholas was an avid collector of ancient manuscripts that seemed to demonstrate the intellectual and religious primacy of Rome. He invited numerous artists and intellectuals to the papal court, including the Florentine architect and writer Leon Battista Alberti (1404–1472). On the basis of his research in topography and reading done in Rome, Alberti wrote his treatise *On Architecture* (1452), the most important work on architecture produced during the Renaissance. It was probably under Alberti's influence that Nicholas embarked on a series of ambitious urban renewal projects in Rome, which included bridges, roads, and a rebuilt Saint Peter's Basilica.

The transformation of Rome had an ideological purpose. As one orator proclaimed, "Illuminated by the light of faith and Christian truth, [Rome] is destined to be the firmament of religion . . . , the secure haven for Christians."[21] Thus, the papal response to critics was to note that Rome and its government were central to political and religious life in Christendom. By reviving the style and organization of classical antiquity, the church sought to link papal Rome to a magnificent imperial tradition reaching back to Augustus and even to Alexander the Great. To papal supporters, only one authority could rule the church. Early tradition and the continuity of the city itself, they assumed, demonstrated papal primacy.

One particular monument in Rome captures most vividly the cultural, religious, and ideological program of the papacy: the Sistine Chapel in the Vatican Palace. The chapel is best known for the decoration of the ceiling by the Florentine artist Michelangelo (see page 408) and for the striking images in his painting of the Last Judgment.

Giving of the Keys to Saint Peter   Pietro Perugino's painting of Saint Peter's receiving from Christ the keys to "bind and loose" on earth and in heaven illustrates the basis of papal claims to authority within the Christian church. This is the central message of the decorative plan of the Sistine Chapel.   *(Scala/Art Resource, NY)*

The chapel, however, was commissioned by Pope Sixtus IV in 1475. It was to be an audience chamber in which an enthroned pope could meet the representatives of other states. In addition, it was expected that the college of cardinals would gather in the chapel for the election of new popes.

The decorations done before Michelangelo painted the ceiling reflect the intellectual and ideological values that Sixtus hoped to transmit to the churches and governments of Christendom. Along the lower sidewalls are portraits of earlier popes, a feature typical of early Roman churches. More significant are two cycles of paintings of the lives of Moses and Christ, drawing parallels between them. To execute the scenes, Sixtus called to Rome some of the greatest artists of the late fifteenth century: Sandro Botticelli, Domenico Ghirlandaio°, Luca

Signorelli°, and Pietro Perugino°. The works illustrate the continuity of the Old Testament and New Testament and emphasize the importance of obedience to the authority of God. The meaning is most obvious in Perugino's painting of Saint Peter receiving the keys to the Kingdom of Heaven from Christ. The allusion is to Matthew 16:18: "Thou art Peter and upon this rock I shall build my church." The keys are the symbol of the claim of the pope, as successor to Saint Peter, to have the power to bind and loose sinners and their punishments.

Directly across from Perugino's painting is Botticelli's *The Judgment of Corah,* which portrays the story of the opponent who challenged the leadership of Moses and Aaron while the Israelites wandered in the wilderness. Corah and his supporters, according to Numbers 16:33, fell live into Hell. Various popes recalled the fate of

---

Ghirlandaio (gear-lan-DIE-yo)

Signorelli (seen-yor-EL-lee)   **Perugino** (peh-roo-JEE-no)

Corah and the rebels. The pope was bound to oppose the council, Pope Eugenius argued, "to save the people entrusted to his care, lest together with those who hold the power of the council above that of the papacy they suffer a punishment even more dire than that which befell Corah."[22]

The effects of Renaissance revival were profound. Rome grew from a modest population of about 17,000 in 1400 to 35,000 in 1450. By 1517 the city had a population of over 85,000, five times its population at the end of the Great Schism. The papal program was a success. Rome was transformed from a provincial town to a major European capital, perhaps the most important artistic and cultural center of the sixteenth century. Visitors to the Sistine Chapel, like visitors to the papal city itself, were expected to leave with a profound sense of the antiquity of the papal office and of the continuity of papal exercise of religious authority. Because the building and decorating were being completed as the Protestant Reformation was beginning in Germany, some historians have criticized the expense of the political and cultural program undertaken by the Renaissance popes. But to contemporaries on the scene, the work was a logical and necessary attempt to strengthen the church's standing in Christendom.

SUMMARY

HE Renaissance was a broad cultural movement that began in Italy in response to a series of crises in the early fourteenth century. It was a cultural and ideological movement based on the assumption that study and imitation of the past was the best method for reform and innovation in the future. Neither the thoughtful world of Petrarch nor the courtly world of Castiglione, however, sparked the origins of modern individualism or introduced a culture radically different from the medieval past. Between 1300 and 1500, however, Europe experienced profound cultural innovation in literature, political and social thought, and art. The attitudes toward the past and ideas about education formed in this period became the model of European cultural life for the next two hundred years. The cultural values of modern Europe were those inherited from the Renaissance.

The impulse for change arose from the belief, shared by thinkers from Petrarch to Machiavelli, that there was a great deal to be learned from study of the Roman past. This was the basis for humanistic innovations in language, history, and politics. Even revolutionary thinkers such as Lorenzo Valla and Niccolò Machiavelli began with the study of classical literature and history. The same transformation is evident among the artists. Early in the fifteenth century, Florentines who experimented with perspective were intent on recovering lost Roman knowledge, and Michelangelo was praised not only for mastering but for surpassing Roman norms.

Issues of reform and renewal were less tied to public life outside of Italy. Moral and spiritual issues were more important. Yet the same movement from imitation to transformation is evident. Erasmus and Dürer assimilated the best of the new art and culture from Italy, but in the *Praise of Folly* and in Dürer's woodcuts, the use of past ideas and models was neither simple nor direct.

The integration of art, literature, and public life was most evident in the ways that art was used by governments. The Gonzaga court and the papacy clearly recognized the value of artistic and literary works as vehicles for explaining and justifying power and influence. The beauty of Mantegna's painting and the power of Michelangelo's frescoes do not obscure their messages about power and authority.

Innovation depended on the study of the past. As humanists came to know more fully the art and history of Greece and Rome, they recognized the extent to which classical culture represented only one source of legal, historical, or moral understanding. Europeans' recognition of other, often competing, traditions would be tested in the sixteenth century, when they came face to face with a previously unknown world.

■ Notes

1. Quoted in J. B. Trapp, ed., *Background to the English Renaissance* (London: Gray-Mills Publishing, 1974), p. 11.
2. Quoted in N. Mann, *Petrarch* (Oxford: Oxford University Press), p. 67.
3. Petrarch, "On His Own Ignorance and That of Many Others," in *The Renaissance Philosophy of Man*, ed. Ernst Cassirer, Paul Oskar Kristeller, and John H. Randall (Chicago: University of Chicago Press, 1948), p. 105.
4. Quoted in Benjamin G. Kohl and Ronald G. Witt, *The Earthly Republic* (Philadelphia: University of Pennsylvania Press, 1978), p. 11.
5. Quoted in M. L. King, *Women of the Renaissance* (Chicago: University of Chicago Press, 1991), p. 194.
6. Quoted ibid., p. 222.
7. Quoted ibid., p. 198.
8. K. R. Bartlett, *The Civilization of the Italian Renaissance* (Lexington, Mass.: D. C. Heath, 1992), p. 314.
9. Quoted in *The Portable Machiavelli*, ed. and trans. Peter Bondanella and Mark Musa (New York: Penguin Books, 1979), p. 128.

10. Quoted ibid., p. 160.

11. Quoted in *The Notebooks of Leonardo da Vinci*, ed. J. P. Richter, vol. 1 (New York: Dover, 1883 and 1970), p. 14.

12. Quoted ibid., p. 129.

13. Giorgio Vasari, *The Lives of the Artists*, trans. George Bull (Baltimore: Penguin, 1965), p. 338.

14. Julia Bondanella and Mark Musa, eds., *The Italian Renaissance Reader* (New York: Meridian Books, 1987), p. 377.

15. I. Origo, *The Merchant of Prato: Francesco di Marco Datini*, 1335–1410 (New York: Knopf, 1957), pp. 155–156.

16. Quoted in A. Rabil, Jr., *Renaissance Humanism: Foundations, Forms, and Legacy*, vol. 2 (Philadelphia: University of Pennsylvania Press, 1988), p. 236.

17. Quoted ibid., p. 229.

18. Quoted in R. M. San Juan, "The Court Lady's Dilemma: Isabella d'Este and Art Collecting in the Renaissance," *Oxford Art Journal* 14 (1991): 71.

19. Unless otherwise noted, quotes of Castiglione are from Baldassare Castiglione, *The Book of the Courtier*, trans. George Bull (Baltimore: Penguin Books, 1967).

20. Quoted in R. W. Hanning and D. Rosand, eds., *Castiglione: The Ideal and the Real in Renaissance Culture* (New Haven, Conn.: Yale University Press, 1983), p. 17.

21. Raffaele Brandolini, as quoted in Charles L. Stinger, *The Renaissance in Rome* (Bloomington: Indiana University Press, 1985), p. 156.

22. Quoted in Leopold D. Ettlinger, *The Sistine Chapel Before Michelangelo* (Oxford: Oxford University Press, 1965), p. 105.

■ Suggested Reading

Brown, Alison. *The Renaissance*. 2d ed. 1999. An excellent short introduction to Renaissance art and culture designed for those with little or no background in the field.

Burke, Peter. *The European Renaissance: Centres and Peripheries*. 1998. A broad account of Renaissance cultural movements in Europe.

———. *The Fortunes of the Courtier: The European Reception of Castiglione's Cortegiano*. 1995. A well-written survey of the influence of Castiglione's ideas.

Goldthwaite, Richard. *Wealth and the Demand for Art in Italy, 1300–1600*. 1993. A thoughtful essay about the social and economic influences on the creation and patronage of art.

Goodman, A., and A. Mackay, eds. *The Impact of Humanism*. 1990. A volume of basic surveys of the arrival of Italian humanistic ideas in the various lands of Europe.

Hale, John R. *The Civilization of Europe in the Renaissance*. 1994. A beautifully written survey of the culture of Europe from the fifteenth to the seventeenth century.

King, M. L. *Women of the Renaissance*. 1991. A survey of the social, economic, and cultural experience of women during the Renaissance.

Stinger, Charles L. *The Renaissance in Rome*. 1985. An engaging survey of the vibrant cultural life at the papal court and in the city during the Renaissance.

Welch, E. S. *Art and Society in Italy, 1350–1500*. 1997. A well-written, well-illustrated discussion of the social context in which artists worked.

Witt, R. G. "*In the Footsteps of the Ancients*": The Origins of Humanism from Lovato to Bruni. 2000. The definitive work on European humanism and the cultural connections between Italy and France.

 For a searchable list of additional readings for this chapter, go to http://college.hmco.com.

The Art of Renaissance Florence

In 1478 or shortly thereafter, Lorenzo di Pierfrancesco de' Medici, a relative of Lorenzo the Magnificent, commissioned Sandro Botticelli to create the painting *Primavera (Spring)*. Since its completion, critics have been fascinated by its composition and lyrical qualities. Notice the figures who make up the picture. At the center is Venus, goddess of love. The group to Venus's left tells the classical myth of the return of spring. Zephyrus, the west wind, who brings the rebirth of springtime, pursues Chloris, a goddess of fertility. Flowers flow from Chloris's mouth as Zephyrus changes her into Flora, the flower-covered goddess of spring, who stands to her right. These figures are balanced by the group to Venus's right—the three Graces, who are dancing beside the figure of Mercury, the messenger and in this context the god of May. We can easily agree with the critics and connoisseurs who praise the grace and enchantment of Botticelli's mysterious grove filled with dark trees laden with oranges and his meadow blanketed with flowers. The work demonstrates Botticelli's great artistic skill and the sophisticated knowledge of classical mythology current in Florence in the last quarter of the fifteenth century. But, you might ask, how much more can it tell us about the culture of Renaissance Florence?

Historians and art historians have struggled to find the best way to use art as a tool in historical studies. In the late nineteenth and early twentieth centuries, art connoisseurs carefully studied brush strokes and coloring so that they could understand and immediately recognize the techniques of the great masters. They believed that knowledge of an artist's technique would allow them to understand why the works of that artist were so widely popular. Modern historians, however, usually approach a work of art in other ways. We can ask, "What did the artist mean to paint?" Or we can ask, "How does Botticelli's *Primavera* compare with other great works of art, such as Pablo Picasso's *Guernica?*" But the most fruitful inquiry is, "What might Botticelli's contemporaries have noticed in the work?"

To answer that last question, it becomes important to know the social and artistic conventions that might illuminate the meanings in the work, where the work was intended to be displayed, and, finally, how the work comments on the social and cultural interests of the people whom the artist expected to view it.

Contemporaries valued Botticelli's brush stroke—that is, his artistic touch. But, surprisingly, they valued just as highly the materials in which he worked. One of the few contracts we have for a work by Botticelli notes carefully the cost and quantities of gold foil and aquamarine blue paint (an expensive and precious color). From this we can see that Botticelli's contemporaries were very aware of color. As Leon Battista Alberti observed critically of fifteenth-century Italians, most people associate gold leaf and deep blue colors with sumptuousness and majesty. Florentines were also very aware of the writings of contemporary humanists—and especially of the humanist belief that classical and Christian wisdom were basically inseparable. Imbuing classical images with contemporary meanings did not seem odd to them. Botticelli's great popularity in Florence actually rested in part on his sophisticated use of classically inspired figures to comment on contemporary issues.

Primavera was meant to decorate the palace of a relative of Lorenzo de' Medici. It was probably designed to be seen by Lorenzo the Magnificent himself, who not only held a position of political and economic importance in the city but was a gifted poet and leader of a *brigata*, or company of poets and humanists. The brigata, in fact, may have been the primary audience for Botticelli's work. Lorenzo and the poets of his circle were actively combining what they believed was the best of their Tuscan culture with the classical philosophy and literature revived by the humanists. Lorenzo once wore on his armor the motto *Le Tems revient*, which loosely translated means "The ages shall be renewed." As we have seen, this renewal was an idea popular among the artists and humanists of Renaissance Italy. In *Primavera* Botticelli uses a number of symbols meant to remind viewers of Lorenzo de' Medici and his cultural interests. Look at the oranges in the trees, for example. They resemble the three balls on the Medici crest. The promising arrival of spring in the person of Flora is precisely the sort of image with which Lorenzo wanted to be associated.

But what of the three Graces? How do they fit into a picture meant to celebrate the merging of old and new in Medicean Florence? For Lorenzo's contemporaries, they may have been the best possible image of the marriage of classical and Tuscan traditions. Lorenzo and his friends knew of the Graces and their association with spring from a variety of classical sources. These particular Graces, however, are Tuscan. The cut of their gowns and their dance would have been recognizable to Lorenzo's friends as typically Florentine. Lorenzo himself had earlier composed a dance, "A Simple Dance Called Venus," which could easily be the dance that they are performing. Next to them stands Venus, the goddess of love. But here she represents spring, flowering (Flora is, after all, the root of the name Florence), and renewal.

Her arm is raised in a gesture of invitation. She is inviting us, or more accurately the Florentines of Lorenzo's time, to join in a dance of celebration and renewal.

What do we finally see in Botticelli's *Primavera*? It is not simply an imitation of either a classical text or any known classical figure. It seems instead that Botticelli created a scene that incorporated numerous themes of classical learning and cultural renewal that were, by the late 1460s and 1470s, widely associated with Lorenzo de' Medici, the cultural and political master of Florentine life. The historian finds in the art of the Renaissance works of great beauty that convey through their materials, composition, and symbols a sense of the values and ideas that animated contemporary politics and culture.

Botticelli: Primavera (*Scala/Art Resource, NY*)

GLOSSARY

This Glossary covers the complete text, Chapters 1 through 30.

absolutism Extraordinary concentration of power in royal hands, achieved particularly by the kings of France, most notably **Louis XIV,** in the seventeenth century. Proponents argued that hereditary monarchy was the divinely ordained form of government. *(Ch. 16)*

Act of Supremacy (1534) Act of the English Parliament during the Protestant Reformation that finalized the break with the Catholic Church by declaring the king to be head of the Church of England. Henry VIII required a public oath supporting the act, which Sir **Thomas More** refused to take; More was then executed for treason. *(Ch. 14)*

Adenauer, Konrad (1876–1967) Leading statesman of post–World War II Germany. As chancellor (1949–1963), he oriented the country toward western Europe and the United States and proved to Germans that democracy could mean effective government, economic prosperity, and foreign policy success. *(Ch. 29)*

agricultural revolution Dramatic increase in food production from the sixteenth to eighteenth centuries, brought about by changes in agricultural practices, cultivation of new crops, greater availability of animal manure, and introduction of the nutrient-rich potato from the Americas. *(Ch. 18)*

Alexander the Great (356–323 B.C.) King of **Macedon** (r. 336–323) and conqueror of the **Persian Empire.** Son of **Philip II** of Macedon, Alexander was an ingenious warrior who, in the course of his conquests, spread Greek civilization to western Asia, Egypt, and India. His despotism and ruler-worship set a precedent for later monarchs, including many Roman emperors. *(Ch. 4)*

Alexandria Mediterranean seaport in northern Egypt founded by **Alexander the Great** in 332 B.C. It was a thriving Hellenistic city with great harbors, marketplaces, banks, inns, courts, shipbuilding facilities, and a renowned library. *(Ch. 4)*

Amarna reform Term for the ancient Egyptian king Amenhotep IV's seizure of power from temple priests by replacing the god Amun-Re with Aten and renaming himself Akhenaten. After Akhenaten's death, the Amun-Re cult regained power. *(Ch. 1)*

Anabaptists Radical religious reformers in Germany and Switzerland during the Reformation. They rejected the practice of infant baptism, believing that baptism should occur only after confession of sin. They also believed that Christians should live apart in communities of the truly redeemed. Mennonites and Hutterites are their modern descendants. *(Ch. 14)*

Antigonids Dynasty of Macedonian rulers founded in 276 B.C. by Antigonus Gonatas, grandson of Antigonus the One-Eyed, a general of **Alexander the Great.** The Antigonid dynasty lasted about 140 years, until the Roman conquest. *(Ch. 4)*

Antioch Greatest of the cities founded by Seleucus, a general of **Alexander the Great.** Located near the present-day Turkish-Syrian border, it became one of the wealthiest and most luxurious of all eastern Mediterranean cities. *(Ch. 4)*

anti-Semitism Centuries-old prejudice against and demonization of Jews. Anti-Semitism became virulent in Europe in the 1880s with the emergence of the ultranationalist and racist "New Right" ideologies and political movements. An essential part of the Nazi world-view, it led to the Holocaust. *(Ch. 24)*

appeasement The term for the policy employed by Britain's prime minister, Neville Chamberlain, to defuse the 1938 crisis with Germany's **Adolf Hitler.** Chamberlain acquiesced to Hitler's demands to annex the Sudetenland portion of Czechoslovakia, which proved a giant step toward the war that broke out less than a year later. *(Ch. 27)*

Aquinas, Thomas (1225–1274) Dominican friar and theologian. In his two most famous works, *Summa Contra Gentiles* and *Summa Theologiae,* he distinguished between natural truth, or what a person could know by reasoning, and revealed truths, which can be known only through faith in God's revelation. No one before him had so rigorously followed the dialectical method of reasoning through a whole field of knowledge. *(Ch. 10)*

Archaic Greece Period of ancient Greek history from around 700 to 500 B.C. Archaic Greece was characterized by artistic achievement, increased individualism amid communal solidarity, and a moving away from divine and toward abstract, mechanistic explanations. The Western philosophical tradition began during this period. *(Ch. 3)*

Arianism Popular heresy advocated by the priest Arius (ca. 250–336), emphasizing that Jesus was the "first born of all creation." It sought to preserve and purify Christianity's monotheism by making Jesus slightly subordinate to the Father. It was condemned by the **Council of Nicaea.** *(Ch. 7)*

Aristotle (384–322 B.C.) Ancient Greek philosopher, student of **Plato** and tutor of **Alexander the Great.** Aristotle emphasized the goal (*telos* in Greek) of change; in his view the entire cosmos is teleological, and every one of its parts has an essential purpose. Aristotle's scientific writings were the most influential philosophical classics of Greek and Roman civilization and remained so during the Middle Ages. *(Ch. 3)*

Armada (1588) Massive fleet of Spanish warships sent against England by **Philip II** but defeated by the English navy and bad weather. The tactics used by the English helped set the future course of naval warfare. *(Ch. 15)*

Assyrians Warlike people who ruled the ancient Near East during the first millennium B.C. Their innovations included using cavalry as their main striking force and having weapons and armor made of iron. *(Ch. 2)*

Augsburg Confession (1532) Document written by Philip Melanchthon (1497–1560), with the approval of **Martin Luther,** that became the most widely accepted statement of the Lutheran faith. It constitutes part of the creedal basis for today's Lutheran churches. *(Ch. 14)*

Augustine (354–430) North African bishop and one of the most influential Christian thinkers. Augustine wrote that all people were sinners in need of God's redemption, that history is the struggle between those who call on divine grace and those who sin, and that learning was useful only to the extent that it equipped individuals to read and understand the Bible's message of salvation. *(Ch. 7)*

Augustus (63 B.C.–A.D. 14) Honorific title of Gaius Julius Caesar Octavianus, grandnephew of Julius **Caesar** and first Roman emperor. After defeating Mark Antony and Cleopatra at the Battle of Actium (31 B.C.), Augustus ruled the empire for forty-five years. His rule laid the foundations of two hundred years of prosperous Roman peace. See also **Principate.** *(Ch. 6)*

Auschwitz-Birkenau The largest and principal extermination center of Nazi Germany's six death camps, all of which were located in what had been Poland. The Nazis shipped Jews from all over Europe to Auschwitz, which killed about twelve thousand people a day at the height of its operation in 1944. *(Ch. 28)*

avant-garde French for "forefront," the term refers to early-twentieth-century artists who, inspired by novel or unconventional techniques, considered themselves precursors of new styles. Avant-garde movements proclaimed idiosyncratic manifestos and constantly called for the rejection of existing forms of expression and the creation of new ones. *(Ch. 24)*

Aztecs Amerindian people that dominated central Mexico from the fourteenth through the sixteenth centuries from their capital Tenochtitlán (present-day Mexico City). Weakened by exposure to virulent Old World diseases, they were conquered in 1521–1523 by Spanish forces led by **Hernán Cortés.** *(Ch. 13)*

Bacon, Francis (1561–1626) England's lord chancellor during the reign of James I and author of a utopian essay extolling science's benefits for a peaceful society and human happiness. His influential works encouraged the empirical method and inductive reasoning. See also **empirical reasoning.** *(Ch. 17)*

barbarian kingship Central institution in a succession of kingdoms (ca. 300–600) ruled by barbarian (non-Roman) leaders, which evolved from former Roman provinces. Most such kings had been political or military leaders under Roman authority before becoming independent rulers. *(Ch. 7)*

baroque Style of European art and architecture popular from the late sixteenth to early eighteenth century. Baroque artists, such as Peter Paul Rubens, modified Renaissance techniques, adding dynamism and emotional energy. Baroque painting used light to portray dramatic illusion, and baroque churches were both impressively grand and emotionally engaging. *(Ch. 15)*

Bauhaus An influential German art school, founded in 1919, that sought to adopt contemporary materials to develop new forms of architecture, design, and urban planning in response to the cultural uncertainty that followed World War I. Though it arguably failed in its immediate German context, the Bauhaus helped shape the whole idea of "the modern" in the West and throughout the world for decades to come. *(Ch. 26)*

Bernard of Clairvaux (1090–1153) Monk, church reformer, and influential adviser to kings and popes. Bernard believed that faith and divine inspiration were more important than dialectical reasoning. He was instrumental in the success of the Cistercian religious order. *(Ch. 10)*

Bismarck, Otto von (1815–1898) Nineteenth-century German statesman. A Prussian aristocrat, Bismarck was the autocratic architect who, through a series of aggressive wars, united Germany and served as the nation's first chancellor. He administered an emperor-controlled country that became the dominant power in Europe. See also **Realpolitik.** *(Ch. 22)*

Black Death (1348–1351) First of a series of epidemics, probably bubonic plague, that raged in Europe and western Asia for three centuries. The Black Death killed about 60 percent of those infected. The huge population decline fueled the economic and social transformations of the late Middle Ages. *(Ch. 11)*

Bolsheviks Members of a faction of the Russian Socialist Party led by **Vladimir Ilich Lenin** (1870–1924), a zealous Marxist who insisted that a revolutionary cadre could seize power on behalf of the working class. The Bolsheviks gained control of Russia in November 1917. *(Ch. 24)*

Bonaparte, Napoleon. See **Napoleon Bonaparte.**

bourgeois century Characterization of the nineteenth century, especially the latter half. In western Europe, the bourgeois elites (middle classes), which had expanded dramatically in the wake of industrialization, helped fashion much of society. *(Ch. 23)*

Brandenburg-Prussia Group of German territories ruled by the Hohenzollern family that became one of Europe's most powerful states in the seventeenth century. Its military strength was supported by its hereditary landowners, who were granted autonomy in their territories. *(Ch. 16)*

Brandt, Willy (1913–1992) Socialist West German chancellor (r. 1969–1974). Brandt's widely popular policy of opening to the East, or *Ostpolitik*, made possible closer economic ties between West and East Germany and broader opportunities for ordinary citizens to interact across the east-west border. *(Ch. 29)*

Brest-Litovsk, Treaty of (1918) Treaty in which Russia accepted its defeat by Germany and its allies in World War I. The treaty forced the Russians to cede much of European Russia to Germany. After Germany's defeat by the Allies later in the year, the **Bolsheviks** recaptured Ukraine and the Caucasus region. *(Ch. 25)*

British blockade Britain's naval blockade of Germany during World War I. By means of this tactic, which cut off supplies to Germany but which also violated several provisions of international law, the British seriously impeded the German war effort. *(Ch. 25)*

Caesar, Gaius Julius (100–44 B.C.) Roman general gifted at war and politics. Named dictator in 49 B.C., he was assassinated by the members of the **senate** in 44 B.C. He introduced to Europe the calendar of 365¼ days. He was succeeded as ruler by his grandnephew Octavian (**Augustus**). Later Roman emperors were also called *caesar*. *(Ch. 5)*

Caliphate Arab empire established by the successors of **Muhammad**; *caliph* means "successor to the prophet." The Umayyad caliphate, with its capital in Damascus, ruled from 661 to 750; the Abbasid caliphate, based in Baghdad, from 750 to 1258. *(Ch. 8)*

Calvin, John (1509–1564) Franco-Swiss theologian and founder of the Reformed Church in Geneva. Calvin's theological writings, most notably *Institutes of the Christian Religion* (1536), were widely disseminated and hugely influential. Calvin stressed the absolute power of God and the need for moral reform of the Christian community. *(Ch. 14)*

canon law Collection of orderly rules for the government of the Catholic Church, based on papal decrees and decisions of church councils. In 1140 the monk Gratian published the *Decretum*, the first systematic collection of canon law. *(Ch. 10)*

Carlowitz, Treaty of (1699) Treaty imposed by the European allies on a weakening Ottoman Empire. The Habsburgs, Venetians, Russians, and Poles gained territory and power at the Turks' expense. *(Ch. 16)*

Carolingian Renaissance Major revival of learning, combined with reform of religious and political institutions, that occurred under **Charlemagne** and his successors. The revival encompassed the founding of schools in religious institutions, production of textbooks, dissemination of early church teachings and of **canon law,** as well as secular reforms such as regularization of royal estates. *(Ch. 8)*

Catherine the Great (r. 1762–1796) Empress of Russia. Through an astute policy of wars and alliances, Catherine expanded her country's borders south to the Black Sea and west into Europe. An "enlightened despot," she advanced the westernizing reforms begun by **Peter the Great.** *(Ch. 18)*

Cato the Elder (234–149 B.C.) Marcus Portius Cato, Roman general and statesman. Known as Cato the Censor because he denounced luxury goods, he was the first Roman historian to write in Latin. *(Ch. 5)*

Charlemagne Frankish king (r. 768–814), crowned emperor in 800. He carried out a program of legal and ecclesiastical reform, patronized learning, and revitalized the western Roman Empire. See also **Carolingian Renaissance.** *(Ch. 8)*

Charles V (r. 1519–1558) Holy Roman emperor and, as Charles I, king of Spain. His empire included Spain, Italy, the Low Countries, and Germany. Though he vigorously opposed the spread of Protestantism during the Reformation, he was forced to sign the Religious Peace of Augsburg in 1555, which acknowledged the right of German princes to choose the religion to be practiced in their territories, Lutheran or Catholic. Charles abdicated his imperial and royal titles the next year, ceding the empire to his brother Ferdinand and his Spanish possessions to his son **Philip II.** *(Ch. 14)*

Chartism Nineteenth-century British political movement whose goal was to transform Britain from an oligarchy to a democracy. The Chartists' demands were contained in the 1838 "people's charter," which called for universal male suffrage, electoral districts with equal population, salaries and the abolition of property qualifications for Members of Parliament, the secret ballot, and annual general elections. The movement failed, but most of its measures eventually became law. See also **Second Reform Bill.** *(Ch. 21)*

Chechnya Small, largely Muslim republic in the Caucasus region of Russia that attempted to declare independence in 1991. Russia intervened in the resulting civil war in 1994. After the Chechens won a substantial measure of autonomy, fighting resumed in 1999. *(Ch. 30)*

chivalry Initially, a medieval code of conduct for mounted warriors, focusing on military prowess, open-handed generosity, and earning a glorious reputation. Later it evolved into an elaborate set of rules governing relations between men and women. *(Ch. 10)*

Christianity Sect originally rooted in Judaism that emerged as a fully separate religion by around A.D. 200. Emphasizing belief in one God and the mission of his son, **Jesus of Nazareth,** as savior, Christianity offered salvation in the next world and a caring community in the present one. A messianic religion, Christianity emphasized Christ's return, leading to the beginning of a heavenly kingdom on earth. *(Ch. 6)*

Churchill, Winston (1874–1965) British prime minister (1940–1945; 1951–1955). As the leader of his country during World War II, Churchill's courage, decisiveness, memorable words, and boundless energy made him widely seen as one of Britain's greatest leaders of the twentieth century. See also **Yalta conference**.

Cicero, Marcus Tullius (106–43 B.C.) Philosopher, writer, and statesman who was Rome's greatest orator. He was crucial in making the Latin language a vessel for the heritage of Greek thought. *(Ch. 5)*

city-state State consisting of an independent city and the surrounding territory under its control. Early examples were the Sumerian city-states in the third millennium B.C. *(Ch. 1)*

civic humanism An ideology, championed by Florentine writers and public officials during the Renaissance, that emphasized their city's classical republican virtues and history. They argued that a moral and ethical value was intrinsic to public life. *(Ch. 12)*

Civil Code Law code established under Napoleon in 1804 that included limited acceptance of revolutionary gains, such as a guarantee of equality before the law and taxation of all social classes. Also known as the Napoleonic Code, it enshrined modern forms of property ownership and civil contracts, enhanced paternal control of families, outlawed divorce in most circumstances, and placed women under the legal domination of fathers and husbands. *(Ch. 19)*

Classical Greece Period of ancient Greek history from about 480 to 323 B.C. Classical Greek culture emphasized public life as the central theme of art and literature, and its sculpture was the most anatomically precise yet. Classical Greece set many standards for modern Western culture. See also **demokratia**. *(Ch. 3)*

Cluny (Cluniacs) A spiritual reform begun in 910 in central France. The movement emphasized strict adherence to the Benedictine Rule, as well as the ideas that the church should pray for the world without being deeply involved in it and must be free from lay control. *(Ch. 10)*

cold war The hostile standoff between the Soviet Union and the United States that began after World War II, when communist governments, relying on Soviet support, took control of most of east-central Europe. The Soviets' first atomic bomb explosion in 1949 intensified the conflict, which shaped world affairs for the next forty years. *(Ch. 28)*

collectivization The program that reshaped agriculture in the Soviet Union under **Joseph Stalin** during the early 1930s. By forcing peasants into government-controlled collective farms, the Soviet regime sought to take control of agricultural production in order better to finance rapid industrialization. *(Ch. 27)*

Columbian Exchange Historians' term for the blending of cultures between the Old World and the New after Christopher Columbus's arrival in the New World in 1492. The Spanish and other Europeans brought their plants, domesticated animals, and diseases to the Americas. The Americas contributed New World crops, most notably maize (corn) and potatoes, transforming the Old World diet. *(Ch. 13)*

Comintern (Third, or Communist, International) An association founded in March 1919 by the communists (formerly **Bolsheviks**) to translate their success in Russia into leadership of the international socialist movement. Its program of tight organization and discipline under Russian leadership produced a schism between communists and socialists in Europe and throughout the world. *(Ch. 26)*

communes Form of government in Italian towns that rose in the eleventh century. Despite numerous local variations, communes involved common decision making by local notables, including both landed aristocrats and wealthy merchants or industrialists. *(Ch. 9)*

Compromise of 1867 Agreement that divided the Habsburg Empire into Austria in the west and Hungary in the east, a dual monarchy under Emperor Franz Joseph called Austria-Hungary. The compromise confirmed Magyar dominance in Hungary. *(Ch. 22)*

congress system System of European international relations in the first half of the nineteenth century in which the major European states cooperated to preserve the balance of power. This system disappeared as political leaders increasingly used force to pursue their narrow interests. *(Ch. 22)*

Congress of Vienna (1814–1815) Conference called by the victorious powers—Austria, Great Britain, Prussia, and Russia—who defeated Napoleon. Guided by the Austrian foreign minister, Prince Metternich, the Great Powers drew new territorial boundaries advantageous to themselves. They also attempted to provide long-term stability on the European continent and restored some of the rulers who had been overthrown. See also **congress system.** *(Ch. 20)*

conservatism Ideology underlying the order established in Europe in 1815. Conservatives emphasized resistance to change and preservation of the existing order of monarchy, aristocracy, and an established church. *(Ch. 20)*

Copernicus, Nicholas (1473–1543) Polish astronomer who initiated the Scientific Revolution by proposing that the earth and other planets orbit the sun, a theory called the heliocentric, or sun-centered, system. See also **heliocentrism.** *(Ch. 17)*

corporative state, corporativism The system established in fascist Italy beginning in 1926 that sought to involve people in public life not as citizens but as producers, through their roles in the economy. A system based on such occupational groupings eventually replaced parliament as the basis of political representation in fascist Italy. *(Ch. 26)*

Cortés, Hernán (1485–1546) Spanish commander who conquered the **Aztecs** and claimed the Valley of Mexico for Spain. Cortés had only five hundred men but was aided by an outbreak of smallpox and the help of Amerindian peoples eager to end Aztec control. *(Ch. 13)*

Council of Constance (1414–1418) Assembly convened by Holy Roman Emperor Sigismund to heal deep religious and civil divisions. The council declared that its rulings were binding even on the pope. Its selection of Pope Martin V ended the **Great Schism.** *(Ch. 11)*

Council of the Indies Body established by the king of Spain in 1524 to oversee Spain's colonial possessions. Located at court, eventually in Madrid, it supervised all legal, administrative, and commercial activity in the colonies until the early eighteenth century. *(Ch. 13)*

Council of Nicaea (325) History's first ecumenical, or "all-church," council, convened by the emperor Constantine. The council condemned **Arianism** and proclaimed key elements of the Nicene Creed, especially the doctrine that Christ was "one in being with the Father," co-equal and co-eternal. *(Ch. 7)*

Council of Trent (1545–1563) Ecumenical council of the Roman Catholic Church during the Reformation. Though rejecting many Protestant positions, the council reformed and reorganized the church partly in response to Protestant criticisms. Its decrees reaffirmed and defined the basic tenets of Roman Catholicism for the next four hundred years. *(Ch. 14)*

covenant As told in the Hebrew Bible, the pact God made with Abraham, the first patriarch of **Israel.** In return for the land of Canaan and the promise of becoming a great nation, the Israelites agreed to worship no other gods. *(Ch. 2)*

Cromwell, Oliver (1599–1658) English Puritan general and statesman. A military genius and leader in the English Civil War, Cromwell governed as Lord Protector during the Interregnum from 1653 to 1658.*(Ch. 16)*

Crusades (1095–1270) A series of largely unsuccessful wars waged by western European Christians to recapture the Holy Land from the Muslims and ensure the safety of Christian pilgrims to Jerusalem. Later, the term came to designate any military effort by Europeans against non-Christians. *(Ch. 9)*

cuneiform First writing system in Mesopotamia, consisting of wedge-shaped impressions in soft clay. Named from the Latin word for "wedge-shaped," it was developed about 3500–3100 B.C. *(Ch. 1)*

Darwinism Profoundly influential theory of biological evolution, first put forth by Charles Darwin (1809–1882). He proposed that all forms of life continuously develop through natural selection, whereby those that are better adapted to the environment have the advantage and are more likely to survive and pass on their beneficial traits to their offspring. *(Ch. 23)*

D-Day The complex Allied amphibious landings in Normandy, France, on June 6, 1944, that opened a second major European front in World War II. In the aftermath of this invasion, American-led forces in the west began moving toward Germany, completing the Soviet effort, which was already forcing the Germans back on the eastern front. *(Ch. 28)*

Decembrists Group of Russian military officers who led the December 1825 rebellion after the death of Tsar Alexander I, seeking to install a constitutional monarchy with Alexander's eldest brother, Constantine, as tsar. They were defeated and executed by Constantine's younger brother, Nicholas. The Decembrists were seen as martyrs by later Russian revolutionaries. *(Ch. 21)*

Declaration of the Rights of Man and the Citizen (1789) Document issued by the **National Assembly** of France in August 1789. Modeled on the U.S. Constitution, the declaration set forth the basis for the new French government and asserted "the natural, inalienable and sacred rights of man." *(Ch. 19)*

demokratia Term coined in Athens in the fifth century B.C. to describe the city's system of direct government. It means "the power *(kratos)* of the people *(demos)."* Athenian society pioneered today's key democratic principles, including freedom, equality, universal citizenship, and the rule of law. *(Ch. 3)*

Descartes, René (1596–1650) French philosopher, scientist, and mathematician. Descartes emphasized skepticism and deductive reasoning in his most influential treatise, *Discourse on Method.* He offered the first alternative physical explanation of matter after the Copernican revolution. *(Ch. 17)*

digital divide A term for the disparity in access to the computing and Internet technologies that seemed essential to compete in the twenty-first-century global economy. It was one way that new technologies were widening the gap between the world's haves and have-nots. *(Ch. 30)*

Directory French revolutionary government from 1795 to 1799, consisting of an executive council of five men chosen by the upper house of the legislature. It was overthrown in a coup led by **Napoleon Bonaparte.** *(Ch. 19)*

Dominic Dominic de Guzman (1170–1221), Spanish priest and founder of the spiritually influential Dominican mendicant order. The order was known for the irreproachable life of its members, its learning, and its desire to emulate the apostolic life of the early church by poverty and preaching. *(Ch. 10)*

Dutch East India Company Commercially innovative Dutch company formed in 1602 that combined government management of trade with both public and private investment. The formation of the company created a permanent pool of capital to sustain trade and resulted in a dramatic expansion of commerce with Asia. *(Ch. 16)*

Edict of Milan (313) Proclamation issued primarily by Emperor Constantine that made Christianity a legal religion in the Roman Empire. Constantine promoted the Christian church, granting it tax immunities and relieving the clergy of military service. *(Ch. 7)*

Edict of Nantes (1598) Edict of Henry IV granting France's Protestants (**Huguenots**) the right to practice their faith and maintain defensive garrisons. They were also guaranteed access to schools, hospitals, royal appointments, and separate judicial institutions. The edict was revoked by **Louis XIV** in 1685. *(Ch. 15)*

Elizabeth I (r. 1558–1603) First woman to occupy the English throne successfully. Elizabeth's adroit rule brought stability to England after the turmoil of previous reigns. She firmly established Protestantism in England, encouraged English commerce, defended the nation against the Spanish **Armada**, and fostered the English Renaissance in poetry and drama. *(Ch. 15)*

empirical reasoning Philosophical view developed by the seventeenth-century English philosophers **Francis Bacon** and **John Locke**, asserting that all knowledge is based on observation and experimentation and that general principles should be derived from particular facts. *(Ch. 17)*

encomienda A Spanish royal grant of protectorship over a group of Amerindians. The receivers of the grants (*encomenderos*) were obliged to Christianize the people under their charge, but instead most forced the natives to work as virtual slaves in mines and on Spanish lands. See also **Bartolomé de Las Casas**. *(Ch. 13)*

enlightened despotism Term for the reform-oriented rule of eighteenth-century monarchs such as **Frederick the Great**, Joseph II of Austria, and **Catherine the Great**. Enlightened despots applied Enlightenment remedies to economic problems, encouraged education and legal reform, and improved agricultural productivity by enabling some peasants to own the land they worked. *(Ch. 18)*

Epicureans Adherents of the Athenian philosopher Epicurus (341–270 B.C.), who taught that the soul is made up of atoms that do not exist after death. Epicureans emphasized the avoidance of pain and the pursuit of intellectual pleasure. *(Ch. 4)*

Erasmus, Desiderius (1466–1536) Prominent Dutch humanist during the Renaissance, best known for his satire *Praise of Folly*. Erasmus's works reinterpreted Greek and Roman wisdom and emphasized tolerance, reason, and faith in the goodness and educability of the individual. *(Ch. 12)*

"ethnic cleansing" A term describing attempts to remove an unwanted ethnic group from an area, which can include forced relocation and mass killing. Beginning in 1991, this tactic was implemented by Yugoslavian ruler Slobodan Milosevic (b. 1941) to unite all Serbs, many of whom lived in neighboring Croatia, Bosnia-Herzegovina, and **Kosovo**. *(Ch. 30)*

Etruscans Inhabitants of twelve loosely confederated city-states north of Rome in Etruria that flourished in the seventh to sixth centuries B.C. They were conquered by the Romans by the early third century B.C. *(Ch. 5)*

euro The common currency launched by the **European Union** in 1999 to eliminate the cost of currency exchange and boost trade and economic interaction. As of January 1, 2002, it replaced the national currencies of the participating countries (the "Eurozone"). *(Ch. 30)*

European Economic Community (EEC) (1957–1967) Common market formed by Belgium, France, West Germany, Italy, Luxembourg, and the Netherlands to promote free trade. The EEC was replaced by the European Community (EC) in 1967. *(Ch. 29)*

European Union (EU) New name for the European Community after the **Maastricht agreement** of 1991. By 2001 the European Union had nine members in addition to the original six members of the **European Economic Community:** Britain, Denmark, Ireland (joined 1973); Greece (joined 1981); Portugal, Spain (joined 1985); and Austria, Finland, Sweden (joined 1995). See also **euro**. *(Ch. 30)*

"euthanasia" program The Nazi program of systematically killing people, overwhelmingly ethnic Germans, whom the Nazis deemed superfluous or threatening to the German racial health. Victims included chronic mental patients, the incurably ill, and people with severe physical handicaps. Initiated in 1939, the program had claimed 100,000 lives by the time it was discontinued in 1941. *(Ch. 27)*

existentialism A philosophical and cultural movement, influential from the late 1940s into the 1950s, that explored life in a world cast adrift from its cultural moorings. Highly influential were the Frenchmen Jean Paul Sartre (1905–1980) and Albert Camus (1913–1960), for whom an authentic human response to an apparently meaningless universe entailed commitment and responsibility. *(Ch. 29)*

factories Centralized workplaces where a number of people cooperate to mass-produce goods. The first factories of industrializing Europe were made possible by the development of the **steam engine** as a central power source. The mechanized production of factories led to huge productivity increases in the nineteenth century. See also **industrialization, mass production.** *(Ch. 20)*

fascism A violent, antidemocratic movement founded by **Benito Mussolini** in Italy in 1919. The term is widely used to encompass Hitler's Nazi regime in Germany and other movements stressing disciplined national solidarity and hostile to liberal individualism, the parliamentary system, and Marxist socialism. *(Ch. 26)*

February Patent (1861) Enactment issued in February 1861 by the Austrian emperor Franz Joseph (r. 1848–1916) that established a constitutional monarchy in the old Austrian Empire. The patent guaranteed civil liberties and provided for local self-government and an elected parliament. *(Ch. 22)*

feudal revolution The societal change in tenth-century France from prince-dominated territories with loyal, reliable, but few vassals to the advent of many locally powerful magnates with numerous vassals whose fidelity was uncertain and who primarily provided military service. *(Ch. 9)*

Five Pillars of Islam The basic teachings of Islam: (1) the profession of faith, "There is no God but Allah and **Muhammad** is His Prophet"; (2) individual prayer five times daily, plus group prayers at noon on Friday; (3) the sunup-to-sundown fast during the month of Ramadan; (4) giving generous alms to the poor; and (5) pilgrimage to Mecca at least once in a person's lifetime. *(Ch. 8)*

Flavians Dynasty of the Roman emperors Vespasian (r. 69–79), Titus (r. 79–81), and Domitian (r. 81–96), whose rule was a time of relative peace and good government. Unlike the Julio-Claudians, the Flavians descended from Italian landowners, not old Roman nobility. Domitian persecuted the nobility and was assassinated. *(Ch. 6)*

Fourteen Points Proposals by U.S. president Woodrow Wilson (1856–1924) to guide the new international order that would follow an Allied victory in World War I. Specifics included open diplomacy, free trade, reduced armaments, self-determination for nationalities, and a league of nations. *(Ch. 25)*

Francis of Assisi (1181–1226) Italian monk and founder of a new order of friars ("brothers," from the Latin *fratres)*. Francis was born wealthy but adopted a life based on the scriptural ideals of poverty, preaching, and service. His apostolate to the urban poor was highly popular. *(Ch. 10)*

Frankfurt Assembly (1848–1849) Popularly elected national assembly that attempted to create a unified German state. The assembly drew up a constitution and offered the German throne to Friedrich Wilhelm IV, king of Prussia, who declined, fearing a war with Austria and not wanting an office offered by representatives of the people. *(Ch. 21)*

Frederick the Great (r. 1740–1786) Autocratic king of Prussia who transformed the country into a major military power, acquired Polish Prussia, and waged three wars against Austria. He participated in and encouraged the study of philosophy, history, poetry, and French literature. *(Ch. 18)*

Freud, Sigmund (1856–1939) Austrian founder of psychoanalysis, a method of treating psychic disorders by exploring the unconscious. Freud believed that people were motivated in part by their unconscious feelings and drives. He helped call attention to the concept that irrational forces play a significant role in human behavior. *(Ch. 24)*

friendly societies Nineteenth-century organizations formed by workers; members pooled their resources to provide mutual aid. Combining business activity with feasts, drinking bouts, and other social functions, friendly societies promoted group solidarity and a sense of working-class identity. *(Ch. 20)*

Galileo Galilei (1564–1642) Italian physicist and astronomer who provided evidence supporting the heliocentric theory of **Nicholas Copernicus** and helped develop the physics of mechanics. His publication of his astronomical observations and his subsequent condemnation by the Catholic Church spurred popular debate and greatly influenced the future of science. *(Ch. 17)*

gentry Class of wealthy, educated, and socially ambitious families in western Europe, especially England, whose political and economic power was greatly enhanced during the sixteenth century. They shared with traditional old-family warrior-aristocrats certain legal privileges, security of landownership, and a cooperative relationship with the monarchy. See also **price revolution**. *(Ch. 15)*

Girondins Political faction during the French Revolution. Republicans and members of the Jacobin Club, the Girondins dominated the French Legislative Assembly when it began to meet in 1791. They favored an activist government but were less radical than other members of the club, called the **Jacobins**. The Girondins were purged from the National Con-

vention in 1793, and many were executed during the **Terror**. *(Ch. 19)*

glasnost Russian term meaning "greater openness." Glasnost was the leading motif in the Great Reforms begun in 1861 by Tsar Alexander II (r. 1855–1881), who sought to strengthen Russia by restructuring its institutions in the wake of defeat in the Crimean War. Glasnost was also part of the reform efforts of **Mikhail Gorbachev** in the Soviet Union during the 1980s. *(Ch. 22)*

Glorious Revolution (1688) Bloodless English revolution in which Parliament replaced the Catholic King James II with William (of Orange) and his wife Mary (James's Protestant daughter). Parliament imposed on the new sovereigns a Bill of Rights that confirmed Parliament's power and protected freedom of speech. *(Ch. 16)*

Golden Bull of 1356 Edict of Holy Roman Emperor Charles IV establishing the method of electing a new emperor. It acknowledged the political autonomy of Germany's seven regional princes. *(Ch. 11)*

Gorbachev, Mikhail (b. 1931) The Soviet Communist Party secretary who, beginning in 1985, attempted to reform the Soviet communist system through arms reduction; liberalization in the satellite states; *glasnost,* or "openness" to discussion and criticism; and *perestroika,* or economic "restructuring." Though widely admired in the West, these measures failed, and Gorbachev ended up presiding over the end of the Soviet communist regime. *(Ch. 29)*

Gothic Period in European architecture, sculpture, and painting from the twelfth to early sixteenth centuries. Gothic architecture was distinguished by the pointed arch, ribbed vault, and point support, which produced a building characterized by verticality and translucency. Examples are the Cathedral of Notre-Dame of Paris and the royal portal at Chartres Cathedral. *(Ch. 10)*

Gracchi Ancient Roman faction led by Tiberius Sempronius Gracchus (163–133 B.C.) and later his brother, Gaius (153–121 B.C.), both of whom were killed by their political opponents. They challenged the conservative **senate** on behalf of the poor. *(Ch. 5)*

Great Northern War (1700–1721) War between Sweden and Russia over control of Baltic territories. **Peter the Great** secured Livonia and Estonia as well as the territory on which he built Russia's new capital, St. Petersburg. Russia became the pre-eminent power on the Baltic. *(Ch. 16)*

"the Great Patriotic War" Term for World War II devised by **Joseph Stalin** to rally Soviet citizens against the German invasion. Stalin appealed to Russian nationalism and recalled past heroic defenses of Russia rather than communist themes. *(Ch. 28)*

Great Reform Bill (1832) British law that broadened the franchise and provided parliamentary seats for new urban areas that had not previously been represented. The bill was a major victory for the government and middle classes over the aristocracy. *(Ch. 21)*

Great Schism (1378–1417) Period during which two, then three, rival popes claimed to rule the Christian Church. The schism ended when the **Council of Constance** deposed all three competing previous popes and elected Martin V as the new pope. *(Ch. 11)*

guilds Merchant groups and associations of crafts and trades established in European cities and towns beginning in the thirteenth century. Guilds expanded greatly during the later

Middle Ages. They provided economic benefits, fostered a sense of community, and served as mutual assistance societies. *(Ch. 9)*

gulag Network of 476 forced labor camps for political prisoners in the Soviet Union. The *gulag* (an acronym for "main camp administration") was first used by Lenin in 1918 but was greatly expanded by **Joseph Stalin** in the 1930s. *(Ch. 27)*

Gutenberg, Johann (ca. 1399–1468) German inventor of movable metal type. His innovations led to the publication of the first printed book in Europe, the Gutenberg Bible, in the 1450s. Printed books and broadsheets played a critical role in disseminating the ideas of the Renaissance and the Reformation. *(Ch. 12)*

Hagia Sophia Largest Christian church ever built, constructed in Constantinople from 532 to 537 for the Roman emperor **Justinian.** The church consists of two intersecting rectangular basilicas that incorporate arches; the whole is surmounted by a huge dome. *(Ch. 7)*

Hanseatic League Late medieval association of over a hundred trading cities, centered on the German city of Lübeck. The league dominated coastal trade in northern Europe from the fourteenth to the fifteenth centuries, until Dutch, English, and south German merchants finally gained shares of the wool, grain, and fur trades. *(Ch. 11)*

heliocentrism Theory advanced by **Nicholas Copernicus** that the earth and other planets orbit the sun. Supported by the scientific and mathematical discoveries of **Johannes Kepler** and **Galileo Galilei**, heliocentrism, which means "sun-centered," won acceptance by the end of the seventeenth century. *(Ch. 17)*

Hellenism Term used to designate ancient Greece's language, culture, and civilization, especially after **Alexander the Great** spread them to other parts of the Mediterranean, western Asia, and North Africa. *(Ch. 4)*

Helsinki Accords (1975) Agreements signed by thirty-five countries in Helsinki, Finland, that committed the signatories to recognize existing borders, to increase economic and environmental cooperation, and to promote freedom of expression, religion, and travel. Dissidents in Soviet bloc countries soon fastened on these provisions to highlight the lack of human rights and to discredit the ruling communist governments. *(Ch. 29)*

Henry IV (r. 1589–1610) First Bourbon king of France, who converted to Catholicism to restore that nation's peace. His **Edict of Nantes** granted rights to the persecuted French Protestants, and he strengthened finance, agriculture, and commerce. *(Ch. 15)*

Henry "the Navigator" (1394–1460) Portuguese prince and director of Portugal's exploration and colonization of Africa's western coast. The Portuguese quickly established trading stations in the region, laying the foundations for their overseas empire. *(Ch. 13)*

Herodotus (ca. 485–425 B.C.) Ancient Greek historian; with **Thucydides,** a founder of history-writing in the West. The word *history* comes from a word used by Herodotus, *historiai*, meaning "inquiries" or "research." In his history of the Persian Wars, Herodotus saw the fall of the Persian Empire as part of a perpetual cycle of the rise and fall of empires. *(Ch. 3)*

Hildegard of Bingen (1098–1179) German abbess who was perhaps the most profound psychological thinker of her age. More than anyone before her, Hildegard opened up for discussion the feminine aspects of divinity. She was also adept in music and biblical studies. *(Ch. 10)*

Hitler, Adolf (1889–1945) The German dictator who, after being legally named chancellor in 1933, militarized Germany and started World War II in 1939, leading the country to defeat in 1945. His enforcement of state-sponsored **anti-Semitism** and racial purity among German people led to the murder of millions of Jews, Gypsies, and Slavic peoples. *(Ch. 27)*

Hobbes, Thomas (1588–1679) English philosopher. In his treatise *Leviathan*, Hobbes asserted that people are made up of mechanistic appetites and so need a strong ruler to hold them in check. However, he also envisioned citizens as potentially equal and constrained neither by morality nor by natural obedience to authority. *(Ch. 17)*

Homer Greatest ancient Greek poet, credited as the author of the epics the *Iliad* and the *Odyssey*, both written during the eighth century B.C. His dramatic stories inspired, moved, and educated the Greeks. *(Ch. 2)*

hominids The primate family *Hominidae*, which includes humans. The modern human being, *Homo sapiens sapiens*, is the only species of this family still in existence. *(Ch. 1)*

hoplite phalanx Battlefield tactic of **Archaic Greece** that relied on a tightly ordered unit of heavily armed, pike-bearing infantrymen. It was the dominant military force in western Asia and the Mediterranean region until 197 B.C. *(Ch. 3)*

Huguenots French Protestants, followers of the teachings of **John Calvin.** Huguenots battled Catholics throughout the sixteenth and seventeenth centuries. Many emigrated to other western European countries and England's American colonies, especially after the revocation of the **Edict of Nantes.** French Protestants gained full religious freedom in the nineteenth century. *(Ch. 15)*

humanism Western European literary and cultural movement of the fourteenth and fifteenth centuries. Humanists emphasized the superiority of ancient Greek and Roman literature, history, and politics, and focused on learning and personal and public duty. See also **Desiderius Erasmus, Francesco Petrarch, Thomas More**. *(Ch. 12)*

Hundred Years' War (1337–1453) Series of conflicts between the ruling families of France and England over territory in France and the succession to the French crown. Sporadic raids and battles devastated the French countryside and checked population growth. The inspirational leadership of **Joan of Arc** contributed to France's eventual success in expelling the English from nearly all of the disputed land. *(Ch. 11)*

hunter-gatherers Food-collecting society in which people live by hunting, fishing, and gathering fruits and nuts, with no crops or livestock being raised for food. During the **Neolithic Revolution**, some hunter-gatherers developed agriculture. *(Ch. 1)*

Hus, Jan (ca. 1370–1415) Czech religious reformer who strongly attacked clerical power and privileges and advocated reform of church practice. His execution for heresy at the **Council of Constance** provoked a civil war in Prague and Bohemia. *(Ch. 11)*

iconoclasm Rejection of, or even the destruction of, religious images in worship. Iconoclasm was the official policy of the Byzantine Empire from 726 to 843 and played a role in the continuing estrangement of Byzantium from the West. *(Ch. 8)*

impressionism Late-nineteenth-century style of painting pioneered by the French artists Degas, Monet, Pissarro,

Renoir, Sisley, and Morisot. Influenced by new theories that images were transmitted to the brain as small light particles, which the brain then reconstituted, the impressionists sought to capture what things looked like before they were "distorted" by the brain. *(Ch. 23)*

Inca A flourishing sixteenth-century empire administered from the mountains of Peru and extending from modern Ecuador to Chile. It was conquered for Spain by Francisco Pizarro (1470–1541), aided by a smallpox epidemic and native peoples seeking to end Inca domination. *(Ch. 13)*

Index of Prohibited Books A list of books banned by the Roman Catholic Church because of moral or doctrinal error. First announced in 1559, it was only sporadically enforced and had little effect. The Index was suppressed in 1966. *(Ch. 14)*

industrialization Beginning in Britain in the later eighteenth century, a system of **mass production** of goods in which specialization and mechanization made manufacturing efficient and profitable. Early industrialization enabled Britain to become the dominant world power in the nineteenth century. See also **factories**. *(Ch. 20)*

information technology (IT) Term for the revolution in information availability and communications resulting from the late-twentieth-century development of personal computers and the Internet. See also **digital divide**. *(Ch. 30)*

Interregnum (1649–1660) Literally "between reigns," the period in English history from the execution of Charles I to the restoration of Charles II. During these years England was a republic—a Commonwealth—ruled by **Oliver Cromwell**, who became Lord Protector in 1653. *(Ch. 16)*

Israel People who settled on the eastern shore of the Mediterranean around 1200 B.C., or perhaps earlier. Their belief in one God directly influenced the faith of Christians, Muslims, and modern Jews. See also **monotheism**. *(Ch. 2)*

Jacobins In revolutionary France, a political club named for a monastic order. One of the most radical of republican groups, the Jacobins purged the **Girondins**, originally fellow members of the club, from the National Convention in 1793. Leaders of the **Terror**, such as **Maximilien Robespierre**, came from their ranks. *(Ch. 19)*

Jesus of Nazareth (ca. 4 B.C.–A.D. 30) Founder of **Christianity**. A forceful preacher and reformer who, to his followers, was Christ, "the anointed one" (from the Greek *Christos*), foretold in the Hebrew Bible as the redeemer of Israel who would initiate the kingdom of heaven. The dynamism and popularity of his teachings led to a clash with Jewish and Roman authorities in Jerusalem and to his crucifixion by the Romans. *(Ch. 6)*

Joan of Arc (d. 1431) Charismatic French military leader during the **Hundred Years' War**. A late medieval mystic, Joan heard "voices" telling her to assist in driving the English from France. She was captured and burned as a heretic by the English. Later she was canonized as Saint Joan, patron saint of France. *(Ch. 11)*

Julio-Claudians Dynasty of Roman emperors founded by **Augustus** and ruling from A.D. 14 to 68. The succession consisted of Augustus's stepson Tiberius, great-grandson Caligula, grandnephew Claudius, and great-great-grandson Nero. For elite Romans, this era was one of decadence and scandal; for ordinary people, it was a time of stability and peace. *(Ch. 6)*

July Revolution (1830) Uprising in Paris in July 1830 that forced King Charles X to abdicate and signaled a victory for constitutional reform over an absolute monarchy. The liberal Louis Philippe was proclaimed "King of the French," with limited powers, by the chamber of deputies. The revolution sparked democratic uprisings in Belgium, Germany, Italy, and Russian Poland and helped persuade British peers to vote for the **Great Reform Bill**. *(Ch. 21)*

justification by faith Doctrine professed by **Martin Luther** that Christians can be saved (justified) only by faith, a free gift of God, and not by penitential acts or good works. Luther's doctrine directly challenged the authority and fundamental practices of the Roman Catholic Church. *(Ch. 14)*

Justinian (r. 527–565) One of the greatest of all Rome's emperors. His comprehensive collection of Roman law is the most influential legal collection in human history. He built **Hagia Sophia**, reformed the imperial administration, and fought constant wars to expand the empire. *(Ch. 7)*

Kepler, Johannes (1571–1630) German astronomer. Kepler developed the three laws of planetary motion, known as Kepler's Laws, which are still accepted, and mathematically confirmed the Copernican heliocentric hypothesis. *(Ch. 17)*

Kosovo Yugoslav province, viewed by Serbs as the cradle of their nationhood but populated overwhelmingly by ethnic Albanians. After Slobodan Milosevic launched a campaign of **"ethnic cleansing"** there in 1999, NATO bombing forced him to agree to allow a UN peacekeeping force to administer the province. *(Ch. 30)*

Kriegsrohstoffabteilung (KRA) The "War Raw Materials Office" that coordinated Germany's World War I economy. The KRA produced synthetic substitute products and created new mixed (private and government) companies to allocate raw materials. This body served as a model for later economic planning and coordination in Germany and elsewhere. *(Ch. 25)*

laissez faire French term meaning "to leave alone," it was applied to the economic doctrine put forward by **Adam Smith** in 1776. Smith advocated freeing national economies from the fetters of the state and allowing supply and demand to shape the marketplace. Laissez-faire ideas contributed to the drive to lower tariffs in the nineteenth century. See also **liberalism**. *(Ch. 21)*

Las Casas, Bartolomé de (1474–1566) First bishop of Chiapas, in southern Mexico. A former *encomendero*, Las Casas passionately condemned the brutality of the Spanish conquests. In 1542 King Charles accepted Las Casas's criticisms, abolishing Indian slavery and greatly restricting the transfer of **encomiendas**. *(Ch. 13)*

Latin Indo-European language of ancient Rome and its empire, from which today's Romance languages developed. *(Ch. 5)*

laws of motion The natural laws of gravity, planetary motion, and inertia first laid out in the seventeenth century by **Isaac Newton**. Newton demonstrated that these laws apply to the solar system and could be used to predict the existence of an as-yet-unseen planet. *(Ch. 17)*

lay investiture Control of church appointments by laymen. Emperor Henry IV (1066–1106) and Pope Gregory VII (1073–1085) disputed who should have this authority in the Christian world. The 1122 Concordat of Worms stipulated that bishops could be invested by kings only after a free church election. *(Ch. 9)*

League of Nations (1919–1946) An international alliance established at the end of World War I without the membership of the United States. Though its covenant called for the peaceful settlement of disputes among member states and for sanctions against a member that went to war in violation of League provisions, it failed to prevent the escalating violence that culminated in World War II. *(Ch. 25)*

legion Innovative and highly successful ancient Roman battle formation. The legion included many flexible, adaptable, and semi-independent groups that broke their enemies' order with javelins at long range, then charged with sword and shield. *(Ch. 5)*

Lend-Lease Act (1941) Act by the U.S. Congress authorizing President **Franklin Roosevelt** to lend or lease weapons or other aid to countries the president designated. A major declaration of American support for the threatened British, lend-lease was later extended to several other countries. *(Ch. 28)*

Lenin, Vladimir Ilyich (1870–1924) Russian revolutionary. Leader of the **Bolsheviks** since 1903, he launched the November 1917 revolution that overthrew the **provisional government**. He concluded the **Treaty of Brest-Litovsk** with Germany and began the establishment of communism in the Soviet Union. See also **New Economic Policy**. *(Ch. 25)*

liberalism Nineteenth-century economic and political theory that called for reducing government powers to a minimum. Liberals worked to impose constitutional limits on government, establish the rule of law, eliminate state regulation of the economy, and ensure a voice in government for men of property and education. *(Ch. 21)*

linear perspective Revolutionary technique developed by early-fifteenth-century Florentine painters for representing three-dimensional objects on a two-dimensional plane. The technique is based in part on the observation that as parallel lines recede, they appear to converge. *(Ch. 12)*

Livia (58 B.C.–A.D. 29) Wife of **Augustus** and mother of Tiberius, his successor. As one of Augustus's main advisers, she intrigued to secure the succession for Tiberius and was suspected of poisoning several family members, including Augustus himself. *(Ch. 6)*

Locarno, Treaty of (1925) Treaty that introduced a new, more conciliatory spirit in international affairs. France and Germany accepted the postwar border between them, and Germany was again accepted as a diplomatic equal and entered the League of Nations in 1926. *(Ch. 26)*

Locke, John (1632–1704) English philosopher. In his influential *Two Treatises on Government,* Locke asserted that the state arises from a contract that individuals freely endorse. Therefore, because sovereignty resides with the people, rebellion against abuse of power is justified—a revolutionary vision of a political society based on human rights. See also **empirical reasoning**. *(Ch. 17)*

Louis XIV (r. 1643–1715) Longest-reigning ruler in European history, who imposed absolute rule on France and waged several wars attempting to dominate Europe. He was known as the Sun King, and his reign marked a great flowering of French culture. *(Ch. 16)*

Loyola, Ignatius (1491–1556) Spanish nobleman and founder of the Society of Jesus, or Jesuits, which has been called the vanguard of the Catholic reform movement. After papal approval of the order, the Jesuits focused primarily on educating Catholics and reconverting Protestants. *(Ch. 14)*

Luther, Martin (1483–1546) German theologian and religious reformer. Luther began the Protestant Reformation in 1517

with the publication of his *Ninety-Five Theses*, which challenged indulgences and Catholic teachings on penitential acts. His translation of the Bible into German in 1522 standardized the modern German language. See also **Augsburg Confession, justification by faith, sola scriptura**. *(Ch. 14)*

Maastricht agreement (1991) Agreement among twelve European Community countries at Maastricht, the Netherlands, to form the **European Union.** The member states agreed to expand cooperation on social, foreign, judicial, and security matters and adopted a timetable for a common policy on workers' rights, a common currency (the **euro**), and a common central banking structure. *(Ch. 30)*

Maccabees Traditionalist Jews led by the Hasmonean family, who in 168 B.C. revolted against Hellenizing laws and influences. Their success is celebrated today during the Jewish holiday of Hanukkah. *(Ch. 4)*

Macedon Weaker, less culturally advanced state on Greece's northern border. It was unified and led to power by **Philip II** and **Alexander the Great**, who became rulers of Greece. *(Ch. 4)*

Machiavelli, Niccolò (1469–1527) Florentine politician and political theorist. His most famous work, *The Prince*, describes the methods a prince can use to acquire and maintain power. Often misunderstood as a defender of despotism, Machiavelli emphasized that a successful ruler needed to anticipate and consider the consequences of his actions. *(Ch. 12)*

Magellan, Ferdinand (1480?–1521) Portuguese-born Spanish explorer who led the first expedition to sail around the world. After finding the South American passage to the Pacific Ocean, he sailed to the Philippines, where he was killed by natives. Survivors on one of his ships completed the circumnavigation. *(Ch. 13)*

Maginot Line A 200-mile system of elaborate permanent fortifications on France's eastern border, named for war minister André Maginot, and built primarily during the 1930s. It was a defense against German frontal assault; in 1940 the Germans invaded by flanking the line. *(Ch. 26)*

Magna Carta (1215) Momentous document that England's barons forced King John to sign. It required the king to respect the rights of feudal lords, not abuse his judicial powers, and consult the barons—in essence, it put the king under the law, not above it. *(Ch. 9)*

manifest destiny Term coined in 1845 for the belief that the expanding United States was destined to occupy the North American continent from coast to coast. The rhetoric of manifest destiny was invoked to justify war with Mexico in 1846 and the acquisition of California and the southwest from Mexico in 1848. *(Ch. 22)*

manor In western Europe, a type of estate that developed under the Carolingians. One-quarter to one-half of the land was set aside as a reserve (or demesne), to be worked on behalf of the landlord; the remainder was divided into tenancies worked by individual peasants for their own support. *(Ch. 8)*

Maria Theresa (r. 1740–1780) Habsburg archduchess of Austria and queen of Hungary and Bohemia. After successfully defending her right to the Austrian throne against attacks by **Frederick the Great** and others, she reformed and centralized the administration of her Austrian and Bohemian lands. *(Ch. 18)*

Marxism Political and economic theories of the two German philosophers and revolutionaries, Karl Marx (1818–1883) and Friedrich Engels (1820–1895), which they called scientific **socialism** and which gave birth to modern communism. Marxism argued that the oppressed working class should and inevitably would rebel against the capitalist owners and build a communist society. *(Ch. 21)*

mass production System in which great numbers of people work in centralized, mechanized **factories** to produce large quantities of goods; an essential feature of **industrialization**. A series of eighteenth-century inventions, culminating in the **steam engine**, enabled Britain to mass-produce textiles and benefit from the resulting increases in productivity. *(Ch. 20)*

Matteotti murder The 1924 killing by fascist thugs of Italian moderate socialist Giacomo Matteotti after he denounced the fascist violence accompanying national elections. The public outcry following the murder eventually led **Mussolini** to commit to a more radical direction, which included the creation of a new fascist state. *(Ch. 26)*

mechanistic world-view Seventeenth-century philosophical view that saw the world as a machine that functions in strict obedience to physical laws, without purpose or will. Experience and reason were regarded as the standards of truth. *(Ch. 17)*

Mehmed II (r. 1451–1481) Ottoman sultan who completed the conquest of the Byzantine Empire by capturing Constantinople in 1453. Mehmed established Constantinople as the Ottoman capital and repopulated the city with a mix of Greek, Armenian, Jewish, and Muslim communities. *(Ch. 11)*

mercantilism Economic policy pursued by western European states in the seventeenth and eighteenth centuries, stressing self-sufficiency in manufactured goods, tight government control of trade to foster the domestic economy, protectionist policies, and the absolute value of bullion. *(Ch. 16)*

Minoans Society that flourished between 2000 and 1375 B.C. on the Aegean island of Crete, where Greece's first civilization appeared. Their sophisticated culture and economy were administered from their magnificent palaces. See also **Mycenaeans**. *(Ch. 2)*

mir Russian peasant commune. After Tsar Alexander II freed the serfs in 1861, the mir determined land use and paid the government mortgages and taxes. Peasants could leave the land only with the mir's permission. *(Ch. 22)*

monasticism Ascetic way of life. Christian monasticism was founded by an Egyptian layman, Anthony (d. 356), who renounced all worldliness and pursued a life of prayer in the desert. A more communal form of monasticism was created by Pachomius (290–346), who wrote the first monastic Rule—a code for daily living in a monastic community. Monasticism quickly spread throughout the Christian world. *(Ch. 7)*

monophysitism Fifth-century theological doctrine emphasizing the divine nature of **Jesus of Nazareth.** The Council of Chalcedon condemned monophysitism and pronounced that Christ had two authentic natures—he was true God and true man. *(Ch. 7)*

monotheism Belief that there is only one God. The Hebrew Bible places this belief as originating about 2000–1500 B.C., when God commanded Abraham to give up Mesopotamian polytheism for belief in one God. *(Ch. 2)*

More, Thomas (1478–1535) Chancellor of England under Henry VIII. More's best-known work, *Utopia,* was highly critical of contemporary European kingdoms. It describes a fictional land of peace and harmony that has outlawed private property and all forms of wealth. More was executed when he refused to take an oath to support the **Act of Supremacy.** See also **humanism.** *(Ch. 12)*

Muhammad (570–632) Prophet and founder of Islam. In 610 he began to receive revelations commanding him to teach all people a new faith that called for an unquestioned belief in one god, Allah, and a deep commitment to social justice for believers. Before his death, he had converted most of Arabia. See also **Five Pillars of Islam, Quran.** *(Ch. 8)*

Mussolini, Benito (1883–1945) Italian fascist dictator. Mussolini founded the fascist movement in 1919 and took power in 1922. He replaced Italy's parliamentary democracy with a **corporative state** and pursued an expansionist foreign policy. He concluded the Pact of Steel with **Adolf Hitler** in 1939 and took Italy into World War II in 1940. Deposed in 1943, he was killed by partisans in 1945. *(Ch. 26)*

Mycenaeans Militaristic people from the Greek mainland who conquered the **Minoans** around 1550–1375 B.C. Mycenaean civilization was a center of Bronze Age culture until its destruction around 1100 B.C. *(Ch. 2)*

mystery religions Popular Hellenistic cults featuring the initiation of worshipers into secret doctrines. Mystery religions replaced the traditional Greek religion of the Olympian gods. Some ancient Egyptian cults were recast as mystery religions, influencing early Christianity. *(Ch. 4)*

Napoleon Bonaparte (1769–1821) Emperor of the French (r. 1804–1815). A French general who took part in a coup in 1799 against the **Directory**, Napoleon consolidated power as first consul and proclaimed himself emperor with the approval of a national plebiscite in 1804. His military conquests exported French revolutionary reforms to the rest of Europe. He was finally defeated and exiled in 1815. *(Ch. 19)*

National Assembly (1789–1791) Legislative body formed in France in 1789 after the Third Estate insisted on being certified as members of the Estates General as a whole. The National Assembly drafted the **Declaration of the Rights of Man and the Citizen** and a constitution that called for a constitutional (not absolute) monarchy. *(Ch. 19)*

National Socialist (Nazi) Party The political party that grew from the movement that German dictator **Adolf Hitler** made his vehicle to power. Originating from the radical right in Munich in 1919, the Nazi Party won voting support during the early 1930s, paving the way for Hitler to be named German chancellor in 1933. *(Ch. 27)*

nationalism Belief arising in the eighteenth century that people derive their identity from their nation and owe it their primary loyalty. The criteria for nationhood typically included a common language, religion, and political authority, as well as common traditions and shared historical experiences. Nationalism was a major force in most of the revolutions of 1848 and in the subsequent unification of Italy and of Germany. *(Ch. 20)*

Nazi-Soviet Pact (1939) Surprise agreement between the Soviet Union and Nazi Germany in August 1939 that each would remain neutral if either got into a war with some other nation. The pact freed Germany to attack Poland a few days later without fear of Soviet reprisal. *(Ch. 27)*

Neo-Babylonians Rulers of western Asia between 612 and 539 B.C. who elaborately rebuilt Babylon, creating the famous Hanging Gardens. They destroyed Jerusalem, deporting many Judeans in what is known as the Babylonian Captivity. *(Ch. 2)*

Neolithic Revolution Human discovery and spread of agriculture, between about 13,000 and 5000 B.C. People first domesticated dogs and other animals and then learned how to cultivate crops. *(Ch. 1)*

New Economic Policy (NEP) (1921–1928) A Russian economic liberalization measure aimed at reviving an economy in crisis. The NEP restored considerable scope for private enterprise and allowed peasants to sell some of their harvest. After initial economic success, it was eventually considered a threat to the socialist state and was replaced by state-controlled central planning. *(Ch. 26)*

new imperialism Era of European overseas expansion launched in the 1880s. In the following decades, Europeans subjugated 500 million people in Africa and Asia—one half of the world's non-European population. *(Ch. 24)*

Newton, Isaac (1643–1727) English physicist, mathematician, and natural philosopher. Newton's mathematical computation of the laws of gravity and planetary motion, which he combined with a fully developed theory of inertia, completed the explanation for motion initiated by **Nicholas Copernicus.** See also **laws of motion.** *(Ch. 17)*

nongovernmental organizations (NGOs) A network of organizations unaffiliated with governments but central to the international community, such as the Red Cross, Amnesty International, and Doctors Without Borders, that had gradually emerged by the early twenty-first century to deal with humanitarian relief and human rights issues. *(Ch. 30)*

North Atlantic Treaty Organization (NATO) An alliance for regional defense, created in 1949 by the United States, Canada, and western European nations, whose members agree to defend one another from attack by nonmember countries. Its original aim was to contain the Soviet Union. *(Ch. 29)*

Nuremberg trials The war crimes trials conducted in Nuremberg, Germany. Most of the twenty-four defendants were convicted of war crimes and "crimes against humanity." *(Ch. 28)*

On the Donation of Constantine Work by Lorenzo Valla (1407–1457) proving that the *Donation of Constantine* was not written at the time of the emperor Constantine. The forged *Donation* purported to record Constantine's transfer to the pope of jurisdiction over Rome and the western half of the empire. Valla's work undermined the papacy's claim to political rule in central Italy. *(Ch. 12)*

Orthodoxy The Catholic Christian faith of Byzantium. It differed from Roman Catholicism by its use of Greek instead of Latin, the inclusion of icons in worship, an adherence to the Greek church fathers, some differences in basic theology, and many differences in customs and practices. *(Ch. 8)*

papacy Name for the institution ruled by the bishop of Rome who, in Roman Catholic tradition, is the successor to Peter, the most prominent apostle. Since Peter was believed to be the leader of the original followers of Christ, his successors, the popes (from *papa* by the fourth century), were believed to be the leaders of the whole church. *(Ch. 7)*

papal monarchy Period during the twelfth and thirteenth centuries when the power of the Catholic Church was increasingly expanded and centralized in the hands of the popes, as papal policy focused on recovering lost lands and rights in central Italy. *(Ch. 9)*

Papal States Beginning in the eighth century, territories held by the popes in central Italy under the protection of the Frankish kings. *(Ch. 8)*

papyrus Paperlike writing material used by the ancient Egyptians, Greeks, and Romans. Made primarily in Egypt from the papyrus plant, it was durable, flexible, and easy to write on. *(Ch. 1)*

Paris Commune (1871) Parisian workers' uprising intended to establish a workers' government under home rule. Stemming from labor discontent and the radicalization of workers during the siege of Paris in the Franco-Prussian War, the commune was suppressed by the army of the conservative French government. *(Ch. 22)*

Parliament English legislative institution whose ancestors were the royal courts that met in 1265 and 1295. The king considered the courts a device to win support for royal agendas; the barons viewed them as opportunities to play a real policymaking role in government. *(Ch. 9)*

paterfamilias Oldest living male in an ancient Roman family, who had supreme legal power within the household. Only the paterfamilias could own property free and clear. *(Ch. 5)*

Paul of Tarsus (d. ca. 67) Christian apostle and saint. A Jew from Anatolia and a Roman citizen, Paul first persecuted the Christians but became a believer around A.D. 36. Paul taught that the life and resurrection of **Jesus of Nazareth** offered all humanity the hope of salvation through faith. Under Paul, **Christianity** began its complete separation from Judaism. *(Ch. 6)*

pax Romana Latin for "Roman peace," the term refers to the period of peace and prosperity in the Roman Empire from A.D. 69 to 180. During this time the emperors emphasized extending citizenship and spreading prosperity throughout the provinces, and Italy was no longer the tyrant of the Mediterranean. See also **Flavians.** *(Ch. 6)*

Peace of Westphalia (1648) Treaty that ended the **Thirty Years' War.** The principalities within the Holy Roman Empire were recognized as virtually autonomous, severely weakening the power of the emperor. Calvinism joined Catholicism and Lutheranism as tolerated faiths within the empire, and the treaty closed the age of religious wars. *(Ch. 15)*

Pericles Leader of fifth-century-B.C. Athens when **demokratia** became entrenched as the government and way of life. Distinguished for his oratory and honesty, he established Athens as a great center of art and literature as well as a great empire. *(Ch. 3)*

Persian Empire Vast, prosperous, and law-abiding West Asian empire, from about 550 B.C. to its conquest by **Alexander the Great** around 330 B.C. The relatively tolerant rule of the Persian emperors represented the greatest success yet of a universal kingship. The Persians also built the first great navy. *(Ch. 2)*

Peter the Great (r. 1682–1725) Russian tsar. Brilliant, energetic, and tyrannical, Peter revolutionized Russian society by his determined efforts to westernize his nation culturally, economically, and politically. He modernized the army and navy, secured seaports, and made Russia into a great power. See also **Great Northern War.** *(Ch. 16)*

Petrarch, Francesco (1304–1374) Influential Italian poet, biographer, and humanist during the Renaissance. Petrarch advocated imitating the actions, values, and culture of the ancient Romans to reform the excesses of the present world. *(Ch. 12)*

Petrograd Soviet The *soviet* (council) of leaders of strike committees and army regiments elected in March 1917, when Petrograd's workers protested in response to severe wartime food and coal shortages. Central to the Bolshevik Revolution of 1917, the soviet eventually became the ruling power in the Russian capital—but only temporarily. *(Ch. 25)*

pharaoh Ancient Egyptians' title for their king, an absolute, all-powerful, and all-providing ruler. It was believed that the ruler represented the ancestors and guaranteed the fertility of the soil. *(Ch. 1)*

Philip II (382–336 B.C.) King of **Macedon.** A brilliant soldier and statesman, Philip conquered the Greek world. He developed a well-trained, professional year-round army and mastered the technology of siegecraft. He was succeeded by his son, **Alexander the Great.** *(Ch. 4)*

Philip II (r. 1556–1598) King of Spain, son of **Charles V.** An avid Roman Catholic, he ruled Spain at the height of its influence. Philip dispatched the ill-fated **Armada** to invade England and attempted to quash the revolt of the Netherlands. *(Ch. 15)*

philosophes Influential group of eighteenth-century French intellectuals, including **Voltaire** and Diderot, who argued that people have natural rights and that governments exist to guarantee and protect those rights. While not advocating violent revolution, they severely criticized the regime's abuses of power. *(Ch. 18)*

Phoenicians Canaanites whose civilization flourished about 1000–750 B.C. in present-day coastal Syria, where they established major trading ports. Master sailors, they planted colonies around the Mediterranean, many of which, including Carthage, became independent states. The Phoenicians exported the civilization of western Asia—including the Phoenician alphabet, derived from **Ugarit**—to the Mediterranean world. *(Ch. 2)*

plantation system Agricultural practices developed by the fifteenth-century Portuguese to produce sugar on their island colonies in the Atlantic using involuntarily transported slaves from Africa. Portugal's prototype—wealthy absentee landlords and masses of forced labor producing cash crops on vast tracts of land—was the model for the New World plantation system. In seventeenth- and eighteenth-century French and English colonies in the Caribbean, large sugar plantations owned by wealthy, often absentee, landlords replaced smaller-scale independent farming. *(Chs. 13, 16)*

Plato (427–348 B.C.) Ancient Greek philosopher, student of **Socrates**. One of Western philosophy's greatest exponents of idealism, Plato believed that the senses are misleading and that truth can therefore be attained only by training the mind to overcome commonsense evidence. In the *Republic*, Plato describes an ideal state in which philosophers rule as kings, benevolently and unselfishly. *(Ch. 3)*

polis Term for an ancient Greek city-state, a system that reached its height around 700–300 B.C. The ideological and political organization of the polis emphasized equality and a shared community life for all citizens, not just the elite. *(Ch. 3)*

popular front A term for antifascist electoral alliances and governing coalitions that communists promoted from 1934 until 1939 to resist the further spread of fascism. Popular front coalitions won control of government in both Spain and France during 1936. *(Ch. 27)*

positivism Philosophy of the French thinker Auguste Comte (1798–1857). Comte asserted that human history progressed through distinct and irreversible stages, leading inexorably upward to the final and highest stage of development, the positive—or scientific—stage. Positivism and its optimistic outlook for human progress were influential in both Europe and Latin America during the nineteenth century. *(Ch. 23)*

Potsdam conference A July–August 1945 meeting held at Potsdam, Germany, between the USSR, the United States, and Great Britain to implement their earlier agreements concerning the treatment of defeated Germany. Many of the agreements reached were later abandoned amid growing hostility between the USSR and the Western democracies. *(Ch. 28)*

Prague Spring The attempt by Czechoslovakian reformers in 1968 to gain freer cultural expression, democratization of Communist Party procedures, and broader participation in public life within the framework of a communist state. The forcible suppression of the movement by Soviet leaders seemed to signal the end of any hope for flexibility and openness within the Soviet sphere. *(Ch. 29)*

price revolution Steady rise in prices in the sixteenth and seventeenth centuries, resulting from population growth and the influx of precious metals from Spain's New World territories. As wages lost one-tenth to one-fourth of their value, people sought new work, protested against taxes, and attacked scapegoats. The price revolution concentrated wealth in fewer hands and contributed to the rise of a new **gentry** class. *(Ch. 15)*

Principate The constitutional monarchy of the Early Roman Empire, from 31 B.C. to A.D. 192. The term comes from *Princeps,* or "first citizen," an old title of respect used in the **senate**. See also **Augustus, Flavians.** *(Ch. 6)*

professionalization Establishment in the nineteenth century of common standards and requirements, especially in medicine, law, architecture, and engineering. Professionalization brought either government or self-regulation to vocations whose prestige rested on the claim of exclusive expertise in their fields. *(Ch. 23)*

proletariat Term used by Karl Marx to describe the new class of industrial workers who owned none of the means of production and were totally dependent on factory owners for their livelihoods. In Marxist thought, capitalists were destined to be overthrown by the proletariat. See also **Marxism.** *(Ch. 20)*

provisional government The body that ruled Russia from March to November 1917, in the wake of the revolution that overthrew the tsarist regime. Originally intended to be a temporary step to an elected constituent assembly, its policies caused discontents that the **Bolsheviks** were quick to exploit. *(Ch. 25)*

Ptolemies Dynasty of Egyptian kings who ruled from 304 to 30 B.C., founded by Ptolemy I, a Macedonian general of **Alexander the Great**. It was the wealthiest, most sophisticated, and longest lasting of the Hellenistic kingdoms. See also **Alexandria.** *(Ch. 4)*

Punic Wars (264–146 B.C.) Three wars during which the Roman Empire eventually destroyed Carthage. The Romans later adopted the Carthaginians' plantation system using massive numbers of slaves. *(Ch. 5)*

Puritans Radical Protestants in late-sixteenth- and seventeenth-century England. Puritans emphasized Bible reading, preaching, private scrutiny of conscience, and de-emphasized institutional ritual and clerical authority. Puritans became a majority in Parliament during the reign of Charles I and led the campaign against the king during the English Civil War. *(Ch. 15)*

putting-out system The production in country homes of thread and cloth by spinners and weavers for an entrepreneur who bought raw materials and "put them out" to be finished by individual workers. This cottage industry system expanded in eighteenth-century Europe as increased numbers of agricultural laborers needed more nonfarm work in off-seasons. *(Ch. 18)*

Quran Islamic sacred writings, which **Muhammad** communicated in the form of "recitations," insisting that he was transmitting a direct revelation from Allah. After Muhammad's death, his followers arranged the recitations into 114 *Suras,* or chapters, containing legal and wisdom literature and moral teaching. *(Ch. 8)*

rabbinic Judaism Main form of Judaism, which emerged during the first century A.D. under the leadership of the rabbis, the spiritual descendants of the Pharisees. Rabbinic Judaism amplified and interpreted the Hebrew Bible to clarify Jewish practice, elevated the oral law to equal authority with the written **Torah,** and enabled Judaism to evolve flexibly. *(Ch. 6)*

Realpolitik Style of governing that uses all means, including war, to expand the influence and power of a state. The best-known practitioner of Realpolitik was Prussian chancellor **Otto von Bismarck.** *(Ch. 22)*

Reconquista Wars of reconquest in the Iberian Peninsula from the eleventh to fifteenth centuries. Spanish and Portuguese rulers seized territories from the weakening Muslim regime. By awarding reconquered lands to their nobles, Christian kings enhanced their own status and power. *(Ch. 9)*

remilitarization of the Rhineland The reoccupation of Germany's Rhineland territory by German troops in March 1936, in clear violation of the **Treaty of Versailles.** When the French and British did not resist the German move, **Adolf Hitler** was emboldened to additional acts of aggression elsewhere. *(Ch. 27)*

res publica Romans' concept of their republic, which uniquely influenced Western political institutions. *Res publica* is Latin for "public thing," as opposed to *res privata,* "private thing," as the Romans characterized monarchy. *(Ch. 5)*

revisionism Late-nineteenth-century argument that **socialism** could and should come about by gradual, democratic means. This idea was a "revision" of Marx's contention that socialism would require a violent revolution. Most European socialists claimed to reject revisionism while at the same time pursuing revisionist policies. *(Ch. 24)*

risorgimento Italian term, beginning in the late eighteenth century, for the political and cultural renewal of Italy. It later came to describe the political and military events that led to the unification of Italy in 1861. *(Ch. 22)*

Robespierre, Maximilien (1758–1794) French lawyer and revolutionary leader. A **Jacobin** who joined the Committee of Public Safety in 1793, Robespierre called for the **Terror** to suppress internal dissent. *(Ch. 19)*

Romanesque Meaning "in the Roman style," this nineteenth-century term characterized the transitional architecture and painting of the period between the waning of Carolingian art and the full emergence of **Gothic** art in the twelfth century. Distinctive features of Romanesque churches are their exuberant decoration and ornament. *(Ch. 10)*

romanticism Artistic movement, prevalent from the 1760s to 1840s, that rebelled against rationalism. Writers, painters, and composers rejected the Enlightenment and its rationalist values, instead praising emotion and sensitivity, and worshiping nature for its inherent beauty. *(Ch. 20)*

Rome-Berlin Axis Alliance between Hitler's Nazi Germany and Mussolini's fascist Italy. Beginning as an informal understanding by 1936, it was cemented by an anti-Comintern agreement and eventually by an open-ended military alliance, the Pact of Steel, in 1939. *(Ch. 27)*

Roosevelt, Franklin Delano (1882–1945) U.S. president who served from 1933 to 1945, through the Great Depression of the 1930s and World War II. His New Deal program, including large public works projects, was an innovative response to the Depression. *(Ch. 28)*

Rousseau, Jean-Jacques (1712–1778) French writer and philosopher. In his 1762 work, *The Social Contract,* Rousseau depicted a hypothetical state with direct democracy in which citizens have inalienable rights to wide-ranging liberties. He was influential as a critic of an elite society still dominated by status, patronage, and privilege. *(Ch. 18)*

salons Regular gatherings in eighteenth-century Parisian private homes, where **Voltaire** and other **philosophes** read and discussed their works in progress, with the exchange of ideas facilitated by female *salonnières* (salon leaders). Anyone with appropriate manners could participate as an equal, enabling conversation to shift from maintaining the status quo to questioning it. *(Ch. 18)*

sans-culottes Ordinary citizens of revolutionary Paris, whose derisive nickname referred to their inability to afford fashionable knee pants ("culottes"). Because of their effective political organization, they were able to influence the direction of the French Revolution through pressure on the government as well as direct action, such as to overthrow the monarchy in August 1792. *(Ch. 19)*

Sappho (fl. ca. 625 B.C.) Ancient Greek poet from the island of Lesbos. Sappho wrote odes, wedding songs, and hymns expressing intimate feelings, including love for other women. She wrote of female sexuality in a male-dominated culture. *(Ch. 3)*

second industrial revolution Interrelated economic changes that resulted in a significant speedup in production in western Europe after 1850. Key factors were the introduction of new products, new methods of manufacture, and new materials such as mass-produced steel, synthetic dyes, and aluminum. *(Ch. 23)*

Second International International socialist organization founded in 1889 that met yearly to debate issues of broad concern. Beginning in 1907, it called for workers to strike and to refuse military service in case of international conflict. *(Ch. 24)*

Second Reform Bill (1867) British legislation that extended suffrage by lowering property qualifications and set equal population requirements for all parliamentary districts. The legislation bolstered the existing system, as the newly enfranchised clerks, artisans, and other skilled workers felt more a part of society. *(Ch. 22)*

Seleucids Dynasty of rulers of Asia Minor from 312 to 64 B.C. Founded by Seleucus (ca. 358–281 B.C.), a general of **Alexander the Great**, the kingdom spread **Hellenism** by establishing seventy colonies throughout the Near East. *(Ch. 4)*

senate In the ancient Roman Republic and Empire, the powerful council of elders that advised the monarchs (Latin: *senatus,* from *senex,* "old man"). Romans spoke of the senate's *auctoritas,* a quasi-religious prestige. *(Ch. 5)*

separate spheres Notion, especially prevalent in the mid-nineteenth century, of two distinct sets of roles—one male and public, the other female and private. While the man was out in the world advancing his career, the bourgeois woman was to run her home, providing her family with an orderly, comfortable shelter. *(Ch. 23)*

show trials Trials staged for ideological and propaganda reasons in the USSR. In the most famous, orchestrated by **Joseph Stalin** from 1936 to 1938, major communist figures were made to confess to trumped-up charges and executed. These trials helped persuade Soviet citizens that a high-level conspiracy was responsible for the USSR's economic woes. *(Ch. 27)*

Sistine Chapel Chapel at the Vatican Palace commissioned by Pope Sixtus IV in 1475, best known for Michelangelo's magnificent paintings of the Creation and Last Judgment. The monument vividly captures the cultural, religious, and ideological program of the papacy. *(Ch. 12)*

Smith, Adam (1723–1790) Scottish economist who developed the doctrine of **laissez faire.** In his treatise *The Wealth of Nations* (1776), Smith argued that an economy regulates itself better without interference by government and without monopolies and other economic privileges. Smith suggested that people's economic activities are often "led by an invisible hand" to benefit society as a whole. *(Ch. 18)*

social Catholics Catholics in western Europe who believed that society bore responsibility for the well-being of the poor. They were following the ideas set out in 1891 by Pope Leo XIII (r. 1878–1903) in his encyclical *Rerum novarum* ("Of New Things"). *(Ch. 23)*

Social Darwinism Theory of social evolution first articulated by Herbert Spencer (1820–1902). According to Social Darwinists, human societies evolve in the same way as plants and animals, and the weak, poor, and improvident are not worthy of survival. Social Darwinism was used to justify callousness toward the poor at home and imperialist conquest abroad. See also **Darwinism.** *(Ch. 23)*

social market economy The late-twentieth-century socially-oriented model of capitalism practiced in continental western Europe, providing a substantial safety net in health care and a commitment to public services such as transportation and day care. It competed with the U.S. model, shared by Britain, which emphasized free enterprise. *(Ch. 30)*

socialism Nineteenth-century economic and social doctrine and political movement that opposed private ownership and control of the means of production. Socialists believed that the "social" or state ownership of property, unlike private ownership, would benefit society as a whole, creating a more just system. *(Ch. 21)*

Society of Revolutionary Republican Women In revolutionary France, a powerful political club that represented the interests of female **sans-culottes.** The society was included in a general ban on political participation by women that the Committee of Public Safety instituted in October 1793. *(Ch. 19)*

Socrates (469–399 B.C.) Ancient Greek philosopher, a founder of the Western philosophical tradition. Socrates changed the emphasis of philosophy from the natural world to human ethics. He believed that no one who truly understood goodness would ever choose to do evil. Accused of being an atheist and corrupting the young, Socrates was executed in 399. Socrates' teachings were recorded and transmitted by his students, including **Plato.** *(Ch. 3)*

sola scriptura Doctrine put forward by **Martin Luther** in *On the Babylonian Captivity of the Church* (1520) that church authority had to be based on biblical teachings. In particular

he argued that the sacraments of the Catholic Church—other than baptism and communion—were not found in the Bible. *(Ch. 14)*

solidarism Late-nineteenth-century policy of conservative and liberal parties to blunt the appeal of socialism. Solidarism emphasized the mutual responsibility of classes and individuals for one another's well-being and led to the passage of laws and benefits to improve the lot of the working class. *(Ch. 23)*

Solidarity A trade union formed from a movement of shipyard workers in communist Poland in 1980. It became the nucleus of widespread demands for change—including independent labor organizations, the right to strike, and freedom of expression. Though forced underground in 1981, the movement eventually proved crucial to the downfall of the communist regime in Poland. *(Ch. 29)*

Solon (ca. 630–560 B.C.) Statesman of early Athens. Appointed to a one-year term as sole archon in 594 B.C., Solon transformed Greek society through mediation, moderation, respect for law, and measures that liberated the poor and downtrodden. His economic reforms sparked a commercial boom. *(Ch. 3)*

Spanish Inquisition Church court that began in 1478 when King Ferdinand and Queen Isabella obtained papal approval to control the grand inquisitor. The Spanish Inquisition investigated and condemned many former Jews and Muslims who were believed to have insincerely converted to Christianity. It became an important and lucrative instrument to expand state power. *(Ch. 11)*

SS (*Schutzstaffel*) Nazi elite troops, led by Heinrich Himmler. Linked to the Gestapo, the secret political police, the SS specialized in institutionalized terror tactics and were responsible for some of the worst atrocities of the Nazi regime. *(Ch. 27)*

"stab in the back" myth The notion, widely held among Germans after their unexpected loss in World War I, that political intrigue and revolution at home had sabotaged the German military effort. It helped alienate Germans from their new democratic government. *(Ch. 25)*

Stalin, Joseph (1879–1953) Soviet dictator. Secretary of the Communist Party since 1922, Stalin outmaneuvered his rivals after the death of Lenin to take control of the Soviet government by 1929. Stalin jettisoned the **New Economic Policy** and instituted a program of crash industrialization and agricultural **collectivization.** He concluded the **Nazi-Soviet Pact** in 1939 but joined the Allies after the German invasion of the Soviet Union in 1941. Victorious in World War II, Stalin sponsored the takeover of governments in eastern Europe by communist regimes, contributing to the development of the **cold war.** See also **"the Great Patriotic War," gulag, Potsdam conference, show trials, Yalta conference.** *(Ch. 26)*

Stalingrad (1942–1943) Decisive World War II battle. The Soviet Union, at immense cost in lives, launched repeated counterattacks on Germany's Sixth Army, stopping it from advancing farther and finally forcing it to surrender. The battle is often considered the turning point of World War II in Europe. *(Ch. 28)*

steam engine Machine invented in England in its modern form by James Watt in 1777. The steam engine provided mechanized power for manufacturing and made **factories** and **mass production** possible. *(Ch. 20)*

Stoics Believers in a philosophical system begun in Athens by Zeno (335–263 B.C.). Stoicism emphasized the pursuit of wisdom, the reliability of sensory experience, and freedom from all passion. Stoics focused on intentions as well as the results of actions. *(Ch. 4)*

Streseman, Gustav (1878–1929) German statesman of the Weimar Republic. Leader of the conservative German People's Party, Streseman served briefly as chancellor in 1923, then as foreign secretary from 1923 to 1929. He secured a reduction of Germany's reparations payments and negotiated the **Treaty of Locarno,** paving the way for Germany's entry to the League of Nations in 1926. His death in 1929 was a blow to hopes for the development of democracy in Germany and peace in Europe. *(Ch. 26)*

Suez crisis (1956) Crisis prompted by Egypt's nationalization of the British-owned Suez Canal. The effort of Britain, France, and Israel to seize the canal prompted a strong negative reaction in world opinion, forcing them to withdraw. The episode demonstrated the newly limited reach of the western European powers in world affairs. *(Ch. 29)*

suffragists Activists who, beginning in the late nineteenth century, organized to win the vote for women. Adopting increasingly violent tactics, English suffragists (often referred to by contemporaries as "suffragettes") endured attacks by male thugs, were arrested, engaged in hunger strikes, and were force-fed. *(Ch. 24)*

Sumerians Dominant inhabitants of Mesopotamia in the third millennium B.C. They established the world's first civilization, thirty flourishing city-states with a common culture, commerce, and tendency to make war on one another. *(Ch. 1)*

summa An encyclopedic compendium of carefully arrayed knowledge on a particular subject. Examples are the two most famous works of **Thomas Aquinas,** the *Summa Contra Gentiles* and the *Summa Theologiae. (Ch. 10)*

surrealism A movement in literature and the visual arts that emerged in Paris in the early 1920s. Though indebted to dada and its mocking defiance of convention, surrealism sought to find something positive by exploring the realm of the subconscious, partly by following some of **Sigmund Freud**'s insights about access to the subconscious. *(Ch. 26)*

Tacitus, Cornelius (ca. A.D. 55–120) Roman historian of the "Silver Age." Tacitus lauded the simple virtues of the German tribes and expressed nostalgia for the Republic. His greatest works were *The Histories,* on the civil wars of A.D. 69, and *The Annals,* chronicling the emperors from Tiberius through Nero. *(Ch. 6)*

Tanzimat Turkish term, meaning "restructuring," for the reform movements in the Ottoman Empire beginning in 1839. Reforms included security of property, equity in taxation, and equality before the law regardless of religion. Government officials were given fixed salaries and subjected to regular inspections. *(Ch. 22)*

Tennis Court Oath (1789) Pledge signed by all but one Third Estate deputy of the Estates General of France on June 20, 1789. The deputies swore to continue to meet until a constitution was drafted. *(Ch. 19)*

Terror (1793–1794) Systematic repression of internal enemies undertaken by revolutionary tribunals across France at the urging of **Maximilien Robespierre.** Approximately fourteen thousand people were executed, including aristocrats, **Girondins,** and **sans-culottes.** The Terror ended with the arrest and execution of Robespierre in July 1794. *(Ch. 19)*

tetrarchy Government ruled by four leaders. Emperor Diocletian established a tetrarchy in about 293 to address the

Roman Empire's political instability, huge size, and complexity, as well as to promote experienced men and provide an orderly imperial succession. *(Ch. 7)*

third-century crisis Period from A.D. 235 to 284, when the Roman Empire suffered barbarian invasions, domestic economic problems, plague, assassinations, and urban decline. Attempting to fend off invasions at opposite fronts, the emperors devalued the currency, leading to massive inflation. *(Ch. 6)*

Third Estate In France, the common people, as distinct from the nobles (First Estate) and clergy (Second Estate). In the Estates General in 1789, it was presumed that the votes of the First and Second Estates would overrule those of the Third Estate, although the commoners vastly outnumbered the nobles and clergy. *(Ch. 19)*

Thirty Years' War (1618–1648) Destructive war, involving most European countries but fought in Germany, resulting from sixteenth-century religious tensions, regionalism versus centralizing forces, and dynastic and strategic rivalries between rulers. See also **Peace of Westphalia.** *(Ch. 15)*

Thucydides (ca. 455–397 B.C.) Ancient Greek historian; with **Herodotus,** a founder of history-writing in the West. A failed Athenian general, Thucydides made a careful study of the Peloponnesian War and prided himself on the accuracy of his account of the prolonged conflict. *(Ch. 3)*

Torah First five books of the Bible. Accepted as sacred by the Hebrews around 425 B.C., it relates the working out of God's pact, or **covenant,** with the Hebrews, his chosen people. *(Ch. 2)*

total war The concept, first associated with World War I, that war requires the mobilization of all a nation's resources and energies. The unexpected need to wage total war during World War I accelerated social and economic processes, from technological development to women's suffrage. *(Ch. 25)*

Toussaint-Louverture, François (1743–1803) Former slave who governed the island of Saint Domingue (Haiti) as an independent state after the slave revolt of 1791. In 1802 French forces captured Toussaint-Louverture, who died in prison. *(Ch. 19)*

trading-post empire Commercial system developed by Portugal in the sixteenth century to dominate trade in the Indian Ocean through fortified, strategically placed naval bases. All merchants were expected to acquire export licenses and ship products through Portuguese ports. *(Ch. 13)*

tragedy Serious play with an unhappy ending. Greek tragedy emerged and reached its height in the fifth century B.C. in the works of Aeschylus, Sophocles, and Euripides. The essence of Greek tragedy is the nobility in the spectacle of a great man or woman failing because of a "fatal flaw," but learning from failure. *(Ch. 3)*

trasformismo System of political manipulation used by Count Camillo di Cavour (1810–1861), Piedmont's prime minister, to create majorities in parliament to support his cabinet. The practice of using cajolery and bribery to transform foes into supporters would continue to characterize Italian government in the late nineteenth century. *(Ch. 22)*

Triple Alliance Military alliance established in 1882 among Germany, Austria-Hungary, and Italy to counter the Franco-Russian Alliance (later the **Triple Entente**). The system of rival alliances contributed to the escalation of international tensions. *(Ch. 24)*

Triple Entente Military alliance between Great Britain, France, and Russia, completed in 1907, countering the

Triple Alliance. The system of rival alliances eventually brought all of Europe into World War I. *(Ch. 24)*

triumph Elaborate procession through the streets of ancient Rome. Triumphs were voted by the **senate** to salute a general's victory over a foreign army. *(Ch. 5)*

Truman Doctrine The U.S. policy of containment, or limiting communist expansion, as outlined by President Harry Truman in 1947. Intended most immediately to deter any communist designs on Greece or Turkey, the doctrine was used thereafter to support any country that the United States considered threatened by communism during the **cold war.** *(Ch. 28)*

Ugarit Cosmopolitan port on northern Syria's Mediterranean coast that was a thriving trading center, especially around 1400–1200 B.C. The alphabet invented by Ugaritic scribes is the source of today's widely used Roman alphabet. *(Ch. 1)*

United Nations International organization of nations founded in 1945 to encourage peace, cooperation, and recognition of human rights. The major powers—China, France, Great Britain, the Soviet Union, and the United States—were given a privileged position as permanent members of the Security Council, each with veto power. *(Ch. 28)*

utilitarianism Political theory of Jeremy Bentham (1748–1832). Bentham argued that the purpose of government is to provide "the greatest happiness of the greatest number" and that the test of government is its usefulness. Democracy was implicit in Bentham's philosophy: the greatest number could ensure its own happiness only by voting for its rulers. *(Ch. 21)*

Vasco da Gama (1460?–1524) Pioneering Portuguese explorer and trader whose voyage from 1497 to 1499 around the Cape of Good Hope to Mozambique and India inaugurated a four-hundred-year-long Portuguese presence in the Indian Ocean region. *(Ch. 13)*

vassal Drawing on both Roman and Germanic customs, vassalage linked two men—lord and vassal—in an honorable, reciprocal bond based on loyalty and service. Eventually leading nobles and their vassals formed a social and political elite. *(Ch. 8)*

Versailles, Treaty of (1919) Peace treaty between the victorious Allies and defeated Germany after World War I. The harsh terms of this dictated peace produced a sense of bitterness and betrayal in Germany. *(Ch. 25)*

Vichy France The term for the repressive French government that followed the Third Republic after France's defeat by Nazi Germany in 1940. Headquartered in the resort town of Vichy, the government collaborated with the victorious Germans, who occupied Paris. *(Ch. 28)*

Victorian morality Nineteenth-century ethos wherein the values of the dominant middle class, which emphasized strict moral principles, especially regarding sex and drink, became the social norms. In Queen Victoria, who reigned for two-thirds of the century, the middle classes saw a reflection of their own values. *(Ch. 23)*

Virgil Roman poet whose works contributed to the Augustan renewal. In the *Eclogues,* Virgil (Publius Vergilius Maro, 70–19 B.C.) describes the blessings of peace under **Augustus**; in the *Georgics,* he glorifies Italian agriculture. His *Aeneid* mythologizes Rome and describes both the burden and glory of empire. *(Ch. 6)*

Visigoths Germanic people who served as allied troops for the Romans. When threatened by the Huns, the Visigoths crossed the Danube and settled in the Balkans. Eventually they sacked Rome in 410 and expanded their rule to parts of Spain and southern France. *(Ch. 7)*

Voltaire (François-Marie Arouet, 1694–1778) Prolific French writer, critic, and reformer who believed that literature should bring about social change. His satires and philosophical critiques targeted Christianity, intolerance, and tyranny. He embodied the spirit of eighteenth-century rationalism: its confidence, its increasingly practical bent, its wit and sophistication. *(Ch. 18)*

Vulgate Bible Latin version of new translations of the Hebrew Scriptures and Greek New Testament written by Jerome (331–420) for Pope Damasus. It was called the Vulgate because it was the Bible for the "people" (*vulgus*), whose language was Latin. *(Ch. 7)*

Warsaw Pact (1955–1991) Military-diplomatic alliance of Soviet bloc countries, created to counter NATO. The pact established a joint military command and mutual military assistance, as well as a new basis for the continuing presence of Soviet troops in the satellite states. See also **cold war.** *(Ch. 29)*

welfare state The concept, especially prevalent in western countries after World War II, that government should adopt large-scale social welfare measures, while maintaining a primarily capitalistic economy. Among the welfare measures usually adopted were a national health service, old-age pensions, and insurance against unemployment, sickness, and disability. *(Ch. 29)*

Weltpolitik Meaning "world politics," the term describes the policy pursued by Kaiser **Wilhelm II** (r. 1888–1918) to make Germany a world power, with colonies, a navy, and major influence among the Great Powers. The kaiser implemented his ambitious agenda with nationalistic appeals and bombastic threats. *(Ch. 24)*

Wilhelm II (r. 1888–1918) German kaiser (emperor) whose aggressive diplomatic, commercial, and military policies helped trigger World War I. His pursuit of *Weltpolitik* severely aggravated international tensions. See also **Weltpolitik.** *(Ch. 24)*

Yalta conference The meeting in February 1945 at Yalta, a Soviet Black Sea resort, between Stalin, Roosevelt, and Churchill. With Allied victory assured, they began outlining plans for the postwar order, including the military occupation of Germany. See also **Potsdam conference.** *(Ch. 28)*

Young Turks Term describing the young intellectuals who wanted to transform the Ottoman Empire into a more modern, Westernized state. Self-exiled in the late 1860s in Paris and London, they overthrew the sultan and seized power in 1908. The expression has subsequently come to designate any group of activists pushing for political change. *(Ch. 22)*

Zionism Nationalist Jewish movement. In the late nineteenth century, faced with growing **anti-Semitism**, some Jews argued that they would be safe only in their own nation. Zionism advocated establishing a Jewish state in the Jews' ancient homeland of Palestine, an idea that became reality with the creation of Israel in 1948. *(Ch. 24)*

Zoroastrianism Religion founded about 1000–550 B.C. by the Persian prophet Zarathustra (*Zoroaster* in Greek). Zoroastrians believe in a supreme deity and a cosmic contest between good and evil within each individual. *(Ch. 2)*

CREDITS

Chapter 1: Pages 19, 20, 24, 33: "King Hammurabi Dispenses Justice," "Heroism and Death in Mesopotamia," "Pharaoh the Divine and Invincible," "Prayers of a Hittite Queen," adapted from James B. Pritchard, ed., *Ancient Near Eastern Texts Relating to the Old Testament,* 3rd ed. Copyright © 1969 by Princeton University Press. Reprinted by permission of Princeton University Press. **Page 30:** "Egyptian Attitudes Toward Foreigners" from *Ancient Egyptian Literature, Volume 1,* by Miriam Lichtheim, University of California Press. Copyright © 1973. Reprinted by permission of the University of California Press.

Chapter 2: Pages 43, 46: "The Banquet of Ashurnasirpal II," "Cyrus and His Subjects' Gods" from James B. Pritchard, ed., *Ancient Near Eastern Texts Relating to the Old Testament,* 3rd ed. Copyright © 1969 by Princeton University Press. Reprinted by permission of Princeton University Press. **Page 46:** Ezra 1:1–3 from *Revised English Bible.* © Oxford University Press and Cambridge University Press 1989. **Page 52:** "The Covenant" from Deuteronomy 5:1–2, 6:1–3, 10:12–19, from *Revised English Bible.* © Oxford University Press and Cambridge University Press 1989. **Page 56:** "Ruth" from Ruth 1:1, 3–6, 8–9, 14–18, 2:1–3, 8–12 from *Revised English Bible.* © Oxford University Press and Cambridge University Press 1989. **Page 64:** "Greeks and Trojans" from *The Iliad of Homer,* translated by Richmond Lattimore. Copyright © 1951 by the University of Chicago Press. Reprinted by permission.

Chapter 3: Page 78: "Aristotle Complains" from *Aristotle, The Politics,* translated by Carnes Lord. Copyright © 1984 by the University of Chicago Press. Reprinted by permission. "Plutarch Counters" from *Plutarch on Sparta,* translated by Richard J. A. Talbert (Harmondsworth, England: Penguin Classics, 1988), p. 24. Translation copyright © Richard J. A. Talbert, 1988. Reproduced by permission of Penguin Books Ltd. **Page 82:** Quote by Sappho from *Ancient Greek Literature and Society,* Second Edition, by Charles Rowan Beye. Copyright © 1987 by Cornell University Press. Reprinted by permission. **Page 87:** "The Debate on Democracy" adapted from Euripides, "The Suppliant Women," translated by Frank Jones in *Euripides IV: The Complete Greek Tragedies,* edited by David Grene and Richmond Lattimore. Copyright © 1958 by the University of Chicago Press. Reprinted by permission. **Page 90:** "The Enemy as Barbarian" from *The Histories* by Herodotus, translated by Aubrey de Sélincourt, revised by A. R. Burn (Penguin Classics 1954, revised 1972), pp. 429, 550. Copyright © The Estate of Aubrey de Sélincourt, 1945. Copyright © A. R. Burn, 1972. Reprinted by permission of Penguin Books Ltd. **Page 92:** "Pericles' Funeral Oration" reprinted with the permission of The Free Press, a Division of Simon & Schuster, Inc., from *The Landmark Thucydides: A Comprehensive Guide to the Peloponnesian War* by Robert B. Strassler. Copyright © 1996 by Robert B. Strassler. **Page 97:** "Plato on Philosopher-Kings" from *Plato's Republic,* translated by G.M.A. Grube. Copyright © 1974 by Hackett Publishing Company. Reprinted by permission of Hackett Publishing Company, Inc. All rights reserved.

Chapter 4: Page 118: "Egyptians versus Greeks in a Temple" adapted from M. M. Austin, ed., *The Hellenistic World from Alexander to the Roman Conquest: A Selection of Ancient Sources in Translation.* Cambridge: Cambridge University Press, 1981. Reprinted with the permission of Cambridge University Press.

Chapter 5: Page 137: From *The Aeneid of Virgil,* trans. Allen Mandelbaum. Copyright © 1971 by Allen Mandelbaum. Reprinted by permission of Bantam Books, a division of Bantam, Doubleday, Dell Publishing Group, Inc. **Page 161:** "Tiberius Gracchus on Rome's Plight" from *Roman Civilization,* ed. Naphtali Lewis and Meyer Reinhold. © 1990 by Columbia University Press. Reprinted by permission of the publisher. **Page 165:** "Caesar on the Gauls" from Julius Caesar, *Seven Commentaries on the Gallic War with an Eighth Commentary by Aulus Hirtius,* translated by Carolyn Hammong. Copyright © 1996 Oxford University Press. By permission of Oxford University Press. **Page 167:** "Cicero in Defense of Milo" from *Selected Political Speeches of Cicero* by Cicero, translated by Michael Grant (Harmondsworth, England: Penguin Classics, 1969), pp. 232–234. Copyright © Michael Grant Publications Ltd, 1969. Reproduced by permission of Penguin Books Ltd.

Chapter 6: Page 177: "Augustus: The Official Story" from *Res Gestae Divi Augusti: The Achievements of the Divine Augustus,* edited by P. A. Brunt and J. M. Moore. Copyright © 1967. Reprinted by permission of Oxford University Press. **Page 178:** "Augustus: A Skeptical View" from Tacitus, *The Annals of Imperial Rome,* translated by Michael Grant (Penguin Classics, 1951, revised edition 1971). Copyright © 1956, 1959, 1971 by Michael Grant Publications Ltd. Reprinted by permission of Frederick Warne & Company (Penguin Books UK). **Page 187:** "Slaves With the Right Stuff" from *As the Romans Did: A Source Book in Roman Social History,* Second Edition, by Jo-Ann R. Shelton. Copyright © 1988, 1998 by Oxford University Press, Inc. Used by permission of Oxford University Press, Inc. **Page 190:** "Syria Between Rome and Persia" from *History of Ancient Iran,* translated by Richard N. Frye, Emeritus Professor of Iranian History, Harvard University (Munich: C.H. Beck'sche Verlagsbuchhandlung, 1984). Reprinted by permission of Richard N. Frye. **Page 196:** "Christian Community and Christian Relationships" from The Letter of Paul to the Ephesians 2:11–17, 5:21–6:9 from *Revised English Bible,* © Oxford University Press and Cambridge University Press 1989.

Chapter 7: Page 208: "A Contemporary View of Diocletian's Reforms" from *Roman Civilization,* ed. Naphtali Lewis and Meyer Reinhold. © 1990 by Columbia University Press. Reprinted by permission of the publisher. **Page 228:** "Basic Principles of Roman Law" from *Justinian's Institutes, 1.1–2.* Edited and translated by Peter Birks and Grant McLeod. Cornell University Press, 1987. Reprinted by permission of the publisher. **Page 234:** "The Moment of Augustine's Spiritual Awakening" from *Confessions of St. Augustine* by St. Augustine, translated by Rex Warner, copyright © 1963 by Rex Warner, renewed © 1991 by F. C. Warner. Used by permission of Dutton Signet, a division of Penguin Putnam, Inc.

Chapter 8: Page 244: "The Message of the Quran" from *The Meaning of the Holy Qu'ran.* New edition with revised translation, com-

INDEX